D0877754

POLICING THE NEW WORLD DISORDER

Peace Operations and Public Security

Policing the New World Disorder
Peace Operations and Public Security

Edited by
Robert B. Oakley
Michael J. Dziedzic
Eliot M. Goldberg

1998

National Defense University Press
Washington, DC

The Institute for National Strategic Studies (INSS) is a major component of the National Defense University (NDU), which operates under the supervision of the President of NDU. It conducts strategic studies for the Secretary of Defense, Chairman of the Joint Chiefs of Staff, and unified commanders in chief; supports national strategic components of NDU academic programs; and provides outreach to other governmental agencies and the broader national security community.

The Publication Directorate of INSS publishes books, monographs, reports, and occasional papers on national security strategy, defense policy, and national military strategy through NDU Press that reflect the output of NDU research and academic programs. In addition, it produces the INSS *Strategic Assessment* and other work approved by the President of NDU, as well as *Joint Force Quarterly*, a professional military journal published for the Chairman.

Opinions, conclusions, and recommendations expressed or implied within are solely those of the authors, and do not necessarily represent the views of the National Defense University, the Department of Defense, or any other U.S. Government agency. Cleared for public release; distribution unlimited.

Portions of this book may be quoted or reprinted without permission, provided that a standard source credit line is included. NDU Press would appreciate a courtesy copy of reprints or reviews.

NDU Press publications are sold by the U.S. Government Printing Office. For ordering information, call (202) 512-1800 or write to the Superintendent of Documents, U.S. Government Printing Office, Washington, DC 20402.

Library of Congress Cataloging-in-Publication Data
Policing the new world disorder : peace operations and public security / edited
    by Robert B. Oakley, Michael J. Dziedzic, Eliot M. Goldberg.
            p. cm.
        ISBN 157906-006-4
            1. United Nations—Armed Forces. 2. United States—Armed
    Forces—Foreign countries. 3. Security, International. I. Oakley, Robert B.,
    1931- . II. Dziedzic, Michael J., 1949- . III. Goldberg, Eliot M., 1969- .
        JZ6377.U6P65 1998
        341.5'84—dc21   97-43986
                                                             CIP
First Printing, May 1998

In Memoriam

On September 17, 1997, a helicopter transporting twelve international officials on a peace mission in Bosnia crashed into a fog-enshrouded mountain, killing all passengers on board.

Among those who perished were six members of the U.N. International Police Task Force in Bosnia and the U.S. International Criminal Investigative Training Assistance Program.

Livio "Al" Beccaccio, United States
Senior Advisor to the Deputy Commissioner
United Nations International Police Task Force

First Lieutenant Andrzej Buler, Poland
Assistant to the Deputy Commissioner
United Nations International Police Task Force

David "Kris" Kriscovich, United States
Deputy Commissioner for Training and Restructuring
United Nations International Police Task Force

Billy Nesbitt, United States
Bosnia Program Manager
International Criminal Investigative Training Assistance Program

Marvin Padgett, United States
Coordinator for Police Training
United Nations International Police Task Force

Dr. Georg Stiebler, Germany
Chief of Local Police Development Section
United Nations International Police Task Force

This book is dedicated to the lives and work of these noble law enforcement professionals who made vital contributions to peace and stability in Bosnia-Herzegovina.

Contents

Foreword

Peace operations have gained international attention in recent years, and many excellent studies have appeared on the role of the military in separating warring factions, enforcing cease-fires, and providing humanitarian relief. Another dimension of peacekeeping has become readily apparent, however: the need to strengthen or rebuild indigenous public security institutions. Without a functioning police force, judiciary, and penal system, any troubled state is further hindered in its attempts to overcome internal crisis.

The Institute for National Strategic Studies at the National Defense University has addressed this growing concern and concluded that rebuilding viable law enforcement capabilities is more central to the success of peace operations than generally appreciated. INSS assembled a core group of experienced civilian and military experts to prepare a series of case studies for discussion. The case studies then formed the basis for a conference held in late 1997 and attended by over one hundred international specialists. This book is the end result of that effort.

Policing the New World Disorder should prove useful in conducting comparative analyses of operations involving international assistance to public security institutions. Chapters contributed by the Dutch, Swedish, Norwegian, Australian, and Austrian experts take a broad view of the subject. A final chapter offers some specific recommendations for consideration by the United Nations, the United States, and other governments in improving the conduct of multilateral operations to assist police forces, courts, and prison systems in troubled states. This effort has already contributed to an increased understanding of this dimension of peace operations among members of U.S. civilian and military agencies as well as international and nongovernmental organizations. This book provides new insights that should help those charged with carrying out such operations become more effective in strengthening public security institutions in troubled countries.

RICHARD A. CHILCOAT
Lieutenant General, U.S. Army
President, National Defense University

xi

Acknowledgments

The Institute for National Strategic Studies' project on Public Security and the New World Disorder originated with a May 1996 conference held by the U.S. Institute of Peace that examined the issue of police functions in peace operations. The resulting important work encouraged us to initiate an intensive year-long project using a series of case studies and involving both U.S. and international participants.

The people whom the editors wish to thank for their participation and valuable insights are so numerous that we used an extensive database to keep track of them. In particular, we thank the U.S. Department of Defense offices of Peacekeeping and Humanitarian Affairs, Strategic Plans and Policy, and Special Operations and Low Intensity Conflict; the U.S. State Department Office of Peacekeeping and Humanitarian Operations; the Global Issues and Multilateral Affairs office at the National Security Council; the International Criminal Investigative Training Assistance Program at the Department of Justice; and the United Nations Department of Peacekeeping Operations and its Civilian Police Unit.

Carnegie Corporation funded the first year of the project, with additional assistance provided by the John C. Whitehead Foundation and the U.S. Institute of Peace. The Carnegie Commission on Preventing Deadly Conflict, the Lester B. Pearson Canadian Peacekeeping Training Centre, and the National Defense University cohosted the concluding conference held September 15-16, 1997, at the National Defense University.

Our final thanks go to the National Defense University Foundation. Their hard-working staff maintained a consistent level of funding for the entire project.

POLICING THE NEW WORLD DISORDER
Peace Operations and Public Security

Introduction

MICHAEL J. DZIEDZIC

The searing image of a U.S. soldier being dragged through the streets of Mogadishu has defined for the American public, perhaps as much as any single event, the troubling character of the contemporary era. "What in the World are we Doing?" the cover of *Time* demanded to know on behalf of an outraged nation.[1] Less than a year later, U.S. troops were again spearheading a multilateral coalition in the midst of chaos in Port au Prince. This time the defining image was an American soldier, pistol drawn, holding a seething Haitian mob at bay. Sprawled on the ground behind him was the intended recipient of popular justice. The photo caption reads, "As Haitian police fade from view, U.S. troops are being drawn into conflict."[2] Two years later, thousands of American peacekeeping troops had been deployed to Bosnia as part of a NATO-led peace operation. Among their duties was providing area security in the strategic Bosnian Serb controlled town of Brcko. In late August 1997, Brcko became the flash point of an internal power struggle in the Serb Republic (RS). Supporters of indicted war criminal Radovan Karadzic, incited by local radio broadcasts and air raid sirens, assaulted U.S. troops positioned there with rocks and ax handles for seeming to side with Karadzic's political rival. Two U.S. soldiers were wounded in the ensuing street violence, and U.N. civilian police (UNCIVPOL) had to be evacuated temporarily to nearby military bases.[3] These jarring images form a mosaic of the post-Cold

---

[1]*Time*, October 18, 1993, cover.

[2]*U.S. News & World Report*, October 10, 1994, 26.

[3]Transcript: Joint Press Conference, Stabilization Force, Land Forces Central Europe (SFOR LANDCENT), August 28, 1997, http://www.nato.int/ifor/landcent/9708280.htm; and "U.S. Troops in Bosnia Leave Bridge: Peacekeepers Abandon Site of Mob Violence," *The Baltimore Sun,* September 5, 1997, 17A.

War era and our reluctant role in it. In tandem with various coalition partners, we are confronting the uncertainties and peculiar challenges associated with policing a new sort of disorder in the world.

Like it or not, contemporary use of the U.S. military instrument in peace operations has very often borne little resemblance to the high-intensity, high-tech battlefields that American soldiers, sailors, and airmen have been so well prepared to dominate. Indeed, the most frequent demands have come from the opposite end of the conflict spectrum, where the skills of the mediator are often more relevant and the essence of the mission is to rehabilitate, not annihilate. Among the more potent therapies for this new world disorder, whether administered prior to a crisis or during an international intervention, is for local institutions of public security—policemen, judges, and jailers—to begin functioning. Most military officers have been in uncharted territory when dealing with these matters, particularly when thrown into this complex task with a host of other international actors with whom they are largely unfamiliar (for example, relief workers, human rights monitors, election supervisors, and police trainers). Much of the early learning was on the job.

Because the factors contributing to the "new world disorder" are unlikely to diminish any time soon, it behooves the United States and the entire community of nations to refine our collective capacity to mount effective multilateral responses. This book is dedicated to the task of increasing international proficiency at coping with the distinctive challenge of restoring public security in war-torn or chaotic societies. There has been a great deal of study devoted to the military aspects of peacekeeping, but little attention has been given to the military contribution to the public security function. Through an examination of relevant recent experiences, we seek to extract useful insights and recommendations for those who must grapple with restoring public security during future peace missions.

Peace Operations and the New World Disorder

Historically, conflict *between* states has been a predominant source of concern for soldiers and statesmen. During the post-Cold War period, however, it has been anarchic conditions *within* the sovereign state that have repeatedly posed the most acute and intractable challenges to international order. Some notable internal conflicts that attracted international attention since 1989 had been exacerbated by superpower rivalry (Nicaragua, El Salvador, Namibia, Angola, Mozambique, Cambodia). More recently, however, the international community has been called upon to act purely in response to dysfunctional or disintegrating states (Somalia, Yugoslavia, Liberia, Haiti, Rwanda, Zaire, Albania). Throughout the present decade, most battlefields have been internal to individual states; very few conflicts have resulted from interstate warfare, the more traditional concern of statecraft.[4]

Domestic disorder, of course, is not new. The essence of this problem in many Third World states is the fragility and decay of governmental institutions, especially those devoted to responding to citizen demands, preserving law and order, and resolving internal disputes. Domestic pressures, brought on by ethnic cleavages, overpopulation, poverty, maldistribution of wealth, environmental degradation, and rapid social mobilization often outpace and even overwhelm government ability to respond. When internal unrest either causes a government meltdown or provokes draconian spasms of repression, the consequences can spill over the border, destabilizing the surrounding region. In turn, transnational forces such as massive refugee migrations, guerrilla movements, and international criminal syndicates have increasingly been unleashed or exacerbated, threatening surrounding states. The humanitarian implications have also become more compelling. The specter of genocide or starvation, televised graphically to global audiences, has the demonstrated capacity to stir world opinion. International politics has thus been turned on its head: instability often tends to emanate today from the

---

[4] "Major Armed Conflict" chapters, *Stockholm International Peace Research Institute Yearbooks* (Oxford: Oxford University Press, 1992-1997), and *Status of Armed Conflicts: 1994-1997* (London: International Institute for Strategic Studies, August 1, 1997), map.

weakest of states (the "failed state") rather than the most powerful. This anomaly has been labeled the *new world disorder*.

The consequences of this disorder for regional and international stability and compelling humanitarian implications have eroded traditional inhibitions against intervention in the internal affairs of states. Unilateral action, however, is not considered legitimate because this could degenerate into the classic pattern of suspicion, and regional/great power rivalry, especially if states were repeatedly allowed to intervene without cost. The international community has preferred to act in concert, under U.N. or other auspices, devoting an unprecedented amount of attention and scarce resources over the past decade to ameliorating this intrastate source of international instability. The challenge for contemporary statesmen is to organize their global community, one which lacks any supranational authority, for the purpose of collectively restoring order in states that are often only marginally viable.[5]

The multinational peace mission has typically been the mechanism adopted. Owing to the need to separate armed domestic rivals while simultaneously restoring law and order, post-Cold War peace operations have increasingly required the participation of both military personnel and civilian police. *International policing*, in this context, involves a flexible combination of participants. The mainstay invariably will be a contingent of policemen recruited from member states by the United Nations (or some other multilateral organization or coalition). When acting under a U.N. mandate, such civilian police are referred to

---

[5]The absence of any supranational authority is the trait that theoretically distinguishes the international system of states from politics within states. Thus, international politics is said to be "anarchic" because of this lack of an authoritative source of order. The state, in contrast, is sovereign within its territory. When the apparatus of the state collapses, however, or dissolves into several armed factions, each claiming the right to sovereignty, then anarchy prevails within that state as well. The first irony of the post-Cold War period is that anarchy within the state has become a more frequent source of disruption for the international system than armed conflict between states. The second is that the anarchic global community must undertake the task of creating order for the sovereign state. It is for this latter reason that international unity of effort during a peace operation is so necessary yet so difficult to attain.

as UNCIVPOL, and they are administered by the Civilian Police Unit within the Department of Peacekeeping Operations (DPKO).[6] Typically supporting UNCIVPOL efforts is an eclectic mix of bilateral law enforcement assistance programs (e.g., the U.S. Justice Department International Criminal Investigative Training Assistance Program, ICITAP), multilateral activities (e.g., U.N. Crime Prevention and Criminal Justice Division), and nongovernmental organizations (e.g., the American Bar Association). Also typically involved with aspects of policing and public security within a U.N. mission are the military contingent, human rights and election monitors, and civilian affairs personnel.[7]

Normally, an international mandate directs the peace mission to establish a secure and stable internal environment. To fulfill this mandate, indigenous institutions of law and order must be coaxed into functioning in rough accordance with internationally acceptable standards. CIVPOL members have been called upon to perform an array of tasks, including monitoring the conduct of local police cadres, training and mentoring police recruits, mediating local disputes, and even maintaining public order themselves. Owing to the complex nature of the public security challenges involved, peace operations since the end of the Cold War have often required sizable CIVPOL contingents.

---

[6]This definition is consistent with that used by Schmidl in his discussion of the origin of UNCIVPOL and with the Norwegian and Swedish chapters (although the Swedish report suggests using "police monitors" and "police mentors" for greater clarity). Some of our case study authors, however, have occasionally used CIVPOL as a synonym for all international policing assistance, bilateral or multilateral, during a peace mission. We prefer the term "international policing" as an all-embracing concept, reserving "CIVPOL" for uniformed civilian police operating under a U.N. mandate.

[7]Both the United Nations and the U.S. Army are apt to have entities involved in a given peace mission that are referred to as "civil affairs."

Size of CIVPOL Contingents in Recent Peace Operations		
Country (Mission)	Peak Personnel	Contributing Countries
Cambodia (UNTAC)	3,600	32
Bosnia (IPTF)	2,015	38
Mozambique (ONUMOZ)	1,086	29
Haiti (UNMIH)	870	12
Haiti (IPM)	821	20
El Salvador (ONUSAL)	341	8

Conceptual Framework

Disorder is the phenomenon certain to be present at the inception of this genre of peace operation. It may be disorder in the form of an appalling incapacity of the state to perform its most basic function—protecting its citizens. In other cases, the "public security" apparatus itself has been the instrument of massive public insecurity, almost to the point of genocide. It is generally the transnational consequences of this disorder that provoke the international community to intervene. Restoring *order* becomes an urgent priority. The initial phase of a typical, post-Cold War peace operation entails separating local armed groups (normally pursuant to a peace accord), restricting them to cantonments or assembly areas, impounding their weapons, and demobilizing many of them. In some instances, one or more of these armed forces may be totally disbanded. Owing to the uncertainty of this process and the firepower available to the disputants, a military peacekeeping force is required to inspire confidence in and verify compliance with the peace process.

The Deployment Gap

The military is a blunt instrument when used alone in this context. It is capable only of imposing a most basic, rigid form of order. An intervening military force can attempt to deter and limit loss of life and destruction of property, but that is about all. Because local law enforcement agencies have either ceased to function or have become oppressive and even murderous, international policing assistance must be mobilized to oversee restoration of this function.

Military forces have a capacity to deploy rapidly in unit strength; police organizations typically do not. Mobilizing a CIVPOL contingent is inherently time consuming because most domestic police forces do not have a significant surge capability, international mobility, or experience in operating beyond national borders. In the early days of an intervention, therefore, the military is often the only source of order. As a practical matter, moreover, CIVPOL in the absence of a credible military backup would be of dubious value and might even be placed in considerable risk.

The local public security force commonly lacks either the capacity or motivation to cope responsibly with civil disorder. Consequently, the international military contingent will likely be faced with a need to perform certain police functions, at least until UNCIVPOL personnel arrive and are able to operate effectively. The lag time between the arrival of the two forces creates a *deployment gap*. It is one of several public security gaps that military peacekeepers are apt to confront. In this case, the gap is temporal in nature.

During this early phase, the peace mission is apt to be tested, and one vulnerable area will likely be the void in public security. If a single soldier errs by using excessive force, the entire mission can be placed in jeopardy because local consent may be squandered. Inaction, on the other hand, risks the loss of credibility and can give the impression the mission is failing. In either case, the peace operation may confront a "defining moment" before it is well postured to respond. The media spotlight will be unavoidable, moreover, since the actions (or inaction) of a deploying peace mission invariably produce dramatic TV news clippings. The consequences for public opinion and the credibility of the peace mission of failing to cope adequately with such challenges can be enduring.

U.S. policy makers received early warning of the pitfalls associated with a deployment gap by virtue of their experiences with the 1989 Panama operation. Although the U.S. intervention to remove General Manuel Noriega was a purely unilateral action, it demonstrated a fundamental point for future peace operations: any intervention force—unilateral or multilateral—that removes or replaces local authority will find itself responsible for maintaining public security. In Panama, no advance provision had been made for this, as described in the paper by Gray and Manwaring.

The intervention in Panama was coincident with the end of the Cold War, and the United Nations was soon being called upon to mop up the vestiges of superpower rivalry in places like Cambodia, El Salvador, Mozambique, and Angola. The U.N. Transitional Authority in Cambodia (UNTAC) was established shortly after the four factions vying for power there agreed to the Paris Accords in October 1991. Although deployment of UNTAC's military contingent required about 5 months, the CIVPOL unit was not fully fielded until November 1992, when the planned 18-month mission was half way to completion. As Farris and Schear have chronicled, this deployment gap contributed to the loss of vital credibility from which the mission never adequately recovered.

In subsequent operations in Haiti and Bosnia, the magnitude of the deployment gap was reduced but not eliminated. Although provisions had been made by the United States to field International Police Monitors (IPMs) in Haiti, during the first chaotic weeks of the intervention, soldiers of the U.S.-led Multinational Force (MNF) were left with the task of maintaining order themselves. When Haitian police began openly brutalizing their own people, the military force was compelled to reassess its rules of engagement (ROE) and assume a law enforcement role. In Bosnia, the first crucial test of compliance with the Dayton Accords involved the transfer of Sarajevo suburbs to Moslem control. Even though the transfer was postponed by 45 days, the International Police Task Force (IPTF) had scarcely begun to become operational when that "defining moment" arrived. The civil disorders that accompanied this process, despite the presence of the IPTF and Implementation Force (IFOR), tarnished the image of the mission and certainly did nothing to diminish the recalcitrance of Bosnian Serb leaders.

The Enforcement Gap

Once sufficient CIVPOL members have been deployed, monitoring of the indigenous police force can begin (assuming the latter remains in existence). The "inner shell" of public security for individual crimes and small scale disturbances, therefore, will usually be provided by some hybrid of the indigenous police force and CIVPOL. The military component normally shifts to a "rapid reaction" mode, thus providing the "outer shell" or area security. At this stage, maintenance of order is normally heavily reliant on external actors.

For society to begin to restore normal activity, however, *law and order* are required. This is the domain of police, judges, and jailers. This phase of the operation, therefore, should be a period of reconstitution for the entire public security apparatus. A common problem is confusion about which legal code applies and who is authorized to enforce it. The parties to the domestic dispute are also intended to reconcile their differences, normally pursuant to an agreement that the peace mission is called upon to verify.

Whereas the deployment gap was about timing, the gap in enforcement is about function. An *enforcement gap* is likely to arise when the peace mission is confronted with the need to perform functions that fall between these inner and outer layers of public security. Typically, these deficiencies relate either to *the basic maintenance of law and order* or *noncompliance with the peace agreement*. When serious lawlessness breaks out or one of the disputants acts to thwart the peace process, the peace mission can be acutely challenged since the capabilities of their military and police contingents to deal with these situations often do not overlap.

In the first case, international police are incapable of dealing with serious lawlessness and violent domestic disorder, especially of the sort that tends to arise during postconflict situations. This applies whether or not they are armed and have arrest authority added to their mandate. The local government is typically characterized by an extremely weak or dysfunctional domestic law enforcement apparatus; the society, in contrast, is awash with automatic weapons and unemployed ex-combatants whose job prospects are extremely limited, at least in the formal economy. While the military intervention force may have great firepower, only specialized units, such as military police (MPs), constabulary units, and special forces (SF), have the training and resources to engage in law enforcement activities. These specialized units may or may not have been included in the peace force. Even when they have been available and the mandate has permitted military involvement in law enforcement, there has sometimes been considerable reluctance by military commanders to use them for this purpose, out of concern this could make it difficult to disengage and possibly incite popular opposition.

The second variant of this gap deals with enforcement of the peace agreement, as opposed to local laws. When one or more of the former disputants is unwilling to abide by or implement aspects of their peace accord, the military contingent may be prevailed upon to compel compliance. To the extent this is done, the peace mission runs the risk of losing consent from at least one of the parties, potentially leading to civil disturbances and more violent forms of opposition to their continued presence. In many cases, moreover, the international community will also be attempting to promote the transformation of the police force from an instrument of state repression into a servant of the people. Policing is inherently political, and such a role reversal for the forces of public security can profoundly affect the domestic distribution of power.[8] This is another area that could precipitate serious local resistance.

Military forces are reluctant to engage in confrontations with civilians because, with the exception of constabulary or military police units, they are generally not trained in the measured use of force, control of riots, negotiating techniques, or de-escalation of conflict. As noted above, CIVPOL is not capable of handling violent challenges, either.

The Cambodian experience reinforced the need to be attentive to political consent, especially when implementation of the peace accord has the potential to alter the internal balance of power. The incapacity

---

[8]Professor David Bayley made this point most persuasively in a discussion devoted to the search for themes and recommendations for this work during a National Defense University conference September 15-16, 1997.

and lack of authority of UNTAC to enforce the cantonment process as specified in the Paris Accord caused a fundamental reorientation at the midpoint of the mission. Military and CIVPOL resources were reconfigured so they could operate jointly, and their mission was reduced to manageable proportions (i.e., providing security for the electoral process).

The Haitian case demonstrates several promising approaches to this issue. Among them is the benefit of unity of purpose for military and police components, premission training, and a comprehensive political-military plan for U.S. Government agencies involved. The experiences of the MNF and the U.N. Mission In Haiti (UNMIH), as documented by Bailey, Maguire, and Pouliot, might serve as a model for achieving smooth transitions and overall unity of effort. In Bosnia, the enforcement challenge was even more demanding and unity of effort was much more difficult to achieve owing, in large part, to the division of international responsibilities among a welter of divergent actors, and the limited mandate for IFOR to support civilian operations such as the IPTF. Although the final word on Bosnia is far from written, the paper by Bair and Dziedzic traces the arduous path traveled by IFOR/SFOR and the IPTF in their struggle to narrow this gap over time. Somalia provides both positive and negative examples of the enforcement gap. The United Task Force (UNITAF) phase provided a remarkable example of the value of a reasonably professional indigenous police force, supported by military peacekeeping forces (in this case, without CIVPOL involvement), in dealing with the enforcement gap. As Thomas and Spataro describe, the Auxiliary Security Force (ASF) was actually capable of functioning in the absence of other governmental structures. The subsequent demise of the U.N. Operation in Somalia (UNOSOM II) is a classic case of the enforcement gap, as the military intervention force sought to apprehend clan leader Mohommad Farah Aideed, becoming a protagonist in the internal dispute without the means or the will to do so. The violence thereby unleashed and the lack of support for the ASF also caused the latter's effective disintegration.

The Institutional Gap

The two gaps discussed above pertain to the relationship between the military and civilian police components of a peace operation. The institutional gap, in contrast, refers to the incapacity of the host government to provide public order, especially when measured against international standards for policing and human rights. Law and order alone do not guarantee sustainable security, since, without justice, the likely result is oppression. That, in turn, could set the stage for another cycle of institutional decay and collapse. *Sustainable security* requires that *law and order* be combined with an adequate measure of *justice* for all. The *institutional gap*, therefore, is the difference in development between a public security apparatus that is responsive to the entire citizenry and one that is dysfunctional (or perhaps not functioning at all). Whereas the deployment gap was *temporal* and the enforcement gap was *functional* in nature, the institutional gap is a matter of *political development.*

Rather than becoming a surrogate for malfunctioning institutions of law and order, the international community aspires to foster their progressive development. Domestic police forces, however, are often ill trained, inadequately equipped, and lacking in discipline. They usually do not command the trust or respect of the citizenry and are often themselves among the more notorious criminal offenders. In addition, ex-combatants may be tempted to join the criminal underworld, and international criminal syndicates may have exploited the previous period of lawlessness to insinuate themselves into the fabric of government and society. The judiciary and penal systems are apt to be similarly overwhelmed. Thus, before local authorities can effectively assume responsibility, a reconstitution of the entire public security system (i.e., police, courts/legal code, and prisons) may be necessary. The international community, including CIVPOL, will need to play an integral role in this institution-building process.

Closing this gap may require that unsuitable local personnel are expunged from the ranks and a new cadre of police and supervisors recruited and trained. Once cadets complete basic training, mentoring (or on-the-job training) will be required for a considerable period. Until the local police force and judiciary have been reconstituted and are able to maintain public security autonomously, there will be a need for continuous international oversight and assistance. This void in institutional capacity can be bridged by effective use of international civilian trainers and mentors, including CIVPOL. This process tends to begin while the military contingent is still present, but it ought to continue well after their departure (5 years is often used as a minimum for such major institution-building projects). Even if the local police force eventually proves to be willing and capable, the entire process will ultimately be of little benefit unless the courts, criminal code, and penal system have also undergone a similar transformation. If these potential deficiencies are not adequately addressed, the likely result will be the re-emergence of conditions that precipitated the peace operation in the first place.

This is, in essence, what transpired in Cambodia. Rehabilitation of the public security infrastructure was not one of its missions. As Farris and Schear conclude, this, coupled with other factors, made UNTAC's contributions "highly perishable" and the political regime it had ushered into existence at great expense was ultimately vulnerable to collapse. In El Salvador, in contrast, the international community undertook to replace the entire police force. In their chapter, Stanley and Loosle capture the spectrum of challenges associated with assembling sufficient human and financial resources from the international community, eliminating incompetent or corrupt former members of the police, developing a leadership hierarchy, and training a new force. Although the Salvadoran case deserves its acclaim as the poster child of successful peace operations, it also serves as a cautionary tale about the damage wrought by neglecting to undertake judicial and penal reform in tandem with enhancements in policing. Similarly, Haiti shows the corrosive effects on a replacement police force, even one receiving substantial ongoing international assistance, when judicial reform lags far behind. The conceptual framework sketched out below seeks to portray the relationship among the three public security gaps over the life-cycle of a peace operation.

Conceptual Framework

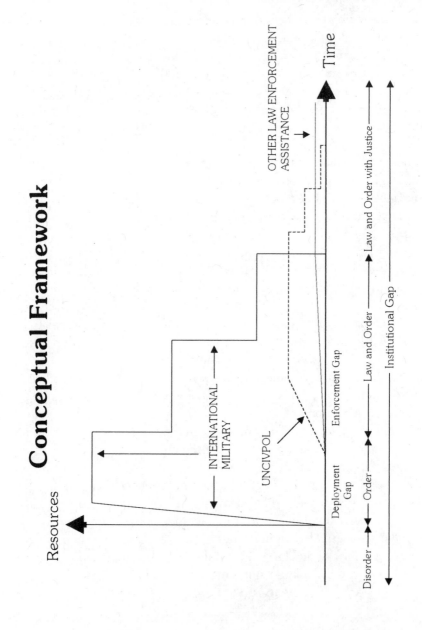

Methodology

In August 1996, the Institute for National Strategic Studies (INSS) at the National Defense University (NDU) hosted its first conference, "Policing the New World Disorder," which involved a team of experienced civilian and military specialists who were assembled to consider this issue and help design the project. The approach that emerged from these deliberations was to conduct an inductive examination of the most instructive post-Cold War interventions using a common analytical framework as a guide. (This framework is included as appendix C.) At a minimum, authors were asked to address five general topics (Background, the Mandate and Resources, the Mission, Coordination and Cooperation, and Evaluations/ Conclusions). Most case studies have been written by a team of authors with an intimate understanding of the specific case but with differing viewpoints (e.g., military and civilian).

After completing an initial draft, each team of authors returned to INSS to discuss their chapter in a workshop including some 15 to 25 key civilian and military practitioners and international specialists having an intimate knowledge of the peace operation involved or who have responsibilities for planning such operations. The authors presented their drafts with particular attention to the public security challenges involved, how these were addressed, and the development of preliminary conclusions. Each group critiqued the paper and helped define the lessons learned. These specialized workshops afforded an opportunity to gather missing data and sharpen analysis. Subsequently, authors, additional civilian and military officials with knowledge of each operation, and editors refined the drafts, in Hegelian manner, through several cycles of thesis and antithesis.

Seven case studies (Panama, Cambodia, El Salvador, Mozambique, Somalia, Haiti, and Bosnia) were completed in this manner and form the foundation for this work. Two chapters are included to describe the origins and functioning of the U.S. Justice Department's International Criminal Investigative Training Assistance Program (ICITAP) and the U.N. Civilian Police. The former is the largest bilateral government program of assistance to law enforcement, the latter a U.N. program; both are prominently featured in the case studies. To place this analysis in historic perspective, Erwin Schmidl introduces the entire work with an overview of pre-1989 attempts to maintain domestic order during external interventions. Lieutenant Colonel Michael Kelly, a lawyer with the Australian Army, contributes a provocative paper on the subject of "legitimacy." Also included in this work are an independent assessment recently completed by the Norwegian Institute of International Affairs and a study done by the official Swedish Commission on International Police Activities.

After the papers had been essentially completed, INSS, the Carnegie Commission on Preventing Deadly Conflict, and the Lester B. Pearson Canadian Peacekeeping Training Centre co-sponsored an international conference at NDU on September 15-16, 1997, which was designed to develop pragmatic approaches to dealing with public security problems typically encountered during post-1989 peace operations. The recommendations growing out of this fertile discussion are presented in the conclusions.

POLICE FUNCTIONS
IN PEACE OPERATIONS:
An Historical Overview

ERWIN A. SCHMIDL

From their beginning in the 19ᵗʰ century and increasingly since the end of the Cold War, many peace operations have included varying degrees of "police activities," ranging from supervising indigenous police agencies to actual law enforcement. Until recently, this aspect of peace operations has often been overlooked or underappreciated in favor of the military, political, and more recently humanitarian components of such missions. This chapter addresses these police functions in peace operations prior to 1989 and the end of the Cold War.

Policing and Peace Operations

Peace operations were not "invented" by the United Nations during the Cold War; they have gradually evolved since the 19ᵗʰ century out of colonial interventions, counterinsurgencies, occupation duties, military assistance to civil administration, frontier operations, and multinational operations. Some of these missions, because of their colonial or hegemonic context, differed considerably from peace operations as we know them today. All these activities, however, did aim at maintaining (or re-establishing) a stable environment. Consequently, most of these missions, especially counterinsurgencies and occupation duties, contained elements of civilian administration and policing. The U.S. Marine Corps *Small Wars Manual* of 1940, for example, included chapters on "armed native organizations," the "formation of a constabulary," and "free and fair" elections, all analogous to contemporary peacekeeping concerns.[1]

As Morris Janowitz noted in his 1960 study, *The Professional Soldier*, "The military tends to think of police activities as less prestigious and less honorable tasks," and therefore has always been reluctant to become involved in law enforcement issues.[2] Within the military establishment, military police have a lower status than airborne or combat troops.

Soldier and cop are different jobs and require different training. Whereas police officers are trained to be flexible on an individual level and adjust their attitudes to the prevailing situation on the streets (including escalating and de-escalating the use of force as needed), the military tends to be less flexible. Different national traditions might play a role, too. Reports from the different military contingents employed in a peacekeeping role in Beirut in 1982-84 suggest that British, French, and Italian soldiers were better able to adjust their behavior to the situation than the U.S. Marines.[3] However, during the 1965 operation in the Dominican Republic, American airborne soldiers managed to cope with similar challenges remarkably well.[4] In peacekeeping, like in counterinsurgency operations, high-quality leadership and cohesion are demanded down to the smallest units: this really is the proverbial "subaltern's" or "corporal's war."

The issue goes deeper than just training for particular tasks. In fact, contrary to some fears to the contrary, professional officers and military forces usually adjust remarkably well to the required "constabulary

---

[1]U.S. Marine Corps, *Small Wars Manual* (Washington, DC: Government Printing Office, 1940). This was reprinted by the service as NAVMC 2890 in 1987, and commercially by Sunflower University Press (Manhattan, KS) in 1989.

[2]Morris Janowitz, *The Professional Solder: A Social and Political Portrait,* 2^d ed. (New York-London: Free Press & Collier-Macmillan, 1977), 418-419.

[3]For more details about this operation, see the papers edited by Anthony McDermott and Kjell Skjelsbael in *The Multinational Force in Beirut 1982-1984* (Miami: Florida International University Press, 1991).

[4]John M. Metz, "Training the Way we Fight or for the Fight: Are Tactical Units Prepared for Post-Conflict Operations?" in *Low Intensity Conflict & Law Enforcement* 5, no. 2 (Autumn 1996): 212-213.

ethic," as Charles C. Moskos noted in his 1975 study of the Cyprus operation: "The data convincingly argue that it would be erroneous to consider the requirements of peacekeeping as a contradiction with military professionalism."[5] But soldiers fear losing their war-fighting capabilities (and war-fighting spirit) by becoming involved in peace operations. As British experiences in peacekeeping and counter-insurgency operations over the years show, soldiers involved might temporarily become less proficient in some specialties, but this is more than compensated by experience gained in the field and added leadership skills, especially among junior and noncommissioned officers. Several crack British units that fought in the Falklands in 1982 and in the Gulf War of 1991 had been employed in Cyprus or in Northern Ireland not long before.[6]

The term "police operations" has often been used for activities "other than war." Britain's "Imperial policing" of her colonies in the interwar years comes to mind, but conflicts like the Korean War of 1950-53, or the Gulf War of 1991, were also known as "police operations." Likewise, the first U.N. force established for the Sinai in 1956 was referred to as a "police force."[7] This is not the meaning

[5]Charles C. Moskos, "U.N. Peacekeepers: The Constabulary Ethic and Military Professionalism," *Armed Forces and Society* 1, no. 4 (August 1975): 399.

[6]In this context, I am indebted to Miss Alex Ward and John C. Harding of the Army Historical Branch (London) for providing me with relevant data. This issue shall be examined in more detail in my forthcoming major study on peace operations. I would also like to mention Laura L. Miller's excellent recent paper, "Should U.S. Combat Soldiers be Peacekeepers? Lessons from Macedonia," which she was kind enough to pass on to me.

[7]The Canadian Minister for External Affairs Lester B. Pearson proposed in the General Assembly the creation of a "truly international peace and police force" on November 2, 1956. See "A Brief History of UNEF" (ca. 1958, U.N. Archives: DAG-1/2.2.5.5.1, Box 9); also Mona Ghali, "United Nations Emergency Force 1: 1956-1967," in William J. Durch, ed., *The Evolution of UN Peacekeeping: Case Studies and Comparative Analysis* (New York: St. Martin's/Henry L. Stimson Center, 1993), 106-130; Joshua Sinai, ed., *United Nations Peace Operations Case Studies* (Washington DC: Library of Congress, 1995), 102-111. Apparently, Pearson's original ideas went beyond simple policing of the armistice. See Nathan A. Pelcovits, *The Long Armistice: UN Peacekeeping and the Arab Israeli Conflict, 1948-1960* (Boulder, CO: Westview, 1993), 123, 167.

associated with the term "police operations" in this work. "Policing" in this context refers to civilian law enforcement functions. To stress this differentiation, and to distinguish the police components from the military police (provost marshal) units employed in the military forces, the United Nations coined the term "civilian police," or CIVPOL for short. However, this acronym is properly used in the U.N. context only, and after 1964. UNCIVPOL are always uniformed, wearing their home countries' police uniforms, with additional U.N. blue berets and badges, just like their military counterparts.

The term "police" has different connotations in different cultures. One country's "Bobbies" are another country's death squads. A study on the U.N. Emergency Force in the Sinai undertaken in the 1960s when this force was commonly known as a "police force" observed that:

> In Egypt, and in many other countries as well, the word 'police' has an extremely negative connotation. It is associated with people who are brutal, who do not refrain from using torture, and in general also are corrupt. . . . For that reason the presentation of the force as a police force is probably not the most happy way of doing it.[8]

The military prefers the term "constabulary," which has a certain tradition going back to *gendarmerie*-type colonial forces, but this lacks clarity. In current U.S. usage, "constabulary" refers to a force organized along military lines, providing basic law enforcement and safety in a not yet fully stabilized environment. Such different institutions as the Mexican "Rurales" or Canadian "Mounties" in their original configuration come to mind. Just as happened with the Royal Canadian Mountain Police, such a constabulary organization can provide the nucleus for a professional law enforcement or police force.

---

[8]Ingrid and Johan Galtung, "A Pilot Project Report from Gaza, February 1964," *Oslo Institute for Social Research,* 14, 4/6 1964, 1314 (U.N. Archives: DAG-1/2.2.5.5.0, Box 12, file 10).

Peace operations often take place inside countries where traditional law enforcement has either broken down or where police lack the apolitical approach typical of the democratic tradition. Anarchic conditions may develop where both the laws and the institutions to enforce them are lacking.[9] This means that restoration of order may require that legal codes and judicial institutions must be rebuilt, as well as police forces.

Depending on the state of law enforcement in the host country, the international role in policing can take different forms. Although it is always dangerous to generalize, one can distinguish among three main aspects of international police missions:

□ Monitoring and supervision of local law enforcement organizations

□ Training and mentoring local police forces

□ On rare occasions, actually performing law enforcement functions.

While some of these functions might overlap (such as monitoring and training), it is important to keep these distinctions in mind to avoid false expectations and adverse public reaction.

It would be wrong to expect an international military operation to take over police work for an extended period. For one, a police organization can function successfully only in the context of long-term stability. While military forces might carry out policing duties in an unstable environment for a short time, to achieve lasting stability and security a local police structure must be either recreated or reformed.

Moreover, "community policing" as we know it now in Western Europe and North America is quite different from military operations engaged in filling the initial public security gap. It can only be performed by officers living in the community who are able to communicate directly with the people—preferably without

---

[9]U.S. Army Field Manual 27-5, *Military Government* (1940), clearly stipulates that in addition to the laws of war, the laws of the country occupied should form the basis for military jurisdiction (section V: Military Tribunals).

interpreters—gaining their trust and confidence. Local laws, customs, and institutions must be understood in their cultural context. Peacekeepers are often hampered by their lack of knowledge of local culture. Language alone can be a serious problem. Interpreters, usually hired locally, are not always perceived as neutral by the population, especially if they come from a different ethnic background.

A good policeman cannot be trained overnight, and there is no substitute for a well-trained and experienced police officer. Just as with civilian administration, it would be wrong to expect the international community to take over these functions completely for a protracted period. When the Allies installed military governments in Germany and Austria in 1945, for example, they had to use suitably vetted local police officers as the core of a new law enforcement system.[10] By monitoring the local structures and training and assisting the "new" police forces, international police officers can help to establish the local population's trust in these institutions and overcome initial difficulties. Police play a crucial role in securing the transfer from war to peace, enabling the people to return to their "normal" lives. Therefore, the selection, training, and supervision of these international police officers are of the utmost importance for the effectiveness of police functions in peace operations.

While international military forces cannot stay forever, advisers might continue after withdrawal of the bulk of the operation. Police advisers, usually provided on a bilateral level, have a long tradition. Before the First World War, international police officers (from the six European Powers as well as Dutch and Scandinavian officers) helped train police forces in the crumbling Ottoman Empire and in Persia.

---

[10]Some data on these aspects can be gained from a recently published case study on the establishment of the U.S. military government in Upper Austria: Kurt Tweraser, *U.S.-Militärregierung Oberösterreich, Band 1: Sicherheitspolitische Aspekte der amerikanischen Besatzung in Oberösterreich-Sud 1945-1950.* (Beiträge zur Zeitgeschichte Oberösterreichs 14, Linz: OÖLA, 1995). For additional information, I am indebted to Lieutenant Colonel Jim Carafano (Center of Military History), who is currently working on a dissertation about American military government in Austria after 1945.

Police advisers and training programs are part and parcel of any activity aiming at improving security conditions.

If we look at various historical examples, three lessons are clear:

☐ International efforts at establishing a stable and secure environment need to be well coordinated and tailored to the circumstances, usually employing both military and civilian police personnel.
☐ The judicial and penal systems as well as the police must be at least minimally operational in order to achieve success.
☐ Providing security and stability is never a short-term task.

Previous Military Involvement in International Law Enforcement

The "new generations" of peace operations introduced since the end of the Cold War involve numerous elements of counterinsurgency operations or military government of occupied territories. Relevant experiences include the execution or supervision of law enforcement as well as the organization or reorganization of police, justice, and prison systems. The involvement of the military in these functions always is an important issue.

The major distinction between the role of the military in a war and other military roles lies in the amount of authority delegated to the armed forces. In a war, the military is in command, whereas it is just one of the actors in a counterinsurgency, in the occupation of a country, or while assisting the civil authorities back home. This parallels the arrangements in peace operations: in "traditional" peacekeeping missions, the force commander is usually in charge, whereas in "wider peacekeeping" or enforcement operations, the military is just one of the branches under the head of the mission.

Although military officers are usually quick to point out that their first and foremost task is to fight—and win—wars, the taking over of essentially civilian tasks—and, in our context, law enforcement functions in particular—has a certain tradition even if this is less well

25

known. For the U.S. Army, previous examples include the use of federal forces in domestic disorders within the United States as well as in operations abroad.[11] Among the more notable cases are the experiences in Latin America and in the Pacific, such as the establishment of the "Garde d'Haiti" during the American administration of that country, 1916-34. Similar local police and constabulary forces were established in the Philippines, Samoa, Nicaragua, and Guatemala.[12]

Although the legal issues involved are still debated,[13] peace operations in "failed states" like Cambodia or Somalia in many respects resemble military government of occupied territory. Typical phenomena include the collapse of existing law enforcement structures and the absence of a functioning administration. These functions have, therefore, to be taken over by the occupying forces. For the United States, the experiences in military government include the involvement in Mexico in 1847 and 1848; in the Confederate States during and after the Civil War; in the Philippines, Puerto Rico, and Cuba after the Spanish-American War of 1898; and in the German Rhineland after World War One. The best-documented case, however, is probably the

---

[11]Two major studies on this subject have been published by the U.S. Army Center of Military History: Robert W. Coakley, *The Role of Federal Military Forces in Domestic Disorders 1789-1878* (Washington, DC: Center of Military History, 1988); and Clayton D. Laurie and Ronald H. Cole, *The Role of Federal Military Forces in Domestic Disorders 1877-1945* (Washington, DC: Center of Military History, 1997).

[12]See M. Dean Havron et. al., *Constabulary Capabilities for Low-Level Conflict* (McLean, VA: Human Sciences Research for Office of Naval Research, 1969), 36-61. This study was done for the U.S. Marine Corps Civil Affairs Branch, to explore the possibility of applying earlier U.S. constabulary experiences from Haiti, the Philippines, Samoa, and Nicaragua to the formation of militia and police units in Vietnam. Another contract study was authored by Joseph F. Coates on "The Police Function in Stability Operations" in May 1968. I found copies of both papers at the U.S. Army Military History Institute Library at Carlisle Barracks, PA. Also see Lester D. Langley, *The Banana Wars: An Inner History of American Empire 1900-1934* (Lexington, KY: University of Kentucky, 1983).

[13]For details, see the article by Michael J. Kelly in this book and also his study, *Peace Operations: Tackling the Military, Legal and Political Challenges* (Canberra: Government of Australia, 1997).

establishment of military governments in Germany and Austria—and Japan—after the end of the Second World War.

The first U.S. Army manual on the subject, FM 27-5, *Military Government*, was issued in July 1940, and preparations for eventual occupation duties slowly began in 1941. Among the consequences was the establishment of the military police branch. In April 1942, a separate School of Military Government was established at the University of Virginia.[14] Later that year, when Allied forces landed in Algiers and Morocco, the Army found itself confronted with civil affairs on a scale it had not contemplated. The pattern established in North Africa—that the military was in control of all functions, including civilian ones, as long as the was lasted—persisted throughout the war.[15] In 1943, the Civil Affairs Division was established, and in cooperation with the British, preparations for the eventual occupation of European territories began. (Along similar lines, plans were made for the occupation of Japan, too.) Drawing in part on British colonial experiences, it soon become clear that transition from wars to occupation was a process rather than a single event.[16] Although the military was not happy with the idea of long-term, essentially civilian duties, it soon became clear that a military government had to be established for the occupied territory.

The need for military government arose in most liberated or occupied countries, but clearly the most important cases were those of Germany and Japan in 1945. For law enforcement, indigenous police were to be used in both countries, under U.S. control on a local (city or town) level, whereas separate U.S. units were established on a regional level. These were U.S. Army units—organized like mechanized cavalry—that received additional training in military government and police duties. Eventually the U.S. Constabulary was formally established on February 15, 1945. It had a peak strength of

---

[14]Earl F. Ziemke, *The U.S. Army in the Occupation of Germany 1944-46,* Army Historical Series (Washington, DC: Center for Military History, 1075), 4.
[15]Ibid., 14-15.
[16]Ibid., 57.

some 31,000 men, organized in three brigades for the three *Länder* (provinces) under U.S. control.[17]

The U.S. Constabulary was a highly motivated force, with a cavalry tradition and special uniforms and insignia. Great care was taken to ensure the integrity of the troops; earlier plans to include nationals from other countries were soon dropped. From their insignia they were known as "Circle C Cowboys," although the Germans usually referred to them as "potato bugs" because of their distinctive yellow, blue, and green insignia and uniform items.[18] As the situation in Germany improved, the U.S. Constabulary was gradually reduced in strength and ceased to exist in late 1952. This experience influenced the thinking of U.S. military planners for a possible operation in Palestine in 1948. They had envisaged a U.N. operation to restore law and order after the expiration of the British Mandate and planned to send constabulary forces as better suited than combat forces for missions involving police duties like crowd control.

Similar arrangements for enforcing the law and backing nascent indigenous police forces existed in other occupation zones of Germany and in Austria. In the context of our study on police operations, three points are important:

□ In "liberated" and "occupied" countries, the military had to take over administration and government functions which could only gradually be relegated to civilian and indigenous authorities as these became available or able to perform these tasks. In law enforcement, military units were employed successfully for backing indigenous police.

---

[17]Ibid, 339. I am also indebted to Dr. John T. Greenwood of the U.S. Army Center of Military History for making available to me two contemporary studies on the subject. *The United States Constabulary* (written in 1947 for the Occupation Forces in Europe Series, now listed under CMH 8-3.1, CA22 CI 1906, Center for Military History, U.S. Army War College, Carlisle Barracks, PA), and James M. Snyder, *The Establishment and Operations of the United States Constabulary: 3 October 1945-30 June 1947* (HQ, U.S. Constabulary, 1947).

[18]See David Colley, "Circle C Cowboys: Cold War Constabulary," *VFW* (June/July 1996): 20-23.

□ Civil affairs and constabulary duties required reliable, well-trained, and motivated personnel. A mature age usually proved an advantage.[19]

□ Good relations with the local population are essential. In Germany in 1945, harsh "retaliation" policies and non-fraternization rules made life and cooperation difficult for occupiers and occupied alike. A more conciliatory approach from the beginning would have facilitated an earlier transition to civilian control.[20]

This last item points to another source of experience analogous to peace missions: counterinsurgency operations. The military recognized quickly the importance of winning the population's "hearts and minds." Therefore, counterinsurgency operations (successful in Malaya, less so in Vietnam) and military administrations (such as in Germany after World War II) always included civilian and police functions.[21]

U.N. Experiences Before 1989

Traditional peacekeeping operations (or, as they should be called "truce-keeping" missions) usually have taken place in narrowly defined border zones and between conventional armed forces to prevent renewed war between states. A major contributing factor to their success has been the general absence of a local population in such areas. It is no coincidence that the more successful operations, like the U.N. forces and later the Multi-National Force and Observers (MFO) in

---

[19]Just as in U.N. peace operations decades later, a more mature age was considered an asset. As many civil affairs officers came from a civilian background, their average age was about 40. The acronym AMGOT—for "Allied Military Government of Occupied Territory"—was thought to stand for "Aged Military Gentlemen on Tour" (see Ziemke, *Occupation of Germany*, 64, 68).

[20]Ibid., 156-157, 160.

[21]An interesting study in this context was written by Joseph F. Coates for the Institute for Defense Analyses in May 1968: *The Police Function in Stability Operations*. See also the U.S. Army's Basic Field Manual 27-5, "Military Government," issued in 1940.

the Sinai, took place in deserts. Therefore, no need arose for policing activities. True, the first U.N. Emergency Force (UNEF), from 1956 to 1967, occasionally had to assist in law enforcement (mainly in the Gaza strip), but this still can be seen in the traditional military role of assisting civilian authorities.[22]

The next major U.N. operation, the ill-fated Opérations des Nations Unies au Congo (ONUC) of 1960-64 was on a totally different scale and much more like what are now called second- or third-generation (wider peacekeeping, peace enforcement) operations. A small police unit from Ghana was attached to the force in 1960. It operated in the capital, Léopoldville (now Kinshasa) but soon became enmeshed in the Congo's internal political confrontations and had to be withdrawn after a few months.[23]

The tasks of this first-ever U.N. police unit included assisting what was left of the Congolese police to maintain civil order. From this experience, the United Nations derived the lessons that "Local Police should be used where practicable, and should be organized if necessary in cadres with U.N. Police personnel."[24] U.N. military troops were also

---

[22]"Brief History of UNEF," part III, 1 and 5; also U.N. Archives: DAG-13/3.11.1.1, Box 6, file No. 7-2 (Ops) vol. 1; and the "Brief of UNEF Functions in the Gaza Strip" (U.N. Archives: DAG-13/3.11.0.0, Box 101, file LE 100); "Summary Study of the Experience Derived from the Establishment and Operation of the Force," Report of the Secretary-General to the General Assembly, A/3943, October 9, 1958, 9. To facilitate cooperation with the local police, UNEF readjusted its battalion boundaries to correspond with the administrative sub-districts of the Gaza strip (Ibid., 28).

[23]Simon Baynham, *The Military and Politics in Nkrumah's Ghana* (Boulder, CO: Westview, 1988), 93, 97, 103, note 44. For the political background, see also Olajide Alunko, *Ghana and Nigeria 1957-70: A Study in Inter-African Discord* (London: Rex Collings; New York: Harper & Row, 1976), 147-148, 154. Ernest W. Lefever, *Crisis in the Congo: A United Nations Force in Action* (Washington, DC: Brookings Institution, 1965), 58-59, mentions that Ghanaian and Guinean members of the U.N. operation were accused by the Kasavubu government of engaging in subversive activities, including an attempt on Kasavubu's life. While the police unit was completely withdrawn, the Ghanaian troops were moved away from the capital, to Kasai province.

[24]See U.N. Archives: DAG-1/2.2.1, Box 75, file U.N. Regulations & Briefing, especially the "General Principles and Methods" for internal security duties issued on August 2, 1960.

used for riot control but were neither trained nor equipped for such duties.

Eventually, a 400-member Nigerian police contingent was sent to the Congo after the withdrawal of the Ghana police, under a tripartite agreement among the United Nations, the Congo, and Nigeria. When the U.N. operation ended in mid-1964, Nigerian police stayed for another year, and "took on some of the duties performed by troops including security of lives and property of the United Nations personnel."[25] The bulk of the Nigerian police contingent was stationed in the capital Léopoldville, with small units in the provincial capitals of Bukavu, Luluabourg (now Kananga), and Stanleyville (now Kisangani). The Nigerians were withdrawn at the end of 1965—partly because Nigeria needed these police officers "in view of the troubled situation in Western Nigeria," and partly because the Congolese Government preferred to go ahead without foreign interference. The U.N. Representative in Léopoldville noted at the time that maintaining the police contingent was "a very costly affair."

The Congo debacle is fairly well known. Another operation of the early sixties, however, quickly faded from memory: The U.N. Temporary Executive Authority (UNTEA) administered West New Guinea (West Irian or West Papua, now Irian Jaya) for 8 months in 1962-63, during the handover of the territory from Dutch to Indonesian rule. The military component, referred to as the U.N. Security Forces (UNSF), was provided by Pakistan and was financed by the two countries involved (Indonesia and the Netherlands).

For law enforcement, the United Nations expected to rely on existing administrative and police structures, and a British officer was put in charge of the Papua police. However, because many Dutch police officers had left early, partly for fear of retaliation by the Indonesians, the United Nations became more involved in police functions than planned. As a U.N. official noted, some of the

---

[25]Because it was not part of the U.N. Force, the Nigerian police officers were not entitled to the U.N. Medal "In the Service of Peace." Osorio-Tafall to Bunche, Léopoldville, November 3, 1961 (U.N. Archives: DAG-1/2.2.1, Box 75, file Nigeria Police; see also file Nigerian Police Agreement).

remaining indigenous (Papua) police inspectors were "above their ceiling," and the United Nations had to recruit additional officers to keep the police force functioning.

> The U.N. Security Forces, whilst ensuring that no large-scale disorders are allowed to develop, can be no substitute for the civil police. If the [military] Security Forces are called upon to act, they will perform their task in a military manner, as they have been trained to do. What the public are entitled to look forward to, and entitled to demand, is that Police Stations throughout the country will continue to function.[26]

To appoint Indonesian officers would have been perceived as biased by the population and by the Papuan police. Thus Philippine police were brought in as a temporary measure. However, not all of them proved sufficiently qualified; a particular problem was their lack of ability to speak the Malay language.[27]

The term "CIVPOL" originated when the U.N. Peace-keeping Force in Cyprus (UNFICYP) was established in 1964. Although this is nowadays considered as a "classic" peacekeeping operation, before the Turkish invasion of 1974, UNFICYP was deployed all over the island to prevent renewed civil unrest between Greek and Turkish Cypriots. In February 1964, José Rolz-Bennett, U Thant's Special Representative (and U.N. Administrator in West New Guinea the year before) suggested including a military police element in the new force. However, U Thant's military adviser, Major-General Indar Jit Rikhye, pointed out that military police normally function only in support of the military.[28] Apparently, it was the force commander, Indian Lieutenant-

---

[26]Memorandum by Chief of Police J. C. Robertson, Hollandia, September 29, 1962 (U.N. Archives: DAG-13/2.1.0.0, Box 1, file ORG 100 [2]).

[27]A. H. Mackenzie to Coates, Manila, note dated October 11, 1962; and George J. Janecek to Robertson, Hollandia, note dated November 9, 1962 (U.N. Archives: DAG-13/2.1.0.0, Box 1, file ORG 100); also Administrator José Rolz-Bennett's reports of September 4, 1962, and December 5, 1963 (U.N. Archives: DAG-1/5.2.2.8, Box 1).

[28]Rikhye's memo to U Thant, February 21, 1964 (U.N. Archives: DAG-1/5.2.2.5.1, Box 1, file "U.N. Force in Cyprus").

General P.S. Gyani (who had been in charge of the Sinai operation for 5 years), who proposed a civilian police component instead. A small detachment of about 30 police officers for every district would be needed to support and supervise the local Cypriot police in order to reassure the population.[29]

It soon became clear that it was far more difficult than expected to find the necessary police officers. Unlike military forces, law enforcement agencies have a continuing peacetime mission, and few police forces, at least in Western countries, ever complain about surplus personnel. To send an existing unit would usually mean to denude a town or district of its police. Therefore, police officers, even from one country, usually are drawn from a wide array of police forces and have highly diverse backgrounds, ranging from small-town police through criminal investigation to elite units. While providing additional expertise, this sometimes creates communication problems, too. In addition, in some countries constitutional issues made it difficult to send police forces abroad. In countries like Australia and Canada, only federal police were eligible for foreign service; provincial police were excluded.[30] Eventually the U.N. civilian police component of UNFICYP (from then on referred to as UNCIVPOL or CIVPOL) became operational on April 14, 1964. By June, 173 civilian police officers had arrived: 40 Australians, 40 Danes, 40 Swedes, 33 Austrians, and 20 New Zealanders. Unlike later operations, civilian police in Cyprus operated as national units, with each contingent being assigned

---

[29]See José Rolz-Bennett's *aide-memoire* of April 13 (U.N. Archives: DAG-1/5/2/2/5/1, Box 1, file "U.N. Force in Cyprus"); George Stergiou Kaloudis, *The Role of the U.N. in Cyprus from 1964 to 1979* (American University Studies IX/107, New York: Peter Lang Publishing, Inc., 1991), 61. A study by Duncan Chappell and John Evans, "The Role, Preparation and Performance of Civilian Police in United Nations Peacekeeping Operations" (Vancouver, B.C.: The International Center for Criminal Law Reform and Criminal Justice Policy, 1997), 21, credits Irish Brigadier Sean McEown with the "invention" of UNCIVPOL, but I have not been able to substantiate this claim from the sources.

[30]At first, Australia and New Zealand refused to participate, citing constitutional problems in this context, while other countries hesitated. See Gen. Rikhye's notes for the files, April 9 and 10 (U.N. Archives: DAG-1/5.2.2.5.1, Box 1).

responsibility for one district. Sometimes officers were exchanged between contingents on a voluntary basis to share experiences and standardize procedures.

The mission of the U.N. police was to establish liaison with the Cypriot police, accompany local police patrols, and monitor checkpoints. Their tasks included "manning United Nations police points in certain sensitive areas . . . where tension exists and might be alleviated by the presence of UNFICYP police elements," as well as "investigating incidents where Greek or Turkish Cypriots are involved with the opposite community."[31] U.N. police officers cooperated with the local police "at grass-roots level," and helped to stabilize the situation—a crucial contribution in an atmosphere like the one in Cyprus where even "ordinary" criminal activities were perceived as part of the ethnic conflict.[32] Also among their functions were investigating cases of missing persons (a major cause for mistrust between the communities) and helping with refugee relief work. The police were organized under the force commander's civilian staff, headed by his police adviser.

The military credited the U.N. police with defusing tension at a very low level. For emergencies, a "quick reaction force" was established at UNFICYP headquarters. According to one Austrian officer, the U.N. police soon became the population's "father-confessor and confidant in one person."[33] With the Turkish invasion and partition of the island in 1974, the character of the U.N. operation changed. In due course, the civilian police component was reduced (currently only 20 Australian and 15 Irish police officers serve in the Cyprus operation).[34]

---

[31]Secretary-General's instructions (U.N. Document S/5679); "History of UNFICYP," 91 (U.N. Archives: DAG-22/Finding Aid).

[32]See Galo-Plaza's comments in the troop-contributing countries meeting of July 23 (Protocol: U.N. Archives: DAG-1/5.2.2.5.1, Box 1).

[33]The experiences of Col. Erich Bäumel as well as of several other Austrian police officers are included in the commemorative booklet edited by Gerald Hesztera, *30 Jahre Polizei-Kontingente im U.N.-Einsatz* (Vienna: BMI, 1994), 10-18. I am indebted to Gerald Hesztera for numerous comments and suggestions over the past years.

[34]U.N. DPKO: Monthly Summary of Troop Contributors as of August 31, 1997. The New Zealand contingent already left in 1967, and the Austrians 10 years later.

Because of the international situation of the seventies and eighties, no new police operations were undertaken by the United Nations. All new missions were either observer or troop-separation operations relating to interstate conflict where there was no need for police monitors. In only one peace operation undertaken outside the U.N. context were police observers employed for a short time: to supervise the transition of Zimbabwe-Rhodesia (the former British colony of South Rhodesia) to independence and majority rule, a 1,500-strong Commonwealth Monitoring Force was deployed from December 1979 through April 1980. In addition, 300 unarmed British police observed the voting stations.

It was only in 1989 that the end of the Cold War led to a new era of U.N. operations in general, and police missions in particular. The operation in South-West Africa/Namibia in 1989-90 is now generally considered the first of the post-Cold War peace operations which included a significant police element.

Military Involvement in Institution Building

When George K. Tanham wrote about the U.S. efforts at nation building in Vietnam in the sixties, he noted, "Strange as it may seem, the military victory is the easiest part of the struggle. After this has been attained, the real challenge begins: the re-establishment of a secure environment opens a new opportunity for nation building."[35] Only after a peace operation succeeds in establishing a stable environment, can the various humanitarian and other efforts hope to achieve a lasting effect.

The tendency to limit a military intervention to a short-term restoration of a "stable environment" is an obvious consequence of the desire, even the urgent need, of western governments to reduce long-term commitments of personnel and resources to a minimum. While an apparently "stable environment" might last as long as intervention forces are present, it might crumble just as easily after the withdrawal.

---

[35]George K. Tanham, *War Without Guns: American Civilians in Rural Vietnam* (New York: Praeger, 1966), 138.

The more successful the international community can be in the restoration of indigenous law enforcement capabilities within an acceptable legal-judicial-penal system, the greater the chance that the conflict will not resurface and therefore that a similar intervention will not be required in the future.

Rebuilding a country structure is a long-term task where both military and police have their proper roles. The equation "peace = order + justice" neatly describes the necessary balance between the various components of society.[36] Whereas the military provides the "order" part of the equation, working police and judiciary systems are needed to guarantee "justice." Likewise, civilian police can never substitute for a military presence if the latter is necessary to guarantee a stable environment or act as a deterrence force.[37] In the words of Colonel Larry M. Forster, the director of the U.S. Army Peacekeeping Institute, the macro- and microlevels of security (represented by military and police components, respectively) are interactive, and both are necessary for the success of an operation as a whole.[38]

A major reason for the reluctance of the military—especially the U.S. Armed Forces—to become embroiled in any long-term nation-building tasks goes back to the Vietnam experience, where U.S. military assistance efforts led within a few years to a major conflict, ending in defeat for the South Vietnamese Government (and the United States). To some extent, this undermined the confidence of the U.S. Armed

---

[36]I am grateful to Colonel Steven Rader for mentioning this equation to me, which he heard from Major General Mark Hamilton on the U.S. Joint Staff. Of course, in the case of a transitional arrangement, the party or parties favoring the status quo ante bellum will focus their demands on the "order" variable in the equation, while their opponents will want "justice" as a first priority. To find the right balance (taking into account the demands of nongovernmental organizations (NGOs) and human rights groups back home) is a challenging task indeed for the peacekeepers!

[37]One of the best studies illustrating this is Jarat Chopra, Age Eknes, and Toralv Nordbo, *Fighting for Hope in Somalia* (Peacekeeping and Multinational Operations 6, Oslo: Norsk Utenrikspolitisk Institutt, 1995).

[38]Colonel Forster made this comment at the NDU workshop on Police in Peace Operations in August 1996. I appreciate his comments on the draft version of this paper.

Forces in their own abilities, as well as in their civilian political leadership at the time, who were blamed for making them fight this war "with one hand tied behind their backs" and engaging in quasi-military activities instead of using all their resources to defeat the North Vietnamese militarily. The U.S. military is geared to achieve victory quickly, with overwhelming force, with as few friendly casualties as possible, in order to free manpower and resources for the next task ahead. In contrast, policing, internal security, or nation-building missions imply a long-term commitment.

Tailoring the Mission to the Task

The lower the host country's capabilities to maintain law and order, the greater the need for intervention forces to fill the institutional gap. Whereas a military intervention can be deployed in a brief time, re-building law enforcement and other local institutions takes much longer (see the Conceptual Framework chart in the Introduction).

The public security role of the international community can be interpreted as providing assistance in training and reorganizing indigenous police forces while maintaining a military and/or police presence. This involvement needs to be carefully adjusted to local conditions. A strong, intrusive intervention may be necessary in certain circumstances, even if it leads to clashes with local forces. However, a major problem can emerge if a strong and dominant intervention hinders local efforts at self-governance. Conversely, a peace operation that lacks the will to address dangerous security conditions may create a vacuum in which those opposed to peace can thrive, either disrupting the ongoing operation or waiting for it to leave before unleashing violence.

One ultimate aim of an international intervention should be to improve local capabilities of self-government. Thus, the level of intervention should be reduced gradually in response to local improvement. From the beginning—this has been a lesson from practically all operations—emphasis must be placed on fostering, reforming, or re-establishing existing structures, including local security and law enforcement institutions. This is also necessary to relieve intervention forces as quickly as possible from policing tasks.[39]

Many peace operations take place after civil wars, insurgencies, or the collapse of oppressive regimes. Existing police forces are often associated with one side of the conflict, or they may simply leave their posts. Paradoxically, in counterinsurgencies military forces tend to become more "police-oriented," because their "enemy" is not a conventional military force, while police forces tend to adopt more "military" attitudes, as their tasks go beyond conventional law enforcement. Effectively, both adopt rather "paramilitary" features. At the end of the insurgency, police forces usually have to be reorganized and "reduced" to their original policing mission. A recent example was the reform of the South African Police—a crucial issue in that country's peace process.

Retraining and rehabilitation are absolute necessities in order to prevent demobilized soldiers and police from being attracted to criminal activities to earn their living. At the same time, separation of internal security from national defense functions is usually considered a prerequisite for a working civil-military relationship.[40]

Police cannot function without the support of a working and humane judicial and prison system. Efforts at re-establishing local police forces must go hand in hand with reforms in other sectors as well. Only then can a lasting effect be achieved. Again, this is by no means new. When the European powers (Austria-Hungary, France, Germany, Italy, Russia, and the United Kingdom) intervened to stabilize trouble spots in the crumbling Ottoman Empire before the First World War, on the island of Crete in 1897, and in Albania in 1913,

---

[39]For an excellent assessment of these problems—and the role the military can play in achieving a long-term solution—see William Rosenau, "Peace Operations, Emergency Law Enforcement, and Constabulary Forces," in *Peace Operations: Developing an American Strategy,* eds. Antonia Handler Chayes and George T. Raach (Washington, DC: National Defense University Press, 1995), 115-135.

[40]William Stanley and Charles T. Call, "Building a New Civilian Police Force in El Salvador," in *Rebuilding Societies After Civil War: Critical Roles for International Assistance,* ed. Krishna Kumar (Boulder, CO: Lynne Rienner, 1997), 107-133.

they created international commissions responsible for law and justice, as well as new police forces.[41]

Conclusions

Looking at the lessons learned from previous experiences—in peace operations and otherwise—the following principles can be derived:

☐ Only the military—always "ultima ratio regum"—has the necessary capacities to fill the initial security gap in unstable situations where indigenous security forces and institutions are unable to function or insufficient to maintain law and order.[42] The delay in fielding a cadre of international police monitors to begin alleviating this burden invariably results in a "deployment gap."

☐ The military is not well adapted to and prefers to avoid civilian police functions, which typically produces an "enforcement gap," during the conduct of the peace operation.

☐ The capabilities of the U.N. civilian police do not go much beyond traditional monitoring, training, or advisory tasks, only occasionally taking on executive functions. While this can improve security conditions considerably, it cannot substitute for law enforcement, when these capabilities are completely lacking in the host country ("the failed state" scenario). Few countries have military police capabilities comparable to the U.S. In most armies,

---

[41]Following the intervention by the European Powers in Crete, the commanding admirals established a proper court system in August 1897, while foreign consuls had a right of appeal. Italian law was used. Likewise, the Powers formed a new police force, after attempts to reorganize the existing *gendarmerie* under international officers failed. International officers were also employed in other Ottoman provinces. When Albania became independent in 1913, the new *gendarmerie* organized by the Powers was to be led by Dutch officers, some of whom had previous colonial police experience in the Dutch East Indies. See my article, "Im Land der Skipctaren: Die internationale Friedensoperation in Albanien 1913-1914," in Österreichische Militärische Zeitschrift 35, no. 4 (July/August 1997): 431-440.

[42]These issues were discussed in depth in a workshop at the National Defense University in Washington, DC, in August 1996.

military police or provost marshal units only fulfil police functions within the military. Although police forces like the Royal Canadian Mounted Police, French or Austrian gendarmerie, and Italian carabinieri were originally formed in the 19th century to fill similar "security gaps," they are now a police rather than a paramilitary force, given the different conditions prevailing in their home countries now compared to the period of their establishment. Therefore, they cannot be automatically expected to be used in a paramilitary role in peace operations.

□   Efforts at re-establishing a stable and secure environment are never short-term tasks, however, there must be a functioning legal system in order to withdraw without a return to the lawlessness and violence which caused their intervention. This is the essence of the "institutional gap."

□   These issues became more evident in the operations after 1989, and will be discussed in more detail in the following pages.

PANAMA:
Operation *Just Cause*

ANTHONY GRAY and MAXWELL MANWARING

Background

Situation that Precipitated *Just Cause*

Unlike other cases included in this comparative study, the intervention in Panama was not a peacekeeping operation. It was a unilateral U.S. intervention in a country where U.S. presence and influence were overwhelming and cultural, social, and economic ties to the United States were inextricable. The lessons that emerged from this operation (as well as from the Somalia action) were to significantly influence the planning of the operation in Haiti.

Operation *Just Cause* was the culmination of a 2½-year effort to remove General Manual Noriega, Commander of the Panama Defense Force (PDF) and de-facto ruler, from power after his indictment in the United States on drug-trafficking charges. U.S. efforts to negotiate Noriega out of power had failed by May 1988. Ongoing economic sanctions only hurt the country and were difficult to enforce (in view of the large U.S. presence). As the crisis progressed, the U.S. military presence steadily increased, as did efforts to pressure the PDF through no-notice exercises and testing of check points. Although a political opposition was slowly coalescing, two coup attempts by the PDF and massive public demonstrations failed to unseat Noriega.

Authors' note: This case study is based upon personal experiences of the authors, interviews with numerous other participants, from both the Washington level and the field, as well as from written accounts. Opinions and accounts vary, a classic case of "where you stand depends upon where you sit."

Events precipitating the U.S. intervention in 1989 included:

☐ A "school bus incident" of March 3 involving the children of U.S. personnel; several low-key PDF incursions onto U.S. installations including the Arraijan fuel tank farm, and periodic shooting incidents at the Jungle Operations Training Center (JOTC)

☐ Nullification of the May 1989 election of President Guellermo Endara, and Vice Presidents Arias Calderon and Billy Ford

☐ The subsequent highly publicized beating of Vice President-elect Ford

☐ A virtual declaration of war against the United States by Noriega on December 15

☐ The brutalizing of a U.S. Navy lieutenant and threats and assaults on his wife, and the killing of Marine Lieutenant Robert Paz on December 16, 1989.[1]

Capacity for Self-Governance

At the time of the intervention, Panama was a self-governing country with functioning bureaucracy, police, judicial, and prison systems. Although it had the trappings of a constitutional democracy until the May 1989 election results were nullified, it was a de facto dictatorship under the control of General Noriega and his PDF. All semblance of democracy disappeared after Noreiga nullified the results of the elections and appointed a President. Despite various economic, political, and social disruptions, including U.S. economic sanctions, Panamanian government institutions continued to function.

Strength of Armed Opposition Groups. The PDF maintained close control throughout the country. The large-scale public opposition or "civil crusade" mounted many demonstrations in Panama City but had no armed capability (see discussion of PDF capabilities for insurgency below).

---

[1] Participant observation; also noted in John T. Fishel, *The Fog of Peace: Planning and Executing the Restoration of Panama* (Carlisle, PA: Strategic Studies Institute, 1992), 1-6.

Condition of Economy and Infrastructure. To keep his government afloat, Noriega exacerbated Panama's already serious financial problems and plunged the country deeper into debt. At the time of the invasion, total government debt was approximately $5 billion; the unemployment rate was about 25 percent; the nation had lost over 2 years of foreign and domestic investment; the international banking sector had suffered severe damage; the number of merchant vessels registered in Panama had declined; and hundreds of businesses had been forced into bankruptcy. Systematic looting of the economy by Noriega and his cronies exacerbated the situation. By 1989, the central government finances had dropped almost by half over the previous 2 years to $598 million.[2]

Extent of Social Disruption. Because of devastation to Panama's economy and U.S. attempts to split the Panamanian public and PDF from Noriega, long-existing class and racial divisions were exacerbated. Traditional norms of political behavior, which had made Panama a relatively nonviolent society, were attenuated. This was manifested in Noriega's creation of "dignity battalions" and the brutality they inflicted. The prolonged crisis created an atmosphere of fear, suspicion, and hatred that could require many years to repair.[3]

Status of Domestic and Public Security Apparatus

PDF Capabilities. Panama's institutions were either tools of the Noriega dictatorship, or they were neglected and dysfunctional. In the decades prior to the U.S. invasion of December 1989, the Panamanian National Guard and its successor, the PDF, had become the main vehicle for power and repression in Panama. The PDF was an amalgamation of the National Guard, the Air Force, the Naval Force, the Canal Defense Force, the Police Force, the Traffic Department, the

---

[2]Congress, Senate and House, *Country Reports on Economic Policy and Trade Practices.* Report submitted to the Committee on Foreign Relations, Committee on Finance of the U.S. Senate and the Committee on Foreign Affairs, Committee on Ways and Means, House of Representatives, by the Department of State. Joint Committee Print, February 1990, 101st Cong., 2d sess.

[3]Ibid.

43

Department of Investigation, and the Immigration Department.[4] In addition to having the capability to control the populace, the PDF was also able to conduct sabotage and stand-off attacks against the Canal and U.S. military installations (such as Quarry Heights, Fort Clayton, Howard Air Force Base, Albrook Air Force Base, and the U.S. Naval Station at Rodman). Confronted by a more powerful intervention force, the PDF planned to retreat into the mountains and jungles of the interior and conduct prolonged guerrilla warfare. At the time of the U.S. intervention, the PDF contained 19 companies and six platoons, numbering some 8,000 men, at least 3,500 of whom were well trained and equipped for combat. Among the major items in their inventory were 29 armored personnel carriers, 12 patrol craft, and 28 light transport aircraft.[5]

During 1988 and 1989, after the termination of security assistance and the imposition of sanctions by the United States, Noriega turned to Cuba, Nicaragua, and Libya for economic and military assistance. Cuba and Nicaragua funneled Communist-bloc weapons and instructors to Noriega and helped develop civilian defense committees (i.e., "Dignity Battalions") for intelligence collection and population control. Libya contributed $20 million in 1989 in return for permission to use Panama as a base to coordinate terrorist and insurgent groups activities throughout Latin America.[6]

Although the PDF was occupied heavily with maintaining civil order and responding to U.S. military efforts to throw it off balance, it continued to function as a police force. By December 1989 the PDF had been on high alert for an extended period. Panama was "not a country with an army, but an army with a country."[7]

---

[4]Richard H. Schultz, Jr., *In the Aftermath of War: U.S. Support for Reconsturction and Nation-Building in Panama Following Just Cause* (Maxwell AFB, AL: Air University Press, 1993), 9.

[5]Ronald H. Cole, *Operation Just Cause: The Planning and Execution of Joint Operations in Panama, February 1988-January 1990* (Washington, DC: Joint History Office, Office of the Chairman of the Joint Chiefs of Staff, 1995), 6-7.

[6]Ibid.

[7]David Adams, journalist, telephone interview by Manwaring, October 18, 1996.

The PDF as an Institution. The PDF was clearly understood to be corrupt. Many of its officers and enlisted personnel were involved in outside business activities, legal and illegal, including drug trafficking. Getting a "turn at the trough" was a method of reward and control. (The PDF itself was a "fee for service" organization. Low pay was supplemented by these rewards.) Along with a reputation for general ruthlessness, the PDF was regarded as an organization that could "get things done, when appropriately motivated," whereas the relatively inefficient civilian bureaucracy could not. This gave Noriega a certain leverage vis-a-vis the U.S. military. The PDF was viewed by many in the lower strata of society as the organization that looked after their welfare and could provide meaningful upward social mobility. Additionally, the business community in general worked accommodations with it, and some prominent business leaders had relatives who became PDF officers.[8]

Condition of the Judicial and Prison Systems. The legal, judicial, and penal systems during the Noriega regime were badly corrupted. Prisoners might languish in jail for months and sometimes literally 3, 4, or 5 years without even a hearing. Jails were crowded, unsanitary, and violent. Any amenities had to be provided by the prisoner's family or friends. The legal system dispensed political control rather than justice. The impact upon the individual depended entirely on the nature of the relationship with Noriega and the PDF.[9]

Planning and Resources

The "Noriega crisis" extended from June 1987, when Noriega was implicated in the murder of prominent Panamanian politician Hugo Spadafora,[10] until the implementation of *Just Cause* in December 1989

---

[8]Interviews by authors; some interviews were conducted with individuals who wish to remain anonymous.

[9]Kaiser Bazzan, telephone interview by Manwaring, October 18, 1996.

[10]Spadafora was a prominent political figure who had fallen out of favor with Noriega and was apprehended, brutally tortured, and beheaded by members of the PDF as he was returning to Panama from Costa Rica.

and spanned portions of two U.S. administrations. Several key players changed with the advent of the Bush administration, as did the Chairmanship of the Joint Chiefs of Staff in September 1989. Many players were also preoccupied by their involvement in the Central American conflicts and the Iran-Contra investigations, and there were different views and objectives being pursued by different agencies. Consequently, from the perspective of those in the field, the planning process had the appearance of being driven by political circumstances "inside the beltway" rather than a clear set of objectives.

Although there was early agreement (summer 1987) that Noriega had to go, there was considerable disagreement about how to depose him. Any lingering doubt about Noriega staying in power was dispelled in February 1988 when he was indicted by the U.S. Justice Department on drug trafficking charges. Any hope that the opposition-instigated "civil crusade" could get rid of Noriega was dispelled on February 25 when President Eric Arturo Delvalle attempted to publicly fire Noriega. In response, Noriega named Solis Palma as Delvalle's successor. The "civil crusade" lacked strong U.S. support and did nothing in response to these events. The U.S. Government continued to recognize Delvalle as the President of Panama and granted him safe haven in the United States, along with a steady flow of political refugees.

In March 1988, a coup attempt gave hope that the PDF could jettison Noriega while preserving itself as an institution. Throughout the crisis there were varying degrees of pressure from some quarters for the United States to take military action. This was resisted by the U.S. Department of Defense. Security assistance was cut off and economic sanctions imposed. A variety of other schemes for ousting Noriega were also examined by the U.S. interagency process. Discussions with exile groups in 1988 and 1989, designed to give the opposition encouragement, probably detracted from a focused U.S. policy, since this raised unrealistic expectations that Noriega could be removed without direct U.S. intervention. In addition, the U.S. Presidential election campaign was at least partly responsible for the apparent void in policy action during the summer and fall 1988.

During 1987-88, the Reagan administration's Panama policy was also hampered by persistent press leaks. The Bush administration handled this problem after January 1989 by placing interagency access to Panama policy matters on a highly restricted basis. While options continued to be examined and economic sanctions remained in place, one objective remained constant: to split Noriega from the PDF. The administration continued to hope that he could be removed without direct U.S. action. This effort intensified significantly in 1989. The U.S. Southern Command (SOUTHCOM) forces began aggressively exercising treaty rights of free passage through Panama by such actions as ignoring road blocks, conducting short-notice "Category Three" exercises and keeping maximum pressure on the PDF, while at the same time complying with the Panama Canal Treaties in order to maintain the legal high ground. U.S. security forces in Panama were steadily increased, the number of personnel living off base was reduced, and dependents were encouraged to return to the United States.

Contingency planning for military intervention began with a Joint Chiefs of Staff (JCS) Planning Order dated February 28, 1988. Known initially as *Elaborate Maze*, it included four major components which could be implemented concurrently or in sequence:

- ☐ Buildup of U.S. combat forces
- ☐ Noncombat evacuation operations
- ☐ Combat operations
- ☐ Restoration of the Panamanian Government and state services in wake of combat operations against the PDF.[11]

In response to the planning order during the first half of 1988, General Fred F. Woerner, Jr., U.S. Commander-in-Chief, Southern Command (USCINCSO) forwarded his plan (code named *Fissures*) to the Joint Chiefs. After receiving no response, Woerner updated *Fissures* on his own initiative, calling it *Fissures II*. The update called for coordinated interagency political-military efforts to split Noriega from the PDF rank and file and the civilian leadership of the regime, resulting

---

[11]Former SOUTHCOM staff officers, interview by authors.

in an internal resolution of the Noriega problem. At the time Woerner forwarded *Fissures II*, he stated it was an integrated, holistic plan that could not be executed piecemeal.

General Woerner was subsequently instructed to execute the plan in individual pieces.[12] Accordingly, *Elaborate Maze/Fissures* was changed to a family of plans later called *Prayerbook*. *Blue Spoon* became the plan for combat operations, and *Krystal Ball*, completed in August 1988, became the plan to provide public security and to restore civilian government in the event combat operations became necessary. Woerner had been told by the President that he did not want to intervene in Panama directly. Combat and postcombat planning was thus considered more an exercise, directed by prudence rather than an immediate requirement. Thus *Krystal Ball* was never discussed with the State Department. The individual plans comprising *Prayerbook* were subsequently put "back on the shelf."[13]

On March 3, 1989, *Prayerbook* came off the shelf. The incident that precipitated this action was the so-called "school bus crisis." On that date, the PDF seized 21 U.S. school buses with children of U.S. military and civilian personnel aboard. U.S. Military Police reacted strongly and the incident was defused within a few hours. However, the incident had a profound effect on the resident U.S. community. A "siege mentality" set in, and calls and letters flooded into U.S. congressional offices asking that something be done to get rid of the oppressive, and now threatening, Noriega regime.[14] *Krystal Ball*, the civil-military operations part of *Prayerbook*, was renamed *Blind Logic* and sent forward to JCS with no recommendations for change.[15]

On May 10, 1989, *Blue Spoon*, the plan for combat operations, became a more serious proposition. The incident that precipitated this was the specter of vice-presidential candidate Ford being brutally beaten by Noriega hoodlums on live TV after the Panamanian elections

---

[12]General Fred F. Woerner, Jr., fomer Commander in Chief, U.S. Southern Command, telephone interview by Manwaring, October 16, 1996.

[13]Woerner and unnamed sources, interviews.

[14]Participant observation.

[15]Woerner and unnamed sources, interviews.

of May 7. The outcome had gone against Noriega, and he had the results nullified. The image of Ford being beaten and bloodied caused revulsion against Noriega not only in Panama but throughout the world.[16]

As part of *Blue Spoon*, a Joint Task Force (JTF) under the XVIII Airborne Corps was established. SOUTHCOM planners assumed that XVIII Airborne Corps would operate in parallel with them and incorporate *Blind Logic*, the civil affairs/public security plan, into their operations planning. However, the XVIII Airborne Corps JTF did not consider that there were any taskings for them in *Blind Logic* and did not perceive *Blind Logic* as an approved plan.[17] In fact, *Blind Logic* had never been approved by the Joint Chiefs.

The Mission

Execution of *Just Cause*
By the time General Powell assumed Chairmanship of the JCS and General Maxwell Thurman assumed command of SOUTHCOM at the end of September 1989, a great deal of planning had already been done. On the basis of this planning, President Bush set four objectives for *Just Cause* on the eve of the invasion:

- Protect American lives
- Ensure implementation of the Panama Canal Treaties
- Bring Noriega to justice
- Restore Panamanian democracy.[18]

The maintenance of public security was a secondary consideration for the overall military operation. To accomplish the President's objectives, however, it would need to be an integral part of restoring democracy. In fact, maintaining public security became a key concern

---

[16]Woerner, Adams, and unnamed sources, interviews; Berta Thayer, journalist, telephone interview by Manwaring, October 21, 1996.

[17]Unnamed sources, interviews, and Fishel.

[18]Fishel, 4.

much earlier than anticipated as a result of widespread looting shortly after the intervention took place.

A sense of urgency came about on October 3, 1989. A coup attempt instigated by PDF Major Moises Giroldi failed, and Giroldi was summarily executed. Ironically, the strategy of trying to separate Noriega from the PDF had worked, but the tactic failed. The United States did not support the coup attempt, and Noriega arrested opposition elements within the PDF. It then became obvious that U.S. military intervention would be required, probably in response to some "threshold event," and revising *Blue Spoon* began in earnest under General Thurman. This took place on two levels—at SOUTHCOM and at the Joint Task Force (JTF)-South component of the XVIII Airborne Corps.[19] The new version of *Blue Spoon* was published at the end of October 1989. Important changes included streamlining command and control by putting all executing elements under JTF-South; shifting combat focus from the center of Panama City to outlying areas which left the U.S. troop presence in the city at a minimum; ignoring the possibility of a public security vacuum and; and placing responsibility for restoration of Panamanian Government functions on U.S. Army South (USARSO) (Major General Cisneros). This latter provision, however, was not properly coordinated.[20]

Leading up to *Just Cause*, the SOUTHCOM J-5, BG Benard Gann, repeatedly tried to present *Blind Logic* to General Thurman; however Thurman's total focus was on planning for hostilities, not posthostilities.[21]

On December 16, 1989, Lt. Paz was killed, and on 17 December President Bush gave the order to execute *Blue Spoon* as Operation *Just Cause*. On the evening of December 19, President Endara and his two vice presidents were sworn into office, and early on December 20, U.S. combat operations against the PDF were in full swing.

---

[19]Unnamed sources, interviews.

[20]Unnamed sources, interviews, and Fishel, 27-28.

[21]Rear Admiral David Chandler (U.S. Navy, Ret.), former Deputy Commander in Chief, U.S. Southern Command, interview by Manwaring, September 24, 1996, Washington, DC.

Although military police were deployed with the 82nd Airborne Division at the outset, planners for *Blue Spoon/Just Cause* had failed to foresee the collapse of the PDF and the resultant need for public security operations.[22] The consequence was seen in looting that took place mostly in Panama City and Colon[23] where the destruction of the PDF left no local police force.[24] The intervention did leave the interior of the country largely unscathed, and the PDF continued to operate there and maintain law and order.[25] In the cities, rules of engagement in force for U.S. military personnel were adequate to avoid a possible bloodbath, but U.S. forces would not shoot looters.

Within the first 2 days of combat operations, looting broke out in the center of Panama City and continued for the next three to four days.[26] As a result of the urgent need to restore order and resume basic government services, *Blind Logic*, the civil-military operations plan, underwent a crash update, was approved by General Thurman and sent to JCS for approval as Operation *Promote Liberty*.[27]

On December 20, Thurman directed BG Gann to move his entire organization to the Panamanian Legislative Assembly building and assist the new Endara government (which consisted of Endara and his two Vice Presidents). The next day *Promote Liberty* was approved by the JCS, and Gann became COMCMOTF (Commander, Civil-Military Operations Task Force) and began to execute the plan for restoration of civil government and public security to Panama. As COMCMOTF, Gann was placed by Thurman under the operational control of the U.S. Charge d'Affairs, John Bushnell.[28] General Thurman also ordered that COMCMOTF personnel be combined with the active duty 96th Civil Affairs (CA) Battalion, expected to arrive on December 22, and 300

---

[22]Had planners anticipated this eventuality, they could have adjusted troop lists and the air movement plan to provide for the early arrival of a critical reserve CA cell, active duty CA personnel and still more MP elements

[23]Woerner, interview, and Fishel, 24.

[24]Participant observation.

[25]Fishel.

[26]Participant observation.

[27]Unnamed sources, interviews; Fishel, 33; Cole, 53.

[28]Unnamed sources, interviews, and Fishel.

reservists who would follow over the next 3 weeks.[29] Because of a misunderstanding of the role that CA personnel were to play, there was initially some resistance within the interagency to this deployment. Some believed that CA personnel would be viewed as "political commissars" directing the Government of Panama instead of facilitating the restoration of essential services.[30]

The looting and chaos were ended when sufficient U.S. infantry and MP forces were brought into the situation to discharge the public security function without excessive use of force. From December 20-25, COMCMOTF worked nonstop to establish security, restore services, assist in the organization of the new government, and coordinate activities of U.S. Government and nongovernment agencies.

Implementation of *Promote Liberty*

The first phase of *Promote Liberty* concentrated on public safety, health, and population control measures. Later, the U.S. country team and the new Panamanian Government took responsibility for civil control, rebuilding commerce, winning the support of the people for reforms, and restructuring the PDF into separate police, customs, and defense organizations.[31]

Restoration of civil government and public order did not get off to a good start. The PDF had been destroyed, and there was no Panamanian entity to replace it. Neither Washington nor JTF-South had contemplated the disappearance of the PDF, counting instead upon a coup by the PDF. Nor was the public chaos problem planned for; no military consultations or coordination had taken place with appropriate U.S. civilian agencies in this regard.[32] Furthermore, *Blind Logic* planners did not address what kind of security force would replace the PDF, since it was predicated upon the assumption of a PDF coup ousting Noriega.[33] In consultation with U.S. authorities, the

---

[29]Cole, 52-53.

[30]Author Gray recollection of events.

[31]Cole, 53.

[32]Unnamed sources, interviews.

[33]Schultz, 45.

Government of Panama (GOP) had determined that a standing army was unnecessary. Lacking other options, the GOP decided to replace it with a police force made up of members of the defunct PDF, after screening out undesirables.[34]

There were several factors that contributed to this lack of focus on civil affairs. Among these were disagreement between the Operations (J-3) and Policy (J-5) SOUTHCOM; lack of an ambassador on scene (Ambassador Dean Hinton arrived a couple of weeks later); lack of interagency focus on this issue; and no political adviser on station at SOUTHCOM. Nevertheless, General Thurman took full responsibility for this oversight and in subsequent years cited it as the greatest mistake in his military career.[35]

As of December 22, four Brigade Task Forces from the 82nd Airborne had been assigned to clear Panama City of hostiles (i.e., Dignity Battalions), enforce a curfew, stop chaos and looting, and assume temporary law enforcement functions. The 82nd Airborne and 193rd Infantry Brigade elements in Panama City were reinforced by additional MP companies. As the former cleared designated zones, the MPs would take over, man the old PDF posts, and undertake active patrols. The presence of the MPs and withdrawal of combat forces had a calming effect upon the population, law and order was restored, and relatively normal activity resumed.[36]

It was not until mid-January 1990 that General Thurman brought command and control of all SOUTHCOM and JTF-SOUTH organizations involved with the civil-military operation under the overall control of Military Support Group—Panama (MSG). At this point the public security mission was being performed on a more routine basis.[37]

To get the United States out of an apparent "occupation" role, three conditions had to be met. First, the Panamanian Government had to place enough police on the streets to undertake joint patrols

---

[34]Ibid.

[35]RADM Chandler interview, and observation of a close friend of Gen. Thurman.

[36]Colonel David Patton, U.S. Army 82nd Airborne Provost Marshall, interview by authors, January 1997, Washington, DC.

[37]Participant observation; unnamed sources, interviews; and Fishel, 34.

with U.S. forces. This required a quick, ad hoc reconstitution of the old PDF into a new Panamanian National Police (PNP). Second, some sort of court/magistrate/judicial system had to be re-established (e.g., the old night-court system). Finally, the penal system had to be reopened. This required a massive reconstruction of old jails and prisons after the looting and destruction in the aftermath of *Just Cause*. This process took several weeks.[38]

Once the decision had been made by General Thurman to implement *Promote Liberty*, Major General Marc Cisneros, Commander ARSO, set up a U.S. Force Liaison Group (USFLG) to advise, train, and equip the new police.[39] A Military Support Group (MSG) became operational on January 17, 1990 and was given the mission of police training. Initially this was conducted by the 18th Airborne Corps' 16th Military Police Brigade. [40] A Judicial Liaison Group (JLG) was also established to advise/assist the Panamanians. This was an ad hoc military response on the ground to an unanticipated situation.

The initiatives instigated by MG Cisneros using ARSO resources got the PNP on the streets, the night-court system operating, and the jails and prisons functioning.[41] Situations not foreseen in *Blind Logic* or not provided for in guidance from Washington were dealt with ad hoc.[42] The establishment of the MSG was the logical extension of *Blind Logic* and the ad hoc effort to institutionalize civil-military operations in Panama prior to the official end of hostilities on January 31, 1990.

Problems arose for the MSG, however, with congressional passage of the "Urgent Assistance Act for Panama of 1990" on February 14. In addition to providing a much needed $43.7M in emergency assistance, it reaffirmed the prohibition on police training by the U.S. military contained in Section 660 of the Foreign Assistance Act. The Act did, however, permit use of residual security assistance funds to

---

[38]Ibid.

[39]Schultz, 29.

[40]Ibid., 46.

[41]Unnamed sources, interviews; Fishel, 36-38.

[42]Participant observation and unnamed sources, interviews.

equip the police force. Negotiations with Congress during January and early February for this legislation were unsuccessful in producing a change in the Section 660 prohibition on police training, in part because the Administration did not foresee the importance of such a change, and in part because the need was not apparent to Congress. However, they did provide authority and limited funding for the Justice Department International Criminal Investigative Training Assistance Program (ICITAP) to train Panamanian police. In addressing the immediate security problem, however, DOD found itself conducting at least what appeared to be police training in violation of the law and took immediate steps to remedy the situation.

Coordination and Cooperation

From a bureaucratic standpoint it became clear to the Department of Defense (DOD) that responsibility for police training should rest with ICITAP, and the general tone of the interagency discussions on policing training reflected "over to you ICITAP." Although ICITAP representatives accepted this responsibility, it was a task for which they had no experience and little capability. ICITAP would eventually do the job, but time was required to respond effectively. One ICITAP official described the task as comparable to standing up a civilian police force in Japan after World War II.[43] This delay presented military forces with several problems.

First, ICITAP, although given the mission to train the PNP and Judicial Technical Police, had no programs or personnel for this purpose, and, therefore, was not immediately able to assemble an adequate training program. During this void, U.S. military personnel, under control of the MSG, carried out patrols and in the process "advised" and acted as "monitors" of training and served as "examples" for the PNP.[44] They also participated in joint patrols, thereby providing the population "with a sense of security."[45] Defense

---

[43]Gray, recollection of discussions.
[44]Participant observation and unnamed sources, interviews.
[45]Schultz, 53.

and State Department officials were concerned lest these activities be perceived to be illegal. In coordination with SOUTHCOM, the Embassy provided a message which described the function of the military as liaison and coordination, not police training. These "rules of engagement" were critical in order to pass the "legal litmus test."[46]

Second, Thurman recognized that a fully coordinated strategy of reinforcing programs would be required if the desired end-state was to be achieved. This had not been accomplished in the *Prayerbook* planning or in the aftermath of *Just Cause* and the creation of the MSG. The MSG would only be one part of a larger program. Absent an approved, cohesive plan emerging from interagency deliberations in Washington, General Thurman engaged a contracting firm to produce an integrated, holistic strategy. Because of illness after June 1990, however, the general was unable to press for and secure approval of his plan.[47]

Third, U.S. proposals had to be approved by the Panamanian Government. This took time. Unity of effort was eventually achieved as a result of ad hoc development of personal relationships between the MSG and General Thurman, Ambassador Hinton, President Endara, and Vice-Presidents Calderon and Ford.[48] Even with good coordination, the Panamanian Government had its own strong views on how the post-Noriega internal security apparatus ought to be strengthened and did not agree with everything the United States wanted.

The Establishment of a New Panamanian Police Force

After the inauguration of President Endara and his two Vice Presidents as the legal government on December 19, 1989, the public security function formally became their responsibility. Yet, the new government had neither a police force nor the resources to create one. U.S. policy favored withdrawal of U.S. military presence as rapidly as possible,

---

[46]Gray, recollection of events.

[47]Participant observation and unnamed sources, interviews.

[48]Participant observation; unnamed sources, interviews; and Fishel, 7-53.

particularly to the extent that it was performing highly visible civilian police functions.

It was essential to get Panamanian police visibly on the streets. One option was to cashier all previous members of the PDF and recruit an entirely new force. This would have taken years to implement properly, and the United States would have been required to maintain the role of an "occupying power" to ensure public order in the interim. This option also risked leaving 14,000 trained, disenfranchised, and disgruntled former military and police without jobs, inviting the development of an organized and violent opposition.[49]

The second alternative was to organize a police force from among former members of the PDF. This option had the advantage of enabling the new Panamanian Government to restore order rapidly while maintaining a measure of Panamanian, rather than U.S., control. Nonetheless, the loyalty of these individuals would be in question, and this approach would be politically unpopular because of general public fear and distrust of the PDF.[50]

The third option was a compromise. The Panamanian Government and its U.S. mentors would employ PDF members as the core of a new police force, the Fuerza Publica de Panama (FPP). This approach was ultimately selected owing to the urgency of the situation.

To implement its decision, the government imposed several conditions:

☐ The leaders of the new FPP, soon renamed Policia Nacional de Panama (PNP), should not be tainted by the Noriega regime.
☐ Known "bad actors" were to be excluded and individuals later found to be unsuitable would be weeded out of the force.
☐ The organization would be divided into several different entities.
☐ The new police force was to be subordinated to civilian authority.[51]

---

[49]Fishel, 67.
[50]Ibid.
[51]Ibid., 67-68.

The new Panamanian Government, with assistance from U.S. civilian and military officials familiar with the PDF, screened former personnel and relieved those known to have been corrupt or abusive of human rights. This process eventually eliminated all colonels, 83 percent of lieutenant colonels, 39 percent of majors, 31 percent of captains, 19 percent of lieutenants, and many of the lower ranks.[52] The remainder were incorporated into the new police forces. Personnel of the old Departamento Nacional de Investigaciones (DENI) formed the new Policia Tecnica Judicial (PTJ), and personnel of the old PDF formed the new FPP/PNP.[53] The PNP became a uniformed police agency responsible for daily law enforcement functions, such as maintenance of order, community patrol, movement of traffic, and initial response to crimes. The PTJ assumed primary criminal investigative responsibilities.

The United States provided a level of assistance sufficient to allow the Panamanians to start to build the new police force, but it was not adequate to prevent continued dependence on the United States or to achieve the thorough professionalization of the organization.[54] Issues related to the equipping and training of the PNP illustrate this problem.

Equipping the PNP with weapons, uniforms, radios, vehicles, and other equipment was accomplished using existing U.S. security assistance funds, U.S. uniforms under the congressional waiver of Section 660, as well as former PDF equipment. Many of the recovered weapons turned out to be "damaged goods," however, so use of security assistance funds was required to outfit the PNP. PDF vehicles were refurbished by U.S. forces using operational funds under the authority of Operation *Just Cause* until January 20, 1990, when DOD directed that this practice cease. Thus, only 40 patrol cars became available to the PNP. Consequently, security assistance money had to be used to obtain surplus U.S. military trucks and new Chevrolet patrol cars. While awaiting arrival of these vehicles, the only way mounted patrols could be conducted under peacetime rules was as joint patrols

---

[52]Schultz, 47.

[53]Participant observation and unnamed sources, interviews.

[54]Participant observation and Fishel, 69.

with U.S. Military Police in the latter's vehicles. Concern for the high U.S. military profile created by patrolling in U.S. military vehicles caused the MSG to lease civilian patrol cars for the joint patrols. Under the law, however, only U.S. personnel could drive them.[55]

A related concern involved the large number of weapons that had fallen into the hands of Panamanian citizens. Hence, an attractive weapons buy-back program was instituted. This program was successful in getting weapons off the street and contributed to public order.[56]

Training the new PNP proved to be a difficult and complex process. ICITAP was tasked to create a civilian police force, impart modern methods of policing, and replace the U.S. military as advisors to the PNP. Its statutory authority was limited to developing criminal investigations, forensics, and administrative capabilities of Latin American security forces and to curriculum development. Its work up until that time had focused on investigative units rather than training "cops on the beat." Nor did it have any previous experience in the design and development of a public security institution-building project, let alone one of the magnitude and complexity of the Panama project.[57]

Nevertheless, in January 1990, ICITAP was tasked to develop a 2½-year plan to restore law enforcement services in Panama. At the time of *Just Cause*, ICITAP was staffed by FBI Special Agents and other civilians with law enforcement investigative experience. The project received a total of $13.2 million from the State Department's Inter-American Affairs Bureau.[58] ICITAP collected information through on-site observations and consultative contacts with senior Panamanian Government and police officials. This was used to assess the training and resource needs of the PNP and subsequently formulate a Panama

---

[55]Fishel, 45.

[56]Gray, recollection of events.

[57]"ICITAP/Panama Police Training Project Evaluation, Final Report" (Arlington, VA: National Center for State Courts, August 23, 1994), 53.

[58]"FBI Panama Project Evaluation Report" (Washington, DC: Federal Bureau of Investigation, Office of Planning, Evaluation and Audit, March 1992), 1, 2.

Program Description and Budget. An initial plan was published in February 1990, but approximately 4 months later, a much more expanded and detailed project plan had been developed and approved.

As a result of the delay in ICITAP startup, Ambassador Hinton made no effort to move the U.S. military out of its relationship with the PNP. Indeed, the PNP called on the MSG to provide a team of reservists who were policemen in civilian life to develop a short, 20-hour transition training course. These military reservists continued for an extended period in a liaison function under the "rules of engagement," discussed above, crafted by Deputy Chief of Mission Bushnell and approved by the interagency process. Ambassador Hinton was generally satisfied with the job done by reserve MPs although he was concerned about the way the military attempted to organize the Panamanian police along military instead of police organizational lines.[59]

Although it recognized the difference in scope and magnitude of the task, ICITAP initially continued the approach it had been using in other Latin American countries, that is, a series of short seminars and courses, taught in English, by instructors drawn mainly from the ranks of retired FBI agents. Those instructors were contracted by ICITAP's "permanent" consulting firm which handled the organizations' logistics. The most important course was the 120-hour "transition" training for former PDF members selected to become part of the new PNP, which included police ethics and community relations. This course replaced the 20-hour course which served as a stop-gap measure until the preparation for the former was complete.

ICITAP's startup problem was compounded by the fact that, for its first 6 months, it had no permanent staff in Panama,[60] although the ICITAP Director and Deputy Director alternated in running the operation there. However, by-mid 1990, ICITAP had established a permanent presence in Panama with several professionals. Its most

---

[59]Ambassador Dean Hinton, former ambassador to Panama, interview by Gray, January 19, 1997, Panama.
[60]Fishel, 50.

successful program was the establishment of a Police Academy in September 1990. The first class of 250 recruits began training in November 1990 and graduated in February 1991. ICITAP also established training centers throughout the country. Forty-eight cadets from the former PDF military academy were selected to form a leadership nucleus for the future PNP. These cadets were provided funding to attend an 8-week program at the Federal Law Enforcement Training Center in Glynco, Georgia.[61]

ICITAP also began providing assistance in 1990 to the reconstituted Judicial Technical Police (PTJ), including instruction, upgraded forensic capabilities, and a new laboratory (completed in September 1991). Some 350 former investigative officials were purged by combined efforts of ICITAP and the new government and were replaced by vetted former PDF members.

By mid-1996, Panamanian instructors, themselves trained by ICITAP, were conducting all cadet training at the PNP Academy. A total of 4,500 new cadets completed basic training courses, and 2,500 officers had taken advanced courses. ICITAP also worked with the Panamanian Government to create a special unit to investigate money laundering and to develop other capabilities designed to cope with the huge problem of narcotics trafficking.

Public Perceptions

At the outset, a majority of Panamanians welcomed and supported the U.S. intervention. The lasting legacy of this action, however, will be greatly influenced by the outcome of U.S.-supported efforts to reform the public security institutions. Over time it has become obvious that incorporating officers and men from the PDF into the "new" Public Force inevitably meant that much of the deviant subcultures and corruption which characterized Noriega's PDF continued to survive. In spite of the resources that were allocated to the re-establishment and sustainment of the police force, much more will be required if Panama

---

[61]Colonel Layton Dunbar, U.S. Army, U.S. Defense Attache, interview by Gray, February 1990, Panama. Also see ICITAP section in this book for further details.

is to have an effective police force with the confidence of the public. This is even more true for the judicial and penal systems that must be in place for the police force to be effective.

The legal, judicial, and penal systems do not function well today—even though this may not distinguish Panama from various other Central American or Caribbean countries. Cases do not get tried; people languish in pretrial detention for months and years;[62] jails continue to be excessively overcrowded and violent. So far as the public is concerned, the failure of law enforcement is exemplified by the fact that 7 years after *Just Cause,* the 1984 Spadafora torture and murder case still had not been brought to trial.

There has been a marked failure to create a professional, nonpolitical PNP and supporting judicial system. U.S. training and support made the organization technically more proficient but did not lessen the institution's propensity for corruption or alter its fundamental hostility toward the democratic process.[63] The police organization has continued to be structured along the same unitary lines as the old PDF. In general, the most competent officers were also the most loyal to Noriega—and tainted. When these were purged, the least competent remained. Ambassador Hinton cites the inability of the PNP to cope with the demonstration against President Bush as an example. On the other hand, a recent State Department visitor to Panama City observed the PNP peacefully clear the streets of a large crowd of angry demonstrators, maintaining discipline and avoiding the use of forceful measures despite the killing of a policeman by a large stone dropped from a nearby building.

An indicator of the level of public insecurity is the large number of private security guards stationed at many commercial and residential properties, a phenomenon common to many other Latin American countries. There are over 100 highly paid private security agencies that

---

[62] An assessment of the Panamanian police performed by ICITAP in mid-1997 estimates that 68 percent of the prison population are pretrial detainees.

[63] Participant observation; Ambassador Eduardo Vallarino (Ret.), interview by Manwaring, September 23, 1996, Washington, DC; Bazzan, interview; and unnamed sources, interviews.

together have nearly as many armed personnel as the entire PNP. Because of the high crime rate, and because businessmen do not trust the police, a whole new set of "private armies" has been created, replacing the "fee for services" system formerly employed by the old PDF. Excessive numbers of PNP personnel are used for static guard duty to protect homes and offices of senior government officials and political figures, contrary to the blandishments of ICITAP. This combination of large numbers of government-sanctioned armed forces has potentially militarized Panamanian society.[64] To date, this has not resulted in armed feuds, however, and Panama is certainly not the only country to be affected by this troubling regional trend.

Summary

The public security mission within Operation *Just Cause* did not unfold gracefully for various reasons. The requirement became apparent only after the intervention was underway, thus the response was ad hoc. Military police from the 18th Airborne Corps, troops from the 193rd Infantry Brigade, and Special Forces troops were used to deal with the general looting and chaos occasioned by the destruction of the PDF and absence of other law enforcement elements in Panama City. Although the plan eventually invoked, *Blind Logic*, included public security measures, it did not envision the immediate vetting of the PDF or its reconstitution as the PNP. U.S. infantry troops were augmented by military police reinforcements and by the quick-fix creation of a "new" Panamanian police force made up of fully screened former PDF officers and men. Use of civilian "jurists" was not originally part of *Just Cause*. They were called upon later (via the U.S. Agency for International Development, AID) but had limited resources and preparation. Joint U.S. military-Panamanian patrols provided public security until they were replaced by the new PNP with limited ICITAP assistance.[65] After the initial delay in getting organized, the ICITAP training program began to function effectively. Congress, by assigning

---

[64]Participant observation; Vallarino, interview; and unnamed sources, interviews.
[65]Participant observation.

ICITAP the mission of training the entire PNP, a mission for which it was unprepared, while prohibiting the military from this mission, unknowingly legislated a security gap. Because of the success of ICITAP's early programs in El Salvador, expectations were unreasonably high on the part of some in the DOD, and this may have contributed to tensions between the military and ICITAP.[66]

Conclusions

The *operational* objectives of Operation *Just Cause* were to protect American lives, to ensure implementation of the Panama Canal Treaties, and to remove General Noriega from power. In an operational sense, however, *Just Cause* was clearly a success.

The *strategic* objective of Operations *Just Cause* and *Promote Liberty* was to help establish democracy in Panama. This was understood by some as simply the inauguration of the *elected* Endara government. In part, this was due to a misperception as to the future role of the PDF (later the PNP) and an overoptimistic view of Endara's ability to take control of the government and transform it into something distinct from the corrupt practices of the Noriega regime and before.

The short-term outcome was that, after about a year, the PNP had no non-PDF recruits (the 48 untainted cadets notwithstanding), corruption had reappeared, and the PNP was unable to provide a level of public security perceived as satisfactory by the Panamanian people. The long-term prospects are perhaps more promising. Some outside observers contend that both the Government and the public security apparatus are suffering a crisis of legitimacy, that while some faces have changed, the Panamanian National Police and the judicial system are today no more committed to the cause of justice than the old.[67] Others see an improved situation, comparable to or even better than some other countries in Central America with similarly troubled

---

[66]Gray, recollection of events.

[67]Dr. Richard Millett, Professor of History and congressional witness, interview by Manwaring, November 4, 1996, Edwardsville, IL.

histories. In Panama itself, a series of six polls conducted between 1993 and 1996 showed that twice as many respondents believed that the PNP had improved under the Endara Government than believed policing had gotten worse.

Factors That Determined the Outcome

The principal issues that plagued the U.S. effort to assist the Panamanian government to establish credible and legitimate public security were failure to anticipate the consequences of intervention (i.e., the deployment gap) and organizational limitations in dealing with the void in public security once it became apparent (i.e., the enforcement gap). These are not completely separate concepts but very much interrelated.

In the long run, however, the more important determinants of the impact on the public security function were the limitations of the Panamanian political process (i.e., the institutional gap).

The Deployment Gap. In this case, the deployment gap consisted of the period between the disintegration of the PDF as a result of the *Just Cause* intervention and the arrival of sufficient military police, Civil Affairs, and regular infantry troops to quell looting and lawlessness in major urban areas of Panama. Moreover, the gap was prolonged by the initial absence of civilian law enforcement programs. This has been attributed to the fact that planning for *Just Cause* was done on a very restricted basis.

Concern for operational security was paramount. During the Reagan administration, proceedings of several highly classified interagency sessions had been leaked to the press, seriously damaging the administration's Panama policy. Because of the large U.S. population living in Panama (40,000) *Just Cause* had to be conducted with the utmost secrecy. The danger of a hostage situation was very real. (In fact, 13 U.S. citizens were taken hostage on December 20; all were subsequently rescued.) The fact that *Just Cause* was carried out without great loss of U.S. troops and only one U.S. civilian being killed was due in no small measure to the security in which the operation was planned. Nevertheless, more key individuals might have been involved in planning so that the appropriate agencies could have developed a coordinated plan for addressing the full range of public security issues raised by this action.

The Enforcement Gap. After order had been restored and civil-military activities had been routinized under the Military Support Group-Panama, the next challenge was to develop an interim Panamanian police force to assume the task of local law enforcement. U.S. military forces are prohibited from conducting police training activities, although Congress did grant a waiver for security assistance funds to be used to equip the new police force. As noted above, no advance planning had been done to fill this void, and the civilian entity belatedly assigned to perform this task, ICITAP, was not designed or staffed for rapid response, nor had it ever undertaken a project of this magnitude. A failure to grasp these limitations caused ICITAP's military counterparts a great deal of consternation and obliged the use of MPs in a quasi-training role. ICITAP developed a 120-hour curriculum to train personnel who would be permanently retained by the PNP as well as other training programs.

The Institutional Gap. U.S. advice and training alone cannot compensate for a paralyzed judicial system, an inadequate legal code, a hopelessly overcrowded penal system, and endless political efforts to manipulate the police and the judicial process. The U.S. Government and particularly ICITAP have been in a constant struggle with the Government of Panama over reforms to the police and judicial systems. Panama has tended to retain habits ingrained over decades.

Rebuilding a civilian police force from a collapsed military establishment, moreover, presents a different set of problems than reconstituting a discrete civilian police force. It is extremely difficult to take a disbanded army and turn some of its personnel into a civilian police force that understands police-community relations, is integrated into society, and is governed by principles of human dignity and respect for the rights of individuals.

Owing to these daunting political, organizational, and cultural challenges, building a stable, well-functioning civilian police institution is a long-term proposition. Enough time must be programmed into such projects to allow for systematic and comprehensive institution-building, including the development of policies and procedures, management capabilities, and administrative infrastructures, as well as the creation of self-monitoring, internal affairs functions.

Given the enormity of the challenges before it, ICITAP has made substantial contributions over time to enhancing the capacity of Panamanian public security forces. Developing policing capacity, however, is a necessary but not sufficient condition to produce a public security establishment capable of providing law, order, and justice. Ultimately, the requisite *political will* must be present to make reform work. Political elites must adopt these goals as their own, otherwise, assistance programs will run the risk of merely making corrupt systems more efficient.

Some significant progress seems to have been made in Panama by dint of sustained efforts by ICITAP and the Panamanian Government, even if important problems remain. However, it is important to realize that U.S. expectations for foreign law enforcement institutions may not be fully achieved, no matter how much help is provided.

Lessons Applicable to Other Operations

The interagency politico-military plan which was used in Haiti and continues to be refined is an outgrowth of both the Panama and Somalia experiences. It must be remembered that with these latter operations as well as Bosnia, secrecy was not a concern. In fact, military movements were intentionally made public.

On a negative note, the weapons buy-back program that was successful in Panama was not successful in Somalia. A lesson here is to look at the culture. Panama has traditionally been a nonviolent society and owning a weapon has no particular significance. In Somalia, owning a weapon is associated with manhood.[68]

The difficulty in pinpointing Noriega's location, sophisticated intelligence notwithstanding, was revisited in Somalia in the attempt to apprehend Aideed, and proved it to be a nearly impossible task.

---

[68]General Anthony Zinni, U.S. Marine Corps, speech at a Center for Naval Analyses conference, October 1995.

Perhaps the most important lesson from *Just Cause* is the recognition of the need for an international civilian police contingent to fill the security gap that neither the military nor ICITAP alone can or should be expected to fill.

POLICING CAMBODIA:
The Public Security Dimensions of U.N. Peace Operations

JAMES A. SCHEAR and KARL FARRIS

Background

During the past quarter century, Cambodia has endured more war, revolution, extremist violence, and sociopolitical collapse than almost any other country on earth. In late 1978, after repeated border skirmishes between the Maoist Khmer Rouge and the Vietnamese army, Vietnam launched an all-out invasion of the country. Hanoi ousted the Pol Pot regime and installed a quisling government in Phnom Penh. For the next 12 years, the Khmer Rouge waged a sporadic civil war against the Vietnam-backed regime from their jungle sanctuaries in loose association with two other Cambodian opposition groups. Throughout this long period, the country remained isolated, destitute, and bitterly contested, with each Khmer faction drawing support to varying degrees from different international patrons.

By the late 1980s, the Cambodian conflict had begun to lose salience internationally. The Soviet Union was retrenching from Southeast Asia and wanted to normalize relations with China; its support for Vietnam's occupation was a major impediment to that objective. The Vietnamese, frustrated by years of futile effort to resolve the Cambodian civil war through military means, were eager to build bridges to their non-Communist neighbors. In April 1989, Hanoi surprised many observers by announcing its intention to withdraw from Cambodia and actually making good on its promise 6 months later. The prospect of Soviet and Vietnamese retrenchment actually pressured the Cambodian opposition factions to negotiate with the Phnom Penh authorities, as a number of Western states appeared to flirt with idea of recognizing the Vietnamese-installed regime. The

Association of Southeast Asian Nations (ASEAN) states, in particular, viewed Vietnam's retreat as a major boost to the resolution of the Cambodian conflict and as a step toward turning Indochina into a prosperous and peaceful region. They upped the pressure on their Khmer allies to negotiate.

None of these outside developments, auspicious as they were, fundamentally attenuated the struggle for power inside Cambodia. Indeed, for all four of the main Khmer factions—the "State of Cambodia" (SOC) in Phnom Penh, led by prime minister Hun Sen; the Khmer Rouge (KR), led nominally by Khieu Samphan (with Pol Pot in the background); the *Front Uni National pour une Cambodge Indépendent, Neutre, Pacifique et Coopératif* (FUNCINPEC),[1] a royalist party led by Prince Sihanouk's son, Prince Ranariddh; and the *Khmer People's National Liberation Front* (KPNLF), a republican non-Communist group—the prospect of peace was somewhat unnerving, because it was unclear how a settlement would affect their positions vis-a-vis the other parties. At the same time, none of them was prepared to accept the onus for stonewalling high-profile negotiations that enjoyed near-universal support internationally. So lacking any better options, they all moved forward, haltingly, toward a comprehensive political settlement, the details of which were finally hammered out in Paris in October 1991.

The diplomacy that produced the Paris Accords spanned a number of years.[2] By the late 1980s, all factions and their sponsors had agreed on the basic elements of a comprehensive settlement: a cease-fire; the permanent withdrawal of foreign forces; the cessation of outside military assistance; the voluntary repatriation of refugees and displaced persons; the creation of a transitional administration; the holding of internationally supervised elections leading to the formation of a new government; guarantees of Cambodia's neutrality, sovereignty, and

---

[1]This translates to English as United National Front for an Independent, Neutral, Pacific and Cooperative Cambodia.

[2]See, for example, Steven R. Ratner, *The New U.N. Peacekeeping* (New York: St. Martins, 1995).

territorial integrity; and international support for the country's rehabilitation and reconstruction.[3]

By far the most contentious issue in the negotiations was the thorny question of power sharing during the transition to a new government. The three opposition factions were adamant that the SOC should cede administrative control to an interim authority composed of the four factions under the leadership of Prince Sihanouk. The SOC accepted the idea of a transitional body but insisted that it be essentially advisory in nature.[4]

Faced with this deadlock, the idea of having the United Nations manage the transition gained popularity. Promoted initially by Australia, the U.N. approach offered a means of uniting the factions on the principle that transitional oversight would be performed impartially and not be in the hands of any Khmer entity. In September 1990, Cambodian factions agreed to form a quadripartite body—the Supreme National Council (SNC)—that would embody Cambodian sovereignty and represent the country during the transition. The SNC would have 12 members, six from SOC and two apiece from the other three factions, with Sihanouk as chairman and its 13th member. The body would then delegate authority to the United Nations to ensure the proper implementation of the settlement.[5]

For all concerned, the experimental character of the arrangement was unmistakable. Delegating contentious jobs to the United Nations helped pave the way for agreement, but how the organization would wield the authority entrusted to it, and how durable the parties' consent to the arrangement would be, remained unclear. The Paris Accords were fragile instruments, a product of intense pressure applied upon the

---

[3]Ministerial Statement on the "Prospects for a Cambodian Peace Settlement," by Senator Gareth Evans, Minister of Foreign Affairs and Trade, Australia, to the Senate of Australia, December 6, 1990.

[4]Ratner, *The New U.N. Peacekeeping*, 144.

[5]General Assembly, *Letter Dated 11 September 1990 from France and Indonesia, as Co-chairmen of the Paris Conference on Cambodia, transmitting a joint statement on Cambodia issued at the end of talks held in Jakarta, September 9-10, 1990*, A/45/490, September 17, 1990.

parties by external powers operating in a climate of cooperation that did not yet exist inside Cambodia.[6]

In broad terms, the Paris Accords sought to end the civil war and restore internationally recognized government to Cambodia. The signatories called upon the United Nations to establish a large, multifaceted peace operation—the United Nations Transitional Authority in Cambodia (UNTAC)—to supervise the implementation of the accords and to undertake a wide variety of military and civilian tasks with the consent and cooperation of the parties.

From the operational standpoint, it is important to stress that UNTAC's mission was neither classical peacekeeping nor "peacebuilding" in the sense of long-term sustainment for reconstruction; rather, it aimed at an intermediate goal—transitional assistance. The operation's purpose was to shake Cambodia's warring factions out of their stalemated civil war and end the country's crippling isolation. It could do these things only by being a large, highly invasive enterprise. UNTAC touched virtually every part of the country. It involved the largest foreign military presence since the Vietnamese invasion of 1978, and its concept of operations called for the largest, albeit voluntary, movement of civilians since the forced evacuation of Phnom Penh and other cites by the Khmer Rouge in April 1975.

Given the nature of the task, public security quickly became a major challenge—if not *the* major challenge—facing UNTAC during its period of operation. In this paper, we examine how U.N. planners sought to address the public security problem; how those plans had to be adjusted in the face of various operational difficulties and backtracking by the Khmer factions, principally the Khmer Rouge and the SOC; and generally how military and civilian resources were utilized in an effort to usher the transition process along to its decisive outcome in September 1993, with the formation of a new royal Cambodian Government.

---

[6]This point is well developed by Ratner and by Julio A. Jeldres, "The U.N. and the Cambodian Transition," *Journal of Democracy* 4, no. 4 (October 1993): 107.

The Mandate

The Security Council expressed support for the Paris Accords in resolution 718 (1991), and it authorized the establishment of UNTAC in resolution 745 (1992) for a period not to exceed 18 months.[7] Shortly before the actual signing of the accords on October 23, 1991, the Council authorized establishment of the United Nations Advance Mission in Cambodia (UNAMIC), initially to monitor the cease-fire and then to initiate mine-clearance training and the repair of roads and bridges to prepare the way for UNTAC's arrival.[8]

Under the Accords, the signatories agreed to confer upon UNTAC "all powers necessary to ensure implementation" of the comprehensive settlement.[9] This expansive delegation of authority came with only one string attached, namely, a decision process for resolving any disputes over implementation that might arise between UNTAC and the local parties; but even these procedures were heavily weighted in UNTAC's favor.[10] An annex to the Paris Accords, along with a plan for implementation developed by the Secretary-General and approved by the Security Council, spelled out a broad range of missions.

Despite the breathtaking scope of UNTAC's involvement, never *at any time* did the Council confer its compulsory Chapter VII authority

---

[7]Security Council, S/RES/718 (1991), October 31, 1991, and S/RES/745 (1992), February 28, 1992.

[8]*The United Nations and Cambodia, 1991-1995* (New York: United Nations, 1995), 10-11. UNAMIC's enabling resolution was S/RES/717 (1991), October 16, 1991.

[9]*Agreement on a Comprehensive Political Settlement of the Cambodian Conflict*, Part I, Section III, Article 6, 10.

[10]Under the Paris Accords, UNTAC was bound to comply with the SNC's "advice," provided there was a consensus among SNC members and provided the advice was consistent with the objectives of the agreement. If the SNC could not reach a consensus, Prince Sihanouk could take the decision on what advice to offer, taking into account the views expressed in the SNC. If, however, Prince Sihanouk could not take a decision, the authority to make decisions would pass to the U.N. Special Representative. In all cases, the authority to determine whether advice was consistent with the Accords would be held by the Special Representative. See ibid., Annex 1, Section A, 17-18.

upon UNTAC to implement its mandated functions. This was somewhat at odds with the tenor of the Paris Accords, under which the Cambodian parties had entrusted UNTAC with powers to do such things as fire or reassign obstructive bureaucrats, seize arms caches, or take corrective action to thwart human rights abuse. In fact, however, no enforcement provisions had been built into the Accords, and it is doubtful the parties would have agreed to the inclusion of such provisions. Nor was there any real support in the Security Council for mounting or sustaining UNTAC on anything but a consensual basis. U.N. leadership was keenly aware of the low tolerance for casualties among UNTAC's troop contributors.[11]

Peace Mission Organization and Resources

UNTAC was structured to perform a wide range of assignments, on both the military and civilian sides. Many of these jobs had either an implicit or explicit public security rationale.

Military Missions

UNTAC's military tasks were the most prominent initially. Thirty-four nations contributed contingents to the 15,568-member uniformed peacekeeping force. It was a diverse organization consisting of 12 infantry battalions, a naval element, an air element, a mine clearance training unit, a robust engineering capability, and a strong medical and

---

[11]James Schear interviews by authors, UNTAC headquarters, Phnom Penh, June 11, 1992. UNTAC's deputy force commander, General Jean-Michel Loridon of France, professed a willingness to risk several hundred casualties in a gambit to challenge the Khmer Rouge for control of their territories. Loridon's criticisms of UNTAC's unwillingness to confront the Khmer Rouge with force created some media waves but his prescriptions were not popular with other troop contributors, nor (apparently) with Paris, and he was soon replaced with a more accommodating successor. Loridon's skeptics wondered how 16,000 U.N. troops could do what nearly 200,000 Vietnamese had been unable to do, namely, dislodge the Khmer Rouge from their sanctuaries.

logistics support structure needed because of the lack of infrastructure support within Cambodia.

Lieutenant General John Sanderson, the Australian Force Commander, summarized the military's mission as supervising the cease-fire and building confidence in the peace process and in UNTAC.[12] Specifically, the Military Component of UNTAC was tasked with:

☐ Verifying the withdrawal and nonreturn of all categories of foreign forces (euphemism for Vietnamese) and their arms and equipment.

☐ Supervising the cease-fire and related measures, including regrouping, cantoning, disarming, and demobilizing the forces of the four warring Cambodian factions.

☐ Instituting a weapons-control program, including monitoring the cessation of outside military assistance, locating and confiscating caches of weapons and military supplies, and storing the arms and equipment of the cantoned and demobilized military forces.

☐ Assisting in mine clearing, including training programs and mine awareness programs.

☐ Investigating complaints from any of the factions; investigating on its own initiative alleged noncompliance with any of the provisions relating to the military arrangements of the Paris Accords.

☐ Providing assistance in the repatriation of Cambodian refugees and internally displaced persons.

In broad terms, the Military Component was expected to canton about 200,000 soldiers, disarm about 450,000 soldiers and militia overall (militia were not to be cantoned for agricultural reasons), securing more than 300,000 weapons of various types and some 80 million rounds of ammunition, and monitoring the borders and territorial waters of

---

[12]*The United Nations Transitional Authority in Cambodia (UNTAC)* (London-The Hague: Kluwer Law International, 1995), 128.

Cambodia. At the same time it had to establish a nationwide mine awareness/training program and assist with mine clearing.

Execution of these tasks was envisioned in two phases. During Phase I, which commenced with signing of the agreement, the factions were to refrain from further fighting and observe a general cease-fire. Phase II would involve the sequential regroupment, cantonment, disarmament, and then demobilization of the factional armies. Plans called for 95 regroupment areas and 52 cantonment areas to accommodate the forces of the four factions.[13]

The core of UNTAC's military capability consisted of 12 infantry battalions, each structured as a light infantry force with about 850 soldiers. Their primary task was to oversee and facilitate the disarmament and demobilization process. For this, Cambodia was divided into nine military sectors corresponding to the locations of the planned cantonment sites. Eleven of the infantry battalions were given responsibility for manning the cantonment sites within the nine military sectors of operations (in two sectors, two UNTAC battalions were deployed). The 12th infantry battalion was stationed in Phnom Penh, acting as a mobile reserve to be deployed on orders of the force commander.

Full deployment of UNTAC's Military Component was planned to be completed by end of May 1992, shortly after which Phase II—the 4-month regroupment, cantonment, and disarmament process of the factional armies—was to commence. At the completion of Phase II, planned for September 1992, at least 70 percent of the factional forces were expected to be disarmed and demobilized. Therefore, with disarmament and demobilization scheduled to be well under way by September 1992, it was thought that civilian-led transitional tasks could be conducted in a stable security environment.

---

[13]Ibid., 40.

Civilian-Led Missions

Outside the military sphere, the lion's share of UNTAC work was performed by six additional components—electoral, civil administration, human rights, repatriation, rehabilitation and civilian police—all reporting directly to the Special Representative of the Secretary-General (SRSG), Yasushi Akashi. (The Force Commander also reported to U.N. Headquarters through the SRSG, though on many issues he dealt directly with New York while keeping the SRSG informed.) In addition, a unit was set up within the Special Representative's office to support UNTAC's needs in the information/education arena.

UNTAC's *Electoral Component* was tasked with organizing and conducting, not simply monitoring, nationwide elections. The range of jobs was enormous: drafting an electoral law and presenting it for consultation by the SNC; conducting civic education in Cambodia's 179 districts and training locally recruited staff; provisionally registering political parties and party agents; registering voters; and planning and conducting the polling and the vote count. All these tasks were to be done within 15 months, with the key task of voter registration starting shortly after the completion of the cantonment of factional military forces.

To help create a level political playing field, UNTAC was given major responsibilities in the area of *civil administration*. The Paris Accords provided that "in order to ensure a neutral political environment conducive to free and fair elections, administrative agencies, bodies and offices which could directly influence the outcome of elections will be placed under direct United Nations supervision or control."[14]

In practice, only SOC had a full-fledged government, and it controlled over 80 percent of Cambodia's territory. FUNCINPEC and KPNLF had virtually no government, and the Khmer Rouge (KR)

---

[14]*Agreements on a Comprehensive Political Settlement of the Cambodia Conflict* (New York: United Nations, 1991), Section III, Article 6.

refused UNTAC access to areas it controlled.[15] Therefore, UNTAC's Civil Administration Component, mandated with "supervision and control" over all existing administrative structures, in practice exercised its responsibilities only over SOC administrations. This asymmetry was bound to create tensions.

Five administrative fields in which UNTAC was to exercise direct control were specified in the Paris Accords: defense, public security, finance, information, and foreign affairs. The term "fields" rather than ministries or departments was used deliberately to avoid any temptation in Phnom Penh to "clone" ministries as a way to evade control.

In defense matters, UNTAC was to scrutinize the administrative structures of the military as well as military expenditures. In finance, UNTAC was to examine fiscal policies and allocation of funds, preparation of budgets, accounting systems, banking, taxation, customs and wage policies. In foreign affairs, UNTAC was to oversee the issuance of passports and visas, and foreign assistance disbursement and accountability. In information, UNTAC was to review printed and broadcast materials and to ensure fair access by all parties to means of information.

In the public security domain, UNTAC's job was to assess the public security procedures of police and other ministries influencing law and order and to examine laws and judicial decisions. To augment its operational oversight, a *Civilian Police Component* was established to supervise and control local civilian police. ("CIVPOL" is discussed in detail in the next section.)

Within the *human rights* area, UNTAC's job was to promote "an environment in which respect for human rights is ensured" and to "prevent a return to the policies and practices of the past."[16] The Human Rights Component was divided into a Monitoring/Investigation Unit and an Information, Education and Training Unit. The Monitoring/

---

[15]Trevor Findlay, *Cambodia: The Legacy and Lessons of UNTAC* (New York: Oxford University Press, 1995), 59.

[16]*Agreements on a Comprehensive Political Settlement of the Cambodia Conflict* (New York: United Nations, 1991), Part III, Human Rights, Articles 15 & 16.

Investigation Unit's principal task was to monitor the existing administrative structures of the Cambodian factions. This was done by visiting prisons and detention centers and investigating any allegations of human rights abuses. The Information, Education and Training Unit was concerned primarily with establishing preventive measures by conducting training workshops in human rights for Cambodian school teachers, university students, and government officials as well as helping to develop human rights curricula for primary and secondary schools.[17]

Initially, the Human Rights Component was to be staffed with only 10 officers, all to be stationed in Phnom Penh. This low figure reflected a judgment that all U.N. personnel would be able to act as de facto human rights monitors, reporting any infractions, and the Human Rights Component would function mainly as a coordination body. This quickly proved unworkable, and the component was increased so that at least one human rights officer would be stationed in each of Cambodia's 21 provinces.[18] Also, UNTAC's Civil Police Component was tasked to serve as human rights monitors.

Paralleling the human rights efforts, UNTAC's Repatriation Component, staffed by the United Nations High Commissioner for Refugees (UNHCR), would oversee the return of roughly 370,000 Cambodian refugees from Thai border camps at a rate of up to 10,000 per week, providing resettlement assistance such as shelter, household kits, and rations for 1 year. Finally, UNTAC's Rehabilitation Component would coordinate the early phases of internationally funded programs to restore basic infrastructure (e.g., transport, telecommunications, roads). In June 1992, acting upon a consolidated appeal by the Secretary-General, an international donors conference

---

[17]Human Rights Component (Phnom Penh: UNTAC Spokesman's Office, March 1993).

[18]Michael Doyle, *U.N. Peacekeeping in Cambodia: UNTAC's Civil Mandate* (Boulder, CO: Lynne Rienner Publishers, 1995), 45-46.

in Tokyo raised $880 million for both near-term rehabilitation and long-term needs.[19]

The scope of UNTAC's activities was enormous, yet a number of missions were *not* included in the mandate that would have given it more of a "peacebuilding" character. There was, for example, no provision for restructuring local police organizations or vetting personnel, and no program specifically focused on judicial reform. The civil administrative work in financial and macroeconomic areas concentrated mainly on oversight rather than technical assistance. The reasons for this, clearly, were political. Opposition parties did not want SOC to benefit politically from such assistance prior to the election. Once the transition was completed, major reconstruction could begin, but that was not UNTAC's job. Overall, the concept of operations foresaw military and civilian activities occurring on largely separate tracks. UNTAC's peacekeepers would help create a secure environment by overseeing an end of the civil war, while the electoral, civil administrative and other components would pave the way for Cambodia's political and economic reconstruction.

Command relationships reflected these largely autonomous activities. An SRSG at the apex ensured a certain unity at the highest level, but at the provincial level UNTAC's military and civilian command chains were quite separate. (Even among various civilian components, while coordination was facilitated by co-location, there were separate "stovepipes" to headquarters in Phnom Penh.) Generally, this division of labor accorded with the basic formula for compromise in the Accords: the Khmer Rouge would agree to end the fighting, while the SOC would demobilize politically. Events, however, quickly conspired to render this strategy untenable.

---

[19]*U.N. Transitional Authority in Cambodia*, DPI/1352 (New York: U.N. Department of Public Information, March 1993), 12.

Public Security Dimensions of the Operation

When UNTAC arrived, Cambodia's public security picture was changing rapidly. Apart from front line provinces, mainly in mountainous northern and western regions, the country was quiet. There was little dissent in SOC-controlled areas, but none was tolerated. The country was isolated; outside the capital, there was little commerce and few foreigners; common crime was not regarded as a major problem, and civil disturbances were rare.[20]

SOC police presence was very pervasive and rarely challenged. Modeled on Vietnam's public security apparatus, SOC police performed a wide range of internal security and paramilitary functions, including border patrolling as well as surveillance of, and action against, anti-regime elements.[21] UNTAC's CIVPOL Commissioner, Klaas Roos, pointed out that there was no longer a criminal justice system as generally understood. Courts, prosecutors, defense attorneys, and prisons had been destroyed by decades of brutal civil strife—justice was arbitrary.[22] How the civil population viewed SOC presence is unclear. The regime consistently portrayed itself as the people's guardian against the Khmer Rouge, but whatever public support it may have won was tarnished by a widespread perception of the regime as corrupt, inefficient, and a tool of Vietnamese interests.

By 1991, a number of stresses in society were growing more acute. Soviet budget support to SOC had dried up. The regime's technique for covering its ballooning public sector deficit was simply to put more

---

[20]But not unknown. When Khmer Rouge's nominal political leader, Khieu Samphan, returned to Phnom Penh for the first time after the Paris Accords, an unruly mob of protesters (most likely orchestrated by elements of the ruling Cambodian Peoples Party) attacked and nearly killed him.

[21]For insights on how these functions continued during the UNTAC transition, see Judy Ledgerwood, "Patterns of CPP [Cambodian People's Party] Political Repression and Violence During the UNTAC Period," in *Propaganda, Politics and Violence in Cambodia: Democratic Transition Under United Nations Peace-keeping*, eds. Steve Heder and Judy Ledgerwood (Armonk, NY: M.E. Sharpe, 1996), 123-5.

[22]See Klaus Roos, "Debriefing of Civilian Police Components. U.N. Transitional Authority in Cambodia," paper presented at Singapore debriefing conference in 1995.

currency in circulation. Inflation was spiraling. Soldiers and civil servants were not being paid; extortion, banditry, and corruption were increasing. With a peace agreement in prospect, there was an influx of foreign visitors, businessmen, and Vietnamese migrant workers into Phnom Penh, stimulating commercial activity but also socioeconomic tensions.

Size and Composition of CIVPOL Component

From the U.N. standpoint, maintenance of law and order clearly was the key not only to the creation of a neutral political environment for elections but to effective implementation of UNTAC's mandate, and it was identified as such.[23] Among other points, Secretary-General Boutros-Ghali noted that the widespread distribution of weapons in the civil population and impending demobilization of soldiers were factors that might lead to a deteriorating security situation during the transition. He also stated that "electoral processes are inherently antagonistic in nature" and might "stretch the existing public order machinery."[24] This was a prescient, if greatly understated, observation.

Under the Paris Accords, responsibility for managing local police organizations lay with each of the factions. UNTAC's job was only to supervise and control the local police, to "ensure that law and order are maintained effectively and impartially, and that human rights and fundamental freedoms are fully protected." It was for this purpose that a civilian police monitoring element was included in UNTAC's organization. The Civilian Police Component was modeled after the U.N. Civilian Police as used in the Namibia operation, where the U.N. police also had to deal with elections-related intimidation and violence.[25] The plan for UNTAC's corps of civil police numbered 3,600 officers, a figure driven by a ratio of one U.N. officer for every 15 local policemen or every 3,000 Cambodian citizens. UNTAC's police came

---

[23]See the Secretary-General's implementation plan, S/23613, February 19, 1992, para. 100.

[24]Ibid., para. 113.

[25]Janet E. Heininger, *Peacekeeping in Transition: The United Nations in Cambodia* (New York: The Twentieth Century Fund Press, 1995), 79.

from 32 different countries. For the United Nations it represented the largest U.N. Civilian Police operation deployed up to that time, and it was also the first time the civilian police were not placed within the structure of the Military Component.

Organizationally, the CIVPOL Component consisted of a Policy and Management Unit located in the capital, Phnom Penh, 21 Civil Police units at provincial level, and 200 Civil Police stations at the district level. Presence at village level was supposed to be maintained by regular patrols from district police stations and by frequent contact with village leaders. Initially UNCIVPOL had no executive authority. They were essentially unarmed monitors, not enforcers, though their ROEs did give them latitude to act where they witnessed acts of violence against citizens.[26] CIVPOL officers, in concert with other UNTAC components, also had roles in investigation of human rights abuse and in provision of security during elections. As the operation progressed, pressures for mission creep quickly set in. Generally, CIVPOL tasks became more diverse and demanding, to include escort and arrest-related activities, some of which the CIVPOL Component was not prepared to undertake.

CIVPOL Relations with Other Mission Components

While CIVPOL was seen as UNTAC's principal instrument in the public security arena, it was not the only component with important public security functions. The Military Component's work in cantonment, weapons impoundment, demining, and vocational retraining was expected to mitigate the social impact arising from widespread demobilization. Similarly, the Repatriation Component's programs for resettlement assistance would help cushion the impact on refugee populations after departure from their well-established camps on the Thai-Cambodian border. Meanwhile, UNTAC's civil administrative supervisors would attempt to deter or weed out top-level sponsorship of crime, corruption and human rights abuse. Human rights personnel

---

[26]Schear interview with UNTAC Police Commissioner Klaus Roos, June 11, 1992, Phnom Penh.

would work on strengthening civil society through local monitoring of police, improving prison conditions, and training police and judicial personnel. Electoral activities would proceed with a number of public security safeguards in place. Even UNTAC procurement policies, in particular its large outlays for prefabricated buildings, stemmed in part from a desire to mitigate negative impacts on local society, including the stimulation of crime, corruption and socioeconomic dislocations.

Although most of UNTAC's components had some role in promoting or maintaining public security, the sheer magnitude of Cambodia's various transitions—from war to fragile peace, from isolation to openness vis-a-vis the outside world, from a command economy to the free market, from a one-party state to multiparty democracy—was too great to be cushioned effectively. As it turned out, public security deteriorated badly once the transition(s) got underway, and UNTAC found it difficult to mount effective responses.

The Implementation Track Record

Even if the mission had unfolded according to plan, the challenges facing UNTAC would have been daunting. Practically from the outset, however, Cambodia's transition did not go according to plan. This added grave complications and gave the impression that UNTAC was lurching from crisis to crisis in its efforts to incubate the creation of a new Cambodian government within a mere 18 months.[27]

The Deployment Gap
UNTAC got off to a terribly slow start. Unlike Somalia or Haiti, it was not preceded by an intervention force. Its military units deployed in a slow, fragmented fashion, with infantry battalions preceding logistics and engineering elements. Even this 4- or 5-month effort was more rapid than the molasses-like pace of civilian components, especially the

---

[27]For a full analysis of the transition, see James A. Schear, "Riding the Tiger: The United Nations and Cambodia's Struggle for Peace," in *U.N. Peacekeeping, American Policy, and the Uncivil Wars of the 1990s,* ed. William J. Durch (New York: St. Martin's, 1996), 135-192.

civilian police element. There was little advance preparation for CIVPOL. In effect, planning and execution occurred simultaneously.

The U.N. Advance Mission in Cambodia (UNAMIC) was deployed in November 1991 to plan for and facilitate the main UNTAC operation. No police element was included, and Commissioner Roos subsequently stated that this "hampered my efforts to set up this largest and most complicated peace operation within peacekeeping."[28] Roos was not appointed until March 1992, 1 week before he arrived for duty, and there were only 200 police by April 1992. Getting U.N. Member States to commit civilian police contingents for UNTAC proved more difficult than recruiting contingents for the Military Component. This is understandable, because few countries have surplus policing capacity, that is, civilian police forces not already operationally committed.[29]

The contingent did not reach full strength until November 1992, only 6 months before the scheduled elections, thus an opportunity to establish early momentum had been lost. Instead, the delays contributed to a sense of uncertainty about the transition and the international community's role in it.

This atmosphere of tension and drift contributed to a situation in which the two main Khmer factions—the Khmer Rouge and SOC—began to backtrack on those parts of the Paris commitments most inconvenient to each of them. For the KR, the military provisions on regroupment, cantonment, disarmament and demobilization were the most constraining. Although there had been numerous field

---

[28]Roos.

[29]For example, the U.N. Secretariat asked Australia to commit 75 officers, but after detailed internal deliberations between Australia's federal authorites and states/territories, only 10 officers were contributed to the operation. As a 1993 report by the Australian Federal Police noted, drawing on highly professional resources is hard for the United Nations. Many countries, the report stated, have a range of "pseudo police services that are not engaged in traditional policing duties and do not have the mix of skills required for an effective peacekeeping operation." It added that "some countries commit police to obtain U.N. funding." See *Peacekeeping Challenges for Civilian Police*, A submisson by the Australian Federal Police to the Defence Sub-committee of the Joint Committee on Foreign Affairs, Defence and Trade, Australia, October 1993, 5.

indications that KR units were preparing to comply in early 1992, their posture grew defiant during April-July as they accused UNTAC and SOC of failing to make good on other aspects of the accords, especially verification of the withdrawal of Vietnamese forces. By October, the Khmer Rouge leadership had moved toward a passive boycott—not cooperating but not violently opposing the process.

That posture, not surprisingly, had a deleterious effect on SOC's incentives to cooperate. The KR boycott seemed to strengthen hard-line elements within SOC. The SOC leadership was desperate to have an election as a way to achieve international respectability, but it also was well aware that the United Nations was not about to cancel the polling in order to penalize any party.

The Law Enforcement Gap

Defiance by SOC was most evident in the public security arena. By late 1992, Cambodia witnessed an upsurge in politically inspired violence and intimidation, aimed largely at the newly resident opposition parties. While the Khmer Rouge were mainly responsible for attacks on indigenous Vietnamese civilians, elements loyal to SOC were widely believed to be the instigators of violence against non-Communist parties.[30] In some of the more unstable provinces, UNTAC personnel saw an expanding pattern of harassment, arrest, or abduction of political activists, bombings of party offices, and execution-style murders. Voter intimidation was also widespread, the most familiar tactic being the "registration" and/or confiscation of voter identification cards by local authorities. These cases provided mounting evidence of the complicity of police and military personnel.[31]

---

[30]The worst of the violence occurred between March and mid-May 1993. During this period, UNTAC confirmed 200 deaths, 338 injuries, and 114 abductions. SOC was suspected of complicity in 15 deaths and 9 injuries, while the Khmer Rouge were thought to be responsible for 131 deaths, 250 injuries and 53 abductions. Press statement by Dennis McNamara, Director, UNTAC Human Rights Component, May 23, 1993.

[31]Philip Shenon, "Cambodian Factions Use Terror Tactics in Crucial Election," *The New York Times*, May 10, 1993, A1.

UNTAC was not oblivious to SOC's role in fomenting violence; what it lacked until late in the process were any means and persuasive arguments to induce SOC to rein in its thugs. The Khmer Rouge boycott put SOC in a sulking mood—"Why should you expect so much from us when the other side is so defiant?" was a common refrain. The problem of political violence also showed tellingly the inadequacies of UNTAC's supervisory apparatus.

As with other components, UNTAC's civil administration unit deployed slowly. UNTAC had designated July 1, 1992, as the date when it would assume control over the five specified areas, but full deployment of the Civil Administration Component was not achieved until October. Planning was also slow. While the mandate specified what was to be controlled, there were no clear guidelines on *how* control should be exercised. The whole effort was highly experimental. It took 6 months for the Civil Administration to develop operational guidelines for the nature and method of "control" UNTAC would exercise in the different domains under its supervision. In reality, the Civil Administration Component was never really structured to permit it to exercise direct control of the SOC ministries. This would have required, among other things, a much larger staff, with greater fluency in French and Khmer, and greater familiarity with local culture and customs.

In the countryside, UNTAC controls were spotty at best and almost nonexistent in some places. Only about five to eight Civil Administration officials were deployed per province. The true nature of SOC's state structure, power relationships, and method of exercising authority from the central government through provincial governors were all recognized too late. Power and decisions in this Communist "party-state" flowed through the interlocking party-government structure and not through the state ministries in which the Civil Administration had positioned itself for control. Finally, the "complex patterns of family, patronage, and political relationships that make up

Cambodian society"[32] made it impossible for UNTAC to gain any control or influence with the entrenched administrations. There were simply too many ways to evade UNTAC's scrutiny. Without a functioning, independent judicial system to investigate, apprehend, and prosecute suspects (something which the Paris Accords left for a post-transition constitution), there was little expectation that criminal acts by public officials would carry any consequences.

With the Khmer Rouge backtracking, and the shortcomings of UNTAC control mechanisms clearly evident, SOC's large assemblage of local party functionaries, hacks, and thugs had little inducement to adjust gracefully to the competitive pressures created by opposition parties. In the best case, it would have been a difficult adjustment, and UNTAC was already some distance away from that objective.

CIVPOL Problems

Conceivably, an effective U.N. Civilian Police operation could have offset somewhat the gaps in UNTAC's civil administrative controls. Unhappily, the Civilian Police Component turned out to be one of UNTAC's least effective overall, despite good work in a few areas by some highly skilled police personnel. The causes were numerous. Slow startup and poor planning were factors. Little training was done to acquaint police officers with the history of the Cambodian conflict or to build a sense of cultural awareness. This is especially critical for mission success, for it impacts on the effectiveness of training, mentoring, and serving as a role model of community policing. International police personnel must understand their environment and establish a good rapport with the local population.

The quality of police contingents provided varied widely. Thirteen of the 14 states that contributed contingents larger than 100 members were developing countries, whose police forces, to some degree, suffered the same problems that afflicted the SOC police: indiscipline,

---

[32]William Shawcross, *Cambodia's New Deal* (Washington, DC: Carnegie Endowment for International Peace, 1994), 37-68.

human rights abuses, and corruption.[33] Many came from constabulary and paramilitary backgrounds and were not particularly adept at community-based policing techniques; some lacked basic policing and investigative skills; and a significant number could speak neither English nor French, the operation's two official languages, let alone Khmer. Roos described rivalries within UNTAC as a whole as well as problems within CIVPOL at the Singapore meeting:

> Between the [UNTAC] components there were tensions for various reasons. Some people felt their component was the most important and therefore CIVPOL should always be ready to assist. These people were not well informed about our mandate. Others held CIVPOL monitors in contempt because of a lack of discipline or professionalism among certain CIVPOL nationalities, which in a number of cases was a correct assumption. I repatriated some 40 monitors on disciplinary grounds.
>
> But also within the U.N. police force we had to deal with problems related not only to general discipline matters but to cultural, religious and professional differences. It is not surprising when you realize that 32 countries contributed to CIVPOL. Here a big responsibility exists both for the United Nations as well as for the countries in preparing and training their policemen for a mission.[34]

There was also confusion about CIVPOL's tasks, which were not precisely explained in the Paris Accords. It quickly became apparent that "supervising or controlling the local police" in a direct sense was an impossible task, given the comparatively small number of police officers available for local operations on a daily basis. Monitoring what Cambodian police officers do outside the presence of CIVPOL would have been a difficult task in any event, but the organization was not established or commanded with a highly intrusive presence in mind. There was no sustained Civilian Police presence at the village level, and patrolling was rarely conducted at night. Beyond this, provincial-level

---

[33]Findlay, 144.
[34]Roos.

coordination with the military and other UNTAC components was erratic.

Unable to perform its core task satisfactorily, UNTAC's beleaguered CIVPOL suffered from an increasing case load and responsibilities—not only monitoring SOC police, but also providing limited training to local police (mainly to FUNCINPEC and KPNLF factional police): investigating human rights complaints, common banditry, and political intimidation, and conducting security operations. To fill the vacuum in local laws and criminal justice, both for UNTAC and Cambodian police a "Guideline for the Conduct of Criminal Justice in Cambodia" was prepared by the U.N. Crime Prevention and Criminal Justice Division and used by UNTAC. This document contained some of the key principles and standards from various U.N. agreements pertaining to criminal justice, but it had little impact on the situation. Security operations were disliked by most civilian police personnel. These operations included providing security for the UNTAC Electoral Component, newly established Cambodian political party offices, and the conduct of polling. This meant putting unarmed CIVPOL up against the very real possibility of armed opposition.

In fairness, the lack of commitment to the peace accord by key parties to the dispute had much to do with CIVPOL's generally lackluster performance. It is difficult to uphold law and order in the midst of a civil war. Cambodia was an anarchic country with no rule of law and no functioning justice system. Each province contained only two prosecutors and three judges, all appointed by the provincial governor and serving SOC interests. SOC simply refused to apprehend or try its members who had been identified by UNTAC investigations as having committed crimes or human rights violations.

The Revised UNTAC Mission

By the end of 1992—9 months into its operation—the United Nations faced three choices: abort the mission, seek a change in the military mandate and attempt to enforce the Paris Accords, or carry on with the elections realizing the work would have to be accomplished in an environment much different than envisioned.

In fact, U.N. planners in Phnom Penh and New York, with Security Council support but without formal action to change the UNSC Resolution, had already begun to flesh out the third option by December 1992. Its elements were to drop the cantonment process as prerequisite to elections, hold the elections without Khmer Rouge participation, if necessary, and take steps to shelter UNTAC electoral preparations from the disruptive effects of a deteriorating public security situation.

This option was risky, but three factors gave it some promise: first, and foremost, the Khmer Rouge were not well postured to obstruct national elections on a large scale. KR soldiers and cadre generally were located in remote jungle areas and were not in a posture of defiance in downtown Phnom Penh, as was the case with Gen. Aideed's forces in Mogadishu, Somalia. Second, UNTAC benefitted from an exceptionally strong mandate and resources in the electoral and information/education areas. Its ability to deliver a technically sound election required a high degree of public enthusiasm, which it achieved, but *not* the active partnership of any political faction. By assuring a secret ballot and mounting an energetic public information campaign, it would create its sought-after "neutral political environment," if not in the country at large then at least in the polling booth. Third, SOC was not without weak points. The question was how to apply pressure to induce restraint in fomenting violence and unrest.

Operationally, the biggest adjustment UNTAC made was to redeploy its Military Component to support the electoral process. Fortunately, there was a clear understanding of the importance of this adjustment at command levels. The Force Commander, Lieutenant General John Sanderson, worked diligently to imbue in his subordinates and the force in general appreciation for the significance of the new mission. This was critical given that support to elections was hardly glamorous work and required active cooperation with civilians.

In this change of mission, the first act was to redeploy UNTAC's infantry battalions. Initial deployment had been designed to accommodate regroupment and cantonment of factional military forces. The new locations corresponded with the borders of the Cambodian provinces and also aligned these units with the deployment of the electoral and other civilian components. Completed by December 31, 1992, the redeployment was intended to make the military more effective in protecting UNTAC activities by conducting escort and patrol operations and ensuring a more rapid response to potential trouble spots.[35]

One immediate and positive result was improved planning and coordination for security operations among the military, the Civilian Police, and the Electoral Component representatives. Regular meetings to discuss each components' plans and requirements were held at the various military battalion headquarters now located in provincial capitals. This helped abate the natural friction between civilians, who tend to want more military protection when the security situation deteriorates, and the military, who prefer that civilians limit their movements to make providing security easier.

The change in mission did have a noticeable impact on how the military interpreted its ROEs. While focused on cantoning and disarming factional forces, the Military Component interpreted its right to use force very narrowly, that is, strictly for self-defense. When the mission changed to protection of elections in which the military did patrolling, performed escort duties, and manned static security positions, the interpretation for the use of force was expanded to cover protection of UNTAC against any person or group that might threaten it with violence. The military thus became more assertive in defending itself and was more ready to return fire when attacked. Throughout Cambodia, UNTAC military installations and positions increased their vigilance and enhanced security measures.[36]

One such measure was weapons control. Instituting a weapons control program was one of the main tasks given to the UNTAC military in the Paris Accords.[37] Habituated to near-constant threats, many Cambodian homes had weapons for self-protection. Automatic

---

[35]*Managing Arms in Peace Processes: Cambodia* (New York and Geneva: U.N. Institute for Disarmament Research, 1996), 67.

[36]Ibid., 71-72.

[37]*The Blue Helmets: A Review of United Nations Peacekeeping,* 3rd ed. (New York: United Nations, 1996), 456.

rifles, rocket-propelled grenades, and hand grenades were easily obtainable and relatively cheap in the black market. At one stage, a weapons buy-back program was considered but dismissed because the supply and availability of weapons was such that speculators would soon dominate the market and get rich.[38]

UNTAC troops initially had no authority to take weapons from individuals other than through the cantonment process, but as violence increased, U.N. Special Representative Yasushi Akashi issued a directive in March 1993 making the possession of weapons illegal without a firearms license from the police force of the relevant Cambodian authority. Those found in possession of a firearm without the appropriate license could have the weapon confiscated. Soon thereafter the military and CIVPOL components, along with local police, began jointly enforcing the directive with weapons confiscation checkpoints.[39] A dip in gun-related crime was reported after UNTAC's weapons directive came into effect.[40]

In taking a more proactive stance, it was clear there were outer limits on UNTAC willingness to take on new tasks. The UNTAC Military Component was not prepared to assume responsibility for protecting party candidates, recognizing (correctly) that VIP security would overwhelm its limited manpower and field intelligence resources. Nor did UNTAC press its prosecutorial powers very far, fearing adverse reactions from SOC.[41] UNTAC's military was unwilling to use force

---

[38]*Managing Arms in Peace Processes*, 75.

[39]UNTAC Spokesman's office, daily press briefing, March 17, 1993 (mimeo).

[40]Starting in April 1993, approximately 14 random checkpoints were set up daily, and an average of 15 weapons were confiscated per day, including AK-47s, rocket launchers, pistols, and assorted ammunition. These measures coincided with a decline in reported crime in Phnom Penh. Security Council, S/25719, May 3, 1993, 19. The assertion of direct cause and effect relationship remained unproved, however.

[41]Heininger, 99. Although a number of arrest warrants were issued (for both SOC and Khmer Rouge suspects), only three arrests were actually made. Moreover, UNTAC could not find a Cambodian judge who was willing to try the cases in accordance with accepted international standards, and it could not rely on SOC jails to reliably detain suspects. The latter issue was resolved when UNTAC established its own facility; the former issue was never resolved. Findlay, 66-67.

when making arrests,[42] and the CIVPOL contingent, which saw its main job as monitoring, was no more enthusiastic about the idea.[43] In the end, UNTAC efforts to establish a Special Prosecutor's office foundered when it became clear that SOC courts would not hear cases brought before them by the Special Prosecutor.

Despite UNTAC adjustments, an atmosphere of crisis lingered. March and April 1993 saw an increase in pre-election violence, with even UNTAC civilians being targeted. During a 2-week period, seven U.N. workers were killed.[44] This led to a near revolt by U.N. electoral volunteers, who threatened to leave the country unless more protection was provided. UNTAC's leadership was compelled to conduct a nationwide stand-down in the electoral process for several days while security procedures were reviewed and electoral volunteers were fully briefed on election security measures. The volunteers were also equipped with U.S. military flak jackets and helmets rushed to Cambodia on American military aircraft. These actions helped to stem the outflow of the electoral volunteers. In the end, only about 60 volunteers out of total of 400 left. However, even this attrition forced UNTAC to backfill for departed U.N. volunteers, using military observers.

As elections neared, polling station security came to be UNTAC's predominant concern. Many feared that the Khmer Rouge, despite their operational weaknesses, could still disrupt the voting by attacking polling stations. A countrywide threat analysis was conducted by the military, with input from other components. Based on this assessment, individual districts received threat ratings (i.e., high, medium, or low). This analysis permitted a more focused allocation of UNTAC security forces, which General Sanderson had admitted to the U.N. volunteers

---

[42]James Mayall, ed., *The New Interventionism: United Nations Experience in Cambodia, former Yugoslavia and Somalia* (Cambridge, UK: Cambridge University Press, 1996), 45.

[43]McNamara, "U.N. Human Rights Activities in Cambodia," 67. McNamara, director of UNTAC's Human Rights Component, argues that UNTAC's prosecutorial effort could have been more effective as a deterrent to political violence had it been used more extensively.

[44]Heininger, 108.

were insufficient to guarantee security for the more than 1,600 static and mobile polling places located throughout the country.

At each site, UNTAC retained responsibility for security and for U.N. personnel and property in the immediate area. Measures included military and CIVPOL fixed guards, mobile patrols, and general area security. Each of UNTAC's infantry battalions established a mobile reserve with the capability to respond to a security situation within 60 minutes anywhere in their area of responsibility. This was further backed up by a force headquarters mobile reserve stationed in Phnom Penh, which could be flown in UNTAC helicopters to any trouble area.

To compensate for UNTAC's insufficiencies, a plan was devised to enlist the military forces of the three Cambodian factions that supported the elections in providing security. By written agreement with the United Nations, these forces were given responsibility for general security in the areas under their control. For this, they were given access to some of the weapons they had turned over to the United Nations for storage before the disarmament process collapsed.

The polling was successful beyond what most had dared hope, with 90 percent of registered voters casting ballots in a festive atmosphere in spite of early monsoon rains. The Khmer Rouge threat did not materialize on any significant scale. While the security situation had deteriorated throughout UNTAC tenure, and a neutral political environment was never established, the elections were technically sound and widely acclaimed, inside the country and out, as a valid expression of popular will. The UNTAC strategic goal was achieved: a new Cambodian Government with international legitimacy was established.

Evaluation

Key Factors Influencing the Outcome

UNTAC military redeployment was a vital step in offsetting a decline in public security. Both operationally and psychologically, it provided valuable protective cover for the process. For the Khmer Rouge, it reduced the number of targets of opportunity, ratcheting up the costs of obstruction. Although it left some military units exposed in remote areas, the shift also helped to keep a reasonable distance between Khmer Rouge-controlled zones and locations where UNTAC planned to concentrate its electoral assets.[45] It also demonstrated a clear resolve to stay the course, bolstering confidence among UNTAC civilian staff, as well as the Cambodian people, that polling could be conducted safely in major population areas. Without the Military Component's direct and active involvement, the elections could not have been held under the tense conditions that prevailed at the time. Yet, it is also true that the Military Component's action alone would not have been enough to deliver a successful result.

UNTAC was able to utilize civilian resources that had a definite value-added from the security standpoint. On the electoral side, UNTAC devised procedures that helped to insulate the process from the corrosive effects of political violence. The ballots listed political parties rather than candidates, which allowed UNTAC to delay the release of the lists of actual candidates in some cases until very late in the campaign. When SOC internal security officials demanded such information, UNTAC refused.[46] Moreover, the balloting and counting procedures were designed to preserve anonymity for localities as well as for individual voters. Prior to counting, returns from a number of districts would be mixed together, so that no one could learn how a given commune had voted (and thus could not threaten reprisals on that basis).[47] To thwart the most common form of political harassment—the confiscation of voter IDs—UNTAC electoral planners adopted a so-called "tendered ballot" procedure, to enable registered

---

[45]Remarks by Lieutenant General John Sanderson to U.N. volunteers, Phnom Penh, April 20, 1993.

[46]The UNTAC Electoral Component told surprised SOC officials that it would honor the request of any party to delay the release of lists of its candidates and registered party members. If SOC wanted to avail itself of that protection, it was free to do so. Schear interviews, UNTAC Headquarters, April 21, 1993. Reportedly, four parties requested such treatment. Security Council, S/25719, 7.

[47]"Confiscation of Registration Cards Will Not Deter Secret Balloting," *Free Choice: Electoral Component Newsletter*, no. 14, February 26, 1993, 7.

voters without their IDs to cast ballots.[48] All these steps helped to ensure that, at least within the polling booth, the environment was conducive to free and fair elections.

There were even some modest successes in dealing with SOC. Unable to penetrate its security apparatus directly, UNTAC sought to attenuate political violence by indirect means. It launched a number of surprise "Control Team" inspections in a number of provinces, to help expose SOC's complicity in political violence. It also deployed static guards and mobile patrols to deter attacks on vulnerable opposition party offices. While efforts such as these hardly solved the problem, they helped to keep political pressure focused on SOC misbehavior. From behind the scenes, the very real threat by non-Communist opposition parties to withdraw from the election because of political violence was exploited by UNTAC and some outside states in efforts to maneuver SOC toward greater self-restraint.

As the election drew closer, these efforts seemed to take effect. The violence that was widely expected during campaign events did not materialize. While campaigning started slowly in the more stable areas, it soon spread throughout most of the provinces. By the end of the 6-week campaign, nearly 1,600 meetings and rallies, involving nearly one million people, had been held around the country without serious incident.[49] It appeared that SOC security forces were finally exercising restraint, perhaps out of a belief that victory at the polls was assured. As it turned out, they were wrong. FUNCINPEC won the May 1993 election, with a sulking SOC coming in second, resulting in a (shaky) coalition between the two, brokered by Prince Sihanouk. The outcome ultimately paved the way for the emergence of the new government.

---

[48]This procedure, in essence, involved placing a marked ballot in a special envelope containing data about the voter which could be verified by a subsequent check of registration records back at UNTAC headquarters. Safeguards were in place to protect the voter's identity. Ibid., 7. During the polling, roughly 244,000 valid tendered ballots were cast. *The United Nations in Cambodia: A Vote for Peace* (New York: United Nations, 1994), 92.

[49]UNTAC spokesman, daily press briefing, May 20, 1993.

Results of the Mission

UNTAC failed to bring about an end to the civil war in Cambodia: the core element of the Paris Accords went unfulfilled, and the Khmer Rouge remained defiant, though diminished. But UNTAC could fairly claim a number of successes. In the face of prodigious difficulties, it organized an electoral process that inspired great public enthusiasm, produced an internationally recognized government and helped to end Cambodia's years of crippling isolation. The operation also brought home hundreds of thousands of refugees, helped to open up Cambodian society in unprecedented ways, and assisted in the unification of three of the factional armies. In steering a shaky transition process forward, UNTAC aided a major realignment of domestic political power, one in which Cambodia's royalist non-Communist opposition party moved into coalition with Hun Sen's Cambodian People's Party (CPP), leaving the Khmer Rouge out in the cold. By codifying Vietnam's disengagement, it played a part in promoting reconciliation between post-Communist Indochina and the ASEAN states.

All these achievements, considerable in their own right, are even more notable for the fact that they were obtained in spite of a public security situation that UNTAC was never able to control. Despite its far-reaching mandate, UNTAC never had the wherewithal to control local police forces effectively. It was deterred from aggressive enforcement action for fear that SOC would either defy the process or unravel internally, producing even more anarchy. Moreover, civil-military coordination was feeble in UNTAC, at least in its initial phases. The civilian and military components were organized as largely separate operations; only the imminent collapse of the mission brought the two camps together.

Lessons Learned

□ In general, it is critically important that mandates for peacekeeping or transitional assistance include not only *general authorities* (e.g., "to supervise and control") but also *explicit authorizations* that the parties accept at the very outset (e.g.,

"CIVPOL will deploy in local police stations by D+30"). Even good operational planning cannot overcome vagueness in a mandate.

☐ There is no substitute for prompt and effective deployment. UNTAC's slow motion entry into Cambodia deprived it of precious momentum early on; it never fully recovered.

☐ Especially in an unstable public security situation, it is critically important for an operation to engage in rapport-building at the grass-roots level. UNTAC's reputation was sullied by misconduct on the part of some of its soldiers and civilians. The Khmer Rouge tried to exploit that problem, casting themselves as the people's protectors against UNTAC's "bad" elements, but this strategy was never really effective. Overall, UNTAC did an excellent job in establishing its good intentions. Its electoral work, information/education programs, repair of roads and bridges, and the repatriation of refugees all inspired great enthusiasm.

☐ Civil-military coordination for multicomponent operations is important. Except at very senior levels, UNTAC was poorly prepared to mount joint operations but was able to improvise reasonably well when deteriorating security conditions required that it do so.

☐ There has to be good coordination with the local factions. In Cambodia, the Mixed Military Working Group, setup under the Paris Accords along with the Supreme National Council, operated effectively as a forum for coordination and escalation control. Gen. Sanderson used the forum to broker agreements on military support for the elections and on the integration of factional command structures. It included all the competing factions, even the Khmer Rouge, and was quick to address any real or alleged violations of agreements.

☐ It is imperative that long-term institution building, or peacebuilding, be incorporated as part of a graceful exit. UNTAC's hefty size and price tag guaranteed not only that it would be a short-lived phenomenon but that its departure would be politically deflationary for Cambodia. Not enough effort was given to scripting the "transition from the transition," thus the institutional gap was largely ignored.

Hun Sen's forceful eviction of the FUNCINPEC leader, Prince Ranariddh, from the ruling coalition in July 1997 makes this point painfully clear. As a short-term intervention, UNTAC's contributions to the Cambodian transition were bound to be highly perishable. The fragile character of the ruling coalition, in particular, was widely seen as a possible Achilles' heel. What was not fully appreciated was how the sharp decline of the Khmer Rouge 4 years later would destabilize CPP-FUNCINPEC relations, as both sides scrambled to gain advantage. In hindsight, a more concerted international strategy for post-UNTAC Cambodia was necessary to keep the ruling coalition on track. Such a strategy, at a minimum, would have required a longer term international presence in the country (albeit much smaller than UNTAC) and more political pressure on the parties. But it was not to be, and the stirrings of civil society begun during UNTAC's 18-month lifespan are now at risk.

Recommendations

☐ UNTAC's difficulties in the public security arena point to the need for an intelligence gathering and analysis capability that focuses not only on military threats, but also on public security issues. If indigenous public security forces cannot or will not provide a secure environment in which the various aspects of the mandate can be carried out, the Military Component will be hardpressed to avoid getting more involved in public security issues and measures. Intelligence is needed to properly focus and apply that effort.

☐ Given the poor premission analysis that plagued UNTAC's efforts, there is a need for a comprehensive assessment of the security situation and potential public security problems as the mission is being organized. This analysis should be used in determining the proper force structure, especially the requirement for military police or military contingents with specific expertise in public security operations. The British are a good example, with their experience in support to police forces in Northern Ireland.

☐ Military contingents deploying into venues such as Cambodia should have a "hip pocket" training program in public security ready so that they can give their contingents in-country training if this becomes a major mission requirement. The U.S. Army in the 1960s and 1970s had such training programs in civil disturbance/riot control missions.

☐ Senior military leaders should keep an open mind regarding public security tasks. The military is understandably cautious about its exposure to these activities. Soldiers in most major national armed forces are not trained for police work. In many volatile postconflict situations, the extensive use of international military personnel for policing tasks tends to run counter to one of the primary goals of a transition assistance mission such as UNTAC—to wit, that local policing ought to be a job for civilians, not for a militarized constabulary.

On the other hand, in situations where fulfillment of the mandate is at stake, it may be necessary for the military to assume some roles prudently and temporarily on the public security side. Whether such involvement constitutes unacceptable "mission creep" depends very much upon the circumstances on the ground and what precisely the military is being asked to do. The critical issues shaping the military's involvement are twofold: whether its involvement would risk a loss of consent (or active defiance) of one or more of the factions, and whether the reallocation of the military's resources to public security tasks would unacceptably impair mission performance in higher priority areas. There are no set answers to these questions; they have to be examined case by case.

Because of its resources, its self-sustaining structure, and its responsive command structure, the Military Component of any given peace operation is generally the most flexible, applying its energy wherever needed. That, inevitably, puts pressure on the military to spread scarce assets and requires it to adopt a skeptical "show me" attitude when other components come calling, hat in hand, to request its assistance. In the end, however, public security remains an indispensable part of complex field operations; and the military's temporary involvement in such functions may be warranted provided the mission is doable and the anticipated payoffs appear to be commensurate with the costs and risks involved. In the Cambodian case, as least, such involvement was a key factor in achieving a decisive and relatively successful conclusion to the operation.

EL SALVADOR:
The Civilian Police Component of Peace Operations

WILLIAM STANLEY and ROBERT LOOSLE

Background

The Situation Precipitating Intervention

In December 1989 the Government of El Salvador and its opponent, the Farabundo Martí National Liberation Front (FMLN) guerrilla organization, independently approached the Secretary-General to request that the United Nations provide its good offices in support of a peace settlement. This initiative by both parties was a good omen for what became one of the most successful peacemaking efforts by the United Nations in cases of internal conflict. It led to 2 years of U.N.-mediated negotiations and eventually a peace accord signed on January 16, 1992. The United Nations verified the accords by means of a multidisciplinary observer mission that included human rights, military, civilian police, and electoral components.

The decision to invite the United Nations to assist came out of a conflict that was "ripe for resolution."[1] Sporadic guerrilla fighting had begun in the late 1970s and had escalated into a full-blown civil war beginning in January 1981. By 1989, after 10 years of warfare, a politico-military stalemate had developed. The Salvadoran military was far superior in numbers and firepower but had proven unable to eradicate the guerrillas, who enjoyed strong popular support in certain areas, diffuse support throughout the country, a de facto sanctuary in border areas disputed by El Salvador and Honduras, and a strong

---

[1]William I. Zartman, *Ripe for Resolution: Conflict and Intervention in Africa* (Oxford, UK: Oxford University Press, 1985).

network of international financial, logistical, and political support. The FMLN had focused its military efforts on economic sabotage and had sufficient weapons, ammunition, and support to continue in this mode for years.

In November 1989 the FMLN attacked and held portions of the capital city for over a week. After being driven out of poor neighborhoods that they had initially occupied, part of the rebel force infiltrated wealthy neighborhoods where the military was reluctant to use its air power. For the newly elected government of Alfredo Cristiani, representing the business-oriented National Republican Alliance (ARENA) party, the ability of the FMLN to bring the war to the capital city confirmed that 10 years of counterinsurgency campaigns had failed to suppress the rebels. Cristiani and moderate sectors of ARENA considered ongoing war and economic sabotage unacceptable.

The political stature of the Salvadoran military was sufficiently weakened by the offensive that they were no longer in a position to veto civilian-led peace initiatives, as they had during the preceding administration of Christian Democrat José Napoleón Duarte. During the offensive, military personnel had murdered six internationally known Jesuit priests and two witnesses at the University of Central America. This action damaged the Salvadoran military's reputation in the U.S. Congress and therefore weakened prospects for ongoing military assistance from the United States.

For the FMLN, the offensive proved that they lacked the urban support needed for popular insurrection. With military victory out of the question, they faced a war of attrition and sabotage. The changing international climate meant that their long-term prospects for international support were declining and that they needed to negotiate while they were still strong.

Negotiations got under way in early 1990 with the United Nations serving as intermediary. Early in the process, the two sides agreed that the United Nations would verify whatever agreements were eventually reached. As the talks proceeded, the United Nations assumed an increasingly important role as mediator, helping in a number of cases to formulate proposals, to the point of drafting the language of several of the most important accords. In multiple rounds of negotiation from

April 1990 through early January 1992, the two sides produced agreements on extensive verification powers for the United Nations; human rights guarantees; constitutional reforms including measures to depoliticize and professionalize the judiciary; a Truth Commission to investigate past acts of violence; an "ad hoc" commission that would identify officers to be purged from the military; constitutional reforms limiting the role of the armed forces; creation of a new civilian police force; formation of a domestic Commission for the Consolidation of Peace (COPAZ) to verify the accords; separation of forces and demobilization of selected military units and of the entire FMLN guerrilla force; distribution of land and other social benefits to demobilized guerrillas, FMLN supporters, and demobilized government soldiers; legalization of the FMLN as a political party; and broad guidelines for a national reconstruction program that would foster national reconciliation and rapid economic recovery.

Status of the Public Security Apparatus

The heart of the peace accords was reform of state institutions, and by far the most important element was wholesale transformation of the nation's public security system. The Army, which had been extensively involved in domestic policing (and in politics), was constitutionally banned from any security function other than national defense, except in cases of national emergency when all other means had been exhausted. The military-controlled public security forces, which included the National Guard, the Treasury Police, and the National Police, were to be demobilized, with their members absorbed into the army (or, in practice, discharged). Rural paramilitary civil defense patrols were also to be disarmed and disbanded. The old constabulary forces were to be replaced by a new civilian police force trained in a pro-democratic and human rights-oriented doctrine at a new civilian police academy. A majority of personnel would come from sources other than the Salvadoran Army or the FMLN. During the transition, one of the old security forces, the National Police (PN), was to remain on duty, while a new National Civilian Police (PNC) was to be trained, organized, and deployed.

The centrality of these reforms reflected the importance of the flawed public security forces in contributing to the conflict in the first place. Military officers had governed the country from 1932 to 1979, with the cooperation of members of the economic elite. Military rule had begun under a personalistic dictator who reined from 1932 until 1944. In 1948, midranking officers had established a more institutionalized form of military governance with corporatist pretensions. This regime survived, with variations, until its collapse in 1979 on the eve of the civil war. Institutional military rule was not always heavily repressive: in the early years it was accompanied by a modicum of democratic political competition and responsiveness to popular demands. But beginning in the 1970s, the system became increasingly rigid, blatant in its use of electoral fraud, and violently repressive.

The most repressive elements of the regime were the three security forces, the National Guard, the Treasury Police, and the National Police, as well as a number of special intelligence units set up within the military. These forces functioned as political police, suppressing dissent while defending elite interests against labor and peasant organizers and other "subversive" influences. At the local level, the relationship between security forces and major landowners was overtly mercenary, with National Guard units housed, fed, and paid bonuses by large-scale commercial farms. The massacre of some 25,000 peasants and workers in 1932 by the National Guard was a landmark for both supporters and opponents of the regime. The security forces periodically carried out crackdowns after that time and turned to extremely murderous conduct during the 1970s and early 1980s. As the military regime deteriorated, all three security forces responded to growing popular opposition to military rule and the emergence of guerrilla organizations by torturing and murdering increasing numbers of citizens. Elements of these same forces also became extensively involved in kidnapping and other crimes for profit.

The brutality of the security forces was a crucial contributing factor in the expansion of support for guerrilla organizations and the eventual outbreak of civil war. While the security apparatus did succeed in infiltrating and imposing great casualties on the guerrilla organizations, thousands of civilians who were merely involved in protest activities were also murdered. The brutality, corruption, and politicization of the security regime created a climate of political exclusion, frustration, and violence that became highly conducive to civil war. More specifically, the growing intensity of represssion by the security forces during the late 1970s and early 1980s, combined with its often indiscriminate targeting, gave thousands of Salvadorans incentives to take arms against the government for self-defense and revenge.[2]

The military withdrew formally from political power following elections in 1982 that brought a new constituent assembly and a provisional president to power. Subsequent elections in 1984 and 1985 helped consolidate this transition to elected civilian rule. But the military remained a powerful and insubordinate actor capable of vetoing the actions of civilian presidents. After an extremely violent period, 1980 through 1983, the military gradually improved its human rights record during the latter half of the 1980s. The security forces were moved into a Vice-Ministry of Defense for Public Security and underwent a gradual purge and reform that dampened their propensity for violence against civilians. Despite these improvements, the security forces and the military as a whole remained politicized, violently repressive, and unaccountable through the end of the war.

Profound reform of this system was a *sine qua non* for achieving peace. In the peace negotiations that got under way in 1990 with U.N. observation and mediation, the FMLN main demands related to reform of the military and accountability for past abuses. Although the FMLN had proclaimed throughout the war that it was fighting for radical socioeconomic reforms, it set these issues aside almost completely during the negotiations, turning to them only in the final months, once the military and public security issues had been largely resolved. Throughout much of the negotiations, the FMLN demanded that government forces be disbanded, or that FMLN combat units be incorporated into the armed forces. Both positions were completely

---

[2]See T. David Mason and Dale A. Krane, "The Political Economy of Death Squads: Toward a Theory of the Impact of State-Sanctioned Terror," *International Studies Quarterly* 33 (1989): 175-198.

unacceptable to the Government. In the September 1991 round of negotiations in New York, the FMLN abandoned these demands in exchange for an agreement that would create a professional, pro-democratic, civilian police force and allow former FMLN combatants to make up as much as twenty percent of the initial cadre. Basic resolution of the military and police issues allowed the talks to proceed rapidly after the New York round, with final agreements reached on the balance of the agenda in just over 3 months.

The Mandate

Unlike other recent U.N. missions, the U.N. Observer Mission in El Salvador (ONUSAL) did not initially face a situation of chaos or collapse of government function, and the mission had only a very limited direct role in maintenance of public order. A serious public security gap developed, however, as a result of postwar social stresses, demobilization of ex-combatants, and the weak transitional public security system. ONUSAL adapted to this problem as it emerged, assisting the existing police forces, engaging in de facto police work in various parts of the country, and providing on-the-job training for the PNC as it began to deploy.[3] ONUSAL also took various steps to prevent the political ramifications of the crime wave from disrupting the peace process, such as pressuring the Government to move ahead with demobilization of the PN. Notwithstanding the effective measures it did take, the U.N. role in public security was deficient in some regards, because of unrealistic planning, personnel shortages, and poor coordination within the mission and with other international actors.

---

[3]As discussed in more detail below, de facto policing means that although ONUSAL CIVPOLs did not have arrest powers and were unarmed, in some parts of the country they carried out many other routine duties of police, including receiving complaints from citizens, investigating cases, dealing with conflicts between citizens, helping citizens prevent crime, and generally maintaining social peace and order. They worked closely with both the old National Police (PN) and the PNC, depending on the Salvadoran institutions to make arrests but often playing a significant role in their own right, guiding investigations, questioning witnesses, and locating suspects.

The CIVPOL mandate of ONUSAL derived from a section of the accords relating to the "transitional regime" for public security:

> The international verification of agreements to be undertaken by the United Nations through ONUSAL shall include the activities of a group of specialists from countries with experience in the organization and operation of civilian police forces. The tasks of those specialists shall include, in addition to cooperating in ensuring a smooth transition and assisting police authorities, that of accompanying officers and members of the National Police in the performance of their duties.
>
> During the progressive deployment of the new force to zones which were traditionally conflict zones during the armed conflict, public security in those zones shall be subject to a special regime to be determined by the Director-General of the National Civil Police. That regime shall, in any case, envisage activities by the group of specialists referred to in the preceding paragraph.[4]

This mandate was quite vague. Nothing in the accords spells out exactly what it should mean for ONUSAL police specialists to "accompany" the National Police, or what tasks the U.N. police should carry out to ensure a "smooth transition." The political understanding behind this phrase was that the U.N. police were to ensure that the National Police did not engage in politically-motivated abusive practices. After reforms in the late 1980s, the National Police had become less repressive in its every day activities. Nonetheless, the PN had a history of operating one of the most active death squads in the country in the early 1980s, and FMLN leaders remained deeply distrustful of the old police.[5] ONUSAL supervision would help ensure that the PN did not operate in ways that might jeopardize the ability of

---

[4]Chapter II, section 7, subsection B, paragraphs e-f, of the Peace Agreement signed at Chapultepec, January 16, 1992. See *El Salvador Agreements: The Path to Peace* (San Salvador: U.N. Department of Public Information and ONUSAL, May 1992), 70-1.

[5]Declassified CIA document, "Existence of Rightist Death Squad within the Salvadoran National Police, Location of Clandestine Prison Used by the Death Squad," March 19, 1983.

the FMLN to demobilize its troops safely and begin to function as a legal political party.

Peace Mission Organization

The U.N. peace operations role began with the establishment of a preliminary human rights observer mission, which began work in July 1991, *before* the cease-fire, verifying compliance with a human rights accord signed in July 1990 in San José, Costa Rica. The U.N. Observer Mission in El Salvador, ONUSAL, expanded once the cease-fire was signed to include military and police divisions. At its peak, it included 317 military observers (of 372 authorized) and 314 police observers (of 631 authorized). These elements were later supplemented by the Electoral Division, which oversaw voter registration, campaigning, and the implementation of elections in March and April of 1994.

The Military Division was responsible for verifying the separation of forces, the demobilization and disarmament of guerrillas, and the demobilization of selected army and security forces units. It operated from January 1992 until early 1993, after which a smaller military contingent stayed on to monitor revisions to military doctrine and education. The Police Division was given the task of assisting in the transition from the old, military-controlled system of policing to a new civilian public security regime. The ONUSAL Police Division's specific duties were to cooperate "in ensuring a smooth transition and assisting police officials," and "accompanying officers and members of the National Police in the performance of their duties."[6]

Size and Composition of the Police Division

To carry out these tasks, the Police Division of ONUSAL was programmed to have 631 police observers, nearly twice the peak authorized size of the Military Division (372 observers). The rationale for this substantial force was that while government and guerrilla

---

[6]United Nations, *El Salvador Agreements: The Path to Peace* (San Salvador: U.N. Department of Public Information and ONUSAL, May 1992), 71.

military forces would be confined to a relatively small number of bases and concentration points, ONUSAL would need to deploy police monitors at all levels of the National Police throughout the country, while also deploying in areas where the "special regime" would apply during the transition. Supervision of the National Police would involve establishing a U.N. presence in the National Police central and regional headquarters and "other decisionmaking and operational levels. Such coverage would extend to as many fixed National Police installations as considered necessary in both urban and rural areas."[7] ONUSAL police would also engage in mobile monitoring, accompanying PN patrols and carrying out random checks of their activities.

The ONUSAL Police Division operated at less than half its authorized strength. Its numbers peaked at 314 and often hovered around 270. The main constraint on the size of the division was the limited number of countries that were willing and able to send contingents, and the rejection by one or another of the Salvadoran parties of certain potential contributing countries, such as Argentina. Spain, Mexico, Chile, France, and Italy provided the largest contingents; the United States did not contribute personnel to the CIVPOL mission.[8] Most of the police arrived with adequate language skills, although some Italians spoke poor Spanish.[9] The nations that did provide contingents did so promptly. Recruitment and selection were accomplished in about 3 months, and the Police Division began its deployment in a timely fashion in March 1992. The selection process was weighted toward police agents from the patrol ranks because the emphasis was on verification and field work. Donor countries selected the personnel, based on criteria provided by the United Nations.

Salaries of CIVPOLs were paid by the sending countries, while the U.N. paid the daily allowances. A few countries, including Spain, France, and Italy, paid their own daily housing and other compensation

---

[7] See *Report of the Secretary-General on the monitoring of agreements by ONUSAL*, January, 10, 1992, 188.

[8] Other contributors included Austria, Colombia, Guyana, Norway, and Sweden.

[9] ONUSAL official, interview by Stanley, December 1992.

in addition to U.N. allowances, a situation that created strong individual incentives for such CIVPOL officials to lobby to remain in the mission beyond their initial tours. These incentives may have had a positive side effect: most countries assigned police to ONUSAL for relatively short periods, resulting in some loss of efficiency as CIVPOL officers were recalled around the time they had gained a working knowledge of the Salvadoran context. Efforts by some officers and national contingents to prolong stays thus helped retain personnel with more experience in El Salvador, although those who pushed hardest to stay were not always the most apt for mission work.[10]

In general, the professional qualifications of the police officers sent to El Salvador were adequate for the "accompaniment" role originally envisioned.[11] It proved difficult, however, to assign duties and establish a command hierarchy. Different police forces had different ranking systems. Even those that used the same nominal categories promoted officers at very different rates. Although the division attempted to assign responsibilities according to preparation and experience, these were not always easy to ascertain. Frictions developed when officers with lower nominal ranks were given authority over officers with "superior" ranks but less experience or training. Some police were reluctant to accept orders from police from other national delegations. Within headquarters, this could be managed to some extent by giving different national delegations different portfolios—for example, Italians took charge of personnel and Spaniards ran operations. This was not always feasible, however, and compromises made to accommodate these sensitivities sometimes produced sub-optimal use of personnel.

Resources

Equipment was rarely a problem for the ONUSAL Police Division. At the time of deployment, U.N. equipment reserves were good, and

---

[10]ONUSAL police and civilian officials, interviews by Stanley, July 1993.

[11]The training and experience level was not always adequate to field training roles that developed in 1993, for which higher rank and greater experience would have been helpful.

vehicles, radios, computers, and other necessities were available from U.N. stores, from the recently terminated the United Nations Observer Group in Central America (ONUCA) mission and from missions in Cambodia and Haiti. As a result, the division had adequate numbers of four-wheel drive vehicles, and the mission as a whole had an effective nationwide radio network.

Relations with Salvadoran Public Security Forces

The shortage of personnel did have an adverse effect on the ability of the Police Division to do its job effectively, largely because it limited the division's ability to monitor activities of the National Police. While CIVPOL supervision of the PN was sufficient to prevent wholesale politically motivated repression or intimidation, it did not prevent the PN from committing significant numbers of human rights violations and outright criminal activity. Reports by the Human Rights Division of ONUSAL showed that the PN continued to commit numerous violations of individual's rights, mainly through excessive use of force and disregard for legal process. Thus while the Police Division was adequate to the task of preventing political bias of the PN from disrupting the peace process, it was not sufficient to motivate the PN to maintain public order adequately during the transition. One result of this public security gap was a tendency for Salvadorans to approach ONUSAL, rather than the PN, to report crimes or other problems.

Cooperation within ONUSAL

The Police Division's responsibility to accompany the PN should naturally have implied close coordination with the Human Rights Division of ONUSAL in the identification and investigation of possible abuses involving the police, military, or politically motivated groups. Indeed, a number of CIVPOLs were assigned to the Human Rights Division as investigators. Too often, however, the police and human rights divisions worked separately and even at cross purposes.[12] The Human Rights Division did not always have access to information possessed by the Police Division. In the worst of cases, the two divisions conducted separate investigations of the same incidents and reached different conclusions.[13]

Part of the problem was that the Police Division had a separate chain of command during the first 2 years of the full, multidivision mission. U.N. police around the country reported to their division director in San Salvador rather than to ONUSAL regional or subregional offices. This created coordination problems and sometimes considerable frustration and resentment on the part of regional and subregional coordinators (who were generally from the Human Rights Division), who were responsible for the overall work of the mission in a given region but lacked control over the police personnel there. Even at ONUSAL headquarters, officials in other divisions complained that the director of the Police Division treated information collected by U.N. police as a proprietary resource.[14] Moreover, Police Division headquarters sometimes failed to use information from the Human Rights Division to press the National Police to dismiss agents who were responsible for repeated human rights violations. Human rights officials in regional offices found themselves having to explain to Salvadoran citizens who had brought complaints forward why known abusers in the PN remained on the job.[15]

The mission was restructured in April 1994 so that police officials were integrated into regional and subregional offices and made

---

[12]Gino Costa, "The United Nations and Reform of the Police in El Salvador," *International Peacekeeping* 2, no. 3 (Autumn): 1995, 381. Costa, who was a senior staff member in ONUSAL's office of the Chief of Mission, writes that the two divisions were often competitive with one another and that this devolved into outright hostility.

[13]ONUSAL official, interview with author, April 1995; Lawyers Committee on Human Rights, *Improvising History: A Critical Evaluation of the United Nations Observer Mission in El Salvador* (New York: Lawyers Committee, 1995), 31.

[14]ONUSAL officials, interviews by Stanley, November 1992 and July 1993.

[15]ONUSAL human rights official, interview by Stanley, April 1995.

responsible to regional coordinators.[16] This improved coordination. However, female ONUSAL officials found that police officers under their authority were sometimes insubordinate and uncooperative.

Part of the explanation for limited collaboration between the human rights and police divisions can be traced to different professional formations. Few members of either division had ever collaborated in joint police/civilian efforts. The Human Rights Division was heavily populated with Latin American human rights attorneys who had had few positive experiences with police institutions in their home countries. The two groups began with mutual suspicions: in some offices, they managed to work out their differences over time. In others, problems worsened. Distrust on the part of Human Rights Division observers was reinforced by their observation that sometimes U.N. police defended, or failed to rigorously investigate, the Salvadoran National Police. When U.N. police and human rights staff worked together toward common goals, they could be highly effective, as in the case of the investigation into the murder of FMLN leader Francisco Velis, in which UNCIVPOL played a key role in locating a witness and persuading her to cooperate in the investigation.

Coordination between the police and military divisions was generally more effective but was also less important. The tasks of the two divisions did not overlap significantly, except insofar as the Military Division, which had a strong presence in many areas of the countryside, was able to pass on reports of crimes to the Police Division. Aside from such reporting, the Military Division did not involve itself extensively in public security roles. Given its lack of armament, there were no provisions to assist the CIVPOL, nor was there any significant logistical interdependence between the two divisions.

According to U.N. officials, some coordination problems could have been ameliorated by stronger steps by the early chiefs of mission to impose a clear, common set of goals for police, human rights, and

---

[16]ONUSAL regional office directors, interview by Stanley, October 1994. See also Costa, "The United Nations and Reform," 381.

military operations. However, this would have required a very active management role from mission leadership that was already heavily taxed by constant, complex political negotiations with the Salvadoran parties. The U.N. Special Representative was involved in constant bilateral and trilateral meetings with the Salvadoran parties, as well as extensive meetings with other international agencies, leaving little time to devote to engendering unity of purpose within the mission. In retrospect internal coordination would have been best served by avoiding institutionalized divisions within the mission in the first place.

The Mission

Phases of the Operation

ONUSAL began human rights verification in July 1991, the Military and Police Divisions deployed following the cease-fire in February 1992, and an Electoral Division operated from late 1993 through the March and April 1994 elections. ONUSAL ended in April 1995, replaced by a small follow-on mission, U.N. Mission in El Salvador, or MINUSAL, which continued to verify remaining aspects of the accords. MINUSAL was in turn replaced by a small monitoring office, the U.N. Verification Office (ONUV), which closed at the end of 1996.

The Enforcement Gap

The accords required the Government to dismantle most of the old security forces; to maintain a fraction of the old system temporarily to keep order until a new civilian police force could be formed; and to train, organize, and deploy a completely new police force, all in fewer than 2 years. This necessarily entailed a temporary but drastic weakening of the public security apparatus. The elimination of the National Guard and Treasury Police abruptly cut available security personnel from 14,000 to about 6,000. Combined with the demobilization of half the Government's Army and all the rebel forces (which had informally policed zones under its de facto control), the end of the war reduced the overall forces of vigilance from roughly 75,000 to around 6,000.[17]

Wholesale transformation of public security forces, essential as it was, proved difficult to carry out and brought with it new public security problems that challenged the capacity of both domestic and international institutions. From 1992 through 1995, El Salvador saw a dramatic increase in crime, which quickly became the primary concern of the majority of Salvadorans. Of particular concern was the rapid expansion of organized crime, ranging from heavily armed rural gangs that robbed and terrorized communities and highway travelers, to highly sophisticated kidnapping and car theft rings. Such organizations were not new to El Salvador, nor was support from and participation by elements of the old security forces and the military a novelty.[18] However, the scope of the problem appeared to expand dramatically with the end of the conflict, fed by the demobilization of tens of thousands of former soldiers, policemen, and guerrilla combatants into a context of inadequate employment opportunities and support services and easy availability of military weapons. The demobilization of a large portion of the public security forces during the transition created a permissive context in which it was relatively easy for criminal organizations to operate.

The generalized climate of violence in the country after 1993 also created uncertainty regarding how much of this was politically motivated. After years of internecine violence, Salvadorans tended to assume that many killings after the cease-fire took effect were politically motivated, especially when the victims were former combatants, political activists, or labor leaders. Investigations by ONUSAL found relatively few cases that were clearly political, but it failed to effectively

---

[17]Subsequent transfers of military and security personnel into the PN raised its numbers to around 8,000, though only about 6,800 of these were regular patrol personnel, with the balance performing administrative and investigative functions.

[18]See "Report issued on 28 July 1994 by the Joint Group for the Investigation of Politically Motivated Illegal Armed Groups (extract: conclusions and recommendations)," *The United Nations and El Salvador 1990-1995,* U.N. Blue Book Series IV (New York: U.N. Department of Public Information, 1995), document 113, 568-74.

publicize these exculpatory findings, leaving much of the public to assume that widespread political violence continued.

In addition to taking over the responsibilities previously handled by three different security forces, the National Police faced a number of institutional constraints. Although the Vice-Ministry of Defense for Public Security had significant numbers of trucks and portable radios, many supplied by the United States, most were retained by the military. The National Police was left with only a few aging police cruisers, an insufficient number of trucks, and very few radios. These equipment shortages greatly reduced the mobility and responsiveness of the roughly 6,000 PN agents. ONUSAL's Police Division helped compensate for this gap by using its communications network and vehicles to help the PN react more effectively to traffic accidents and reports of crimes. Without U.N. help, the National Police would probably have been completely overwhelmed.

Although crime-fighting was not an explicit aspect of ONUSAL's mandate, its broader responsibility to ensure a "smooth transition" required that it assist wherever it could in controlling crime. Furthermore, many ONUSAL police engaged in de facto police work, investigating crimes and dealing with various public order problems. UNCIVPOL lacked arrest authority and depended on the Salvadoran police to request judicial actions and make arrests. Activities varied across different ONUSAL offices and depended on individual proclivities. In a number of instances, ONUSAL police greatly exceeded their nominal mandate, accepting complaints from citizens, carrying out investigations, questioning witnesses, locating suspects, and effectively commanding newly trained PNC personnel on the job. As one U.N. official put it, "In many parts of the country, ONUSAL police *were* the police."[19] Another U.N. official remarked that the involvement of CIVPOL in investigations was not really surprising; as professionals accustomed to taking an active role, their accompaniment and verification functions in El Salvador left them bored and restless.[20]

---

[19]U.N. official, interview by Stanley, April 1996.
[20]ONUSAL official, interview by Stanley, November 1992.

CIVPOL investigative work was never formally authorized, except in human rights cases, and it is unlikely the Government would have agreed to such an intrusive role. The de facto involvement of some CIVPOLs in active police work at the local level, however, although uncoordinated and inconsistent across different parts of the country, helped to fill this temporary law enforcement gap and does not appear to have produced negative consequences.

ONUSAL police were unarmed, and there were no arrangements for support from the Military Division, which was also unarmed. This limited the policing roles UNCIVPOLs could take on in El Salvador's heavily armed and violent environment; however, most agreed that the decision to be unarmed was a wise one. ONUSAL police were not targeted by any organized group and therefore had no need to defend themselves. CIVPOLs in the field necessarily acted cautiously in situations in which they might have come under fire, such as Salvadoran police operations against criminals known to be armed or demonstrations that turned violent. This enforced caution may have prevented casualties. Given their small numbers, ONUSAL police, even if armed, would not have made a significant additional contribution to fighting violent crime. One of their more important roles was to mediate the dozens of potentially volatile confrontations that occurred between police and various groups of citizen demonstrators, such as former combatants dissatisfied with government benefits packages, and organized labor, peasant groups, and FMLN supporters protesting land issues. In these situations, the moral authority and neutrality of ONUSAL police were enhanced by the fact that they were unarmed. If mediation failed and violence broke out, ONUSAL police withdrew. Having armament in such situations would not have furthered the CIVPOL mission and might well have jeopardized it if ONUSAL police had resorted to force.[21] When they

---

[21]There was a strong negative public reaction to a number of traffic accidents in which ONUSAL vehicles ran over and killed children on the highways. This is a common type of accident in El Salvador, but the incidents involving ONUSAL drivers led to complaints about speeding and arrogance on the part of ONUSAL monitors. Had ONUSAL police possessed arms, it is possible that they would have had cause to

carried out de facto police work or engaged in on-the-job training with new PNC police, their ability to function effectively without being armed helped de-emphasize the use of physical force and highlight effective human relations, use of information, and mediation.

The inconsistent involvement of CIVPOL in direct police work was symptomatic of a general lack of uniformity, direction, and clarity regarding how they were to go about their job. Because the mandate of the Police Division was so vague, it was particularly important to have clear guidelines regarding how they should go about gathering and using information and how this work should be integrated with other aspects of the mission. Neither the Chief of Mission's office nor Police Division leadership provided the required guidance: as a result the Police Division was not used to fullest effect to manage the public security crisis and its various political ramifications.[22] Throughout the transition to the PNC, there were serious problems in organization, operation, and conduct of the PN involving human rights abuses, inefficiency, low morale, corruption, and outright criminality. The Police Division constituted a significant resource for gathering intelligence on patterns of crime, yet this information was not exploited to allow ONUSAL to analyze the nature of the crime problem effectively and to identify and seek remedies to problems within the PN.[23] Nor was information on police misconduct comprehensive enough for the United Nations to use it consistently in its public reporting.

The lack of a coherent criminological data base contributed to a failure by ONUSAL leadership to acknowledge the severity of the crime problem and to anticipate its likely political consequences. ONUSAL human rights reports in late 1992 and early 1993, relying on crimes

---

use them, which in light of the readiness of some Salvadorans to condemn the mission for even accidental killings, would likely have produced very negative political consequences for the mission.

[22]ONUSAL official, interviews by Stanley, December 1992, July 1993, April 1995. See also Costa, 382.

[23]U.N. officials, interviews by Stanley, December 1992, July 1993. See also Costa, 382.

reported in the media, argued that homicide rates were essentially stagnant during 1992, following major increases during the final years of the war. From this, ONUSAL concluded that much of the public concern about crime was a result of postwar psychology and the media's spectacularized (though factually accurate) reporting of crime, which seemed designed to heighten public anxiety.[24]

Yet evidence from other sources does show a public security crisis underway already in 1992 and 1993, centered on an extremely high incidence of armed robbery and on the apparent randomness of homicides associated with these robberies. A February 1993 survey by the Central American University's Public Opinion Institute (Instituto Universitario de Opinión Publica, IUDOP) showed that 73.2 percent of the those surveyed considered crime the main problem of the country, 88.6 percent thought crime had increased, and 68.1 percent were afraid of being assaulted in their own homes. According to the same poll, 76 percent of crime victims did not notify the police. Most significantly, 34 percent of respondents from urban areas said they or an immediate family member had been robbed in the past 4 months, clearly an extraordinarily high rate.[25] Public fear was stoked by the fact that crimes, mainly armed robbery, increasingly involved the use of military weapons, including M-16 and AK-47 rifles, and grenades. The lethal weaponry, combined with the callousness of criminals, many of whom appear to have been former combatants inured to violence, led to what ONUSAL acknowledged was "a trend toward fatalities for relatively trivial causes or reasons."[26]

---

[24]See Report of the Director of the Human Rights Division of the United Nations Observer Mission in El Salvador up to January 31, 1993 [sixth report], annexed to U.N. Document A/47/912, S/25521, 5 April 1993. The Ministry of Justice reported that crime increased by 83 percent between 1990 and 1991, prior to the signing of the final accords. Se El sector justicia de El Salvador en números (San Salvador: Ministerio de Justicia, 1993).

[25]IUDOP, "La delincuencia urbana," Estudios Centroamericanos 534-545 (April/May 1993), 471-79.

[26]Report of the Director of the Human Rights Division of the United Nations Observer Mission in El Salvador up to April 30, 1993 (seventh report), annexed to U.N. Document A/47/968, S/26033, July 2, 1993.

Indeed, crime statistics for 1994 through 1996 show El Salvador with the highest homicide rate in Latin America, exceeding that even of Colombia, long notorious for its high murder rate. According to government statistics, 7,673 people were murdered in El Salvador in 1994, a rate of 138.2 per 100,000 persons, compared to 85 per 100,000 persons in Colombia. Among countries with reasonably reliable crime statistics, only South Africa reports a higher rate. Some observers estimate that criminal gangs have as many as 12,000 armed members, greater than the size of the FMLN guerrilla army during the war.[27]

The prevalence of military weapons in civilian hands reflected the laxness of controls by both sides. ONUSAL's Military Division was responsible for collecting and overseeing the destruction of FMLN weapons. The FMLN lied to the United Nations regarding its weapons inventory, retaining major caches of arms in El Salvador and neighboring countries. Many of these weapons were finally turned over and destroyed after an apparently accidental explosion at an FMLN weapons cache in Nicaragua in May 1993 exposed the extent of the FMLN deception. The discovery was so politically damaging to the FMLN, coming less than a year before the 1994 elections, that it led to a more thorough process of disarmament than would otherwise have taken place.[28] In the long run this probably helped reduce availability of military weapons in subsequent years.[29] On the government side, the Ministry of Defense did a very poor job of maintaining control over its own weapons. Large numbers of the military's own M-16 rifles had been distributed to relatives of military personnel, family friends, civilian officials, business people, and bodyguards of military personnel and wealthy civilians. Neither the military's own weapons nor arms

---

[27]Serge F. Kavaleski, "Murders Soar in El Salvador Since Devastating War's End," *Washington Post*, October 1, 1997, A22. El Salvador's murder rate rose to 7,877 in 1995 a rate of 138.9 per 100,000 persons, then declined in 1996 to 6,792, or 117.4 per 100,000.

[28]FMLN political analyst, interview by Stanley, July 1993.

[29]U.S. embassy official, interview by Stanley, October 1992.

captured from the FMLN during the war were properly inventoried.[30]
Under the peace accords, the legislature was to pass laws restricting the
weapons that could be possessed by civilians, and the Ministry of
Defense was required to collect all "military use" weapons in private
hands. These provisions were never effectively implemented, and PNC
officials complained in interviews in 1994 that the Ministry of Defense
continued to distribute military weapons, unlawfully, to former soldiers
and other associates of the military.[31] Under the Salvadoran
constitution, the Ministry of Defense retains ultimate authority to
regulate the possession of arms, although the PNC has enforcement
authority. The problem of weapons in private hands was compounded
by the fact that it was not uncommon for uniformed soldiers to commit
crimes, particularly armed robbery, in areas outside the capital city,
using their duty weapons.[32]

The Special Regime for Ex-Conflict Zones

A "special regime" in former conflict zones was necessary because the
FMLN and their supporters distrusted the National Police and were not
willing to allow that force to establish a presence in their areas of
political and military strength. Details of the special regime were to be
determined by the director of the PNC. Unfortunately, the first PNC
director, José María Monterrey, was not appointed until July 1992, 6
months after the beginning of the cease-fire. In the interim there was
a public security vacuum in the former conflict zones. As residents
expressed alarm about the lack of any public security force, the FMLN
deployed armed patrols to police these areas. This was, of course, a
violation of their agreement to concentrate their forces in specific areas,
as required to ensure positive separation of government and guerrilla
forces.[33] While these patrols did not lead to any clashes with
Government forces, they did result in protests from the Government.

---

[30]Salvadoran army officer, who related a number of examples of poor
administrative control over weapons, interview by Stanley, May 1995.

[31]PNC officials, interview by Stanley, September 1994.

[32]ONUSAL and PNC officials, interview by Stanley, March 1995.

[33]U.N. and Salvadoran military officials, interview by Stanley, August 1992.

In October 1992, a special regime was put into place with the deployment of "Auxiliary Transitory Police" (PAT) units, made up of cadets from the new civilian police academy commanded by ONUSAL police officials. The PAT units did not have full police powers: they could not investigate crimes and could make arrests only in cases of *in fraganti delito*. They were required to notify judicial authorities of crimes they became aware of, and ONUSAL was to assist in arranging for National Police investigations of such cases. Thus the PAT role was mainly one of crime prevention and maintenance of public order, and ONUSAL's role therein did not encroach on sovereignty.[34] PAT units were generally considered successful in providing rudimentary public security, and the young PAT cadets were well accepted by the population. This was crucial because it helped set the stage for favorable public response to the new PNC as it deployed in former conflict zones. PAT cadets also received useful on-the-job training from experienced foreign police officers.[35]

Institution Building and the New Police Force

The exit strategy of the U.N. mission was to oversee a simultaneous process of democratization, social reintegration of former guerrillas, and institutional reforms to the state that would create conditions for lasting peace. A central piece of this process was the formation of a new National Civilian Police. The United Nations was deeply involved in the conception, design, and fielding of the PNC, in conjunction with other international players. A special U.N. mission visited El Salvador in October 1991 and wrote detailed recommendations regarding the makeup, design and doctrine of the new force, as well as initial drafts of enabling legislation for the PNC and the civilian police academy— Academia Nacional de Seguridad Pública (ANSP). These recommendations, though modified somewhat in response to input from the Salvadoran protagonists as well as other international experts,

---

[34] "Regimen especial de seguridad en zonas ex-conflictivas; Policia Auxiliar Transitoria (PAT) Lineamientos." ONUSAL document, undated.

[35] Interviews with PNC agents, July and August 1993.

formed the core of the institutional design, doctrine, and legal framework for the ANSP and PNC.[36] A revised version of the Organic Law for the PNC was annexed to the final peace accords and ratified by the Legislative Assembly early in 1992.

The peace accords gave ONUSAL overall responsibility for verifying the formation of the ANSP and PNC. The U.N. Development Programme (UNDP) was responsible for soliciting and coordinating international technical and financial contributions to the project. Initial plans for formation of the ANSP were drawn up by a technical team made up of Spanish, U.S., and Salvadoran police specialists. Once the ANSP was established, a Principal Technical Advisor (ATP) was appointed, nominally directing instructors and advisors from Spain, the the United States, Chile, Norway, and Sweden. Of these national contingents, Spain, Norway and Sweden coordinated their assistance through the UNDP, while U.S. and Chilean contingents served under bilateral agreements.

ONUSAL's role at the ANSP was limited. Liaison with the international technical team was maintained via weekly meetings between ATP and the ONUSAL Chief of Mission. This did not always provide an adequate flow of information between ONUSAL, which was monitoring performance of PNC personnel in the field, and the international trainers at the ANSP.[37] Initially, technical assistance to the PNC itself took two forms: high-level advising by the U.S. ICITAP program, and an on-the-job field training program carried out by

---

[36]See "Informe de la misión de las Naciones Unidas sobre la cración de la Policía Nacional Civil," annexed to interoffice memorandum from Alvaro de Soto to the Comisión Negociadora del Gobierno de la República de El Salvador, October 29, 1991. The mission was made up of Jesús Rodés, Escola de Policia de Catalunya in Spain; Sarge Antony, French National Police; Juan Manuel Mayorca, Central University of Venezuela; Pierre Rémillard, Police Institute of Quebec; Gösta Melander, Stockholm police; and Angela Knippenberg, Office of the Secretary-General's Personal Representative for the Central American Peace Process. In retrospect, the mission's recommendation that the ANSP and PNC be separate entities was probably a poor one. Coordination problems have plagued the academy and police, suggesting that combining both in the same legal and organizational structure might have been better.
[37]Costa.

ONUSAL police observers. Subsequently, UNDP developed a number of technical assistance projects for the PNC, and Spain provided assistance under the rubric of the European Union.

Even this level of international support was not considered sufficient as far as the Salvadoran Government was concerned. Salvadoran officials claimed they had been assured during negotiations that the international community would bear all costs associated with transforming the public security system. In fact, international support for police projects was markedly weaker than for other aspects of post-conflict reconstruction and reform. While the international community funded 26 percent of overall reconstruction activities for 1993, it financed only 12 percent of anticipated public security related development expenses in 1993 and 9 percent for 1994.[38]

Despite repeated international requests by the U.N. Secretary-General, additional funds were slow in coming. There are several explanations for this. First, police aid is not generally a popular form of assistance, especially to police institutions in countries with a history of human rights violations. Relatively few donor countries have programs in place to provide such assistance. The Salvadoran Government contributed to this poor response by manifesting what appeared to be a weak commitment to carrying out the PNC project. It initially failed to allocate even the most rudimentary start-up costs for the new academy. It did not require the military to hand over any of several possible appropriate sites. When the military finally did cede a small facility (the police technical school in Santa Tecla), it first stripped the building of anything of value that could be removed, increasing the costs of preparing the site. The Government failed to allocate funds for renovation of the facility or for uniforms, food, shoes, and other basic necessities of police academy cadets. Norway came forward with funds

---

[38]See Charles Call, "Recent Setbacks in the Police Transition: El Salvador Peace Plan Update #3" (Washington, DC: Washington Office on Latin America, 1994); Presidencia de la República de El Salvador, Requerimientos de cooperación internacional para el funcionamiento de la Academica Nacional de Seguridad Publica, San Salvador, June 1993; and Requerimientos de cooperación internacional para el funcionamiento de la Policía Nacional Civil (San Salvador, June 1993).

to be quickly disbursed to get the ANSP going, but other donors may have been dissuaded by this lack of commitment.[39] Furthermore, the Salvadoran Government was inexplicably slow in preparing requests for international assistance and estimates of what funding it would need. One U.N. official remarked that he thought these delays were deliberate efforts to sabotage the creation of the new police.[40]

Because of funding and other obstacles and an unrealistic time table, the ANSP opened 3 months late but thereafter achieved an impressive record of producing graduating classes of new police agents in a timely fashion. The ANSP had a curriculum developed by the international technical team in conformance with the doctrine and legal framework set out in the accords. Instruction was provided mainly by international faculty from the United States, Chile, Spain, Norway, and Sweden. The first double-size class of 600 PNC agents entered the academy in August 1992 and graduated in February 1993. Subsequent classes of approximately 300 graduated monthly thereafter. The goal set out in the accords was to train 5,700 basic police agents and 240 officers in 2 years.

The first PNC delegations were deployed to departments in the north where much of the fighting had taken place during the war. They also replaced the PAT units in former conflict zones covered by the special regime. The new PNC delegations were led by provisional commanders who had been trained in an accelerated course at a police academy in Puerto Rico.[41] ONUSAL police observers conducted on-the-job training and the Human Rights Division provided legal training and assistance in development of procedures. The initial deployments were highly successful, despite serious organizational shortcomings, severe shortages of even the most basic equipment and facilities, and a lack of national-level leadership and coordination. This reflected the dedication of the PNC agents and officers themselves, as well as the strong support they received from a hopeful public.

---

[39]William Stanley, *Risking Failure: Neglect of the Promising Civilian Police Project in El Salvador* (Washington, DC: Washington Office on Latin America, 1993).

[40]U.N. official, interview by Stanley, July 1993, El Salvador.

[41]PNC officers who participated in this program uniformly praised it.

The balance of PNC deployment proceeded department by department through late 1994, when takeover of public security duties was completed nationwide. The deployment process was phased to allow the PNC to build experience in relatively quiet rural communities before taking on urban areas and portions of the western part of the country where organized crime was stronger. Beginning in 1994, the PNC developed specialized units dealing with financial crimes, borders and customs, arms and explosives, protection of VIPs, environmental protection, and motor vehicles. According to guidelines set out in the accords (which reflected the views of U.N. police planners), the PNC would be able to carry out these diverse functions, nationwide, with a force of 5,940 agents and officers. This force size proved seriously deficient, and the government committed itself to ongoing expansion of the PNC with an eventual target of 20,000.

Threats to Police Reform

Salvadoran actors had many reasons to delay or resist the formation of the new police and to attempt to influence its formation in ways that were inconsistent with the doctrinal and legal guidelines laid out in the peace accords. Many members of the ruling party and the administration initially distrusted the untried new institution. Members of the business and national security elite were concerned the FMLN might gain control of the new force by packing it with political cadre who were not registered with ONUSAL as former combatants, thereby circumventing their quota of 20 percent of the force.[42] The military remained concerned that the FMLN might not really abandon armed struggle, a view that was not entirely groundless in view of the FMLN's retention of major weapons caches. A minority of the military leadership resented the institution's loss of its role in public security.[43] These political considerations combined with the postwar crime problem to produce a series of decisions by the Cristiani administration

---

[42]Private sectors leaders, interviews by Stanley, June and July 1993.

[43]Salvadoran army officers, interviews by Stanley, October and December 1992, July 1993.

to preserve more of the old security system until the new system had been adequately tested.

One of the Government's first responsibilities was to demobilize the National Guard and Treasury Police. Rather than doing so, it merely renamed these units as Border Guards and military police, respectively, with legislation that failed to definitively end their public security roles. This was subsequently corrected but only after intense pressure from the United Nations. The Government transferred hundreds of members of the Treasury Police, National Guard, and an elite Army battalion into the National Police, sometimes keeping entire companies intact and merely changing their uniforms.[44] The Government also continued to operate the old National Police academy and train new agents, raising questions about whether it ever intended to demobilize the old police force. In 1993 the Government began deploying military units in quasi-public security roles, patrolling the highways and assisting in protection of the coffee harvest. These measures, which apparently enjoyed popular support, were nonetheless viewed by the FMLN and its supporters as potentially threatening and not carried out in accordance with constitutional requirements that the Executive declare a public emergency and notify the legislature of exceptional military deployments.

While the Government seemed to move slowly on demobilization of the old public security structure, the PNC faced budgetary starvation. As the PNC began to take over policing of more and more areas of the country, the budget of the PN continued to be larger relative to its size than that of the new force, notwithstanding PNC need to equip itself from scratch.[45] The PNC was forced to function without needed vehicles, radios, uniforms, and investigative equipment. PNC salaries were kept at a level lower than originally planned, a fact that made recruitment of qualified people more difficult and increased the risk of corruption.

---

[44]Although individuals could be reassigned from one organization to another, the wholesale redesignation of entire units was a circumvention of the peace accords.
[45]Costa.

The United States and the United Nations applied consistent pressure on the Government to prepare a plan for demobilizing the PN and stick to it. This yielded some progress toward demobilizing the PN during 1994, but ultimately it required a change of presidential administrations, and an embarrassing incident apparently involving criminal activity by PN forces, to turn the tide decisively against the old system. Incoming President Armando Calderón Sol ordered an accelerated demobilization of the PN following a widely televised armored car robbery allegedly carried out by uniformed PN agents. With the PN on the way out, and crime continuing to grow, the Calderón administration and the Legislative Assembly committed increasing resources to the PNC, whose budget expanded dramatically in 1995 and 1996. The main equipment shortages were subsequently resolved, and the budget was also sufficient to enable the PNC to continue to expand, passing the 14,000 mark by 1997.

Recruitment efforts were generally successful, and the PNC was not forced to lower its formal standards in order to maintain its growth rate. Basic recruits were initially required to have a 9th grade education. This was subsequently raised to 12th grade after it became clear that educational deficiencies among some of the first graduates of the academy were interfering with their ability to learn the penal code and adopt correct procedures. Roughly 7 percent of the new force is female, a significant innovation in comparison with the old security forces. In the long run, it may prove difficult for the PNC to continue to expand while maintaining quality. PNC members have made considerable sacrifices, accepting salaries lower than originally expected and facing a staggering casualty rate of roughly 1 percent since 1993.

More important in the long run than the Government's slowness to commit financial resources and resistance to dismantling the PN were numerous internal threats to civilian control, accountability, and respect for human rights. As with measures to extend the life of the old institutions, these actions stemmed from the political and sometimes parochial interests of domestic actors. In late December 1992, the Government and the FMLN agreed, against the recommendations of the United Nations, to transfer into the PNC two law enforcement units made up largely of military personnel—the Special Investigations Unit

(SIU) and the Executive Anti-Narcotics Unit (UEA). These units would form the core of the Division of Criminal Investigations (DIC) and the Anti-Narcotics Division (DAN), respectively, of the PNC. The FMLN apparently took this position because they were concerned that the Government might otherwise form a completely separate investigative service outside the PNC, an arrangement permitted by the constitution but at odds with the organic law of the PNC. The deal did at least require that members of these two groups be screened and given a short training course at the ANSP.

Neither the screening nor even the minimal training requirements were fully implemented, and some enlisted men in the two units, who lacked requisite education and training for leadership roles in the civilian police, were made officers upon entering the PNC. By late 1993, a number of ex-UEA officers had assumed command positions outside their area of specialization, bypassing the academy training and educational requirements for PNC officers entering through regular channels. They quickly became a corrosive, self-aggrandizing influence within the new force. Ex-UEA agents and officers emerged as the most frequent violators of human rights within the PNC. The ex-SIU members of the Criminal Investigations Division performed poorly, and some were implicated in criminal activities, including the murder of a prominent FMLN leader, Francisco Velis.

ONUSAL responded to this deteriorating situation by adopting an increasingly firm position in 1994 that ex-UEA officers could work only within the PNC Anti-Narcotraffic Division and that all ex-UEA and ex-SIU personnel would have to attend a full course of training at the academy. When the Government finally agreed to these requirements in late 1994, most members of both groups went on strike and eventually resigned from the force.

This entire episode might have been avoided had ONUSAL and major bilateral donors, such as ICITAP, opposed the integration of these units. However, ONUSAL found it difficult to oppose something that both parties had agreed to, and the United States had invested heavily in training and developing both units and therefore had reason to believe they would function professionally. The UEA, in particular, had a reputation as one of the few successful antidrug units in Latin

America and had demonstrated independence from the military hierarchy by arresting military officers.

Another threat to the PNC was the appointment of a former Army captain, Oscar Peña Durán, as Sub-Director for Operations in August 1993. Peña had directed the UEA and had the confidence of President Cristiani and of the U.S. Drug Enforcement Administration (DEA). In part because the PNC director at the time was a businessman with no police experience, Peña managed to amass de facto control over the PNC. He placed loyalists from the UEA in key command positions throughout the PNC, severed the PNC's relationship with ONUSAL, and replaced ONUSAL field training advisors with UEA agents. Peña was actively hostile to the human rights doctrine taught at the ANSP and advised his agents to disregard that orientation. These measures promptly led to a deterioration in the human rights performance of the PNC, which for the first time was reported to have used torture. Peña also undermined the apolitical character of the new force by encouraging former military and PN officers within the PNC to monitor the activities of former FMLN members in the police. Peña was eventually forced out in April 1994 by a combination of international diplomatic pressure and effective use of aid conditionality by the U.S. Embassy, which held up delivery by ICITAP of essential equipment for the police until Peña was gone.

With Peña's departure, it became possible once again for ONUSAL to provide on-the-job training for PNC agents. By this time the PNC was much larger, however, and the ONUSAL Police Division was in the process of drawing down. It was not possible, therefore, to go back to the kind of individual hands-on field training program of 1993, although ONUSAL did provide some technical assistance on legal and procedural matters.[46]

ONUSAL and its successor mission, MINUSAL, continued to play an important role from mid-1994 onward as a result of a pair of

---

[46]A contributing factor in the nonrenewal of the ONUSAL field training program was that the entire mission was only renewed for 6 months at a time. This made it impossible to make an agreement with the Government for a longer period, and thus opened the door to the Government to refuse to renew the field training program.

agreements with the Salvadoran Government to carry out detailed analyses of the conduct of the PNC and to make recommendations.[47] This more intrusive role—which went well beyond what was called for in the peace accords—helped focus international attention on how the PNC was developing and increased the ability of the United Nations to influence specific decisions, such as the question of retraining ex-UEA and ex-SIU personnel. The second of these U.N. assessments was followed by an ambitious 5-year plan known as Plan 2000, drawn up by U.S., Spanish, Chilean, and Salvadoran advisors. The plan encompassed hundreds of institutional, structural, legal, and doctrinal issues. It set out a timetable for completion of important measures and included recommended changes to the organic law of the PNC, as well as formation of a National Council on Public Security to be made up of prominent civilian opinion leaders with strong pro-democracy credentials who would advise the president on law enforcement policy.

The timing of these evaluations, after the 1994 elections when U.N. leverage could be expected to be diminishing, points to the importance of cooperation between the United Nations and bilateral donors. By May 1994, ONUSAL and ICITAP were making greater efforts to coordinate their positions and ICITAP's use of aid conditionality. This reinforced incentives for domestic actors to cooperate with the U.N. agenda for the PNC. President Cristiani wanted to leave office with a clean bill of health from the international community. With the elections finished and ARENA's hegemonic political position well established, Cristiani no longer needed to worry about offending ARENA's more conservative and nationalistic constituents by making concessions on public security. Moreover, incoming President Calderón Sol needed to refurbish his somewhat negative international reputation

---

[47]In the May 19, 1994, "work program," the Government and FMLN asked ONUSAL to evaluate both PNC and ANSP efforts to date. A year later, the new Calderón Sol administration asked outgoing U.N. Chief of Mission Enrique Ter Horst for a report on pending issues in the implementation of the accords and an evaluation of the PNC. The United Nations delivered two detailed assessments of the PNC, in July 1994 and September 1995.

and therefore had incentives to make concessions to U.N. concerns about the police.

Other measures by government officials were potentially harmful to the development of the PNC. The Ministry of Defense was extremely uncooperative in providing ONUSAL with records to identify whether applicants to the PNC had been in the military and, if they had, the nature of their past performance. The Ministry of Public Security, the State Intelligence Agency (Organo de Inteligencia del Estado—OIE), and the PNC all operated irregular investigations groups. For example, the ministry had a special kidnappings investigation team made up of individuals who had not been trained at the ANSP and who operated outside the PNC structure. Besides raising serious problems of accountability and coordination, they lacked legal status and could therefore contribute nothing to legal arrests and prosecutions. This has since been shut down. Its extensive files were temporarily held by the OIE until being transferred to the PNC. The PNC itself has had special intelligence and investigations groups operating outside proper channels. Although these organizations at least had legal standing as police, they had the potential to disrupt orderly and accountable investigations by the Division of Criminal Investigations (DIC). The tendency to form special groups has undermined international donor efforts to help institutionalize the PNC and has reduced donor confidence in the project.

It is a credit to the United Nations and bilateral donors that these problems have not derailed the PNC. Although international pressures could not prevent unfortunate measures from being adopted in the first place, in most cases the combination of diplomatic pressure, private and public criticism, and aid conditionality have led domestic actors to reverse damaging policies, or at least to moderate them. Much of the international community's success with respect to the PNC is attributable to coordination among the mission and donors. There is concern, however, that with the departure of ONUV in 1997 and the failure of some donors to communicate effectively to others what they are doing, coordination and cooperation among international donors and the United Nations may suffer. The UNDP is taking positive steps to promote donor cooperation, but the departure of the last of the peace verification missions necessarily reduces the stature of the United Nations and may limit its ability to wield diplomatic pressure—with both the government and donors—on public security questions.

Institution Building and the Judicial System

El Salvador's judicial system was deeply flawed prior to the conflict and deteriorated further during the war. Provisions of the accords and subsequent reform initiatives have only partially remedied these problems. In contrast to the very detailed language on the police and military, the accords are quite vague on judicial reform. This oversight was an understandable consequence of the negotiation process and the priorities of Salvadoran actors, but it resulted in an imbalance between the highly reformed police system and a resistant and often ineffective judiciary.[48]

Among the main flaws were partisan selection of Supreme Court justices, highly centralized control of the entire court system by the Supreme Court, extremely low levels of professional qualifications among judges, and a generally ineffective and politicized prosecutor's office. The accords provided for a somewhat less partisan procedure for selecting justices and raised the training standards for judges. Few of these measures could be implemented during the term of the sitting Supreme Court, however, whose president, Mauricio Gutiérrez Castro, was openly contemptuous of the peace accords and the United Nations.

Accusations of corruption within the court system led to repeated calls for a purge of judges between 1994 and 1996. A gradual purge began in 1995 after Gutiérrez's term in office ended and a new

---

[48]As one close observer of the peace process remarked, "It was hard to spark discussion of technical legal issues in a context of war and negotiations" under intense time pressures. Neither the FMLN nor the Government representatives to the peace talks had a comprehensive vision of how the judiciary could have been reformed. In contrast to police reform, in which the United Nations provided extensive technical guidance to the parties in formulating the accords, U.N. mediators placed less priority during the negotiation on shaping the content of the accords with respect to judicial reform.

president had been installed. The courts refused to publicly acknowledge rampant corruption, however, despite accusations by the Minister of Public Security and bluntly worded statements by U.N. chief of mission Enrique Ter Horst. The Attorney General's office also remains grossly understaffed and ill equipped.

During the first 2 ½ years of the mission, ONUSAL carried out only a few seminars for judges, with little apparent effect. Only after the election of a new Supreme Court in 1994 that was more receptive to reform and cooperation with the United Nations was it possible for ONUSAL to begin a more substantial program of assistance to judicial institutions. By the time ONUSAL had access to work with the courts, however, the mission was already downsizing and lacked the personnel to carry out extensive technical assistance. ONUSAL was criticized for not cooperating more closely with AID, which already had considerable experience in judicial reform in El Salvador.[49] More recently, AID and UNDP have been coordinating more effectively in this area. The United States and other international donors have put in place thorough training programs for developing new judges and prosecutors. A judicial training school was supported by UNDP and AID and implementation of essential legal reforms was closely monitored by both U.S. and international donor agencies.

The poor performance of the judiciary was an obstacle both to police reform and to effective management of the crime problem. Particular tensions arose as the PNC deployed to new areas and began pressuring judges to issue judicial orders promptly. PNC officers complained that judges too often let suspects off on technicalities and voiced suspicions that some were corrupt. They anticipated that

---

[49]AID had major judicial reform projects in El Salvador dating from the 1980s. These efforts were constrained in their effectiveness by the power of the Supreme Court and the general politicization of the judicial system. AID's more recent efforts have contributed, among other things, to the development of a new criminal procedure code, movement toward an adversarial trial system, and other procedural and institutional changes. Recent AID efforts have depended heavily on the expertise of experienced Latin American jurists. See Margaret Popkin, *Peace without Justice: Obstacles to Building the Rule of Law in El Salvador* (State College, PA: Pennsylvania State University Press, forthcoming).

frustrations with the judicial system would contribute to vigilantism on the part of police, a phenomenon that did in fact become visible in 1995 with the emergence of the "Black Shadow" vigilante organization in which PNC officers and agents were alleged to have participated.[50]

The police are an auxiliary of the justice system, and its performance in this area has been mixed at best. ONUSAL evaluations revealed that the PNC failed to carry out an extraordinarily large number of judicial orders, including arrest warrants. Moreover, a high percentage of PNC arrests involved individuals who were supposedly caught in the act, yet records reveal the police had not witnessed the vast majority of these crimes and merely made arrests on the basis of witness statements. Most human rights violations committed by the PNC appear to result from poor knowledge of law and procedures, despite efforts by the ANSP to reinforce these elements of training.

The state of the prison system was, and remains, deplorable, and the problems are in large part a result of the extremely slow and inconsistent functioning of the judiciary. A high percentage of prisoners has not been tried, and many have not even been formally charged. Bail is not generally available except for the wealthy, with the result that many wrongly accused individuals languish for months in squalid conditions without effective recourse. The prison population has grown dramatically as a result of increased crime and arrests, combined with the inability of the judicial system to keep pace with, or sometimes even to keep track of, the accused. Resulting overcrowding has made the prisons increasingly inhumane and volatile. These conditions led to a number of violent revolts and other incidents in the prisons. Recently, the Inter-American Development Bank has agreed to provide funds to the Ministry of Justice for improvements in this area, but it is unlikely that the prison crisis can be resolved until the judicial system develops the ability to indict and try prisoners in a timely fashion.

---

[50]PNC officers, interviews by Stanley, July and August 1995.

Conclusions

Success of the Mission

The Salvadoran peace process required establishment of a climate in which state institutions no longer preyed on the population, in which police did not use political affiliations and beliefs as grounds for persecuting citizens, and in which there was at least some progress toward the rule of law. Given the history of Salvadoran public security forces, achieving these conditions entailed wholesale transformation of the public security system, a process that required time and extensive financial, technical, and material resources. The experience of El Salvador suggests that such extensive reform of the public security system, even if ultimately successful, can be fraught with hazards. The demobilization of existing security forces, inadequate interim security forces, an undermanned and sometimes uncoordinated U.N. police monitoring effort, and inadequate attention to "social reinsertion" of former combatants combined to create conditions for a major crime wave. Public outcry about the crime situation fed politically expedient measures by the Government that had the potential to undermine the extent of reform and the institutional consolidation of the PNC.

Despite the crime problems, the peace process appears to be largely consolidated, producing a transition to democratic rule and significant reform of state institutions. Elections were held in 1994 and 1997 that produced significant representation for the FMLN party. FMLN members won a significant minority position within the legislature in 1994 and nearly matched ARENA in the legislative race in 1997. The FMLN also won the mayoral office in the capital city in 1997.

These political successes for the left have not resulted in any significant backlash of electoral violence, notwithstanding isolated incidents of violence that appeared politically motivated. Despite delays, the PNC did take over full control of all public security functions in 1994 and subsequently has received adequate budget support for its continually expanding force, which exceeded 15,000 by late 1997. In 1995, the Government responded to public pressures by issuing a temporary emergency police law that expanded police search and arrest powers. This measure was only marginally effective and raised

138

serious questions about potential violations of constitutional protections and due process. In mid-1997, public insecurity, lack of confidence in the police and the judicial system, and public support for elements of the old order remain among the most difficult issues facing the nascent Salvadoran democracy.

The main role of the CIVPOL division was to prevent the PN from acting in an openly politicized and abusive manner during the peace process and to assist in maintaining public safety in former conflict zones. It carried out these functions successfully. Its general mandate to ensure a "smooth transition" implied a broader role for the United Nations in helping to diagnose and solve public security problems as they arose, as well as assisting the new PNC in its development. Although the United Nations may not have been totally successful in this capacity, the fielding of an entirely new police force was a remarkable achievement that has brought closure to a brutal era. The remaining challenges are of a different sort—the consolidation of El Salvador's nascent institutions of democracy and public safety.

Lessons

◻ The United Nations should not underestimate the likely extent of crime, especially organized crime, that can develop during a transition to new police institutions, especially in countries that have experienced prolonged civil conflict and a tradition of impunity. Planning for the transition to new institutions should provide for sufficient personnel, equipment, mobility, and communications to avoid creating a vacuum. Estimates should take into account the demobilization of large numbers of former combatants from both sides, lack of employment, and pervasiveness of military arms. Furthermore, U.N. planning should take into account the likely low morale and corruptibility of existing forces whose members anticipate demobilization and unemployment. In El Salvador, the prompt demobilization of the Treasury Police and National Guard may have been politically unavoidable. If possible in future cases, however, it may be preferable to retain more of the old forces through the transition, subject to more intense and systematic U.N. scrutiny, so that a vacuum is avoided. As an alternative,

UNCIVPOL forces could play a more active and direct role in policing, deploying sufficient forces to make this feasible. When a new force is being created a central goal should be to ensure that it does not face overwhelming challenges after deployment that may distort its development and rob it of legitimacy.

☐ Police monitoring and human rights verification will be more effective if closely integrated. Rather than creating separate divisions, human rights and police should operate as a single mission, under close political guidance from the office of the Chief of Mission. Regional office directors or coordinators should have full authority over both police and human rights monitors in their area, and information obtained by both types of personnel should be combined, systematized, and reported through a single channel to mission headquarters. Before deployment, police observers should receive an orientation to prepare them for the possibility that they may be commanded by female civilian U.N. officials.

☐ In constructing new public security forces, close cooperation between the United Nations and donor nations involved is crucial. There is almost certain to be political resistance to police reform. To a large extent, the international community can counteract these impulses if it is able to speak with a uniform voice and apply effective aid conditionality according to political criteria. This may require major bilateral donors to back some U.N. mission recommendations that it does not fully support. In El Salvador, the advantages to be obtained through unity and coordination generally outweighed the costs associated with conceding differences in narrow policy preferences.

☐ Previous investments by bilateral donors in existing public security units may lead to reluctance to see those units demobilized and a tendency by donors to support their integration into new forces. The experiences with the UEA and SIU suggest that it may be better to sacrifice experience and technical expertise if there is significant risk that incorporating elements of old forces may undermine the goals of creating an accountable, human rights-oriented, prodemocratic police force. If the decision is made to transfer members of old forces into the new one, it is essential that they undergo detailed screening, be treated as individuals rather than as a group, be fully retrained in the civilian police academy, and not be given preferential treatment in the allocation of assignments.

◻ The gradual phase-out of U.N. presence through a succession of smaller verification missions was an effective approach that reduced the likelihood of reversals of institutional reforms. As the UNDP expands its role in institution building in the area of public security, greater thought needs to be devoted to how it can develop some of the political leverage associated with peacekeeping missions and how it can manage aid conditionality and coordination with donors more effectively.

◻ The United Nations and other international donors need to ensure that reform and development of the public safety system is addressed as a whole, including police, prosecutors, courts, and the penal system. All four elements need to develop concurrently with one another, to avoid imbalances that can undermine the reform of other elements or the effectiveness of the system as a whole during the crucial transition phase. The United Nations and other international actors can contribute significantly to the eventual development of effective and coordinated rule-of-law institutions by providing extensive guidance and technical assistance to the parties during negotiations, followed by assistance during implementation. Parties to a civil war may find it difficult to envision a functioning justice system: a crucial role for international actors is to help provide that vision, along with the technical assistance needed to draw up and implement workable and locally adapted blueprints for institutional reforms. Any such efforts will necessarily be constrained by the constitutional autonomy of judicial institutions and their relative insulation from international pressures and influence. International efforts to assist judicial reform must be based on realistic assessments of the international community's leverage in a given context.

MOZAMBIQUE:
The CIVPOL Operation

JAMES L. WOODS

Background

The Civil War

The following account addresses three early UNCIVPOL efforts, all taking place in southern Africa from 1989 on, focusing primarily on the operation in Mozambique, and including comparisons with the Angolan and Namibian missions. The three CIVPOL efforts described here were sizable, costly affairs and involved personnel from dozens of contributing countries. Their importance must be considered not only in terms of their contributions to the respective operations but also their learning and doctrinal value at this early point in the development of UNCIVPOL operations.

Beginning with independence in 1975, Mozambique struggled for nearly two decades under the weight of a primitive but deadly civil war. The Communist-backed FRELIMO party, which came to power after independence, was opposed by the RENAMO[1] rebels—initially formed

Author's note: A number of persons made contributions or suggestions to me for use in the preparation of this report, and I should particularly like to thank the following: Colonel Harry Broer, Deputy Police Advisor, U.N. Department of Peacekeeping Operations; Ambassador Cameron Hume, Minister-Counselor for Political Affairs, USUN; Lieutenant General Daniel I. Opande, Nairobi, Kenya; Richard Synge, Associate, African Studies Centre, University of Cambridge, and consultant to the United Nations; Dmitry P. Titov, Principal Officer, Africa Division, U.N. Department of Peacekeeping Operations; and Malachy Nugent of Harvard University, a most diligent and helpful research associate. For errors and omissions, I take all responsibility.

[1]The Resistência Nacional Moçambicana (RENAMO) was the leading opposition group to RENAMO and received substantial assistance from neighboring countries and the West. Frente de Libertação de Moçambique (FRELIMO) led the war of liberation against Portugal. Upon independence FRELIMO took control of the government and

and supported by Rhodesia and later given modest support by South Africa and apparently also by some western private groups. Their conflict left a bloody legacy of a million dead, three million internally displaced, and the infrastructure of the country destroyed. By 1989-90, the two sides had finally reached exhaustion and stalemate. Serious peace negotiations followed in 1991, supported by several African countries (including South Africa) plus the United States, the United Kingdom, Italy, Portugal, and the United Nations; in October 1992 a General Peace Agreement (GPA) ending the conflict was signed in Rome.

The two parties approached the peace process with very different views and expectations. The Government felt it should both govern and supervise the electoral process; it was not fully comfortable with the leading role of the United Nations and specifically objected to the concept of introducing a CIVPOL element. RENAMO, however, was looking to the United Nations to protect both the process and itself.

The United Nations was given responsibility for implementing or supervising the most difficult aspects of the peace, including demobilizing former combatants, reintegrating them into civil society, and organizing national elections. At the same time, but independent of any provisions of the Peace Agreement, the United Nations designed a civilian policing (CIVPOL) mission as a way to monitor the conduct of the indigenous police force during this delicate time in Mozambique's history. Although a robust CIVPOL mission was advocated from the beginning by RENAMO, the Government was equally adamant in its opposition. This disagreement led to an initial impasse, and then to a long delay in approving the inclusion of a CIVPOL element in the operation, as well as restrictions on its mandate. This was notwithstanding obvious major deficiencies in Mozambique's existing police structure and capabilities.

---

soon declared itself to be a Marxist-Leninist party. They received assistance from Moscow and Havana.

The Police

The need for improved civil policing in Mozambique was great. The public security system had deteriorated by the early nineties.[2] Mozambique's cities, which had been renowned for their lack of crime even during the height of the civil war, were caught up in a crime wave against which the local police seemed almost powerless. Several factors had contributed to the increased crime rate:

☐ Economic liberalization had increased the amount of consumer goods in shops but did nothing to increase the public's purchasing power.

☐ Thousands of migrant workers had lost their jobs and returned home to Mozambique when East and West Germany reunited.

☐ Thousands of decommissioned soldiers and rebels had no jobs and no prospects.

☐ The remaining armed forces were increasingly desperate and undisciplined.

☐ Army and rebel guns began finding their way into criminal hands.

☐ Social constraints simply broke down after 15 years of civil war.

As a result of these various strains on the social and labor systems, violent crime in Mozambique soared, and public confidence in the police was virtually destroyed. Along with their inability to control crime, the police force was also considered highly corrupt by most Mozambicans.[3] As crime increased, the police became almost irrelevant to the public, and citizens took the law into their own hands. Often, the consequences were very violent. Alternatively, when the

---

[2] See Ruth Ansah Ayisi, "Fighting the Crime Wave," *Africa Report*, November-December 1991, 66-68.

[3] Paper by Ambassador Dennis Coleman Jett, "Mozambique: A Temporary or Lasting Success Story?" Harvard International Relations Council, April 1995, 9.

police did act, it was sometimes with such excessive force that suspects were killed.[4]

Explaining the operational foundation for the CIVPOL mission, the Secretary-General cited the following difficulties facing Mozambique:

> The population of approximately 16 million people had endured almost 16 years of a devastating civil war, which resulted in approximately 1 million deaths and 4.5 million refugees and displaced persons. The protracted hostilities in Mozambique have disrupted infrastructure to a great degree, contributed to the existence of armed banditry and created conditions for lawlessness in some parts of the countryside. Between May and September 1993 alone, the number of reported crimes in Mozambique included 167 homicides, 726 armed robberies and hundreds of cases of physical assault, rape, etc. . . . It is obvious that among their functions, United Nations police observers will need to encourage the Mozambican police to improve the protection of citizens and property. . . . A number of additional factors should also be taken into account. There is no efficient arms control system in place, and estimates put the total number of assorted types of weapons in "non-official" hands at approximately 1 million.[5]

The Judicial System

The judicial system was also in trouble in the early nineties. Despite constitutional provisions establishing strong, independent courts, Mozambique's judicial system was hampered by several factors:

☐ A de facto lack of judicial independence from the ruling FRELIMO party

☐ A lack of capable district and provisional judges

---

[4]As an example of how far the situation had deteriorated, after witnessing one particular case of police brutality, bystanders in turn beat the police, killing one and sending another to the hospital.

[5]United Nations, *Report of the Secretary-General on ONUMOZ*, S/1994/89, Add.1, January 28, 1994.

146

- ☐ A lack of lawyers in general[6]
- ☐ A severe lack of funding.[7]

The Prison System

The prisons also suffered from a lack of resources. Some were greatly overcrowded, sometimes holding four times the prisoners they were designed for. Prisoners were often fed only once each day.[8] The majority of prisoners were being held on remand, and they complained that it could take up to a year to hear their cases. Despite these difficulties, some prisons fared better—they were less crowded and therefore less resource-constrained than others—and prison officials systemwide were generally commended for doing the most with what they had.[9]

Police Relations with Local Power Structure

Relations between the police and other elements of the local power structure were very uneasy. The Minister of the Interior (who had responsibility for the police force) was detained in late 1991 as a suspected coup plotter. Cooperation between the military and police forces was the exception rather than the rule. One such exception was a joint police and military operation in September 1991 which led to the arrest of over 800 criminal suspects.[10]

Size and Structure of the Police Force

In January 1994, shortly after the initiation of the first phase of UNCIVPOL operations, the Secretary-General reported on the size and structure of Mozambique's police force:

---

[6]Jett, 9. In 1995, there were only 100 lawyers in Mozambique, a country of 17 million people.

[7]Ibid.

[8]In some prisons, relatives were permitted to supplement prisoners rations if they could.

[9]U.N. Operation in Mozambique, daily SITREP no. 22, April 13, 1994, and U.N. Operation in Mozambique, weekly SITREP no. 40, May 9, 1994.

[10]Ayisi, 67.

The current strength of the Mozambican police (PRM) is 18,047, with the command structure of national headquarters in Maputo, 11 provincial headquarters and over 200 stations and posts in the districts. There is a quick reaction police force numbering several thousand as well as various private security companies and agencies.[11]

The Mandate

The U.N. Mission in Mozambique (ONUMOZ) mandate specified the following tasks:

□ Monitor and verify the cease-fire, the separation and concentration of forces of the two parties as well as their demobilization, and the collection, storage, and destruction of weapons
□ Monitor and verify the complete withdrawal of foreign forces
□ Provide security in the four transport corridors; monitor and verify the disbanding of private and irregular armed groups; authorize security arrangements for vital infrastructures; and provide security for United Nations and other international activities in support of the peace process.[12]

The parties agreed that legislative and presidential elections would be held simultaneously 1 year after the date of signature of the agreement. Elections could be delayed only if warranted by prevailing circumstances. The ONUMOZ Electoral Division was to monitor and verify all aspects of the electoral process, which would be organized by the National Elections Commission.

The agreement also set two objectives for international and humanitarian assistance: to serve as an instrument of reconciliation, and to assist the return of people displaced by war and hunger,

---

[11]Report of the U.N. Secretary-General, S/1994/89, Add. 1, para. 7.
[12]*The Blue Helmets: A Review of United Nations Peace-Keeping,* 3ᵈ ed. (New York: United Nations Department of Public Information, 1996), 324.

whether they had taken refuge in neighboring countries or in provincial and district centers within Mozambique.

Even though the Secretary-General was personally convinced of the desirability of a CIVPOL mission, initially he could not persuade the Government to accept one. The General Peace Agreement does discuss the indigenous police force in Protocol IV (Military Questions), Point V. This protocol addresses several points: guidelines for police conduct; selection; basic tasks; appointment of Commander and Deputy Commander; and establishment of a National Police Affairs Commission (COMPOL) to verify conduct. However, there is no mention either of international police or a role for the United Nations specifically.

The official request for U.N. involvement in Mozambique came on October 4, 1992 in a letter from President Chissano to the Secretary-General, in which he wrote:

> Accordingly, I would like to request Your Excellency to take appropriate action in order to ensure the participation of the United Nations in monitoring and ensuring the implementation of the General Peace Agreement and in assisting the Government by providing technical assistance for the General Elections and in monitoring these elections.[13]

This broad initial request was directed at U.N. military and electoral assistance to implement the GPA. While civil policing was a part of the agreement, the section dealing with policing does not suggest a role for the United Nations. President Chissano requested the United Nations to chair the newly created Supervision and Control Commission (CSC) and its subcommissions, the Cease-fire Commission (CCF) and the Reintegration Commission (CORE). Indeed, in the GPA paragraphs that create these commissions, a U.N. role is explicitly stated.

---

[13]This letter is reproduced as document S/24635, in "The United Nations and Mozambique, 1992-1995" (New York: U.N. Department of Public Information, 1995), 105.

On the other hand, the text creating the National Police Affairs Commission (COMPOL) in Protocol IV does not mention a role for the United Nations, nor did President Chissano request such a role when he asked for U.N. chairmanship of the other three Commissions. Likewise, in his report to the Security Council on the details of the General Peace Agreement, the Secretary-General outlined the U.N. role in Mozambique but only spoke of the CSC, CCF, and CORE. "In essence," the Secretary-General wrote, "the United Nations is asked to undertake certain specific functions in relation to the cease-fire, the elections, and humanitarian assistance."[14] Again, there was no mention of a policing function.

The Secretary-General himself requested a CIVPOL mission in his report to the Security Council on the establishment of ONUMOZ. In this report, he outlined the need for a policing element based on prior experience:

> While the agreement [GPA] does not provide a specific role for United Nations civilian police in monitoring the neutrality of the Mozambican police, experience elsewhere suggests that this could be desirable in order to inspire confidence that violations of civil liberties, human rights and political freedom will be avoided. Throughout the peace process, but particularly during the electoral campaign, the presence of a United Nations police component could be most useful, although agreement on this point was not reached in the Rome negotiations.[15]

He also outlined a proposed structure for such a CIVPOL effort:

> If agreed by the two sides, such a component could be headed by an Inspector General, and consist of up to 128 police officers, deployed in the regions and provincial capitals. It would work in close cooperation with the National Police Affairs Commission and provide technical advice to this body as required. I believe that such a unit would be a valuable addition to ONUMOZ and I therefore intend to

---

[14]Report of the U.N. Secretary-General, S/24642, II, para. 9, October 9, 1990.
[15]Report of the U.N. Secretary-General, S/24892, V, para. 29, December 3, 1992.

ask my interim Special Representative to reopen this matter with the parties and seek their concurrence.[16]

There was no suggestion that the United Nations should act as the chairman of COMPOL, though the United Nations served as Chair of the other Commissions. On October 15, the day the peace agreement came into effect, an advance team of 21 U.N. observers arrived to verify the withdrawal of foreign troops and assess the general situation. On November 4, 1992, the CSC held its first meeting and appointed the main subsidiary commissions: Cease-Fire (CCF), Reintegration (CORE), and the Joint Commission for Formation of the Mozambique Defense Force (CCEADM).

On December 16, 1992, the Security Council approved Security Council Resolution (SCR) 797, creating ONUMOZ along the lines suggested by the Secretary-General. The mission included a civilian police component of 128 people, *contingent* upon a request from the Mozambicans for CIVPOL. Such a request did finally come, nine months later and after much negotiation. After receiving that request, the Secretary-General, in his report on ONUMOZ, wrote:

> The parties have agreed to request the United Nations to monitor all police activities in the country, public or private, to monitor the rights and liberties of citizens in Mozambique and to provide technical support to the Police Commission (COMPOL). The proposed United Nations police contingent would be responsible for verifying that all police activities in the country are consistent with the General Peace Agreement. The Government has agreed to provide a list of *materiel* in the possession of the police, as well as other information necessary to verify the activities of the police.[17]

However, he also noted in the same document that "It appears that at least one of the parties has in mind a much larger police force than that envisaged in the initial operational plan for ONUMOZ."

---

[16]Ibid., V and VIII (c). See also para. 48.
[17]Report of the U.N. Secretary-General, S/26385, Add. 1, September 10, 1993, para. 3.

ONUMOZ was fully deployed and its military infrastructure established in all three operational regions by the beginning of May 1993. However, the establishment of the National Elections Commission and the Commission of State Administration was still pending, as was the cantonment and demobilization of troops and the formation of the new army.

Concerned about the pace of implementation, the Secretary-General presented a revised timetable that took as its point of departure resumption of the work of the Joint Commissions beginning on June 3, 1993, concluding 16 months later with elections in October 1994. The phased concentration and demobilization of Government and RENAMO troops was expected to take 8 or 9 months.[18]

Following the signing of the General Peace Agreement, the CIVPOL mission in Mozambique evolved from a policy controversy into an operational reality, with the first CIVPOL personnel deploying on the ground in September 1993. A month later, in October, the parties reached agreement on the function of all Commissions, including COMPOL, allowing these to begin their work as well. After this agreement had been reached, the Security Council, in February 1994, authorized creation of an expanded police component of ONUMOZ,[19] along the lines described by the Secretary-General in his report a month earlier.[20]

The Secretary-General outlined the CIVPOL mandate, listing seven separate points:

□ To monitor all police activities in the country, including those of PRM [Mozambican police] and any other police and security agencies and verify that their actions are fully consistent with the General Peace Agreement

---

[18]*The Blue Helmets*, 324-326.

[19]Security Council Resolution 898, February 23, 1994.

[20]Report of the U.N. Secretary-General, S/1994/89, Add. 1, para. 9, January 28, 1994.

Comparison with Namibia and Angola

The mandate for a similar CIVPOL mission in *Namibia* was less broad, focusing on ensuring that the South West Africa Police (SWAPOL) fulfilled their duty of maintaining law and order in an efficient, professional and nonpartisan way. CIVPOL was a part of the U.N. mandate in Namibia from the very beginning. The Settlement Proposal agreed to in April 1978 and UNSC Resolution 435 of September 1978 allowed for the U.N. Special Representative to ensure the good conduct of the indigenous police force, and United Nations personnel were to accompany the Namibian police forces in the discharge of their duties. UNSC Resolution 632 of February 16, 1989 updates and clarifies the role of UNTAG (U.N. Transition Assistance Group) and within it, CIVPOL. The UNTAG mandate authorized what was essentially a political operation, ensuring that free and fair elections could be held in Namibia. Creating the conditions for such elections, however, required UNTAG to carry out a wide variety of tasks, many of which went well beyond those previously undertaken by more traditional peacekeeping operations. UNTAG had to monitor the cease-fire which was supposed to come formally into effect on the first day of the mandate (but which tragically did not do so). It had to monitor the rapid reduction and eventual removal of the South African military presence in Namibia, which was an essential condition for free and fair elections and the subsequent transition to independence. It had the difficult task of ensuring that the remaining security forces, SWAPOL, carried out their duties in a manner which was consistent with free and fair elections.*

Therefore, public security, especially monitoring SWAPOL, was an initial responsibility of the U.N. mission in Namibia, though the size of the CIVPOL contingent grew to be more than four times its initial projection (from 360 observers to a final total of 1,500) during the course of the mission. This growth could be considered a failure to assess accurately the resources necessary to fulfill the CIVPOL mission. It also had an added responsibility of assisting with elections. Significantly, the counterinsurgency "Koevoet" unit was formed (by South Africa) after the Settlement Proposal was signed. As a result, this unit was not mentioned in the Proposal and did not fall under its authority, though it became one of the most serious public security challenges facing UNTAG and CIVPOL in Namibia.

The Blue Helmets, 209.

In *Angola*, the CIVPOL element developed over time. There was no civil policing mandate in U.N. Angola Verification Mission (UNAVEM I), which lasted from January 1989 until June 1991. In UNAVEM II, which was scheduled to last from May 1991 until the day after elections, the role of monitoring the neutrality of the indigenous police was one of the "other tasks" for the United Nations, after the primary function of monitoring the cease-fire. UNAVEM III, established on February 8, 1995 by UNSC Resolution 976, explicitly listed policing as a major part of its mandate. The Lusaka Protocol, signed in November 1994, provided the basis for the UNAVEM III mission. It included neutrality of the national police as one of its five major issues (the others were military, political, humanitarian, and electoral). The stated CIVPOL mandate in Angola was to monitor the neutrality of the Angolan National Police, disarming of citizens, quartering of the Government rapid reaction police, and security arrangements for the National Union for the Total Independence of Angola (UNITA) leadership. They were also to verify the whole process of integration of 5,500 UNITA personnel into the National Police.

In Angola, the CIVPOL mission grew over time from nothing under UNAVEM I to major prominence under UNAVEM III, six years later. However, considering each UNAVEM mission as a separate response to a distinct set of circumstances, civilian policing could be considered an explicit, initial responsibility of UNAVEM III (perhaps also of UNAVEM II, to a degree).

☐ To monitor the respect of rights and civil liberties of Mozambican citizens throughout the country
☐ To provide technical support to the National Police Commission
☐ To verify that the activities of private protection and security agencies do not violate the General Peace Agreement
☐ To verify the strength and location of the government police forces, their materiel, as well as any other information which might be needed in support of the peace process
☐ To monitor and verify the process of the reorganization and retraining of the quick reaction police and their activities, as well as to verify their weapons and equipment

☐ To monitor, together with ONUMOZ components, the proper conduct of the electoral campaign and verify that political rights of individuals, groups and political organizations are respected, in accordance with the General Peace Agreement and relevant electoral documents.[21]

Though this public security gap needed to be filled, the Secretary-General also wrote, in the context of the CIVPOL mission, that "responsibility for the maintenance of law and order will clearly remain with the Government. All violations of the Criminal Code will be investigated by the Mozambican police, with the possibility of parallel investigations being conducted by CIVPOL, when the latter considers it appropriate."[22]

Size of the Component

Once the Mozambicans had agreed to a civilian policing mandate, the Secretary-General proposed that the strength of the expanded CIVPOL contingent be set at 1,144 police observers (inclusive of the initial 128). He broke down the contingent as follows:

☐ The Chief Police Observer, with the rank of Inspector General
☐ The Deputy Police Observer
☐ 29 police observers at the component headquarters in Maputo
☐ 30 police observers comprising a special task force to monitor and evaluate the quick reaction police and to be available for unforeseen exigencies
☐ 12 police observers in *each* of the three regional headquarters
☐ 327 police observers to be deployed at 11 provincial capitals, including those to be formed into stationary and mobile teams to service surrounding areas

---

[21]Ibid., para. 14.
[22]Report of the U.N. Secretary-General, S/1994/89, Add. 1.

□ 720 police observers in other locations throughout the country.[23]

The Security Council approved 1,144 police observers but mandated that an appropriate number of military observers be drawn down in order to keep the overall cost of the ONUMOZ mission the same.[24] Ultimately, 1,086 CIVPOL officers deployed in Mozambique, coming from 29 different countries.

Comparison with Namibia and Angola
In *Namibia*, the initial CIVPOL strength of 500 officers was increased by 500 in order to deal with ongoing difficulties in the north of the country, and then again by another 500 to provide sufficient coverage during the election, for a total of 1,500 officers from 25 countries. In *Angola*, UNAVEM II was slated to have up to 90 civilian police monitors, eventually raised to 126; for UNAVEM III CIVPOL, 260 police observers were authorized from 39 countries.

Organizational Structure

As planning for the CIVPOL mission in Mozambique matured, the Secretary-General outlined its organizational structure:

□ The *headquarters component* would be headed by the Chief Police Observer at the rank of Inspector General and would consist of his deputy and chiefs of staff for operations, liaison, investigations, logistics and personnel. A headquarters team would also liaise with and provide technical assistance to the Police Commission.

□ A *special task force* would be stationed in Maputo for monitoring and verification of the quick reaction police force. This

---

[23]Report of the U.N. Secretary-General, S/1994/89, Add. 1, para. 16.
[24]Security Council Resolution, S/Res/898, paras. 2, 3, 1994.

group would also monitor security arrangements for the leadership of RENAMO. In addition, it would be on call to respond to any exigencies that might arise in other parts of the country.

☐ Three compact *regional headquarters*, whose tasks would primarily be coordination of activities spanning several provinces. Each of these headquarters would be headed by a regional chief police observer.

☐ Eleven *provincial headquarters* would each be headed by a provincial chief police observer and would include a deputy, an operations officer, an investigations officer, a logistics/personnel officer and several patrol and investigation teams, which would cover the provincial capital and as much of the surrounding area as possible.

☐ One hundred and eighty *United Nations police stations and posts* would be established throughout the country in remote and isolated locations, near Government police facilities.[25]

The CIVPOL operation was established as a separate component within ONUMOZ. Its commander, the Chief Police Officer, reported directly to the Secretary-General's Special Representative in Mozambique. It worked closely with existing electoral, military, humanitarian and administrative components of ONUMOZ. After a period of difficulties, appropriate liaison arrangements were established with the national police at all levels, and CIVPOL itself had a presence at all strategic locations throughout the country. Despite some resistance, especially at the initial stages of the operation, it sought unrestricted access to the general public. It conducted all its own investigations and, when necessary, recommended corrective action.[26]

Training of CIVPOL Personnel
There was little initial training for CIVPOL officers beyond an "induction program" to explain the mission. Officially, qualifications for

---

[25]Report of the U.N. Secretary-General, S/1994/89, Add. 1, para. 15.
[26]*The Blue Helmets*, 329.

participation were command of English and the ability to drive U.N. vehicles.[27] However, even these basic requirements were often not met: in mid-1994, the U.N. Police Commissioner in Maputo reported that 255 CIVPOL officers (about 36 percent of the total contingent at the time) could not drive or did not speak English, or both.

As the mission progressed, two special training programs were developed for officers already deployed. One training session dealt with human rights, the other with electoral observation. In each case, a small number of CIVPOL officers were trained to recognize violations; these trainees in turn trained other officers to do the same.[28]

Deployment, Activity, and Withdrawal of Personnel

Deployment of the CIVPOL observers was staggered, starting with the topmost layers of the hierarchy and proceeding progressively downwards as the elections approached. Specifically, the Secretary-General suggested:

> The initial phase, during which the central headquarters and regional and provincial capitals' teams would be fully established, should be completed by mid-March 1994. The second phase would coincide with the voter registration process from April to June 1994, during which up to 70 per cent of CIVPOL's posts and stations throughout the countryside would become operational. The remainder of the component would be deployed by no later than one month before the beginning of the electoral campaign, which is scheduled to begin on 1 September 1994.[29]

By April 18, 1994, 278 U.N. police observers had been deployed around the country and 10 CIVPOL outposts had been established. By the end of April, CIVPOL had investigated 36 cases of police

---

[27]Spanish or Portuguese language proficiency was considered a plus, but was not required. Initially, it was recommended that 50 percent of the CIVPOL contingent come from Portuguese-speaking countries, though this target quickly proved impractical. UNCIVPOL staff memoranda, 1993.

[28]Weekly SITREP no. 62, October 9, 1994.

[29]Report of the U.N. Secretary-General, S/1994/89, Add. 1, para. 18.

misconduct, and had communicated these cases to COMPOL and the Mozambican Police Command for remedial action, where necessary.[30]

By July 4, 1994, 817 U.N. police observers had been deployed around the country and 29 CIVPOL outposts had been established. CIVPOL had received a total of 47 complaints of police misconduct, 35 of which had been investigated and resolved, while 12 were still under investigation. These cases fell into three categories: illegal detention of civilians; abuse of detainees' civil rights; and criminal investigations involving possible political motives.[31]

By August 22, 1994, 905 police observers from 26 countries had been deployed and 44 field posts had been established. CIVPOL had received a total of 91 complaints, 78 of which had been resolved, with 13 still under investigation.[32]

Overall, a total of 1,086 U.N. police observers from 29 countries were deployed to 83 field posts, plus the national and provincial capitals. They investigated 511 complaints, 61 of which were related to human rights violations. CIVPOL also monitored the conduct of the election campaign and the polling.[33]

The elections were held on October 27-29, with roughly 2,300 international electoral observers present, 910 from the United Nations. The Special Representative of the Secretary-General stated that they had been conducted peacefully, were well organized, and were without any major irregularities or credible charges of fraud or intimidation. The ONUMOZ mandate was extended by the U.N. Security Council from November 15 until December 15, with residual activities to be completed by January 31, 1995. The UNSC called upon all concerned to respect the election results. The new Parliament was installed, President Chissano took office on December 8, and the ONUMOZ mandate official ended on December 9. By November 17, 1994, 32 police observers had been withdrawn from Mozambique; 566 were gone by December 18, 1994, and the remainder left by December 31,

---

[30]Report of the U.N. Secretary-General, S/1994/511, IV, April 28, 1994.
[31]Report of the U.N. Secretary-General, S/1994/803, IV, July 7, 1994.
[32]Report of the U.N. Secretary-General, S/1994/1002, IV, August 26, 1994.
[33]Report of the U.N. Secretary-General, S/1994/1449, III, December 23, 1994.

1994 (except for a group of about 20, to remain in Mozambique until mid-January, 1995).[34]

Comparison with Namibia and Angola

In *Namibia*, the first 500 officers were deployed by May 1989, the second 500 between June and August, 1989, and the third from mid-September through October 1989. Most were repatriated quickly after independence in March 1990 (some officers stayed in Namibia for several months under bilateral arrangements). Almost two-thirds of the CIVPOL strength was concentrated in the northernmost quarter of the country where incidents between South African forces and SWAPO were the most numerous.

In *Angola*, CIVPOL was not a part of the UNAVEM I operation (1989 to 1991), but was added to UNAVEM II, with initially 90 personnel deployed from May 1991. In May 1992 this was increased to 126 for the run-up to the elections, but in the fall, after UNITA's rejection of the outcome of the elections and renewed heavy fighting, the CIVPOL mission was slashed to 18. In October 1994, with the return of relative peace, the strength was returned to 126. In February 1995, with the installation of UNAVEM III, the contingent was increased to an authorized strength of 260, but only 185 actually arrived. It remained at this level until the gradual phaseout of UNAVEM III in the summer and fall of 1997.*

*Monthly and total expenditures for the Mozambique, Namibia, and Angola CIVPOL missions are summarized in the attached tables. They reflect the timing and number of personnel deployed. The total cost was $28 million for ONUMOZ, $55 million for UNTAG, and $20 million for UNAVEM II and III.

The Mission

The CIVPOL mission got off to a slow start. In his February 1993 letter to the Foreign Minister of Italy on the status of ONUMOZ, the Secretary-General reported that the National Police Affairs Commission (COMPOL) had not yet been established. The delay resulted from RENAMO's refusal to name representatives to the commission because

---

[34]Ibid.

of claims that the Government had integrated military officers into elements of the police force. As a result of the delay, allegations of human rights abuses by the police were not being investigated, a primary function of the commission. Agreement on the various commissions was not reached until October 1993, 1 year after the signing of the General Peace Agreement, after which time COMPOL could begin work (it was February 1994 by the time COMPOL was fully staffed and actually began functioning). The public was generally pleased to see the CIVPOL officers arrive, though they were perceived first as "guarantors of human rights" and then as providers of public security.[35]

However, in a further complication, the United Nations announced in November 1993 that it was running out of money for the CIVPOL effort in Mozambique. Because of the growing number of U.N. commitments around the world, the Secretary-General notified the parties in Mozambique that the United Nations could not fund any expansion of CIVPOL beyond the 128 officers initially authorized, that COMPOL would need to use local units wherever possible, and that the mission would be limited geographically. The Government and RENAMO were also asked to establish local subdivisions of the National Police Affairs Commission in order to shoulder some of the civilian policing burden. Eventually, though, the CIVPOL mission was able to field 1,086 police observers (out of 1,144 eventually authorized) without increasing overall ONUMOZ costs, primarily by shifting resources from cease-fire observation which was proceeding at a much lower cost than initially expected.

Election Monitoring

Another goal of the CIVPOL mission was to instill confidence among the public in the appropriate conduct of the elections. This goal entailed direct observation of the process, together with U.N. electoral observers, as described by the Secretary-General:

---

[35]*Mozambique Peace Process Bulletin,* issue 8, February 1994, published by AWEPA, the European Parliamentarians for Southern Africa.

With the concurrence of the Mozambican parties, United Nations police observers would assist the electoral observers of ONUMOZ in monitoring the registration process and the electoral campaign. In this context, they would also monitor security at the polling stations, including the security arrangements for the storage, counting and transporting of ballot papers and other election materials.[36]

From the beginning, CIVPOL observers were assigned to assist ONUMOZ election observers during each phase of the election—voter registration, political campaigning, and voting. CIVPOL was also responsible for assisting with security at polling sites, including during counting and transporting of ballot papers. Some CIVPOL teams apparently also provided logistics support (mainly transportation), facilitating both registration and the conduct of the elections.

Human Rights Monitoring

Another prominent goal was to teach the Mozambican police force to conform to international standards of conduct, to respect human rights, and to act professionally in protecting citizens and their property. Regarding such a mentoring role, the Secretary-General wrote:

> It may be necessary to familiarize local police with the international concepts of rights, civil liberties and fundamental freedoms, as well as the codes of conduct the political parties might agree to observe during the electoral process.[37]

The U.N. Centre for Human Rights provided human rights training for CIVPOL monitors. Amnesty International was also very involved in monitoring human rights during the ONUMOZ operation and provided reports and checklists to help guide the CIVPOL efforts. The Centre trained 30 CIVPOL officers to identify human rights abuses. These trainees were then sent out both to monitor human rights and to train

---

[36]Report of the U.N. Secretary-General, S/1994/89, Add. 1, para. 14.
[37]Ibid.

other CIVPOL officers, government officials, and NGO workers to do the same.[38]

The Centre was not asked to provide training until 4 months after the first CIVPOL officers arrived in Mozambique, and the subsequent training program had to be adapted to minimize the effect of the delay. The U.N. High Commissioner for Human Rights later expressed his desire to see such training incorporated into CIVPOL missions from the beginning.[39]

CIVPOL officers had no authority to act on human rights violations. Instead, they reported violations to COMPOL, which in turn reported them to the Ministry of Interior, which was then responsible for taking action to redress the violation. This system was, however, problematic. There was a lack of COMPOL offices at the provincial level to which CIVPOL could file reports, and even when reports did make it through this system, CIVPOL would not be informed of the action taken.

Often civilians decided it was faster to go directly to the Ministry of Interior themselves, rather than reporting human rights violations to CIVPOL. Nonetheless, the very presence of CIVPOL officers in the country was thought to have the effect of mitigating some police excesses, and their presence at political rallies was credited with keeping the police from behaving in a partisan manner.[40]

CIVPOL authorities did report several serious violations of human rights by the PRM, ranging from deaths of individuals while in PRM custody or while being apprehended, to attempted assassination. In these more serious cases, after referring the matter to the Mozambican Government, CIVPOL authorities also sent reports directly to the U.N. High Commission for Human Rights.[41]

---

[38]Amnesty International Report, *Mozambique: Monitoring Human Rights—The Task of U.N. Police Observers,* AFR 41/3/94, London, 1994.

[39]Letter from the U.N. High Commissioner for Human Rights, Jose Ayala Lasso, to Kofi Annan, U.N. Under Secretary-General (Peace-Keeping), July 13, 1994.

[40]Amnesty International Report, AFR 41/03/94.

[41]Interviews by author, United Nations, June 1997.

Comparison with Namibia and Angola
No similar training in human rights was conducted in *Namibia*. In *Angola* (UNAVEM III), although there was a somewhat similar project, prepared with the Centre for Human Rights and supported by the European Union, to train Angolan nationals involved in human rights education, this training was not provided to CIVPOL officers. The Mozambique human rights training, limited as it was, thus stands as one of a kind in these efforts.

In general, CIVPOL was most effective at policing human rights at posts far from headquarters, where local policemen were less aware of CIVPOL's lack of authority for redress and were fearful of having their misdeeds reported to their superiors. CIVPOL was also more effective in situations where its officers had developed good personal relationships with the local police force.[42]

Weapons Verification and Disarmament

The ONUMOZ mission overall was very involved in demobilizing combatants and collecting weapons. Under the terms of the specific CIVPOL mandate, the Government was required to report all police weapons, but there was disagreement about the extent to which CIVPOL was allowed to verify weapons depots. Often, CIVPOL officers were denied access to police sites.[43]

CIVPOL officers were also available to help disarm private security forces and the public, an important role given the estimated one million weapons in "non-official" hands. The Secretary-General had written of the CIVPOL disarmament function:

---

[42]Amnesty International Report, AFR 41/03/94.
[43]U.N. DPKO staff, interviews by author, June 1997, New York.

Special attention would be given to the systematic verification of weapons and equipment in the possession of the national police and of private agencies and to monitoring the activities of the quick reaction police force, whose facilities would also be visited on a regular basis; ONUMOZ would also examine the latter's role and structure. Given the scope of arms proliferation among the general population, teams of United Nations police observers would be available to collect any weapons and ammunition that may be surrendered by individuals or irregular forces throughout the country.[44]

In the end, however, ONUMOZ CIVPOL elements made only very limited progress in meeting any of these goals, given the difficulty of the tasks, lack of cooperation, and a general shortage of means and time.

The General Peace Agreement called for the Government and rebel armed forces to be combined to create a new army, but, RENAMO having no police, there was no need for a similar provision for the Mozambican police force. Rather, the existing police force, the 18,000-man PRM, was to extend its operations to include RENAMO areas. The role of CIVPOL in this extension was critical, because RENAMO authorities did not trust the PRM and would not let them into rebel-held territory without a CIVPOL chaperone.[45]

Over time, it became increasingly clear to CIVPOL officers that government military troops and equipment were being transferred to the police, especially to the Presidential Guard. These transfers were especially worrisome to RENAMO, who filed complaints about the weapons. The Government contended that because the Presidential Guard was neither a military nor a police unit, it was outside the scope of ONUMOZ and CIVPOL mandates. Consequently, CIVPOL was denied the authority to verify weapons claims.[46]

CIVPOL officers were sometimes denied access to sites where military personnel and equipment were suspected of being converted

---

[44]Report of the U.N. Secretary-General, S/1994/89, Add. 1, para 13.

[45]Mozambique Peace Process Bulletin, Issue 12, September 1994. Published by AWEPA, the European Parliamentarians for Southern Africa.

[46]U.N. DPKO staff, interviews.

to police use. In one case, a visiting Security Council delegation was inadvertently shown an undeclared police training camp where police recruits were being trained in machine-gun use. Later, CIVPOL officers were denied access to the camp when they asked to verify the report.[47]

In order to accomplish this variety of tasks, the Secretary-General detailed the following guidance:

> CIVPOL's functions would be carried out by stationing United Nations teams in the vicinity of the Mozambican police stations, posts and by extensive patrolling. In order to monitor certain activities, police observers would be deployed at various national police headquarters. At the same time, ONUMOZ would have unrestricted access to the general public and would be able to gather information as well as to receive complaints from individuals and organizations. CIVPOL would conduct its own investigations, on the basis of such complaints, as well as independently, into politically motivated offenses and, when necessary, recommend corrective action. Information about such investigations would be provided promptly to the National Police Affairs Commission and the national authorities.[48]

Coordination and Cooperation

Local Police

The relationship between CIVPOL officers and the Mozambique police was complex. It incorporated elements of monitoring, mentoring, joint patrolling, passive observation, and some training. Though the Mozambican police had full authority to investigate crimes, CIVPOL could, at its discretion, conduct its own investigations alongside the indigenous force.

There were problems of coordination and cooperation with the local police force, especially where access to information and visits to police stations and prisons were concerned. These difficulties, especially acute at the provincial level, were attributed to a lack of information provided to local police commanders concerning the tasks

---

[47]U.N. DPKO staff, interviews with author.
[48]Report of the U.N. Secretary-General, S/1994/89, Add. 1, para. 12.

of CIVPOL. As a result, a seminar was held in February 1994 at which CIVPOL, the Police Affairs Commission, and the National Police worked out a *modus operandi* that improved the situation. There were also cases of government police refusing to accompany CIVPOL officers into RENAMO territory, and other instances when RENAMO officials denied access to government police, all of which hindered CIVPOL's ability to exercise its mandate.[49] On the other hand, CIVPOL teams in some cases were the first to "open up" territory in the countryside, loosely controlled by RENAMO, where government police and civil authorities dared not go.

As the mission progressed, there was concern about the fact that most cases investigated by CIVPOL and referred to COMPOL were not being acted on. In August 1994, the Secretary-General reported:

> It is a matter of concern that the National Commission for Police Affairs has not yet ruled on the cases referred to it by CIVPOL. Obviously, the deterrent effect of CIVPOL observation would be diluted if no corrective or preventive action follows CIVPOL investigations.[50]

Given the short duration of the full CIVPOL mission, its focus mainly on the electoral process, and its rapid withdrawal after elections, this issue was never successfully resolved and can be considered a major shortfall in CIVPOL accomplishments.

Other U.N. Components

In the first addendum to his January 1994 report on ONUMOZ, the Secretary-General suggested that CIVPOL share resources, infrastructure, and administration with the military and other civilian components of this mission but that some local employees be hired to work for CIVPOL specifically as needed:

---

[49]Report of the U.N. Secretary-General, S/1994/511, April 28, 1994, and S/1994/803, July 2, 1994.

[50]Report of the U.N. Secretary-General, S/1994/1002, para. 17, IV, August 26, 1994.

To the extent possible, United Nations civilian police observers would be colocated with the military and other civilian elements of ONUMOZ and would rely on the existing military and administrative infrastructure of the Mission, including transport and communications facilities. However, given the fact that these elements would be widely spread throughout the country, CIVPOL would require additional support in terms of administrative personnel, such as interpreters and translators, as well as adequate transportation and other equipment, accommodation facilities, etc. It is estimated that a total of 4 international staff and 35 locally recruited personnel would be required.[51]

In practice, the CIVPOL operation was conducted as a separate function of ONUMOZ, independent of the military peacekeeping mission.[52] The option of fully integrating into the military command structure seems never to have been seriously considered; however, the failure to achieve such integration seems not to have substantially affected the performance of either CIVPOL or the military component. The lack of training for CIVPOL officers was a much bigger problem.

Evaluation

Successes

Most commentators believe CIVPOL had a limited but positive impact in curbing abusive police behavior, especially in the more remote areas. More importantly, the elections were generally peaceful, without reports of serious violations by the local police. The CIVPOL mission can be judged as successful in contributing, psychologically as well as substantively, to this positive outcome.

---

[51]Report of the U.N. Secretary-General, S/1994/89, Add. 1, para. 17.

[52]Dennis C. Jett, "Lessons Unlearned or Why Mozambique's Successful Peacekeeping Operation Might Not be Replicated Elsewhere," *Journal of Humanitarian Assistance*, http://www-jha.sps.cam.ac.uk/a/a075.htm (December 1995).

Comparison with Namibia and Angola

In *Namibia*, SWAPOL remained ultimately responsible for the maintenance of law and order, while the role of CIVPOL was to monitor the activities of SWAPOL. United Nations officers accompanied SWAPOL on patrols (when SWAPOL would cooperate), and to political rallies and other election-related activities. Eventually, however, the CIVPOL role in Namibia grew, and its officers often patrolled on their own and were seen at political rallies without corresponding SWAPOL officers. However, it had no power of arrest nor did it have a training or monitoring mission for SWAPOL. CIVPOL was present at the 70 voter registration centers and helped the 110 mobile registration teams. Some 1,000 CIVPOL were assigned to duties assisting elections.

In *Angola*, the CIVPOL mission and functions varied substantially over time, adapting to the very violent and turbulent situation there. In UNAVEM II, the focus was to be on monitoring the neutrality of the Angolan police during the cease-fire and elections; to encourage the creation of joint police monitoring groups; and to oversee the integration of selected UNITA military personnel in the new national police force. In the expanded UNAVEM III operation, CIVPOL had a broad array of responsibilities, "focused on monitoring the neutrality of the Angolan National Police, the general law and order situation, the free circulation of people and the provision of assistance to the mission's Human Rights Unit. In addition, the component verified and monitored the quartering of the rapid reaction police and provided the quartered police with training. UNAVEM III police observers also closely monitored the activities of the Angolan National Police in providing security to UNITA leaders residing in Luanda."*

*The Blue Helmets, 263.

Shortcomings

Allegations of human rights abuse by the police continued after the CIVPOL mission concluded. By mid-1996, there were also allegations that the police had been taken over by organized crime.[53] It appears that CIVPOL had only a minor impact on curbing abusive tendencies of the Mozambique police. Even this impact rapidly waned after completion of the CIVPOL operation.

The most serious technical criticism of CIVPOL concerns a perceived lack of proper training for CIVPOL personnel. Many of the police who participated in the mission were not properly prepared to meet the enormous challenges they would face in Mozambique. This failure included differences in experience and a lack of such basics as being able to communicate with the local police or even to drive a vehicle. Though attempts were ultimately made to deal with the worst of these shortcomings, the experience has led some to question whether policemen are the most appropriate CIVPOL monitors in the first place. Trained human rights monitors (integrated into the existing U.N. military peacekeeping hierarchy) might be more effective.[54]

Conclusions

Despite its shortcomings, the CIVPOL operation in Mozambique can be termed a qualified success. It contributed substantially to creating a stable environment in which elections could be peacefully conducted. CIVPOL reporting is also considered to have contributed substantially to the curbing of police abuses, including abuses of human rights, especially in the countryside, even though most CIVPOL complaints were not formally acted on by the Government.

As one of the early UNCIVPOL operations, the Mozambique experience also made it very clear that there would have to be higher standards in personnel selection, to include serious attention to such basics as language and driver qualification. The experimentation with human rights training for CIVPOL monitors also proved positive and

---

[53]For example, see "Mozambique Rights Body Accuses Police of Torture," *Central News*, Maputo, December 2, 1995; and "Government Probes Police Links to Organised Crime," SAPA-AFP report from Maputo, July 8, 1996.

[54]Jett, "Lessons Unlearned."

would exert influence for similar but expanded training in future operations.

Nevertheless, the operation would have had a more substantial and long-lasting impact had it been started much earlier. Owing to this deployment gap, the peace process was already in an advanced and critical stage. CIVPOL's role was largely constrained to opening up territory and providing a neutral presence during electoral registration and conduct. This was an important political contribution, but it prevented CIVPOL from having much impact on civil rights abuses by Mozambique police units.

Further, had there been the political will at the United Nations to investigate more actively and act on at least the more egregious reports of abuse filed by CIVPOL, this might have led to earlier and more sustainable corrections by the Government. Shortcomings in this area seem to have preoccupied the U.S. Embassy in particular. In retrospect, those sharp criticisms seem to miss the mark by failing to give weight to the broader CIVPOL contribution of political and psychological reinforcement to the peace process, and especially to the critical phase of the run-up and conduct of the elections.

CIVPOL Composition and Costs

	NAMIBIA (UNTAG)	ANGOLA¹ (UNAVEM II)	ANGOLA¹ (UNAVEM III)	MOZAMBIQUE (ONUMOZ)
U.N. Mission Duration	4/89-3/90	5/91-2/95	2/95-6/97	12/92-12/94
CIVPOL Duration	4/89-3/90	5/91-2/95	2/95-6/97	9/93-12/94
U.N. Mission Cost	$368,584,324	$175,802,600	$366,523,900²	$471,199,200
CIVPOL Cost³	$54,975,205	$3,577,972	$17,338,362	$30,199,824
CIVPOL Strength⁴	Initially 500 6/89 raised to 1,000 8/89 raised to 1,500	Initially 90 5/92 raised to 126 11/92 lowered to 18 10/94 raised to 126	260	Initially 128 2/94 raised to 1,144⁵
Countries Contributing CIVPOL Personnel	Austria, Bangladesh, Barbados, Belgium, Canada, Egypt, Federal Republic of Germany, Fiji, German Democratic Republic, Ghana, Guyana, Hungary, India, Indonesia, Ireland, Jamaica, Kenya, Netherlands, New Zealand, Nigeria, Norway, Pakistan, Singapore, Sweden, Tunisia	Argentina, Brazil, Ireland, Malaysia, Morocco, Netherlands, Nigeria, Sweden, Zimbabwe	Algeria, Bangladesh, Brazil, Bulgaria, Congo, Egypt, Fiji, France, Guinea-Bissau, Hungary, India, Italy, Jordan, Kenya, Malaysia, Mali, Namibia, Netherlands, New Zealand, Nigeria, Norway, Pakistan, Poland, Portugal, Republic of Korea, Romania, Russia, Senegal, Slovak Republic, Sweden, Tanzania, Ukraine, United Kingdom, Uruguay, Zambia, Zimbabwe	Argentina, Australia, Austria, Bangladesh, Bolivia, Botswana, Brazil, Canada, Cape Verde, China, Czech Republic, Egypt, Finland, Ghana, Guinea-Bissau, Guyana, Hungary, India, Indonesia, Ireland, Italy, Japan, Jordan, Malaysia, Nepal, Netherlands, New Zealand, Nigeria, Norway, Pakistan, Portugal, Russia, Spain, Sri Lanka, Sweden, Switzerland, Togo, United States, Uruguay, Zambia

CIVPOL Mission			
"Ensure that the South West Africa Police fulfilled their duty of maintaining law and order in an efficient, professional, and non-partisan way"[6]	"Monitoring the neutrality of the Angolan police during the cease-fire"[7]	"Verify and monitor the neutrality of the Angolan National Police, the disarming of civilians, the quartering of the Government rapid reaction police, and the security arrangements for UNITA leaders"[8]	Monitor all police activities and verify consistency with the Agreement, monitor respect of citizens' rights and civil liberties, provide technical support to the National Police Commission and verify that activities of private security agencies did not violate the Agreement, verify strength and location of Government police forces, monitor and verify reorganization and retraining of rapid reaction police and assist the other ONUMOZ components in monitoring election campaign and respect for political rights[9]

1. UNAVEM I, which lasted from 1989 to 1991, did not have a CIVPOL component.
2. Cost through May 8, 1996.
3. Rough estimates taken from U.N. Secretary General Reports to the Security Council.
4. Authorized strength; in most cases, actual deployment was very close to the authorized strength.
5. Actual deployment was 1,086.
6. *Blue Helmets*, 213
7. Ibid., 239
8. Ibid., 256
9. Ibid., 329

Cost of CIVPOL Missions

Month	ONUMOZ	UNTAG	UNAVEM II	UNAVEM III
1	677,220	4,518,510	219,750	184,512
2	699,794	4,669,127	227,075	178,560
3	699,794	4,518,510	227,075	184,512/
4	632,072	4,669,127	205,100	184,512
5	699,794	4,669,127	59,923	(1-8) 47,616 (9-20) **338,760
6	677,220	4,518,510	57,990	** 525,078
7	3,110,757	4,669,127	59,923	** 508,140
8	3,010,410	4,518,510	57,990	** 525,078
9	3,110,757	4,669,127	59,923	** 508,140
10	3,110,757	4,669,127	59,923	** 647,652
11	3,010,410	4,217,276	(1-15) 28,995 (16-30) *29,295	** 647,652
12	3,110,757	4,669,127	* 60,543	** 626,760
13	(1-15) 1,505,205 (16-30) **965,685		* 58,590	** 647,652
14	** 1,995,749		* 60,543	** 626,760
15	** 1,995,749		* 60,543	** 647,652
16			* 54,684	** 647,652
17			* 60,543	** 605,868
18			* 58,590	** 647,652
19			* 60,543	** 626,760
20			* 58,590	** 647,652
21			** 58,187	** 626,760
22			** 58,187	** 647,652
23			** 56,310	** 647,652
24			** 58,187	** 626,760
25			** 56,310	** 647,652
26			(1-15) **28,155	** 626,760
27				** 647,652
28				** 647,652
29				** 584,976
30				** 647,652
31				** 626,760
32				** 647,652
33				** 626,760
Total Cost	$28,312,336	$54,975,205	$2,022,334	$18,456,960
Size	1,086	1,500	90	260
Cost per	$26,070	$36,650	$22,470	$70,988

* Estimated expenditure (i.e. estimated from a past period)
** Cost estimate (i.e., estimated for a future period)
Source: The figures were derived from the Secretary General's financial reports of CIVPOL costs or, if those numbers were not available, from the estimates of costs for future periods. (Note that figures reported by period have been divided into months for comparison purposes; they do not strictly reflect actual expenditures in a given month.) November 1993 (month 1) was the first month for which ONUMOZ numbers were available. In May 1994 (month 7), the CIVPOL costs spiked, increasing by about 4½ times for the 6-month period up to (and including) the October elections (month 12). The CIVPOL mission was complete and its personnel repatriated by mid-January 1995 (month 15).

PEACEKEEPING AND POLICING IN SOMALIA

LYNN THOMAS and STEVE SPATARO

Background

The international community's intervention in Somalia began in April 1992 and ended in March 1995. The intervention included three distinct U.N. operations with different mandates and sets of resources. Public security is a recurrent issue in all discussions about this intervention. The lack of it contributed heavily to the widespread starvation and refugee flows that prompted the intervention. Throughout the 3-year period of the intervention, public security problems underlying each operation aggravated a fragile situation in Somalia characterized by the lack of national authority. Disagreement and difficulties in addressing public security issues ultimately undermined the international effort and helped bring it to an end. Responsibilities for this are shared by the United Nations, the United States as the principal power in the international effort, and by other participating states. The fundamental responsibility, however, was that of the fractious, power-driven, clan-divided Somali "leadership."

Situation Precipitating Intervention

General Mohammed Siad Barre ruled by force for 20 years during the Cold War, and Somalis suffered a standard of living ranked as one of the lowest in world. Somalia was strategically important, and Barre exploited this to his advantage receiving huge amounts of aid, arms, and military equipment from the Soviet Union in the early 1970s, and then from the United States after Moscow switched support to his rival, Ethiopia, in 1977. He suppressed clan loyalty by forcing fealty to himself in a single-party structure while manipulating clan rivalry through the distribution of weapons and other perquisites based on affiliation with his clan.

Somalia's history and nomadic, clan-based society are not conducive to nation-state organization. Civil war erupted during the 1980s and worsened between 1989 and 1990; and on January 26, 1991, Barre fled Mogadishu. After a few months two Hawiye clan warlords, Ali Mahdi Mohammed and General Mohammed Farah Hassan Aideed, became locked in an inconclusive battle for control of Mogadishu. Struggles among other factions and subclans occurred elsewhere in the country. In May, northern Somalia declared independence. Once Barre's authoritarian rule was broken, the already fragile unity of Southern Somalia also collapsed, as did state institutions.

The pre-civil war police "as an organized element of society . . . provided one of Somalia's most stabilizing influences."[1] Historically, Somalis had made a clear distinction between their police and military. The army had been trained by the Soviet Union and had been used by Barre as an instrument of repression. The police forces, in contrast, were Western trained (principally by the United States, Italy, and West Germany), generally respected, well administered, and relatively apolitical. The police forces had an undisputed reputation for professionalism.

By the end of Barre's regime in January 1991, Somalia's police force totaled approximately 15,000 members, with almost 200 police stations located throughout 18 regional districts.[2] When Barre fled, the police, along with all government institutions, ceased to exist. Police returned to their clans. If they were not residing in their home regions, they stopped performing police functions for their own safety. Most members, especially senior police officers, sought to avoid involvement

---

[1] Irving Kaplan et al., *Area Handbook for Somalia* (Washington, DC: Government Printing Office, 1969), 380.

[2] Martin R. Ganzglass, "The Restoration of the Somali Justice System" in *Learning from Somalia: The Lessons of Armed Humanitarian Intervention,* eds. Walter Clarke and Jeffrey Herbst (Boulder, CO: Westview Press, 1997), 20-21.

on one side or the other during the civil war in spite of the risk this entailed.

Capacity for Self-Governance

Since 1991 there had been no government in Somalia.[3] After Barre fled, the nation languished in a political vacuum for almost a year. More weapons poured into the country. Hundreds of thousands of Somalis moved to refugee camps in Kenya and Ethiopia or fled to Yemen; wealthier Somalis went to Western Europe, the United States, and Canada. With no leadership and instability spreading beyond its borders, Somalia was positioned to benefit from outside mediation.[4] The United Nations, and specifically the Secretary-General and the Security Council, did not intervene during 1991, although they had the justification to do so.[5]

By April 1992, Somalia was a nation in name only with no ability for self-governance. There was little physical infrastructure and no formal local, regional, or national governmental systems. There were, however, a number of local and a few regional administrative arrangements built upon traditional clan and subclan foundations.

Military and paramilitary forces included ethnic-based factions (nine major ones) that had ousted Barre, as well as armed gangs aligned with the factions or operating on their own. The fighting factions comprised in part men from the former Somali Army; for example, Mohammed Said Hersi "Morgan" had a well-organized force of 1,000 former

---

[3]For discussion of Somali efforts to form one during 1991, see John Drysdale "Foreign Military Intervention in Somalia: The Root Cause of Shift from U.N. Peacekeeping to Peacemaking and its Consequences," in Clarke and Herbst, *Learning from Somalia*.

[4]Drysdale, 3,4, 119-120. See also Terry Atlas "New Activism Underscores U.N.'s Failures" *Chicago Tribune*, January 10, 1993, final ed.: Perspective 1.

[5]Under Chapter V, Article 24, the Security Council has the primary responsibility for maintaining international peace and security; at minimum, under the authority of Chapter VI it could have begun role in the peaceful settlement of disputes. Throughout the history of the United Nations, the Secretaries-General have taken the initiative and use their implied power in Chapter XV, Article 99, to keep the peace through the Secretariat's Good Offices using informal contacts and diplomatic efforts.

soldiers.[6] Although not as well organized, Aideed and his allies had the largest force and controlled more territory than any other faction.

The Intervention

UNOSOM I

During Somalia's second year without a government, the unfolding natural catastrophe of drought, massive refugee migration, and the specter of pandemic starvation compelled the United Nations and its members to confront Somalia's plight and consider a response.

Between January and August 1992, the Security Council passed five resolutions pertaining to Somalia. The uniqueness of the situation was acknowledged in each resolution. "In passing Resolutions 733, 746, 751, 767, and 775, the Security Council recognized the special nature of the Somali situation and noted that the magnitude of the human suffering posed a 'threat to international peace and security.'"[7]

Yet the actions called for in each resolution appeared irrelevant. Resolution 733 imposed an arms embargo with no effective mechanism for enforcement. In April, the Security Council passed Resolution 751, establishing the U.N. Operation in Somalia (UNOSOM I) and calling for the development of a 90-day humanitarian aid plan. In July, Resolution 767 reaffirmed Resolution 751's action authorizing 50 observers to monitor a cease-fire whose existence was debatable at best, a committee to monitor an arms embargo that was meaningless to begin with, and a 500-member U.N. military force to provide security in this country of 6 million people (and 1 million refugees) whose warlords had already killed 4,000 people and wounded 20,000.[8] Four weeks later, the Security Council passed Resolution 775 which

---

[6]John L. Hirsch and Robert B. Oakley, *Somalia and Operation Restore Hope: Reflections on Peacemaking and Peacekeeping* (Washington, DC: U.S. Institute of Peace, 1995), 76.

[7]Rajendra Ramlogan, "Towards a New Vision of World Security: The United Nations Security Council and the Lessons of Somalia," *Houston Journal of International Law* 16 (1993): 242.

[8]"Somalia: Pause to Bury," *The Economist,* February 1, 1992, 44.

increased the number of authorized military forces to 3,500 just as the first 500 had been given reluctant permission by Aideed to deploy. According to U.N. Special Representative for Somalia, Mohamed Sahnoun, this infuriated Aideed.[9]

In September, 500 Pakistani troops finally arrived; they were pinned down at the airport, unable to move, much less provide protection to humanitarian agencies. They were lightly armed, authorized to use their weapons only in self-defense. The additional 3,000 troops never went to Somalia. Generally, Aideed and other faction leaders never fully accepted these Security Council Resolutions or cooperated fully with U.N. operations.

UNOSOM I eventually made some progress in providing humanitarian assistance and organizing political reconciliation, but there was no effective component to address public security. Thus, UNOSOM operated in a void with no means to address factional feuds and banditry, fueled by massive numbers of weapons in the country.[10]

---

[9]U.N. Security Council Resolution 751 also authorized Mohamed Sahnoun as the U.N. Special Representative for Somalia. For 6 months he worked tirelessly throughout the country with a wide spectrum of citizens and leaders to achieve political reconciliation. Early on Somalis asked Sahnoun to use former police to provide security assistance to U.N. forces; although supported by Sahnoun, the idea never received approval from the U.N. Secretary-General. In August, Sahnoun negotiated an arrangement with Somali factions that allowed for arrival of the 500-person force but restricted any further increase. Ignoring his efforts, the Security Council authorized the additional 3,000 military personnel almost immediately after the agreement had been negotiated. Sahnoun, who had not been notified in advance, believed he had been deliberately double crossed by the U.N. Secretary-General. Aideed proposed that some of his forces work *with* the Pakistani peacekeepers to secure the port. U.N. Force Commander General Imtiaz Shaheen declined. Aideed's forces then kept the Pakistanis immobilized at the port. Sahnoun earned the respect of Somalis and international aid providers while struggling to garner sufficient resources from the United Nations and Member States to operate under these conditions. He was forced to resign by the Secretary-General in October because of his direct public criticisms of the U.N. system and indirect criticism of the Secretary-General.

[10]With regard to weapons, from 1963 to 1976 "Somalia was the principal aid recipient of the Soviet Union in sub-Saharan Africa" according to the Congressional Research Service Report to Congress 93-934F *Somalia: Arms Deliveries* authored by Richard F. Grimmett, October 27, 1993. Most of the aid was military. The United

In August the United States organized and implemented an emergency airlift of food into Somalia from Mombassa, Kenya. Operation *Provide Relief* delivered over 28,000 tons of relief supplies from August 1992 to March 1993.[11] By December 1992, when UNITAF arrived, substantial work had begun to develop a U.N. humanitarian aid plan.[12] Primarily because of lack of security, it was never implemented during UNOSOM I.

Before the international intervention, security was a problem for the few humanitarian organizations that had remained. Others, including U.N. agencies, had pulled out. Aid workers hired armed Somalis (dubbed "technical assistance" or technicals) for protection, then it became impossible to get rid of them. In effect, the organizations paid extortion to local warlords in exchange for use of vehicles and armed guards. These "security guards" were normally members of a local warlord's militia, or members of an armed gang associated with the

---

States provided "most of its combat weaponry to Somalia in the 1980s . . . the combined value of all lethal weapons and ammunition delivered from the U.S. between 1981 and 1991 was over $35 million." Citing separate U.S. Arms Control and Disarmament Agency documents, the Report to Congress identifies the total value of arms deliveries from all countries in the 1970s and 1980s (including the United States, Soviet Union, Italy, France, China, and others): 1973-1977—$300 million; 1978-1982—$675 million; 1981-1985—$365 million; 1985-1989—$160 million. Since 1991, it is safe to say that the Middle East and Persian Gulf region have been a significant source of small arms and ammunition to Somalia. See also Jeffrey Alan Lefebvre, *Arms for the Horn: U.S. Security Policy in Ethiopia and Somalia 1953-1991* (Pittsburgh: University of Pittsburgh Press, 1991).

[11]SCR 767 authorized the airlift which the United States called Operation *Provide Relief.*

[12]At a U.N.-sponsored meeting in Geneva, "The 100-Day Action Programme for Accelerated Humanitarian Assistance for Somalia" was launched on October 12, 1992; it identified eight target sectors, including agriculture, basic health services, the building of civil society, clean water, and livestock; see United Nations [UNOSOM], *Review of the 100-Day Action Programme and Beyond: Key Issues for Somalia* (New York: U.N. unpublished document, December 1992).

warlord.[13]   Throughout the entire intervention the protection of humanitarian relief workers remained a problem.

Many Somalis saw the United Nations as a whole rather than an assortment of different organizations, viewing it as having abandoned them when its agencies moved to Kenya in 1991 because of security concerns. When the United Nations finally attempted to provide assistance and high local expectations were not met, its reputation suffered further because of mismanagement and from an inability to take action to suppress violence.[14] By November 1992, over 300,000 Somalis had died and some 1,500,000 Somalis were refugees or internally displaced persons.

UNITAF

On December 3, 1992, the Security Council unanimously passed Resolution 794 authorizing a Chapter VII peace-enforcement operation. Called Unified Task Force (UNITAF), the operation would be led by the United States with a mandate to enforce peace by using "all necessary means to establish as soon as possible a secure environment for humanitarian relief operations in Somalia."[15] The resolution also

---

[13]Many of these security guards were members of the warlord's militia, or Morions—young male Somalis each warlord armed to attack other warlords' militia and people. Morions received weapons, women, and khat from their warlord and were allowed to keep whatever they stole. The warlords established these groups of marauding bandits because they believed it to be an effective yet inexpensive force to distract their opponents. The problem was many of the Morions owed their allegiance to no one, and often attacked their own sponsoring warlord's people. They were very difficult to control and became a problem for all: warlords, the Somali people, and members of the international community.

[14]Boutros-Ghali became U.N. Secretary-General in January 1992. He immediately began calling for active U.N. involvement in Somalia; however, Security Council members—notably the United States—urged limiting U.N. involvement to humanitarian aid and diplomacy; see Woods, 4. Somalis generally disliked Boutros-Ghali himself; they viewed him as having supported Siad Barre while Boutros-Ghali was Egypt's Deputy Foreign Minister. Aideed personally distrusted Boutros-Ghali who similarly, disliked Aideed and became deeply involved in managing U.N. activities in Somalia.

[15]United Nations, Security Council Resolution 794 (1992), December 3, 1992.

established a separate trust fund to accept voluntary contributions for the operation.[16]

By December 1992, when this second operation began, Somalia was in chaos. With some estimates of 2,000 or more people dying per day during the fall, an unprecedented humanitarian crisis had erupted in this completely broken society. The country was inundated with weapons, and open air arms markets flourished. Food was being used as a weapon by the warlords, particularly Aideed, who controlled the port, but also by Ali Mahdi, who shelled the port to stop Aideed from using it. As early as 1991, relief supplies were being looted, stolen, and extorted. By December 1992, thousands of tons of food were stuck at ports or being stolen by the armed groups. The U.S. Air Force airlift (*Provide Relief*) helped, but much of the food was taken over by the factions who controlled the airfields. For 2 years prior to UNITAF there had been no law in Somalia. When relief aid was brought to a standstill for lack of security, the United Nations recognized the situation as "the most extensive looting and extortion ever experienced by relief operations."[17]

Prior to the war, the population of Somalia was estimated at about 7.5 million. By December 1992, between 300,000 and 500,000 people were estimated to have died, including about 25 percent of all children; 1.5 million people were at great risk; and 4 million were in need of some form of assistance.[18] By the end of 1992, many Somalis felt they had been forsaken by the world. The feeling was reinforced by the 8-month U.N. effort that had done nothing to address the overriding problem of security. When the media, general public, and the U.S. Congress demanded action, policymakers agreed the only way to stop

---

[16]The resolution "calls on all Member States which are in a position to do so to provide military forces and to make additional contributions, in cash or in kind . . . and requests the Secretary-General to establish a fund through which the contributions, where appropriate, could be channeled to the States or operations concerned." Security Council Resolution 794 (1992).

[17]United Nations, UNOSOM, *Relief and Rehabilitation Programme for Somalia Covering the Period 1 March to 31 December 1993* (Mogadishu: UNOSOM, February 8, 1993), 1 and 20.

[18]Ibid.

the violence was to bring in the world's military superpower to end the anarchy rapidly and allow food to reach the starving population.[19]

UNITAF was the international community's first effective effort to assist Somalia. Under the command of Lieutenant General Robert Johnston, the UNITAF coalition comprised over 38,000 troops from more than 20 countries and was dominated by 28,000 U.S. troops. By authorizing UNITAF, the military component to the international intervention, the international community provided both credibility and a means to stabilize a situation which was out of control. UNITAF effectively superseded UNOSOM I, although the latter remained nominally in existence.

The international community's largely symbolic efforts through UNOSOM I did not effectively address security conditions. In stark contrast, security was a fundamental reason for the intervention under UNITAF and this concern affected every element of the intervention. SCR 794 had passed unanimously and "marked the first-ever U.N. sanction for the use of force to ensure the delivery of humanitarian relief."[20] Boutros-Ghali described the situation as a "paradox . . . without security, relief assistance will continue to be severely constrained, but without relief assistance programmes, the prospects for security are at best precarious."[21]

In a broad sense, public security as a responsibility of the peace mission was not a controversial issue in Somalia. It was *the purpose* of the intervention—delivery of humanitarian aid had become impossible because of the lack of security. There was fundamental

---

[19]Individual members of Congress, especially Senators Nancy Kassebaum and Paul Simon, were instrumental in finally getting effective assistance to Somalia. As early as April 1991, a Senate resolution introduced by Kassebaum requested that the U.S. President lead a humanitarian effort and that the United Nations give the crisis top priority.

[20]Security Council members distinguished the situation in Somalia as one that required "an 'approach different from the usual form of peacekeeping operation' . . . warranted by the 'exceptional circumstances of anarchy and human suffering.'" United Nations, "U.N.-Mandated Force Seeks to Halt Tragedy: Operation *Restore Hope,*" *U.N. Chronicle* 30, no. 1 (New York: U.N. Dept. of Public Information, 1993): 13.

[21]Ibid.

disagreement, however, on the interpretation of that responsibility. This concerned two issues: disarmament of the warring factions and re-establishment of local security (vice security provided by international forces).

During the period leading up to UNITAF, decisions and communications concerning disarmament were (and still are) intensely disputed. SCR 794 "did not *require* [emphasis added] the Unified Task Force to disarm the Somalis, but Boutros-Ghali subsequently argued that he had an understanding with U.S. President George Bush that the force would disarm the Somali gunmen."[22] The Secretary-General claimed the creation of a "secure environment" presupposed disarming the gunmen and that this would be necessary for a lasting cessation of civil strife, as well as for a U.N. mission to replace UNITAF. President Bush argued that "there was no consideration of disarming the various Somali factions."[23] The United States and UNITAF believed disarmament would require the forces to police Somalia, which would have involved many more forces, increased the threat to the troops, and diverted them from the primary mission of protecting humanitarian operations.

UNITAF viewed its mission as limited and the disagreement on security did not hamper military operations. The multilateral forces were under the command of a U.S. general and command and control as well as support systems were highly effective. Somalis respected the kind of authority exemplified by the U.S. military (although they also knew the U.S. commitment was of limited duration, so they could wait, if need be, until the United States left).

The UNITAF mission had three phases: secure the Mogadishu airfield, seaport, and areas within the capital city; secure the towns identified as relief centers—Baidoa, Belet Weyne, Gialassi, and Oddur—as well as areas in the south including Bardera, the route from Baidoa to Bardera, the port cities of Kismayo and Merca, and

---

[22]Samuel M. Makinda, *Seeking Peace From Chaos; Humanitarian Intervention in Somalia* (Boulder, CO: Lynn Rienner Publishers, Inc., 1993), 71.

[23]John R. Bolton, "Wrong Turn in Somalia," *Foreign Affairs* 73, no. 1 (1994): 58-59.

Baledogle which had one of the largest runways in Africa; and provide for the transfer of responsibility for maintaining a secure environment to a follow-on U.N. peacekeeping force.[24] Contingents from participating countries were assigned specific geographic areas of responsibility where they established Humanitarian Relief Sectors (HRS) and protected the delivery of humanitarian goods and services.

Many believe that the UNITAF Rules of Engagement (ROE) were responsible for UNITAF's early success. Heavy weapons in areas where UNITAF forces were operating were to be confiscated, destroyed, or placed in designated storage areas. Light weapons were not to be carried on the streets but were not confiscated.[25] Bandits and militias respected UNITAF strength and willingness to use it when warranted. During the civil war, "technicals" were the primary vehicles used by Somali factions and one of the most visible potential threats to UNITAF forces. UNITAF was "authorized to use 'all necessary force' to confiscate and demilitarize" the technicals and disarm individuals. Especially with the technicals the question arose whether this meant "'shoot on sight' . . . Johnston decided it did not and directed commanders to challenge and approach the technicals, using all necessary force if the weapons were not voluntarily surrendered."[26] By

---

[24]See also four phases of UNITAF in Hirsch and Oakley, 44.

[25]"Crew served weapons are considered a threat to UNITAF forces and the relief effort whether or not the crew demonstrates hostile intent. Commanders are authorized to use all necessary force to confiscate and demilitarize crew served weapons in their area of operations. . . . Within areas under the control of UNITAF forces, armed individuals may be considered a threat to UNITAF and the relief effort whether or not the individual demonstrates hostile intent. Commanders are authorized to use all necessary force to disarm individuals in areas under the control of UNITAF. Absent a hostile or criminal act, individuals and associated vehicles will be released after any weapons are removed/demilitarized." UNITAF Rules of Engagement (ROE), quoted in Colonel F.M. Lorenz, "Rules of Engagement in Somalia: Were They Effective?" *Naval Law Review* 42 (1995): 62.

[26]Kenneth Allard, *Somalia Operations: Lessons Learned* (Washington, DC: National Defense University Press, 1995), 36, 37. Using Clausewitz's terms, the culminating point of victory involved a recognition of the center of gravity by the UNITAF commander. That is, in order to provide for the delivery of humanitarian relief, UNITAF had to neutralize the Somali warlords without directly threatening their

January 1, 1993, there were almost no weapons on the streets of Mogadishu or in other HRS.

UNITAF was a significant military operation in conjunction with and actively assisting a complex relief operation. There was an unprecedented degree of interaction among the military, political, and humanitarian communities. In December 1992, just days prior to the arrival of UNITAF, the international community, Somali political leaders, and clan elders met in Addis Ababa, Ethiopia. This led to a January 1993 U.N. conference at which Somali political leaders agreed to a "nationwide cease-fire, general disarmament and a national reconciliation conference to be held on 15 March 1993."[27] A U.N. Relief and Rehabilitation Program was developed, submitted to the Security Council and approved in March 1993.

During UNITAF, Humanitarian Operations Centers (HOCs) and a Civil-Military Operations Center (CMOC) were created to organize military support for humanitarian operations.[28] The HOC in Mogadishu

---

individual political ambitions; both Aideed and Mahdi's primary goal was to become the new leader of Somalia. The culminating point of victory incorporated the ROE. In light of this potentially volatile use of force authorized by the world community for a humanitarian objective, in an operation other than war, to be carried out by the world's most powerful military, the ROE could determine the success or failure of UNITAF. The culminating point of victory occurred with General Johnston's interpretation of the ROE and his decision on when to use force with respect to the "technicals" and armed individuals. For a detailed discussion on UNITAF ROE see Lorenz.

[27]Makinda, 34. Numerous cease-fires were negotiated (none held); the first was in March 1992.

[28]Kevin Kennedy, "The Relationship Between the Military and Humanitarian Organizations in Operation Restore Hope" in *Learning from Somalia.* U.N. Manager of Humanitarian Aid Dr. Phillip Johnston directed the establishment of HOCs as a novel coordinating mechanism to involve Somalis and the entire international community in developing and implementing the Relief and Rehabilitation Programme on a regional basis: "By January, thanks to Kevin Kennedy's efficient work, we had transformed the Department of Humanitarian Affairs in Mogadishu into the Humanitarian Operation Center (HOC). The HOC in Mogadishu would work so well matching the NGOs' needs to military support that HOCs were set for the major cities in southern Somalia." Philip Johnston, *Somalia Diary* (Atlanta, GA: Longstreet Press, 1994), 100.

was housed at UNOSOM headquarters. The CMOC was at UNITAF headquarters. The HOC in Mogadishu had as its coordinator the U.N. Manager of Humanitarian Aid, Dr. Philip Johnston, with the director of the CMOC serving as military deputy, and the U.S. Disaster Assistance Relief Team chief as civilian deputy. The degree of coordination in the HOCs of each of the HRSs varied from region to region depending on the strategy employed by HRS commanders.

The re-establishment of local security, in the form of Somali police, was included as a target sector of the U.N. Relief and Rehabilitation Program developed during UNITAF. After Sahnoun's departure, the possibility of U.N. support for local police was raised again during UNOSOM I. Relief workers and Somalis from Hargeisa and Kismayo asked the United Nations to provide food to local Somali police forces that had been working voluntarily in those regions. U.N. headquarters determined this was outside the Security Council mandate.

The U.S. military was equally hesitant to support local police development. Following interagency decisions in Washington, the U.S. Central Command (CENTCOM) was charged with implementation. Civil affairs personnel and police training was considered but not included.[29] UNITAF was viewed as a limited humanitarian mission that would be concluded within a short period.[30] Although not part of the mandate, UNITAF decided after deployment to help re-establish the Somali police because it did not want to do policing itself. Somali police would help protect the troops and would accelerate the transfer to UNOSOM II.

As UNITAF forces began to secure distribution routes and food storage locations, problems developed in dealing with the Somalis. The soldiers could not communicate effectively, nor did they

---

[29]Lieutenant Colonel S.J. Whidden, "United States Civil Affairs Support to UNOSOM II During 1993-1994," in Learning from Somalia. Whidden discusses the fact that the Civil Affairs Brigade in the original Op Order was deleted by CENTCOM and the Joint Staff. This was consistent with the U.S. policy of limiting the scope of the operation to humanitarian assistance only.

[30]Walter Clarke "Uncertain Mandates in Somalia: Can External Intervention Revive Failed States?" in Learning from Somalia.

understand Somali customs and traditions.[31] On an ad hoc basis, former Somali police officers began to assist UNITAF forces with certain operations. At some intersections in Mogadishu, they directed traffic as a purely voluntary activity. In Mogadishu and elsewhere they joined elders and judges in performing rudimentary neighborhood police and judicial functions. U.S. Special Envoy Robert Oakley recognized the utility and effectiveness of voluntary efforts by former Somali police and concluded that some sort of institutionalized police operation might be feasible and would certainly be useful.

In late December 1992, the UNITAF Provost Marshal Lieutenant Colonel Steve Spataro explored the possibility of hiring a contract security force of former Somali police officers to perform various security functions around UNITAF compounds and on UNITAF convoys. The UNITAF leadership soon realized that without a functioning Somali-led police force to begin re-establishing a safe society, UNITAF would have merely created an "artificial" safe haven for the provision of humanitarian aid, but no more. After several exchanges by Lieutenant General Johnston and Ambassador Oakley with CENTCOM and authorities in Washington, DC, fears of "mission creep" were set aside because of the enhanced force protection the Somali police could provide.[32] UNITAF was authorized in late

---

[31]During confrontations between UNITAF and Somalis, UNITAF had taken detainees. While UNITAF leaders and CENTCOM debated how to handle the legal status of the detainees, Somalis attempted to report crimes to UNITAF in the hope that UNITAF would apprehend and jail the offenders. UNITAF quickly developed "civilian detainee" policies and procedures; they were not effective, however, nor were commanders and soldiers comfortable in applying them. Among other stop-gap measures, UNITAF established a temporary holding facility for detainees.

[32]Oakley sent a cable to the National Security Adviser arguing that Somali police were ready to undertake potentially dangerous tasks such as patrolling in back alleys and guard duty on public streets being conducted by U.S. soldiers. The day it arrived in Washington, the first U.S. soldier was shot when he happened across a robbery in a back alley. The response to the cable was approval for use of local U.S. resources to start a police force. There was no financial or personnel assistance from the United States to assist in the process for fear of violating congressional restrictions. Later, in October 1993, after the U.S. decision to withdraw militarily, waivers of these restrictions were sought and obtained, and over $45 million was allocated for the Somali police.

December 1992 to provide assistance (but not training) to the police from local resources only. No official U.S. Government assistance was provided. This U.S. unwillingness to provide assistance during the initial, formative period, when coupled with the refusal of the United Nations to provide assistance, seriously weakened the development of the Somali police force.

There was no legal precedent or mandate for UNITAF to recreate police forces except to establish security as called for in SCR 794. It emerged as an attempt to achieve sustainable security and Somali control of their society. UNITAF, therefore, sought to establish an interim Auxiliary Security Force (ASF) that would enforce locally agreed upon laws and be controlled by the community: in essence, a community police force.

A Local Security Force

To encourage dialogue among the warring factions, a political committee comprising representatives of the Aideed and Mahdi clans began meeting in Mogadishu in early January under the guidance of Oakley. The paramount issue of security was a topic in every discussion, whether it was the resettlement of refugees or the re-establishment of market places. Oakley pursued the idea and feasibility of establishing interim forces of Somali police to work with UNITAF in providing security. Initially, Somali committee members doubted it could be done. Eventually, they decided it would be possible with international support. Oakley also approached the Islamic Higher Council, a traditional organization and an important segment of Somali society which supported the idea outright. The political committee came up with 10 names to serve on a police committee. Oakley personally obtained approval from Aideed and Mahdi. The warlords agreed to the establishment of the police committee and the nonpolitical interim police force specifically limited to the Mogadishu region. Individuals on the committee were supposed to be apolitical former police colonels or generals with good human rights records.

Although four members of the police committee failed to meet all the standards hoped for by UNITAF (two were former Army officers, one was the former chief of the hated secret police, and one was an engineer), they remained on the committee because it had the approval of Aideed and Mahdi. Time was short, and security was essential to the intervention's success. There was no time to renegotiate. The police committee first met in the neutral territory of the U.S. Special Envoy Office (USLO) in mid-January 1993. Representatives from each sector of the international intervention—political, military, and humanitarian—attended the meetings.[33] Those who had not been police officers were initially more interested in political aspects and gaining control of the committee for Aideed or Mahdi. With U.S. and U.N. support, they were ignored by the former police officers who did not want political leaders to interfere in what they were trying to do. The former police took charge of discussions on how best to revive the police, focusing on the practicalities involved in standing up an interim force.[34] They expressed concern that the police could not make the law, enforce the law, and convict and punish those who break the law. Establishment of a police force had to be done in conjunction with the formation of a court system. Within 2 weeks the committee had identified the number of personnel needed, a list of qualifications, an acceptable vetting procedure, physical plant needs, and training and equipment requirements for the ASF.[35]

---

[33]Questions posed by the international community representatives and answered by subcommittee members characterized the first committee meetings: What did you do before the civil war? How were the former Somali police organized? What was the reporting structure? How were police selected? What kind of training did police get? Who was armed and with what? What laws did you use? Although Spataro already knew many of the answers, this process would help determine the credibility of the individuals on the subcommittee.

[34]These discussions addressed questions such as: How many could stand up in Mogadishu? What minimum materials and support would they need? How should they be selected? What kinds of activities could they perform?

[35]One of the two subcommittees worked on training and equipment; the other on operations. Old training manuals and law books were found, reproduced, and provided along with identified trainers. The UNITAF, USLO, and U.N. representatives worked with the Somalis in determining resource requirements and then providing UNITAF and U.N. support. Somalis gave old uniforms to the UNITAF, USLO, and U.N. representatives to use as samples in order to procure new ones. Somali construction engineers worked alongside UNITAF engineers to design and rebuild

These developments evidenced the commitment of most committee members to a nonpolitical and effective effort toward sustainable rehabilitation. After this constructive beginning, a complexity of disagreement brought work to a standstill. For different reasons the warlords and some members of the committee wanted a national police force. Mahdi and Aideed each believed that by controlling the police committee they could control the establishment of a national police; in turn, whoever controlled the national police could claim legitimacy as Somalia's leader.[36] Others believed that only a national police force could permanently end the civil war. General Ahmad Jama, the last commander of the Somali National Police and generally respected by all clans, argued that a properly armed national police force could enforce a cease-fire, disarm the militias and bandits, and enforce agreed-upon laws.[37]

Local U.S. leadership, on the other hand, was working to establish the ASF—a 5,000 person interim, regional, auxiliary force (3,000 in Mogadishu, and 2,000 in other regions). The professional relationship between the Somali police and the staff of the UNITAF Provost

police stations. Four operational divisions comprised of 13 police stations and one prison in Mogadishu were established. Somalis and the international community identified leadership and a chain of command for the operation of the divisions and stations. Committee members signed written agreements on procedures and policies.

[36]That is one reason why Oakley and LTG Johnston issued strict instructions to USLO and UNITAF representatives that all parties understand the distinction between this interim security force and a national police force. The name of the interim force was carefully chosen to help clarify that distinction in the minds of all Somalis. And UNITAF pointedly refused to guarantee members of the ASF automatic membership in any future national force.

[37]Jama claimed that the interim force would not be successful because it was incapable of forcing the militias and clans to stop fighting. He envisioned a sufficiently armed National Police Force that could enforce a cease-fire, disarm the militias and bandits, and enforce agreed-upon laws. He believed that Somali police officers would put their clan differences aside to work for a National Police Force and the Somali people—as they had in the past. Jama further claimed that Somalis respected the Americans and believed in the Americans' commitment to help the Somali people. He felt that the Somali police chief must be a foreigner, specifically American. Later Somali jurists also called for foreign leadership believing that foreign judges with no clan ties were the only ones capable of being impartial.

Marshal (PM) was important to developing a credible ASF. The PM's staff consisted of 22 Marines and Army Military Police to provide interim assistance. The United States was walking a very fine line because there was no U.N. mandate to establish police, and U.S. law required a wavier before military assistance could be provided to foreign police.[38] The UNITAF position was that the local populace would more likely support the ASF if it were under local control and that this would lead to Somalis assuming some responsibility for handling their own problems. Ultimately, when the U.N.-led UNOSOM II operation assumed responsibility, a new national police force could be established.

At the suggestion of police officers on the committee, religious and other community leaders were brought into the discussions. They became convinced that re-establishment of police, courts, and jails was necessary to security, stability, and economic recovery. Their support, combined with pressure from Oakley and UNITAF commanders finally convinced Aideed and Mahdi to drop their objections. The effort to establish the ASF won full community participation, the logjam broke and the process continued. The committee agreed that it would become the supervising authority for the ASF, representing the Somali people, with the advice and assistance of UNITAF and the United Nations.

The vetting procedure started with the establishment of a list of qualifications: Somali citizen; no tangible offense against Somali society; police officer with 2 years experience prior to January 26,

---

[38]Section 660 of the Foreign Assistance Act of 1961 prohibited U.S. forces from training, equipping, advising, or providing financial support to foreign police, prison, or other law enforcement forces. The law was specifically designed to ensure that the United States not support countries that are using their law enforcement assets as instruments of oppression against legitimate opposition individuals or movements. Section 660 was repealed in an amendment to the Foreign Aid Reduction Act of 1995. Nevertheless, Title X, Section 164, and Title 22, Section 2420, U.S. Code, still limit U.S. military involvement in re-establishing a law enforcement force.

1991; no handicap; and retain rank held prior to January 26, 1991.[39] The discovery of personnel files of the former national police reduced the time required for proper vetting. A midlevel manager from police headquarters had secured almost all personnel files in his home when faction militias and bandits looted police headquarters. After former police organized the files,[40] a week-long employment fair was held. Individuals were verified with the help of former commanders and photographs from personnel files.

The police were assigned basic functions designed to meet immediate needs of traffic control; crowd control; neighborhood patrols; security of food distribution sites; and security of airfields and seaports. Police were unarmed while on routine duty, but weapons were available in police stations, both for protection from attack and for use on special joint patrols with UNITAF.[41]

UNOSOM, UNITAF, U.N. agencies, and the warlords provided funding and equipment. The United Nations funded the purchase of uniforms, personal police equipment, office equipment (i.e., typewriters and furniture), and building supplies to rebuild and operate police

---

[39]The date January 26, 1991, was significant because it marked the day that the Somali police institution ceased. The committee wanted officers with experience and 2 years' experience was also the probationary period for former Somali police. They also wished to avoid having members of faction militias infiltrate the police. No handicap was included because the committee felt that an officer without a leg or arm would be ineffective. Determination of what constituted a "tangible offense" would be made by the committee and the local community; if someone accused a former police officer and could prove that he or she had committed atrocities during the war, the individual would not be admitted. The former Somali police included women and some joined the ASF.

[40]The training and equipment subcommittee took on this responsibility with the assistance of Spataro; committee members knew where to find the former personnel as well as what was required to ensure a satisfactory vetting process.

[41]These simple tasks were essential to establishing a stable and secure environment. It also ensured that Somalis were dealing with Somalis rather than an "occupation force" in assuming responsibility for advancing their society. Wherever the Somali police provided these basic functions, commerce flourished, schools opened, and life began to return to pre-civil war normalcy.

stations. The United States supplied vehicles and radios.[42] The Italians supplied additional uniforms. UNITAF and Somali engineers refurbished police stations.[43] The World Food Program (WFP) supplied food for police officers and their families. UNDP and UNOSOM I each provided $2.4 million for salaries. Eventually the United Nations provided money for a communications network. Under pressure from UNITAF, the warlords donated specific pieces of equipment (e.g., Mahdi provided rifles). Confiscated militia vehicles were refurbished and painted to serve as patrol vehicles, and in outlying areas, weapons came from the warlords' weapons storage sites.

Initial plans called for the ASF to begin in Mogadishu and eventually expand to all areas covered by UNITAF. By the time of the transfer to UNOSOM II, the ASF was established in 17 cities and towns.[44] Spataro traveled to all UNITAF HRS to brief them on the formation of the ASF and to explain the program to senior former national police officers and elders in those areas. All supported the program, although some were more dynamic and effective than others. The HRS commanders' representatives and community leaders traveled to Mogadishu to observe the vetting process there and discuss requirements. Using the same guidelines, local communities submitted former police officers' names for vetting.[45]

Representatives from the Somali police training and equipment subcommittee, UNOSOM I, and UNITAF wrote an ASF handbook with administrative, training, and operational guidelines regarding UNITAF

---

[42]U.S. provisions included 3 repeaters, 40 Motorola handheld radios, chargers, and 40 batteries; UNOSOM immediately provided 3 repeaters, 50 mobiles, 100 Motorola hand-helds, 200 batteries, and 13 base stations. From excess stocks in Saudi Arabia, the United States also provided 24 vehicles that had been contributed by Japan for use in *Desert Storm*.

[43]In Mogadishu, UNOSOM contracted with a Somali engineering firm; in outlying areas, UNOSOM provided the materials and UNITAF engineers did the work.

[44]These included Mogadishu, Bardera, Baidoa, Belet Weyne, Matabaan, Giolossi, Giolar, Baclad, Bullo Barde, Oddur, Wageed, Teeglo, Afgooye, Wanla Weyne, Merka, and Kismayo.

[45]To ensure control of the remaining police records, all vetting was accomplished in Mogadishu. This led to delays in vetting for outlying locations and in some instances to falsification of records from some locations.

and UNOSOM I support to the ASF. Its purpose was to inform UNITAF HRS commanders about ASF functions, responsibilities, and organization and the command relationship with the ASF. UNITAF and UNOSOM I oversight officers used the handbook in their monitoring of administrative and technical operations of the ASF.[46] The 10-chapter manual also served as an agreement with the Somalis that UNITAF and UNOSOM I supported the ASF.

The ASF showed promise in Mogadishu after just 2 weeks of very basic training.[47] The forces included 3,000 men and 50 women, four

---

[46]The handbook included annexes containing information on administrative requirements, equipment issue/availability, supply accountability, food-for-work program, monetary payments, weapons issue and use procedures, patrolman's handbook, administrative handbook, and criminal code/proceedings and reports. UNOSOM provided some funding and equipment; UNITAF provided technical and administrative oversight. In early February UNOSOM CA, Doug Manson, instructed Spataro to work with the UNOSOM procurement and finance chiefs; the process of coordination was documented in the handbook.

[47]UNITAF and the political committee were attempting to resettle refugees across what was called the "Green Line"—a DMZ during the civil war. U.S. Marines, charged with securing the crossing sites, were being stoned by both sides as both clans fought against each other. Oakley asked that the Somali police be called to duty, although they had no equipment, no uniforms, and Spataro felt that he would be setting them up for failure.

The police commander in the area estimated that he would need 100 police officers. That night the word was spread for 100 officers to report for duty the next day at the new police training center. Spataro expected 10 at most. The next morning 95 policemen and 5 policewomen appeared in rags—old police shirts, pants, and their old blue berets. The police commander formed two companies, issued orders, and dismissed them with instructions to get their equipment. They scurried around picking up sticks and breaking branches to serve as batons—a well-recognized part of their uniform before the civil war; they then climbed onto trucks that would take them to the staging site. As the trucks passed through the neighborhoods, the police officers stood on the trucks singing. People in the street were waving, smiling, and jumping up and down. Upon arrival at the staging site, the police disembarked. As Spataro walked with the police commander to the crossing site, they could hear occasional gunfire, and rocks from both sides rained down on them. The commander completed his final reconnaissance, saluted Spataro and returned to his men and women. Spataro recalls feeling sick to his stomach; here were U.S. Marines in full combat gear, unable to control a very volatile situation, and Spataro was sending a bunch of ragtags to slaughter. A few minutes later, Spataro heard the calling of cadence and the slapping operational divisions, three special divisions (Criminal Investigative Division, traffic, and customs), 13 stations, and one prison. There were approximately 30 people in each of the divisions and 175 total in each of the 13 stations; an additional 150 people were assigned to the prisons. UNITAF conducted joint patrols with the ASF, and UNITAF military contingents were co-located with each division HQ and station. This provided extra communications and logistics support, protection against attacks by heavily armed factions, and psychological support.

The ASF became very popular with the local population in Mogadishu, Baidoa, and other locations. In Mogadishu, shortly after uniforms were issued and the police organized into units, they were assigned the duty of protecting 35 feeding stations that were to be opened by the international community (e.g. WFP, U.N. Children's Fund, AID, Irish Concern, and OXFAM) and operated by Somali women. The program generated substantial political controversy and threats of organized as well as spontaneous violence. However, all 35 stations opened as scheduled, with unarmed Somali police present and UNITAF military backup nearby. An average of 4,000 extremely hungry persons were fed by each station each day, peacefully and without incident. This did wonders for the morale and health of the city population as well as the morale and reputation of the ASF. On several occasions, the latter stood their ground in protecting the people against armed bandits, often suffering casualties, until UNITAF could arrive, further enhancing their standing.

UNITAF was capable of guiding the establishment of the ASF, because of its military structure and the fact that security was such an urgent and fundamental issue. However, neither the U.N. Secretary-General, the Security Council, the United States, nor other

---

of sandal feet on the pavement as the police crested the hill. The rocks stopped falling and it became very quiet as the police moved between the factions. The formation stopped, the officers quickly issued orders, and the police moved to their posts. As they did this, the crowds on both sides began applauding and shaking hands with the officers. The resettlement process proceeded without incident. Spataro was stunned and realized for the first time that with UNITAF support the ASF could really work in carrying out limited operations.

governments actively advocated establishment of a nationwide judicial system. (Australia did help establish one in its limited HRS of the Bay Region.) With no government, elders and religious leaders in communities throughout Somalia determined what law the police would enforce. In most situations, Islamic law and local customs combined with the 1962 Somali Penal Code (which was Somali law prior to Siad Barre's reign) to serve as the local legal code.[48]

Lacking official recognition and funding, and without a parallel effort to establish judicial and penal systems that would have strengthened the work of the ASF, the success of the ASF varied from region to region. Among the more than 20 nations contributing to UNITAF, only Australia brought civilian police advisors. The Australian unit arrived in January, having had time to study the situation. It integrated police advisors and judicial experts into its force (see paper by Michael Kelly). The United States, Italy, and France had military police personnel and units. Each of these nations used its MPs differently in support of ASF. Police officers in the ASF were most effective when integrated as equal partners into a military commander's strategy for providing security.[49]

---

[48]A former police officer provided a copy of the Penal Code. UNITAF made copies, and these were distributed to the ASF and Somali judges. The code was included in the ASF handbook signed by Zinni and Manson. UNITAF decided to leave the decision as to which law would be enforced up to the individual community (elders, women's groups, councils). In areas where Islam was strong, Islamic laws were enforced. In other areas it was a combination of Islamic law and the Penal Code.

[49]See Ganzglass, in Clarke and Herbst, *Learning from Somalia*, 9-10. In the Bay region the Australian UNITAF contingent completely integrated the police and judiciary into their security program from the outset. The Australians provided materiel and moral support to both institutions and generally created an environment whereby local Somalis felt that they controlled their own destiny. The capture and prosecution of Gutaale, the leader of a particularly vicious local bandit group, illustrate how and why the ASF worked so well. Gutaale operated brothels and a profitable extortion ring; he had personally raped and killed many Somalis. During one incident, he drove an armored vehicle into a crowd of people; he then backed up and ran over those he had already knocked down, killing many. The local ASF captured him and the community-selected judges tried him for murder. The local populace testified (without fear of reprisals from Gutaale's followers) and convicted Gutaale. This successful process of re-establishing law and order would not have occurred prior to the arrival of the

In addition to the question of what the ASF would do with persons it detained, there was the question of what laws UNITAF military personnel would apply when serious crimes (e.g., armed theft, murder) were committed in their presence and what to do with any Somali detained. These issues were not addressed in Security Council Resolution 794, endorsing UNITAF, or in the UNITAF ROE. These issues had to be decided on the ground and were subject to varying approaches by the various national contingents of UNITAF. UNITAF Headquarters put out general guidance that any prison facilities must be up to minimum standards for POWs, for temporary detention of fewer than 48 hours based upon *prima facie* evidence. After the initial period, prisoners were released or sent to Mogadishu's UNITAF detention center for no more than 72 hours. Thus, in practice, detainees were released or handed over to the ASF, which, in turn, relied upon an ad hoc mixture of courts and justices, with widely varying degrees of fairness and political influence. This imperfect system was the best UNITAF could do under the circumstances.[50]

Australians and their subsequent support of the ASF. Gutaale's capture and trial with the participation of the local community was a watershed event in the region. It put bandits on notice that the community supported the ASF and the judiciary, that the community was taking charge, and they would no longer be intimidated by the bandits. The police station/court house became the town center where all judicial proceedings took place. The ASF increased their patrolling thereby reducing the need for the Australians to patrol. Commercial and social activities flourished in this region. Markets were re-established, schools opened, and sense of normalcy began to take hold. The Australians provided oversight and a big-brother approach that worked.

In Kismayo, the police were ineffective because the military commander refused to provide support. The police were afraid to leave their station. Former militia formed a rival police group and attacked the ASF police. Although UNITAF quickly took charge after this incident, both the ASF and UNITAF lost credibility.

[50] Interestingly, when the Australian contingent assumed responsibility for the HRS centered at Baidoa, it came prepared to assist in rebuilding the local court system. It also determined that the international laws of military occupation (i.e. Fourth Geneva Convention) applied and that conditions in the Bay Region, around Baidoa, satisfied all requirements of the Fourth Convention. Following meetings at Oakley's HQ and then at UNOSOM HQ under the leadership of UNITAF JAG Colonel Rick Lorenz (U.S. Marine Corps), a technical committee of Somali jurists was established. This committee advised the Australian contingent in selecting Somalis to re-establish courts

Eventually the populace viewed the international community's presence and functions as legitimate. For 2 years, Somalis had watched the international community collectively abandon them; they had to be convinced that UNITAF was a genuine and effective effort. The re-establishment of a Somali authority—the police—with the help of the international community helped legitimatize the effort.

UNOSOM II

In March 1993 the Security Council set another precedent with Resolution 814, which established UNOSOM II as a Chapter VII peace-enforcement operation under the command of the Secretary-General. Security remained a priority and was combined with an expressed mandate to assist the rehabilitation of Somalia. SCR 814 also dealt specifically with disarmament, charging UNOSOM II troops with the task of seizing small arms from all unauthorized armed elements. The mandate expanded the territory to be covered by U.N. forces and included a direct reference to the role of Somali police. The Security Council concluded that UNOSOM II would cover the whole country, whereas UNITAF had been responsible only for the southern third. Furthermore, they reasoned the mission could be accomplished with 10,000 fewer troops than UNITAF because of the help of a re-established Somali Police Force. While SCR 794 (UNITAF) had established a trust fund for voluntary contributions, under UNOSOM II the fund was authorized to *receive* contributions for the police, although it initially received none. The measure of success for UNOSOM II was very unclear.

Although UNITAF was a U.S.-led operation and UNOSOM II a U.N.-led operation, UNOSOM II had the political support and involvement of the United States. Political and military officials from

---

in the Bay region. This was the only such system in Somalia. It was not replicated elsewhere or endorsed by UNITAF and UNOSOM. Baidoa and the Bay region also had very well organized, effective ASF contingents established with help from UNITAF PM Spataro based on the model used for Mogadishu. See Michael J. Kelly, *Peace Operations: Tackling the Military Legal and Policy Challenges* (Canberra, Australia: Australian Government Publishing Service, 1997), 8-13 to 8-19.

the United States worked closely with U.N. officials to draft the mandate, concept of operations, and ROE for UNOSOM II.

Planning and implementation for UNOSOM II suffered badly from a lack of appreciation by the United States, other U.N. Member States, and the Security Council of the resources required and time it would take to deploy. A broad range of delays undermined the transfer of assets and responsibilities from UNITAF to UNOSOM II. The inclusion of public security and disarmament as mission elements meant a much greater challenge for UNOSOM II whose forces were far inferior to UNITAF. The original disagreement on disarmament was still evident in April 1993, with no plan to implement the new mandate. Forces did not arrive when expected, and some did not have necessary equipment. UNOSOM II did not have anywhere near the same resources, yet it had a much broader, more intrusive, and potentially explosive mandate vis-a-vis various factions, especially Aideed's.[51] U.N. structure provided no effective command and control, with much of the burden falling upon the Deputy UNOSOM II Commander (and U.S. Force Commander) Major General Thomas Montgomery.[52]

A considerable amount of detailed planning went into that section of the mandate authorizing a program for local security. A U.N. evaluation of police requirements was conducted in February 1993. In March, a team from the ICITAP conducted its own review of the ASF and the potential for re-establishing a Somali national police.[53] They concluded that the ASF was an effective force and, with training and equipment, could form the basis for re-establishment of a national police force utilizing former members of the Somali National Police. Subsequently, Ann Wright of the UNOSOM II Justice Division developed a $45 million budget and strategy to re-establish the Somali

---

[51]Aideed had earlier shown his opposition to UNOSOM I and had been able to neutralize and humiliate 500 Pakistani soldiers who made up UNOSOM I.

[52]See John Gerard Ruggie, "Wandering in the Void: Charting the U.N.'s New Strategic Role," *Foreign Affairs* 72, no. 5 (1993): 28, for discussion on the limitations of a peace-enforcement operation under the command of the Secretary-General. See Lorenz for discussion of the complexity of UNOSOM II command and control.

[53]Havekost and Ganzglass.

police, corrections, and judicial systems. This program envisioned establishing a Mobile Quick Reaction Force of 2,000, plus 8,000 more police officers throughout the country. Seventy police stations would be renovated, and modest transportation and communications systems would be provided. UNOSOM sector military commanders would maintain operational control of the police until a 152-person CIVPOL organization assumed control. Operational control would pass to Somali Government authority as soon as it was capable of assuming such responsibilities. The plan called for a court structure similar to that in place in 1962 in addition to "21 District Courts, Regional Courts in seven regions, and two Courts of Appeal." A more "modest program" called for the rehabilitation of two prisons, one in Mogadishu and one in Hargeisa.[54] The most basic problem was the lack of resources to implement the plans. U.N. Headquarters were not working in sync with UNOSOM II in preparing for implementation of the plan.

UNITAF transferred command to UNOSOM II on May 4, 1993, despite strong reservations expressed by the U.N. Secretary-General that the United Nations was not ready. The Secretary-General's new Special Representative in Somalia, Admiral Jonathan Howe, believed he had received concept approval for the Wright plan during a May 16, 1993 meeting in Mogadishu with Kofi Annan, Director of the U.N. Department of Peacekeeping Operations (DPKO). Howe and his staff assumed DPKO would implement the staff and funding for the justice program approved by Annan. Unbeknownst to Howe, Annan and the Secretary-General did not request donor country contributions for police instructors, funding, or equipment. They believed the United Nations should wait until there was a real political agreement among the Somalis and when they had set up local district and regional councils to assume control over the police and judiciary.[55] Moreover, at this time there was little prospect of substantial donor contributions, since the need was not perceived. (The United States was not prepared to make a contribution to the United Nations. Nor was it prepared to assist bilaterally.)

---

[54]Ganzglass, in Clarke and Herbst, *Learning from Somalia*, 12-13.
[55]Ibid., 13-15, for an explanation of the disparate views.

After UNOSOM II assumed control, the ASF program floundered. UNOSOM II did not have any CIVPOL on its staff to manage the ASF and had no funds to pay them. Military personnel were removed from the ASF stations and joint patrolling ceased just as factions brought weapons out of hiding into Mogadishu and resumed escalating violence. Outgunned by the militia and organized bandits and demoralized by the loss of military support, the ASF became incapable of performing viable missions except in the Bay Region where they received strong Australian support. Concurrently, confrontations began to arise as in Mogadishu as Aideed began to test U.N. forces. UNOSOM II Commander Lieutenant General Cevik Bir responded by changing the ROE to authorize forces to engage "organized, armed militias, technicals and other crew served weapons . . . without provocation."[56]

The UNOSOM II Deputy Provost Marshal was given the title of Officer in Charge of the Somali police program and ordered to hold the program together until the UNOSOM II Justice Division assumed control.[57] During a May staff meeting, senior UNOSOM II commanders determined that the Somali police was not a military mission but the responsibility of UNOSOM II Justice Division.

On June 5, less than 1 month after UNOSOM II accepted command, Aideed's forces responded to an armed inspection of a critical installation containing stored weapons and the vitally important faction radio station. In an attack that killed 24 Pakistani peacekeepers, Aideed retaliated for UNOSOM II's failure to obtain his agreement for the inspection. One of his lieutenants who was notified by UNOSOM specifically warned against the inspection. UNOSOM II had not anticipated the change in Aideed's reaction to the U.N. inspection, since UNITAF inspections had not been challenged. The following day the Security Council passed Resolution 837 condemning the attack and calling for the "arrest and detention . . . of those responsible for the armed attacks." On June 17, Howe called for the

---

[56]Lorenz, 3.
[57]Major Mark Inch, interview by Spataro, November 5, 1996.

arrest and detention of Aideed while the investigation continued.[58] UNOSOM II's focus upon arresting Aideed upset the military, political, and humanitarian balance.[59]

In July the UNOSOM II Justice Division finally began to act on the aforementioned police plan.[60] However, to manage the Somali police program were only six police monitors who worked strictly with the police in Mogadishu, in a very limited capacity. The CIVPOL cell, composed of three police monitors, was a subcell of the Justice Division. They never left Mogadishu, and their contact with the police committee, minimal from the start, further decreased. Unlike UNITAF, the U.N. military forces had no role with the police in Mogadishu. Equipment and funding identified for the ASF by UNITAF and UNOSOM II never made it to the ASF. The old ASF handbook was not updated, and CIVPOL was unfamiliar with it. Military and humanitarian leaders in the field lacked definitive guidance and adequate resources.

The Secretary-General in summer 1993 again placed police as a top priority calling for the expansion of the forces to 5,000, promising $6 million in support, claiming that an interim judicial system using the 1962 code would be in place by October 1993. Yet, no new guidance was issued to the field until September 1993, and no funds were provided. On the ground in Mogadishu, the focus was almost entirely on the conflict with Aideed and his forces. Moreover, the head of the

---

[58]"The United Nations investigation of the recent events has continued to progress, with evidence mounting in support of the premise that there was an SNA [Aideed's Somali National Alliance] conspiracy to commit premeditated acts of violence against UNOSOM II on June 5." *Report of the Secretary-General on the Implementation of Security Council Resolution 837*, S/26022, paras. 31 and 32 (New York: United Nations, July 1, 1993).

[59]This was in direct contradiction to the spirit of peacekeeping, peacemaking and peace-enforcement interventions. In the broad context of U.N. intervention, "The requirement of impartiality is fundamental, not only on grounds of principle but also to ensure that the operation is effective. A United Nations operation cannot take sides without becoming a part of the conflict which it has been set up to control or resolve." Frederic L. Kirgis, Jr., *International Organizations in Their Legal Setting*, 2nd ed., American Casebook Series (St. Paul, MN: West Publishing, 1993), 718.

[60]Michael Sheehan, interview by Spataro, November 6, 1996.

Justice Division diluted and factionalized the reasonably effective Somali police committee by appointing additional members proposed by Aideed, Mahdi and other faction leaders. This misguided attempt to obtain support effectively neutralized and demoralized the police committee by bringing partisan political maneuvering to the fore and rendering ineffectual the previously dominant core of professional policemen who ran the committee and supervised the ASF.[61]

In August, the Secretary-General identified "the re-establishment of the police, judicial, and penal systems" as the "key to establishing security and law and order in a system managed by Somalis."[62] His report included an extensive review of what had been accomplished with the police to date and an equally extensive strategy for what was needed. It presented the plan that those in the field had been ready to implement 4 months earlier.

In summary, after UNITAF left in April 1993, the ASF rapidly deteriorated. Without pay or UNOSOM II military support, morale and discipline fell sharply. Moreover, the ASF was defenseless in the face of heavily armed militias who had again taken control of Mogadishu and other centers. Throughout the summer Somali militias fought each other, especially in Mogadishu and the Kismayo area, and Aideed fought UNOSOM II. The Security Council continued to call for re-establishment of the police, judiciary, and prisons in order to restore security and stability, but few resources were provided.

The October 3 fight between U.S. troops and Aideed's militia marked the end of any comprehensive support from the United States. Eighteen U.S. soldiers were killed, 78 wounded, and one taken hostage; over 1,000 Somalis were also killed. The Secretary-General's Report of November 12, 1993, assessed UNOSOM II's effectiveness as follows:

---

[61]Berkow and Sheehan, interviews.

[62]United Nations, Security Council, "Further Report of the Secretary-General Submitted in Pursuance of Paragraph 18 of Resolution 814," S/26317, III, para. 18, August 17, 1993.

UNOSOM II's record of general progress throughout most of Somalia has been seriously marred by the incidents that took place between 5 June and 3 October 1993. These incidents challenged the cause of disarmament and reconciliation in Somalia, created a situation of instability in South Mogadishu and stimulated factional elements elsewhere to prepare for a future of renewed fighting.[63]

With the passage of SCR 885 on November 16, 1993, this was acknowledged.[64]

After the events of October, there was increased interest in the withdrawal of U.S. forces by March of 1994. A functioning Somali police force was seen as an important part of the "exit strategy" and necessary for any hope of stability following withdrawal of U.S. troops. ICITAP, which had seen no interest on the part of the United Nations to support the police program it had outlined in March or the Justice Division's detailed plan, was called back to Somalia to develop an implementation plan for re-establishing a Somali police force. In November, an ICITAP team consisting of four people, led by ICITAP Director David Kriskovich, conducted an assessment of the status of the ASF and the requirements for re-establishing a police force. In December, a detailed plan was submitted to the U.S. Department of State, which approved the bilateral U.S. effort. Funding of $11 million was reprogrammed from the ICITAP Haiti project.

During a visit to Somalia in November 1993, former UNITAF PM Spataro met with the police committee in Mogadishu and with all the ASFs UNITAF had established in the field. They complained that UNOSOM II CIVPOL had not visited them. Many of the UNOSOM II

---

[63]United Nations, "Further Report of the Secretary-General Submitted in Pursuance of Paragraph 19 of Resolution 814 (1993) and Paragraph A5 of Resolution 865," S/26738, para. 49 (New York: United Nations, November 12, 1993).

[64]"The efforts to find and arrest Aideed [ended]. The Security Council made this official on November 16 when it called for the establishment of a commission to investigate the attacks on the Pakistani peacekeepers. Emphasis returned to brokering a political solution that would include Aideed and his followers." Richard N. Haass, *Intervention: The Use of American Military Force in the Post-Cold War World* (Washington, DC: Carnegie Endowment for International Peace, 1994), 46.

military commanders in the field did not understand the purpose of the ASF or that they had any responsibility for the ASF. For good reason, many commanders did not trust the ASF; in Merca, Kismayo, Baidoa, and Bardera, the original ASF had been ousted, and militia members had become the police. In Mogadishu, patrolling had ceased, and many police stations were no longer in use.

In December 1993, the United Nations announced a "new" task for UNOSOM II: to "re-establish" the Somali police. The detailed plan envisioned a 10,000 member force by the end of 1994. This was seen as a way to compensate for the loss of U.S. and other major military units, a means toward a U.S. "exit strategy," which might enable the operation to succeed without the U.S. military. Following the October clash between Aideed and U.S. forces, President Clinton announced that U.S. forces would leave Somalia by March 1994. The United States then shifted its focus almost entirely to public security, offering $12 million in support of the police and judiciary and $25 million in Department of Defense (DOD) equipment and services for the police. However, at that time the United States had not yet delivered on its pledge, made 2 months earlier, of $2 million for police salaries. Very little of the U.S.-provided equipment, advisors, or funds was in place before the withdrawal of all U.S. forces in March 1994. This meant that psychologically, the international intervention had lost its advantage and was at a disadvantage vis-a-vis the aggressive Somali factions that saw it as a spent force and were awaiting its total departure. Thus the resources bilaterally committed to the police had little effect in reversing their demoralization and ineffectiveness.

In January 1994, Japan announced a contribution of $10 million for the training and operation of the Somali police. It eventually provided $4,759,899 to the police program and $4,750,000 to the judiciary program.[65] From March 1994 to March 1995, however, the United Nations suffered from a chronic shortage of funds to pay police salaries.

---

[65]Provided by the Japanese Embassy, Washington, DC.

On February 27, 1994, Congress approved a U.S. bilateral program for the Somali police, and ICITAP immediately dispatched Project Manager Michael Berkow and a team of trainers to Mogadishu. However, by the time ICITAP was authorized to begin development activities, U.S. forces were withdrawing. The security situation had so deteriorated that they could not use the Somali Police Academy and instead had to establish a provisional training center inside the U.N. compound. A second provisional training center was established in Baidoa and work had begun for a joint ICITAP-CIVPOL training center at Calcaio when ICITAP was ordered to withdraw. ICITAP also provided assistance to help rebuild police stations in the Indian sector. ICITAP conducted three 21-day "refresher" courses for former Somali National Police officers and nine specialized training courses before the program was suspended in June. ICITAP left police training materials and equipment that was used by UNCIVPOL until the withdrawal of all U.N. forces.

Frustration with the slow pace of the UNOSOM II Justice Division deployment was not limited to the United States. Within the UNOSOM II military there was a great deal of resentment at the inability of the Justice Division to provide necessary support to Somali police; the efforts of UNITAF had created certain expectations and laid a foundation for the ASF that required continued assistance. The result was the establishment in the spring of 1994 of a Military Police Liaison Cell. The military began to develop a series of courses for the Somali Police: marching, weapons handling, and other basic skills. This program became closely connected with and supported by the ICITAP program.

Both the ICITAP and the new UNOSOM II military programs came to naught. By the time they began, the last U.S. forces were leaving. It was evident that UNOSOM II would not attempt to re-establish authority by force, and that Aideed would continue to ruthlessly pursue his ambitions in many parts of the country, including the Bay Region. This meant there was little utility in the belated police assistance programs. Surprisingly, most of the vehicles and weapons delivered by the United States at this late stage of the police program were successfully removed and used by UNCIVPOL elsewhere (e.g., Angola and Haiti).

Conclusions

Much of the planning and implementation in Somalia required the establishment of new rules and guidelines for interventions on an ad hoc basis. The United States, which was clearly the dominant power behind UNITAF and UNOSOM II, had not previously been a direct participant in major peace operations. Somalia, with a civil war but without governmental institutions, was *terra incognita*. This resulted in isolated successes, particularly for UNITAF; the initial humanitarian mandate of UNITAF was successfully implemented. The end result, however, was not successful in restoring public security or achieving political agreement.

Insurmountable internal problems grew from ineffective coordination between off-site planning and on-site implementation, a lack of resources, and a misreading of the political and security situations. A basic obstacle was the inability of the Somalis to come together in any sort of peaceful consensus. The mandate for the intervention changed, and changed drastically, with each phase or operation; it was also so vague as to require interpretation during operational planning and implementation. The direction of implementation changed so drastically during UNOSOM II that key participants such as France, Italy, Zimbabwe, and Botswana ordered their forces on the ground not to participate in the hunt for Aideed and his lieutenants.

The initial results of ASF operations were successful despite several handicaps: an absence of advance planning; no agreed, detailed UNITAF-wide plan; shortage of resources; and uneven application of general guidelines by different UNITAF major component commanders. The ASF took a community policing approach by communicating and working with the local population. The ASF had strong UNITAF support (especially in the most difficult area, Mogadishu) and their assigned tasks were within their capabilities. When the ASF was vetted by the community, it was successful. The community participated in selecting the leadership, the laws, courts, and patrol operations. Mogadishu illustrates good ASF policing on a large scale. However, even here there was no assistance for the restoration on improvement of judicial and penal systems which were in a state of disarray. Baidoa was the best example of overall law enforcement success because it included UNITAF planning and assistance with courts and prisons, as well as policing.

Despite singular agreement by the international community and the Somali people, with grudging acquiescence of the factions, on the effective role that the Somali police could play, adequate emphasis on and support for its long-term development never materialized. Disagreement on how to address the problem of security plagued planning and implementation of all phases of the international intervention.

The transition from the regional ASF established by UNITAF to a national police force planned by UNOSOM II did not succeed because UNOSOM II was not provided with the personnel, physical and financial resources, and political will to continue the program. There was no Somali political consensus and the overall security environment turned hostile for the police, which was deprived of UNITAF's military backup.

Lessons Learned

❑ The purpose of any successful peacekeeping operation is to achieve a peace agreement truly accepted by the warring parties. This was never achieved during the intervention in Somalia. The intervention was fundamentally flawed and doomed to failure when Aideed's political ambitions and increasing assertiveness were met by a confrontational U.N. response. Eventually, a de facto state of war developed between Aideed and the United Nations that the United States and other troop-contributing states were not prepared to sustain and win.

❑ If the objective is to provide sustainable stability and eventual rehabilitation, it is unrealistic to launch a humanitarian operation into a civil war and not address long-term political issues. Yet this is what UNITAF did, leaving the issues of political and physical reconstruction to the subsequent U.N. phase. When UNOSOM II replaced UNITAF, it failed to understand the basic political issues or the limitation of its military power in the peculiar Somali political environment.

□   CIVPOL can only operate effectively in an environment where the belligerents agree at least not to fight.   In an insecure environment, international police (CIVPOL) and local police must be attached to military units or have the full backing of the military in order to be effective. Police are trained in the minimum use of force to protect citizens and public order. The resumed fighting did not allow CIVPOL or the Somali police to do their jobs in most parts of Somalia (although they performed reasonably well in the Indian sector).

□   Police officers from multiple nations can be extremely problematic. In Somalia, some groups of trainers could not even communicate in a common language with other police trainers. Even more important, there were fundamental differences in operating styles among the contributing nations, yet they were expected to develop training and technical assistance—throughout the country—that would ultimately result in a uniform national police force. These differences are exacerbated with paramilitary contingents (e.g., the Italian carabinieri). One could argue that the carabinieri or the French gendarmerie are more suited for a mission like Somalia; the problem is the attempted integration of these paramilitary policing agencies with other "softer" civilian police agencies.

□   There must be a clear understanding of the roles, missions and limitations of the civilian police agency receiving the support. During the UNOSOM II period, there were unrealistic expectations for the Somali police. This resulted in strong pressure from the United States and UNOSOM II military to release weapons and vehicles to the Somalia police before they were ready for them. It also resulted in the mistaken expectation that the Somali police could be made strong and cohesive enough, both militarily and politically, to act effectively after the departure of U.S. forces and in the absence of political agreement amongst the much more powerful factions and even to undertake military action against the latter.

□ Public education by U.N. Members' constituencies can help create the political will necessary to achieve a successful intervention. As it was, neither the United Nations nor the United States did an adequate job of disseminating information to the public about the purpose and progress of the intervention. Media coverage—of starving children in the fall of 1992 and of American soldiers being dragged through the streets in the fall of 1993—marked the beginning and end of effective action by the international community. According to a former U.S. Defense Department official, there is a need for more

> effective programs of political consultation, of dialogue with national legislatures, and of a forthcoming and proactive public affairs posture. The Somalia operation was poorly understood in large part because it was very poorly explained, whether to the public or the U.S. Congress, or the German Parliament.[66]

□ A local police force can benefit military peacekeepers through its knowledge of the indigenous culture and the political situation—down to the neighborhood and gang level. It has in most cases established means of dealing with potential problems without the use of force, which are popularly understood and accepted (even if not always liked). By using local police in a cooperative mode, the military peacekeepers can avoid unwanted incidents with the local population due to lack of mutual familiarity (e.g., language, customs), and due to the difference in approach by military and police forces (e.g., crowd control and patrolling troublesome neighborhoods). Local police forces can also assume missions such as static protection which would otherwise require the use of military personnel.

---

[66] Woods, 29.

☐   The use of military peacekeepers, particularly military police in a liaison role, can not only substantially enhance the effectiveness and behavior of local police forces, but avoid problems such as U.S. law regarding foreign police training and taking command of police forces. Military personnel serving in a liaison capacity can assist with monitoring, training, and gaining greater respect for local police forces from the population. The provision of logistics support (including transportation and communications) can enhance the influence of military peacekeepers over the police, and help in the coordination of police and military activities. However, care must be taken in troubled states, where the period immediately after an international intervention is often uncertain and potentially violent; military support of this kind can go a long way to prevent incidents between the local police and the population.

☐   Establishment of a functioning, generally accepted local police can reduce the length of time required for the presence of military peacekeepers. Although this idea of local police to complement and then replace military peacekeepers was eventually accepted by the United Nations and Member States, it came too late to be implemented successfully.   In the absence of a political understanding among major combatants, the police cannot be expected to fill the enforcement gap over the long term.

☐   Initial military support for local police is warranted even if international civilian support for local police forces arrives later. During the danger period, the presence of international civilian police monitors and trainers is not an adequate deterrent against violence. Likewise, there is almost always a delay in the arrival of international civilian police monitors and adequate logistic support. The supplemental military support at the beginning is often essential for the long-term success of a program to assist police in assuming a major role in public security.

☐   International civilian support for local police, judiciary, and prisons is essential in most cases if long-term indigenous stability and security are to be established. Assistance for police alone, while courts, legal codes, and prisons are neglected, is not a viable long-term approach.   Arbitrary or politicized sentencing and degrading or brutal prison conditions quickly corrode and undermine whatever benefits come from better policing. Planning for such support needs to be an integral part of the peacekeeping plan and included in the military plan when there is no integrated military-civilian plan. Planning should include adequate human and material resources that are available as early as possible after the intervention; it should provide for civilian support for the long haul, even after the end of military peacekeeping; and it must include replacement of any military support as soon as conditions permit. In Somalia, the initial success in rehabilitating local police was undermined by the failure to include police support in U.S. or U.N. planning, the inadequate priority by the United Nations for the police plan later developed, the lack of judicial and penal assistance (except for the Australian contingent's brief stay in the Bay Region), and only belated U.S. material support for the police program.

□ Each international intervention is different. In Somalia, unlike most countries, the police had not been involved in political repression—that role was played by an entirely separate force, the army. It had taken sides neither during the civil war to oust President Siad Barre nor in the conflict over power once he left Somalia. Although the Somali police needed protection from heavily armed politico-military "factions" and criminal gangs that had come to dominate the country during the pre-intervention period, the police were welcomed by the populace. The absence of any indigenous institutions or accepted political framework into which the police could fit was another unusual element of the Somalia situation. It created major difficulties for the authority, activities and development of the police, even with external support. The police were thus organized temporarily and regionally rather than as a permanent, national agency. The absence of any national institutions, as well as the absence of a plan for international civilian police support, also resulted in regional police being formed and supported by whatever national military contingent had responsibility for that region. This produced widespread variations in the capability and behavior of the regional police forces. In Mogadishu and some outlying areas (such as the

French and particularly the Australian sectors), the police performed reasonably well during the UNITAF period. In other areas, they performed poorly, even being controlled by local warlords. Nowhere but in the Bay Region was there any serious support for judiciary or penal rehabilitation. During the UNOSOM II period, police performed well in the Indian sector but the functioning system established in Mogadishu collapsed under pressure of renewed factional fighting and political confrontation.

□ Consistency and continuity are key aspects of a successful police program. Part way through the intervention in Somalia, security broke down and the civil war returned. At the same time, a shift in U.N. and U.S. policies essentially deprived the local police of international military protection. These developments seriously damaged the successful work that had been achieved in rehabilitating the police and stabilizing public security.

HAITI:
Military-Police Partnership for Public Security

*MICHAEL BAILEY, ROBERT MAGUIRE,
and J. O'NEIL G. POULIOT*

Background

Capacity for Self-Governance

In December 1990, Jean Bertrand Aristide, a Catholic priest and political populist, was elected President of Haiti, winning some two-thirds of a massive voter turnout. Aristide's internationally monitored election came 4 years after the 1986 demise of the 29-year Duvalier family dictatorship and a subsequent series of military-dominated governments. Aristide's election seemed to offer Haiti a chance to join other nations of the region in developing modern, democratic institutions and achieve a more equitable distribution of wealth in the Western Hemisphere's poorest nation.

Eight months following Aristide's February 7, 1991, inauguration—the first of a democratically elected president in Haiti's turbulent history—the enormously popular President was overthrown by a violent military coup d'etat and forced to flee to the United States. The late September 1991 coup set in motion a chain of events that would eventually lead to a U.N.-sanctioned and U.S.-led military intervention in Haiti almost 3 years later.

Aristide's free and fair election and his brief, pre-coup tenure ran against the grain of Haiti's political tradition. For most of its history it had been ruled by autocrats. Since winning its freedom from the French in 1804, Haiti had 21 constitutions and 41 heads of state, 29 of whom were assassinated or overthrown. Haiti's history of autocracy and political instability had begotten a society highly polarized on the basis of race, class, and geography, with a small group of French-speaking, urban-based elites completely dominating the country's social, economic and political institutions, reducing both the Creole-speaking urban poor and the demographically dominant Creole-speaking peasantry to positions of second-class citizenship.

Over time, Haiti's increasingly impoverished masses eked out survival on smaller and smaller farm plots or as members of an expanding urban underclass. As the country's population grew, and Haiti's leaders failed to invest in its human resources or to provide new opportunities for sustained economic growth, tremendous pressure was placed on the country's limited natural resources, leading to severe environmental degradation. With their resource base shrinking, Haiti's poor became desperate for change, as evidenced by significant increases in internal and external migration commencing in the 1970s. As much as the 1986 demise of the Duvaliers provided hope for many, it posed a grave threat to those who benefitted from this repressive and corrupt system.

As Haiti entered the 1990s, shared political power and the rule of law had not emerged. Power remained in the hands of Haiti's tiny elite, with the Haitian Armed Forces (FAd'H) serving as the country's enforcer and political arbiter, dominating the series of governments that succeeded Jean-Claude Duvalier. As such, institutions of the state continued to oppress the people rather than serve them, and the entire public security apparatus (police, courts, and prisons) functioned to control the population and preserve the status of the elites in exchange for the spoils of governance.

With the coup, Haiti reverted to its long tradition of authoritarian rule and political corruption, with no truly functioning judicial system and no tradition of public service or integrity on the part of those in government service at any level. Further, international intervention came only after the perennially weak economy had virtually disintegrated under the pressures of governmental corruption and an international economic embargo was imposed to dislodge the coup leaders.

216

Status of the Public Security Apparatus

Haiti's police remained integrated within its Army even though the 1987 Constitution passed overwhelmingly by a popular referendum mandated their separation, with the police to be placed under civilian authority within the Ministry of Justice. Intimidation of the population by the uniformed military and allied paramilitary thugs who functioned with complete impunity was the norm, with no official or legal recourse available to average Haitians, who had no illusions that the state's security apparatus would serve or protect them.

In this void, citizens had little choice but to acquiesce to fear and intimidation, or to take matters into their own hands. Particularly following the demise of the Duvaliers, the acquiescence of the past gave way to heightened confrontation between state authorities and citizens seeking change. As a result, incidents of "popular justice" increased, with groups of frustrated, angry, usually poor Haitians replicating the system that repressed them by reacting in a harsh and violent manner toward those believed or alleged to have abused power or committed other crimes. In the absence of a police or a judiciary that applied mandated legal practices, frenzied crowds sometimes beat, stoned or even necklaced with a burning tire suspected or confirmed criminals. Political scores were settled similarly, with impunity for all the norm.

The Situation Precipitating the Intervention

During President Aristide's brief, precoup tenure, Haiti's profile of violence and impunity was challenged by initiatives to apply constitutional law, separate the police from the Army, and reform the security apparatus. With the coup, however, those nascent reforms were immediately swept aside and old practices restored. As the reformers fled the country or went into hiding, more than 1,000 Aristide supporters, primarily in the slums of Port-au-Prince, were murdered by Haiti's army.

The immediate response to the coup by the United States was to condemn it, demand the restoration of President Aristide to his legitimate office, and initiate diplomatic efforts—reinforced by economic sanctions—toward achieving that goal. The Organization of American States (OAS) and the United Nations kept apace with the U.S. response as a quick reversal of the coup seemed assured. Unevenly applied sanctions and ineffective diplomatic pressure, however, helped to prolong the crisis that had in the meantime become beset with another element, particularly troublesome for the United States: massive outmigration. As military rule tightened, tens of thousands of poor, frightened Haitians took to the seas on rickety boats to seek a safe haven, primarily in Florida. This element of the crisis quickly involved not only the U.S. Coast Guard but also U.S. Armed Forces based in Guantanamo, as they intercepted, housed, processed, and returned refugees.

By July 1993, unrelenting, albeit uneven, international pressure on the de facto Haitian Government led by Lieutenant General Raoul Cedras, the commander of the Haitian Armed Forces, managed to bring the junta to Governor's Island in New York to negotiate an end to the stalemate. The resultant Governor's Island Accords established steps for the eventual return of President Aristide to Haiti by October 30, 1993, and the almost immediate removal of economic sanctions.

The accords called for the introduction of a small multinational peacekeeping force to assist in the transition to Aristide's return. On October 8, 1993, however, when the USS *Harlan County* attempted to dock in Port-au-Prince to land those lightly armed peacekeepers, a small but rowdy, gun-carrying mob affiliated with the Front for Haitian Advancement and Progress (FRAPH)—a paramilitary organization that had coalesced from disparate elements in 1993 and was closely linked with the de facto government—occupied the dock to protest the landing. Recalling recent events in Somalia where U.S. military peacekeeping personnel were killed by an armed mob, the Clinton administration decided to turn the ship away rather than to face a confrontation for which the small force was not prepared.

The *Harlan County* incident was quickly followed by more FAd'H/FRAPH violence against Haitians and heightened intimidation of foreigners, particularly those attached to the joint U.N./OAS International Civilian Mission (MICIVIH), which deployed to Haiti in early 1993 primarily to monitor human rights violations. On October

13, international sanctions lifted in August were reimposed, effectively acknowledging the death of the Governor's Island Accords. Two days later, the United Nations evacuated all personnel from Haiti, including MICIVIH. Correctly sensing that nothing short of armed force would convince the Haitian military to relinquish control of the government, a decision was then made by U.S. policy makers to begin planning for a possible military intervention to restore President Aristide to office.

By July 1994, as conditions in Haiti worsened, planning for a forced military entry into the country was relatively advanced, with parallel preparations for entry in either a permissive or semi-hostile environment were also underway. On July 31, the U.N. Security Council passed Resolution 940 calling for the application of "all necessary means" to dislodge the de facto government and restore the duly elected Aristide to office. The use of military force was thus legitimized. The resolution envisioned the Multinational Force (MNF), composed primarily of U.S. military forces, under U.S. command, that would unseat the de facto government, followed by a smaller peacekeeping force under U.N. command, after a safe and secure environment had been established by the MNF.

The potential opposing force in Haiti consisted of an ill-equipped, ill-trained army/police of about 7,000 regulars and an unknown number of irregulars referred to in general as attaches and including paramilitary personnel affiliated with FRAPH. On September 19, 1994, following the last-minute success of a diplomatic mission led by former President Carter and deployed to Haiti by President Clinton to achieve a negotiated departure of General Cedras and other key de facto leaders, U.S. forces quickly shifted their mission from a forced entry to a permissive one. Immediately, the first contingent of an eventual 21,000 strong armed force moved into Haiti as part of Operation *Uphold Democracy*.

The Mandate

U.N. Security Council Resolution 940 authorized the use of all necessary means, including military force, to secure the departure of the de facto military regime from Haiti, restore the legitimate government to power, and create a secure and stable environment that would allow both Haiti's democratic political processes to advance and its shattered economy to recover. It established the mandate for the predominantly U.S.-manned MNF to intervene. The resolution also called for a U.N. peacekeeping force (U.N. Mission in Haiti, UNMIH) to replace the MNF once a safe and secure environment had been established. UNMIH was to remain in the country until free and fair presidential elections and a peaceful transfer of power had occurred. In addition, it also provided for civilian International Police Monitors (IPM) to assist the MNF and, subsequently, for U.N. Civilian Police (CIVPOL) to replace the IPMs during the UNMIH phase.

The operational guidelines for the IPM and CIVPOL (similar to military ROE) were the vital ingredient in UNMIH's ability to accomplish the mission successfully. CIVPOL's guidelines were essentially the same as those established by the MNF for the IPMs and were also more robust and proactive than normal CIVPOL guidelines. Under the 1993 Governor's Island Accords, the IPM and CIVPOL were authorized to carry weapons (a first for a U.N. police contingent), to enforce Haitian laws when no local security forces were present, to use the minimum force necessary under carefully prescribed conditions, and to intervene to prevent loss of life or disruption of a "safe and secure" environment. In addition, CIVPOL was charged with monitoring the performance of the Haitian public security forces and serving as mentors for the HNP.

The U.N. mandate authorizing the MNF was translated by the U.S. Atlantic Command (ACOM) into three primary military objectives:

☐ Neutralize armed opposition and create a secure environment for restoration of the legitimate government.
☐ Preserve or restore civil order.
☐ Be prepared to pass responsibility for military operations in Haiti to UNMIH.

Regarding the public security function, U.N. Security Council Resolution (UNSCR) 940 authorized assistance to the Government of Haiti (GOH) in the creation of a separate police force and in establishing an environment conducive to free and fair elections that would be monitored by the United Nations and the OAS. Although the Security Council resolution did not explicitly call for military personnel to provide direct assistance to the IPMs, CIVPOL, Haitian security forces, or judicial and penal systems, by its nature the mandate created unity of effort by ascribing the same mission to all entities participating in the operation. The United States and the United Nations were very cognizant of the need to integrate the three main aspects of the operation: military/security, diplomatic, and humanitarian relief/economic revitalization. In particular, this led to synchronization of actions by military and civilian police elements first of MNF, and then of UNMIH. In general, the U.S. military provided the overall organizational and support framework for the entire military-civilian operation. The initial military emphasis was on stopping violence and restoring stability by use of the MFN (10th Mountain Division followed by 25th Division) with emphasis on developing an indigenous capability to sustain stability in a democratic framework.

Public security was a requisite for success and a principal objective of both the MNF and UNMIH. To fill the public security void while a new Haitian National Police (HNP) force was trained and fielded, the U.S. interagency community, working in collaboration with the United Nations and other concerned nations, developed a comprehensive plan prior to the intervention of the MNF calling for an Interim Public Security Force (IPSF). The IPSF would consist primarily of former Haitian soldiers vetted by the United States and restored Haitian authorities, excluding from participation those with a record of extreme abuse or corruption. Those selected for inclusion in the IPSF would subsequently be subjected to reorientation training. Their performance was to be monitored by the IPMs, followed by CIVPOL. As mandated in Haiti's Constitution, the new HNP would be an separate entity under civilian authority. However, less consideration was given to the need for rapid judicial reform or prison conditions.

IPM Resources

The decision was made in advance of the September 19 landing to create an IPM force to work with Haitians, in conjunction with the MNF. As 821 International Police Monitors from 20 separate countries were deployed to Haiti, a partnership developed among the military police, the IPMs, and the IPSF through extensive combined patrolling. The IPMs were commanded by Ray Kelly, former Commissioner of Police for New York City, who reported to and was supported by the MNF Commander. Kelly had a staff provided by the MNF that coordinated logistics, communications, and operations.

Once Kelly overcame the initial command disorganization, the three greatest limitations on the IPM were that of quality of personnel, experience, and language. As with any multinational group, some national delegations were stronger in police skills than others. During the first UNMIH phase, this constraint was addressed by mixing national CIVPOL contingents to assure a core group of mature, experienced French and Canadians in each contingent to provide leadership and policing skills. During the earlier MNF phase, however, national contingents of IPMs remained intact, to do either a good or bad job, based upon their respective skills.

Complicating the problem posed by differences in experience and methods of policing were delegations originating from countries with diverse systems of civil and common law. Further, delegations tended to have pre-conceived notions on how to police based on their national experience. In an attempt to provide consistent mentoring and monitoring of police activity, the U.S. Justice Department's International Criminal Investigative Assistance Program (ICITAP) provided each IPM with a full set of lesson plans that were to be used in training the IPSF so that they could directly reinforce the training, as it had been given. Later, ICITAP provided the CIVPOL contingent with full sets of HNP basic recruit lesson plans for the same reason. Giving police monitors standard lesson plans that were designed specifically to be consistent with Haitian law allowed the monitors to support the training effort in a consistent manner nationwide.

The third major problem, language, was evident from the very start of U.N. operations. Most IPM and CIVPOL contingents spoke English; few spoke French; several spoke neither English nor French; and Creole-speakers were a rare asset. The majority of both the IPMs and CIVPOL officers, therefore, could not communicate directly with the IPSF, at least not in French, let alone Creole. During the IPM period, national police contingents were deployed intact, despite their uneven capabilities and language limitations. During the CIVPOL period, experienced French and Canadian police were mixed with other contingents in order to deal with language problems and enhance capabilities generally.

This host of limitations linked to international police contingents was not just a sobering reality for the Haiti U.N. mission, but also underscored the fact that most contributing countries did not abide by the basic personnel requirements. As a result, the entire concept of working closely with the IPSF and of training HNP cadets in the field was seriously handicapped. Enormous pressures were exerted on the United Nations to supply more interpreters, but mostly in vain. The relatively few bilingual CIVPOL members were unavailable to conduct the concurrent, language-sensitive tasks that had to be carried out, namely, to be partnered 24-hours a day with CIVPOL members who did not meet French language requirements; to be involved with the recruiting efforts of ICITAP; to be involved in security planning for elections in their respective areas; and to instill the principles of community policing everywhere. Often these individuals found themselves required to provide translation while attending meetings between Government of Haiti officials and MNF commanders and, later, U.N. personnel. Out of an identified minimum requirement of 359 interpreters, the U.N. administration informed CIVPOL on the eve of the UNMIH's April 1995 takeover that only 100 were available.

The Mission

The successful deployment of the MNF and the avoidance of casualties resulted from flexible advanced military planning and skillful exercise of coercive diplomacy. Once the 11th-hour diplomacy of the Carter

Mission, which also included Senator Sam Nunn and former Chairman of the Joint Chiefs of Staff General Colin Powell, secured assurances that Haiti's de facto leaders would step aside, the MNF rapidly shifted from a forced-entry scenario to a plan predicated on more permissive circumstances. Rules of engagement (ROE), already prepared for this option, were quickly verified and disseminated.

The Deployment Gap

According to the Carter Agreement, security was to have been achieved through the joint cooperation of international forces and existing Haitian public security personnel. Initially, efforts were made by ACOM to work with Haiti's existing public security forces, still under the command of General Cedras, and joint patrols were established. Although the MNF plan did not originally call for U.S. soldiers to take on a police role, it quickly became evident that existing Haitian security forces could not perform public security functions according to accepted international norms. Continued incidents of FAd'H/FRAPH violence toward Haitian citizens in the immediate aftermath of the intervention, matched by repeated citizen protests against the maintenance of authority by those who had so recently repressed them, made joint cooperation a particularly difficult mission to accomplish. In this setting, the International Police Monitors could not provide the presence needed to deter violence, particularly since they were slow to deploy and had an uncertain initial command and support structure. Creating a secure and stable environment thus required a degree of both oversight and presence by MNF military forces in addition to the presence of the IPMs.

Within 3 days following the arrival of its forces, the United States made a major change in policy, spurred in part by televised reports of unarmed Haitian citizens being beaten (and killed) by uniformed Haitian personnel while U.S. soldiers looked on because their ROE precluded involvement in such violence. Fearing that a repetition of such incidents would embolden the FAd'H and turn the populace against U.S. forces, a revised ROE interpretation was issued allowing U.S. forces broad police-style powers to detain and, if necessary shoot, people committing serious criminal acts (e.g., homicide, aggravated

224

assault, rape, robbery). This specifically applied to Haitian-on-Haitian violence. Michel Francois, Haiti's then-Chief of Police, was told in no uncertain terms that police violence was to stop. This ultimatum, combined with more aggressive U.S. patrolling, significantly reduced the level of violence against the local population.

While initial efforts were made to work with the existing police element, it was always understood that a new, professional police corps would have to be created in order to have legitimacy with the Haitian people. Two incidents hastened that process—a shoot-out in Haiti's second largest city, Cap Haitien, between the FAd'H and U.S. Marines on September 24, 1994, that left 10 Haitians dead, and an armed attack several days later by FRAPH on peaceful, unarmed protest marchers in Port-au-Prince that left 5 dead. In rapid succession, the FAd'H virtually ceased to exist in northern areas within the vicinity of Cap Haitien, the FRAPH was declared illegal by the legitimate Haitian government, and the MNF closed FRAPH offices around the country. Concurrently, the MNF continued to disarm the FAd'H.

Following another violent incident involving Haitian Army personnel in December 1994, President Aristide moved in January 1995 to disband the FAd'H immediately. Most disappeared into the streets or their homes, without pay but with real grievances. By late May 1995, all that remained of the erstwhile repressive force was a 50-member marching band. After disbanding the FAd'H, Aristide gave grudging permission for the United States to conduct a demobilization program aimed at reintegrating ex-soldiers into Haitian society by providing them 4 months of training in such marketable skills as mechanics, carpentry, electrical repairs, plumbing, and computer operations. As the IPSF was displaced by the newly trained Haitian National Police (HNP) personnel commencing in March 1995, these former FAd'H also became eligible for the reintegration program (except for the small number of former FAd'H who were deemed eligible to enter HNP training or take positions with the Presidential and Palace Security Units). Of an estimated 6,250 demobilized soldiers, 5,482 (88 percent) registered for the retraining program.

While in training the former soldiers received a stipend, but upon graduation they were on their own to compete in Haiti's largely informal job market. Although 4,867 former soldiers graduated from the program, only 304 found jobs through its job referral service. Unable to secure permanent jobs in the formal sector, most have joined the informal economy, competing for scarce jobs with others in Haiti's vast manpower pool, thus undermining the effectiveness of the program and leaving some graduates disillusioned, still more angry, and prone to engage in disruptive activities.

Concurrent with the demise of the FAd'H, MNF authorities moved quickly to stand the Interim Public Security Force in order to fill the glaring deployment gap. U.S. and restored GOH officials collaborated in vetting the records of Haitian military personnel who were identified for possible incorporation into the force with the intention of eliminating known human rights abusers and criminals. Some 3,000 former FAd'H personnel were incorporated into the IPSF. ICITAP provided 6 days of orientation and training prior to redeployment. In addition to the former FAd'H, 950 overwhelmingly pro-Aristide Haitian refugees at Guantanamo who had been given 21 days training by ICITAP were incorporated into the IPSF. This cadre of former FAd'H and returned Guantanamo refugees provided public security until the new civilian HNP could be recruited and trained by ICITAP.

From the day the IPSF was created, it was planned that it would be phased out as the HNP gradually deployed between June 1995 and February 1996. However, IPSF members who passed the rigid acceptance standards for the HNP would be permitted to apply for entry into its training program. Few IPSF met that criteria. The United States had originally planned for a vetted, smaller army as well as a national police force, in good part to keep former soldiers off the streets and out of trouble. However, Aristide's action made this impossible. He also resisted for several months the use of retrained FAd'H for the IPSF, wanting to replace them with Aristide loyalists whose names his lieutenants kept adding to IPSF rolls while the U.S. Embassy and the MNF kept striking them off.

The Royal Canadian Mounted Police (RCMP) also trained 100 Haitians in Canada for inclusion into the IPSF. Manipulation of the selection of the Regina cadre by Aristide supporters, however, and the cadre's subsequent, favorable treatment (e.g., salaries at least triple the standard Haitian police and better weapons than others in the IPSF) were viewed as an attempt to create a group of elite loyalists who could be used to assert control over the nascent HNP. Not all 100 of the Regina cadre chose to deploy to Haiti. Ultimately, President Rene Preval, who was elected in December 1996 to succeed Aristide, cashiered the most politicized individuals because of criminal misconduct and other problems, including the fact that many Regina recruits had actually become American or Canadian citizens.

The MNF Role in Public Security

With Port-au-Prince and Cap Haitien considered "operational centers of gravity" for the MNF mission, urban security operations were especially important for establishing and sustaining the "secure and stable environment" necessary for eventual transition to UNMIH. By October 15, 1994, the 10th Mountain Division had seven infantry battalions stationed around Port-au-Prince and Cap Haitien. The 16th MP Brigade had two military police battalions in the urban areas. They were supplemented by a Caribbean Command battalion and 327 IPMs.

The MNF conducted scores of separate day-and-night mounted and presence patrols in Port-au-Prince and had a Quick Reaction Force (QRF) on standby at all times. The military police conducted an average of 160 joint patrols per day with the IPMs and the IPSF. Frequent and highly visible MNF mobile patrols provided a psychological deterrent against violent outbursts between Haitian civilians and elements of the de facto regime.

Concurrently, a small detachment of MPs with good communications capability was stationed at each police station. Together with IPMs, they provided initial training at the police stations on subjects such as patrolling, desk operations and use of force. The MP approach was "watch what I do." Problems that the MPs had to overcome included the absence in police stations of an office for citizens to file complaints. In addition, most police officers were unfamiliar with the necessary forms to receive complaints.

The MNF and UNMIH also employed Psychological Operations teams. To assuage U.N. sensitivities, the name was changed to Military Information Support Teams (MIST). Deployed throughout Haiti and challenged to work in the relatively obscure language of Haitian Creole, they were crucial in shaping a favorable public reaction to the MNF, as well as in contributing to the pacification of unruly protesters. Because television is limited to the capital city and radio coverage is uneven, wild rumors are often a prime source of information. Initially, MIST was the only vehicle available to the GOH to communicate and provide accurate information to the country's widely dispersed population. MIST also helped the police development effort by providing materials for recruitment and testing process.

In rural areas, where approximately two-thirds of Haiti's 7 million people reside, there were Special Forces (SF) teams stationed in 27 separate locations, with patrols to 866 towns and villages. While disaffected and criminal elements were cowed by their presence, the general populace was converted into enthusiastic supporters through the SF teams' presence and their creative use of community development projects (often in conjunction with the AID Office of Transition Initiatives). In an environment of weak, nascent local government capabilities, SF teams fulfilled a variety of essential tasks, not only facilitating order but performing such varied tasks as public health and socialization into democracy. Included on the SF teams were civil affairs and psychological operations personnel.

By virtue of their joint activities with the IPSF, MNF personnel were operating within the context of Haitian law. When necessary, MNF commanders used the mandate of UNSCR 940 to arrest and detain Haitians unilaterally, but this was minimized especially because the judicial and prison systems were in such bad shape. By putting MPs in police stations and on patrol with the IPSF, the situation in the cities was stabilized. In the countryside, Special Forces and the IPSF conducted similar combined patrolling. This demonstrated to ordinary citizens both that the legitimate Haitian Government was beginning to function again and that earlier abuses and lawlessness would not be tolerated. The morale, discipline, and leadership of the IPSF increased markedly, both on patrol and in the station houses, because of the standards set by the IPMs and U.S. forces. Also contributing to effective policing were the communications and logistics support supplied by the MNF. Detracting from morale and discipline, however, was concern that most IPSF members would soon be laid off, with virtually no hope of joining the HNP.

Arms reduction and arms control also contributed to the pacification process. Although the MNF did not disarm all Haitians through door-to-door searches for weapons, it acted immediately to seize heavy weapons from the Haitian Armed Forces, to confiscate weapons caches as they were discovered, and to keep all weapons (even machetes) off the streets. The MNF quickly seized large weapon stocks at major Haitian military bases. A weapons buy-back program, initiated in late September 1994, garnered 13,432 weapons by May 1995, including mortars, antitank weapons, artillery pieces, and machine guns. Together, the number of weapons purchased and confiscated by the MNF exceeded 30,000. The main effect of the arms reduction and control program was to break the power of FAd'H and its allies and discourage any thoughts of organized resistance. The program also helped both to convince the general populace that they had little to fear and to create a climate more propitious for establishing civil order.

In addition to arms control, the IPM/IPSF, with MNF backup, conducted operations to protect power plants and other vital civil installations. They also played a very important role in ensuring both a limited but regular supply of electricity in Port-au-Prince—a commodity equated by Haitians with improved security. By means of assigning civil affairs personnel to key ministries, the MNF aided the restoration of normal government functioning, replacing the de facto government's patterns of abuse and corruption. This effort was designed to begin to return the country to a sense of "normalcy" and correctly justified as being a plus for force protection.

Institution Building and the Haitian National Police

Prior to the 1994 intervention, ICITAP prepared a Haiti Police Development Program based upon a 5-year commitment with two overlapping phases to help the GOH address its most pressing law enforcement needs. The first phase called for rapid action. It involved separating police functions from those of the FAd'H, defining the role of police in the context of Haitian society and local needs, and instituting a basic training program that provided vetted members of the FAd'H with immediate policing skills so that they could perform as interim police for the maintenance of law and order. Simultaneously, armed International Police Monitors would be trained and deployed, with ICITAP assistance, as a method of deterring violence during the transition period. The police monitors would also serve as an informal training resource for basic policing functions until HNP personnel could be trained and deployed.

The second phase of ICITAP's mission would focus on institution building. This stage, central to the development of a professional civilian police force, included training and assisting in developing police administrative and managerial capabilities and specialized skills, such as investigative policing and forensics.

During the pre-Harlan County period, ICITAP coordinated planned activities with CIVPOL Commander LeMay. Given the rupture of the Governor's Island Accords, the CIVPOL/ICITAP collaboration produced nothing. However, renewed collaboration got into full swing during the summer of 1994, when RCMP Chief Superintendent Pouliot was named UNMIH CIVPOL Commander. Joint planning efforts were developed between ICITAP and RCMP and between ICITAP and CIVPOL. The RCMP assigned three officers to ICITAP Washington Headquarters to assist in the development of the basic recruit curriculum and lesson plans. In addition, an outline of the field training officer manual was developed, based on U.S. and Canadian models, for use by police monitors following the deployment of the HNP after basic recruit training.

After the MNF landed, ICITAP refurbished the FAd'H's former heavy weapon battalion complex at Port-au-Prince into a police academy. It had initial help from MNF logisticians, and engineers (for design and minor construction). The three RCMP members detailed to Washington were among the core of instructors involved in the ICITAP HNP training effort. At one point there were 20 RCMP and 3 French trainers assigned to the basic recruit training effort at the Police Academy in Port-au-Prince. The number of U.S. trainers grew to over 100, most of whom were active duty state and local police from throughout the country.

A major role of CIVPOL during the period of deployment of the new HNP personnel would include acting as field training officers (FTOs) for the fledgling police force. This task would include joint patrols, mentoring, and using standardized reporting forms to evaluate performance and effectiveness of training. Because UNCIVPOL was part of the U.N. advance team in Haiti, planning and coordination with Commissioner Pouliot continued during the entire MNF period. Because of a delay in full deployment of CIVPOL, ICITAP had to deploy some FTOs for Class 1 of the HNP from its instructor cadre. Once CIVPOL was in place, however, it began to fully implement the FTO program using the FTO manual that was jointly drafted by ICITAP and the RCMP.

The new Police Academy was staffed by ICITAP with experienced U.S. Government and civilian contract trainers plus Royal Canadian Mounted Police and French police personnel. It opened its doors January 30, 1995, with an initial class of 375. Cadets were given basic instruction over a 4-month period in a wide variety of skills, including making arrests, handling firearms and protecting civil rights. The salaries of the Haitian National Police were high by local standards, as was the level of education. Almost all recruits were in their late teens or early twenties and were carefully vetted for previous human rights abuses. CIVPOL, in consultation with ICITAP, developed a Field Training Guide for HNP and CIVPOL Trainers. The guide provided specific tasks to be accomplished by the cadet in the field to test in a real life situation how he/she put in practice what was learned at the Academy. The guide included an evaluation by the trainers for each of the field training stages. A further monthly performance evaluation system was designed for the 3,050 IPSF personnel. This would form the basis for future consideration for their integration into the HNP.

To establish an operational 5,000-member police force in time to replace the United Nations when its mandate expired in February 1996, ICITAP increased the training capacity to 3,000 by establishing an auxiliary training center at Fort Leonard Wood, Missouri. The final class of new police cadets graduated in February 1996, putting the total HNP complement at 5,243 officers.

Public Security Transition

To initiate on-the-ground planning for the transition from the MNF to UNMIH and from the IPSF/IPM to HNP/CIVPOL, an UNMIH Advance Team including military and civilian planners and 13 civilian police officers arrived in Haiti on October 4, 1994. By December 19, the team had increased to 40, with members deployed to Port-au-Prince, Cap Haitien, Gonaives, Les Cayes, Jacmel, and Jeremie. The Advance Team studied conditions around the country, with a view toward establishing initial community policing principles with the population and organizing community consultative groups (CCG).

The Advance Team had to determine the requirements for the operation such as vehicles, equipment and fuel. At the same time, CIVPOL contributed significantly toward the establishment of minimum standards for the selection of HNP applicants. They also supplied personnel to assist the MNF and ICITAP in selection of HNP applicants and administration of entry exams and fitness tests. As CIVPOL personnel undertook these duties, they developed operational concepts to execute the mission's mandate: to train and monitor the IPSF and later the HNP; and to assist both in the maintenance of a safe and stable environment and in the conduct of free and fair elections.

On April 1, 1995, following the visit to Haiti of President Clinton, a seamless transition from the MNF to UNMIH was completed. U.N. Secretary-General Special Representative (SRSG) Ambassador Lakhdar Brahimi and his core headquarters personnel, both civilian and military, had been on the ground since October 1994, working with the MNF and undergoing advanced training. By the time of the transition, 95 percent of the military forces for UNMIH were already in place, either as part of the MNF, or as new personnel to replace departing MNF units. With the U.S. 25th Division replacing the 10th Division, Major General Joseph Kinzer became the UNMIH Force Commander with a total force of 6,000 troops, 2,500 of which were U.S. personnel. Brigadier General Tom Hill of the 25th Infantry remained as Commander of the U.S. contingent. U.S. Special Forces were still deployed in the countryside, reinforced by several UNMIH national contingents. Two hundred U.S. MPs remained in Port-au-

Prince, reinforced by a 120-man MP company from India. A Guatemalan MP company was deployed in Cap Haitien. All MPs were under the command of the U.S. 504th MP Battalion.

A crucial factor contributing to the smooth transition and UNMIH's successful mission accomplishment was exceptional cooperation among the key players particularly Ambassador Brahimi and Major General Kinzer. They and other senior officials regularly conferred together and with GOH authorities. Brahimi held twice-weekly meetings with his component heads to ensure synchronization of effort by the multidisciplinary U.N. team. The ROE for UNMIH, operating under a Chapter VI mandate from the UNSC, were robust enough to enable UNMIH to take appropriate actions to protect themselves and carry out the mandate. Though all MNF vehicles were eventually painted white to signify the change from the MNF to UNMIH, U.S. forces remained under U.S. Command and maintained their own uniforms and a high profile presence. These last factors contributed to Haitian perception that reality had not changed as a result of the transition. Indeed, UNMIH continued active patrolling in Port-au-Prince and Cap Haitien.

As part of UNMIH, the United Nations deployed 870 Civilian Police monitors under the command of RCMP Chief Superintendent Neil Pouliot, who, on the mission's organizational chart, was coequal with Kinzer. Both men reported directly to the SRSG. CIVPOL headquarters, its operations center, and its logistics support units were co-located with UNMIH military forces. This, along with a shared communications system, complemented deployment of forces, joint patrolling and integrated planning, to maximize collaboration between the two. This collaboration created the conditions that actually reduced the requirements for military presence.

The fact that both CIVPOL and the IPM were armed and had rapid military backup meant that they were more confident and less threatened in potentially dangerous environments where small-scale theft and violence were common. They were not subjected to having vehicles stolen or to being abused as had been the case with CIVPOL in Cambodia and elsewhere. They were also able to carry out arrests as well as encourage a more pro-active effort by the HNP than would have been the case had CIVPOL not had a more robust mandate and permission to carry arms.

Until the HNP was fully staffed with trained personnel and at least nominally capable of operating without direct military support, UNMIH MPs remained in Port-au-Prince police stations providing liaison and technical assistance. Initial CIVPOL reservations about the continued presence of MPs were overcome because their communications capability meant that UNMIH was able to monitor the evolving security situation accurately and respond more effectively when called upon by CIVPOL or the HNP.

UNMIH military patrols continued throughout the country as a deterrent against criminal activities or political violence. The main responsibility for security in the countryside remained with SF units, whose activity continued as before, although aided by UNMIH military units who were deployed to more rural locations than had been the case with MNF. The QRF, based in Port-au-Prince, remained ready to respond to any incident which posed a threat.

As the Haitian National Police gradually assumed responsibility for public security, the role of international military personnel diminished accordingly. U.N. Civilian Police monitors provided on-the-job training and mentoring for the HNP. Additionally, patrolling U.N. military forces monitored the conduct of the HNP, providing feedback to CIVPOL as necessary.

The Haitian National Police

Following his inauguration to succeed Jean-Bertrand Aristide as elected President of Haiti in February 1996, Rene Preval nominated Pierre Denize as Director General of the HNP. Noted for his record of honesty and dynamic action in the drug rehabilitation field, Denize's nomination was quickly approved by the Haitian Parliament. Subsequently, recruitment began to fill supervisory positions, and ICITAP received authority to fund training programs for supervisors and to provide funds for communications and transportation. Only 35 of 257 HNP supervisors were in place when Preval took office, because of the limited pool of talent from which to draw and Aristide's reluctance with a few notable exceptions to rely upon former members of the FAd'H.

In spite of progress made under Denize, the HNP continued to manifest shortcomings that flow from inexperience, insufficient training, and inadequate supervision. This included occasional episodes of excessive use of force, cases of poor discipline, and even abuse of human rights. Even though the Director General of the HNP moved responsibly to address these inherent problems, this did not completely quell Haitian and international concern. A July 1996 report issued by the U.N./OAS International Civilian Mission (MICIVIH), for example, stressed the role of the Inspector General (IG), set up to monitor police infractions but not fully functional when Denize took over.

Although a USIA-sponsored poll in November 1996 indicated three-quarters of the population had a good opinion of the HNP, international scrutiny and concern over HNP shortcomings continued to mount. In late 1996, the Clinton administration and Congress agreed to suspend $5 million in U.S.-funding for specialized training by ICITAP and for communications and transportation support. This was precipitated by the aforementioned shortcomings and also the assignment of a number of former FAd'H personnel to the HNP and the Palace and Presidential Security Units. By January 1997, as the Office of the IG became more robust and other actions were taken to assuage congressional concerns, half the withheld funding was released. Subsequently, the remainder was made available to ICITAP for its programs as former FAd'H members were removed and the IG continued to demonstrate improvement. By May 1997, more than 100 members of the HNP accused of abusing their positions had been dismissed at the behest of the IG, a fact unprecedented in the history of Haitian policing.

Parallel to these developments, other key institutional enhancements were made. In mid-1996, ICITAP organized four examinations in collaboration with the United Nations that yielded 54 commissaire (supervisory) recruits from the FAd'H, Haiti's university milieu, and HNP commissaires already in place. These candidates received a 3-week orientation to the HNP and its management systems, as well as basic leadership skills. In 1997, a fifth round of recruitment assembled 23 additional *commissaires* who were promoted from HNP inspector ranks after completion of a 5-week training program. In addition, the Government of Canada, in coordination with other members of the international community, started a bilateral enforcement assistance program in August 1996 to develop midlevel supervisors.

ICITAP also conducted specialized training on a continuing basis for classes of 200 to 300 officers at the Haitian National Police Training Center (HNPTC) in instructor development, criminal investigation, narcotics enforcement, crowd control, SWAT, coast guard operations, dignitary protection, border patrol, and airport security. In addition, ICITAP began to provide in-service training in firearms, use of force limits, judgment, and respect for human rights.

To help the HNP define its own institutional needs, ICITAP worked with the Ministry of Justice's Secretary of State for Public Security, the HNP Director General, the Chief Inspector General, and their respective staffs. Fashioned out of this collaboration was an HNP Development Plan to the year 2000. The plan constituted perhaps the most significant tangible innovation in Haiti's law enforcement development process. The GOH and the international community have relied on the plan as the blueprint for all collective efforts. A *Support Group for HNP Development Plan Implementation* was created to consolidate efforts and accelerate HNP organization and development. The group meets regularly to verify compliance with stated objectives as well as to articulate needed resources for implementation and to identify potential donors.

The Judiciary and Prisons

To have lasting impact, improvements in law enforcement need to be accompanied by similar developments in the courts and prisons. This was particularly the case in Haiti, where the judicial system had been corrupt, largely dysfunctional, and devoid of legitimacy. Rebuilding the judicial system has proven a formidable task, with progress lagging far behind the police. As performance and efficiency of the police have improved, matching improvements in the judicial system, from the courts and prosecutors to the prisons, became even more urgent.

Further complicating the situation is the fact that Haitian law mandates officials of the judicial system, not the police, to conduct criminal investigations.

Following international intervention, the judicial system could not adequately process individuals arrested by the IPSF and the HNP. Prisons were constantly overcrowded, and riots were numerous. To rectify this, the international community began to provide resources to start training the judges. Nevertheless, the dysfunctional state of the judicial system became a major source of frustration for HNP efforts to stop criminal activity as arrests were not met with adequate handling of suspects and other required judicial actions.

Almost 3 years after the intervention, Haiti's judicial system remained virtually unchanged, unable to respond effectively either to the population's desire for legal reform and uniform application of the law or to the HNP's reformed role in law enforcement. CIVPOL officers reported HNP comments that they would rather get into a gunfight and kill a "bad guy" than turn him over to the judicial system because that was tantamount to release. Failure of judicial reform undermines police reform, therefore, and breeds attitudes that could lead to replication of traditional abuses carried out by Haitians.

International actors were aware of this imperative. In pre-intervention planning by the United States, the Agency for International Development (AID) was given responsibility for training and reform of the Haitian judicial system, paralleling the ICITAP role with the police. AID prepared a project proposal and eventually awarded a contract to an international firm. Congressionally mandated AID procedures, however, were so cumbersome that it took over 6 months before activity actually began. Recognizing the dangers this delay posed, the U.S. military took interim action to jump start judicial reform.

In February 1995, the U.S. Atlantic Command, and the U.S. Army Civil Affairs and Psychological Operations Command under Major General Donald Campbell, instituted a Judicial Mentors Program in February 1995. Campbell and his team provided copies of Haitian laws to judges and undertook an inventory of all courts and prisons, cataloguing the qualifications and capabilities of magistrates as well as needed commodities. In May 1995, the AID Administration of Justice

Project (AOJ) was expanded to a 4-year, $18 million effort involving the U.S. Department of Justice (DOJ) and other agencies as well as the AID contractor. The program began with the renovation of the former Military Academy in Port-au-Prince as the site for the National Magistrates School.

The DOJ, the Haitian Ministry of Justice, and the Haitian State University's law school faculty developed a judicial training curriculum for a series of 2-week training courses for justices of the peace, prosecutors, investigating judges, and trial judges. From July 3, 1995, through October 11, 1996, an emergency training program was conducted for 439 incumbent judicial personnel by the DOJ and the Haitian National Center for State Courts. The Magistrates' School became a resource center to provide technical assistance for judicial officers, and an Office of Judicial Supervision was established within the Ministry of Justice to monitor the performance of judges and prosecutors throughout the country.

Further reforms were enacted when the DOJ assigned two attorneys to work with the AOJ program with a particular focus on Haitian prosecutor's offices (or "parquets") that handle cases usually referred by local justices of the peace or by magistrates. These DOJ attorneys worked to improve investigative capability, judicial competence and case management in six of Haiti's fourteen parquets. In October 1996, at the request of the National Security Council, the DOJ developed a more robust effort to be executed and managed by its Office of Professional Development and Training (OPDAT) in a manner similar to the ICITAP effort with the HNP.

When AID funding ($1.9 million) for the 6-month program was approved, OPDAT instituted a Phase I project to expand the model parquet program to Port-au-Prince, and to add seven new attorneys (five Haitians, two Americans) to support the effort nationwide. The Haitian attorneys were assigned as full-time mentors in the parquets while the U.S. attorneys advised the Port-au-Prince parquet and worked on judicial curriculum development and training at the École de la Magistrature, and on legislative reform, including judicial standards. To coordinate the programs for the police and prosecutors/investigating magistrates, DOJ programs are managed from Washington, and the field managers for the police and AOJ projects are co-located in Port-au-Prince.

Achievements through January 1997 include the completion of an inventory of all pending cases in the seven jurisdictions, the validation of prison registers and matching case files, and selection of a sample of cases from each parquet for detailed analysis to determine remedial case management procedures. They also include completed seminars for prosecutors and magistrates on managing complex investigations, joint investigative training with HNP Judicial Police investigators, and draft legislation to establish judicial selection and retention criteria. Delays in the elections of the territorial assemblies that are mandated to nominate local judicial officials and the resultant absence of fresh faces in local judicial offices are among the key factors that have slowed the pace of judicial reform.

In January 1997, the DOJ presented AID with a Phase II proposal to expand the model parquet program to all remaining jurisdictions, to conduct full judicial training for all new personnel whose appointments are anticipated following territorial elections, and to provide in-service training for all current judicial personnel who are retained. As an interim step, U.S. Army Civil Affairs Military Assistance Teams (MATs) assisted in expanding the standardized case tracking system to all remaining parquets.

Despite this progress in training and reorganization, the judicial system in many ways has continued to operate as in the past, still a prisoner of ignorance, corruption, intimidation, and impunity. It has failed to perform up to the expectations of the public and this has had especially negative consequences with regard to the HNP. With the HNP Office of the Inspector General now functioning more robustly, the Director General has approved the jailing or dismissal of over 100 HNP members for a variety of offenses. Unfortunately, jailed HNP officers have not been prosecuted, and the HNP can take no action stronger than dismissal. The failure of the judicial system to proceed with prosecution of HNP personnel gives the impression that Haiti's new police can also act with impunity.

Another problem confronting judicial reform efforts is the rise of crime and corresponding vigilante acts by citizens who have no faith that the system will deliver justice. Particularly in urban milieux, armed car jackings, robbery, and burglary, perpetrated by individuals and gangs with weaponry that can match or exceed that of the police, have become commonplace. Shootouts with criminals have resulted in the deaths of at least 20 members of the force. Sensing a return of insecurity, citizen groups have begun to take matters into their own hands. In several extreme cases, vigilante groups have attempted to remove suspects from HNP custody forcibly, and suspected criminals have been killed when the HNP was loath to fire upon frenzied crowds to rescue alleged criminals. Until the public gains confidence in a reformed and functioning justice system, problems such as these will persist.

The National Penitentiary, the Cap Haitien prison, and other prisons throughout the country were in a state of almost complete disrepair when the de facto regime was dismantled and were incapable of meeting even minimal international health or human rights norms. Early in the MNF mission, these conditions gained international attention through the case of Captain Lawrence Rockwood, a U.S. military officer who disobeyed orders and attempted to visit the National Penitentiary late at night to conduct an investigation of conditions there. All jails and prisons in urban areas had already been inspected by MPs within 1 week of the landing. Reports on the horrible conditions were filed, but the air and sea lift then underway did not include resources for the penal systems. Although Rockwood was later court-martialed, the United States and the United Nations responded to the heavy publicity by taking emergency measures, including hands-on involvement to provide basic repairs to the National Penitentiary and other prisons. In February 1995, prison riots and Haitian inability to cope with them caused the MFN to assume control of prisons, begin training guards, etc. U.S. Army engineers and Special Forces were used for urgently needed repairs. A special prison was established for women and juveniles in Port-au-Prince to separate them from adult male prisoners, and weekly coordinating meetings on prison conditions were established by MFN, AID, MICIVIH, and interested nongovernmental organizations (NGOs).

CIVPOL created a partnership with a Haitian NGO, the Bureau of Nutrition and Development, to supply food for the prisoners in Haiti's 28 jails scattered nationwide. Outside Port-au-Prince, food was delivered by CIVPOL. Although not part of its mandate, CIVPOL took charge of administering 27 of the 28 jails.

Haiti's penal system, though improved over conditions in 1994, continues to pose obstacles to public security reform programs. More than 75 percent of inmates are in pretrial detention. The average time served by these detainees is 1 year. Most have never seen a magistrate in spite of requirements to do so within 48 hours of detention. This intolerable reality underscores the slow progress of judicial reform and its detrimental impact throughout Haitian society.

Effective action to establish judicial recruitment, retention and training standards (as recommended in the OPDAT legislative proposal) and establishment of an appropriate pay scale for judicial personnel, would improve the system. The United States, Canada, France, and other members of the European Union continue to participate actively in judicial assistance programs. The election of regional bodies mandated to name new judicial officials, coupled with vetting of existing judicial personnel and selection of qualified personnel to fill judicial vacancies and with internationally sponsored judicial training, could result in significant improvements over time.

Public Security and Elections

Between President Aristide's return to office on October 15, 1994, and the end of his term in February 1996, the Haitian electoral calendar called for the election of 399 municipal council members and 1,692 other local officials, 18 members of Haiti's 24-member Senate, all 83 members of the Chamber of Deputies and, finally, Aristide's successor. In all, Haiti conducted five nationwide elections (including runoffs) in a 6-month period. The successful completion of this electoral cycle was central to U.S. "exit strategy." Despite numerous concerns that the campaigning or balloting would be marred by violence, the electoral process unfolded without serious incidents thanks to the orderly environment established by UNMIH and its planning and logistical support role, along with that played by a multitude of governments and electoral observers, including MICIVIH.

In the midst of this hectic electoral calendar, other tasks confronted UNMIH, CIVPOL, and the nascent HNP. In the summer of 1995 Haiti was to host the annual General Assembly meeting of the Organization of American States (OAS). CIVPOL developed and implemented a security plan for the meeting, which would bring numerous heads of state, other diplomats and dignitaries to Haiti. CIVPOL coordinated the security components of the HNP, UNMIH, and other personnel seconded to CIVPOL for the occasion. Around the same period, CIVPOL also provided firearm training to Presidential and Palace Security Guards that had been organized by the MNF and conducted a security needs analysis and security screening for the Truth Commission that had been established by the GOH to look into human rights abuses perpetrated under the de facto regime.

It was the task of organizing elections, however, that posed the greatest logistical, political, organizational, and security challenges. A variety of governments and international organizations collaborated to confront them. UNMIH military forces, including U.S. MPs and Special Forces, were crucial to this process, providing logistical and security planning assistance to distribute and collect ballots and assisting in maintaining security during the voting process. The United Nations provided technical assistance to the Provisional Electoral Council (CEP), funded largely by the United States. The Government of Canada contributed several million dollars worth of ballot boxes and equipment. Most international electoral observers came under the sponsorship of the MICIVIH. A variety of NGOs funded by AID assisted with ballot procedures, training poll workers, public education, voter mobilization, and electoral observation. UNMIH, CIVPOL, IPSF, and HNP all played a role in providing a secure and stable environment.

The first round of elections, though free and fair, was flawed by major operational deficiencies on the part of the CEP. By the time of the December 17, 1995, presidential election, however, these irregularities had been almost totally resolved, owing to extensive international technical assistance and plenty of practice. As a result, the consensus view of the 400 international observers was that the December 1995 Presidential election was free and fair. Equally important, it was unblemished by the bloodshed and intimidation that had traditionally accompanied elections in Haiti.

Following the 1995 Presidential Elections and the impending end of the UNMIH mandate, CIVPOL began a transition from an operational to a training mode, and proceeded to downsize from 900 to 300 members. Remaining CIVPOL personnel were all French-speaking officers dedicated to training the HNP in the field. While previously developed Principles of Community Policing were being taught by CIVPOL officers, consultations with local community consultative groups became more exclusively the domain of the HNP.

UNMIH to UNSMIH: Extensions and Transition

With the impending end of the U.N. mission set for March 1996, including departure of all U.S. military personnel, the fledgling HNP was far from ready to assume sole responsibility for Haiti's public security. HNP personnel simply did not have the on-the-job experience needed to develop a leadership capability. Additionally, the force did not have the necessary cadre of trained supervisors; nor had it fully trained and deployed such specialized units as riot control, SWAT, or counterdrug operations.

Given this situation, the Haitian Government, supported in the United Nations by the "Friends of Haiti," requested a 6-month extension for UNMIH. The UNSC approved only a 4-month extension, however, until August 1, 1996, for a force of 1,200 military personnel and 300 Canadian, French, and West African CIVPOL (160 French and 100 Canadians) in what was officially labeled the U.N. Support Mission in Haiti (UNSMIH). The Canadian Government agreed to provide, at its own expense, an additional 700 troops, while the United States extended its presence in UNMIH until April 1996, when the Canadians would be in place and thus able to take command. At the start of UNSMIH, France assumed command of CIVPOL and introduced a different approach based upon French national police and gendarmerie traditions, with less presence and training in the police stations and less participation in joint patrols.

243

The transition to UNSMIH and the resulting change in leadership of CIVPOL resulted in changes in both CIVPOL philosophy and capabilities. The French command took a different view toward mentoring, viewing its role as advisors at the executive level and limiting its work with basic recruits to stationhouse lectures and readings from manuals. French gendarmerie were specialists in tactical control, not general "beat cops," in contrast to the French Police Nationale assigned to the UNMIH I planning cell who had been very useful in earlier development of concepts for basic police mission and deployment.

Many RCMP officers, particularly those in outlying districts, continued to perform familiar mentoring activities. This mentoring/leadership role was later re-enforced with the arrival of U.S. CIVPOL. Despite these individual initiatives, the official FTO program ceased to exist with the transition to UNSMIH. The impact of this change, coupled with a lack of HNP experience and supervisory personnel, would contribute to later cases of police misconduct and poor decision making during critical incidents. Moreover, it was not until January 1997, with 122 of the 150 police *commissaires* selected, trained and deployed, that the elements for leadership at the district level were in place.

A significant problem that emerged during the period following the international intervention—that of the multiplicity of "official" (as opposed to private) Haitian security forces—remained into 1997. Most prominent among these have been the Palace and Presidential Security Units (PSUs). Although formally placed under the HNP by executive order, these units continued to operate autonomously. It was not until ICITAP made it a condition for continued training in October 1996 that the responsibilities of the PSUs and their relationship to the HNP were defined by General Directive. And even then, HNP control over the units was nominal and de jure, with real control resting in the hands of former elements of the FAd'H and of Aristide-era appointments. Not until the PSUs were purged, with U.S. assistance, following the October directive was the Preval-Denize chain of command clearly established. Another discrete group consists of 950 former Guantanamo refugees who had been recruited for the IPSF. Primarily pro-Aristide, they now work in such posts as ministerial guards and have not been through HNP basic recruit training. They cannot receive full HNP status without being subjected to vigorous human rights vetting, testing and intensive training. In general, the Preval Government has continued to struggle in defining its relationship with the HNP vis-a-vis recruitment of new personnel and reporting relationships.

As the August 1996 UNSMIH-extended mandate drew down, increasing socioeconomic strains, an unresponsive economy, unresolved political problems, and the need for more time to provide the HNP on-the-job training, to weed out undisciplined members, and to put trained supervisors in place meant that an international presence would still be required. Indeed, conventional wisdom among those working to improve Haiti's public security institutions suggested that police mentors would be essential for several more years. Accordingly, in late June 1996 the U.N. Security Council again extended the UNSMIH mission, this time to November 30, 1996.

For its third extension, UNSMIH consisted of 600 troops and 300 CIVPOL monitors. An additional 700 troops participated in the mission, funded directly by member states (the United States and Canada). The two main military contingents came from Pakistan and Canada, with a Canadian general in command of all forces except those from the United States The United States maintained a highly visible Support Group, with rotating units from the United States, consisting of up to 500 personnel at any one time. Oriented as a training mission, the rotational units of the support group carry out engineering/public works and public health projects, and provide additional presence. Nevertheless, perceptions of a less robust international CIVPOL and military presence during UNSMIH raised the potential for both criminal and political violence.

By the end of the third extension of the UNSMIH mandate, the politico-socioeconomic environment was still not conducive to shifting complete responsibility for public security to the HNP. The failure of the economy—shattered by the corruption and mismanagement of the Cedras era plus tough international economic sanctions—to respond to the population's high expectations and desperate needs translated to a growing level of discontent accompanied by continued high unemployment and a resultant susceptibility to cynicism and violence. Powerful criminal groups, some allegedly linked to contraband and drug trafficking, vied with "unofficial" political groups for control in the streets. Ordinary citizens lamented the return of insecurity for the first time since the intervention.

In Parliament, divisions emerged between hard-core supporters of former President Aristide and those favoring Preval's policies of economic modernization. As a result, economic reform legislation became delayed or blocked, holding back release of much needed financing from international financial institutions. The political struggle weakened the Preval government, prolonged Haiti's economic stagnation, led to increasing agitation by the unemployed (including former FAd'H) and created disillusionment with the idea of democracy. These factors all contributed to continued popular unrest and a growth in criminal activity.

Accordingly, as November 30, 1996, drew near, the Government of Haiti, joined again by the U.N. "Friends of Haiti," requested an 8- to 12-month extension of UNSMIH, including CIVPOL. The primary purpose was to provide the HNP more time to function under U.N. tutelage. Granted an 8-month extension until July 31, 1997, this iteration of UNSMIH included 45 Haitian-American CIVPOL members drawn from major metropolitan police force's throughout the United States. Working in the FTO mold, they blended cultural and professional skills to help members of the HNP refine their abilities as street cops.

More recent political developments highlighted continuing uncertainty. In March 1997, Prime Minister Rosny Smarth was called before the Chamber of Deputies to answer questions on the issue of privatization, to which he and the President were committed but which Aristide opposes. This was followed by a vote of approval led by his party, the Lavalas Political Organization (OPL). (There is also a pro-Aristide party, Lafanmi Lavalas, created in early 1997.) The Government, however, failed to build on this victory.

Although elections in April for one-third of the Senate, two seats in the Chamber of Deputies, and thousands of members of local assemblies were held without incident, less than 10 percent of the electorate voted. Afterward, the Electoral Observer Mission of the Organization of American States (OAS-EOM) cited irregularities and "attempts to manipulate the results" in some jurisdictions (a reference to pro-Aristide elements). This caused some of the parties to withdraw from the process just prior to the second round. Attempts by the international community to resolve the situation have thus far failed. The second round was postponed, and some in Haiti began to blame the international community for the country's continuing difficulties. Some popular organizations that strongly support Aristide publicly opposed what they term a "foreign occupation," even calling for an armed struggle to "liberate" the country.

In June, Prime Minister Smarth resigned saying he had been hamstrung by tensions within the ruling coalition and lamenting certain developments surrounding recent elections. Smarth noted continued criticism by "some sectors" which had not accepted the Parliament's decision and wanted to force the Government to "resign under pressure of the street" (another reference to pro-Aristide elements). By December, no prime minister had been named, the deadlock on privatization still blocked economic recovery, and the socioeconomic-criminal situation was worse.

Parallel to these developments, growing concern has emerged among U.N., U.S., and GOH officials regarding new and more sophisticated forms of organized crime. Smuggling has burgeoned, particularly of drugs and vehicles. If the fledgling HNP becomes more effective in combating this traffic, violent confrontations with criminal organizations could increase.

As July 31, 1997, drew near and Haiti's political and economic conditions had not improved, UNSMIH's mandate was extended for a final time to November 30, 1997 and was renamed the U.N. Transition Mission in Haiti (UNTMIH). The HNP is assessed as having made real progress, it remains at a modest level of development. On the other hand, law enforcement is still very badly handicapped by the embryonic level of development of the judicial system. The UNTMIH mandate was not renewed after November 30, 1997, but ICITAP and 150 CIVPOLs will continue their programs with the support of 150 armed Argentine gendarmes to protect U.N. personnel. The separate bilateral U.S. military support unit will remain.[1] (See chart for a representation of the public security timeline in Haiti.)

Conclusions

Seven broad lessons are suggested:

☐ Each peacekeeping mission is unique. International actors must carefully analyze the context, identify required resources, and apply appropriate lessons learned from other settings. In the case of Haiti, the political problems and security situation were unlike Cambodia, Somalia, and Bosnia. Haiti was not a country being torn apart by warlords. It was a dysfunctional state where most citizens, including an unarmed poor peasantry and urban underclass, had been grievously exploited by their own government and its allied security forces.

☐ It is difficult to escape the gravitational pull of past political culture and economy to rebuild a country in accordance with new norms. Often those norms are perceived as alien, especially by those with vested interests in the old system. Where conditions offer relative prosperity or at least economic promise, it is much easier to reduce significantly the generalized unrest that threatens public security. Unfortunately, Haiti had neither relative prosperity nor economic promise. The military and civilian public security effort was initially accompanied by large-scale humanitarian relief including food distribution and temporary job creation. However, after the first year, this program was cut back substantially while the economy failed to move ahead to create new jobs.

☐ Unity of effort by international peace forces, including police, is important. U.N. Security Council Resolution 940 was the one strategic document that provided a framework for every aspect of the international operation linked to security objectives—political,

---

[1]For a more recent report on the status of the HNP, see *Can Haiti's Police Reform be Sustained?* (Washington, DC: Washington Office on Latin America and the National Coalition for Haitian Rights, January 1998).

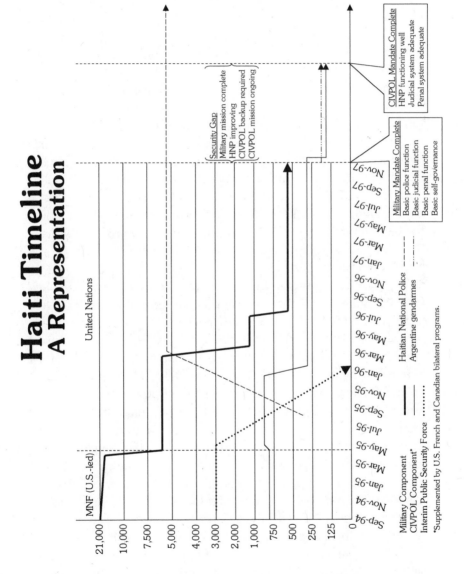

Haiti Timeline
A Representation

military, civilian police, and diplomatic. With one common goal, a single overall commander on the ground (for both the MNF and UNMIH) and the civilian police and military components equally charged with creating a secure and stable environment, mutually supporting plans could be developed. Strategic and operational headquarters were co-located, and the communications systems were shared and interoperable.

A corollary to this lesson is that U.N. civilian police should be given the resources and mandate to conduct limited law and order functions under some circumstances. The approach in Haiti was a break from past U.N. operations. Monitors were armed, carefully deployed, and authorized to conduct limited law enforcement operations (they could arrest people). Having both a "real" police mandate and the required resources, U.N. civilian police were empowered to compel compliance with the mandate. This enabled the UNMIH military force to concentrate more on military tasks.

□ The military can and should be mandated under some circumstances to participate in the execution of public security tasks, especially during the initial period of operations while CIVPOL are getting organized and the security situation is usually more threatening. In Haiti, the Special Forces and the military police made significant contributions. These unique forces were employed in a manner that filled a security vacuum and thus enhanced the limited numbers and capability of the International Police Monitors. These forces are capable of providing critical links among the population, local police force, international police monitors and the U.N. military force in the conduct of day-to-day security/stability operations. Additionally, as the supplementary force, these units can be utilized in situations that the police are not able to control and prevent these situations from threatening the mission. A related point is the importance of at least initial military logistics support for the law enforcement program. Given the slowness of the latter to mobilize, plus a common situation where the military initially controls or at least prioritizes access by sea and air for supply purposes (military or civilian), logistics support can be essential in getting CIVPOL established and operating effectively, thereby reducing more rapidly the longer-term involvement of the military. As part of the intervention, Haiti's seaports and airports were under complete military control. ICITAP therefore placed a field representative at ACOM in Norfolk, Virginia, to coordinate the shipment of materials to refurbish a training center, fuel for generators, and the fullest array of equipment for the police on military craft destined for Haiti.

□ The actors in the realm of international law and order assistance other than the United Nations can play a useful role. International Police Monitors played a critical role during the initial stages of the intervention. This force filled a severe public security gap between the time that the MNF dismantled the existing police force and the short-term Interim Public Security Force could be reoriented and deployed in sufficient numbers to maintain security with IPM assistance. Bilateral assistance from the United States (in the form of ICITAP and the DOJ and "Haitian-American cops") and Canada and France (in the form of the RCMP and gendarmes) also played important roles. These programs were closely coordinated by CIVPOL so as to ensure continuity.

□ Neither CIVPOL nor bilateral assistance programs were effective during the first 2½ years in significantly improving the decidedly dysfunctional judiciary and got off to a slow start in improving terrible prison conditions. Therefore, it is important to assess and work to improve concurrently all three elements of the public security triad: police, judiciary, prisons. Each must be recognized in advance as needing attention, with planning for early action on all three appropriate to the local culture, available resources, needs, and the magnitude of the task.

□ When the international community decides to conduct an operation of this magnitude, it must carefully assess the time and resources needed to reach the desired endstate. These are not short-term undertakings. At some point, the international community will turn its attention and resources to another significant problem. By the time that inevitability arrives, the transition process toward the point where new or reformed public security mechanisms can take over and sustain themselves must be sufficiently achieved. Premature withdrawal risks reverting to square one.

BOSNIA AND THE INTERNATIONAL POLICE TASK FORCE

MICHAEL J. DZIEDZIC and ANDREW BAIR

Background

After the death in 1980 of Yugoslavia's erstwhile ruler, Marshal Josip Broz Tito, and the disintegration of the Soviet empire in the late 1980s, forces that had held Yugoslavia's fractious peoples together were no longer present. When Serbian leaders sought to unify their nation into a greater Serbia, the Republics of Slovenia and Croatia began moving toward independence. After several failed attempts at peaceful transition, Croatia and Slovenia unilaterally declared independence in June 1991. In response, the Yugoslav Army (JNA) moved to secure Slovenia's external borders. In fewer than 3 weeks, Slovenia succeeded in surrounding JNA armored columns, capturing a sizable number of tanks and troops. By early July, the European Community (EC) had mediated a truce and a 3-month moratorium on further steps toward independence. Slovenia's subsequent declaration of independence met no significant resistance, but the Croatian announcement triggered an immediate attack by Serb-dominated JNA

Authors' note: We wish to acknowledge the careful scrutiny and incisive suggestions we received on earlier versions of this chapter from former International Police Task Force (IPTF) Deputy Commissioner Robert Wasserman, UNPROFOR CIVPOL Commissioner Michael F. O'Reilly, Major Donald Zoufal, U.S. Army Reserve, Colonel Larry Forester, U.S. Army, Jim Hooper, Lynn Thomas, Joe Drach, and Glenn MacPhail. In addition, as primary researcher for this chapter, Mike Dollenger was indefatigable, lending much greater precision and substance.

troops. The battle for Serb-populated areas in Croatia took place between July and December 1991, with the Serbs gaining control over 27 percent of Croatian territory.

Active involvement by the United Nations began in September 1991, when the Security Council unanimously adopted Resolution 713 calling for an embargo on deliveries of arms and military hardware to Yugoslavia. At the request of the Yugoslav Government, the Secretary-General subsequently began preparing to deploy a peacekeeping force to areas of Croatia with sizable Serb populations. The U.N. Protection Force (UNPROFOR) was established in Croatia for an initial period of 12 months by Security Council Resolution 743 (February 21, 1992). In what proved to be a crucial deficiency, the Serb leadership never gave its complete approval to the operation or to the countries that would comprise the force.

In March 1992, UNPROFOR infantry units began deployment to three U.N. Protected Areas (UNPAs): Eastern Slavonia, Western Slavonia, and Krajina (see map). Their mandate: to monitor withdrawal of JNA forces from Croatia and to oversee demilitarization and administration of the UNPAs. UNPROFOR was authorized to control access to the UNPAs. It also had 900 unarmed CIVPOL personnel to monitor local police compliance with human rights standards and to facilitate the return of refugees and displaced persons. By mid-June, UNPROFOR was almost fully operational.

Although JNA and Croatian National Guard units generally withdrew as agreed, irregular forces were absorbed into local territorial defense militias or community police forces. In many cases, local Serb paramilitary units acquired heavy weapons from the JNA as they withdrew. Fighting among irregulars continued until the Croatian Army seized the Krajina and Western Slavonia in the summer of 1995. During its 3½-year history, UNPROFOR's CIVPOL contingent was essentially powerless against these well-armed local military and paramilitary organizations.[1]

---

[1]For example, scores of CIVPOL vehicles were highjacked, typically at roadblocks, by such heavily armed forces.

Even though the situation in Croatia stabilized after the UNPROFOR deployment, the contagion of ethnic distrust and polarization had already spread to Bosnia-Herzegovina. When President Alija Izetbegovic declared Bosnia's independence on February 29, 1992, conflict erupted among Bosnia's three major ethnic groups.[2] Violence quickly spread, creating a desperate humanitarian situation. At the end of May, U.N. Security Council Resolution 757 demanded unimpeded delivery of humanitarian supplies to destinations in Bosnia. UNPROFOR established a security zone encompassing Sarajevo and assumed operational control of the airport. The conflict continued to escalate, however, despite incessant mediation by the United Nations and the European Community. UNPROFOR was thus forced to conduct its operations in and around the airport in a militarily active and hostile environment.

During the summer, some relief supplies were distributed, but the requirement vastly outstripped supply. That fall, Bosnian Serbs resorted to a deliberate policy of rape, torture, and mass murder to purge ethnic minorities from territory they sought to control. By late 1993, the Bosnian Serb Army, under the command of General Ratko Mladic, had 75 percent of Bosnia under its sway. Owing to a considerable Serb advantage in tanks and artillery, Bosniac and Croat forces were very much on the defensive.[3]

---

[2]The CIA estimated the demographic distribution of Bosnia's prewar population as consisting of 44 percent Muslim, 33 percent Serb, and 17 percent Croat; *The World Factbook 1992* (Washington, DC: Central Intelligence Agency, 1992), 43. Four years later CIA statistics indicated a Serb plurality of 40 percent, followed by 38 percent Muslims, and 22 percent Croats; ibid., 54. Those Bosnians of whatever ethnic background who sided with Izetbegovic to support an independent Bosnia-Herzegovina later became known as "Bosniacs."

[3]After 1993, Bosniac forces (the Army of Bosnia-Herzegovina, or ABiH) were able to exploit their advantage in manpower to mount a credible defense of the territory remaining under their control. At the end of the war, their forces numbered 200,000, compared to the Army of the Serb Republic (VRS) at 90,000 and the Bosnia Croat Army (HVO) with about 45,000 troops. The VRS and HVO had the advantage of vastly superior firepower and the support of well-armed patrons as a strategic reserve. *Bosnia Country Handbook Peace Implementation Force (IFOR)* (Washington, DC: Department of Defense, May 1996), 8-1 to 8-5.

In June 1993, the Bosnian Croat Army (HVO) turned its sights on the Bosniacs, compelling them to defend a second front, primarily in areas bordering Croatia. By March 1994, the United States and key European nations had brokered a cease-fire and formation of a Federation between Bosniacs and Croats. This new alliance laid the foundation for expansion of UNPROFOR into Sectors Southwest and Northeast (see map). After this expansion, the United Nations also enlarged its CIVPOL activities in Bosnia, by opening a detachment in Tuzla, adding to its existing activities in Sarajevo, Srebrenica, and Mostar. The CIVPOL presence in Bosnia began in Sarajevo in June 1992, with 40 personnel assigned to the airport to monitor the flow of relief supplies to preclude the abuse of this process to smuggle weapons into the enclave. After Srebrenica was declared a "safe area," 16 CIVPOL personnel were sent there in April 1993 in an attempt to restrict abusive behavior by local police and to regulate the influx of refugees and relief supplies. Shortly thereafter, a similar contingent was introduced into Mostar for the purpose of limiting police misconduct.[4]

Ultimately, UNPROFOR proved incapable of preventing continued ethnic purges, mostly directed at Moslems.[5] An attempt to bring pressure on Bosnian Serbs using air strikes in May 1995 resulted in the further discrediting of the mission when Serb forces retaliated by taking hundreds of UNPROFOR troops hostage for several weeks. World opinion was horrified when Serb forces under General Mladic overran U.N.-protected enclaves of Srebrenica and Zepa in July 1995, slaughtering thousands of defenseless Moslem males. The Croatian Army, bolstered through a clandestine arms program, launched an offensive in August aimed at evicting 150,000 Serb inhabitants of the Krajina. Coupled with retaliatory NATO air strikes in late August and September, this shattered the myth of Serb invincibility and

---

[4]UNPROFOR Commissioner Michael F. O'Reilly to Colonel Michael Dziedzic, facsimile dated April 2, 1998.

[5]The conflict claimed the lives of an estimated 250,000 persons, some 150,000 of which were Moslem. "Death Toll Remains Vague," Associated Press, February 16, 1996.

Bosnia After the Dayton Accords

dramatically altered the balance of power. Bosnian Croat and Bosniac forces took advantage of this to drive the Serbs from 20 percent of the territory they had occupied in central and western Bosnia, eventually threatening to overrun Banja Luka, the largest Bosnian Serb population center. This reversal in conditions on the ground created an opportunity to negotiate a settlement to the ethnic conflict. The Dayton Peace Accords (DPA) were signed in Paris on December 14, 1995, and deployment of the Implementation Force (IFOR) commenced under the authority of U.N. Security Council Resolution 1035 (December 21, 1995).

Capacity for Self-Governance

The absence of a formula for governance acceptable to each of Bosnia's ethnic constituencies is the fundamental source of dysfunction. Until this primordial issue is resolved, no amount of international largesse, infrastructure repair, or specialized training will suffice to put Bosnia back together again. Thus the central issue is the lack of consensus about whether Bosnia should be a unitary state or partitioned, not lack of governing capacity.

If a workable political formula ultimately emerges, there are numerous secondary factors relevant to governing capacity that will likely play a crucial role in shaping Bosnia's ultimate destiny (e.g., economic resources; reintegration of refugees, displaced persons, and former combatants into productive society; and the link between governing elites and organized crime).

The Economy

Bosnia's economic challenges would have been daunting even without the convulsions of civil war. The shock of exposing the centrally planned economy to the discipline of global competition would have been harsh enough, given Bosnia's relatively primitive level of development, even by East European standards. By 1989, when the Berlin Wall collapsed, the Bosnian economy was in deplorable condition. Inflation exceeded 1,000 percent, and per capita foreign debt for all Yugoslavia was the highest in Europe.[6] Compounding the task of economic adjustment, roughly half the 1990 federal budget for

---

[6]"Economy Section," *Yugoslavia, A Country Study* (Washington, DC: Library of Congress, December 1990). In 1986, 1987, and 1988 inflation rose from 190 to 419 percent and then to 1,232 percent. "International Financial Statistics," *International Monetary Fund* 45 (November 1992): 556, 748-49; as quoted in Susan Woodward, *Balkan Tragedy: Chaos and Dissolution After the Cold War* (Washington, DC: The Brookings Institution, 1995), 96.

Yugoslavia was consumed by the military.[7] Lacking the means to continue propping up noncompetitive state-run enterprises, the Government slashed subsidies. Unemployment skyrocketed. The economic devastation subsequently wrought by the war reduced the economy largely to smuggling and distribution of humanitarian supplies. Industrial activity in Bosnian-Moslem areas fell to an estimated 5 percent of prewar levels.[8]

The infrastructure was also a shambles, with Bosniac areas suffering the greatest devastation. By autumn 1995, 75 percent of Bosnia's oil refining capacity had been destroyed, electrical generation was down 80 percent, and coal production was less than 10 percent of prewar output. Almost one-fifth of all houses had been destroyed and another two-thirds damaged, 50 percent of schools had been gutted, 30 percent of roads and bridges had been damaged or destroyed, and more than $1 billion of damage had been inflicted on railroads.[9]

By mid-1997, 18 months after the Dayton Accords had come into effect, economic activity within the Federation was growing at a 50 percent annual rate, and unemployment had fallen to 50 percent. The bulk of this, however, was being driven by foreign reconstruction assistance.[10] Since only a trickle of external aid had gone to the Serb Republic (RS), its economy had not yet begun the postwar recovery process.

---

[7]CIA figures indicate total Yugoslav government expenditures for 1990 were U.S. $6.4 billion; *CIA Factbook 1991* (Washington, DC: Central Intelligence Agency, 1991), 344. Yugoslavia's 1990 defense budget approximated U.S. $3.52 billion; *The Military Balance 1991-1992* (London: Institute for International Strategic Studies, 1991), 96.

[8]*Economic and Infrastructure Overview for Bosnia*, Central and Eastern Europe Business Information Center (Washington, DC: Department of Commerce, March 1995), 1-2.

[9]Ibid.

[10]*This Week in Bosnia,* Bosnia Action Coalition, http://world.std.com/~slm/twib0504.hfml, May 4, 1997, 3.

Social Disruption

A further consequence of the war, waged largely against civilian targets, was massive emigration.[11] A million Bosnians, 20 to 25 percent of the prewar population, fled the country. These refugees came disproportionately from the ranks of professionals and skilled laborers, causing a "brain drain" but also creating a potential source of remittances useful for recovery after the conclusion of the conflict.[12] In addition, more than a million inhabitants remained displaced by the conflict inside Bosnia.

Organized Crime

The exigencies of the war drove political leaders from all three warring factions to rely on the criminal underworld to perform various essential functions. Owing to the international arms embargo and their need to fashion a military establishment from the ground up, the Bosniacs desperately needed to smuggle military contraband across international boundaries. Criminal organizations based in Sarajevo helped to meet this requirement. Revenue to fund the war effort was particularly vital for the Serbs, which was in part satisfied through smuggling and black marketeering in consumer goods and primary products. This continues to be essential for de facto Bosnian Serb leader, Radovan Karadzic, and his ability to maintain a grip on power.

Another common phenomenon was reliance upon local thugs and armed gangs to prosecute the war effort at the local level, including perpetration of some of the most brutal instances of "ethnic

---

[11]In the domestic census of 1991, the population of Bosnia and Herzegovina was placed at 4,377,033. AID estimated the 1995 population to be 3,400,000, while the CIA estimated the July 1995 population at 3,201,823. Susan L. Somers and Thomas Reeves, *A Functional Review of the Criminal Justice System in Bosnia and Herzegovina*, unpublished joint study conducted by ICITAP and CJ-CIMIC, Sarajevo, October 28, 1996, 15.

[12]Some $3 billion may have been repatriated in 1996 alone. U.S. Embassy Country Team briefing, Sarajevo, May 14, 1997.

U.N. Protection Force Sectors

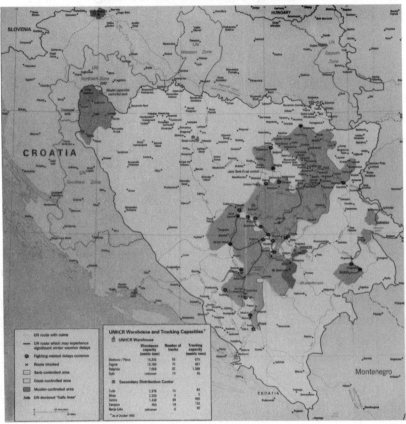

cleansing."[13]   Among the more notorious were the Serb "Arkan" around Brcko, and Croats "Tuta" and "Stela" in Mostar. Certain of these individuals have been indicted as war criminals; however, in their local ethnic communities they are regarded as war heroes. Owing to their intimate links with local elites, this criminal element will be an

---

[13]Noel Malcolm, *Bosnia: A Short History* (London: Macmillan London Ltd., 1994), 252.

especially severe challenge for those seeking to establish the rule of law in Bosnia.

Public Security Apparatus

Throughout most of its recent history, including the Tito regime, the public security apparatus—the judiciary, police force, and penal system—served as a fundamental instrument of state control. Yugoslavia's disintegration into ethnically defined entities during the first half of the 1990s had the further effect of converting many local police organizations into agents of intimidation and brutality against those of different ethnic origins.

The Courts and Judiciary

The basic features of the legal system have remained relatively constant in spite of political upheavals in the region.[14] Prior to the war, the judiciary in Bosnia-Herzegovina consisted of some 970 judges and 250 prosecutors distributed among a Supreme Court, 7 Higher (or appellate) Courts, and 61 Basic Courts at the municipal level. Each court is presided over by a president and a panel of trial judges that varies in size according to the level of the court. Cases are assigned initially to an investigating judge who is responsible for conducting an inquiry to determine if sufficient evidence exists to warrant a trial. Unlike the "adversarial" process in the United States, which seeks to establish truth via competing arguments of prosecuting and defense attorneys, the Bosnian system is inquisitorial. The trial judge, therefore, conducts an examination of the facts in the courtroom.[15]

The Constitution contained in Annex 4 of the DPA establishes two political entities, the Federation and the Serb Republic, and endows each with separate responsibilities for administering a system of justice. In practice, however, there were three discrete systems operating at the

---

[14]*Report by the Legal Advisor Headquarters Allied Command Europe Rapid Reaction Corps into the Functioning of the Legal System in Bosnia Herzegovina as at 01 October 1996,* unpublished NATO document, October 10, 1996, 2, sec. 1.2.1.
[15]Ibid., 3 sec. 2.2.2.

end of the Bosnia conflict, one for each ethnic group.[16] All three shared the same basic structure, and they functioned similarly in that the courts were highly politicized.[17] In similar fashion, the role of the prosecuting attorney has been exploited by those in power. Other factors having a negative impact on the judicial system are a shortage of trained personnel, meager salaries, lack of basic resources (e.g., transportation, computers, reference books, and a centralized database), and a legal code that was designed to maximize state power at the expense of individual liberty.

The Police

During the Communist era, the police force was a basic instrument of state control in Yugoslavia's autocratic, single-party regime. Their formal functions were state security, major criminal investigation, traffic regulation, executive protection, intelligence, and border/customs services. In addition to municipal police forces, a key element of state security was the Ministry of Interior Special Police (commonly referred to as MUPs). During times of war or martial law, these paramilitary units were assigned to support territorial defense and maintain control of the interior of the country. MUPs were armed with rocket-launched grenades, large caliber weapons (including mortars and antitank guns), light armor (including armored personnel carriers, or APCs), and, in some cases, tanks and anti-aircraft guns. During the 1992-95 war, MUPs in all three ethnic communities were used heavily, performing a range of paramilitary functions.

The typical mode of police interaction with the population was the traffic checkpoint attended by some four or five armed policemen. Citizens were required to produce mandatory documents, and the

---

[16]Somers and Reeves identified a total of 118 Basic and High courts functioning in 1996 (53 Moslem, 48 Serb, and 17 Croat), 27.

[17]*Report by the Legal Advisor*, 14, sec. 6.1.3. Glenn Curtis also observed, "The judiciary lacked sufficient independence to ensure impartial justice for all citizens. Judges were subject to party discipline by the League of Communists of Yugoslavia (LCY), through which they had reached office." *Yugoslavia: A Country Study*, in Somers and Reeves, 26.

function served was population control. Police harassment was common, and during the Bosnian conflict checkpoints were exploited to restrict freedom of movement and intimidate ethnic minorities. Police forces lacked patrol cars and radios, so the checkpoint was a tactic well tailored to their meager means and overall mission of state control.

Most officers began police training in high school and subsequently followed a professional career path. Owing to the character of the Bosnian conflict, all ethnic communities sought to preserve internal security by expanding their police cadres. This was accomplished through an influx of personnel with little or no police training. An IFOR study conducted in 1996 indicated that over 80 percent of Federation policemen had fewer than 6 years' experience, and in many cases their background was of a paramilitary nature.[18] The ranks were swollen with individuals having predominantly military preparation, and the flow of personnel between police and military units became quite fluid (the standard uniform for the police was the fatigue uniform of their military counterparts, and their basic weapon was the AK-47).

Prior to the war, municipal police forces in the larger urban areas, Sarajevo in particular, were reasonably multiethnic; however, the outbreak of conflict quickly produced three ethnically segregated forces. In December 1995, a U.N. advance mission determined that 44,750 police officers were on active duty in Bosnia: 29,750 in Moslem-controlled areas, 3,000 in Croat areas, and 12,000 in the RS.[19] Police strength, in proportion to the civilian population, was several times higher than the European standard (1:330), owing to the wartime expansion.[20] After deployment of IFOR and the IPTF, the Federation agreed to reduce their forces to 11,500. The Serb Republic, in

---

[18]"This particular group of police appears to have none of the formal police academy training which existed in prewar Yugoslavia. The educational level of approximately 80 percent of these officers includes some high school but not necessarily graduation." Somers and Reeves, 22.

[19]*Report of the Secretary-General Pursuant to Security Council Resolution 1026,* S/1995/1031, December 13, 1995, 6, para. 22.

[20]Ibid., 6, para. 22; Somers and Reeves, 19.

contrast, persistently refused to participate in such a normalization process. Until February 1997, when the first canton was restructured in the Federation, Bosnia continued to have three completely discrete and autonomous police forces.

Police of Bosnia-Herzegovina

The regular police are headquartered in Sarajevo and are subordinate to the Ministry of Internal Affairs. Prior to 1997, the police force was geographically divided into seven districts (Sarajevo, Zenica, Doboj, Bihac, Tuzla, Mostar, and Gorazde). At present, the organization is being realigned on a cantonal basis under the Federation restructuring program.[21] Functionally, the force is organized into motorized patrols, traffic patrols, criminal investigation units, and state security services, including presidential protection. The traffic and motorized patrol police are more akin to "street cops" and were meant to control the local population and rural areas.

Prior to the restructuring program, the MUPs also constituted a major element of the Ministry of Interior. They were equipped with automatic weapons and light armor and thus were similar to a constabulary force. Although they fell under the day-to-day administration of the Ministry of Internal Affairs, when required for national defense they came under the command of the Ministry of Defense. In some cases, these police conducted patrols and engaged in actual combat along the confrontation line during the Bosnian conflict, but they were intended chiefly for rear area security. The main Bosniac element of the MUPs, the Black Swans, have been disarmed and demobilized.

The Bosnia-Herzegovina Government also has Border and Customs units, but they are largely vestigial, because the government lacks control over most of its international border. The Croats still control border crossings in the south and west, Serbs control the north and east, and the Bosnian Army's Fifth Corps provides border security in the Bihac area. In reality, these police have collected customs and

---

[21]The Federation is divided into 10 cantons.

fees on commodities in transit through the interior of the country. Border and Customs belongs to the Ministry of Internal Affairs.

The Bosnian Agency for Investigation and Documentation (BAID) is the main Bosniac intelligence organization. Known for ruthless intimidation and political assassination during the conflict, the BAID served as an arm of the Bosnian Presidency and is populated by hard-line members of the governing Party for Democratic Action (SDA). The BAID's influence in Bosniac politics has been greatly reduced since implementation of the Dayton Accords, and the agency has been restructured as a result of the Split Agreement of August 1997.

Police of the Croatian Republic of Herceg-Bosna

Patterned after the police of Croatia, the primary functions of the police of the Croatian Republic of Herceg-Bosna (CRHB) have been state security, criminal investigation, traffic regulation, special operations and intelligence, and border and customs services. Although the CRHB was in theory disbanded on January 10, 1996 under terms of the Dayton Agreement, there was no immediate mechanism to provide a substitute police force. The subsequent Petersburg and Federation Forum (Sarajevo) Agreements called for integration of Croat and Moslem police forces, which began to take place, canton by canton, during the latter half of 1997. Since Bosnian Croat police control border crossings along the primary trade routes between Bosnia and Croatia, they provide a major source of revenue via collection of customs fees. Prior to Federation restructuring, CRHB police had been deployed in eight districts: Mostar, Livno, Travnik-Vitez, Derventa, Zepce, Kiseljak, Jajce, and Orasje.

During the Dayton-mandated transfer of territories from the RS to the Federation, MUPs from Croatia deployed into areas south of Mostar to assist their Bosnian Croat counterparts. IFOR successfully expelled the Croatian MUPs. Throughout most of the Federation, therefore, the Special Police have come under IPTF monitoring and have been incorporated into the police restructuring program.

Police of the Serb Republic

The RS police were exploited during the war as an instrument of population control and genocide, and they continue to be used as the principal defense against infiltration or incursions by other ethnic groups. Their training and functions were similar to the other police forces, but greater emphasis has recently been placed on state security, special operations, and border control. Thus, even at the municipal level, police also perform intelligence and paramilitary activities and were active during the conflict in "ethnic cleansing" operations. Among the functions performed by Special Police throughout the RS in the aftermath of the conflict has been to provide bodyguards for indicted war criminals.

Revenue to meet the payroll of municipal police and the Interior Ministry has been generated from monopolistic control exercised by Radovan Karadzic over imports and distribution of consumer products throughout the Serb Republic. Karadzic has exploited his control over the police to repress both ethnic minorities and his political opponents. Although officially subordinate to the Ministry of Internal Affairs, command of local police can easily be handed over to the RS Army General Staff in a crisis. When required, the RS military also assumes command of key border units and Special Forces police. Headquartered in Pale, major RS police stations are located in Banja Luka, Prijedor, Brcko, Bijeljina, Foca, Trebine, and Han Pijesak.

The Penal System

Bosnia has eleven prisons, five of which are Bosniac (Sarajevo, Tuzla, Bihac, Zenica, and East Mostar) three Serb (Bijelina, Banja Luka, Doboj), and three Croat (Travnik, Busovaca, Mostar/Rodac).[22]

The Cultural Context

The historic relationship between state and society in the Balkans placed very little emphasis on abstractions like individual rights or

---

[22]Somers and Reeves, 28.

responsiveness to citizen demands. Power has traditionally been concentrated in the hands of a monarch, a marshal, or similar monolithic authority figure. Law and order have historically been imposed on subjugated masses in the interest of the state. The police role has been to maintain control on behalf of whoever wields power. (Currently, the reins of power in each ethnic community are dominated by a faction of the former Communist Party.) Thus, the notion of policing as a public service is alien both to the police and the populace.

Routine procedures in such basic functions as traffic control and criminal investigation illustrate the traditional role of the police and the expectations that have been shaped in the public mind. The most likely form of interaction with the average citizen during the communist era was the police roadblock or checkpoint. This would afford police an opportunity to review documents, collect customs fees, inspect for weapons or other contraband, and intimidate members of other ethnic groups. The purpose was regulation and control of individual conduct, as opposed to protection of the public against criminal activity.

When crimes were committed, evidence gathering was largely confined to rounding up witnesses and suspects for questioning under police custody. Interrogation was both a verbal and physical process, sometimes even for the hapless witness. Little or no emphasis was placed on using forensic techniques to gather physical evidence to establish guilt or innocence.[23] Given that these police practices have persisted over generations, they have become deeply ingrained in the political culture and conform to expectations of the average citizen.

The Mandate

The purpose of the intervention resulting from the Dayton Peace Accords (DPA) differed fundamentally from UNPROFOR, which was largely humanitarian and directed at facilitating delivery of relief supplies and shielding Moslem enclaves in territory surrounded by Serb

---

[23]It was rare for police to have even a fingerprinting kit or other aids to process evidence at the crime scene. Major Donald Zoufal, U.S. Army Reserve, IFOR Civil Affairs officer assigned to assist IPTF operations, unpublished manuscript, 2.

forces. In discharging their numerous mandates, UNPROFOR commanders had to consult political authorities in both NATO and the United Nations before force could be used. U.N. authorities were very reluctant to authorize forceful measures. Consequently, this unwieldy, "dual key" command and control arrangement rendered UNPROFOR powerless to respond to tactical developments. The Contact Group countries (the United States, the United Kingdom, France, Germany, and Russia), especially the United States, insisted that IFOR would not operate under the same emasculating constraints. To discharge its responsibilities under Annex 1A of the DPA (ensuring separation of forces, their confinement to cantons, and downsizing), IFOR would be endowed with a single chain of command (NATO), executive powers, robust rules of engagement, and overwhelming force.

U.N. Security Council Resolution 1035 (December 21, 1995) articulates the mandate for both IFOR and the International Police Task Force (IPTF). As with IFOR, however, the real basis for the IPTF originates in the DPA. Annex 11 of the DPA explicitly states that responsibility for maintaining a "safe and secure environment for all persons" rests with the signatories themselves.[24] However, to assist in discharging their public security obligations, the Parties requested that the IPTF be created and that it perform the following functions:

☐ Monitor and inspect judicial and law enforcement activities, including conducting joint patrols with local police forces
☐ Advise and train law enforcement personnel
☐ Analyze the public security threat and offer advice to government authorities on how to organize their police forces most effectively
☐ Facilitate law enforcement improvement and respond to requests of the parties, to the extent possible.

---

[24]Dayton Peace Accords, *General Framework Agreement for Peace*, Article 1, Annex 11, *Department of State Dispatch* 7, supplement no. 1, March 1996, 50.

The IPTF was not armed and was not empowered to enforce local laws. Because its purpose was to help already established law enforcement agencies maintain public order and assist them in adopting methods of policing consistent with international standards, the IPTF could function effectively only with the consent of the Parties. In the absence of such collaboration, the IPTF possessed neither the mandate nor the resources to preserve public order independently. The dilemmas this would generate for IPTF officials do not appear to have been anticipated or well understood by drafters of this annex. The IPTF's first Deputy Commissioner, Robert Wasserman, offers the following insights into this situation:

> It appears the framers of Dayton perceived that the IPTF would somehow simply monitor local police to see they didn't get out of hand and then advise willing parties on how to professionalize the police with modern practices. There was no thought given to the fact that the ethnic rivalries meant there was no functioning police to protect minorities after Dayton. And Annex 11 used the term 'internationally accepted standards of policing,' which are non-existent. There are internationally accepted human rights standards, but policing reform required something far more descriptive.[25]

In circumstances where implementation of Dayton ran counter to interests of one of the Parties (e.g., the transfer of Serb-held suburbs of Sarajevo to the Federation or the resettlement of Moslems to strategic locations in the Zone of Separation), local police either withdrew or became active protagonists. In such instances, IFOR was compelled to become involved. While IFOR could provide "area security" or reinforced patrolling to deter lawlessness, its forces were not trained or equipped for riot control or law enforcement tasks. Nor was it considered prudent to engage in activity that smacked of policing. Thus, when the police force of one of the Parties refused to cooperate with the IPTF—because doing so would have damaged their vital interests—an "enforcement gap" arose. There were no effective

---

[25]Observations provided in response to an earlier draft.

sanctions available to the IPTF to punish noncompliance, and this gap was never bridged during the life of the IFOR mission.

Peace Mission Organization

By establishing IFOR under NATO auspices, the "dual key" problem suffered by UNPROFOR was resolved for purposes of implementing the military provisions of Dayton, but the consequence was to fragment implementation of civilian aspects. The two international actors concerned with maintaining a safe and secure environment, IFOR and the IPTF, were divided from each other organizationally, with the IPTF falling under the U.N. Mission in Bosnia-Herzegovina (UNMIBH). Yet another actor, the High Representative (HR), was delegated a coordinating role by the DPA, but without authority over any other entity. The IPTF Commissioner was simply directed to consult with the High Representative. Responsibility for organizing the pivotal national elections, moreover, was assigned to the Organization for Security and Cooperation in Europe (OSCE), which itself regularly spoke with contradictory voices.[26] In addition, the U.N. High Commissioner for Refugees (UNHCR), the World Bank, numerous other international organizations and several hundred NGOs had vital, independent contributions to make to various aspects of the peace building process.

During the first crucial months, the HR made no effort to promote coordination among the various civilian entities (such as convening regular meetings of the "principals" or heads of the other key international organizations operating in Bosnia). Only after the mission was well under way was the HR ultimately prodded into conducting weekly "Principals Meetings" to bring a measure of coherence to the

---

[26]On September 25, 1996, Ed van Thijn, Coordinator for International Monitoring, publicly asserted that the postponed municipal elections should be put off for at least 4 more months until the minimal essential conditions could be satisfied. In contrast, OSCE Mission Chief, Ambassador Robert Frowick insisted on going forward with the elections in late November. In fact, they were ultimately postponed until September 1997. "Monitor Wants Bosnian Elections Postponed," *Washington Times*, September 25, 1996.

peace operation.[27]   Obtaining strategic unity of effort out of this fragmented structure, therefore, could only be achieved by dint of considerable exertion and continuous attention to cooperative action. At the operational level, the national and municipal elections compelled the IFOR/SFOR, the OSCE, IPTF, and the Office of the High Representative (OHR) to establish a Joint Elections Operations Center for more timely exchange of information and coordination of responses.

Size and Composition of CIVPOL

In the wake of Security Council Resolution 1026 (November 30, 1995), a U.N. assessment team was dispatched to Bosnia in early December by the Secretary-General to establish the requirements for the forthcoming CIVPOL mission. The determination of the number of required IPTF personnel was based simply on a mathematical calculation (one monitor for 30 local police). Since the assessment team determined the total strength to be 44,750, the IPTF was authorized 1,721 monitors.[28] Their organization scheme was simply to replicate the deployment of the various police forces in Bosnia. Because there were 109 police stations, IPTF monitors were originally to be disbursed among 109 stations of their own. No consideration was given to the implications of the other tasks assigned to the IPTF in

---

[27]The "Principals" were the High Representative, IFOR/SFOR commander, IPTF commissioner, and Special Representative of the Secretary-General, who heads UNMIBH. In addition to this core group, when the issues of the day concerned the OSCE or the U.N. High Commissioner for Refugees (UNHCR), the heads of these organizations were also included.

[28]This comes out to 1,492 monitors. Presumably the additional 229 monitors were added because of a planning assumption that roughly 13 percent would be on leave, sick, or otherwise unavailable for duty. U.N. Security Council Resolutions 1103 (March 31, 1997) and 1107 (May 16, 1997) added an additional 186 officers to allow for creation of a super-station in Brcko after the March 1997 decision to place that contested city under international administration. By June 1, 1997, a full contingent of 258 officers had been deployed there. *Report of the Secretary-General of the United Nations Mission in Bosnia and Herzegovina (UNMIBH)*, U.N. Doc. S/1997/468, para. 8, 2, June 16, 1997.

Annex 11, such as advising, training, and restructuring local law enforcement agencies. In part, this was driven by external constraints, specifically concerns that the United Nations could neither recruit nor finance a larger force.

On December 24, 1995, the U.N. Secretary-General issued a verbal invitation to U.N. Member States to contribute to the newly established monitoring mission. Over 40 countries responded, and the first contingent of monitors began to deploy a month later. These were added to the residual UNPROFOR CIVPOL contingent that retained some 200 monitors. Rather than following the original deployment scheme, which would have required an inordinate number of intermediate management layers, the IPTF Commissioner reduced the number of stations from 109 to 54, which resulted in a corresponding reduction of district offices to 14. Initially, there were three regional headquarters (Tuzla, Banja Luka, and Sarajevo), with the IPTF headquarters also situated in Sarajevo.

In keeping with previous U.N. practice, the requirements to serve on the first IPTF mission were fluency in English, the ability to drive, and 8 years of experience in policing (as policing was defined in the contributing country). No consideration was given to recruiting personnel with skills essential for tasks other than monitoring (e.g., field training officers, police academy administrators, specialists in management or police reform). During the initial stages of deployment, however, it was not uncommon for IPTF members to fall short of even these basic standards. Of the three requirements, the most vital was competence in English. Without the ability to communicate, personnel were unable to make any contribution to the mission. In addition, the long-range objective was to reorient Bosnia's various police agencies to operate in accordance with international standards. Police monitors from autocratic regimes that themselves fail to conform to these standards could scarcely be expected to imbue such ideals in their Bosnian counterparts.

It quickly became apparent that screening potential CIVPOL volunteers for English fluency and driving skills in the donor country prior to deployment would be much more cost-effective. The IPTF was able to convince the United Nations to begin doing this with a few donor nations as early as March 1996. Prior to recruiting the second rotation for duty as of December 1996 (a normal tour in Bosnia being 1 year), the United Nations began routinely sending Selection Assistance Teams to screen volunteers in various source countries before deployment. To evaluate the English competence of incoming personnel, the IPTF Training Unit developed an English aptitude test (speaking, reading, and writing). To avoid compromise of the exam, the IPTF insisted that a member of their training staff accompany the teams administering the qualifying exams. This significantly enhanced the quality of incoming IPTF personnel. The quality of the force was also greatly enhanced during recruitment of the second rotation by specifying to donors the spectrum of skills required to staff the organization. Once the United Nations established specific guidance regarding the type of expertise and level of experience required, most contributing countries responded positively, producing personnel with the desired capabilities.

Prior to deployment in the field, newly assigned police monitors underwent a 1-week screening and orientation course at the IPTF training facility outside Zagreb, Croatia. In addition to being tested on their English language and driving ability, incoming personnel received specific information pertaining to the mission in Bosnia. Once again, the IPTF began with a generic U.N. formula and transformed it into a program well tailored to mission requirements. This also entailed inviting the U.N. Centre for Human Rights to offer human rights training retroactively to 900 previously deployed IPTF monitors and to help incorporate this subject into the curriculum at the Zagreb training facility. Among the other topics covered were the mandate, IPTF reporting forms, computer literacy, attributes of the mission area, mine awareness, and an orientation to IFOR/SFOR. After the second rotation, the training unit began conducting in-service training to provide additional skills that posttraining surveys had indicated were lacking. When more training time was available, as occurred with the contingent destined for Brcko in early 1997, the IPTF experimented with instruction in Serbo-Croatian. Many monitors did achieve some fluency in the local language on their own initiative during the mission.

Resources

When UNPROFOR transferred the Bosnia operation to IFOR, all participating forces came under NATO operational control. UNPROFOR also transferred the existing U.N. logistical and communication infrastructure to the NATO-led operation. This made it possible for IFOR to begin operations immediately and to reach its full complement of over 60,000 troops expeditiously. No consideration was given to the needs of the IPTF, however, even though it was to be a U.N.-supported activity just like UNPROFOR had been.

After IFOR absorbed mission-essential U.N. assets in theater, the IPTF had to build its entire operation from the ground up. Consequently, the deployment gap typically associated with CIVPOL missions was greatly compounded. The Security Council Resolution authorizing creation of the IPTF (as well as the U.N. Mission in Bosnia-Herzegovina to manage it) was approved in late December 1995. Organizers then had to confront the Herculean task of procuring essential resources via the U.N.'s plodding logistic support system. Recruiting more than 1,700 qualified police monitors from around the world was also a protracted process.[29] Even the United States was delayed in fielding its contingent,[30] and as of the first week of March 1996, the IPTF had only 392 monitors in-country.[31] The result was considerable delay in bringing the IPTF up to operational status, and a serious gap in readiness when the Sarajevo suburbs were transferred to Moslem authority in February-March 1996 (see chart).

The operational capability of the IPTF was seriously hampered during the IFOR phase of the peace operation owing to deficiencies in logistical support. While improvements were made with the passage of time, shortcomings in transportation, communications, and interpreters

---

[29]*Bosnia-Hercegovina—No Justice, No Peace: The United Nations International Police task Force's Role in Screening Local Law Enforcement, Human Rights Watch/Helsinki* 8, no. 15(D), September 1996, 5.

[30]Kevin F. Mc Carroll and Donald R. Zoufal, "Transition of the Sarajevo Suburbs," *Joint Force Quarterly*, no. 16 (Summer 1997): 50-53.

[31]*Bosnia-Hercegovina—No Justice, No Peace*, 5.

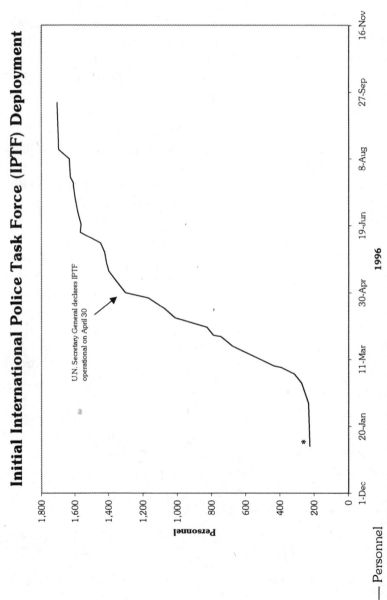

Initial International Police Task Force (IPTF) Deployment

Personnel

1996

U.N. Secretary General declares IPTF
operational on April 30

— Personnel

*Remaining CIVPOL from U.N. Confidence Restoration Operation and U.N. Protection Force were transferred
over. The United Nations authorized 1,721-member IPTF on December 21, 1995.
Source: "Weekly Summaries," Implementation Force, Sarejevo.

continued to plague the mission well into the SFOR phase.[32] As of the end of July 1996, for example, deficiencies in communications equipment had become chronic, with shortfalls of 25 percent in handheld radios, 29 percent for vehicle radios, and 65 percent for satellite links.[33] Transportation was another major limitation. The IPTF had received 516 vehicles as of July 30, yet only 454 were operational. This constituted a 21 percent shortfall from the 574 required to carry out mandated responsibilities.[34] UNMIBH made no provision to replace total losses in spite of regular attrition, a problem that was accentuated by the recurring failure of donor countries to ensure all their monitors could drive.[35] Even simple items such as snow tires and chains began to loom large in late September 1996 after the UNMIBH Chief Administrative Officer (CAO) refused repeated IPTF requisition requests. This was in spite of the fact that 75 percent of IPTF vehicles had bald tires, and November is one of the snowier months in Bosnia.[36] This had serious operational implications, because municipal elections were slated at the time for November 22, and this electoral process was

---

[32]Deputy Chief Logistician to IPTF Commissioner, memorandum dated late July 1996; it portrayed the problem as follows:

> As of 29 July, the required communications, vehicles, reasonable fuel supply, EDP [Electronic Data Processing], and medical support has [sic] not been completed. . . . Based upon the IPTF subordinate relationship to the UNMIBH, the IPTF has no organic assets. All logistical support is to be provided by UNMIBH. The general level of support by UNMIBH has been inadequate. . . . The current IPTF logistical status to support the mandate is unacceptable, and unless rectified prior to 15 August 1996, may cause the IPTF to fail in all or part of the critical mission requirements.

Memorandum for the Record, Subject: "UNMIBH Logistical Support to IPTF," D/Chief Logistics Officer to IPTF Deputy Commissioner, July 29, 1996; and enclosure to memorandum, 1 and 8.

[33]"All shortages reflect the minimum number to marginally accomplish the mission using common assets, and presuming no equipment failures, losses, or repairs." Ibid., enclosure, 9.

[34]Ibid., 9.

[35]Ibid., 3.

[36]Ibid., 6.

expected to be contentious, involving efforts by tens of thousands of prospective voters to cross the Inter-Entity Boundary Line (IEBL).

Two fundamental constraints compounded the IPTF's logistical woes, one procedural and one administrative. As a standard procedure, the United Nations based its resource allocations for essential items like vehicles and communications gear on standards developed during previous missions involving use of CIVPOL as monitors only. In the U.N. mission assessment, no consideration was given to the added requirements associated with training, advising, or restructuring law enforcement agencies in Bosnia. Thus, the United Nations authorized a single vehicle for every three IPTF personnel, for example, when the needs of the mission dictated a ratio of at least one for every two policemen.[37]

Most of these logistical deficiencies were exacerbated by UNMIBH's first Chief Administrative Officer. This individual ensured that top priority for vehicles, computers, communications equipment and other perquisites was given to UNMIBH headquarters personnel in Sarajevo. Their needs were fully satisfied before many IPTF personnel in the field even began to be supported.[38] Summarizing the situation as of mid-1996, a senior IPTF logistician asserted, "During formal and informal discussions with IPTF Monitors, from the IPTF Stations, Districts, and Regions, almost without exception all have indicated that UNMIBH logistical support has been unresponsive, or totally inadequate."[39] This changed dramatically at the end of the IPTF's first year when the CAO was replaced. After a more mission-oriented CAO took charge, many of the more troubling logistical difficulties were eventually alleviated.[40]

---

[37]Observations on an earlier draft provided by former Deputy Commissioner Robert Wasserman.

[38]In part, the CAO accomplished this by refusing to process IPTF requests for support prior to the arrival of each influx of personnel. Because personnel deployments extended over a 6-month period (March-August), a persistent delay was built into the process of achieving operational status. See note 34, enclosure, 3 and 7.

[39]Ibid., 6.

[40]Observations made by IPTF Deputy Commissioner David Kriskovich at a conference sponsored by the National Defense University, June 26, 1997.

This second constraint illustrates the crucial importance of placing the right people in key posts.

It was perhaps inevitable that the IPTF would turn to IFOR to ameliorate shortcomings in mission support. As the operation was being established, the IPTF sought assistance with medical care, fuel, maps, security for its vehicle maintenance facility, and access for its personnel to military stores. With the exception of maps (readily available) and post exchanges (which were not), the support the IPTF sought was decentralized and available only by negotiating directly with one or more of IFOR's 34 contributing countries.[41] This scattershot approach proved to be particularly inappropriate for purposes of medical care.[42]

The U.N. medical staff had assumed that IPTF personnel would be able to rely on IFOR's medical support system. IFOR did agree to provide emergency medical evacuation. For other medical support, the United Nations was directed to approach each national contingent possessing medical units to make arrangements. Even though nations such as Norway allowed IPTF personnel to use their medical services on an informal, space available basis, this still left many gaps. As late as mid-1996, UNMIBH had not made any formal arrangements for medical support, other than emergency evacuation.[43]

In mid-1996, IFOR agreed to formalize a "Logistics Support Package" involving co-location of communications antennas and diesel fuel storage sites, and, in emergencies, to provide fuel, medical care,

---

[41]Chief of the Supply and Services Division to the Director, Joint Logistics Operations Centre, memorandum dated January 27, 1995, "Support to the U.N. Mission in B-H (UNMIBH)." All 16 NATO countries and 14 Partnership for Peace nations contributed personnel to IFOR (and later to SFOR), as well as Egypt, Morocco, Jordan and Malaysia.

[42]Fax No. 151-2275, from Chief Medical Officer, U.N. Transitional Office for Operations in the Former Yugoslavia, to SRSG UNMIBH Sarajevo, "Medical Support to U.N. Personnel UNMIBH/UNIPTF, March 15, 1996.

[43]In the view of a senior IPTF official, this situation "jeopardizes the IPTF operationally, and more seriously, from a personal safety aspect." Memorandum for the record, subject: UNMIBH Logistical Support to IPTF, footnote 32, 1.

water, rations, and shower facilities.[44] This alleviated the more extreme implications of IPTF logistical shortcomings. Thus, as the IPTF entered its second year, logistic support had improved considerably, as arrangements with IFOR were put in place, as UNMIBH itself became more responsive, and as logistics pipelines began operating predictably with the simple passage of time. Nevertheless, its operational capacity continued to be impeded in particular by inadequate transportation owing to an aging vehicle fleet that required excessive maintenance and was not adequate for the IPTF's multiple tasks in the first place.

The Mission

Phases of the Operation

The Dayton Peace Accords (DPA) establish the authority for both the IPTF (Annex 11) and IFOR (Annex 1A). The only reference to duration pertains to IFOR, stating that the Parties "welcome the willingness of the international community to send to the region, for a period of approximately one year, a force to assist in the implementation of the territorial and other militarily related provisions of the agreement as described herein."[45] Although Annex 1A had been fulfilled well ahead of schedule, crucial civilian aspects of the DPA (e.g., refugee returns, municipal elections, status of Brcko, war criminals) remained outstanding. Accordingly, a subsequent military force, the Stabilization Force (SFOR), was authorized by NATO and the United Nations. SFOR's expected duration was 18 months, until June 1998. The IPTF mandate was also extended, but only for a year, until December 1997, with subsequent extensions likely as long as a NATO force is present.

Owing to the crucial role performed by Ambassador Richard Holbrooke in forging the Dayton agreement, the State Department was the lead agency for orchestrating the U.S. role in implementation. As a result, a political-military plan was not developed to guide the U.S.

---

[44]Ibid., 6.
[45]*The Dayton Peace Accords*, Annex 1A, Article I, para. 1.

contribution to this effort at its inception. In essence, Dayton itself was the formula for implementation, even though it made the former warring factions responsible for implementing civilian aspects of the accord.

During the IFOR phase of the operation, the IPTF focused on monitoring local police authorities for compliance with internationally accepted standards in their daily operations and treatment of minorities. They also assisted with the September 1996 national elections. During the SFOR phase the focus shifted to vetting, training, and restructuring local police forces so their future conduct would conform to norms of democratic policing (see "Guiding Philosophy of the IPTF Mission").

The Deployment Gap

The first real test for the IPTF came when neighborhoods surrounding Sarajevo were transferred from the Bosnian Serbs to the Federation in early 1996. The Dayton agreement directed that control of certain high ground and buffer zones around Sarajevo, areas fiercely contested during the war, be transferred to the Federation so the city would not be as vulnerable to Serb artillery fire in the future. Over 100,000 ethnic Serbs populated these suburbs. Many were not permanent residents but had themselves been displaced by the fighting from other locations in Sarajevo. The transfer of these seven municipalities (i.e., Vogosca, Centar, Novi Grad, Ilijas, Hadzici, Ilidza, and Grbavica) was scheduled to take place, simultaneously, on February 4, 1996, 45 days after implementation of the DPA had begun.

As the date approached, the IPTF was not yet functional. The Commissioner and Deputy Commissioner would not arrive until mid-February, fewer than 400 monitors were on hand, and very few field stations had yet been opened. Other crucial deficiencies were described by two IFOR public safety specialists assigned to assist the IPTF during this early period:

> In addition to manpower difficulties and almost no command and control structure, IPTF faced other critical deficiencies. Habitable office space was at a premium. Also scarce were phone links, for

example, between IPTF headquarters and IFOR, the support base in Zagreb, and field stations. In addition, radios, base stations, vehicles, and petroleum products were in short supply.[46]

In addition to the unpreparedness of the IPTF, the Office of the High Representative (OHR) had not done any detailed planning for the transition. Consequently, on February 4 the High Representative and the IFOR commander announced that the transfer would be delayed. The concept would also be changed to a phased process occurring over a 6-week period ending in mid-March. This adjustment provided an opportunity for the IPTF to become partially operational and for IFOR to render crucial assistance with planning, logistics, and communications. Bosnian Serb authorities took advantage of the delay, however, to prepare a sweeping evacuation of the suburbs and to pressure Serb residents to leave.[47] Residents thoroughly ransacked fixed property so that incoming Federation citizens would inherit little more than a wasteland.

In mid-February, as the OHR, IPTF, and IFOR began to conduct the first transfer, Serb authorities implemented their own plan to relocate ethnic Serbs into the Serb Republic. They employed local Serb police and marshaled Bosnian Serb Army vehicles and logistics infrastructure to facilitate movement of inhabitants and their belongings. From late January through mid-March, some 100,000 Serbs fled Sarajevo for RS territory. At least some of the dwellings being evacuated belonged to their Serb occupants, and therefore, the claim could be made that the electrical wiring, plumbing fixtures, and window frames being carted off were rightfully theirs. In the absence of an authoritative mechanism to establish legitimate ownership, the international community was powerless to prevent homes and apartments from being gutted. In addition, various buildings and

---

[46]McCarroll and Zoufal, 8.

[47]This demonstrates the central role of public information during peace operations. In this case, the assets available to incite fear in Serbs living in the affected suburbs vastly exceeded the capacity of the IFOR Information Campaign and other public relations elements of the peace mission.

industrial facilities were either set ablaze or booby-trapped. This turmoil created an impression of lawlessness, especially when these images were captured, and to a certain extent magnified, by international news coverage.

The transfer of Sarajevo suburbs was a "defining moment" for the entire peace mission. Although the limited assets available to the IPTF were skillfully employed, the organization would clearly have been much better equipped to handle the exigencies of this crucial event if it had been more nearly operational. Indeed, experience made a significant difference. Even though planners had specifically reserved the more troublesome locations until the end, each successive transfer was handled more smoothly than the previous ones, and the relationship with IFOR became more supportive. In general, the IPTF was more successful at managing the behavior of local uniformed police forces than they were at controlling the conduct of vandals and provocateurs from both sides of the ethnic divide.

An evaluation of whether the peace mission met this defining moment successfully depends on the yardstick used. If measured against the number of persons killed (one) in this volatile operation, then the transfer could be considered a remarkable accomplishment. Much more was at stake, however, as this event set the tone for the entire operation. If Dayton was to work, Serbs and Moslems had to have confidence that they could live together in relative safety. The message derived from this experience was that even under the cognizance and apparent protection of international military and police forces, it was not safe for Serbs to remain in Moslem neighborhoods. The international community could not dissuade the Serbs from fleeing en masse. Nor could they prevent significant destruction of property and intimidation aimed at compelling others to flee when they otherwise might have remained. This event also revealed a serious enforcement gap that would persist throughout the operation. IFOR would not engage in law enforcement, and because the disruptions did not constitute an imminent threat to life, IFOR did not initially consider the circumstances to warrant a military response. The IPTF, on the other hand, had neither the authority nor the firepower to act forcefully.

As each suburb was transferred, Federation authorities took political and administrative control, an accomplishment for the Dayton Accords. IFOR had just established its presence in Bosnia, however, and all parties were anxious to gauge what this would signify. While the outcome could clearly have been much worse, it was not quite reassuring either, and IFOR would not have another "window of opportunity" to create a stronger impression on the Bosnian Serb leadership.

IPTF Relations with Entity Police Forces

Annex 11 of the DPA describes functions that the IPTF is to perform, which essentially amount to monitoring, restructuring, and mentoring the law enforcement apparatus in Bosnia.[48] Although the parties theoretically requested such assistance, the Serb Republic did not participate in negotiating the Dayton Accords and did not freely consent to such intrusions. Thus, from the very start, the relationship between the IPTF and police forces of the RS was far less constructive than it was with the Federation.

During the earliest days of the mission, IPTF monitors found police in all three ethnic communities engaged in the traditional practice of erecting checkpoints to maintain internal control. This was in direct contravention to Dayton (Freedom of Movement). Federation police forces were the first to accept the need to change their mode of operation and restructure their police forces in conformance with principles of "democratic policing" (the Bosniacs doing so more convincingly than the Bosnian Croats). RS police remained unwilling to submit to the IPTF restructuring formula until late 1997, but the differences were narrowed to two items over time. First, the RS rejected the IPTF limit of 6,000 policemen, insisting on a force equal in strength to the Federation (11,500). The second contentious issue was the requirement to provide the names of all RS policemen so they

---

[48]*The Dayton Peace Accords*, Annex 11, Article III. In addition, the Secretary-General's report prior to the deployment of the IPTF states "International Police Task Force monitors may be involved in local mediation if conflict arises as a result of actions by local police." U.N. Doc. No. S/1995/1031, para. 27, 7.

could be vetted against the International Criminal Tribunal's list of indicted war criminals.

When not subject to IPTF monitoring, RS police loyal to Radovan Karadzic continued to engage in conduct contrary to the DPA. Thus, the relationship with the RS was not one of collaboration, and at times it became confrontational (e.g., especially after the internal rupture between RS President Biljana Plavsic, with whom the international community sided, and Karadzic erupted in June 1997). In contrast, within most of the Federation, IPTF monitors were normally able to establish a professional working relationship, and this served as a catalyst for combining Bosniac and Bosnian Croat police forces into integrated entities at the municipal, cantonal, and Federation level.

In performing its monitoring function, the IPTF suffered from an enforcement gap that hindered the entire peace operation. Abuse of ethnic minorities by policemen continued to take place in all three ethnic communities.[49] Certain municipal police chiefs, moreover, were notoriously corrupt and enmeshed in networks of illicit activity along with their political mentors. Under certain circumstances, the IPTF could call upon IFOR/SFOR to back them up to compel compliance with the DPA. This was a suitable mechanism for dealing with unfolding or existing activities, such as roadblocks, weapons caches, or illegal detention of ethnic minorities. After the fact, however, the IPTF was reduced merely to conducting investigations and imploring

---

[49]The following incident, summarized by Somers and Reeves, is illustrative:

> An example of such a violation is the groundless, ethnically motivated arrest of the Bosniac police chief of Jablanica by Croat police officers on 18 July 1996 after having been brought to Croat dominated territory for an official police coordination meeting. The Chief was immediately arrested and detained by Croat authorities in West Mostar. An investigative judge commenced criminal proceedings while the Chief remained in detention. IPTF was required to standby [sic] helplessly and attempt to negotiate his release from this ethnically motivated human rights violation perpetrated upon a high ranking Bosniac police officer by high ranking Croat Criminal Justice Officials. No form of police disciplinary action or prosecution against these Croat officials has resulted from this incident.

Somers and Reeves, 23.

appropriate authorities to act in accordance with their own laws.[50] As the authors of a 1996 study of Bosnian jurisprudence concluded, these entreaties tended to have only superficial effect:

> IPTF monitors often become aware of human rights abuses or other misconduct by police officers of the Entities. Reports of these activities are usually generated and passed up the chain of command. . . . Generally, in the Entities, such conduct is condoned or overlooked and the officer is transferred, not dismissed.[51]

It remains to be seen whether efforts to restructure and reform the police (see below) will have a profound and lasting impact on police accountability to the general public and, in particular, on their treatment of minorities.[52]

Another serious constraint was lack of credibility for those monitors who were not proficient as policemen. Local Bosnian police cadres tended to regard themselves as superior to such IPTF personnel. Lack of funding also severely limited police restructuring. Only about 30 percent of the $100 million required for the 2-year program had been pledged by late 1997, almost all of which had come from the United States.

---

[50]The premission assessment prepared by the United Nations notes that IPTF "effectiveness will depend, to an important extent, on the willingness of the Parties to cooperate with it in accordance with Article IV of Annex 11 to the Peace Agreement." U.N. Doc. S/1995/1031, para. 27, 7.

[51]Somers and Reeves, 23

[52]The IPTF Commissioner's Guidance calls upon Bosnian police forces to investigate police misconduct and discrimination scrupulously, use external auditors to ensure that written policies are enforced in practice, and establish an independent review mechanism for allegations of police misconduct. Peter Fitzgerald, *The Commissioner's Guidance for Democratic Policing in the Federation of Bosnia-Herzegovina* (Sarajevo: U.N. Mission in Bosnia-Herzegovina, May 1996), Part 1, page 2; Part 2, pages 9, 16, 18.

Vetting and Restructuring of Indigenous Police Forces

The agreement on restructuring Federation police forces (also known as the Petersberg Declaration) was signed on April 25, 1996, in Bonn-Petersberg.[53] This agreement obligated the Federation to reduce its police establishments to 11,500. Even though this left a ratio of policemen to inhabitants that is nearly double the European standard, it nevertheless reduced their forces by almost two-thirds.[54] This was agreeable because government expenses would be reduced, it would bring the parties a step closer to conformity with the European model of community policing, and it would thereby afford their public security forces access to international assistance. The Petersberg Declaration also mandated a new uniform for all Federation police officers; anyone found in the old uniforms would be subject to arrest.[55]

The IPTF was a central player in cajoling the Federation and the RS to restructure their forces.[56] In April 1996, the IPTF Deputy Commissioner proposed the creation of a Commission on Restructuring for each entity for the purpose of exchanging information about the restructuring process and gaining cooperation from the relevant authorities. Although the RS stonewalled, the Commission dealing with Federation restructuring was able to make gradual progress. The membership included the Federation Minister of Interior (a Bosniac), the Deputy Minister of Interior (a Bosnian Croat), and senior IPTF and IFOR officials. The Commission agreed that all personnel allowed to remain in the Federation's police forces should meet the following requirements:

□ Educational background in policing and a performance review showing no evidence of improper conduct

---

[53] *Agreement on Restructuring the Police*, 2.

[54] With 11,500 policemen and roughly 2 million inhabitants, the Federation has a ratio of about 1:175; the European standard is 1:330.

[55] *Agreement on Restructuring the Police*, 2.

[56] Major Fred Solis, member of the IPTF Special Projects Division, which had responsibility for the vetting program, interview by author Dziedzic, September 1996.

□ No evidence of psychological disorders and a passing score on the police knowledge examination

□ Completion of induction training involving an introduction to international standards for policing, human rights, and the structure of the Federation police force.

The IPTF crafted a 40-question, multiple-choice exam designed to test comprehension of the new Bosnian Constitution, the new Police Code of Conduct, and the role of policing in a democratic society. In addition, each aspirant had to take a written psychological test. The latter was conducted by an IFOR psychologist seconded to the IPTF for this purpose. The multiple-choice exam was printed by IFOR (to avoid compromising the exam) and administered by IPTF members, with assistance from members of the Ministry of Interior.

Screening was conducted by canton, with the first exams administered in August 1996. Federation authorities sent only those applicants for testing whom they felt were qualified, thus accomplishing the first phase of "downsizing" themselves internally.[57] Out of the first batch of 1,350 taking the exam, only 29 failed the multiple-choice portion, and only one was ultimately found to be mentally imbalanced. All those vying for a position in the Federation were also screened against the files of the International Criminal Tribunal. After the exams were administered in the first several cantons, the entire process was suspended because the multiple-choice test had been compromised, and those affected were required to take a second test.

In late 1996 the IPTF recognized that the focus of its mission needed to evolve, with more emphasis given to training and the restructuring process and less to monitoring. Accordingly, they created a second Deputy Commissioner's position with specific responsibility for restructuring. In recruiting the second contingent of monitors,

---

[57]The "re-vetting" process as an IPTF function is found in *The Commissioner's Guidance, Part 1*, page 5. This document specifically states that all police officers "not selected for duty in that Canton or its Opstinas, or selected for duty at the Federal level, will be demobilized."

moreover, the IPTF sought personnel with skills relevant to the task of restructuring.

To train police officials at all levels in the Federation in the principles of democratic policing and human rights, the IPTF collaborated with bilateral programs from the United States (ICITAP), Germany, and Austria. This entailed leadership training seminars in these countries to familiarize Federation police officials with law enforcement principles such as community policing and to expose them to investigative and enforcement techniques for dealing with transnational challenges such as drug-trafficking, organized crime, and smuggling. In addition, the United States and other interested countries collaborated with the United Nations to provide basic police equipment.

The certification process for all Bosniac personnel in the Sarajevo Canton was completed in February 1997. Eight of the 10 cantons comprising the Federation, along with the 1,000-member police force of the Federation itself, had completed the certification process by December 1977. Initially only Bosniac personnel were certified because there were no Bosnian-Croat volunteers. As of August 1997, however, this barrier had been overcome in three cantons (Sarajevo, Gorazde, and Mostar), and joint Moslem-Croat police forces were formed in almost all the municipalities of these cantons. A U.S. Embassy assessment noted as of August 5 that, "Since the integration of police in Sarajevo and Gorazde Cantons and in Mostar, we note that there have been few problems among the police themselves, and joint patrols are becoming the norm."[58] Another positive step was taken in December 1997 with the inauguration of an IPTF-administered police academy with 110 cadets from all three ethnic populations. All 11,500 Federation policemen were slated to complete the 4 weeks of induction training by August 1998.[59] Assuming this process continues to progress

---

[58]AMEMBASSY SARAJEVO Message, Date-Time Group 051727 AUG 97, UNCLASS SARAJEVO 005266.

[59]The training consisted of a one-week "Human Dignity" course and a 3-week introduction to international policing standards and the reorganized Federation police structure. IPTF Workshop conducted at the National Defense University on June 26-

as planned, the IPTF anticipates there could be a viable, integrated Federation police force before the year 2000.[60]

Until September 1997 the RS had received training that served only the broader purposes of the peace mission, such as election security and VIP protection. Other programs were confined to the Federation until Biljana Plavsic agreed to permit restructuring to begin among those RS police units that were loyal to her (about a quarter of the force).

Demobilization

In spite of concerns that policemen thrown out of a job by the restructuring process would become a source of social disruption, this does not appear to have occurred in the Federation. If, in fact, the vetting process worked as intended, those who lost employment were not career policemen in the first place, but rather the minimally skilled recruits added to police ranks during the war. This outcome is probably in line, therefore, with what most of those involved expected to happen. To the extent these vetted individuals had a previous skill or trade, they presumably have attempted to return to that; this would undoubtedly include those who had been involved in criminal acitivity as well.

Judicial and Penal Reform

At least until late 1997, the Communist-era Code of Criminal Procedure and Bosnian Penal Code remained in force, and they were still being applied by many of the same judicial authorities as before the war.[61] Transforming these ingredients into a system of jurisprudence

---

27, 1997.

[60]Remarks made by Deputy Commissioner David Kriskovich at the IPTF Workshop conducted at the National Defense University June 26-27, 1997.

[61]According to a 1996 IFOR assessment of the Bosnian judiciary, "It was clear that the majority of judges we interviewed were well qualified for the positions they held. All were graduates of one of three law schools (Belgrade, Sarajevo and Banja Luka) and the majority had practiced law before their appointments." *Report by the Legal Advisor,* 14, sec. 6.1.1. According to the director of the American Bar Association's

that functions in rough conformance with internationally accepted standards, such as the European Convention on Human Rights (ECHR), is one of the basic requirements if sustainable security is to be attained in Bosnia.

IFOR's 1996 evaluation of the judiciary indicated that "approximately 50 percent of judges from Republika Srpska and Bosnian Croat courts were not aware of the European Convention on Human Rights and the fact that the fundamental freedoms set out in it were to be incorporated into the legal system."[62] In part, therefore, this transformation will require a process of education for the legal profession. The more intractable problem, however, will be to remove judicial authorities from the ambit of political elites who exploit them to perpetuate their monopoly on power.

The first step taken by the international community to address these challenges was to study the issue. This took place during the first phase of the intervention, while the IPTF was concentrating on monitoring the various police forces of Bosnia.[63] As the IPTF turned its attention to the task of police restructuring in 1997, a broad spectrum of projects has also sprung forth in the judicial realm, many based on European legal traditions and expertise.[64] In January 1997, the Minister of Justice for the Federation launched a full-scale reform of the Criminal Procedure and Penal Codes with the assistance of UNMIBH, the OHR, and the American Bar Association's Central and Eastern European Law Initiative (ABA/CEELI). By mid-1997, a draft had been presented to the Council of Europe, and that body had also become directly involved in the reform effort. When the process is complete, the

---

program in Bosnia, however, there are no established standards for judicial appointments, and the entire process is dominated exclusively by the ethnically based parties that dominate Bosnian politics. Presentation by Charles Rudnick at the American Bar Association, Washington, DC, December 12, 1997.

[62]*Report by the Legal Advisor,* 15, sec. 6.1.1.

[63]It is likely the United Nations and IPTF will give increasing attention to these issues.

[64]We are especially indebted to Lynn Thomas, who worked on legal reform issues in the U.S. Embassy during 1997, for the factual data contained in this section.

proposed amendments will be introduced into the Federation Parliament for legislative action.

Judicial reform was addressed by a range of initiatives, but these efforts were severely constrained by lack of funding. An Association of Judges was formed within the Federation in late 1996, and in mid-1997 this body collaborated with ABA/CEELI and the Federation Ministry of Justice to conduct a conference on the issue of nurturing an independent judiciary. This produced a continuing campaign for judicial autonomy and for a judicial training institute to educate judges in the new criminal code, constitution, and international conventions that have either come into force recently or are expected to in the future. One product of this effort was a formal robing ceremony for Federation Justices, the intent of which was to burnish the image of judges and lend prestige to their office. Indicative of the distance still to be traveled, though, the Constitutional Court for Bosnia-Herzegovina was one of the last institutions of the Dayton Accords to be established. While it formally came into existence in April 1997, it had heard no cases as of late 1997. A Constitutional Court had also been created for the Federation. It had just begun to accept cases dealing with some of the most sensitive interethnic issues, such as cantonal privatization laws and symbols used for cantonal flags, as of December 1997. Trial activity within other courts throughout the Federation and the RS is continually monitored by the Office of the High Representative.

Initiatives specifically directed at lawyers and prosecutors include an education program regarding the ECHR and other measures to democratize the legal process run by the International Human Rights Law Group. On their own initiative, prosecuting lawyers have established the Federation Prosecutors Association.

To guide reform of the corrections system, the Crime Prevention and Criminal Justice Division of the U.N. Development Program has developed a procedural manual. Finally, educational programs addressing democratic rights and responsibilities serving both legal professionals and the general public have been provided by the OSCE Rule of Law program.

While each of these discrete international programs is beneficial, as yet there is no formal mechanism to coordinate or integrate them into a coherent reform program. To fill in this void, ABA/CEELI began convening ad hoc monthly meetings open to interested parties as a means of sharing information and informally coordinating efforts. Although the Office of the High Representative would appear to be the logical body to perform this function, during the first 2 years after the DPA was signed, it had neglected to do so.

Support for Elections

To monitor the September 14, 1996, national elections effectively while preserving the capacity to respond to potential disturbances, the IPTF developed a plan allowing for a more flexible deployment posture. Only 600 of its roughly 1,700 personnel were left to man static positions (i.e., at IPTF headquarters, Regional and District headquarters, and IPTF stations). The remainder were formed into 400 two-man Mobile Patrol Teams (providing coverage of 19 voter routes and 4,000 polling places), with a reserve comprised of a dozen strategically located "Hot-Spot" teams, each having 25 personnel.[65] The IPTF collaborated with IFOR to identify the most likely trouble spots and then established coordinated patrolling patterns for these areas. A number of OSCE officials were also incorporated into IPTF patrols on election day.

The IPTF gave particular attention to Inter-Entity Boundary Line (IEBL) crossing points along voter routes. Their function was to monitor local police as they searched vehicles and occupants for weapons and contraband. During the election, only wanted criminals could be detained by local police forces. After the search was completed at the crossing points, drivers received a certificate, signed by both the local police and IPTF, exempting them from further searches that day. Prior to the elections, IFOR assigned military communications specialists to IPTF headquarters, and on election day,

---

[65]Pre-election briefing in CIMIC headquarters by IFOR Liaison Officer assigned to the IPTF, September 13, 1996.

senior IPTF officials were incorporated into the IFOR command post. The intent was to ensure rapid communications with IFOR should IPTF patrols encounter a hostile situation requiring a response.[66]

In contrast to the controversy swirling around other aspects of the elections (e.g., intimidation of opposition candidates during the campaign, restrictions on their access to the media, and manipulation of the voter registry for municipal elections by the RS), the actual conduct of elections on September 14 was remarkably free of incidents. Several factors contributed to the absence of serious disruptions, but the *sine qua non* was the cooperation of governing elites in all three entities. Postponement of the municipal elections removed contention from the process, because the national-level elections then became contests over who would govern within each of the ethnically defined entities. In all three cases, nationalist leaders, exploiting the advantage of incumbency to the fullest, expected to be victorious. Thus, elections would confer a mantle of legitimacy on them that was useful for their aims. This prospect motivated Interior Ministers from each of the entities to work with the IPTF in developing a security plan for the election and instructing local police to implement it.

The IPTF Commissioner sought to ensure compliance in the field by personally visiting each anticipated trouble spot and obtaining the commitment of the local police chief to cooperate with the election security plan. As one experienced observer noted: "The IEBL crossing plan developed by the Interior Ministers is an excellent example of strategic instructions issued to local police for the accomplishment of a sensitive mission and the local police executing the instructions in a calm and competent manner."[67] Without this, the efforts of the international community would merely have served to limit damage caused by inevitable confrontations and protests.

While the collaboration of local authorities was pivotal, prospects for tranquility on election day were certainly enhanced by the extensive

---

[66]They still had to depend on their own communication net: 73 base radios with a 10-mile radius, and 178 handheld radios of 1-mile range.

[67]Lieutenant Colonel Mike Bailey to Ambassador Robert Oakley, memorandum dated October 3, 1996: "To provide you with thoughts regarding the IPTF."

planning and coordination undertaken by the IPTF and its counterparts, especially IFOR and the OSCE. The IPTF's advanced preparations were assessed by a veteran U.S. military peacekeeper, as follows:

> The IPTF had a superb plan to assist the local police as it prepared for the September 14 elections. The IPTF prepared a comprehensive duties and responsibilities handbook for the local police as well as established a national election planning cell to facilitate planning and coordination in support of the elections.[68]

It was also vitally important that members of the international community with electoral responsibilities (OSCE, IFOR, and IPTF) had made extensive efforts to coordinate their actions. IFOR, in particular, provided crucial support in the form of Civil Affairs planning specialists for the OSCE and the IPTF, as well as logistic support for distribution and postelection collection of ballots.

When the oft-postponed municipal elections were subsequently held in mid-September 1997, the IPTF again played a crucial role in ensuring the support of ministry-level and local police authorities. The same basic approach was taken to maintaining order on election day as had been used a year earlier, with a similarly peaceful outcome. Shortly after these elections, however, the IPTF suffered a tragic loss in a helicopter accident that claimed the lives of Deputy Commissioner David "Kris" Kriskovich and four other senior IPTF officials.

Coordination and Cooperation

Guiding Philosophy of the IPTF Mission

Perhaps the most enduring contribution this mission has made to the conduct of future CIVPOL operations has been the articulation and operational enactment of the concept of "democratic policing." A step beyond the "community policing" approach adopted in Haiti, this

---

[68]Lieutenant Colonel Mike Bailey to Michael Arietti, memorandum dated September 26, 1996: "Bosnia Trip Report."

model explicitly links reform of the police with transformation of the political context. The essence of this innovative approach to policing is captured in the IPTF "Commissioner's Guidance Notes for the Implementation of Democratic Policing Standards:"

> For Bosnia-Herzegovina, the police must realign their missions from the protection of the state to the protection of citizen's rights. Service to the public must become the police's calling. . . . A democratic police force is not concerned with people's beliefs or associates, their movements or conformity to state ideology. . . . Instead, the police force of a democracy is concerned strictly with the preservation of safe communities and the application of criminal law equally to all people, without fear or favor.[69]

The "democratic transition of the Federation" thus became more than a byproduct of IPTF activities.[70] In the words of Commissioner Peter Fitzgerald, "It is a mandate."[71] To execute this mandate, the Commissioner directed that action be taken in three essential areas:

☐ Affirmative police activities by public security establishments to demonstrate that their role is public service, not state control
☐ Acceptance of a democratic Standard for Policing by which each policeman's performance would be measured
☐ Demobilization of superfluous personnel and "re-vetting" of the force to ensure that those with backgrounds incompatible with democratic policing were discharged.[72]

While the detailed articulation of this concept in a 40-page document was a major advance, devising an effective scheme for implementation is an even more vital, and challenging, matter. That

---

[69]"Commissioner's Guidance Notes for the Implementation of Democratic Policing Standards in the Federation of Bosnia-Herzegovina," in *Commissioner's Guidance, Part 1*, 1-2.

[70]Ibid., 1.

[71]Ibid.

[72]Ibid.

remains a work in progress as of our publication date, but clear progress has been made within the Federation. Very little substantive interaction with RS police had been possible until September 1997 due to the recalcitrance of the Pale leadership. As a result of a power struggle between RS President Biljana Plavsic and de facto Bosnian Serb power broker, Radovan Karadzic, police forces loyal to Plavsic agreed to participate in the restructuring program in September 1997.

Relationship Between the Military and CIVPOL

International responsibility for security matters is divided in the Dayton Peace Accords between the IPTF and IFOR. Annex 11 confers the tasks of monitoring, inspecting, training, and assisting Bosnia's law enforcement and judicial systems to the IPTF. Military aspects of DPA are treated separately in Annex 1A (e.g., separation of the Former Warring Factions, establishment of the Zone of Separation, and cantonment of heavy weapons). Within the confines of their respective mandates, both IFOR/SFOR and the IPTF performed well. When called upon to support implementation of "civilian" aspects of Dayton, however, acute difficulties periodically arose. Some of the key provisions of Dayton (e.g., freedom of movement, refugee return, apprehension of war criminals, municipal governance, and the status of Brcko) regularly revealed an "enforcement gap" that remained largely unresolved well into the second year of the peace mission.[73]

Freedom of Movement. One of the more egregious examples of interference with freedom of movement occurred in Mostar in February 1997. The Bosnian Croat Deputy Police Chief from West Mostar and numerous other Croatian police officers were observed by IPTF monitors firing point blank into a group of Moslems seeking to visit a Moslem cemetery located in the Croat sector. One Moslem was killed and 21 were wounded. Contributing to this outcome was an apparent failure to inform SFOR of the impending event and the subsequent lack of military backup for the IPTF. In spite of an IPTF investigation and

---

[73]We are indebted to Dr. Ivo Daalder for this approach to conceptualizing the problem of implementing the Dayton Accords.

indisputable evidence of police misconduct (including photos), the international community was unable to ensure more than token accountability for these actions. Only after intense international pressure had been applied was the Deputy Police Chief removed from his position.[74]

On a more routine basis, freedom of movement was regularly impeded because policing had traditionally been equated with the use of traffic checkpoints/roadblocks. Unless authorized by the IPTF, this practice was forbidden but difficult to control owing to the ease of establishing impromptu checkpoints. Unarmed IPTF monitors, moreover, were not always sufficiently compelling to persuade local police to cease such activity. The IPTF was thus dependent on IFOR/SFOR to provide the muscle to compel compliance. It was not until the early stages of the SFOR mission that a checkpoint policy was established that routinized military support to the IPTF. The policy required local police to request authorization to set up checkpoints, and when necessary, unauthorized checkpoints were dismantled with SFOR assistance.

Refugee Return. A severe test of IFOR and the IPTF regarding this issue arose during the fall of 1996. Targeted for resettlement by Moslem authorities were communities located in the Zone of Separation (ZOS); however, these areas also tended to be strategic high ground overlooking vulnerable RS choke points. Consequently, each incursion by a large group of Moslems into the ZOS provoked a hostile response from the RS, typically involving MUPs. Since the IPTF had no capacity to control such encounters, IFOR/SFOR were repeatedly thrust into the midst of ugly confrontations between Moslems and Serbs. The most serious of these clashes, at Mahala in August 1996, was aggravated because the RS reacted to an influx of

---

[74]Three Bosnian Croat officers were also suspended from duty, but their prison sentences were voided after conviction for criminal maltreatment in what amounted to a "show trial." LANDCENT transcript of press briefing: February 26, 1997, NATO/SFOR web page, www.nato.int/ifor/landcent/t970226a.htm. Also, *This Week in Bosnia-Hercegovina*, Bosnia Action Coalition, http://world.std.com/~slm/twibo223.html, February 23, 1997, 1, and March 24, 1997, 1.

Moslems by sending armed MUPs to the scene in flagrant violation of the Dayton Accords. After IFOR detained and disarmed the offending policemen, RS authorities nearby in Zvornik responded by surrounding the local IPTF station with a surly crowd of demonstrators and effectively holding IPTF personnel hostage for 6 hours until the situation could be defused.

Control of RS Special Police. The challenge of asserting international control over MUPs in the RS reflects many of the difficulties associated with implementation of Dayton. Throughout the first 18 months of the peace process, RS Special Police obstructed implementation by hindering freedom of movement for non-Serbs, preventing return of refugees and displaced persons to their homes in the RS, and provoking the international community, including IFOR and the IPTF, with threatening incidents. RS Internal Affairs Minister Dragan Kijac stonewalled on police restructuring, asserting that even the number of police employed in the RS was a state secret. The unarmed IPTF was powerless to deal with MUP strong-arm tactics and obstructionism.

The Special Police, however, were included under provisions of Article 1-A of the Dayton Accords, along with regular military forces, as follows:

> Each party shall ensure that all personnel and organizations with military capability under its control or within territory under its control, including armed civilian groups, national guards, army reserves, military police, and the Ministry of Internal Affairs Special Police (MUP) (hereinafter "Forces") comply with this Annex.[75]

When IFOR oversaw the process of confining heavy weapons to cantonment areas, it did so for all units possessing such items (whether Special Police or regular military). This did not address the status of MUP personnel, however. Within the Federation, the IPTF

---

[75]The Dayton Peace Accords, Article 1, Annex 11, para 1, *General Framework Agreement for Peace.*

restructuring program eliminated the MUPs, but the RS was another matter.

For some 18 months, MUPs in the RS flouted Dayton by carrying long-barreled rifles, grenades, and other weapons and acting as a local enforcement arm of the RS government and the Serb Democratic Party (SDS) under the control of Radovan Karadzic. They organized much of the continuing "ethnic cleansing" in the RS that occurred after Dayton implementation began in December 1995. They also played a key role in coercing the exodus of Serbs residing in Sarajevo during the transfer of Serb-occupied suburbs to the Federation in early 1996.

After Biljana Plavsic was elected RS President in the September 1996 national elections, the stage was set for an internal RS power struggle. Eventually, Plavsic began to focus on the police, and on Kijac in particular, as a source of smuggling, black marketeering, and graft. She also accused Karadzic of misappropriating millions of dollars in tax revenues from state coffers. In June 1997, Plavsic suspended Kijac, sparking a confrontation with Karadzic. This provided the international community an opportunity to act against the MUPs. In July and August, SFOR formally asserted control over these personnel as provided in Annex 1-A. SFOR began regularly inspecting their stations (e.g., Banja Luka and Doboj), confiscating illegal weapons and equipment, and cashiering unacceptable personnel. Movements of MUP personnel were subject to careful SFOR scrutiny. This significantly curtailed their capacity in the RS to engage in paramilitary activities inimical to Dayton.[76]

War Criminals, Brcko, and Municipal Governance. Each of these issues has defied full implementation as envisaged by the Dayton Accords, placing extraordinary demands on IFOR and the IPTF. To date, only three operations have been conducted to apprehend war criminals militarily (Prijedor, Vitez, and Eastern Slavonia); however, the quest for a solution has included consideration of mobilizing an international gendarmerie for this purpose. Similarly, the status of

---

[76]MUPs in the Federation had effectively been brought under IPTF authority via the police restructuring program (see "Status of Public Security Apparatus," above).

Brcko remains unresolved. Instead of deciding the status of that strategic city, international arbitration placed it under OHR administration in March 1997 for at least a year. To support this administration, the authorized strength of the IPTF was increased to 2,027, and an IPTF superstation with over 250 monitors was established in Brcko. In August 1997, after RS police became enmeshed in the Plavsic-Karadzic power struggle, SFOR troops were portrayed by RS media as attempting to take control of the Brcko station on behalf of Plavsic. This provoked an uprising among the Bosnian Serb populace, compelling the evacuation of IPTF personnel and leaving SFOR troops face to face with a hostile mob. Two soldiers sustained injuries, and SFOR ultimately resorted to use of tear gas to control the situation.

The Dayton-mandated election of municipal councils may also result in future enforcement dilemmas. In a handful of cases (e.g., Srebrenica and Brcko), a nonresident ethnic population voted their candidates into office, but their capacity to govern a community openly hostile to their presence remains to be seen.[77] The attempt to implement this aspect of the DPA will also test the resources and ingenuity of SFOR and the IPTF.

The issues cited above illustrate several aspects of the "enforcement gap" in Bosnia. First, these gaps in enforcement pertained to implementation of Dayton, not enforcement of local law. Police forces in each of Bosnia's ethnic communities were capable of maintaining order and applying local law, even though their procedures did not necessarily conform to principles of due process and equal protection. Second, the police were one of the major instruments used by obstructionists in the RS to thwart implementation of the Dayton Accords. In part this was by default, because military activity was highly circumscribed by the DPA and the presence of IFOR/SFOR. Third, IFOR initially sought to remain aloof from law enforcement functions, both out of a desire to avoid a mission for which their units

---

[77]Bosnian Serbs have threatened to arrest any of these elected officials who attempt to occupy their elected posts.

were neither trained nor equipped and in keeping with the division of responsibility in the peace treaty. The dependence of the IPTF on military back-up and the absence of other sources of international leverage, however, meant that the military contingent inevitably had to respond to serious breaches of Dayton. Whereas the initial IFOR posture was to deny that they were the "911" for IPTF emergencies, after several months the inevitability of this role was explicitly acknowledged. It was not until the SFOR phase of the mission, however, that this support became routinized.[78] Finally, when the parties were at least willing to acquiesce to implementation of certain provisions of Dayton (e.g., the elections of September 1996 and 1997), the IPTF and IFOR/SFOR were able to collaborate effectively to maintain order.

Military assistance, principally in the form of Civil Affairs police specialists, was also invaluable in establishing an operational capability for the IPTF and reducing the initial "deployment gap." Their role was especially crucial in planning for the pivotal transfer to Moslem control of Sarajevo suburbs. To help the IPTF begin functioning as expeditiously as possible, IFOR detailed a half dozen Civil Affairs officers with backgrounds in planning, operations, training, and logistics. Among their contributions were the following:

□ Establishment of the IPTF Command Center, including the overall design, operational procedures, and communication net linking IPTF Headquarters with stations in the field and with IFOR

□ Secondment of a logistics specialist to serve as acting Chief of Logistics to manage the influx of personnel and procurement of radios, vehicles, and facilities so monitors could begin performing their duties

---

[78]As recounted by Jock Covey, Special Assistant to the President for Implementation of the Dayton Peace Accords at the National Security Council, during a presentation to a conference, "Bosnia: U.S. Options after June 1998" conducted by the Congressional Research Service and General Accounting Office, November 6, 1997.

☐ Secondment of a senior police administrator to serve as Special Assistant to the Chief of Staff, in particular to draft the plan for transfer of the Sarajevo suburbs and to coordinate IFOR support for the IPTF during this operation

☐ Secondment of a training specialist to the training base at Camp Pleso, Croatia to provide curriculum assistance and classroom instruction to meet the initial surge of 200 incoming police monitors per week.

Once the IPTF had become fully operational, Civil Affairs personnel provided liaison between the two organizations, ensuring that operationally relevant information was exchanged daily. IFOR also provided certain forms of logistic assistance (see Logistic Support, above). Another IFOR responsibility was to be prepared to evacuate IPTF personnel, if necessary. Civil Affairs personnel were responsible for coordinating these procedures between the two organizations. In addition to their daily function of exchanging operational information, they also provided the interface between IFOR and the IPTF in preparing for and supporting national and municipal elections and monitoring and dealing with the organized crime threat.

Relationship with U.N. Headquarters

In addition to the U.N.'s inherent bureaucratic lethargy, the IPTF faced an uphill battle for resources because of its unfortunate parentage. This CIVPOL mission was a creature of the U.S.-brokered Dayton Accord, which arose after many in the United States had heaped condemnation on the United Nations for the demise of UNPROFOR. Yet, when it came to finding a sponsor for the IPTF after the Dayton Accords had been drawn up, the United Nations was the only viable alternative. It took time for the IPTF to recover from the animus that had developed between the United States and the United Nations. Nor was the United Nations blessed with surplus funds to commit to this unanticipated contingency, a condition the United States certainly had a hand in creating.

Conclusions

Success of the Mission

The publication of this book occurs while the peace operation in Bosnia is far from completed, therefore any observations regarding the success of this mission must be regarded as preliminary. If we measure progress against the goal of sustainable security, however, there is clearly a considerable distance yet to travel. Implementation of Annex 1A by IFOR and the IPTF police restructuring and training programs will not provide sufficient prophylaxis against a resumption of conflict in Bosnia. To tout these commendable achievements too vocally at this stage would risk declaring the operation a success even though the patient (i.e., a multi-ethnic Bosnia) would almost assuredly perish if taken off life-support any time soon. The peace that prevailed under IFOR and SFOR was deceptive because it was a product of external intervention.

There can be no confidence that peace will be self-sustaining because the core issue in dispute—integration vs. partition—has not been resolved. Without consensus among the parties on the question of Bosnia's identity, many matters integral to the DPA, such as refugee returns, municipal governance, the status of Brcko, or the disposition of war criminals, will continue to be regarded as matters of national survival. The outcome of each will heavily influence Bosnia's ultimate destiny. The various police forces will be crucial players in the process that determines the outcome of each of these critical disputes. The most basic deficiency is not one of police capabilities, but rather, how those capabilities are employed. As long as xenophobic political leaders command the allegiance of police forces, the public security apparatus will continue to be exploitable as an instrument of repression and nationalistic policies.

Respect for Human Rights

This issue is at the core of the quandary in Bosnia. Ethnic populations were the targets of violence during the war, more so than opposing armies. The outcome was "ethnic cleansing," and the carnage stopped just short of its ultimate objective. For Bosnia's three nations to live peaceably together in a single state, respect for minority rights must become integral to its political and judicial processes. Abuse of minorities continues to be a chronic concern,[79] however, and no ethnic group had a totally unblemished record in this regard. A study conducted in 1996 provided the following assessment:

> The animosities that grew out of the war continue to smolder. Police officers act out these animosities with impunity. There continues to be no accountability for lawless or improper actions at any level in the police structure. Interviews of IPTF monitors in both Entities corroborate the attitude that a Serb police officer only recognizes as criminal an act against a Serb victim, a Bosniac police officer only recognizes as criminal acts against a Bosniac and a Croat officer only acknowledges crime where Croats are the victims.[80]

The Police

Until recently, intimidation (or worse) by police against members of other ethnic groups was likely to be equated with the promotion of public safety by the majority in their communities. The ethos of police officers from all three groups, at least until 1996, had been devoid of precepts such as equality before the law and respect for the rights of minorities.[81] Initial indications from three cantons that had been restructured in the Federation by late August 1997 were positive, but the RS was still lagging far behind. If restructuring is to have an

---

[79]"The human rights abuses take many forms, ranging from willful blindness toward enforcing laws to overt criminality. A common form of misconduct is police participation and/or complicity in the kidnapping of members of ethnic minorities in order to amass candidates for the prisoner exchanges which occur on a regular basis with the full knowledge of the international community, including IPTF." Somers and Reeves, 33.

[80]Ibid., 20.

[81]Characteristic "abuses in the present criminal justice system are carried out by the police. The abuses range from affirmative acts perpetrated upon citizens to dereliction of duty. Some misconduct is carried out individually, other conspiratorially. Much of the misconduct is ethnically motivated. It is unclear whether or not it is the result of individual prejudice or of official orders and institutional, systemic ethnic hatred." Ibid., 32.

enduring effect, policemen at the municipal level would have to be held accountable for their conduct, and leadership at the Ministry of Interior and senior political levels would have to refrain from trampling on minority rights in premeditated actions ordered from above. It would not be sufficient, therefore, to convert the police into a public-service-oriented agency for the majority population alone. It is even more crucial, and demanding, to gain acceptance for concepts such as due process and human rights for all, without regard for ethnic origin.

The Courts, Legal Code, and Prison System

The IPTF's path-breaking democratic policing initiative will need to be replicated in judicial and penal realms, because these are also chronically prone to abuse.[82] One aspect of the system that appears to merit particular scrutiny is pretrial detention. This is a major concern given the preference of police for interrogating suspects, as opposed to the tedium of gathering physical evidence. There are numerous areas where safeguards are weak, disregarded, or lacking. These include manipulation and abuse of the supposed 3-day limit on police detention, the regular failure to notify detainees of their rights, and the lack of prohibitions against use of illegally obtained evidence.[83] These serious flaws in Bosnian jurisprudence were not resolved by the DPA, as the Legal Advisor for the HQ ACE Rapid Reaction Corps concluded:

> Although GFAP (the General Framework Agreement for Peace or Dayton) contained provisions related to the Constitution, Human Rights and Policing, insufficient attention was, in our view, given to the administration of justice and the development of a system of laws

---

[82]"The political manipulation of police, prosecutors, the judiciary and corrections personnel which was prevalent in authoritarian states has not been substantially diminished by the independence of Bosnia and Herzegovina. The democratic principles set forth in the ECHR have not as yet taken root. . . . An independent judiciary which is essential to rule of law taking hold, however, has not yet evolved. The same can be said of the office of the prosecutor." Ibid., p. 38.

[83]"The pretrial period of the criminal process is, in most cases, subject to abuse, fails to conform to the European Convention on Human Rights, and requires the most immediate corrective measures." *Report of the Legal Advisor*, 18, sec. 7.1.3.

which not only comply with Human Rights but also and more importantly ensure that they are protected. In this respect GFAP and the Constitutions of both entities seem to have created an unwieldy structure of Human Rights Courts and subsidiary organizations which sit on top of a system which is almost certainly fundamentally flawed. While breaches of Human Rights will almost certainly be identified by this system, they will be difficult to rectify unless a properly functioning, independent system of justice, at all levels is developed to protect them.[84]

Even the most well-conceived judicial reform plan can be confident only of resolving deficiencies in skills, knowledge, and materiel. Absent the political will to permit the intended democratic transformation to take place, the result will merely be a legalistic mirage. As long as the courts continue to respond to political direction from above, the judiciary can be expected to serve more as a barrier to police reform than as a watchdog over police conduct. To date, an autonomous judiciary and independent prosecutor's office have not yet evolved, and detention of uncharged individuals persists within the penal system.[85] Important measures have been taken within the Federation to oxygenate a democratic rule of law. This process has scarcely begun in the RS, and ultimately the outcome will be determined by the amount of political will that emerges for a viable Federation and a multiethnic Bosnia.

The Federation and the RS, vestiges of a Communist-era police state now bereft of an ideology to lend them a whiff of legitimacy, are political regimes in transition. Municipal police chiefs and Ministers of Interior have operated as agents of public control for the leadership of their respective ruling parties. The only outcome compatible with a multiethnic state would be a democracy that preserves minority rights

---

[84]Ibid., 24, sec. 11.1.1.

[85]"Incidents involving the police chief of Jablanica and the four abducted Serbs who turned up in Sarajevo's Centar jail indicate that all components of the criminal justice system in post-Dayton Bosnia and Herzegovina are still willing to use the power of their office to compromise the interests of justice in favor of advancing a political agenda or for personal advantage." Somers and Reeves, 38.

while practicing majority rule. Human rights monitoring organizations, such as the Commission on Human Rights created by Annex 6 of the DPA (including the Ombudsman and Human Rights chamber) need to be nurtured so they can perform a watchdog function over formal institutions of government. Sustaining them will require long-term international engagement, especially by entities with ECHR-based legal traditions. Bosnian human rights organizations, in turn, must develop robust linkages with counterparts internationally. All this will require an arduous process of institutional development coupled with a campaign to educate the citizenry so they understand their rights and obligations in a democracy. This represents the peace-building phase of a peace operation, and it will take many years to complete. It is not yet certain, however, that Bosnia is solidly headed down this path.

Lessons Learned

Even though an overall evaluation of the success of this mission would be premature, the IPTF has accumulated nearly 2 years of experience with the process of mobilizing and operating a CIVPOL mission. Drawing upon this experience, it is possible to highlight some innovations that ought to be continued, and it is also possible to identify persistent deficiencies that ought to be remedied.

Mandate

The foundation for any peace operation is the mandate. In this case, Annex 11 of the DPA serves this purpose, establishing the IPTF's functions and authority. The factor that determines whether the mandate can be executed successfully is the extent to which the parties actually consent to ends that CIVPOL seeks to serve. At the core of the "enforcement gap" was the fiction that all the parties consented to full implementation of the DPA. Compounding this, Annex 11 clearly makes the parties themselves primarily responsible for maintaining law and order.[86] When they failed to do this, the typical response from the international community was to restate this responsibility emphatically and insist that the parties meet their obligations. The issue, however, was not a lack of clarity about the meaning of the DPA. There were no effective sanctions to close the gaps in either law enforcement or compliance with the DPA, other than compellance by IFOR/SFOR, and this also had its constraints.

Clearly, the international community needs to develop instruments that can give it greater leverage in such circumstances. Economic conditionality risks being overburdened, and it is not always a precise instrument. To deal with police misconduct, the clout of the IPTF to carry out its mandate has been strengthened by giving it authority over which personnel would be retained in public security forces in Bosnia. Anyone decertified for police duty would be subject to removal if they seek to continue functioning in a police capacity, with the IPTF backed by the military contingent, as required. The military contingent might be better positioned to support such IPTF enforcement action if constabulary or gendarme units were to be incorporated into the force mix for this purpose. To make this effective, the IPTF should bolster its capacity to conduct investigations, including those for corruption and organized crime. Additionally, the international community should consider whether it ought to become the paymaster for municipal, cantonal, and national-level police forces until public security in Bosnia is self-sustaining.

Premission Assessments

In December 1995, the U.N. assessment team focused essentially on numerical factors such as the total number of personnel and police stations in the forces of each ethnic community. This was inadequate for several reasons. First, it was sufficient only to determine the

---

[86]"The Parties shall provide a safe and secure environment for all persons in their respective jurisdictions, by maintaining civilian law enforcement agencies operating in accordance with internationally recognized standards and with respect for internationally recognized human rights and fundamental freedoms, and by taking such other measures as appropriate." DPA, Annex 11, Article 1.

number of monitors required, neglecting the other missions assigned to the IPTF by Annex 11 of the Dayton Accords (e.g., training, advising, and restructuring Bosnian police forces). Second, it failed to take into account the extent to which the IPTF would confront "enforcement gaps" as it attempted to carry out its mandate owing to the evident lack of political commitment from Bosnian Serbs and Croats to Dayton. Thus, without advanced planning or coordination with IFOR for such contingencies and lacking resources to respond, treaty enforcement became a major deficiency. The credibility of the IPTF suffered considerably, especially with IFOR. Future assessments, therefore, should take into account the manning and resources needed to perform all CIVPOL missions, as well as the extent to which limited political consent among the disputants might constrain the CIVPOL mission.

Recruitment of CIVPOL Monitors
The Bosnia experience highlights four deficiencies in the CIVPOL recruitment process:

☐ An inordinate delay in mobilizing personnel. This is one of the primary factors that aggravated the "deployment gap" (the other being logistics). The IPTF did not reach full strength until about 5 to 6 months into the operation, the military aspect of which was initially scheduled to end after a year.[87] This is a systemic problem that was compounded in this case by a lack of advance notice and by constraints on the capacity of the IPTF to conduct premission training which meant that only 200 monitors could be fielded per week.

☐ The caliber of monitors. The approach to recruitment has been ad hoc, yet the requirement to field a mission has normally been immediate. This has not been conducive to producing only top-flight volunteers. All too often misfits have crept in because they

---

[87]When the number of deployed personnel reached 1,300 at the end of April 1996, the Secretary-General declared the mission "operational." Personnel strength did not rise above 1,600 until July 1996. Authorized strength was 1,721.

were the ones most readily available. Thus, various contingents, including the United States, had to repatriate a number of monitors because they were unqualified. Other nations had particular difficulty producing monitors fluent in English and, to a lesser extent, policemen who could drive. This has had a corrosive impact on mission capabilities, exacerbating the challenges associated with treaty enforcement and police reform. To rectify this, the United Nations began to send Selection Assistance Teams to contributing countries to screen volunteers prior to their departure for Bosnia. This markedly improved the quality of subsequent CIVPOL cadres and should become standard U.N. practice.

☐ The mix of ranks and skills required to perform the CIVPOL mission. During the first months of the operation, the principal task was monitoring, and special skills were not a particular concern. Once the focus shifted to training and mentoring, however, there was a need for special expertise, such as field training officers. When the second IPTF contingent was recruited, therefore, countries were asked to fill specific personnel needs. This is another innovation that ought to become standard practice in future missions. Rank is also an issue because an overabundance of senior officers can flood the headquarters and generate endless squabbles over relative seniority while billets in the field are shortchanged.[88]

☐ The capacity of the IPTF to recruit monitors from democratic nations capable of imparting the necessary skills of democratic policing. The ability of the IPTF to nurture a democratic transition in policing is proportional to its success in attracting monitors of this caliber. This issue will become even more crucial for the third rotation that will assuredly be needed after the current mandate expires in December 1997. The constraint in this regard is not the United Nations, which has shown commendable flexibility, but

---

[88]CIVPOL assignments may be regarded as sinecures in some places because the level of remuneration may be vastly superior to the pay scale back home.

rather the capacity to recruit additional personnel from stable democracies, especially from Europe. This will happen only if the nations involved understand this to be a priority.

Premission Training

Several IPTF training innovations are worthy of replication. First, all monitors were given human-rights training. This is vital if monitors are to understand clearly the fundamental standards they are expected to enforce and actually do so in a consistent manner. Second, a program of in-service training was initiated during the second rotation to address shortcomings that the training unit had identified by surveying IPTF personnel and supervisors. Given that CIVPOL contingents will always contain an eclectic mix of skills and abilities, one way to enhance and standardize their capabilities is through in-service training. Presumably this might help to return CIVPOL personnel to their local police forces with enhanced capabilities, serving everyone's purposes.

Logistics Support

The "deployment gap" in the Bosnian case was exacerbated by the failure to consider the future needs of the IPTF when U.N. assets were transferred to IFOR. While the acquisition of UNPROFOR's communications systems, vehicles, and equipment by IFOR clearly accelerated its timelines, this also retarded IPTF ability to field an operational contingent. Because it was not incorporated into the military logistics system, the IPTF was left to build its own operation from the ground up even thought its predecessor, UNPROFOR, had been the dominant international organization in Bosnia before Dayton. Because it was under UNMIBH auspices—as opposed to being part of an integrated mission with combined military and CIVPOL components—logistical limitations became a chronic operational concern. The inevitable delays and shortfalls only aggravated the "enforcement gap" with IFOR, which ultimately had no other choice but to provide essential assets, such as communications capabilities, so the two organizations could work together. Even though the situation has gradually improved, the IPTF continues to be hampered logistically, especially by a shortfall in reliable transportation.[89] As the peace operation evolves, the military presence will presumably diminish, and the significance of the IPTF will correspondingly increase. Thus, the "enforcement gap" between the two organizations could easily grow unless the IPTF develops an adequate logistics support system.

IPTF Relationship with the Military Contingent

After strong initial reservations about the IPTF, which persisted during much of the IFOR phase, most military commanders and planners eventually came to recognize the centrality of the IPTF for the accomplishment of their own mission and to the creation of conditions propitious to a military end state. From an operational standpoint, daily IPTF reporting of conditions throughout Bosnia was a potentially invaluable data source. If properly exploited, this could help anticipate trouble spots and provide a more sophisticated understanding of the organized crime threat. Even though unarmed, the IPTF can make vital contributions to implementation of Dayton by restructuring local police forces, monitoring their conduct (especially toward minorities), and assisting military forces in their efforts to bring RS Special Police under Annex 1-A of the DPA. For the IPTF to be credible and viable, however, it was essential to have military reinforcement available. Rather than constituting a drain on scarce military resources, an effective relationship between the military contingent and IPTF can serve as a peace multiplier, minimizing the number of occasions when military force must actually be applied. It was not until the SFOR phase, however, as the IPTF became a more competent organization and military commanders became more amenable to collaboration, that the potential benefit of military-CIVPOL interaction was more fully realized.

---

[89]Even the vehicle the Deputy Commissioner was driving in June 1997, presumably one of the best in the fleet, had over 50,000 miles. Comment by Deputy Commissioner Kriskovich at a National Defense University workshop, June 26-27, 1997.

Objective Standards for Democratic Policing

Perhaps the most significant contribution the IPTF will make to the conduct of future peace operations is the articulation of specific, observable standards for democratic policing. IPTF commissioners found existing international standards of policing to be so general that they were of no use. Accordingly, they developed and operationalized the concept of "democratic policing." A major stride forward will have been taken if these principles become recognized as "the international standards of policing."

This emphasis on standards is an explicit recognition that merely supplying the capacity to perform policing functions (i.e., via training programs, academies, and material) is insufficient. The more crucial issue is the function served by police. The same instrument can be used either to repress freedoms or to protect them. Thus, it is vital that future CIVPOL operations be armed with a clear standard of conduct to serve both as a goal for the international community's efforts to fill the "institutional gap" and as a tool to evaluate the conduct of the indigenous police force. This is particularly vital in the context of a U.N. activity that casts its recruitment net globally and will inevitably include monitors from a wide array of regimes with an equally disparate understanding of the policing function.

INSTITUTIONAL LEARNING WITHIN ICITAP

CHARLES T. CALL

Introduction

With the end of the Cold War, police forces have found a new place in international security. Drawn into a plethora of internal conflicts, the major Western powers are dialing 911 more and more frequently. As a result of providing humanitarian relief in Somalia's failed state, ousting dictators in Panama and Haiti, and keeping the peace in Bosnia and Rwanda, the big powers are recognizing the importance of an effective and humane police force to provide the internal security linked to international peace. The United Nations has deployed a growing number of international civilian police in peacekeeping operations; their number grew from 35 in 1988 to 3,600 in 1997. International assistance to foreign police forces has risen while military aid programs have shrunk.

U.S. policymakers now view professional, accountable, civilian police forces as serving several U.S. interests: fostering the rule of law and human rights in new democracies, promoting democratic civil-military relations abroad, confronting expanded international criminal and drug-trafficking networks, as well as providing order in unstable countries. One entity has come to play a central and widening role in U.S. efforts to train and develop foreign police forces: the International Criminal Investigative Training Assistance Program (ICITAP).

Author's note: The research and writing of this paper were funded by the U.S. Department of Justice ICITAP program. The author is grateful for the generous access to ICITAP personnel and files for this project. Research conducted as a Peace Scholar of the U.S. Institute of Peace and as a National Security Education Program Fellow was helpful in the preparation of this paper.

315

ICITAP was created in 1986 to help gain prosecution in key human rights cases in El Salvador and to bolster the criminal investigative capacity of Latin American security forces. Beginning with Panama in 1990, however, ICITAP became the principal U.S. agency involved in filling the "institutional gap," restructuring of the entire law enforcement apparatus of countries in transition.

As the U.N. role in police monitoring and training during peacekeeping operations has expanded over the past several years, ICITAP collaboration with U.N.-sponsored police monitors (CIVPOL) from around the world has grown as well. Although the ICITAP mandate prevents it from doing actual policing in postintervention scenarios, its capacity to build local police forces is increasingly viewed as the ticket to quick military withdrawal following interventions or peacekeeping missions. As the scope of ICITAP activities has widened, so has its geographic reach. In 1996 alone, ICITAP initiated new projects in Rwanda, Bosnia, Kazakhstan, Kyrgyzstan, Belarus, Ukraine, Uzbekistan, and the Croatian province of Eastern Slavonia, with new projects set for Brazil, Albania, Belize, and Liberia.

With the transformation of ICITAP into the most significant bilateral police aid program in the world, an analysis of its past work and the lessons it has learned is warranted. This paper describes the history of ICITAP and how it operates. It then examines in more detail four of its most significant projects: Panama, El Salvador, Somalia, and Haiti, describing ICITAP's activities and the lessons it drew from each experience. It concludes with some general observations about the possibilities and constraints faced by ICITAP that might inform thinking about police assistance programs more generally.

ICITAP in Historical Context

Before the 1960s, U.S. civilian police generally played a minimal role in U.S. attempts to build and shape foreign police forces. Federal law enforcement agencies such as the Federal Bureau of Investigation (FBI) performed limited activities abroad, and these were focused on catching criminals rather than training foreign cops.[1] Furthermore, during this time U.S. law contained no means to compensate local U.S. cops who advised or trained foreign police, thus the State Department arranged training contracts exclusively between foreign governments and private U.S. police specialists, such as the New York City patrolman who advised and trained the Panamanian police in the early 1900s.[2] Consequently, U.S. police training abroad was carried out almost exclusively by U.S. military and intelligence agencies. Between 1898 and 1930, the U.S. Marines created paramilitary constabulary forces in Panama, Nicaragua, the Dominican Republic, Cuba, Puerto Rico, Haiti, Liberia, and the Philippines.[3] In some cases, U.S. officers served as the initial leadership for these forces. After World War II, the military dominated U.S. efforts to create new civilian police forces in Japan, Korea, and West Germany.

In 1962, the Kennedy administration created a civilian foreign police training program whose legacy would shape the creation of ICITAP. The Office of Public Safety (OPS) was established as a semi-autonomous agency within the U.S. Agency for International Development (AID) to improve the capabilities of civilian police and paramilitary forces through "training, technical assistance and equipment."[4] During OPS' 13-year tenure, it would train over a million

---

[1]Ethan A. Nadelmann, *Cops Across Borders: The Internationalization of U.S. Criminal Law Enforcement* (University Park, PA: Penn State Press, 1993). Recent research—see Martha K. Huggins, "Political Policing: Internationalizing Security Through U.S. Assistance to Latin American Police" (Durham, NC: Duke University Press, forthcoming)—has documented anew the FBI's foreign police training in Latin America during the 1940s and 1950s.

[2]Huggins.

[3]Thomas David Lobe, "U.S. Police Assistance for the Third World" (Ph.D. diss., University of Michigan, 1975). Also Huggins, ibid.

[4]U.S. Department of State, "Interdepartmental Technical Subcommittee on Police Advisory Assistance Programs," *Report of the Interdepartmental Subcommittee on Police Advisory Assistance Programs,* June 11, 1962 (declassified April 2, 1981), cited in Michael McClintock, *The American Connection,* vol. 1 (London: Zed Books, 1975), 54.

cops and send some $325 million in equipment overseas.[5] OPS approaches foreshadowed those of ICITAP two decades later: it drew mainly on U.S. civilian police for trainers and advisers; emphasized the separation of police and military functions; and explicitly conceived of its work as long-term "institution building."[6]

Yet its mission was explicitly ideological, seeking to counter communism by offering courses in subjects such as communist tactics and ideology.[7] Its director came from the CIA, and building covert intelligence networks was part of its work, often in countries whose security forces abused human rights.[8] Based on reports that OPS-provided equipment was used in serious human rights abuses, Congress shut down the program in 1974 and a year later banned all police assistance, with certain exceptions, in Section 660 of the Foreign Assistance Act.[9] For the next several years, U.S. foreign police training was very limited, consisting mainly of anti-narcotics training.

ICITAP's authorization grew out of a number of congressional waivers to Section 660 which the Reagan administration sought in the 1980s principally to combat Communist insurgencies in Central America and the Caribbean. These waivers were often the result of hard-fought battles with members of Congress determined not to repeat the OPS experience. Exemptions included authorization for police aid to Costa Rica and the eastern Caribbean, to El Salvador and

---

[5]Michael Klare and Cynthia Arnson, *Supplying Repression* (Washington, DC: Institute for Policy Studies, 1981).

[6]See Lobe.

[7]Lobe; Martin Edwin Andersen, "International Administration of Justice: A New American Security Frontier," *SAIS Review* (Winter-Spring 1993): 95. OPS' stated objectives were twofold: to assist friendly governments "to enforce the law and public order" and to "counter Communist inspired or exploited subversion and insurgency." See McClintock, 55.

[8]McClintock; Lobe. The CIA had personnel "integrated in AID police programs in ten of the 27 countries in which AID has programs," according to the U.S. State Department report cited .

[9]See A.J. Langguth, *Hidden Terrors* (New York: Pantheon Books, 1978), for an account of the kidnapping and killing of one OPS adviser in Uruguay by leftist Tupamaros guerrillas. They believed him to be a CIA agent.

Honduras, and "antiterrorism assistance" to deter international terrorist acts such as bombings and hijackings.

In 1983 the administration obtained a congressional waiver of Section 660 for the first "administration of justice" (AOJ) program to be administered by AID. Designed to improve the overall systems of justice in Latin America, the AOJ program responded largely to pressure for prosecution in cases where security forces receiving U.S. military assistance were accused of murdering American citizens. Fay Armstrong, a judicial specialist with the State Department in 1985, recounts:

> We had the case of the four churchwomen in El Salvador and other cases which especially involved American victims, and there was a need to pursue these cases and push them forward. . . . But the judicial systems simply didn't work.[10]

The first "administration of justice" assistance sought to create a small Judicial Protection Unit to protect jurors, judges and witnesses in sensitive political trials in El Salvador. This did nothing, however, to ensure the collection and presentation of evidence to the courts. One State Department official recalls:

> As we began trying to get cases through the system, it became obvious that we needed to address evidence collection. But we came up against Section 660, and we asked how to get around that section.[11]

As a result of negotiations in mid-1985 involving mainly Jim Michel, on behalf of the State Department's Inter-American Bureau, and Rob Kurz, a staff member of the House Subcommittee on Western Hemisphere Affairs (chaired by Rep. Michael Barnes, D-MD), Congress expanded the administration of justice waiver of Section 660 to include

---

[10]Fay Armstrong, AOJ Officer, Inter-American Bureau, Department of State, interviews by author, March 21 and March 26, 1997.

[11]Ibid.

"programs to enhance investigative capabilities conducted under judicial or prosecutorial control."[12]

This legislation, Section 534(b)(3) of the Foreign Assistance Act (FAA), became the authorization used to establish ICITAP on January 6, 1986. Reflecting congressional concerns about the potential abuse of police aid, ICITAP's legal mandate was initially limited to developing criminal investigative capabilities only. By late 1987, however, Congress had become sufficiently comfortable with ICITAP to expand section 534(b)(3) to two other critical areas: police management generally and police academy curriculum development. ICITAP was still not to provide direct training in sensitive enforcement areas (such as arrests and use of force) that had been issues in the OPS program, but it could work to ensure that proper curricula were in place in these areas. Beginning in 1990, statutory authority was extended on a country-specific basis to all areas of civilian police development in high visibility situations, such as Panama, El Salvador, and Haiti. This broader authority, now codified as FAA section 660(b)(6), permits assistance "to reconstitute civilian police authority and capability" in nations "emerging from instability," authorizing ICITAP training of "cops on the beat" and all specialties within a police force.

The particular conditions that gave rise to ICITAP have heavily shaped its activities and structure: its staff until recently was drawn almost exclusively from personnel from U.S. investigative agencies (e.g., the FBI and DEA) rather than local police; its work has focused on Latin America and the Caribbean; it remains sensitive to congressional concerns about human rights; and developing criminal investigative and forensics capabilities remains the core of most of the smaller country projects, which are not discussed in detail here.

How ICITAP Works

ICITAP has been something of an orphaned child of the U.S. bureaucracy. Partly because of the negative image of its old OPS program, AID remained deeply reluctant throughout the 1980s to be

---

[12]Rob Kurz, interview by author, March 18, 1997; Armstrong, interview.

affiliated with police assistance programs, even in the face of the Reagan White House's repeated attempts to expand police aid.[13] Thus in contrast to OPS, ICITAP was not housed within AID. Yet this situation created a dilemma. The Pentagon was prohibited from engaging in foreign law-enforcement training, and the State Department had limited operational capabilities to deliver foreign aid, AID's purpose.[14] Furthermore, the FBI declined when asked to oversee the new police component of the administration of justice program, reportedly because its officials feared association with another OPS experience.[15]

Consequently an unusual arrangement was adopted whereby a small program, ICITAP, would report directly to the Deputy Attorney General. In an arrangement which continues to date, ICITAP was placed under the administrative and operational authority of the Justice Department, receives its funding from AID channeled through the State Department, and receives policy guidance from the State Department.[16] Because of this institutional arrangement, ICITAP responds to numerous pressures and bureaucratic tendencies. In the words of one congressional staff member, "It's not as if ICITAP has its own agenda. It's always being driven by everyone else's agenda, pulled and pushed by various political factions usually on a very short-term basis."[17] Moreover, there are important differences in interests, cultures and commitment among the various agencies which have some voice in

---

[13]Armstrong, interview; Kurz, interview; David J. Kriskovich, interview by author, March 18, 1997.

[14]See Ethan Nadelmann, Cops Across Borders (Pennsylvania State University Press, 1995), for an account of how State Department's operational capabilities, especially those focused on drug control, have grown.

[15]Kriskovich, interview. In 1985, Kriskovich was an FBI Inspector-in-Charge.

[16]Initially, ICITAP received its policy guidance from the Bureau of Inter-American Affairs of the State Department. In 1994 ICITAP was administratively shifted to the Justice Department Criminal Division, headed by an Assistant Attorney General.

[17]Marian Chambers, professional staff member, House International Relations Committee, comments in a review session at National Defense University, May 28, 1997.

ICITAP's activities: the State Department, the Justice Department, AID, the FBI, and ICITAP itself.[18]

ICITAP fundamentally implements policy rather than formulating it. Decisions to initiate or end ICITAP projects generally lie with policymakers outside ICITAP, and there are no formal guidelines for such decisions. In large projects linked to high-profile U.S. foreign policy initiatives (such as Panama, Somalia, Haiti, and Bosnia), ICITAP has sought a role and helped shape its own activities, but the timing and nature of ICITAP's programs derive principally from interagency discussions involving the White House, the Defense Department, the State Department, and the Justice Department. For lower-profile projects such as those in the Andes, the Eastern Caribbean, and much of Central America, the original impetus for ICITAP involvement might come from local government officials, the U.S. Embassy, ICITAP's own proposals, AID, or the State Department, but ultimately some agreement between State and Justice must materialize. In all cases, local governments are consulted, and a process of harmonization occurs between what the U.S. Government is willing and able to provide and what the host government is interested in receiving.

ICITAP is the only U.S. program established specifically to address the developmental and training needs of foreign law enforcement agencies. Yet it is not the sole provider of U.S. police assistance. Under some dozen exceptions to the Section 660 ban, myriad U.S. agencies conduct foreign law enforcement training, including the Drug Enforcement Administration (DEA), the FBI, the State Department Diplomatic Security Service, the U.S. Customs Service, the Federal Aviation Administration, the Coast Guard, the Defense Department, and the U.S. Marshals. The number and complexity of U.S. police assistance programs make it impossible to calculate how much money is spent or how many students are trained in any given year. In the most comprehensive attempt yet to account for U.S. police aid, a U.S. General Accounting Office study found that 125 countries received at least $117 million in police training from U.S. agencies in fiscal year

---

[18]Ibid.

1990.[19] While ICITAP often coordinates with other U.S. agencies, it has only recently begun to conduct joint training and development activities in conjunction with other agencies of the U.S. Government.

Nor is ICITAP necessarily the largest U.S. provider of police aid. In the General Accounting Office study, the ICITAP FY 1990 budget was $20 million; State Department's antinarcotics aid totaled over $45 million; antiterrorism assistance was $10 million; and the Defense Department spent over $11 million in military assistance for training police forces in Central America and the Caribbean, plus $30 million for training and equipping antidrug police in Mexico and the Andes.[20] These other programs tended to be extremely technical and operational, focused on specific U.S. military or law enforcement objectives. Whereas many ICITAP projects are similarly technical in content, it is capable of having a more far-reaching impact by addressing the overall structure, management, doctrine and curriculum of national police forces, especially in larger projects.

ICITAP Expansion

Since its inception, ICITAP work has expanded greatly in size and scope. It opened with only a director and a deputy director, grew to 6 program staff by 1988, to 22 by late 1990, and to 51 by 1997, including staff based abroad.[21] ICITAP staff also reflects a healthy degree of diversity: of its 51 employees, 23 are women, including the current ICITAP director, and 20 are of minority races and non-U.S. nationalities. ICITAP opened its first field office in Panama in 1990, and by 1997 had seven such offices in Panama, El Salvador, Bolivia, Colombia, Haiti, Guatemala, and Honduras. In addition, ICITAP drew on a growing number of short-term and long-term contractors and sub-contractors who perform the bulk of ICITAP's training and advising

---

[19]U.S. General Accounting Office, *Foreign Aid: Police Training and Assistance*, Report GAO/NSIAD-92-118 (Washington, DC: U.S. Government Printing Office, March 1992).

[20]Ibid.

[21]Figures provided by ICITAP personnel director, current as of March 26, 1997.

around the world. For instance, at the height of the biggest ICITAP project to date, it employed some 300 people in Haiti including advisers, instructors, interpreters, and support staff. Subcontractors are generally selected by ICITAP staff and hired through contracting agencies on the basis of their background in federal, state, or local law enforcement as well as their language skills and areas of expertise.

In its first year, 1986, ICITAP received $1.52 million for its regional (known as "Latin American and the Caribbean," or "LAC regional") projects. The LAC regional Administration of Justice (AOJ) authorization for ICITAP was broadened in 1987 to three principal missions: enhancement of professional capabilities to carry out investigative and forensic functions; assistance in development of academic instruction and curricula for law enforcement personnel; and improvement of administrative and management capabilities of law enforcement agencies, especially those pertaining to career development, personnel evaluation, and internal discipline procedures.

As security priorities evolved with the decline of the Cold War, ICITAP was increasingly called upon. Pursuant to the *Anti-Drug Abuse Act of 1988* and the *International Narcotics Control Act of 1990*, ICITAP initiated specialized training and assistance in Bolivia, Colombia, and Peru. The *Urgent Assistance for Democracy in Panama Act of 1990* contained funds for ICITAP to provide civilian law enforcement training in Panama. That authority was continued under Section 124 of *Public Law 102-266* and extended to El Salvador by Section 122, authorizing ICITAP to develop a new, national civilian police force, a central requirement of the 1992 Peace Accords. The *East European Democracy Act of 1989* and the *Freedom Support Act of 1992* provided the authority for ICITAP to conduct projects in the newly established and developing democracies of Eastern Europe and the former Soviet Union. Congress has authorized other ICITAP programs as well.

In 1996, the ICITAP annual budget topped $30 million, a 20-fold increase from 1986 (see chart). In 1996, new projects were approved for South Africa, Liberia, Belize, and Brazil. Proposals were pending for new projects in Albania, Cambodia, Estonia, Jordan, Mexico, and Lebanon. Ongoing work continued in Bolivia, the English-speaking

ICITAP Funding History
Funding by Fiscal Year ($ million)

Project Description	1986	1987	1988	1989	1990	1991	1992	1993	1994	1995	1996	Project Totals
Albania Project											0.1	0.10
Alien Smuggling Training Alternative											0.5	0.50
Brazil Project											0.21	0.21
Bolivia Project						0.25	0.55	0.75		1	1.4	3.95
Bosnia Project											3	3.00
Cambodia Initiative											0.09	0.09
Colombia Judicial Protection Program				1.75								1.75
Colombia Justice Sector Reform Project						2.6	3.5					6.10
Colombia Project										0.85		0.85
Eastern Slovenia Transitional Administration											2.47	2.47
El Salvador Academy and Police Development							12			8		20.00
El Salvador CID Project								1.4	0.8	0.75	0.4	3.35
El Salvador Police Development Project											3.5	3.50
El Salvador Procurement Project								5.75				5.75
El Salvador Project											0.25	0.25
El Salvador SIU Project					0.3							0.30
Guatemala Project										0.3	0.75	1.05
Haiti Project								4	7	27	12.7	50.70
Haiti Project											0.1	0.10
Honduras Project											1.5	1.50
Latin American Countries Regional Program	1.5	2.75	6.4	5.55	6.97	4	4.9	4	3	2	2	43.07
Mexico Initiative										0.05		0.05
Newly Independent States Projects										1.35		1.35
Panama Project					13.2		10	2		3.95	3	32.15
Peru Project						0.5						0.50
Somalia Project									4			4.00
South African Initiative											0.5	0.50
TOTAL	1.5	2.75	6.4	7.3	20.47	7.35	30.95	17.9	14.8	45.25	32.47	187.14

Caribbean, Colombia, Costa Rica, the Dominican Republic, El Salvador, Guatemala, Haiti, and Panama.

ICITAP Early Years: 1986-1989

Early ICITAP projects reflected the experience and abilities of its influential founding director, FBI Inspector-in-Charge David J. Kriskovich. On loan from the FBI until his retirement from ICITAP in 1994, Kriskovich was hired based on his experience in developing a 4-week course in criminal investigations known as the "Caribbean Police School" in 1981 and his experience training the Special Investigative Unit in El Salvador in 1985.[22] ICITAP's original activities were limited to Central America, the Dominican Republic, and the English-speaking Caribbean. Activities were divided between "training" and development." By 1989, the agency was conducting training off a menu of approximately a dozen courses, including criminal investigations and interview techniques, forensics, police management, and violent personal crimes.

ICITAP "development" activities included the transfer of equipment, the sponsorship of regional police or forensics conferences, the provision of internships to serve for 2 or 3 weeks with law enforcement agencies or forensics facilities in the United States, and the bolstering of foreign police departments' institutional procedures. In the Caribbean, for instance, ICITAP assisted efforts to get police forces in locations such as Barbados and Jamaica to comply with the standards of the Commission on Accreditation of Law Enforcement Agencies.

During this early phase, ICITAP developed a reputation for quick action and professional delivery of courses. Kriskovich was a tireless organizer of regional networks of police investigators and information exchange. He also maintained a willingness to discuss ICITAP programs openly with Congress and nongovernmental organizations at any time. Given the highly charged atmosphere in Washington over

---

[22]Kriskovich, interview, March 18, 1997. The Defense Department funded early training for the SIU, and Kriskovich was funded by AID during 1985.

U.S. policy in Central America throughout the 1980s, this accomplishment was no small feat. As Rob Kurz, who was instrumental in drafting ICITAP's mandate in 1985, said in 1997:

> Remember that at the time our purpose was to prevent the U.S. government from making the profound error of engaging in a direct relationship with the death squads which were operating within the Salvadoran security forces.
>
> So Kris Kriskovich, to his enormous credit—and even though we got off to a rocky start I have the highest respect for him because he did what we thought was impossible: He created a police training program which allowed the best American values, that is respect for the rule of law, to prevail and avoided contaminating the U.S. integrity by working with murderers and torturers.[23]

Although human rights groups maintained a skeptical attitude about ICITAP at the time, their skepticism was due mainly to the nature of the public security forces and governments with which the U.S. Government was affiliated rather than actions of ICITAP.[24] ICITAP's reputation as a "clean" agency also derived from the exceptional congressional scrutiny to which its operations were subjected.[25]

As time passed, ICITAP shortcomings became more apparent. Its design, planning, and evaluation of programs were very poor. According to one State Department official:

> Kris [Kriskovich] was really good in the early years, chatting people up at AID and in the NGOs so they would not be afraid of police officers and police aid. But when it came to designing projects with well-defined goals and objectives ICITAP was allowed to wade into situations with no plans at all. Certainly this was the case with Panama, but also with the smaller projects. There was a kind of "anti-planning."[26]

---

[23]Kriskovich, interview, March 18, 1997.

[24]Rob Wiener, Lawyers Committee for Human Rights, interview by author, March 25, 1997.

[25]Ibid.

[26]U.S. State Department official, interview by author, March 1997.

Second, insufficient attention was paid to the legal and cultural context in which training took place. While ICITAP used Spanish-speaking instructors, most courses were simply translated versions of courses taught in U.S. law enforcement academies ("off-the-shelf" courses). Thus ICITAP gave instruction on combating "crimes" that turned out to be legal activities in the country in question and courses that reflected the accusatorial U.S. legal system while the legal systems involved were inquisitorial, drawn from Spanish and French traditions. In the latter systems, judges, rather than police officers, play a dominant role in criminal investigations.

Third, much of the training took place outside a context of institutional development. During ICITAP's first few years, "development" was conceived narrowly as improving material conditions for recipient criminal investigative units (e.g., better equipment), enhancing police standards, and providing professional career development for police trainees.[27] In practice, this meant ICITAP tended to offer discrete courses from its menu at the request of host governments. But, such activities could be blind to the broader context, and their benefits washed away by factors outside the specific training program itself.[28] As ICITAP's current deputy director puts it, "We learned that just going out and doing a couple of courses doesn't work because when you go back 6 months later you may not find a trace of the training that was done."[29] ICITAP would later adopt an "institutional development" approach involving local police leadership to ensure that training fit into an overall plan, that standard operating procedures existed and corresponded to training, and that the overall

---

[27]This concept is reflected in the activities cited in the "development" section of ICITAP's early quarterly reports. The most oft-cited are the provision of equipment and participation in conferences and workshops.

[28]For example, ICITAP trainees in criminal investigative skills were often promptly transferred to street beats where their training proved irrelevant (such transfers occur with trainees of other U.S. agencies such as the FBI, the DEA, etc.). ICITAP resolved the problem by obtaining a commitment beforehand that trainees would not be transferred for a certain amount of time so that their skills could be utilized.

[29]Comments by Robert Perito during review session at the National Defense University, May 28, 1997.

institutional environment would preserve rather than undermine the training. In 1990 such an approach was, in the words of ICITAP's current director, "not yet invented."

Panama: ICITAP's First "Whole-Force" Development Program

The biggest and most difficult shift in ICITAP's institutional history commenced with the U.S. invasion of Panama in December 1989. U.S. troops defeated Manuel Noriega's Panamanian Defense Forces (PDF), and the elected government of President Guillermo Endara chose not to reconstruct the military but instead to build a civilian-controlled "Public Force" consisting of an air corp, naval corp, and a new civilian police force. As described in this volume by Gray and Manwaring, U.S. policymakers were eager to remove U.S. troops from public security roles but faced a lack of public order following the invasion. Without any advance notice, ICITAP was tasked in January 1990 to draw up a 2½-year plan to assist in development of police services in Panama. Special congressional authority was quickly approved in the Urgent Assistance for Democracy in Panama Act of February 7, 1990, which authorized ICITAP for the first time to train street cops. The Inter-American Affairs Bureau of the State Department subsequently granted ICITAP $13.2 million for the initial project.

ICITAP was wholly unprepared for the tasks thrust upon it and received intense criticism, especially from the U.S. military. At the time the agency consisted of only a small staff of FBI agents on loan and a few regional language specialists. ICITAP staff backgrounds centered on criminal investigations and police management. None of the staff specialized in city policing, rural policing (a major requirement in Panama), midlevel police management, erecting a training academy, or designing the curriculum, policies, procedures, and selection criteria for any cops other than detectives. In fact, ICITAP's mandate had precluded it from engaging in providing training in patrolling and use of firearms that would be required in Panama. Expecting ICITAP to help reduce the "deployment" and "enforcement" gaps, U.S. military officers were shocked to discover that ICITAP would have fewer than ten staff in Panama, far from the number required to place police advisers and mentors in cities and provinces around the country.

ICITAP's job was complicated by decisions about the composition of the new Panamanian police forces. Panama was the first country after the Cold War in which U.S. policymakers confronted the "demobilization dilemma" common to transitions from authoritarian rule. Because pre-existing security forces are generally associated with the prior authoritarian regime, they often lack popular legitimacy or have been involved in repression and human rights violations. This was precisely the case in Panama. Preserving such a force can sully the reputation of a new civilian regime and perpetuate problems of police corruption, human rights violations, and an authoritarian or militarized law enforcement approach. Yet demobilizing such a force brings its own problems. Creating a new security force from whole cloth takes years and money, and periods of transition are often accompanied by a dramatic rise in violent crime. Furthermore, former policemen and soldiers, organized and trained in the use of firearms, might easily turn to crime and destabilize a nascent democracy whose new police lack experience. This "dilemma" has no cost-free answers.[30] The Endara Government, facing imminent U.S. troop withdrawal, chose to address the dilemma by cashiering many senior-level PDF officers, transforming the remaining soldiers into the cops of the new police force, and opening a civilian training academy whose graduates would, over a period of several years, gradually supplant former military personnel.

ICITAP began its work, therefore, by developing a 3-week "transition" course to orient the majority of former PDF personnel toward basic policing skills for a democratic society. For the long term, ICITAP created a new Police Academy, provided instructors, and helped organize the new Panamanian National Police (PNP) and a

---

[30]The "demobilization dilemma" is somewhat different from the "public security gap" which has been generally conceived of as the lack of an effective public security forces which follows international military interventions. The "dilemma" concerns regimes in transition, whether or not international actors are involved, although it can coexist with a "public security gap."

separate criminal investigations service known as the Judicial Technical Police (PTJ). ICITAP sought to address corruption and abuses by creating an Office of Public Responsibility (OPR) for the new police forces.

Because of ICITAP's lack of preparedness for the tasks in Panama, the U.S. military played an important role in maintaining public security and in standing up the new police force in the first months of 1990. U.S. infantry and military police units began to provide public order a few days after the invasion. In January 1990, a U.S. Military Support Group was activated and the 16th Military Police assigned to train the new police. U.S. policymakers sought to remove the military from these roles, and their frustration grew because ICITAP was extremely slow to organize transitional training for the new police, even slower to organize an academy, and was never able to provide field training in the cities and countryside. The 3-week transition course for former PDF members was not initiated until May 1990, and the 1991 target of 5,000 course recipients was not met until September 1992. ICITAP had no permanent project director in Panama until June 1990.

Consequently, U.S. forces did the bulk of the work with the vetted and renamed Panamanian police in the first months after the invasion. Prohibited by the Urgent Assistance for Democracy in Panama Act from conducting training in Panama, U.S. Special Forces and reservists patrolled rural areas and conducted joint patrols with Panamanian police in the two main cities, serving as an important means of monitoring and evaluating police performance.[31] The Defense Department also provided vehicles and other equipment for the police.

ICITAP drew many lessons from this experience. Despite its poor start, ICITAP laudably maintained a firm conviction that institution building cannot be done effectively overnight. It recognized the need for long-term support in Panama, although the program's duration

---

[31]Frequent joint exercises (mainly medical and engineering exercises) between the U.S. Armed Forces and the Panamanian Public Forces continue to date. Telephone interview with John Fishel, former officer of the U.S. Forces Liaison Group, June 4, 1997. Operation *Promote Liberty*, aimed at restoring civil government and public order, continued until 1995. See also Gray and Manwaring in this volume.

(now in its 8th year) has recently drawn criticism for lack of its own "exit strategy."[32] ICITAP had to make many adjustments in the course of the program (e.g., a "Model Precinct" program was terminated, and a scarcity of academy candidates from rural areas forced a relaxation of selection standards). The agency also learned the benefits of establishing internal control units to maintain the quality and credibility of police counterparts. The OPRs of both the PNP and the PTJ have dismissed some 150 officers and turned their cases over to judicial prosecutors. Later in the project, AID and ICITAP began integrating PTJ detectives and prosecutors in a pilot project aimed at improving criminal case management.

Panama's approach to the "demobilization dilemma" showed ICITAP the problems of utilizing former members of militarized and corrupt security forces. Although popular acceptance of the PNP has improved in recent years, Panamanians knew that the police were the same personnel as before, only with different uniforms. One 1992 poll showed that 64 percent of all Panamanians distrusted the police, while only 26 percent held confidence in them.[33] Although corruption within the new police force is reportedly not as institutionalized as under Noriega, it remains widespread. In addition, U.S. military troops were forced in December 1990 to help suppress a coup attempt led by former PDF officers which the PNP was unable to handle.[34] Whereas the PNP handling of riots has improved,[35] both the new police and the academy suffered from extremely high turnover of leadership—six and five directors, respectively—in their first 4 years.

The Panama experience also revealed the importance of field mentoring in whole-force police development and ICITAP inability to provide sufficient experienced cops to accompany and guide newly

---

[32]Debra McFarland, AID, interview by author, March 27, 1997. MacFarland has worked on the Panama Administration of Justice program since its inception.

[33]Poll cited in Richard H. Shultz, Jr., *In the Aftermath of War: U.S. Support for Reconstruction and Nation-Building following Operation* Just Cause, unpublished manuscript, 54.

[34]Ibid.

[35]Memo from ICITAP Project Manager Mike Youngs to ICITAP HQ, February 13, 1997.

deployed police officers. In most countries with established police forces, newly trained officers benefit from pairing with experienced officers who provide ongoing on-the-job training. Some police departments have field training officers who instruct rookie cops. Wholly new forces obviously lack such experienced "mentors." Panama revealed for the first time the importance of field training in filling the institutional gap facing U.S. policymakers in peace operations: the U.S. military is neither an appropriate nor a politically acceptable tool for conducting sustained field training; ICITAP resources, mandate, and history leave it ill prepared to do so; and no U.S. agency could readily locate the hundreds of police field trainers with the requisite language skills and availability. UNCIVPOL can probably best provide the numerous personnel required for this role. However, they are selected more for the monitoring skills needed for the enforcement gap than for mentoring skills, and are often withdrawn anyway before the institutional gap is adequately filled.

For ICITAP, the Panama experience also showed the limits of training outside an "institutional development" context. Building police institutions demands more than delivering technical skills. It requires attention to the legal framework, organizational leadership, and the development of institution-wide policies. According to current ICITAP Director Janice M. Stromsem:

> Panama is what showed us that this [off-the-shelf approach, without attention to the institutional, legal and social context] didn't work. It became clear that this was not the best approach. But the answer wasn't yet clear either. When I came to ICITAP in 1992, Kris [Kriskovich] was just starting to use the term "development." It took a while to learn what changes to make.[36]

To ICITAP's credit, it would incorporate many of the lessons of Panama in its programs in El Salvador and Haiti.

---

[36]Janice M. Stromsem, interview by author, March 18, 1997, Washington, D.C.

El Salvador and ICITAP

Shortly after the Panama invasion, ICITAP had the opportunity to apply these lessons in a second "whole force" development project in El Salvador. U.N.-mediated peace accords signed in January 1992 ended the civil war between the U.S.-backed Salvadoran Government and the leftist Farabundo Marti National Liberation Front (FMLN) guerrillas. A central part of the accords was reform of the armed forces, including their removal from public security functions. Three military-controlled security forces with reputations for human rights abuses were dissolved and replaced by a single new police force, the National Civilian Police (PNC). A separate National Public Security Academy (ANSP) was also created. In an unusual arrangement crucial to convincing the guerrillas to lay down their weapons, 20 percent of the new force could be composed of former FMLN combatants and an equal number could be vetted members of the former National Police. The remainder would be new recruits with no combat history.

Although ICITAP had provided assistance since 1986 to detectives from various security forces, the accords created vastly expanded roles for the agency.[37] First, ICITAP participated in a commission with Spanish police advisers and Salvadoran government representatives to design the curriculum for the ANSP. ICITAP trained half the first class of PNC supervisors in Puerto Rico in 1992 and contributed the bulk of international aid (some $10 million out of $13 million in the first 2 years) to the costs of materials and instruction at the ANSP.[38] ICITAP continues to fund several instructors at the ANSP, including retired

---

[37]This training included members of a controversial Special Investigative Unit (SIU), the director and several members of which were later implicated in committing or covering up political murders. Other U.S. agencies (the Defense Department, the State Department, and AID) were involved in funding or providing the training for the SIU in the 1980s. See Lawyers Committee for Human Rights, *Underwriting Injustice: AID and El Salvador's Judicial Reform Program* (New York: April 1989); and Teresa Whitfied, *Paying the Price* (Philadelphia, PA: Temple University Press, 1995); and interviews with author, 1995-96, El Salvador.

[38]See William Stanley, *Risking Failure* (Washington, DC: Washington Office on Latin America, September 1993).

federal and local U.S. law enforcement agents and a few Chilean carabineros. ICITAP also provided technical advice to the leadership of the PNC which continues to date, as well as a separate project in support of the new criminal investigations division of the PNC. As of March 1997, ICITAP maintained an FBI project manager in El Salvador, five U.S. teaching fellows who provided training or advice on instruction, five Chilean carabinero instructors, and five advisers to various divisions of the PNC.

ICITAP accomplishments were significant, and its role was viewed positively by the government as well as the former guerrillas.[39] ICITAP helped recruit, vet, and train the target number of 5,700 basic recruits and 240 officer-level candidates, roughly meeting an ambitious 2-year transition timetable. ICITAP continued supporting an accelerated training pace at the ANSP, and as of March 1997, ICITAP had trained over 12,000 recruits, 200 supervisory level officers, 2,000 trainees in specialized courses, 30 instructors, 800 field training officers, and 40 forensic lab technicians. Ultimately, ICITAP was critical in the creation of a self-sustaining academy, which has served as a model for neighboring countries. ICITAP also played a crucial role in developing policies and procedures for the PNC and contributed more than any other donor to PNC material needs such as vehicles and communications equipment. Although ICITAP helped initiate an Inspector General for the PNC and two internal control units, these were not fully effective. Some human rights groups argue the United States might have done more to prevent the corruption and abuses that emerged after full PNC deployment.[40]

The El Salvador project represented ICITAP's first extensive collaboration with the United Nations. In general, the relationship proved positive. Police issues were included in weekly coordination

---

[39]In 1995 and 1996 the author conducted numerous interviews with Salvadoran government officials; with PNC officers drawn from the National Police, from the FMLN, and from the civilian sector; and with top FMLN officials.

[40]Rob Weiner, Lawyers Committee for Human Rights, interview by author, March 25, 1997; and William Stanley, *Protectors or Perpetrators* (Washington, DC: Washington Office on Latin America, January 1996).

meetings between the U.S. ambassador and the U.N. head of mission. ICITAP and U.N. instructors achieved a division of labor in instruction at the ANSP, as did ICITAP and European Union advisers to the PNC. Additionally, some 300 UNCIVPOL provided field training for newly deployed PNC agents where ICITAP did not have the manpower.

The relationship was not without tensions. ICITAP was familiar to the Salvadoran Government through its prior training. In addition, the United States was a more significant donor to the police project than all others combined, providing $25 million through ICITAP between 1992 and 1997, with $7 million more obligated as of this writing. Yet the accords named the United Nations the transitional coordinator of international support. ICITAP placed its instructors at the ANSP via a bilateral agreement rather than through the United Nations, and U.N. officials complained that ICITAP did not cooperate enough with the U.N. principal technical adviser.[41] One well-placed U.N. official subsequently suggested that international efforts to develop the police would have benefitted if all assistance had been channeled through the United Nations and that the international community might thus have spoken with one voice in exercising leverage with the Government.[42] The United States, and particularly ICITAP, held a significant financial stake in the project, sometimes disagreeing with U.N. positions, and sought to avoid being subject to the notoriously slow U.N. bureaucracy. In the end, these problems did not alter the fact that the ad hoc relationship worked acceptably well.

El Salvador yielded several lessons for ICITAP. First, the project underscored how important the political aspects of ICITAP's work are and how important politically skilled project managers can be. The attention and contention surrounding the development of the ANSP and the PNC within the Salvadoran peace process placed unusual demands upon ICITAP. Like Haiti after it, El Salvador had a high profile in U.S. politics, and members of Congress and human rights

---

[41]Spanish instructors at ANSP and U.N. officials, interviews with author, July and November 1993, San Salvador.

[42]See Gino Costa, "United Nations and Reform of the Police in El Salvador," *International Peacekeeping* 2, no. 2 (Autumn 1995): 365-390.

groups scrutinized these two projects like no others. ICITAP learned the benefits of its open-door policies, winning critical praise for its work in both countries from international human rights groups.[43] The fact that the ICITAP project manager from 1991 until 1996, FBI agent Robert Loosle, was not only technically skilled but also politically astute proved extremely helpful in dealing with obstacles to police development which were quite often political in nature.[44]

ICITAP also learned the importance of exercising, as part of the U.S. Embassy team, diplomatic and political leverage in its dealings with local government officials. It is difficult to walk the road between heeding the judgment of local officials on the one hand, and ensuring that propitious conditions for police development prevail on the other. In El Salvador, elements of the Government itself were resistant to agreed-upon police reforms. As the paper by Stanley and Loosle shows, without exercising some leverage, the international community could well have squandered its substantial investment in the PNC and the ANSP. Because ICITAP project manager Loosle occupied the post for 6 years, the U.S. ambassador was able to take advantage increasingly of his experience and judgment on such matters. Such longevity and influence have their risks as well, of course.

The presence of other bilateral donors and the United Nations provided ICITAP with an opportunity to examine its own advantages and disadvantages with respect to these actors. ICITAP learned the value of having language-capable field monitors and trainers who can provide on-the-job training, capabilities ICITAP does not possess. It also benefitted from hiring long-term foreign instructors for the first time. According to Stromsem, El Salvador was also the "first time we saw the difficulties of working with CIVPOL and the U.N." The

---

[43]See, for example, reports by the Washington Office on Latin America on El Salvador in 1993 and 1996, and on Haiti in 1995 and 1997; reports by Human Rights Watch on Haiti in 1995 and 1997; and comments by Martha Doggett of the Lawyers Committee for Human Rights at a November 1994 conference co-sponsored by WOLA, Johns Hopkins SAIS, and the North-South Center in Washington DC.

[44]See section in this volume by Stanley and Loosle on those obstacles.

inefficiency and lack of top quality CIVPOL personnel led to less than desired results.

At the same time, the United Nations generally proved more agile in detecting political and human rights problems, in part due to its mandate and staffing advantages in these areas. In the case of the integration of the Special Investigative Unit (SIU) and the old Anti-Narcotics Unit into the PNC, the United States and ICITAP clung to units in which they had a vested interest longer than they should have, as Loosle and Embassy officials now acknowledge.[45] While the United States turned out to be better positioned to weigh in with Salvadoran officials on these problems, the United Nations was quicker to recognize them.

ICITAP also drew lessons from the nature of the peace process in El Salvador. The presence of a detailed peace agreement had its advantages and disadvantages. According to ICITAP's Stromsem:

> The accords were good because they provided a clear road map for reforms. But the degree of specificity was also bad. Deadlines left little flexibility. And the accords forced the government to do certain negative things, such as separate the academy from the PNC.[46]

ICITAP's next big project, Somalia, would show the negative side of not having a peace agreement.

Building a Police Force in Somalia

ICITAP involvement in Somalia illustrates the importance of political context in the failure or success of police training programs. Its involvement in Somalia came late in the international community's 1992-95 high-profile intervention, only after the Clinton administration had announced its decision to pull out all U.S. troops following the killing of 18 U.S. Army Rangers in October 1993. Prior to ICITAP

---

[45]See Stanley and Loosle section; U.S. Ambassador to El Salvador Alan Flanigan, interview by author, September 1995.

[46]Stromsem, interview.

involvement, the U.S.-led United Task Force (UNITAF) had taken steps to reconstruct a police force that had numbered over 15,000 before civil war broke it apart, leading to informal, regionalized, clan-dominated policing.[47] By March 1993, a 5,000-member "Auxiliary Police Force" comprising former Somali National Police members had been reassembled in the southern UNITAF-controlled zone, reporting to a Police Committee named by the main Somali factions.[48]

ICITAP's first involvement was a 5-day evaluation of the Auxiliary Police Force in March 1993. Like the 2-week U.N. evaluation conducted a month earlier by a police technical team, the ICITAP evaluation concluded that the auxiliary force enjoyed a "positive reputation" and could form the basis for a reconstituted national police force comprised of former members of the Somali National Police force.[49] Unlike police forces in Panama, El Salvador and Haiti, the Somali force had enjoyed widespread legitimacy among diverse groups, had relatively modern equipment, and was seen as professional and apolitical.[50] However, the ICITAP March evaluation cautioned that the potential to rebuild the police force was contingent upon three factors: high levels of international funding for equipment, buildings and training; reconstitution of the other elements of the justice system, which were wholly inoperative at the time; and a change in the dangerous security environment prevalent in Somalia.[51] In the end these conditions were not met before police assistance was undertaken.

---

[47]For a detailed analysis of the international peacekeeping operations in Somalia, see John L. Hirsch and Robert B. Oakley, *Somalia and Operation Restore Hope* (Washington, DC: U.S. Institute of Peace, 1995).

[48]See Martin R. Ganzglass, "Restoration of the Somali Justice System," *International Peacekeeping* 3, no. 1 (Spring 1996): 118; Thomas and Spataro section in this volume; and Hirsch and Oakley.

[49]See report by Lang and Havecost, "Evaluation of the ASF Somalia," ICITAP (Washington, DC: Department of Justice, March 5-10, 1993); see Ganzglass on the U.N. team report.

[50]The two abovementioned evaluations and another by Ganzglass concurred on this point. Also see Thomas and Spataro paper in this volume.

[51]See Lang and Havecost, 4.

No action was taken by ICITAP until U.S. policy shifted in response to the killing of 18 U.S. Rangers in October 1993. At that time the Clinton administration announced U.S. forces would withdraw by March 1994, and U.S. policymakers called in ICITAP to ensure that a Somali police force would function after U.S. forces departed. In December 1993, the United States pledged $12 million for a 1-year ICITAP police training program, $6 million for the judiciary, and $25 million in Defense Department excess equipment, mainly vehicles.[52] Unfortunately, it was not until Congress approved authority for the Somalia police program on February 27, 1994, that ICITAP project manager Mike Berkow could depart for Somalia and begin the program.[53] By then U.S. troops were packing to leave, and the Auxiliary Police Force, now nominally totaling 8,000, had suffered setbacks. The outbreak of renewed conflict had rendered the Police Committee more politicized and less effective. In Mogadishu and other regions, an initial high degree of motivation and discipline had given way to demoralization and significant disintegration of the force.[54] In some provincial areas the police continued to function, producing a bizarre situation of fairly effective police working with no elected national government and weak or nonexistent local councils.[55]

Part of the problem was UNOSOM II's insufficient attention to reconstituting the Somali police. Although the resurrection of a police force had been the international community's "ticket out" of Somalia from the beginning,[56] the police were a low-level U.N. priority with little U.S. involvement after UNITAF handed over the peacekeeping baton

---

[52]Ganzglass, 128.

[53]Berkow had conducted a second assessment in November 1993, drawing up a two-phase ICITAP plan.

[54]Comments to the author from Ambassador Robert Oakley, May 1997.

[55]Peter Vrooman, then-political officer of the U.S. Embassy in Somalia, interview by author, June 27, 1997; and Berkow, interview, May 26, 1997.

[56]The phrase was used by the Special Representative of the U.N. Secretary-General under UNOSOM II, Admiral Howe, cited in Ganzglass, 125.

to UNOSOM II in May 1993.[57] Total CIVPOL in Somalia grew from three in May 1993 to only 22 by March 1994, when ICITAP arrived. Although their primary task was training rather than monitoring, CIVPOL personnel were unable to carry out any significant activities because they lacked the funds for classrooms, teaching materials, transport, food, and housing for students.[58]

ICITAP threw itself into reconstituting the Somali National Police and considered its activities positive. Yet the plug was pulled on the ICITAP program in June 1994, only 4 months after it had begun. ICITAP built a provisional training center in Baidoa and another at the U.N. compound in Mogadishu, carried out three 21-day "refresher" courses for some 176 police officers, and completed nine other courses in arms-handling, convoy escort, and police station administration.[59]

The context called for unusual skills from ICITAP staff. In claiming portable buildings for classrooms that had been abandoned by the U.S. Air Force, project manager Berkow had to dodge factional gunfire, negotiate away three trailers in exchange for perimeter security from Romanian U.N. troops, and locate a forklift and a truck to personally load and haul away the buildings.[60] ICITAP also began refurbishing police stations with invaluable assistance from U.N. military forces, who also provided all transportation to police students attending ICITAP courses.[61] Such ad hoc collaboration between ICITAP and the United Nations, however, was largely at the initiative of ICITAP staff and individual U.N. military field commanders. Overall coordination between U.N. and U.S. efforts in Somalia was poor.[62]

---

[57]Ambassodor Walter Stadtler, then-head of Pentagon Somalia Task Force, interview by author, May 29, 1997; U.S. political officer Peter Vrooman, interview by author, June 27, 1997. See also the Thomas and Spataro paper for more details.

[58]Berkow, interview, June 26, 1997.

[59]ICITAP "Briefing on Somalia Program Status," June 23, 1994; and Berkow, interview, April 3, 1997.

[60]Berkow, interview, April 5, 1997.

[61]Berkow, interview, April 6, 1997.

[62]Colonel Harry Broer, Deputy Police Adviser to the U.N. Secretary-General, interview by author, May 28, 1997; Berkow, interview, June 26, Vrooman, interview, June 27, 1997.

In the end, ICITAP did not complete much of its 1-year program. It spent less than one-fourth of its $12 million budget and never initiated longer term activities such as establishment of a permanent academy or development of specialized units. According to Berkow, "We never accomplished half of what we had planned. We never got to long-term institution building. We were using two provisional stations which everybody recognized were only temporary."[63] Over three-fourths of ICITAP's Somalia budget was transferred to the Haiti project. The $25 million of excess stocks from the Defense Department, including 353 vehicles, 5,000 M-16s, 5,000 .45-caliber pistols, and 1.2 million rounds of ammunition, sat in a warehouse for months, not claimed or distributed by UNOSOM by ICITAP's departure in mid-1994.

ICITAP training programs were closed because the security situation made them unsustainable.[64] At the time, instructors wore flak jackets and dodged stray bullets that whizzed through their classrooms. Following a 3-day firefight near the police training center in Mogadishu, the United States pulled all nonessential personnel from the country, including all ICITAP personnel.

The ICITAP Somalia program was unusual in that it sought to rebuild a pre-existing police force rather than create a new force. Presumably this task should have been easier; however, this proved not to be the case because of a second unusual aspect of the Somalia operation: it was an attempt to construct a police force in the absence of a government or legitimate political authority. Perhaps too late, it was determined that an internationally supported police force, no matter how professional and popularly accepted, is unsustainable in the absence of a governmental structure to support it.

---

[63]Berkow, interview, April 6, 1997; Ambassador Walter Stadtler, head of the Pentagon's Somalia Task Force, interview by author, May 29, 1997.

[64]Berkow, interview, June 27, 1997; Vrooman, interview, June 28, 1997.

Haiti and ICITAP

The remaining funds for Somalia were quickly transferred to the next crisis spot, Haiti. ICITAP involvement in Haiti began in 1992, when it was asked to draw up plans for a long-term police development project should a political settlement be reached to restore civilian rule. In January 1993, ICITAP drew up a 5-year plan to develop a completely new civilian police in Haiti, where a corrupt and unpopular military had long controlled public security. In August 1993, after the Governors Island Accord was reached between exiled President Jean-Bertrand Aristide and the de facto military government, then-Associate Director Jan Stromsem and two other ICITAP advisers went to Haiti and helped Justice Minister Guy Malary draft a police law for a planned new police force. After Malary was gunned down by military henchmen in October 1993, ICITAP left the country to await the ouster of the military government.

In September 1994, 2 days after U.S. troops landed in Haiti, ICITAP began the largest program in its history when Stromsem and four other ICITAP personnel arrived by military transport. In contrast to Panama, ICITAP involvement in Haiti was carefully planned in advance. Determined not to repeat the Somalia debacle, Pentagon officials hosted interagency working group meetings on Haiti starting in August 1994 that included ICITAP representatives. The Joint Staff would allow no military "mission creep" into institution-building functions or policing duties in Haiti. The Defense Department wanted no U.S. casualties if force was to be used at all and as speedy a departure as possible.

Consequently, the State Department, working with ICITAP, developed a plan to provide interim public security should U.S. intervention render the Haitian Armed Forces inoperative. ICITAP's long-term plan for a new police would not address the deployment or enforcement gaps. Based on its experience in Panama, ICITAP strongly preferred to avoid the use of former army personnel for the new Haitian National Police. The working group recommended a three-step program. U.S. forces would neutralize the Haitian Armed Forces and fill the initial deployment gap, field an Interim Public

Security Force (IPSF), and develop a permanent, new Haitian National Police (HNP) force to fill the institutional gap. President Aristide directed that no more than 9 percent of the new HNP could be composed of former army personnel.[65]

U.S. and Haitian policymakers addressed the demobilization dilemma by using mainly vetted members of the Haitian Armed Forces for the IPSF and by discouraging their membership in the basic level of the new HNP. Some 3,000 IPSF members were drawn from the 7,000-member army, vetted by two groups of Haitian and U.S. Government officials (including ICITAP) and sent through a 6-day transition course developed and delivered by ICITAP. In addition, ICITAP designed and delivered a 21-day course for 1,089 refugees in Guantanamo, Cuba, 900 of whom were incorporated into the IPSF along with ex-army members.

The State Department organized a force of 920 International Police Monitors (IPMs) from 26 countries to perform monitoring tasks that are often carried out by UNCIVPOL. Former New York Police Commissioner Ray Kelly headed this force. ICITAP provided a 3-day orientation to the IPMs and their 300 interpreters in Puerto Rico prior to their deployment. When the U.S.-led Multinational Force gave way to the UNMIH in March 1995, some 300 CIVPOL took over the monitoring function.

At the same time ICITAP was carrying out the transition course, it was selecting a site for the new HNP Training Center and devising a recruitment drive with the Aristide Government. Between February 1995 and February 1996, ICITAP would train more than 5,000 basic-level cadets, drawing upon instructors from France and Canada as well as the United States. Concerns by U.S. policymakers about the admission of former army soldiers were eased when only some 20 or 30 met the entrance requirements of the ICITAP-run academy, although ultimately some 730 IPSF members drawn from the army

---

[65]Former officials of the Aristide Government and ICITAP staff, interviews by author, April-August 1996, Port-au-Prince.

were passed into the HNP by Aristide.[66] Because of the rush to deploy the HNP before the then-scheduled departure date for UNMIH of February 1996, the United States decided to open an ICITAP-run training center at Fort Leonard Wood, Missouri, to expand upon the limited space of the HNP Training Center.

ICITAP expressed its deep reservations about the symbolism of conducting training at a U.S. military base. Nevertheless, the program was carried out, with the positive result that training was completed more quickly and the negative result that many Haitians suspect that HNP cadets somehow came under the influence of U.S. military or intelligence services.[67] At its peak, the Haiti effort employed over 300 ICITAP trainers and interpreters and other personnel on the two campuses, with over 3,000 cadets in training. In 1996, ICITAP completed courses for senior-level and midlevel supervisors. It also initiated specialized training in crowd control, narcotics, criminal investigations, and SWAT team tactics. Several of these courses involved collaboration with UNCIVPOL instructors. ICITAP also provided advisers to the HNP Director, the Inspector General, and other divisions of the HNP, and helped develop policies and procedures for the new force. ICITAP assistance included vehicles, communications equipment, and other materials.

As in Somalia, the U.S. military both facilitated and posed difficulties for ICITAP's work. As ICITAP trained the IPSF and began setting up the police academy for the long-term police force in late 1994, U.S. Special Forces and U.S. Military Police filled the immediate deployment gap. They supervised, monitored, accompanied, and offered minimal arms training to IPSF members. ICITAP was also heavily dependent upon the military for logistics support, relying upon

---

[66]Many of these 730 soldiers resigned or abandoned their positions in the IPSF. Thus, after the IPSF was incorporated into the HNP, ex-army personnel comprised less than 10 percent (probably less in fact) of the total forces officially under the HNP structure. As of March 26, 1997, 46 of 166, or 28 percent, of top uniformed command positions (*commissaires*, both principal and municipal commissioners) were former army officers.

[67]Haitian academics, NGOs, and political figures, interviews by author, March-April 1996 and July-August 1996, Haiti.

military transport for concrete, building materials, and a truck to haul pre-fab trailers for housing at the police academy. Despite inevitable breakdowns in logistics, the coordination between the Pentagon and ICITAP was improved in Haiti over prior operations.[68] For example, ICITAP placed a staff member in Norfolk at the U.S. Atlantic Command headquarters to coordinate shipments of materials. On the other hand, Joe Trincellito, ICITAP/OPDAT Haiti Operations Director, described how the "exit strategy syndrome" undermined institutional-building objectives:

> First we were forced to shorten the planned training from six months to four months. Second we had to create a SWAT team in Haiti months before we felt they were ready for that kind of training and function.[69]

Circumstances in Haiti and the effective management of the enforcement gap helped avert a widely feared repeat of the Somalia debacle. Attacks on U.S. personnel were few, and public order was generally well preserved during the period of heaviest international involvement: the period of U.S. operational control (September 1994-March 1995) and the full U.N. peacekeeping operation (March 1995-February 1996). This period coincided with both the remainder of the Aristide presidency and the tenure of the Interim Public Security Force, although the IPSF held little legitimacy in the eyes of the public. Many failed to show up for work or stayed in the stations for fear of public wrath. As Trincellito said:

> It was really the [U.S.] military that was guaranteeing public security. The reason the IPSF could go out and direct traffic was because there was a humvee behind them; otherwise they might have been dead.[70]

---

[68]Ibid.

[69]ICITAP/OPDAT Haiti Operations Director Joe Trincellito, interview by author, March 26, 1997.

[70]Ibid.

Some 20 alleged political killings occurred in this period, some of which implicated members of the IPSF and the Palace guard. These grave human rights violations nevertheless represented a vastly lower number than during the military regime. Later, human rights groups praised the aggressive work of the new HNP Inspector General's office, describing it as part of "revolutionary" efforts to exact police accountability.[71] Drawing on the experiences of places like El Salvador, ICITAP made a concerted effort to erect an internal oversight unit quickly. ICITAP officials report that the Inspector General's office is more developed and functional than the internal oversight mechanisms in Panama and El Salvador at comparable stages.[72]

More difficult than filling the enforcement gap was the construction of a new institution capable of handling public security without significant international back-up. Although a CIVPOL force of roughly 300 and a military presence of some 1,300 U.N. soldiers remained in Haiti from March 1996 though late 1997, the HNP increasingly assumed responsibility for public security during this time. The new force is considered more trustworthy and humane than its predecessor, but it was deployed throughout the country with insufficient training and a dearth of equipment such as radios, vehicles, and even paper and pencils. Human rights groups point out that the police force has not won the full support and trust of the population and that its members are responsible for dozens of unjustified killings and instances of torture and beatings of prisoners.[73] On the other hand, people clearly recognized the improvement over the previous military-run "police" who engaged in systematic brutality and carried out deliberate political murders.

A significant negative factor in the HNP's performance was the deployment of all 5,200 recruits before midlevel supervisors or senior police directors had been trained. ICITAP had planned to select and

---

[71]See National Coalition for Haitian Rights/ Washington Office on Latin America/ Human Rights Watch, *The Human Rights Record of the Haitian National Police*, January 1997, 17.

[72]Trincellito, interview.

[73]National Coalition for Human Rights.

train midlevel supervisors from among the best and most educated of the recruits; however, other recruits did not respond well to supervision from their peers with whom they had just completed basic training. A lack of discipline and supervision was prevalent. After deployment, some entire rural delegations initially abandoned their posts for the city. ICITAP was prepared to train top-level commanders, but the Haitian government failed to fill many of these positions, and it was unclear whether those appointed would remain on the job long. ICITAP staff foresaw the negative consequences of this leadership vacuum, and its Director now believes that the agency should have been more forceful in articulating the consequences of this decision to the Haitian government and other U.S. authorities.[74] Ultimately it was not until April 1996, after President Rene Preval took office and appointed a new director of the HNP, that ICITAP training for senior commissioners began.

One of the results of the Haiti project is that ICITAP was left in a better position to influence U.S. policy decisions regarding police development. It was involved in higher level meetings than at any time in its history. It was also given a seat on the NSC-led interagency Executive Committee which coordinated preparations for the U.S. intervention and subsequent assistance. As Stromsem reported, "Because our judgment often proved correct on the Haiti project, now they [U.S. policymakers] tend to listen to us when we identify a problem."[75] "Whole force" police reform opportunities are rare, however, and ICITAP's ability to shape both police development and U.S. policy are likely to be diminished in their absence.

One area where ICITAP judgment proved prescient was its refusal, prior to the 1994 intervention, to train a Presidential Security Unit (PSU) that would provide President Aristide personal bodyguard service. ICITAP, citing the lack of professional qualifications of many members who had been handpicked by President Aristide for their personal loyalty, "screamed bloody murder" at the pressure to train the

---

[74]ICITAP Director Jan Stromsem, interview by author, March 18, 1997.
[75]Ibid.

unit, according to one ICITAP official.[76] In the end, the unit was trained by State Department Diplomatic Security personnel in the United States and, after Aristide's return, given follow-on advice and training by a U.S. advisory unit stationed in the presidential palace and funded by the State Department. In August 1996, the head of the PSU and several other members were implicated in the murders of two right-wing opponents of the government. Moreover, President Preval reported being powerless to fire those accused, and a special U.S. contingent was flown in to provide security for Preval while a purge of some 20 PSU members was undertaken. ICITAP refusal to train the PSU before certain conditions had been met illustrates its own learning from prior situations and shows the costs of delivering training out of expediency.

The Presidential Security Unit illustrates another lesson drawn by ICITAP from the Haiti experience: the difficulties of fostering discipline and accountability in a new force when there exist multiple police units, separate selection procedures and different lines of authority. Haiti's police law created a single national police force, the HNP. But the process of Aristide's restoration to power led to factions within the HNP and units outside the control of the HNP's director. Tensions over integration and authority occurred among several identifiable groups: the 5,200-plus ICITAP-trained Haitian National Police; the 100 "Regina police," trained at the Royal Canadian Mounted Police center in Regina, Canada, of whom less than half remain in the HNP; the roughly 730 ex-military members who remained in the IPSF when it was transferred by decree in December 1996 into the HNP; the 900 "Guantanamo" police who remained in the IPSF; and the Presidential Security Unit.[77] For example, many of the ex-military and Regina police were more loyal to their political allies than to their HNP commanders. ICITAP has argued consistently for unified hierarchical control, merit-based selection standards, and the extension of the

---

[76]ICITAP official, interview by author, October 1996.
[77]Other groups exist as well, such as the National Palace Guard Unit.

Inspector General's authority to all security forces. Yet the difficulties of integrating these multiple groups and units continue.

Despite some problems in coordination, the relationship among ICITAP, the United Nations, and other bilateral donors has probably been as smooth in Haiti as anywhere. Initially there was confusion over the division of labor between the United Nations and ICITAP; as Stromsem put it, "We thought we were doing training, and so did they." For the first time, ICITAP attempted to deploy its own field trainers with the first deployed group of cadets. However, ICITAP ultimately would not have been able to field sufficient personnel, and UNCIVPOL assumed the job as planned. ICITAP and other U.S. agencies have complained that since the French delegation assumed command of the CIVPOL unit in February 1996, CIVPOL became less aggressive in "mentoring" new agents in the field, preferring classroom training instead.[78] But in general, a high degree of communication and coordination was worked out, especially after HNP Director Pierre Denize assumed strong leadership in coordinating international donor meetings. As Trincellito describes it:

> One thing we carried from the Somalia experience was to control our own destiny. That is, to have a plan and be prepared to work with the U.N., but to be our own masters.
> We were very fortunate at the beginning to have a CIVPOL commander with whom we could work, Neil Pouliot. We were able to draw lines where the U.N. and the U.S. could do complementary work without stepping on each other's toes. In Haiti that meant that we were responsible for the basic training of the new police, and CIVPOL was responsible for field training.[79]

Recent Developments in ICITAP Work

As the ICITAP Haiti project adjusted to a less frenetic pace in 1996, it was besieged with projects in a number of other countries. Most

---

[78]ICITAP officials and State Department officials, interviews by author, October 1996, January 1997, and March 1997.

[79]Trincellito, interview.

prominently, ICITAP became increasingly involved in Bosnia. Annex 11 of the 1995 Dayton Accords provided for the training of civilian police forces in accordance with international human rights standards and deployment of a 1,721-member, U.N.-run International Police Task Force (IPTF). In early 1996 the IPTF deployed. It developed and distributed guidelines and standards for "Democratic Policing." Although ICITAP expected to be increasingly involved in training and development for the Bosnian police, most of its initial activities supported the IPTF. In 1996 ICITAP provided training in roles and mission for the entire IPTF and drafted standard operating procedures and policies. It also conducted a needs assessments of the judicial system, of equipment for the police, and of specialized units such as traffic control and internal affairs.

ICITAP is working more intimately with the United Nations in Bosnia than in previous projects, initiating no activities without the IPTF commander's authorization. It is too early to assess the Bosnia operation, although ICITAP staff express frustration at the slow pace of police development and believe that their capabilities have been underutilized thus far. In April 1997, ICITAP founding director David Kriskovich was named the IPTF's Deputy Commissioner for Development, the top American post within the IPTF.[80]

ICITAP's expanded portfolio of projects does not necessarily mean more "whole-force" development projects. In Bosnia the project does not entail creating a new police force but reforming existing police forces. The bulk of ICITAP current projects involve specific training and institution-building objectives. In Liberia, for instance, ICITAP's initial task was to develop the capability of the police to provide security for national elections. In the Caribbean, one of ICITAP's main objectives was to harmonize the institutional policies and training goals of twelve small police forces so that joint training can be institutionalized. In Kazakhstan, ICITAP was developing a model precinct program rooted in the principles of community-oriented

---

[80]Commissioner Kriskovich, one ICITAP staff member, and four other IPTF personnel were killed in a helicopter crash while serving in Bosnia on September 17, 1997.

policing for replication in other localities. In Honduras, ICITAP work has recently focused on training, equipping, advising, and establishing an academy for a newly formed criminal investigations force separate from the military.

One of the most interesting and positive areas of training pioneered by ICITAP is its "Human Dignity" course, developed jointly with the John Jay College of Criminal Justice in New York. Aimed at improving police officers' understanding and protection of human rights, the course begins with police officers' own personal experiences and observations, requires them to develop their own definitions of rights, and takes them through numerous role-playing scenarios. Above all it seeks to instill a notion of human dignity that is common to all persons, including cops, that should be preserved under all circumstances. The human dignity course has been given in most Latin American countries and is now being delivered at the International Law Enforcement Academy in Budapest, Hungary.

Lessons for International Police Aid

Several broad conclusions can be drawn from the experiences of ICITAP over the past 11 years. First, overall political conditions often limit what is possible. In countries where armed conflict has not been resolved, or which are not "ripe" for resolution,[81] it is extremely difficult to develop new government institutions, especially ones that reflect democratic norms of community orientation, accountability, and representativity. ICITAP's experience in Somalia and the first phase of El Salvador illustrate this limitation. ICITAP's learning process was evident in its refusal to initiate a project in Burundi because requisite political conditions were absent. In contrast, the peace process in El Salvador, and perhaps now in Guatemala, show that a climate of political reconciliation is highly beneficial. Likewise, domestic economic constraints in countries such as Haiti and Rwanda limit the potential of police development programs.

---

[81]On the concept of "ripeness" for negotiation, see William I. Zartman, *Ripe for Resolution*, 2nd ed. (New York: Oxford University Press, 1989).

Similarly, wherever political will for change and institutional development has been lacking, police training programs have had little or no success. International actors such as ICITAP and CIVPOL may use pressure, but they cannot create political will where none exists. No matter how solid the international planning and implementation, if conditions on the ground are not permissive, then international efforts will founder. One former employee praised ICITAP for its attention to this point: "[In inter-agency discussions on Haiti,] I heard [ICITAP's Director] repeatedly raise the issue of whether political will was present, whether the government was committed to the project, but she was often overruled."[82] "Whole-force" police development projects such as Haiti tend to occur with a certain degree of political support; smaller assistance programs to existing forces may face a lack of will more often, particularly in larger countries where international influence is limited.

In addition, international actors must approach police assistance as more than a technical process. ICITAP disinclination to start a Burundi project and to use reviled ex-soldiers for policing in Haiti are illustrative of a broader point. Reforming or creating foreign police forces is not simply a technical matter whereby international actors can deliver training, deploy a new cadre of police and then leave. It is inevitably a political process, whereby certain groups are legitimate in society and others are not, and whereby religious, class and ethnic groups feel better protected if they are incorporated into the police and if it responds to their needs. Police advisers must ensure that they do not leave behind a Somoza-style police force in the hands of one political party, a single individual, or the military. Many ICITAP employees, seeking to work as technical experts and avoid politics, have favored utilizing existing security forces as the most expedient means of quickly establishing an effective tool for maintaining order.[83] However, ICITAP's leadership has displayed some sensitivity to these political

---

[82]Former ICITAP employee, interview by author, March-April 1997.

[83]William Stanley, *Protectors of Perpetrators: The Institutional Crisis of the Salvadoran Civilian Police* (Washington, DC: Washington Office on Latin America and Hemispheric Initiatives, January 1996).

questions, both in the peace process in El Salvador and in the general preference for nonmilitary recruits in Haiti. The lesson here, perhaps not fully learned by U.S. policy makers, is that international decisionmakers must pay attention to these highly political issues, often balancing them against technical ones.

Other conditions affect the success of police assistance. The effectiveness of the judicial system is perhaps the most relevant. In case after case, police reform efforts have outstripped the impact and pace of judicial reforms. In part this is because training and deploying a cop are easier and quicker than training a judge or a prosecutor who requires longer and more complex technical preparation before starting work than a police officer who will learn a great deal on the job once deployed. Basic-level cops generally have no more than a high-school education, whereas a law degree is often necessary for an officer of the court. Furthermore, the checks and balances imbedded in constitutional democracies, while imperfect in practice, generally mean that judges and judicial processes are more insulated from broad political changes than executive-controlled police forces. Ineffective international efforts in these areas have also made a difference, pointing to another lesson.

The effectiveness of police assistance is constrained and shaped by the overall international engagement with a country. ICITAP is just one U.S. agency, and its efforts must be viewed within the context of its relation to other international efforts. If one views police as only one leg of the "three-legged stool" of the criminal justice system which also includes the judiciary and the prison system, then one recurring problem is that U.S. police assistance has not been conceived or implemented in coordination with judicial assistance. For instance, ICITAP separation from AID judicial reform programs has deepened the gap between police development and judicial reform. AID has been oriented toward a longer time horizon and has felt less pressure to produce operational results quickly. It has also relied more upon contractors whose approaches and strengths vary.

Recent changes in U.S. bureaucratic organization have enhanced coordination of judicial and police assistance programs. In 1996, ICITAP offices and administrative staff were united with those of the

Justice Department's aid program for foreign judges and prosecutors, the Overseas Prosecutorial Development, Assistance, and Training (OPDAT). For Haiti, where judicial shortcomings have drawn much attention, responsibility for both the ICITAP and OPDAT U.S.-based operations is now unified under one person. And in Colombia, OPDAT and ICITAP jointly trained thousands of judges, police, and prosecutors in groups across the country in preparation for a wholly new judicial system. Also, policymakers are more willing to take strong measures aimed at harmonizing these two sides of the administration of justice: the State Department suspended the ICITAP program in the Dominican Republic in 1996 mainly because corresponding judicial reforms were not forthcoming.[84] Yet because police development can be achieved more quickly than developing judges, prosecutors and public defenders, newly deployed police officers are likely to continue confronting unresponsive courts.

Other examples abound of the limits the U.S. policymaking structure places upon ICITAP. For example, ICITAP involvement in a country is most often initiated as part of an overall U.S. policy decision. Often the circumstances requiring ICITAP services are precisely those that impede its effectiveness. The use of ICITAP as part of a frantic "exit strategy" in Somalia is an excellent example. ICITAP has some influence over when and how it carries out projects (e.g., the decision not to train the Haitian PSU), but this influence is limited.

The most prominent constraint in larger ICITAP projects has been the imperative to withdraw military forces from a country as quickly as possible and to shield them from public security functions—the "exit strategy syndrome." In situations such as Somalia and Haiti a military presence has been essential for filling the deployment gap so that meaningful international assistance programs can be initiated. Yet an overriding concern with the military exit has undermined efforts to build police, judicial and other institutions necessary to ensure security and to reorient attitudes and conduct. Rather than letting the exit strategy drive police development decisions, the performance of the police

---

[84]State Department ARA official, interview by author, March 25, 1997.

should shape the exit strategy. Long-term interests in security and conflict-prevention might best be served by basing the timing of troop withdrawal partly on whether the local public security force is capable of maintaining order and enjoying legitimacy and support.[85]

Perhaps the clearest lesson ICITAP has learned is that piecemeal training efforts are often squandered if not carried out in the context of long-term development and institutional strengthening. The initial tendency to provide whatever discrete courses were picked from a menu by recipient governments has been discredited, as this comment by ICITAP's deputy director illustrates:

> One of the lessons that ICITAP has taken out of the Panama, El Salvador and Haiti experiences is that even when we have a very small amount of money, we try to take a development approach. Now we never just go out and do a couple of courses in a vacuum. We try to put a technical adviser in at the beginning and try to create an environment in which training will make sense and then do the follow-on.[86]

Evidence suggests that other police assistance organizations such as the United Nations are largely unaware of and poorly organized for long-term institutional development.[87] Yet as one former staff member said, ICITAP confronts two very different sorts of situations:

> One is a situation like Colombia where police forces are up and running. . . . The other is a crisis case where a state has failed or a government is collapsed or is being rebuilt. These require very different personnel, different approaches, and a different logic.[88]

---

[85] I am grateful to Rachel Neild of the Washington Office on Latin America for this observation.

[86] Robert Perito, interview by author, March 18, 1997, Washington, DC.

[87] See Charles T. Call and Michael Barnett, "Looking for a Few Good Cops: Peacekeeping, Peacebuilding and the U.N. Civilian Police," paper presented at the International Studies Association conference, Toronto, Canada, March 1997.

[88] ICITAP official, interview by author, March-April 1997.

In smaller projects where existing forces are not being reconstituted, it is difficult to create an "institutional development" context.

Nevertheless, ICITAP has begun to find ways to do so. In Bolivia, for example, ICITAP was asked for limited assistance in training the investigative police unit. An ICITAP project manager arrived and found that broader problems of corruption and low quality stood in the way of successful training. Prepared to leave the country, he suggested broader reforms, and within a month obtained ministerial approval for such reforms and housecleaning. Within 7 months the old unit was disbanded, and within 1 year a new unit had been formed under new selection criteria with new procedures. Moreover, suggested changes in the police educational system subsequently led to improved upward mobility and higher educational levels for the main Bolivian police force. While such opportunities are not universal, ICITAP has pressed to identify them.

The limits of ICITAP's current capabilities and its small size have also become more apparent through recent "whole-force" programs. ICITAP cannot fill the deployment gap that immediately follows an international intervention. It is not configured to deploy massive numbers of personnel as a short-term international police monitoring force. As a result, other forces—be they reluctant military troops, scarce military police personnel, paramilitary (non-U.S.) gendarmerie forces, or a hypothetical standing international police rapid-deployment unit—must be relied upon to provide public order during the early stages of peace operations.

The U.S. Government is only beginning to put into place an interagency mechanism to address this problem. The challenge remains to find means to fill these public security gaps without exposing soldiers to unnecessary risk or detracting from other defense requirements. Currently there is no institutionalized coordination between the Defense Department and the Justice Department regarding peace operations and public security issues,[89] and many Pentagon officials do not

---

[89]Lieutenant Colonel Mark Haselton, Joint Staff, interview by author, May 29, 1997; Ralph Novak, Office of Inter-American Affairs, Office of the Secretary of Defense, interview by author, May 28, 1997.

understand the capabilities and limits of ICITAP. Planning occurs ad hoc around each crisis situation, when military planners and representatives of ICITAP and other agencies are brought together.

If ICITAP is unable to fill the deployment or enforcement gaps, it also needs help from the U.S. military and the United Nations to address the institutional gap. ICITAP cannot match the U.S. military's "surge" capacity for moving materials, people, and supplies necessary to set up a public security force quickly after an intervention. Nor does ICITAP have the resources to deploy monitors and field trainers all over a country, even one as small as Panama. Peacekeeping operations require UNCIVPOL or comparable forces (such as the U.S.-led International Police Monitors in Haiti) to provide vital field training and mentoring for newly trained and freshly deployed police. In its large-scale projects, ICITAP has focused instead on activities where small numbers might have broad institutional impact, such as developing doctrine and institutionalizing training curriculum and standard operating procedures. Multinational efforts such as CIVPOL are the only means of marshaling the manpower required for monitoring interim security forces until permanent forces are up and running, and for field training of those permanent forces.

The United Nations can also benefit from ICITAP experience. The United Nations currently has no organization dedicated wholly to the institutional development of police forces. UNCIVPOL has neither the resources nor the organization to have a standby pool of experienced police development specialists (as opposed to police monitors) who can dedicate a few years to erecting academies, developing standard operating procedures, and advising the leadership of new police forces.[90] U.N. Headquarters has only one full-time police adviser and four bilaterally-funded police staff to guide the selection, deployment, and logistics of some 3,600 CIVPOL around the globe. Bilateral programs such as ICITAP are needed to supplement the U.N. police monitoring function with coherent institution-building expertise and financial commitment.

---

[90]See Call and Barnett for a more detailed discussion of these issues.

One lesson gleaned from ICITAP experiences is that the demobilization dilemma is a genuine dilemma, but its effects can be mitigated by stringent selection criteria, effective oversight units, and broad public education about citizen-oriented policing. ICITAP has generally found that relying upon too many former members of militarized or politicized security forces can undermine the ability to foster changes in organizational culture and public image. Even technically sound and careful selection procedures may not resolve deep legitimacy problems. At the same time, a total exclusion of former security forces personnel en masse may lead to a backlash. A sense of unjust discrimination and lack of alternative job opportunities have facilitated the transformation of some ex-cops into ringleaders of organized, violent crime in several posttransition settings.

ICITAP has also found that members of existing security forces can be an important means of providing order on an interim basis. Despite fears by some observers in Haiti that unqualified ex-soldiers on the interim force would find their way into the permanent force, events showed that interim arrangements do not necessarily constrain decisions about permanent composition. Of course, vetting police-force members for human rights violations and criminal involvement is important to ensure the integrity of a new force. Given the limitations on data for vetting processes, however, ICITAP has learned the value of institutionalizing external and internal mechanisms for continuous accountability checks by the new force itself.

Even careful, well-planned, and amply funded attempts to develop accountability and diversity (e.g., the inclusion of women in police forces) will have limited impact absent an active and informed civil society. In former military regimes such as Haiti, the population has known security forces that only repress rather than protect them. Police reforms have limited effect unless large-scale education about human rights and police roles transforms citizen expectations. This applies for both accountability for abusive behavior and the incorporation of marginal groups. In general, unless civil society is broad based and well organized, efforts to enhance the representation of women and marginalized political or ethnic groups are likely to be disappointing.[91] Such efforts have received inadequate attention.

ICITAP has been slower to learn other lessons, such as the need for appropriate personnel. Because the ICITAP mandate focuses on criminal investigation, ICITAP initially relied principally upon law enforcement personnel from U.S. Federal agencies, especially the FBI. Starting with the first ICITAP director, the agency's main program positions were filled principally with FBI special agents whom it "rented" by renewable short-term contracts.[92] As ICITAP grew rapidly in the 1990s, it hired and advanced more "civilian" (i.e., nonlaw enforcement) staff. It also expanded a longstanding practice of hiring retired or active agents on loan from other federal law enforcement agencies to conduct training: the Drug Enforcement Agency, the Border Patrol, the U.S. Marshals, the U.S. Park Police, and Customs agents.

Beginning with Panama, ICITAP extended its training beyond investigators. Over time the agency learned that "whole force" projects require different sorts of skills and experience than they had originally possessed. Recognizing that the FBI has no experience in walking a beat, riot control, traffic control, rural patrols, or community-oriented policing, the agency began recruiting retired or active-duty state and local cops in the mid-1990s.[93] Somalia's Berkow was the first project manager drawn from a local police force, and he relied mainly upon active-duty local police officers there.[94] In addition, the great bulk of

---

[91] I am grateful for conversations with Professor Tracy Fitzsimmons in clarifying my thinking on this issue.

[92] This arrangement derived from several factors: (1) the agency's original mandate limiting it to investigative policing; (2) the absence of a national administrative police in the United States, and the status of the FBI as the biggest and best national criminal investigative force; (3) the experience of FBI agents in foreign embassies as law enforcement liaisons; and (4) the FBI's interest in furthering ICITAP's work in order to develop allies abroad in its own U.S. enforcement tasks.

[93] Over 90 percent of the instructors used in the Haiti project had local law enforcement backgrounds. Although roughly six FBI agents on loan to ICITAP between 1990 and 1997 continued to dominate the main project manager slots (including Panama, El Salvador, Haiti, Guatemala and a Deputy Director slot in 1997), the agency grew from 22 to 51 people in that time.

[94] Berkow, interview, April 5, 1997.

contract trainers in the field are active or retired local police. Yet ICITAP continues to rely principally upon persons with federal law enforcement backgrounds, in part because they are generally more available than cops from smaller, cash-strapped local U.S. forces. As of March 1997, only three of ICITAP's 51 permanent employees had backgrounds in local law enforcement. Consequently, some human rights groups point out that ICITAP, like other international bilateral programs and U.S. programs, has drawn upon national-level models that underemphasize community policing, local participation, and local means of accountability such as civilian review boards.[95]

Finally, ICITAP illustrates an important evolution of bilateral U.S. police assistance: it is possible to overcome the problems of association with human rights abuses that plagued OPS. Although ICITAP-trained individuals have been implicated in human rights violations in places such as El Salvador and Haiti, ICITAP has not been accused of responsibility for these incidents. Instead, local human rights groups in those countries have generally attributed abuses to factors beyond the control of international police trainers.[96] Although the possibility of abetting abuses is ever present, the experience of ICITAP shows that, given a carefully constructed mandate, close monitoring by both the executive and legislative branches, support for mechanisms of accountability, and a willingness to avoid training in certain circumstances, bilateral police aid can avoid furthering human rights abuses and even be perceived as contributing to the protection of human rights.

Part of avoiding the OPS fate derives from ICITAP interaction with human rights groups. Rob Weiner of the Lawyers Committee for Human Rights described the evolution of human rights groups' attitude about ICITAP as passing from "suspicion" in the late 1980s, to an "ICITAP-neutral" phase, and then to a third phase since the mid-1990s, where there is "a limited desire by ICITAP to hear what human rights

---

[95]Rachel Neild, Washington Office on Latin America, to author, letter dated April 24, 1997.

[96]Human rights groups, interviews in El Salvador, November 1995, January 1996; and in Haiti, spring/summer 1996.

groups have to say, to do what it can to avoid problems and to incorporate the input of groups from civil society."[97] In Haiti, for instance, ICITAP invited speakers from human rights, business, and popular groups to weekly open fora with HNP cadets at the academy. At the same time, human rights groups point out that ICITAP has engaged in very limited consultation with the nongovernmental human rights groups of the countries where programs are carried out.[98]

Conclusions

Organization theorists have long noted the inertia with which organizations respond to change in their environment, and academics generally believe that institutional learning is rare in the field of U.S. police and military assistance. Conventional wisdom holds that starry-eyed police advisers and reformers commit the same well-intentioned (or not so well-intentioned) mistakes abroad that prior reformers committed. Certainly many of the same constraints that faced U.S. police assistance during the days of OPS and prior decades continue to vex ICITAP operations. Operational and planning problems clearly persist.

Yet as the end of the Cold War ushered in a new wave of global police assistance efforts, ICITAP adaptation to changing circumstances is instructive. As one State Department official mentioned in an offhand remark upon hearing of this research project, "ICITAP has always shown an unusual willingness to examine its own warts." Many of the lessons learned by ICITAP—an orientation toward institutional development over short-term training, an ability to recognize when police training would be unwise, etc.—have not been learned by other U.S. agencies or by other bilateral or multilateral police aid providers such as the United Nations.[99] As a congressional staff member stated,

---

[97]Weiner, interview, March 24, 1997.

[98]Neild, interview, April 1997. In general the increased importance of the human rights movement and international human rights norms has certainly shaped the environment in which police assistance occurs.

[99]See Call and Barnett.

"Despite all of ICITAP's problems, which are numerous, it is the best effort in the world right now, practically alone. Other countries won't touch this stuff [police aid], and the U.N. has been very slow in coming on-line with this."[100] Police assistance programs will always run the risk of imposing inappropriate models, squandering resources where training is unwelcome, and abetting abusive practices. Political authorities bear the responsibility of minimizing these risks, and they have sought to do so with ICITAP, with more or less success. ICITAP history demonstrates that police assistance can improve the effectiveness and conduct of the government forces which are often most in contact with citizens around the world.

---

[100]Comments made at the National Defense University review session, May 28, 1997.

CIVILIAN POLICE IN U.N. PEACEKEEPING OPERATIONS

HARRY BROER and MICHAEL EMERY

Introduction

We prepare for war like precocious giants and for peace like retarded pygmies.

Lester B. Pearson

So wrote former Canadian Prime Minister Lester B. Pearson in his Nobel Peace Prize acceptance speech in 1957. Although Pearson's words may be considered inappropriate in the politically correct 1990s, the implication is strikingly relevant in the post-Cold War era, particularly in the context of postconflict peace building. As with many problems facing an increasingly global community today, the causes of conflicts may be clearly identified, but the solutions are much harder to come by. In his 1992 report, "An Agenda for Peace," former U.N. Secretary-General Boutros Boutros-Ghali suggested, "Peacemaking and peacekeeping operations, to be truly successful, must come to include comprehensive efforts to identify and support structures which will tend to consolidate peace and advance a sense of confidence and well being among people."[1] Indeed, the international community has become increasingly aware that without a fair, functioning, and transparent criminal justice system, of which law enforcement agencies are an essential part, there is little chance for meaningful lasting peace in divided communities.

With the end of the Cold War and the dissolution of the Soviet Union, threats to peace have taken on a new character. The fear of

---

[1]Boutros Boutros-Ghali, *An Agenda for Peace: Preventative Diplomacy, Peacemaking and Peace-keeping* (New York: United Nations, 1992), 32.

nuclear war, which ironically imposed an awesome stability on the international system, has been replaced by unpredictable "brush-fire" conflicts, which are much more likely to be intrastate than interstate.

This transformation of the international system had obvious implications for the role of U.N. peacekeeping. The traditional function of "holding the line" between opposing forces and supervising a truce has been superseded by more complex and more risky roles. Almost all peacekeeping operations before 1989 involved relatively simple situations where the potential combatants were easily identifiable, and the task of policing a buffer zone was relatively straightforward.[2]

Today, peacekeepers are called upon to serve in a complex, often tense milieu of domestic conflict, one largely characterized by civil war and ethnic rivalry. The roles of peacekeepers have come to include a wide range of confidence-building measures, such as holding of elections and restructuring government institutions.

As a vital part of this challenge to restore and nurture confidence and well being among people in divided communities, the UNCIVPOL are responsible for monitoring, reconstructing, and restructuring some of the elements of the national criminal justice system. From local police forces to the courts to even the prison systems, a fair and effective justice sector is at the heart of civil society and as such is now often the focus of U.N. peacekeeping efforts.

UNCIVPOL in a Peacekeeping Mission

Philosophy of CIVPOL

Each U.N. Civilian Police Mission is guided by a similar objective: ensuring that local law enforcement officers and institutions are respecting human rights and fundamental freedoms.

In "first-generation" peacekeeping operations, U.N. personnel were deployed as impartial referees. During these missions, only U.N. military troops were deployed, and they frequently assumed police

---

[2]For further information, refer to *The Blue Helmets: A Review of United Nations Peace-keeping*, 3rd ed. (New York: U.N. Department of Public Information, 1997).

duties, including riot control. Only two peacekeeping operations prior to 1989 contained U.N. civilian police components, both dating from the early 1960s. The U.N. operation in the Congo (1960-64) drew on Ghanian and Nigerian police for a few months, and the Cyprus operation (1964 to the present) originally included a 175-person U.N. civilian police unit,[3] which was the first to come under the now familiar term "UNCIVPOL," but which was reduced to 35 by the late 1970s.[4] By and large, therefore, most operations focused on monitoring the military forces of opposing states. Thus, U.N. peacekeeping operations were composed of "blue helmets" rather than "blue berets."[5] Since 1990, however, a CIVPOL component has become an integral part of most U.N. operations, and in the case of Bosnia, it is the primary focus of U.N. involvement.[6]

The "classic" UNCIVPOL concept was to draw experienced police officers from Member States, deploy them to troubled areas and, through various mandated responsibilities (some more realistic than others), expect them to perform a host of ostensibly impartial activities aimed at creating the law and order conditions necessary for lasting peace.

Unlike military personnel, CIVPOL usually work and live in the local community, in many cases sharing accommodations with a local family; hence, in many ways, they are the eyes and ears of the peacekeeping operation. UNCIVPOL has their own command structure within the overall context of the mission headed by a U.N.-appointed Commissioner (with the exception of U.N. Peackeeping Force in

---

[3]Ibid., 152.

[4]Ibid., 170.

[5]The term "blue helmets" refers to armed military components of a United Nations peacekeeping force; "blue berets" refers to the unarmed civilian police component of peacekeeping operations even though, on most occasions, the military, military observers, and civilian police all wear the U.N. blue beret.

[6]In December 1995 the Security Council adopted Resolution 1031, which created the 1,721-strong International Police Task Force for Bosnia-Herzegovina. The main peacekeeping responsibilities for the theater shifted from the(UNPROFOR to a NATO-led IFOR, hence shifting the primary focus of U.N. involvement to the civilian police component.

Cyprus, where UNCIVPOL comes under military command). In the planning stage of the U.N. Angola Verification Mission III (UNAVEM III), bringing the CIVPOL component again under the Military Force Commander was considered. In hindsight, this would have been an incorrect decision.[7]

Although both civilian police and the military form the uniformed part of peacekeeping operations, there are significant cultural differences between them. The traditional role of the military is to provide territorial security against armed attacks from outside. They are unit and group oriented, with emphasis on purely military operations. In peacekeeping operations, their role is mainly related to demobilization of forces; supervision on cessation of hostilities; and disarmament of warring factions and providing security for the mission.

The traditional role of a police force is to provide internal security by enforcing law and order. The focus of CIVPOL activity centers primarily on relationships with local police and civilians and requires a different mindset. The role of police in peacekeeping is almost the same as traditional local policing, with one important exception: CIVPOL in a peacekeeping operation (PKO) normally has no law enforcement powers. There are very good reasons why CIVPOL normally is not responsible for the enforcement of law and order: this is par excellence a responsibility of local authorities. Neither they nor CIVPOL-contributing governments are inclined to accept that such responsibilities be assumed by the United Nations; the costs would be prohibitive; and the risks of casualties and escalation would be great. However, when "civilian police" arrive in a war-torn country where the local institutions of law and order are not working properly, there is an understandable tendency for the local population to expect CIVPOL to assume an authoritative role and correct the situation. This perception must be addressed by ensuring that the local population understands the limitations of the CIVPOL mandate.

---

[7]The civilian police component of UNAVEM III was and is considered to be vital in achieving a lasting peace in Angola and hence warranted the status and autonomy of an independent police component within the overall structure of the mission.

Notwithstanding their lack of law enforcement authority, CIVPOL can and do undertake tasks that place them in difficult and dangerous situations. CIVPOL often have to operate outside the bounds of normal community policing and are thus exposed to confrontation with one or more of the parties. An example is the checkpoint policy introduced by the U.N. IPTF in Bosnia in order to ensure implementation of the freedom of movement provisions of the Dayton Agreement.[8] Under this policy, IPTF requires the removal of unlicensed checkpoints established by the parties and, if they do not comply, calls in the NATO-led SFOR to remove the checkpoints, by force if necessary. This policy has an obvious advantage and an obvious risk: it will be good for the peace process if the parties can be persuaded by IPTF to permit freedom of movement rather than being forced by SFOR to do so; but when IPTF is obliged to ask SFOR to use force, it puts at risk its relations with the local police force concerned and thus its ability to carry out other parts of its mandate that require the daily cooperation of that force. Thus, a decision has to be taken on whether higher priority should be given to local police reform or to enforcement of freedom of movement.

Another reason for not giving UNCIVPOL law enforcement powers is that the police are part of the justice package (public administration, police, prosecutor, judges, prison system). If one of those five institutions is not in place, which is often the case in a troubled area, there is a huge problem. In the last phase of the mission in Cambodia, U.N. police were given powers of arrest, with a special U.N. Prosecutor and a prison that was built and secured by personnel of the U.N. Transitional Authority in Cambodia (UNTAC). However, no judge was prepared to sentence Cambodians. As a result those individuals were put in prison, sometimes for more than 3 months, without being brought before a judge, which obviously is a significant violation of

---

[8] As outlined in the tasks set out in the Dayton Peace Accords, Annex II, Department of State, *Dispatch Supplement* 7, supplement number 1, March 1996.

369

human rights and led to allegations of abuse against the United Nations.[9]

Mandates and Tasks of CIVPOL

Mandates of UNCIVPOL have varied widely, although the overriding objective has not altered. The most common and successful CIVPOL mandates have included:

☐ Monitoring local law and order forces to ensure that they perform their duties in a manner consistent with the agreement
☐ Training local police forces
☐ Ensuring free and fair elections
☐ Supporting programs for the reform of local law and order forces or for creation of a new police force
☐ Investigating alleged violations of human rights either in the context of their monitoring function or in support of the human rights component
☐ Assisting nations in institution building, specifically law enforcement institutions.

The primary duty of U.N. police is monitoring, which means ensuring local police carry out their tasks without discrimination against any individual and with full respect for human rights of all persons in the mission area. Tasks evolving from the monitoring function are:

☐ Observing the conduct and performance of local police and judicial investigative authorities in arresting, detaining, and interrogating criminal suspects, handling prisoners, and searching residences
☐ Accompanying local police on patrols
☐ Attending the scenes of crime

---

[9]Brigadier General Klaas C. Roos, UNTAC Commissioner, interview by author, July 1997, New York.

☐ Conducting investigations as required, where inquiry by the local investigative body is seen to be inadequate due to bias, indifference, or a deliberate intent to mislead the course of justice

☐ Conducting independent patrols and observing the presence or absence of local police

☐ Observing and monitoring movements of refugees, displaced persons, returnees and the exchange of prisoners of war and the bodies of those killed in the conflict

☐ Observing gatherings, rallies, and demonstrations

☐ Visiting prisons and observe treatment of prisoners

☐ Following investigations against minorities, through the judicial system and monitor the final results

☐ Assisting humanitarian aid agencies and the United Nations Civil Affairs component

☐ Helping defuse intercommunal tensions

☐ Recording and reporting incidents, as directed

☐ Ensuring tranquillity and insisting on the maintenance of law and order in the vicinity of and within voter registration offices and polling stations

☐ Ensuring that no person is denied entry into the aforementioned centers for the purpose of registration and/or voting

☐ Assisting in the establishment and training of the local Police Force.

Implementing a UNCIVPOL Mission

It was with the 1964 UNCIVPOL concept in mind that the United Nations initiated in Namibia in 1989 its first large-scale civilian police deployment. In essence, the U.N. Transition Assistance Group (UNTAG) mandate was to monitor the local police forces and to assist in creating the necessary conditions for the March 21, 1990, elections. Unlike the U.N. Forces in Cyprus (UNFICYP) mission, where the United Nations had the relative luxury of only 35 well-prepared monitors, the sheer size of the Namibia operation (drawing 1,500 police from 25 countries[10]) required assistance from Member States with little or no experience of policing in a U.N. peacekeeping domain. Although in general the UNTAG mission was considered relatively successful, it clearly illustrated that without adequate preparation deployed civilian police were often functionally ineffective. Unfortunately, the lessons identified with the large-scale UNTAG deployment were to be repeated with successive large-scale police deployments in the early mid-1990s.[11]

Because there has been a major change in the types of conflicts that the United Nations is being enlisted to confront, most peacekeeping operations since 1989 concern not the monitoring of politics across borders, but rather the politics within borders. Whereas once peacekeepers were situated solely between two combatants who had agreed to a cease-fire and were rarely engaged in offensive action, "second-generation" operations are involved in a variety of activities associated with nation building and peace enforcement.

Reflecting this change, there has been a sharp expansion in the presence and responsibilities of U.N. civilian police. Because most of the recent peacekeeping operations have involved an attempt to foster political reconciliation and to establish democratic law enforcement institutions, the role of the U.N. civilian police has grown in importance.

In February 1995 there were 1,325 police officers deployed in various U.N. Missions.[12] This number increased to 2,998 by July 1997,[13] drawn from 53 countries and deployed in seven missions. The largest mission is UNIPTF in Bosnia-Herzegovina with an authorized strength of 2,027.[14]

---

[10]*The Blue Helmets*, 210.

[11]In particular, Cambodia (UNTAC), Angola (UNAVEM I, II, and III), the missions in the Former Yugoslavia (UNPROFOR, UNCRO, UNPREDEP), and Mozambique (ONUMOZ).

[12]U.N. Department of Peacekeeping Operations, Personnel Statistics Unit, Monthly Peacekeeping Personnel Statistics, February 1995.

[13]Ibid., July 1997.

[14]Ibid., 18.

General View

At the end of July 1997, the President of the U.N. Security Council made a statement emphasizing the increasing role and special functions of civilian police in U.N. missions.

In this statement, the following important aspects are worth mentioning:

    ☐ The Security Council encourages Member States to look for further means to enhance the way civilian police components are set up and supported.

    ☐ Civilian police perform indispensable functions in monitoring and training national police forces and can play a major role in restoring civil order, supporting the rule of law, and fostering civil reconciliation.

    ☐ Civilian police play an increasingly important role in building confidence and security between parties and among local populations in order to prevent conflict, to contain conflict, or to build peace in the aftermath of a conflict.

    ☐ The Council underlines the importance of recruiting qualified civilian police from the widest possible geographic range and expressed the importance of recruitment of female officers.

    ☐ The Council encourages Member States, individually or collectively, to provide appropriate training of civilian police for international service and encourages the Secretary-General to provide assistance and guidance to Member States in order to promote a standardized approach toward their training and recruitment.

    ☐ The Council encourages Member States to make available to the United Nations, at short notice, appropriately trained civilian police, if possible, through U.N. standby arrangements. It welcomes the role of UNCIVPOL Selection Assistance Teams.

    ☐ The Council underlines the necessity for UNCIVPOL to be trained as required to render assistance and support in reorganizing, training and monitoring national police forces and to help defuse tension on the ground through negotiations.[15]

This statement underlines the demanding challenges facing UNCIVPOL. To meet these challenges several issues, discussed below, must be addressed.

Recruitment Standards

During the last few years, recruitment standards have been strengthened to include the following requirements:

☐ A minimum of 5 years, or for more difficult missions at least 8 years, of active policing experience
☐ Ability to drive 4 x 4 vehicles
☐ Oral and written fluency in the working language of each particular mission.[16]

Further, recruitment efforts are now targeted toward specialized skills in a variety of fields, like judges, lawyers, investigators and computer specialists.

Language Problems

Probably the most glaring issue confronting UNCIVPOL has been monitors having little or no English language fluency. Although the United Nations required that monitors "had the ability to communicate in the official mission language"[17] (usually English[18]), this requirement has often been ignored. It was not uncommon for monitors to arrive in the theater of operations barely able to write their names on the

---

[15]Security Council Presidential Statement, July 14, 1997.

[16]Michael Emery, *Selection Standards and Training Guidelines for United Nations Civilian Police* (New York: U.N. Department of Peacekeeping Operations, 1997), 18.

[17]Ibid., 18.

[18]Other official mission languages have included Spanish and French.

forms required for their identification cards.[19] The reasons behind this were many and varied ranging from Member States (and individual monitors) simply unable to afford expensive English language training courses to monitors being sent on mission as political favors regardless of their language ability. On a recent visit to Nepal, a U.N. Selection Assistance Team (SAT) discovered that, in an attempt to meet required English language standards, some police officers were spending the equivalent of a full year's salary enrolling in English language courses.[20] The lack of fluency in the mission language translates directly into lack of effectiveness on the ground, which has seriously hampered successive UNCIVPOL missions. Monitors lacking the necessary language skills found it difficult to write even the simplest of reports, often sending in copies of previous reports reading "situation calm, patrolling proceeding as normal" or "NTR"—nothing to report— regardless of the situation on the ground. These same monitors had difficulty understanding spoken and written instructions and were largely unable to communicate with the local population through interpreters. In addition to problems with the official mission language, some monitors even had difficulty communicating in the official language of their home country, further complicating an already unsatisfactory situation.

Various attempts have been made to address the language issue. In 1994, UNCIVPOL Commissioner for the UNPROFOR, Michael O'Reily, RCMP, initiated a simple English language test (consisting of a number of multiple choice questions) that monitors had to pass on arrival in Zagreb.[21] Although the test was a step in the right direction, it was not long before contingents were arriving with memorized answers, and cheating during the testing procedure was not

---

[19]Jane Adams, Chief of the Pass and Identification Unit for the U.N. Missions in the Former Yugoslavia, interview by author, June 1997, Australia.

[20]The average salary for a Nepalese police officer in 1997 was barely U.S. $200.

[21]Chief Superintendent Michael O'Reiley, RCMP (Ret.), Commissioner UNPROFOR, interview by author, April 1996, Canada.

uncommon.[22] All too often the real work in police stations was left to those monitors possessing adequate language skills, which tended to create resentment toward those without, who either did the best with their limited skills or tended to withdraw both personally and professionally in the station.[23]

Driving Problems

The second major issue confronting civilian police in the 1990s was poor driving skills. In every mission, from UNTAG in Namibia to IPTF in Bosnia-Herzegovina, there has been a significant disparity in driving abilities ranging from excellent to absolutely appalling. As with poor language skills, this has seriously hindered monitors ability to perform in the mission area. Not only have they posed a safety risk to themselves and others, they also added extra strain to fellow monitors who had to assume driving responsibilities. In addition, frequent accidents have created extra burdens on already "thin" logistical resources. In the current IPTF mission, as many as one-third of vehicles are out of order[24] largely because of traffic accidents. Some monitors have arrived without even knowing the basic rudiments of driving. As with language skills, the reasons for poor driving are varied, ranging from an acute lack of access to vehicles in some Member States, to driving in unfamiliar vehicles and conditions, to driving on a different side of the road, to having driven only with a police-provided chauffeur. Unlike language skills, however, poor driving skills can be, and often are, life threatening. From the inception of the U.N. missions in the former Yugoslavia until December 1995, over 250 United Nations personnel were killed and 1,900 injured—slightly over one-

---

[22]Robert Pettigrew, UNPF civilian police examination officer, interview by author, October 1995, Zagreb.

[23]Chief Superintendent. Karl-Georg Andersson, U.N. Department of Peacekeeping Operations Civilian Police Unit, interview by author, May 1997, New York.

[24]Inspector Mohamed Ali Bin Jamaluddin, Chief Transport Officer, IPTF, interview by author, February, 1997, Malaysia.

third were from traffic accidents.[25] Compounding this driving problem is the poor quality of many U.N. vehicles.

Cultural Tension

There have been tensions caused by mixing police from many different cultures. Often there have been as many as 15 to 20 different nationalities working in the same station, bringing with them differing policing traditions, religious belief systems, working ethics, hygiene standards, eating habits, and agendas. In a training needs assessment (TNA) conducted by the UNPROFOR Training Management Unit in September 1995, many monitors identified the issue of working within a multicultural station environment as the most pressing issue that needed to be addressed through training at a station level.[26] One Finnish monitor interviewed as part of the TNA was appalled when, upon visiting a police station in Knin, Croatia, he witnessed the local Serb militia beating a detainee. His UNCIVPOL partner at the time was not fazed by the beating, seeing it as a necessary part of the interrogation process. Another interview revealed toilet habits as a source of frustration in one particular station, with one monitor continually cracking the toilet seat as a result of standing and squatting instead of sitting.[27]

Planning

While Member States must assume much of the responsibility for poor language and driving skills of the monitors, U.N. Headquarters has also been found deficient in its own UNCIVPOL premission planning and logistical support. This has been, in part, because of the Department of Peacekeeping Operations (DPKO) sailing in uncharted waters, with the enormous growth in global peacekeeping responsibilities in the early 1990s, and also in part because of a lack of importance attached

---

[25]U.N. Peace Forces (formerly UNPROFOR) Medical Office, Weekly Casualty Statistics, Zagreb, December 1995.

[26]Belinda Goslin and Rob Pettigrew, *Training Needs Assessment for United Nations Civilian Police* (Zagreb, 1995), 47.

[27]Ibid., 48.

to the civilian police concept at a strategic planning level. In UNTAC, for example, UNCIVPOL Commissioner Brigadier General Klaas Roos noted at an extensive debriefing session held in Singapore in December 1995,

> The largest, most expensive and most complicated CIVPOL mission [to date] had suffered in particular from very poor preparatory planning; from inadequately prepared and qualified personnel; from insufficient resources and powers to deal with the tasks assigned; and from tensions and problems within and between the various components of UNTAC.[28]

Roos also noted that no police element was included in the U.N. Advanced Mission in Cambodia (UNAMIC), which was deployed to Cambodia in November 1991 to facilitate the later arrival of the UNTAC mission. Roos himself was only officially appointed Commissioner 1 week before he left for Cambodia in March 1992, and it took the United Nations almost 8 months to achieve the peak staffing level of just over 3,300 UNCIVPOL monitors.[29]

It was not until May 1993, after the UNTAG and UNTAC experiences, that a separate Civilian Police Unit was established as part of DPKO (containing only one funded position, that of Police Adviser, with minimal administrative support). A further problem was the lack of attention given to other crucial criminal justice elements. The UNTAC and UNMIH missions were good examples of this where inadequate judicial and penal support proved a hindrance to the newly established and trained Cambodian and Haitian police forces, respectively.

---

[28]Duncan Chappell and John Evans, "The Role, Preparation and Performance of Civilian Police in United Nations Peacekeeping Operations," unpublished report (Vienna: U.N. Crime Prevention and Criminal Justice Division, 1997), 31.
[29]Ibid., 32.

Quantity and Quality

Another problem is the inadequate survey of police officers to serve as UNCIVPOL. It has both a quantitative and a qualitative aspect. The quantitative problem is that governments do not have at their disposal police officers who are not already engaged in important functions in their own country. Soldiers can normally be made available for U.N. peacekeeping service without impairing their governments' ability to defend the national territory. Most police forces, however, are already stretched and are, therefore, reluctant to spare good officers for U.N. service. Sometimes political pressure from one Member State on another is needed to get the numbers of police officers required for a peacekeeping operation. In many countries, constitutional factors make it difficult for the central government to order them to do so. Recent experience in Bosnia has demonstrated the hazards of recruiting retired officers unless candidate backgrounds are meticulously checked.[30]

The qualitative aspect arises from the nature of CIVPOL work. It involves daily interaction not only with local police but with the ordinary people of the country, sometimes in trying circumstances and usually through interpreters. This requires personal skills of an even higher order than those expected of police officers dealing with their compatriots in their own country in their own language. They differ from skills required of U.N. military officers, even military observers, who usually deal with their fellow-soldiers. The organization's practice therefore has been to seek rather senior officers for CIVPOL missions, both because of the delicacy of their tasks and the clout needed vis-a-vis their local counterparts. This adds to the quantitative problem. A further complication is the wide variation in the qualifications required to attain a given rank in different police forces. This problem exists to some extent with military officers, too; the education, training, experience, and military skills to be expected in a lieutenant colonel will

---

[30]The U.S. civilian police contingent deployed to IPTF was largely made up of retired officers recruited via a personnel contracting company (DynCorp) and hence were contractually linked to the company, not the national government. The U.S. contingent had the highest desertion rate of any contingent in the IPTF mission.

vary somewhat from army to army, but planners can nevertheless design a mission headquarters, for instance, in the knowledge that they can count on a certain minimum level of qualifications in an officer of that rank.

To compensate for this wide variation in skills, the police commissioner (PC) in a U.N. mission must be able to identify those police officers who have the skills required to perform senior management roles, taking into account a global distribution of functions. In requesting police officers for a PKO, the CIVPOL Unit in DPKO makes it clear to Member States that it is the prerogative of the PC to select his management team.[31]

Weapons

The success of CIVPOL operations depends largely on the support and cooperation given to it by international military forces, and there must be a clear understanding of the roles played by CIVPOL and the military. After almost 30 years of operations, it must be clear that CIVPOL is not a security force. In most cases, CIVPOL is unarmed and does not have executive law enforcement authority.

A major point of discussion at the startup of a CIVPOL mission is whether CIVPOL should be armed or unarmed. UNCIVPOL are generally unarmed with the notable exceptions of UNMIH in Haiti, the U.N. Guards Contingent in Iraq (UNGCI),[32] and for a short time, UNTAC in Cambodia. Hence, the security of the CIVPOL relies largely on the moral authority of the blue beret. At the Singapore CIVPOL conference in December 1995,[33] discussions on this topic were lengthy and intense. The positions correspond also to the national tradition of the police, some being armed at home, others not. Views were varied

---

[31]Chief Superintendent Om Prakash Rathor, Chief, U.N. Department of Peacekeeping Operations Civilian Police Unit, interview by author, July 1997, New York.

[32]The UNGCI were a lightly armed, quasi-civilian police contingent not administered by the Civilian Police Unit in New York.

[33]Conference conducted by IPS/UNITAR on The Role and Function of Civilian Police in Peacekeeping Operations.

but, in general, there was consensus that while some missions could warrant the need for carrying arms, in most cases this was not welcome; being unarmed remained one of the particular features that distinguished civilian police from the military, for example.

In the former Yugoslavia, some monitors were of the firm belief that they needed sidearms for self-protection in the often volatile Yugoslav theater.[34] However, these monitors were in the minority, with most realizing that they were much less of a threat and therefore much less at risk while unarmed. This point was well illustrated when, in 1995, in an attempt to combat a spate of U.N. car-jackings, armed U.N. military escorts were assigned to civilian drivers. In the first week after this initiative was introduced, a Kenyan soldier and Czech civilian found themselves in a car-jacking. The Kenyan was shot dead, the Czech was shot through the ankles, and the U.N. vehicle was stolen.

The first discussion of arming CIVPOL arose when the Namibian operation (UNTAG) was set up in 1989. To bridge differences of opinion, a compromise allowed those national contingents normally armed in their home country to bring their sidearms and ammunition to the mission area and keep them in storage there. Despite this arrangement, UNTAG still faced problems. One national contingent brought AK-47s, claiming this was a regular police weapon in the home country.[35] Two other contingents unilaterally decided to issue the stored sidearms when some of their contingent members felt insecure at a certain point in the mission.

It took Commissioner Stephen Fanning and his Chief of Operations Colonel Klaas Roos (later Commissioner of CIVPOL in UNTAC) quite a bit of discussion and negotiation with contingent commanders, as well as diplomatic representatives, to restore the U.N. policy concerning unarmed CIVPOL. Three years later, in Cambodia, Roos again had problems regarding the issue. As a confidence-building measure, Roos had ordered CIVPOL monitors to patrol local communities 24 hours a

---

[34]As articulated by several participants in a workshop conducted by the U.N. Crime Prevention and Criminal Justice Division at Wiener Neustadt, Austria, in December 1995.

[35]Brigadier General Klaas Roos, interview by author, July 1997, New York.

day. Because of the presence of groups of undisciplined armed soldiers and armed bandits, the commissioner requested a security backup from the U.N. military component. Some of these military contingents, however, were reluctant to leave their compounds at night. Instead of trying to convince these contingents otherwise, the Military Force Commander requested the SRSG to arm the CIVPOL so that they could act more efficiently as a security force. The CIVPOL Commissioner, however, fiercely opposed this idea and strongly advised the SRSG against it. Similarly, certain CIVPOL contingents even suggested they would withdraw from the mission if ordered to arm themselves.[36]

In the end, the SRSG decided not to arm CIVPOL. There is solid evidence to indicate this is a prudent policy. In large CIVPOL missions, (e.g., UNTAG at 1,500; UNTAC at 3,600; and UNMIBH/IPTF at 2,000) no CIVPOL lives have been lost as a result of the unarmed status of U.N. police officers.[37]

When he was Chief of Operations in Cambodia, Peter Fitzgerald outlined several reasons why CIVPOL should not be armed:

□ The objectives of arming the CIVPOL would be to provide us with self-protection and to allow us to control the situation. It would do neither, as CIVPOL could not match the "firepower" in a country where a PKO is deployed.

□ I can think of no situation in which CIVPOL have been involved to date that being armed would have helped: on the contrary we have been shot, threatened, detained, robbed, and generally abused, not killed, and in none of these situations would a sidearm have helped.

□ Unarmed we do not pose a threat to any person and so can perform our duty more effectively. Our best protection is the professional performance of our duty in a neutral, impartial manner.

---

[36]Ibid.

[37]U.N. Department of Peacekeeping Operations Medical Support Unit., *Cumulative Statistics, 1989-1997.*

☐ We have gained the confidence and respect of the people by being unarmed. This will be damaged if we suddenly become an armed force and will create a feeling of unrest and a belief among the people that things are worse than they are.

☐ There are already too many guns in circulation, and this is what has created the problem; arming CIVPOL will only add fuel to the fire.

☐ I would be very concerned about the competence of many of our police to possess, carry and use firearms.

☐ Those that would shoot us can do so at any time at present but can never use the excuse that they did so in self-defense. This lack of motive is a further protection for us.

☐ Possession of firearms would mean possession 24 hours a day. CIVPOL houses would become targets as a means of obtaining weapons. Further to this they would be carried on and off duty and so I believe would create problems in bars, restaurants, etc.

☐ I am convinced that no Police Force can succeed by force of arms or indeed by force of numbers but only on their moral authority as servants of the people and answerable to the people they serve. The United Nations name and emblems provide us with that moral authority.[38]

Another argument could be added: in UNCIVPOL operations the police generally do not have law enforcement powers, and sidearms are mainly for self-defense in situations in which the police have to make an arrest.

The overriding opinion of civilian police leadership, both past and present, is that the U.N. policy *not* to arm the police is the correct one.

International Standards

Another issue arises in the context of CIVPOL monitoring of, and advice to, local police forces. What standards of policing should

---

[38]Peter Fitzgerald (Chief of Operations), Evaluation Report, UNCIVPOL, UNTAC Cambodia, Phnom Penh, 1993.

CIVPOL insist on? Should they be "international standards" and, if so, how defined? Or should they be standards commonly applied in the region concerned? Partial answers can be found in the international human rights instruments to which the country in question is party and in the country's existing legislation, assuming that it conforms with those instruments. The Crime Prevention and Criminal Justice Division in Vienna has prepared a handbook with criminal justice standards for peacekeeping police.[39] It attempts to provide a compact overview of relevant international standards and norms, and it is designed to serve both as a basis for reporting on activities of local law enforcement officials and as a reference source to work with them. The "Blue Book" regulates the following 10 areas:

- Arrest
- Force and firearms
- Trials
- Victims
- Detainees and prisoners
- Torture and cruel treatment
- Illegal execution
- Genocide
- Humanitarian rules
- Refugee protection.

It has been used in several training courses for civilian police components of U.N. missions and has been translated into Arabic, French, Spanish, and Serbo-Croat.

Furthermore, the U.N. Centre for Human Rights has provided training in international human rights standards and criminal justice to CIVPOL in ONUMOZ and UNPROFOR in recent years.[40] It is also

---

[39]U.N. Crime Prevention and Criminal Justice Branch, U.N. Criminal Justice Standards for Peacekeeping Police, UNOV, 1996.

[40]U.N. High Commissioner for Human Rights, *Human Rights and Law Enforcement: Field Guide for International Police Task Force Monitors of the Peace Implementation Operation in Bosnia-Herzegovina and CIVPOL Officers of the United*

preparing a manual on human rights and field operations. Answers may also be found in the peace agreement that provides the basis for the U.N. operations. In Bosnia, for instance, guidelines on "democratic policing" were prepared on the basis of the Dayton Agreement and issued by the IPTF Police Commissioner.[41]

Logistics

One of the most common problems identified by many police commissioners at the Singapore Conference in 1995 was the lack of sufficient logistical support caused by what they called the U.N. "Blue Tape."[42] Usually military troops arrive in the mission area with their own equipment whereas the CIVPOL forces are deployed only with their own national uniform. They are dependent on logistical support provided by the United Nations, but lack of adequate equipment, communication systems, and transportation arrangements has been problematic in many CIVPOL operations.

In Singapore, the recommendation was made that U.N. Headquarters develop the capacity to be more responsive to specific requests made by the team in the field with regard to logistics. Authority, and subsequent accountability, should be delegated to the U.N. Police Commissioner in the field. It is unlikely that this suggestion will be implemented because of the accounting processes incorporated in United Nations regulations, but the Lessons Learned Unit in DPKO has made several recommendations to address logistical problems:

☐ Operational and logistics plans should be fully integrated and developed together. As soon as a "concept of operations" is formulated, a "logistics concept" should be developed, followed by

---

Nations Transitional Administration in Eastern Slavonia (Geneva: United Nations, 1996).

[41]These guidelines were issued by Commissioner Peter Fitzgerald via the CIVPOL Support Unit in Zagreb in March 1997.

[42]*The Role and Function of Civilian Police in Peacekeeping Operations,* conference conducted by IPS/UNITAR, December 1995, Singapore.

a comprehensive operational plan which would include a logistics plan to support it.

Joint operational and logistics planning as well as integrated planning with other components is being done. This approach was followed during the planning for UNAVEM III, UNMIH, and UNTAES.

□ The mission logistics infrastructure should be set up, if possible, before the arrival of UNCIVPOL contingents to ensure smooth induction and establishment of the mission. This would entail early budgetary allocation, selection, recruitment and positioning of essential logistics staff, finalization of services and supply contracts and procurement action. Procedures for the above should be ensured to minimize delays. Budgetary and procurement procedures have been streamlined to minimize delays. A roster of suitable logistics personnel for mission service is being maintained to ensure early positioning of essential staff in the mission area.

□ Vehicles and stores dispatched to missions from the U.N. Logistics Base in Brindisi, Italy, or transferred from other missions should be in serviceable condition. The Brindisi Logistics Base is being provided adequate resources to ensure that vehicles and stores warehoused there are in serviceable condition before being dispatched to missions. Efforts to improve material management and inventory control continue, including establishment of mission startup kits to offset procurement delays of critical operational material during the initial deployment phase.

□ The budget cycle needs to be regularized to overcome financial difficulties caused by short mandates. Early budgetary allocations are needed so that a peacekeeping operation is not constrained in its initial stages by lack of funds. The budget cycle for peacekeeping operations was regularized early in 1997 and now runs from July 1 to June 30. Previously, the budget cycle was tied to the mandate and could cover different periods, some of which lasted only a few days. This meant that, in the past, budgets could appear throughout the year. The new arrangements should reduce the workload in the Secretariat, the Advisory Committee on Administrative and Budgetary Questions and the Fifth Committee, thereby increasing their capacity to focus on the details of a peacekeeping budget.[43]

In the startup phase of every peacekeeping mission in which UNCIVPOL is deployed, there is an immediate need for transportation and communications. Therefore, it is essential that the Logistic Base in Brindisi maintain a reserve stock of the most essential equipment required to set up a new mission.[44]

Measures Taken

Introduction

The UNCIVPOL picture painted so far is fairly bleak, primarily because the focus has been on recent shortcomings. Nevertheless, there have also been many successes and positive lessons identified for UNCIVPOL since 1989. Not the least of these were the intangible benefits to local populations in war-torn communities of the calming presence of international police. UNCIVPOL also has a long list of more tangible achievements. BG Roos noted following the UNTAC mission:

> Despite the problems and deficiencies I mentioned . . . the mission was a success to the extent possible. Given the natural and unavoidable limitations every international operation presents, we dare say that CIVPOL contributed positively to the success of several missions. One should not only focus on the minority of policemen that didn't meet the required quality, but let's think of all the very good police monitors that made it possible to train 10,000 Cambodian policemen, who worked diligently to protect human rights, who contributed to free and fair elections, who made it possible that 365,000 refugees could peacefully resettle after

---

[43]*Recommendations to Address Logistical Concerns in United Nations Peacekeeping Operations* (New York: U.N. Department of Peacekeeping Operations, Lessons Learned Unit, 1997).

[44]In 1994, the United Nations established a logistics base at a former Italian Air Base near Brindisi to handle usable equipment from liquidated U.N. missions.

repatriation and through their day and night patrols gave a feeling of security among the population.[45]

It would be fair to say that these sentiments could be echoed for UNCIVPOL missions undertaken in the past decade. Nonetheless, the progress made to strengthen the United Nations' capacity has resulted from initiatives undertaken by a variety of parties: the United Nations, specialized agencies, and Member States.

CIVPOL Unit in DPKO

One response to the massive increase in both the number and relative importance of UNCIVPOL operations was to establish a separate Civilian Police Unit as part of DPKO in May 1993. The Unit was made responsible for "all CIVPOL officers deployed to U.N. peacekeeping operations, including advice on implementation of the mandate, preparation/selection of qualified officers and discipline in the field. It provides information to Member States via the Permanent Missions. The Unit prepares/reviews SOPs and Guidelines for CIVPOL on mission assignment, as well as training materials, e.g., manuals and handbooks for CIVPOL training."[46] The evolution of the Civilian Police Unit has been a difficult struggle. The November 1994 Report of the Secretary-General stated, "In order to enhance the current role of the [Civilian Police] Unit and respond to the present and future demands placed on it, bearing in mind the various missions in which United Nations Civilian Police are currently involved, it is proposed that the Unit be strengthened by the provision of one D-1 post,[47] for a Chief of Unit, and one General Service post." Even today, with UNCIVPOL

---

[45]Duncan Chappell and John Evans, *The Role, Preparation and Performance of Civilian Police in United Nations Peacekeeping Operations*, Vienna, unpublished internal U.N. document, 1997, 36.

[46]U.N. Department of Peacekeeping Operations, *Civilian Police Unit Strategic Plan* (New York: United Nations, 1997).

[47]D-1 refers to "Director Level 1" in the U.N. Civil Service Professional Categories.

accounting for 12-15 percent[48] of all U.N. peacekeepers in the field, the Civilian Police Unit still has only the one Support Account funded position and five on-loan, Government-provided personnel to assist the Police Adviser.[49]

The staffing situation of the unit will be further complicated by the reform proposals from the Secretary-General, which call for a plan to phase out the use of gratis personnel in the Secretariat at the earliest possible date. It is recognized, however, that this can be achieved only by consolidating the existing capacity in DPKO and with a budget that reflects DPKO's real personnel requirements for DPKO.

Cooperation with Other Institutions

The Civilian Police Unit in DPKO is being aided in its efforts to address UNCIVPOL shortcomings with the assistance of other institutions interested in improving policing standards in peacekeeping operations. The IPS/UNITAR "Conference on the Role and Functions of Civilian Police in Peacekeeping Operations" held in Singapore in December 1995 brought together some of the world's most knowledgeable CIVPOL minds to examine the "lessons learned" in peacekeeping operations in the first half of the 1990s. Soon afterward in Washington in June 1996, the U.S. Institute for Peace conducted a similar exercise, "Police Functions in Peace Operations," broadening the scope to include non-U.N. international policing in troubled communities.

On a more operational level, between 1994 and 1995, the U.N. Crime Prevention and Criminal Justice Division, based in Vienna, facilitated three workshops for UNCIVPOL leadership personnel from the U.N. missions in the Former Yugoslavia. These workshops were funded by the Austrian Government and held at a gendarmerie training school in Wiener Neustadt. The workshops examined substantive issues confronting and frustrating UNCIVPOL operations on the ground. The

---

[48]U.N. Department of Peacekeeping Operations, Personnel Statistics Unit, Monthly Peacekeeping Personnel Statistics, July 1995-July 1997.

[49]On-loan government-provided personnel refers to personnel provided free of charge to the United Nations to assist with specific areas within the peacekeeping domain, usually for a period of 2 years.

third of these also drew on recommendations from the recently completed *Training Needs Assessment*, conducted by the Training Management Unit in Zagreb.[50] Together, these recommendations largely shaped the conceptual development of the UNCIVPOL Support Unit in Zagreb.[51] Of particular importance was the induction course that ensured that all monitors received basic instruction in safety and security issues, human rights training (initially conducted by the U.N. Centre for Human Rights), computer training, personnel issues, winter-driving training, as well as briefings about policing in the mission area. Monitors completing the induction course in Zagreb in 1996 and 1997 had never been better equipped to "hit the ground running" in a peacekeeping operation.[52]

Training Guidelines Before Deployment

While the Support Unit in Zagreb was testing and training monitors (repatriating 80 monitors in the first three months of 1996[53]), recommendations from the third workshop in Vienna and interest generated by the massive deployment of monitors to UNIPTF created a new sense of urgency to develop more concrete predeployment selection and training guidelines for UNCIVPOL monitors. In response, the DPKO Training Unit, the Civilian Police Unit, and the Lester B. Pearson Canadian Peacekeeping Training Centre conducted a seminar aimed at establishing clear guidelines for Member States to follow in

---

[50]Belinda Goslin and Rob Pettigrew, *Training Needs Assessment for the United Nations Civilian Police,* internal U.N. document, Zagreb, 1995.

[51]The UNCIVPOL Support Unit in Zagreb was developed in December 1995 to enhance the capacity of the United Nations to screen, induct and deploy civilian police monitors arriving in the former Yugoslavia. The Unit supported the UPTF, UNTAES and UNPREDEP Missions.

[52]Helen Webber, OIC Training Section of the Support Unit in Zagreb, comments to author, March 1996.

[53]Rob Pettigrew, *Report of the Selection Assistance Team Visit to Nepal and India,* internal U.N. document, Zagreb, 1996, 3.

the selection and preparation of their monitors.[54] They concluded that the minimum requirements for UNCIVPOL service would be as follows: monitors must be a citizens of their home country; monitors needed to be sworn, serving members of the police force in their home country; monitors had to have at least 5 years (recommended 8 years) active community policing experience; monitors must meet established U.N. health requirements; monitors needed a valid 4 x 4 driving license and the ability to operate a 4 x 4 vehicle in any conditions; monitors must be able to communicate effectively (in writing and orally) in the official mission language and in the official language of their home country; if necessary, monitors must be competent in the care, use and discharge of personal issue firearms and; monitors must have impeccable personal and professional integrity.[55]

In addition to establishing selection standards, the seminar also addressed generic, mission-specific, and in-theater training guidelines for Member States to follow when preparing monitors to go on mission. The selection standards and training guidelines have been combined in a DPKO Training Unit publication, "Selection Standards and Training Guidelines for United Nations Civilian Police," which has already been communicated to many Member States contributing civilian police. This document complements the other three U.N. Civilian Police publications produced by the Training Unit since 1995 (The United Nations Civilian Police and Peacekeeping Training Curriculum: United Nations Civilian Police Course, English Language Course for United Nations Civilian Police, and the U.N. Civilian Police Handbook). However there remains a significant lack of appropriate resources to assist civilian police trainers in Member States.

---

[54]The Seminar brought together over 30 participants, including three former Commissioners, former and current UNCIVPOL monitors, and representatives from the Permanent Missions in New York. These included Chief Superintendent Michael O'Reily, RCMP (Ret.) (UNPROFOR), Brigadier General Klaas Roos (UNTAC), and Chief Superintendent Neil Pouliot, RCMP (UNMIH).

[55]Michael Emery, *Selection Standards and Training Guidelines for United Nations Civilian Police* (New York: U.N. Department of Peacekeeping Operations, 1997), 3.

In conjunction with the DPKO Civilian Police Unit, the DPKO Training Unit has also played a major role in raising the global status of civilian police in peacekeeping training. In addition to the above mentioned publications, the Training Unit has included a major Civilian Police component in both its U.N. Training Assistance Teams (UNTAT) and the Training Course for Military and Civilian Police Trainers, Peacekeeping, Human Rights, and Humanitarian Assistance held biannually at the Training Centre in Turin, Italy. The UNTAT concept is to gather Military and Civilian Police Trainers from a grouping of Member States and enhance their capacity to develop and conduct coordinated and uniform predeployment mission training. The most recent of the UNTAT Seminars was held in Ghana where representatives from 23 countries (including eight Civilian Police specialists) gathered in Accra for a week of intense training assistance. Similarly, the course in Turin aims to enhance the capacity of civilian police trainers, particularly in the field of Human Rights. It was interesting to note that in the 12 countries visited by SATs in 1997, seven of these had participated in the Turin course and all seven had initiated, within the past 12 months, a human-rights training component as part of their premission training.[56]

Selection Assistance Teams

The creation and strengthening of the Civilian Police Unit have enabled other issues to be addressed, the most important being the language and driving skills of monitors deployed to missions. At the beginning of 1996, with large numbers of monitors being deployed to the newly created IPTF in Bosnia, it soon became apparent that some Member States had again largely ignored the language and driving criteria communicated to them by the United Nations via their Permanent Missions. By mid-March 1996, 1,075 monitors had been sent to the IPTF mission and undergone English and driving tests. These tests had been significantly improved from the previous multiple choice test

---

[56]National trainers in Indonesia, interviews with author, 1997, Malaysia, Nepal, Pakistan, Jordan, Egypt, India, Bangladesh, Chile, Argentina, Senegal, and Ghana.

initiated by Commissioner Mike O'Rielly during the UNPROFOR mission. They included reading and listening comprehension (and an oral interview retest if monitors failed the first two), which better determined if incoming monitors would meet the language necessities of the mission. Of the 1,075 monitors tested, 57 failed to meet the required English standard, and a further 23 failed to meet the required basic safety standard in driving.[57] These monitors were repatriated at the Member States' expense; however, the initial travel costs and mission subsistence allowance (MSA) incurred before repatriation had to be borne by the United Nations. This amount was considerable, given the number of monitors repatriated. The average cost to the United Nations of a monitor arriving in the mission and failing the English test was $3,060.[58] The average cost of passing the English test but failing the driving test was $4,500 (those monitors failing the driving test were allowed additional days to take driving lessons and given three attempts to pass the test).[59] Of the 80 monitors repatriated, 50 came from just 5 countries. To avoid repatriation costs and facilitate recruitment of qualified monitors, the Civilian Police Unit and the Civilian Police Support Unit in Zagreb, supported by Member States, developed the Selection Assistance Team (SAT) concept.[60] Initially, the concept was to send U.N. representatives to Member States prior to deployment to test potential UNCIVPOL candidates. The first SAT was deployed to India and Nepal mid-March 1996, saving an estimated $527,360 for the United Nations. There were many other spinoff benefits, however, for the individual monitors, the United Nations, and Member States through use of the SATs. Of the more tangible was the direct savings to Member States. Under U.N. guidelines for repatriation of monitors who do not meet the language and driving criteria, the

---

[57]Robert Pettigrew, *Report of the Selection Assistance Team Visit to Nepal and India,* Zagreb, U.N. internal document, 1996, 3.

[58]Calculated on an average stay in the mission area of 13 days x $120 MSA and $1,500 travel expenses.

[59]Based on an average stay in the mission area of 25 days x $120 MSA and $1,500 travel expenses.

[60]Ibid., 2.

Member State is responsible for return travel as well as for all travel costs for the replacement, often amounting to over $3,000 for each monitor repatriated.

In several Member States, police authorities responsible for selection and training of potential CIVPOL monitors are often under considerable pressure to favor candidates who are politically well connected. The use of SATs in these countries has greatly reduced pressure on selection personnel, who are able to distance themselves from the results of the impartial SAT. That said, in several countries the SAT has been requested to "reconsider the results of some unsuccessful candidates" by senior police leadership, a request that invariably has been rejected on the basis of "protecting" the failed candidate on safety grounds. This spinoff also sent a very clear message to Member States to refrain from sending unqualified or inappropriate personnel to mission.

By testing monitors prior to deployment, the SAT also saves unsuccessful monitors a great deal of in-country humiliation and heartbreak suffered in repatriation. In recent conversations with several monitors who had been deployed to the former Yugoslavia, only to fail the English test on arrival in Zagreb, they all expressed the most distressing aspect of the exercise was facing families and professional colleagues again, when only weeks previously they had said their farewells.

A further tangible benefit for Member States, and to a certain extent the United Nations, is the inclusion of a training specialist as part of the SAT. The role of the training specialist is to enhance the pre-mission training capacity of Member States by conducting a "training exchange" with local selection and training personnel, exchanging training ideas, concepts, resources, and U.N. policing trends. The training specialist encourages good practice and makes recommendations pertaining to premission selection and training of candidates in the light of what is already being done and the track record of monitors from that particular country. This concept was first successfully tested with a SAT visit to Argentina in May 1996 and has been a regular feature of subsequent SAT visits to other Member States. This process has proved very successful, with several countries developing comprehensive premission training courses. Jordanian police, for example, have initiated a 12-week training course including 192 hours of immersion English training, 56 hours of computer training, first-aid procedures, human-rights training, radio communication training, UNCIVPOL duties and responsibilities, police administration skills, map reading, and briefings from UNHCR and the ICRC.[61] The training exchange also serves the purpose of establishing key contact personnel in each of the Member States, and may, in the future, lead to the creation of regional multilateral training assistance to support countries new to the UNCIVPOL domain.

The SAT, whose composition normally includes experienced police testers from the mission area, allows potential monitors the opportunity to ask questions about the mission, usually in a briefing session held at the conclusion of the English and driving testing. In the first 6 months of 1997, 12 major UNCIVPOL-contributing Member States requested SAT assistance. SATs deployed to these Member States tested 1,985 potential UNCIVPOL candidates in English and/or driving, with 804 monitors meeting the selection criteria. Criteria used in 1997 were slightly more difficult than in 1996, reflecting the increasingly complex nature of UNCIVPOL missions. The new criteria included a reading and listening comprehension test; writing a police report based on a video presentation; an oral interview where candidates were asked five questions and assessed on the time it took to develop the answer; and grammar, pronunciation, and the amount of information contained in their answers. Candidates needed to achieve a grade of 60 percent or better to be eligible for UNCIVPOL service.

The use of SATs has vastly improved the level of English and driving skills of monitors deployed to various UNCIVPOL missions, (particularly in the former Yugoslavia). This contributes to successful achievement of mandated responsibilities, a vast improvement in the "public image" of UNCIVPOL, fewer fatalities resulting from accidents

---

[61]Colonel Mahmood Abbas Al Hadid, Director of the Public Security Directorate, interview by author, Jordan, March 1997.

and has generated an estimated saving to the United Nations of over $3.5 million.[62]

Conclusions

Certainly, these seminars, round tables, and workshops have contributed to the enormous progress made on some problems identified in the early 1990s. Many challenges, however, continue to confront the United Nations and the international community. Foremost among these challenges are the ever more complex mandates being assigned to peacekeeping operations with civilian police components. In addition to normal monitoring duties, UNCIVPOL has moved from monitoring electoral processes, to supporting and training local police, judiciary, and penal systems. The current mandate of the UNIPTF mission in Bosnia-Herzegovina involves the total overhaul of a criminal justice system[63] involving police officers, judges, and other officials from three different ethnic groups in an atmosphere of delicate peace. These challenges call for increasingly specialized civilian police. To a certain extent, the United Nations has begun to meet this challenge by issuing specialized job descriptions to Member States in advance of new deployments or rotations. These "position descriptions," developed by UNIPTF Headquarters in Sarajevo, detail the duties, responsibilities, and experience required for 12 specialized positions ranging from Director of Local Police Training and Assistance to Human Rights Officers/Investigators.

In his "Blue Book," former Australian Foreign Affairs Minister, Senator Gareth Evans recommends development of Justice Packages for future U.N. peacekeeping missions:

> The building of a functioning criminal justice system is a particularly crucial priority if the gains of a peacekeeping operations are to be

---

[62]Michael Emery, *Report on the Selection Assistance Teams 1997,* New York, U.N. internal document, 1997, 3.

[63]Refer to U.N. Security Council Resolutions 1031 (1995), 1035 (1995) and 1088 (1996) (New York: United Nations).

consolidated and a relapse into conflict is avoided. We support the idea, advanced by lawyers in Cambodia troubled by their inability to effectively implement UNTAC's human rights mandate, that United Nations' Justice Packages be part of any peacekeeping and post conflict peace building exercises in countries where the rule of law, and the institutions needed to support it, have manifestly broken down. Elements of such a package would include provision, as appropriate, of a body of criminal law and procedures, drawing on the universal principles; civilian police, with training as well as law enforcement responsibilities; a panel of judges, prosecutors, and defenders able to work with available local professionals during the transitional period, again with the obligation to train their local successors; adequate correctional facilities and personnel to staff them while developing local replacements. Basic as all these requirements may be, no viable government or social order can be built without them, and there will be situations where only the authority of the United Nations is capable of delivering them.[64]

To this end, UNCIVPOL must be viewed as a necessary component of most, if not all, peacekeeping operations. This is particularly true with respect to the long-term rehabilitation of a war-torn society. In his 1992 "Agenda for Peace," Boutros Boutros-Ghali stated that peacekeeping operations, to be truly successful, must include comprehensive efforts to identify and support structures which will consolidate peace and advance a sense of confidence and well-being among people.[65] This should include the restoration of law and order, and hence, there is need for the United Nations to provide technical assistance, particularly with respect to the transformation of deficient national structures, such as the judicial system in all its aspects.

At the 51st session of the General Assembly, the Special Committee on Peacekeeping Operations has stressed the need to further enhance cooperation between peacekeeping operations and other related U.N. activities and has requested that the Secretary-General continue to look

[64]Gareth Evans, *Cooperating for Peace: The Global Agenda for the 1990s and Beyond* (Sydney: Allen & Unwin, 1993), 56.

[65]Boutros-Ghali, 32.

into ways of ensuring this cooperation. The U.N. Development Program (UNDP), the Centre for Human Rights, and the Criminal Justice and Crime Prevention Division (CJCPD) should be included in the consultative process when defining the scope and nature of a proposed operation, especially regarding the role of CIVPOL. Close cooperation should be maintained with these agencies for the duration of the operation to ensure that after the withdrawal of CIVPOL there is no collapse of law and order institutions within the country in transition.

In Haiti, UNDP is already running a technical assistance project by providing technical advice to everyday operations of the Haitian National Police. The CJCPD could be involved in judicial reform programs, helping to redraft criminal and procedural codes and other legislation if needed, plus training criminal justice personnel (i.e., judges, prosecutors, prison officers) and rebuilding correctional services. The Centre of Human Rights, together with the High Commissioner for Human Rights, must be involved to coordinate human rights field work in the context of peacekeeping operations.

Postconflict peace building is the best guarantee to the international community that the sacrifices it has made in a peacekeeping operation will not be wasted by the return of violence. This must involve restructuring and rehabilitation of the whole judicial system. It requires time and coordination, but it offers the best hope of turning tenuous agreements into lasting peace.

LEGITIMACY AND THE
PUBLIC SECURITY FUNCTION

MICHAEL J. KELLY

Peacemaking and peace-keeping operations, to be truly successful, must come to include comprehensive efforts to identify and support structures which will tend to consolidate peace and advance a sense of confidence and well-being among people. Through agreements ending civil strife, these may include disarming the previously warring parties and the restoration of order, the custody and possible destruction of weapons, repatriating refugees, advisory and training support for security personnel, monitoring elections, advancing efforts to promote human rights, reforming or strengthening governmental institutions and promoting formal and informal processes of political participation.

U.N. Secretary-General Boutros Boutros-Ghali[1]

In most peace operations the public security function will be assumed in varying degrees by the intervening military force, which poses problems for the selection and preparation of troops and force structure. Of particular concern are the collapsed-state phenomenon and the role public security issues play in the long-term resolution of conflict. Examination of the methods adopted by Australian forces in dealing with these problems, including those in Somalia, Bosnia, and the Middle East, reveals a number of common key issues. These include the primary issue of legitimacy as relates to the action that the peace operation wishes to take, in what often amounts to an intervention into areas usually the specific preserve of the sovereign state. An example of a legitimacy "tool" is the law of occupation, which was employed to good effect in the context of Operation *Restore Hope*

---

[1]Boutros Boutros-Ghali, *An Agenda for Peace* (New York: United Nations, 1992), 32.

in Somalia in 1993 by the Australian contingent. What often emerges in these operations is the need for a robust approach to get at fundamental problems that if not dealt with will only serve to constitute the seeds for further conflict or instability.[2] The robust approach must be tempered by cultural sensitivity and the forging of an alliance with the people and their responsible leaders. A possible approach to various aspects of the application of force in this context is also discussed.

The Context

The issue of public security in peace operations has arisen because the context in which they take place has more and more frequently been one of internal conflict. These internal conflicts have resulted in or been a product of the disintegration of a "civil society." A common feature in the cause of conflict has been the insecurity felt or attacks endured by one particular ethnic, religious, or national group. This is often because the group has lost confidence in the administration of justice to secure their human rights, protect their cultural identity, and guarantee their physical security. In these cases, or in the case of rebellion against an authoritarian regime, the problem has been that the mechanisms of "justice" have been the instruments of repression in the first place. Addressing the issue of the administration of justice therefore goes to the heart of the conflict resolution objective of a peace operation.

In addition, the peace operation should be focused on leaving behind a viable state entity whose institutions will be self-sustaining and from which the intervening forces can depart as quickly as possible. Justice reconstruction issues are centrally tied to this objective. An effective public security environment encourages responsible leadership to step forward and enables economic activity to develop. No one will work when they know that the fruits of their labor will end up in the hands of a rapacious bandit organization or be siphoned off by a corrupt administration. Another common feature of these conflicts is

---

[2]Cambodia is an example.

property disputes, which should be addressed by an appropriate dispute resolution forum. If this is not done, the seeds will be sown for future conflict.

In order to deal with the public security function, a peace operation must be provided with a framework of legitimacy tailored to the particular circumstances of the operation. Without this legitimacy, a peace operation can rapidly lose credibility, focus, rationale, and support both internationally and locally. Without a framework, the forces will be left to flounder and will be prone to descend to summary justice measures as occurred in certain notable instances in Somalia. To begin with, a mandate from the United Nations is clearly required, although it would be limited by certain factors. It would be of necessity a brief "warrant" that establishes the basic legitimacy of the presence of the force and sets out its goals in broad terms. These bare bones ought to be provided with flesh in the form of either a detailed framework agreement or some other international law source as a point of reference to justify their actions to the international community and the local population. The other key limiting factor is that a U.N. mandate cannot override the provisions of existing international law, which would be beyond its power under the U.N. Charter.[3]

Once the framework is settled, it is necessary to determine how the mission will be structured. In theory, in rebuilding a justice system it would be logical to attempt to mobilize civilian experts in the field. Certain factors tend to preclude this, at least in the initial phases of an operation. The environment may be such that the security threat is still beyond that which civilian police forces could cope with. States generally do not have a spare capacity of civilian policing, as these personnel are fully engaged in daily policing at home. As a consequence the police contribution may be of the wrong category (i.e., border police) or from jurisdictions with an inferior human rights record. It has proven difficult to recruit civilian police for peace operations. Even more difficult is the problem of what to do about the

---

[3]See M.J. Kelly, "Peace Operations—Tackling the Military, Legal and Policy Challenges"(Canberra, Australia: Australian Government Publishing Service, 1997), 4-21, para 434.

other arms of the justice administration, such as the judiciary and prisons. The judiciary in particular presents a major problem, because judges and magistrates cannot be trained and employed within the same time frame as a police force. This aspect must be addressed, however, as a functioning police force cannot exist without a judiciary to serve.

Many important opportunities are lost in the early phases of an operation as a result of the inability to come ready to address these issues. The military offers certain institutional advantages for quickly establishing administrative and technical functions. These advantages include potential speed of mobilization, greater logistic capability, and equipment capability and spare capacity as troops are often engaged in ongoing training rather than operations. Some countries are also equipped with a military capability, which can be enlisted to assist in justice reconstruction. This could include military police, judges, courts, and lawyers, in either an advisory or emergency and interim substitutive role. The United States, for example, has an excellent military police and civil affairs capability geared for the possibility of dealing with public security and rehabilitating administrative functions of this type. If this is considered undesirable, then greater effort needs to go into establishing a call up list of civilian volunteer specialists or a body that can coordinate the speedy recruitment of such volunteers, bearing in mind that the harshness of the operational environment or security threat may not permit this option. The reality is, however, that such an option is unlikely to meet the need.

If the military is the best source for the short term in addressing public security issues, this does not mean that they are perfectly adapted for it. This is merely to say that the potential is there. In order for that potential to be maximized the troops must have appropriate rules of engagement and operating guidelines, they must be properly trained, and the force must be properly structured with the public security function in mind. This may involve placing the emphasis on military police, engineers, civil affairs, psychological operations, and special forces.

Legal Framework

Having noted the problems in the context of collapsed states in particular, what are the possibilities in terms of legal frameworks to establish the legitimacy of the actions a peace operation may be required to take to restore an efficacious regime of public security? One regime under general international law is particularly relevant and useful in the worst case scenarios, that being the law of occupation, which is embodied in the Fourth Geneva Convention of 1949.

Application of the Convention

There are 185 States party and signatory to all four Geneva Conventions of 1949 making them the most universally adopted international humanitarian law codes.[4] The questions that arise in relation to the Convention are: (a) in what circumstances will the Convention apply and in particular does it apply to peace enforcement under Chapter VII of the U.N. Charter?, and (b) when does the Convention cease to apply?

The introduction of the Fourth Convention was intended to radically alter the application and shape of the legal regime regulating military presence in foreign territory. It would no longer be accurate to refer to the law of belligerent, or nonbelligerent, occupation.[5] This resulted from the expansion of the convention coverage to all forms of nontreaty occupation, regardless of whether there was an armed conflict. The new Convention was designed to regulate the relationship between foreign military forces and a civilian population where the force exercises the sole authority or is the only agency with the

---

[4]As of August 18, 1995. Figures from the International Committee of the Red Cross, "Geneva Conventions of 12 August 1949 and Additional Protocols of 8 June 1977—Signatures, Ratifications and Successions," communique DDM/JUR 93/940-CPS/11 30 June 1995 and Addendum DDM/JUR 95/3500-CPS/15a, August 18, 1995. The only U.N. members not yet party are Eritrea, Lithuania, Marshall Islands, Micronesia, Nauru, and Palau.

[5]A distinction based on whether the occupation occurred in the context of war or peace.

capacity to exercise authority in a distinct territory. As Adam Roberts puts it:

> One might hazard as a fair rule of thumb that every time the forces of a country are in control of foreign territory, and find themselves face to face with the inhabitants, some or all of the provisions on the law on occupations are applicable.[6]

How does the Convention produce this result and what did the framers have in mind when they so expanded this area of law? The answer to the first question lies in an analysis of Article 2 of the Convention where the application of the laws set out in the Convention is defined. To appreciate the Convention fully, it must be understood that it has different levels of application. The four Conventions of 1949 were drafted with the object in mind of addressing all forms of armed conflict in some way, as by that time the experience of undeclared and civil wars had already been evident.[7] For example, common Article 3 to all the conventions addresses all forms of armed conflict not of an international character, while paragraph one of common Article 2 applies the remaining provisions in the Conventions to all international armed conflicts, whether a state of war exists or not. We also can see that certain nonconflict situations were to be addressed in the Fourth Convention in particular, dealing as it does with the protection of civilian populations and their relationship with foreign armed forces. The Conventions also create certain peacetime obligations. It is important at this point to set out the exact wording of Article 2:

> In addition to the provisions which shall be implemented in peacetime, the present Convention shall apply to all cases of declared war or of any other armed conflict which may arise between two or

---

[6]A. Roberts, "What is a Military Occupation," *British Yearbook of International Law* 55 (1984), 250.

[7]D. Plattner, "Assistance to the Civilian Population: the Development and Present State of International Humanitarian Law," *International Review of the Red Cross,* May-June 1992, 258.

more of the High Contracting Parties, even if the state of war is not recognized by one of them.

The Convention shall also apply to all cases of partial or total occupation of the territory of a High Contracting Party, even if said occupation meets with no armed resistance.[8]

Paragraph two of the Article contains the key formula, providing the expanded coverage of the provisions regulating occupations. The wording to note here is the expression, "The Convention shall *also* apply," meaning that it also applies to the following outlined circumstances *other than* a state of war or armed conflict between or among High Contracting Parties as mentioned in paragraph one. The additional application is to, "*all* cases of *partial or total* occupation of the territory of a High Contracting Party, *even* if the said occupation meets with *no armed resistance*."[9] The language adopted in the "Report on the Work of the Conference of Government Experts," convened by the ICRC in Geneva in 1947,[10] would have made this clearer, as it stated that the Convention should apply "also in the event

---

[8]"The Geneva Conventions of August 12, 1949" (Geneva: International Committee of the Red Cross Publications, 1994), 153-154.

[9]This was not intended to discourage armed resistance to an invader or reflect a belief that it was improper to expect civilian populations to resist, as such action was given legitimate belligerent status, provided certain qualifications were met, in Articles 13 (2) of Geneva Convention I and 4A (2) of Geneva Convention III. The absence of the requirement for resistance reflected only the desire to simplify the de facto qualifications for the application of the Convention to ensure the protection of civilian populations in the widest range of relationships with foreign armed forces in positions of authority. G. Schwarzenberger, *International Law as Applied by International Courts and Tribunals,* vol. 2 (London: Stevens and Sons, 1968), 325-327.

[10]This conference was convened to review draft reworkings developed by the ICRC in 1937 of the earlier Geneva Conventions and was an important preliminary step toward the final drafting of the Geneva Conventions of 1949 at the Diplomatic Conference of that year. *Report of the Work of the Conference of Government Experts for the Study of the Conventions for the Protection of War Victims (Geneva, April 14-26, 1947)* (Geneva: International Committee of the Red Cross, 1947).

of territorial occupation in the absence of any state of war."[11] The report elaborated its intention in this respect by its commentary on the draft provision, stating, "This Article was adopted in order to make the Convention applicable to . . . every occupation of territories, even should this occupation not be forcible."[12] Nevertheless, as Pictet states regarding paragraph two of Article 2 of the 1949 Geneva Convention:

> The sense in which the paragraph under consideration should be understood is quite clear. It does not refer to cases in which territory is occupied during hostilities; in such cases the Convention will have been in force since the outbreak of hostilities or since the time war was declared. The paragraph only refers to cases where the occupation has taken place without a declaration of war and without hostilities, and makes provision for the entry into force of the Convention in those circumstances.[13]

This general category of occupation is distinct from occupations occurring as a result of armistice or capitulation, which is covered by paragraph one of Article 2. The Pictet commentary explains the distinction as follows:

> (A) simultaneous examination of paragraphs 1 and 2 leaves no doubt as to the latter's sense: it was intended to fill the gap left by paragraph 1. The application of the Convention to territories which are occupied at a later date, in virtue of an armistice or a capitulation, does not follow from this paragraph, but from paragraph 1. An armistice suspends hostilities and a capitulation ends them, but neither ends the state of war, and any occupation carried out in war time is covered by paragraph 1.[14]

---

[11]Ibid., 272. J.S. Pictet, *The Geneva Conventions of 12 August 1949: Commentary: IV Geneva Convention Relative to the Protection of Civilian Persons in Time of War"* (Geneva: International Committee of the Red Cross, 1958).

[12]Report of the Work of the Conference of Government Experts for the Study of the Conventions for the Protection of War Victims (Geneva: International Committee of the Red Cross Publications, April 14-26, 1947), 272.

[13]Pictet, 21-22.

[14]Pictet, 21-22.

It was clear therefore that the Convention was not concerned with the *circumstances* of the coming together of military forces and civilian populations foreign to each other in a relationship of authority and submission, but with the *fact* of its occurrence. As Roberts states, "The broad terms of common Article 2 establish that the 1949 Geneva Conventions apply to a wide range of international armed conflicts and occupations—including occupations in time of so-called peace."[15] The practical effect is that, for the parties involved, the Convention will apply to a wide range of situations that were hitherto not within the contemplation of the formal codes or that would have been covered by the less prescriptive law of nonbelligerent occupation.[16]

The test is whether the force present is not just passing through, is not engaged in actual combat, and is, in effect, the sole authority capable of exercising control over the civilian population, or if any remaining authority requires the approval or sanction of the force to operate. The test is not based on whether the force has established a formal administrative framework or military government; this would be contrary to the intention of Article 4 of the Convention, which defines protected persons, in relation to whom the rights and obligations of the Convention relate, as those simply "in the hands" of the occupying power.[17] The whole thrust of this law is that the situation is temporary, seeking only the regulation of the relationship between the force and the population while the force is present.

Given the transformation that has been wrought by the Fourth Convention it now seems possible to identify the circumstances which will attract the application of this body of law. Adam Roberts has set out four basic elements in this respect:

(i) there is a military force whose presence in a territory is not sanctioned or regulated by a valid agreement, or whose activities there involve an extensive range of contacts with the host society not

---

[15]Roberts, 253.

[16]E. Benvenisti, *The International Law of Occupation* (Princeton, NJ: Princeton University Press, 1993), 170-171, 173.

[17]Pictet, 47, 617.

adequately covered by the original agreement under which it intervened;

(ii) the military force has either displaced the territory's ordinary system of public order and government, replacing it with its own command structure, or else has shown the clear physical ability to displace it;

(iii) there is a difference of nationality and interest between the inhabitants on the one hand and the forces intervening and exercising power over them on the other, with the former not owing allegiance to the latter;

(iv) within an overall framework of a breach of important parts of the national or international legal order, administration and the life of society have to continue on some legal basis, and there is *a practical need for an emergency set of rules to reduce the dangers which can result from clashes between the military force and the inhabitants* [emphasis added].[18]

These elements were to be found in reference to the UNTAC operation in Cambodia, the IFOR/SFOR operation in Bosnia (although those operations were governed by formal agreements), and, in particular, in the UNITAF and UNOSOM operations in Somalia. Other recent situations that have often contained these elements are "safe haven" operations, which involve a force being deployed into a clearly demarcated area. Within the safe haven the deployed force may be required to undertake the restoration and maintenance of public order. The force may find itself the predominant authority, with the varying degrees of break down in civil authority, including the total lack thereof, that may occur in these areas. Clearly, for example, the Convention applied to the safe haven in Northern Iraq during Operation *Provide Comfort* and to South-West Rwanda in Operation *Turquoise*.

There is nothing specified or implied in either the Fourth Geneva Convention, or the customary law of occupation that *requires* the force

---

[18]Roberts, 300-301.

to remain. It is not, for example, a requirement that the force must remain until normal civil life or order is restored. The force is only required to work toward this end as far as it is within its capacity for the period during which it is in the territory. The force is free to depart at any time of its own pleasing and all its legal obligations with respect to that territory end with this departure.[19] The only circumstance where the force may be obliged to remain is where a genocide is occurring, in which case there may be an obligation on the force, and indeed the international community at large, under the Genocide Convention to take preventative action.[20]

There is a gradation of application provided for in the Fourth Convention based on the changing nature of the military presence. Article 6 specifies that in the case of occupied territory occurring in a conflict situation, the general application of the Convention ceases 1 year after the close of military operations.[21] While the occupation continues, however, and to the extent that the occupying power exercises the functions of government, a number of articles remain

---

[19]"Belligerent occupation is, after all, a question of fact. It seems to the writer that an occupation would be terminated at the actual dispossession of the occupant, regardless of the source or cause of such dispossession." G. von Glahn, *The Occupation of Enemy Territory: A Commentary on the Law and Practice of Belligerent Occupation* (Minneapolis: University of Minnesota Press, 1957), 29.

[20]*Convention on the Prevention and Punishment of the Crime of Genocide*, U.N. Treaty Series, vol. 78, no. 1021 (1951): 277. Article 1 of the Convention states, "The Contracting Parties confirm that genocide, whether committed in time of peace or in time of war, is a crime under international law which they undertake to prevent and to punish." The prohibition of genocide will be binding on all states regardless of whether they are signatories to the Convention as this prohibition has attained the status of *jus cogens*. There were 118 states party to the Convention as of November 1995.

[21]Article 6. "The present Convention shall apply from the outset of any conflict or occupation mentioned in Article 2. . . . In the case of occupied territory, the application of the present Convention shall cease one year after the general close of military operations; however, the Occupying Power shall be bound, for the duration of the occupation, to the extent that such Power exercises the functions of government in such territory, by the provisions of the following Articles of the present Convention: 1 to 12, 27, 29 to 34, 47, 49, 51, 52, 53, 59, 61 to 77, 143. . . . Protected persons whose release, repatriation or re-establishment may take place after such dates shall meanwhile continue to benefit by the present Convention."

applicable. This then poses the question as to what provisions apply to a nonbelligerent occupation, whether the application of the provisions change at any point and when they cease altogether. Pictet comments on this issue:

> Article 6 does not say when the Convention will cease to apply in the case of occupation where there has been no military resistance, no state of war and no armed conflict. This omission appears to be deliberate and must be taken to mean that the Convention will be fully applicable in such cases, so long as the occupation lasts. [22]

This produces the result that more provisions continue to apply for an occupation which begins as nonbelligerent, while fewer provisions would apply in relation to an occupation begun in a conflict situation, even though it may have acquired the same character as a nonbelligerent occupation 1 year after the cessation of military operations. This anomaly was addressed by Protocol I. For those states party to it, the Protocol altered the termination provisions of Article 6 of the Convention by clearly stating, without qualification or elaboration, in Article 3(b) that the relevant provisions of the Protocol and Convention will cease to apply "on the termination of the occupation."[23]

Political Misapprehension

The utility of the law of occupation is extensive in relation to the public security issue, including guidelines for dealing with the local law and the parameters for departing from this law when necessary. It also provides well for the temporary administration of justice where there is no local capability. The measures for security of the force and relief operations

---

[22]Ibid., 63.

[23]Article 3 (b), "the application of the Conventions and of this Protocol shall cease, . . . in the case of occupied territories, on the termination of the occupation, except . . . for those persons whose final release, repatriation or re-establishment takes place thereafter. These persons shall continue to benefit from the relevant provisions of the Conventions and of this Protocol until their final release, repatriation or re-establishment."

410

are clearly spelled out as is the authority for reconstructing the local justice administration.[24] Any apprehension that may be felt concerning possible obligations under this law should be dispelled by a closer reading of the manner in which the law is worded and a look at the reality of the modern operating environment. The convention only obliges the force to assume responsibilities for the population in terms of health, sustenance, and welfare to the extent that it has the spare capacity to do so, beyond what it needs to deal with operational demands, and only to the maximum extent feasible. The role of meeting the needs of the population is more than adequately met by simply allowing the array of NGOs to do their job in these environments as they will always be present.[25]

The United States could have relied on this law to meet the problem it had with its Foreign Assistance Act (FAA) in supporting the standing up of the Somali police force during UNITAF's Operation *Restore Hope*. The FAA prohibited the United States from supporting foreign police forces, which forced UNITAF to label the reviving Somali police force as an "Auxiliary Security Force" and limited the extent of U.S. involvement. Citing its obligations under the law of occupation, the United States could have overridden the limitations of the FAA in this respect. In debates UNITAF had with aviation authorities over control of the airspace in Somalia, they could have overcome the concern these authorities felt over whether the U.N. mandate was suitably elastic to cover this by once again citing the force's rights and obligations under the law of occupation.[26]

The Current Status of Nonbelligerent Occupation

Recent examples of pacific occupation[27] by agreement include the UNTAC experience in Cambodia. The Paris Agreement under which the U.N. forces deployed constituted the temporary transfer of key

---

[24]See Kelly, chap. 5.

[25]Ibid., paras. 518-27.

[26]Ibid., 7-29 to 7-36.

[27]This is where the presence of a force which is assuming certain sovereign functions is regulated by a specific treaty with the host state.

areas of sovereignty to the United Nations.[28] As we have seen, however, there were many areas that remained the source of much contention and uncertainty under the necessarily broad terms of the Agreement. The customary law of pacific occupation will fill any such voids left by an Agreement of this sort and certain fundamental principles can be applied to help clarify uncertainties.[29] One example of an area the customary law can illuminate is the right of the force to take measures for its own security.[30] Another of the principles discussed above that would also be applicable in the case of occupation by agreement relates to the aspect of control. For example, in the case of UNTAC, the U.N. force was never able to exert its authority in the areas controlled by the Khmer Rouge, who were clearly a force exercising sole control over a part of Cambodia and carrying out sustained and concerted military operations.[31] The customary laws of pacific occupation therefore did not apply to that particular area of Cambodia, as the occupying force had no control there.

Another recent experience of pacific occupation was that established by the Dayton Agreement, which involved the warring parties in the Former Republic of Yugoslavia, NATO, OSCE, and the United Nations.[32] This agreement provided for the deployment of a large NATO IFOR for a period of 1 year pursuant to U.N. Security

---

[28]*Agreement on a Comprehensive Political Settlement of the Cambodia Conflict, Agreement concerning the Sovereignty, Independence, Territorial Integrity and Inviolability, Neutrality and National Unity of Cambodia, October 23, 1991*, Australian Treaty Series, no. 40 (1991).

[29]See Kelly, chapter 3, paras. 343-69.

[30]Ibid. See also para. 309 and note 24.

[31]Cambodia did not accede to Protocols I & II until 14 January 1998 (see the ICRC International Humanitarian Law database maintained at the ICRC website, www.icrc.org). The test is used here as an indicative guide for determining when effective control by the occupant ceases.

[32]General Framework Agreement for Peace in Bosnia and Herzegovina, November 21, 1995, executed in Paris on December 14, 1995. Full text provided courtesy of the Office of Public Communication, Bureau of Public Affairs, U.S. Department of State.

Council authorization and Chapter VII of the U.N. Charter.[33] IFOR was empowered to "take such actions as required, including the use of necessary force, to ensure compliance with the . . . [agreement] and to ensure its own protection," a point to be emphasized throughout the document.[34] There were a number of other provisions assigning authority to the IFOR commander and various agencies, approximating an occupation condition.

Of particular interest was the development of the role of an International Police Task Force building on the experience in numerous recent deployments. The management of this operation was assigned to the United Nations and headed by a Commissioner appointed by the Secretary-General in consultation with the Security Council. It was coordinated by and came under the guidance of the High Representative. The Commissioner was permitted to receive and request personnel, resources, and assistance from States as well as from international and nongovernmental organizations.[35] In carrying out their functions they were to act in accord with international standards but were to respect local laws and customs.[36]

The tasks of the IPTF included monitoring, observing, and inspecting law enforcement activities and facilities, including associated judicial organizations, structures, and proceedings; advising law enforcement personnel and forces; training law enforcement personnel; facilitating, within the IPTF's mission of assistance, the Parties' law enforcement activities; assessing threats to public order and advising on the capability of law enforcement agencies to deal with such threats; advising governmental authorities in Bosnia and Herzegovina on the organization of effective civilian law enforcement agencies; and

---

[33]Annex 1-A, Articles I (1) and VI (1). U.N. Security Council Resolution 1031 of 15 December 1995 subsequently provided full authorization for the Agreement under Chapter VII. including U.N. responsibilities arising from the International Police Task Force and the High Representative for relief matters.

[34]Annex 1-A, Article I (2).

[35]Annex 11, Article II, 2.

[36]Article II, 5.

assisting the Parties' law enforcement personnel as they carried out their responsibilities, as the IPTF deemed appropriate.[37]

To fulfill these tasks the IPTF was to have complete freedom of movement and be allowed access to any site, person, activity, proceeding, record, or other item or event in Bosnia and Herzegovina. This was to include the right to monitor, observe, and inspect any site or facility at which it believed police, law enforcement, detention, or judicial activities were taking place.[38]

Clearly pacific occupation is alive and well and is finding new modes of application and relevance as it is employed by the international community to meet the challenges of the diverse security crises that threaten international peace and stability. This is clearly being driven by the need to address the source of this threat which is not primarily that of tackling cross-border invasions but internal disintegration and violence. It is important, however, that the terms of a pacific occupation be sufficient to allow a robust approach to establishing an efficacious public security administration. Both the Paris Accord in particular and to a lesser extent the Dayton process have not fully measured up to this test. It is only through action that equates to occupation that such internal strife can be effectively addressed, if addressed at all. It also requires a realization that process requires engagement of one form or another, depending on the circumstances, over a number of years.

The treaty approach is certainly the best option to pursue where possible. One of the problems that may be experienced with the treaty approach, however, is that it is sometimes not feasible to do any kind of deal with the factions, or some of them, as they may be unworthy partners, unrepresentative, or too chimerical. In strictly legal terms, any agreement with an internal armed faction that cannot be described as representing "the State" has no status in international law. Such an agreement, then, can only acquire such status through its endorsement and enforcement by the U.N. Security Council.

---

[37] Article III.
[38] Article IV, 3.

The Proper Use of Force

The dilemma that faces any peace operation is the appropriate use of force in dealing with the public security aspect. This becomes an even more complicated issue when there is no law enforcement agency of any form or civil authority capable of enforcing a code of law. The troops will often in these circumstances be caught between the force appropriate for combat situations and something more akin to civil policing.[39] This difficult circumstance places emphasis on two aspects of military preparation: the training of the troops and the rules of engagement. It was clear in Somalia that some troops were better prepared for the complexity of the operation than others.[40] The Canadian Airborne Regiment Battle Group (CARBG) was able to achieve much good work in the Belet Weyn area, but its reputation was tarnished by the inappropriate manner in which the unit dealt with the issues of base security and crowd control. This deficiency was a consequence of disciplinary problems within one of the subunits; poor leadership and command attitude in relation to ROE standards; inadequate training of at least one subunit and the lack of a proper framework for effecting the ROE.[41]

---

[39]M. Maren, "The Tale of the Tape," *The Village Voice*, August 24, 1993, 23-24.

[40]M. J. Mazar, "The Military Dilemmas of Humanitarian Intervention," *Security Dialogue* 24, no. 2 (June 1993): 158.

[41]The Board of Inquiry into the CARBG of August 31, 1993, the Toronto Star investigative piece of July 10, 1994, and Canadian Television (CTV) investigative reports revealed the extent of the disciplinary problems of 2 Commando of the Airborne Regiment. These included challenges to the authority of unit and subunit formal leadership, inappropriate initiation rituals, racist attitudes and practices, steroid usage, and a tendency to unharnessed aggression. 2 Commando's preparation was not ideal. It was put through what amounted to a collective punishment exercise in an attempt to correct its discipline problems and had suffered a high turnover in junior personnel. It fell behind 1 and 3 Commandos in specific mission training for Somalia as a result, focusing instead on "general purpose combat training." In an attempt to remedy the training deficiency 2 Commando was put through a one week crash course immediately prior to departure for Somalia.

Once in Somalia a number of training, leadership and ROE issues arose. The troops began referring to the Somalis using derogatory epithets and this was not stamped out by the unit leadership. Despite the use of force regime laid out by the

It is not advisable to deploy assault units of this kind into a situation like Somalia without careful supplementary training. This was recognized, for example, in the preparation of the 1st Battalion, Royal Australian Regiment (1 RAR), before it deployed to Somalia. While this unit was also trained for intense and aggressive combat, in the 2 years prior to the Somalia deployment it had been coming to grips with more complicated mission concepts. These revolved around low-level conflict scenarios in Northern Australia and Services Protected Evacuations of Australian citizens in circumstances such as internal conflicts and the disintegration of law and order. In the course of this training the soldiers learned to deal with varying levels of threat and the discriminating use of force. The training was in reference to two simple states of restraint based on a "red" and an "amber" card. The cards are plastic and carried permanently in the soldier's basic pouch. The cards themselves would be meaningless, of course, without appropriate training. Training might consist of taking a rifle platoon and having members of the platoon play act a scenario with props in an outdoor setting. The remainder of the platoon would observe as the scene was played out. Afterward, the soldiers would be queried as to appropriate responses and given the opportunity to ask questions and discuss the issues. The scenarios would then be varied to present gradations of the

---

UNITAF ROE, the commanding officer on January 28, 1993, issued instructions that any Somali caught in the perimeter stealing equipment was to be shot. Major Seward, the 2 Commando Officer Commanding (OC) wrote in his diary concerning this instruction that, "he has amended the rules of engagement ordering us to open fire on individuals pilfering the camp. These individuals are teenaged Somalis." Later instructions were issued by the sub-unit leaders, including Major Seward, to physically "abuse" captured intruders in order to deter them. This resulted in the torture and death of a Somali. On February 17, 1993, there was a demonstration by some Belet Weyn inhabitants against LTCOL Mathieu's selection of locals for reconstruction committees which excluded some clans from representation. In handling the demonstration 12-gauge shotguns were fired into the crowd by the Canadian troops killing one Somali and critically injuring three others. See CARBG Board of Inquiry, Phase I, National Defence Headquarters, Ottawa, August 31, 1993, vol. 11, 3287, 3306-3310, 3313-3318, 3321, 3328-3329, 3345. CTV news reports and video recordings provided to author by CTV up to January 1995. P. Cheney, "Death and Dishonor in Somalia," *The Toronto Sunday Star*, sec. F, July 10, 1994.

problem. In subsequent exercises the troops would be exposed to civilians, sometimes their own families, who had volunteered to participate. Also encountered would be delegates of the ICRC who have been incorporated into major Australian exercises since 1989.

This soldier-level regime of standard response is called orders for opening fire (OFOF), to distinguish it from higher level ROE reserved for commanders in control of significant weapon systems which focus more on the strategic implications of conflict. The OFOF training emphasizes certain key elements of the soldier's decision making reference. The first is the clear identification of the target. This was a fundamental discipline in Somalia to which the soldiers adhered exceptionally well.[42] This concept places soldiers under the stricture that they must be able to identify the target to be fired upon as hostile or the source of a hostile act (depending on the circumstances) and not open fire indiscriminately or engage, for example, in "reconnaissance by fire."[43]

The element emphasized and debated most extensively in the training is the issue of self-defense and proportionate or necessary force. Here, through demonstration and discussion, the soldier is made intimately familiar with the concepts of this legal standard and the parameters set by the courts. The goal here is threefold: reduce the hesitation of the soldier that might otherwise result in his death or the death of a person it is his duty to protect; minimize the risk to innocent bystanders; and equip soldiers with the means of explaining and accounting for their actions in any subsequent review.

In training, the concept of the proportionate use of force is carefully explored. The focus here is providing soldiers with guidelines as to the options they might use when confronted with particular situations. The first distinction drawn is whether the soldier faces a lethal or nonlethal threat. If they face a nonlethal threat that nevertheless has the potential to cause physical injury, then methods of responding are canvassed

---

[42]Review by author of all casualty-producing incidents caused by the Battalion in Somalia.

[43]This term refers to clearing an area in front of troops by massive use of fire power without regard to what may be under the fire.

such as the use of batons, warning shots, or Riot Control Agents. The force they are instructed to apply in this circumstance must be no more than is required to neutralize the threat; it must not kill or cause more bodily harm than is absolutely necessary. In response to a lethal threat, soldiers are authorized to use whatever means they can to counter the threat including the employment of lethal force subject only to the requirement to attempt to minimize the risk of death or injury to innocent bystanders.

When 1 RAR was warned for deployment to Somalia, the troops were put through refresher OFOF training, which was modified according to the known facts about the operational environment, the specific ROE for the mission, and the law and order role. They were permitted to employ the level of firepower considered necessary to neutralize the threat, restricted by consideration of the proportional risk to civilians. In this respect the training of the soldiers in the Laws of Armed Conflict and discussion in the acted out scenarios assisted them in judging the issue of proportionality. This training and the command philosophy of the commanding officer also highlighted the individual responsibility of the soldier and the standards of behavior expected of them when dealing with civilians. This training was validated when members of the contingent reportedly observed violations of these standards committed by members of another contingent resulting in disciplinary action.[44] Any reports of an inclination to lack respect for the local population were quickly acted upon by the commanding officer. The combination of training, realistic ROE, command philosophy, the creation of a law and order regime relying on the law of occupation and a civic action program explains the remarkable good will enjoyed by the Australian contingent with the local population. No progress in rehabilitating the public security function can be made without maintaining the good will of the population.

It is therefore imperative for common standards to be developed in the application of force and the Laws of Armed Conflict for all troops

---

[44]The Australian contingent commander Colonel W. J. A. Mellor reinforced this by writing to the soldiers concerned, commending them for their actions.

who are nominated to become part of a peace operation with a public security dimension. To this end, it is a matter of some urgency that a training package be created and adopted by the United Nations and by regional military cooperation organizations that focus on the essential elements of behavior and the application of force for peace operations. This package should then be provided to every prospective troop contributing nation, and a training regime commenced for those forces who have been nominated as part of the standby force arrangements between the United Nations and participating countries.

The United Nations should have a permanent training officer who can advise on the implementation of this training and monitor the standards attained. The advice of this officer could then be obtained as to whether a contingent being offered for a mission had achieved a satisfactory level of training in this respect, measured against the type of operation. Such a package could form the basis of a general standard to apply to all armed forces in the same manner as U.N. rules relating to standards of criminal justice.

Training should also be put into effect to prepare troops to operate in accord with the particular ROE for a given mission. When ROE are promulgated to supplement or alter original ROE, then the onus is on commanders to ensure there is proper briefing and training for troops expected to adapt to new operating conditions,[45] as explained by Colonel Kenneth Allard, U.S. Army:

> A single unwise tactical move by a soldier on patrol can instantly change the character of an entire operation and, when broadcast by the ever-present media pool, can also affect strategic considerations.[46]

---

[45]F. M. Lorenz, "Rules of Engagement in Somalia: Were They Effective?" paper submitted for publication in the *Naval Law Review,* January 1995. M.S. Martins, "Rules of Engagement for Land Forces: A Matter of Training, Not Lawyering," *Military Law Review 143* (1994): 3-160.

[46]Kenneth Allard, *Somalia Operations: Lessons Learned* (Washington, DC: National Defense Unversity Press, 1995), 6, 37-38.

It is a fundamental prerequisite that the military force be well disciplined and led by forceful and moral leaders. This basic soundness prevented contingents like the U.S. and Australian troops from experiencing the extent of the problems other contingents had in Somalia and on other operations. This is not enough, however. It is also important that the commanders of the contingents examine carefully the management of the application of force in peace operations.[47] In this respect the commanders must appreciate the differing circumstances of operations so that they will understand that most peace operations are closer in nature to what used to be termed "counterinsurgency" operations, now given the generic term Low-Intensity Conflict.

Those commanders who are not sensitive to the subtleties of such operations should not be appointed. This was one of the major lessons to emerge from the Canadian experience in Somalia, much of the explanation for which stems from the attitude of the Airborne Regiment leadership at the time. The employment of firepower must also be highly selective and confined. The circumstances of peace-enforcing occupations and humanitarian interventions dictate a standard higher than would apply in a state of war and therefore it is incumbent on commanders to adopt tactical options that offer a more surgical approach. This once again places emphasis on the need for the assets to open up such options, including special forces and intelligence.

Justice Reconstruction and Interim Measures

We have seen how important an effective justice reconstruction program was to the overall success the Somalia intervention hoped to achieve and how this was not reflected in the urgency, resources, or efficiency with which the issue was approached. The recurrence of this central problem in peace operations requires that the international community find a way of addressing it at the outset of the contemplation of a mission.

---

[47]Ibid., 8-9.

The two crucial aspects of creating an effective international response are funding and physical capability. First, the program in Somalia suffered because funds to support it could not come from the peace-keeping budget for the mission, but had to come instead from donors. Perhaps the United Nations may have had greater success in raising funding support had it used the argument that the troop-contributing countries had obligations in this respect under the laws of occupation. In missions of this type in the future, where it is clear that the re-establishment of a justice regime is going to be involved, an estimate should be provided as to the costs involved. This cost should then be factored into the determination by the Security Council and contributions assessed against Member States in accordance with their assessed proportional contributions to the United Nations in general. In "contracted out" operations, which appear to be the most likely for the foreseeable future, participating states should be required in the authorizing resolution to organize an effective means of dealing with such reconstruction issues in tandem with the United Nations and other agencies.

Second, having noted the difficulty of quickly deploying civilian experts in a peace operation, what is the interim solution? It is essential that some nations who are intending to offer standby forces to U.N. operations develop a deployable civil affairs capability geared to address the restoration and maintenance of law and order. Such units could deploy rapidly, at less cost, and in harsher environments than civilian alternatives. Once circumstances permit, these units could either hand over control to civilians or to local authorities who had resumed functioning. They would have the capability to establish interim measures such as military courts to hear cases involving major offenders against the force and public order. It would also be equipped and staffed to conduct investigations to support the work of international criminal tribunals or assist local prosecution efforts against major violators of international humanitarian law. These units could use as their reference the provisions of the laws of occupation and international standards established by conventions, general principles, and published U.N. rules. Under these authorities a basic code could be drawn up that could serve as an interim regime in the worst case of

421

no local code capable of application. Primarily the focus should be on rehabilitating pre-existing local codes pursuant to the obligations of the law of occupation. The world is predominantly divided into criminal law traditions derived from the Napoleonic Code, English Common Law, and/or Sharia Law. The nation called upon to contribute a civil affairs unit to a mission could be selected on the basis of a tradition or capability matching the assisted country so that familiarization on deployment will be quicker. The NGO community could also be drawn into such efforts.

Apart from the failure of UNOSOM to deal effectively with justice reconstruction for reasons of funding and capability, it was critically undermined by the approach taken during the UNITAF phase to the issue and the restoration and maintenance of order in general.[48] This stemmed from the reluctance to recognize the need for a framework for the interim administration of justice and the rejection of the laws of occupation for this purpose. One option in this early phase, according to the former head of the Somali police force, Brigadier Ahmed Jama, would have been to have foreign judges come in to operate courts until a transitional government was formed and enough judges found, trained, and vetted to take over. He believed this was necessary at least in Mogadishu, where it would take some time for the people to accept that a Somali judge would not be clan biased. He believed the foreign judges would have been required for at least a year,[49] which would have created problems for UNITAF and UNOSOM because of the uncertainty both experienced over the authority for taking such action. This authority was clearly available under the law of occupation. This option has been partially adopted in the pacific occupation arrangements of the Dayton Agreement where nonnationals have been nominated to the role of Human Rights Ombudsman and on the panel of the Human Rights Chamber.

The failure to establish any form of effective law and order regime by either UNITAF or UNOSOM led directly to the frustration that

---

[48]I. Alexander, "There Oughta Be a Law," *National Review*, February 7, 1994, 32-33.

[49]Brigadier Ahmed Jama, interview by author, Washington, DC, January 3, 1995.

emerged among the troops of contingents where no alternative had been attempted similar to the Australian initiatives. This frustration led to incidents that would only further alienate the troops from the population and seriously damaged the international image of the operation. The frustration of troops who have their initial motivation to help restore order checked, plus the loss of faith of a population with high expectations of what the force will do to restore security to their lives, combine to produce a tragic atmosphere of bitterness, futility, and the decay of morale. There was also confusion among the commanders trying to come to grips with the complexity of the operation. In considering the detainee issue, the Canadian Board of Inquiry into the CARBG made what was a common error in Somalia—looking for guidance on the handling of detainees in the Third Geneva Convention of 1949 Relative to the Treatment of Prisoners of War, rather than in the Fourth Convention.[50] All troop-contributing governments and the United Nations have a responsibility to ensure that the men and women of their armed forces are never placed in such a position again. No mission into a failed state or to establish a safe haven should proceed without an interim administration of justice plan and a concept of operations with the appropriate resources and assets for the longer term restoration of the local capability.[51]

---

[50] CARBG BOI, 3332.

[51] Ibid., 3281-3282:

2 Commando was also given the task of re-creating the local police force. This was a part of the normalization process and supported the UNITAF Phase Three integral task of re-establishing non-partisan institutions at the local level as the basis for a return to effective government. Although the task of training the Somali police force was assigned to the Battle Group by UNITAF through the CJFS (Canadian Joint Force Somalia) headquarters, there were major policy deficiencies and potential legal command and control problems associated with this project. These problems could have been resolved only at the U.N./UNITAF level.

Ibid., 3288:

It was to be expected that Operation *Deliverance* (the Canadian name for its participation in UNITAF) would at some point lead to the detention of Somalis. This was contemplated in the ROE in that they specified that detainees would be handed over to the appropriate military authorities. UNITAF Headquarters were formally queried the first week of

Such plans do not necessarily imply the commitment of vast sums of money and personnel. The Australian experience in Baidoa proved that much can be achieved with little; in fact, the best approach is to rely as much as possible on what can be gleaned locally. For example, it was not necessary to bring large numbers of police trainers to Somalia. In many cases the trainers that were brought in had inferior training to the formerly highly competent Somali force and were an insult to the locals. The Australian approach of locating survivors from the old police academy and putting them to work doing the training in coordination with members of the former Somali Criminal Investigation Division (CID) and Somali judges was the better and would have saved much time and money. Similarly, weapons could have been issued from the confiscated stock and buildings restored from the least damaged available. The police could have been equipped with vehicles from confiscated technicals or the vehicles of bandits. All that may have been needed then was some basic office equipment, stationery, communications gear, generators, and uniforms to supplement what was salvaged from Somali stock in Kenya.

January 1993, as to the procedures necessary to comply with this direction, but no practical solution was provided. There were, in fact, significant jurisdictional problems which were beyond the authority of the in-theater commanders to resolve.

Ibid., 3331:

This was peacemaking, which might informally be described as falling somewhere between peacekeeping and low-intensity war. As noted in the statement by the Board, there was no government in Somalia, and no administrative, legislative or judicial structures in place. This new challenging environment posed problems to all levels of command who had not, in the opinion of the Board, fully contemplated, nor provided the required policy direction. This did have an effect on the actual application of the ROE in theater.

For example, the ROE clearly anticipated the requirement for the detention of Somali persons. They directed that detainees be handed over to "appropriate military authorities." However, within the CJFS, clear legal authority to detain Somali persons on a long term basis did not exist. A detainee was certainly not a prisoner of war because Canada was not at war with Somalia, nor could the detainee be considered subject to The Criminal Code of Canada, or the Code of Service Discipline. The Commander CJFS' attempt to obtain clarification from UNITAF, his next higher headquarters in the operational chain of command, resulted in a verbal response to simply avoid detaining Somali persons for any length of time. The Board concludes that this was an indication that the same problem was recognized at that level.

Another measure that should have been adopted to help finance the operation in terms of pay for the police and judges was the commencement of some form of rudimentary taxation, once the markets, farms and livestock trade were functioning again in areas where councils were established. The Somali Democratic Movement (SDM) council in Baidoa had wanted to commence taxation for this purpose toward the later period of the Australian presence. As the justice system was providing a secure environment for the economy, to revive the measure would have had moral logic. The authority that could have been used to provide a framework for taxation was the law of occupation. Under these provisions the force may gather revenue for the administration of the territory and take measures necessary for the welfare of the population. As long as the taxation was applied solely for paying local personnel, it would have been easily justified. In this way the officials would be paid in accordance with what the economy could bear and there would be no difficulty of sustainability after U.N. departure or lowering of expectations, and one less string to the cycle of dependency could be severed. To avoid any acrimony within the population from the United Nations gathering the revenue, re-established councils acting in accord with U.N. guidelines and under U.N. supervision and financial monitoring could have collected the actual monies.

Perhaps the key issue a law-and-order regime would have had to contend with is the position to be taken toward the warlords. Prosecution action greatly assisted the long-term objectives of the Australian contingent in Baidoa. It was advocated in some quarters that all the warlords who had been guilty of committing grave atrocities during the civil war should have been arrested en masse and placed on trial.[52] What would have been the correct approach? For the seizing of the warlords to have been effective, in the sense of being seen to be evenhanded and preempting conflict with any particular faction, all the warlords would have had to be arrested simultaneously. Clearly this would have been extremely difficult and fraught with great risk. There

---

[52] "The Bandits on Their Donkeys," *The Economist*, May 1, 1993, 40-41.

is also the important consideration that there ought to be some evidence connecting particular individuals with specific acts, in the possession of the seizing force, that would justify every arrest if it was intended to bring the warlords to trial. Such evidence would not have been available, if at all, until after careful investigation. More legally sustainable would have been the detention of the warlords on the grounds of the threat they represented to public safety and the safety of the force. This would still have carried grave operational risk and would have been difficult to execute.

A more feasible approach would have been the establishment, once the force was effectively and securely established, of a humanitarian law violations investigation operation to gather evidence of atrocities committed during the civil war. Initially, regional bandits such as Gutaale in Baidoa and Jess and Morgan in the south could have been targeted for possible prosecution (as opposed to the approach taken in the hunt for Aideed). Once sufficient evidence had become available, the warlords could have been arrested, when the opportunity presented and without announcing beforehand that these individuals were being sought. Targeting the lesser regional figures would have sent a powerful message to the major faction leaders to cooperate lest the same fate befall them. It would have had the added benefit of eroding the regional support for these main players. This proved to be the case with the warlord Gutaale, who was tried and executed in Baidoa and whose demise resulted in a reduction in revenue and support for Aideed.

International Tribunals

The idea of an international tribunal to try such figures is fine in theory. However, the difficulty in establishing the Rwanda and Former Yugoslavia tribunals indicates that these instruments cannot be rendered operable within at least a year. The other problem with a tribunal in the Rwandan circumstance is that it focuses attention and funding on an external legal mechanism rather than on reviving the local system. The Rwandan Tribunal could only prosecute at best a small number of perhaps the key figures in the genocide. In the meantime, 100,000 languish in appalling conditions in Rwandan prisons awaiting trial. Many of these people have had accusations leveled against them that have not and will not be supported by further evidence but who have been nominated by the word of a single complainant who may have had particular motives for making the accusation, such as acquiring the land of the accused.[53] While the trial of the key figures by the tribunal is desirable, the real problem is the inability of the system to handle the languishing thousands. An Argentinian team working in Ethiopia[54] concentrated on enabling the Ethiopians themselves to handle the investigation and prosecutions relating to the atrocities committed by the Mengistu regime.[55] In

---

[53]Information supplied by Majors B. Oswald and C. McConaghy, the legal officers attached to the Australian contingent in Rwanda, 1994-95. See also the Australian ABC Television *Foreign Correspondent*, investigative report, "Rwanda Justice," by Jonathon Holmes on the prison situation in Rwanda and the Rwandan International Tribunal, June 6, 1995.

[54]From 1974 to 1991, the Dergue regime, led by now-exiled Colonel Mengistu Haile Mariam, was responsible for human rights violations on a massive scale. Tens of thousands of Ethiopians were tortured or murdered or "disappeared." Tens of thousands of people were killed as a result of humanitarian law violations committed during Ethiopia's many internal armed conflicts. Many others, perhaps more than 100,000, died as a result of forced relocations ordered by the Mengistu regime. These violations are documented in Human Rights Watch/Africa's 1991 book-length report, *Evil Days: 30 Years of War and Famine in Ethiopia.* In May 1991, the Ethiopian People's Revolutionary Democratic Front (EPRDF) and the Eritrean People's Liberation Front (EPLF), overthrew the Mengistu regime. Human Rights Watch/Africa report, *Accountability and Justice of Transitional Government,* December 12, 1994.

[55]See Australian ABC Television *Foreign Correspondent*, broadcast of investigative report, "Terror on Trial," from BBC Assignment program on Ethiopian atrocities investigation, July 19, 1994. See also U.S. State Department, *Report on Human Rights in Ethiopia,* for 1995:

> On October 25, the Special Prosecutor's Office (SPO) handed down long-awaited indictments against the first group of defendants to be tried for serious crimes, including for crimes against humanity during the "Red Terror" and forced resettlement and villagization, committed during the Mengistu dictatorship from 1974 to 1991. The SPO was established in 1992 to create an historical record of the abuses during the Mengistu government and to bring to justice those criminally responsible for human rights violations and corruption. The trial of the first 66 defendants began on December 13 (1994). In this first group, the Government is trying 21 of the 66 in absentia, including the former president, Colonel Mengistu Haile Mariam, who is in exile in Zimbabwe. It may eventually charge and try more than 3,000 defendants in connection with these crimes; some

Somalia, the priority should have been in equipping Somalis to prosecute the bandits and warlords. Major figures beyond the capability of the locals to handle could have been tried by the domestic courts of one of the troop-contributing states where there was evidence of such persons having committed grave breaches of common Article 3 of the Geneva Conventions of 1949. With no Somali sovereignty left to offend, and these figures having passed into the hands and authority of the occupying power, this would have been justifiable.

More robust but still limited action was taken by SFOR in support of the Hague Tribunal in Bosnia. Once again the question arises of whether such action is wise in the context of establishing the momentum of a peace process, with the hope of moving away from confrontation and recrimination. However, this is really a question of timing, building confidence, equitable dealing, and demonstrating the value of due process as opposed to summary revenge or stored grievances for a later conflict. In this respect apprehension and trial of offenders should be, where possible, evenhanded. In other words, if a Serb is to be arrested, then attempt to also arrest a Croat or Muslim suspect. In particular focus should be on the prime instigators. Once again, the emphasis should be on ensuring that the internal processes

---

government officials expect the trials to go on for 3 to 5 years. In 1994 the Government arrested 25 former Air Force personnel for having bombed civilian targets during the civil war. Over 1,600 suspects remained in detention without charge at year's end, some of whom have been detained for more than 3 years.

Human Rights Watch /Africa Report:

The people of Ethiopia and the international community have waited many years for the process of accountability and justice to begin in Ethiopia," said Paul Hoffman, one of the report's authors and a member of the California Committee of Human Rights Watch. "It is essential that those accused of serious human rights crimes be brought to justice under internationally recognized fair trial procedures as a foundation for the creation of a judicial system in Ethiopia based on the rule of law. These trials offer a unique opportunity for national reconciliation and remembrance that should contribute to the development of democratic institutions in Ethiopia.

Unfortunately the new government is beginning to evince characteristics that suggest it may not be committed to furthering human rights standards in its own dealings (see U.S. State Department Report).

428

of justice in Bosnia are efficacious and eliminate the suspicions of ethnic groups.

There may be established in the future a permanent international criminal court before which may be brought major violators against international humanitarian law. Notwithstanding this possibility, the priority of effort should always be in enabling the assisted country to conduct its own trials in missions seeking to salvage and revive collapsed states. This approach is better for the long-term viability of such states and is a better investment than spending large sums of money to support international tribunals conducting trials outside of the assisted country.

Property Disputes

Justice reconstruction should not focus solely on the issue of maintaining order, however. As the Australian experience in Baidoa and the operations in Haiti and Rwanda have demonstrated, an integral factor in laying the foundations for long-term order is the need to address the attempted usurpation of ownership of land and property, often accompanied, as in Baidoa, by genocidal activities.[56] It is essential to include a mechanism for resolving land and property disputes in many operations, and this may include establishing a special tribunal. The same logic as was discussed in relation to crimes tribunals applies here in that effort should be directed primarily at creating an indigenous capability to deal with these matters, albeit perhaps with close supervision. This can help take the heat out of potentially explosive situations.

The Long-Term View

The mission in Somalia could have achieved a great deal more had the international community been fully committed to the long-term view,

---

[56]L. V. Cassanelli, "Somali Land Resources Issues in Historical Perspective," in W. Clarke and J. Herbst, eds., *Learning From Somalia: The Lessons of Armed Humanitarian Intervention* (Boulder, CO: Westview Press, 1997), 67.

finally expressed in U.N. Security Council Report 814, from the first day the troops hit the beach and sent in assets capable of carrying it out with them. In principle it is possible to restore a Somalia, a Rwanda, a Liberia, an Ethiopia, or many other situations like them. The world learned how to go about such a task in Germany and Japan after World War Two and is relearning in Haiti and Bosnia. Internal civil wars and/or social breakdown pose much greater difficulties, but they are not insurmountable. Resolution of such conflicts depends on the ability of the intervening force to manage and begin the resolution of inherent grievances, to guarantee security, and to create mechanisms that will give all parties confidence that this guarantee will continue on the departure of the force.

When dealing with the public security issue in a collapsed state scenario, the idea that laboratory solutions produced in Western think tanks can be automatically and inflexibly applied should be dispelled. Similarly the concept that all developing states should be made over in the image of Western economies and societies is destructive of the social fabrics that must be built upon for long-term results and usually cannot be sustained by the environment or resources of the assisted country. The failure of the instant "short sharp shock" remedies applied to some post-Cold War Eastern Bloc countries has demonstrated the counterproductive consequences of this approach. An intervention should deploy with a capability and with experienced staff in key positions but should be prepared to be flexible and imaginative, adapting the mission to the circumstances and being as inclusive of the local population and sensitive to their culture and laws as possible. It must also be prepared to remain engaged in one form or another for an extended period, with 5 years being a suggested conceptual planning figure.

From the perspective of the military it is critical that the public security function in peace operations be addressed in planning for the early phases of a deployment and force structures adjusted accordingly. Where a public security function is likely to be significant, it is advisable that a Civil Affairs Task Force be formed to include sizable units of military police, engineers, and civil affairs specialists in the areas of administration and law, including the three aspects of police, prisons, and judiciary. The public security function is a thorny nettle, but it is one that can be grasped if we properly equip ourselves for the task. It is worth the effort to do so, for if the issue is dealt with effectively, the cultivation of a lasting peace has a brighter prospect.

RESPONSE

The U.S. Perspective of
Operation *Restore Hope*

F. M. LORENZ

Lieutenant Colonel Michael Kelly makes a strong argument for the application of the law of occupation to situations like those faced by the Unified Task Force Somalia (UNITAF) in 1992. Each mission is different, and the legal basis for the operation must be carefully developed in advance, but peace support operations typically involve some level of host-nation sovereignty for the duration of the deployment. Government institutions such as the police and the courts may need rehabilitation, but they are not displaced by the peacekeeping force. In Bosnia, the NATO force operates in a sovereign state under the terms of the Dayton Peace Agreement negotiated by host nations leaders as well as other states. The law of occupation should be used with caution, because it may narrow the options of the force commander. Moreover, the United States and most other governments are very reluctant to invoke and apply the Fourth Geneva Convention and the law of occupation, as was done with Germany and Japan after WWII. The political, economic and legal ramifications of taking over the functions of sovereignty and administration of another state are enormous. The local conditions may be present for applying the Fourth Geneva Convention, but governments will still avoid doing so. This was the case with Somalia.

In December 1992, CENTCOM took the lead in establishing UNITAF, as the military element of Operation *Restore Hope*. The I Marine Expeditionary Force (I MEF) from Camp Pendleton assumed the responsibilities as the command element, and the Staff Judge

Advocate of I MEF was in daily contact with the CENTCOM Legal Advisor in the early stages of the operation.[1] In the early days of the operation it was important to establish the legal basis for the expedition and for UNITAF commanders to understand their responsibilities and obligations under the law.

Restore Hope presented a situation that had not been encountered before by U.S. personnel in the field. After 2 years of civil war, all Somali civil and political institutions had collapsed, and anarchy had replaced the rule of law throughout the country. The U.N. Security Council had just passed Resolution 794, which authorized "all necessary means" to provide security for the delivery of relief supplies. This was a narrow mission that did not include rebuilding civil institutions or remaking Somali society. The UNITAF commander made it clear that the force was in Somalia only temporarily and that he was not seeking new missions that were outside the scope of the original mandate.

Before the operation began, UNITAF and CENTCOM lawyers discussed the application of the Fourth Geneva Convention and the law of occupation to the operation in Somalia. At the outset they determined that the law of occupation would not apply. Resolution 794 provided solid authority for *Restore Hope* under Chapter VII of the U.N. Charter. This gave the commander of UNITAF the flexibility to use force when necessary to perform the mission, without creating any legal requirements to provide for the civilian population. In their view, the Fourth Geneva Convention was designed to cover those situations where the host-nation government is displaced by an invading army.

If the law of occupation applied, this could mean that all the other provisions of the Geneva Convention might apply, such as the responsibility to provide schools, sanitation, and a new civil government, and the Bush administration did not want to accept such a degree of responsibility for Somalia. CENTCOM made a conscious decision not to deploy major U.S. Civil Affairs assets because the

---

[1]The CENTCOM Legal Advisor was Colonel Walt Huffman, later promoted to Major General and now serving as the Judge Advocate General of the Army.

United States considered *Restore Hope* as a security mission and not a nation-building one. After the United States gave up command to the United Nations in May 1993, the mission changed, and the results are history. The U.N. Security Council mandates in Resolutions 814 and 837 for UNOSOM II came close to the Fourth Geneva Convention in the authority given U.N. forces. The issue was not the adequacy of authority for the international intervention, but how it was used by the United Nations, the United States, and other troop contributors. Here, history speaks for itself.

During *Restore Hope,* the Australian and U.S. contingents both were successful in accomplishing the mission assigned. The difficulties encountered later by the United Nations should not detract from the initial success. The U.S. and Australian contingents may have had different legal interpretation on the application of the law of occupation, but this made no practical difference in terms of performance in the field. UNITAF Commander Lieutenant General Robert Johnston allowed a considerable degree of autonomy for the commanders in charge of different Humanitarian Relief Sectors, so long as each respected the basic mission requirements. This was certainly the case with the Australian contingent. The Canadian, Belgian, and Italian armies were shaken by allegations of abuse and violations of rights of the local population. The U.S. and Australian contingents were better trained, disciplined, and made better use of their noncommissioned officers in the field. Success in these difficult operations requires the right force, a clear mandate, and achievable objectives. If one looks at broad mandates such as Haiti, Cambodia, and Bosnia, the difficulty of achieving long-term success is evident.

NORWEGIAN EXPERIENCES WITH U.N. CIVILIAN POLICE OPERATIONS

ESPEN BARTH EIDE and
THORSTEIN BRATTELAND

Introduction

This paper is a Nordic perspective of the increasing role of international public security support. After briefly placing the subject in the wider context of peace operations, it outlines the experience of a small, but active U.N. Member State, Norway, and the way in which it is adapting to the changing demands in this specific field. From there it goes on to discuss some of the major questions in the public security debate in light of the Norwegian (and Nordic) experiences with this type of operation. It concludes with a few comments on how the UNCIVPOL system could be further strengthened in the years to come.[1]

The public security project emphasizes the importance of looking into the "microsecurity" dimension of modern, complex peace operations. It is widely recognized today that in order to be able to assist a country torn by internal strife in its transition from war to peace, the emphasis cannot solely be with the military element, however

---

[1] The paper is a preliminary offshoot of the project, *Civilian Police in Peace Operations,* currently conducted at NUPI with financial support from the Norwegian Ministry of Justice. When it refers to "Norwegian experiences" and conceptualizations, it is to a large extent based on a number of internal government documents, mission reports, and discussions with a number of individuals working in this area within the Ministry and various police institutions. The authors particularly want to thank the U.N. Co-ordinator at the Royal Norwegian Ministry of Justice, Halvor Hartz, and the Norwegian Institute of International Affairs military adviser, Vegard Hansen, for their valuable support and insights in writing this paper.

important, nor exclusively with the various humanitarian and developmental efforts aiming at reconstruction and reconciliation. As has been pointed out elsewhere, a public security gap frequently arises between the two. Where one used to apply peacekeeping troops to monitor a negotiated border between two distinct statelike units, the challenge was to maintain the respect for that new international border, not to assist the internal law and order mechanisms of the two parties. Where a political settlement has to take place internally, however, such simple demarcation lines are seldom applicable, or at least not the main problem. In post-civil war communities, groups that were recently fighting are now expected to live together.

This has a series of new implications for an international peace operation. Over and over again, we have seen that when the artillery surrounding a city is silenced, the security challenge to the individual citizens is not removed but rather transformed. Crime, rampage, and demands for revenge flourish in such a climate. Frequently, demobilized fighters who come back to civilian life meet a harsh reality of rejection, unemployment, and loss of status compared to that which they enjoyed as combatants. In many areas of the world, these are among the first to become involved in criminal activity, together with political leaders who got their power through the conflict and are more than reluctant to give it away.

Simultaneously, such immediate post-civil war societies are often characterized by lack of an appropriate and benign native police force and judiciary. In some cases the functions of the former state system may have collapsed altogether; in other cases it might be intact but associated with the "old regime" and perceived as part of the problem rather than part of the solution.

This type of climate is extremely hostile to long-term development initiatives. Without a basic feeling of security among civilians, few efforts will be channeled into reconstruction and fresh investment. It is hardly surprising that an individual—for instance, a refugee who has just returned from abroad—will think twice about investing scarce capital into something that is likely to be taken away the next day by armed bandits. At the end of the day, the many individual decisions that citizens make under "normal" conditions—such as building a house, investing in local industry, marrying, or raising children—are always taken with some kind of calculation about the future in mind. If one does not believe in a peaceful future where a minimum of security for life and property is ensured, people will not focus on these decisions. Thus, a vicious circle is introduced where peace does not come along because people do not believe it will come. In such situations, much of the capital locally available is saved for the eventuality of having to escape from a return to hostilities, and thus even existing capital is not circulated into the local economy. Nor are such climates particularly attractive to foreign capital investments. Much of the link between security and development lies here. The security-first approach often referred to in African contexts addresses precisely this problem. The path back to "normalcy" passes through the (re)establishment of public security in the form of police forces designed for public service, independent judiciaries, and penal systems.

The recognition of this particular dimension of complex peace operations has led to a "new wave" of international police efforts over the last 7 to 8 years. Since the UNTAG operation in Namibia in 1989-90, the United Nations has rapidly increased its emphasis on international police and judiciary support.[2] The current number of police personnel serving with the United Nations is approximately 3,000. In addition, lawyers and criminal investigation experts serve in field missions or assist national judiciaries.

At the United Nations, this has led to the establishment of a dedicated CIVPOL unit within the Department of Peacekeeping Operations (DPKO), which, together with the UNDPKO Training Unit, is responsible for the selection and preparation of officers for deployment as U.N. civilian police. As will be argued later in the paper, a more dedicated approach to both selection and training has brought a clear improvement over the last few years, after some quite obvious

---

[2]UNTAG is here seen as the first example of the "new wave" of U.N. police operations, but it is not the first. In the 1960s, there were police elements in the operations in the Congo (ONUC) as well as in Cyprus (UNFICYP). These were, however, more enforcement-type operations where the role of the police and that of the military were not as clearly separated as in the "new wave" of U.N. police support.

mistakes had been made at earlier crossroads, particularly in the field of recruiting the right personnel.

Likewise, individual contributing countries are adapting and developing their own systems of selection and training of police officers for international service. This paper intends to look closer at Norway's efforts in this respect. In doing that, we are not arguing that Norway represents a unique model. Rather, the paper should be seen as a specific case-study of a more general development. Much of what will be said about Norway's model here will in broad terms also be valid for a series of other small and medium-sized Western countries, not the least the other members of the Nordic family.[3]

Norway's Commitment to U.N. Peacekeeping

Norway is a long-standing contributor to international peacekeeping operations. It has contributed since the very beginning of U.N. peacekeeping. Over the almost 50 years that have passed, Norwegian troops or observers have participated in around half the U.N. peacekeeping operations. The total number of Norwegians who have served as military servicemen and women in U.N. uniform exceeds 55,000. As recruitment has taken place from all over the country, one will hardly find a village where no one has served with the United Nations. In other Nordic countries, figures are roughly the same, hence, peacekeeping has become a household word. In addition, there are

---

[3]The Nordic community consists of five countries: Finland, Sweden, Denmark, Norway, and Iceland. The Nordic countries chose different security arrangements after the second World War, ranging from NATO membership (Denmark, Norway, and Iceland) to neutrality (Sweden and Finland), the latter with a "treaty of friendship and co-operation" with the Soviet Union. Despite this, political co-operation has been extensive, not the least in the field of U.N. matters. Iceland does not have a military force but has participated with other Nordic countries' contingents with, among other resources, medical personnel. When we refer to the Nordic countries' military U.N. experience, therefore, we are primarily referring to the four countries that maintain military forces: Finland, Sweden, Denmark, and Norway. Although we will refer most specifically to Norway, many of the observations will be valid also for the rest of the Nordic community.

large numbers of people who have participated over the years on related missions, such as humanitarian relief operations. On the civilian side, the Norwegian Refugee Council handles a system of rapid deployment of humanitarian relief personnel. Currently, some 300 to 400 people are "on call" on the Norwegian team list of experts; many are ready to go to a crisis situation on 72-hours notice.

In Norway, support of the United Nations is widespread and almost an apolitical topic. In fact, there is no political party in parliament that has suggested substantial cuts in either financial or personnel contributions to U.N. peacekeeping.

For the Norwegian Armed Forces, peacekeeping has increasingly come to be understood as an integral part of their *raison d'être*. From initially viewing peacekeeping as an activity on the side of the "real" tasks of the military, the Armed Forces have adapted to the post-Cold War by increasing their efforts in training and other preparations for peace operations and through establishing an International Competence Center with specific responsibilities in this respect. Similar processes have taken place in other Nordic countries. The country that most enthusiastically has adapted, however, is Denmark, which is undergoing a major restructuring of its military forces in order to make international operations their prime rationale.

For decades, the Nordic countries have co-operated in the field of peacekeeping, particularly with respect to training activities. Through the Nordic Committee of U.N. (peacekeeping) Co-operation (NorSamFN), the training tasks have been divided in such a way that Finland has trained the military observers; Norway, the logistics officers; Denmark, the military police; and Sweden, the staff officers.

Over the last few years, this co-operation has increased. In the Balkans, there has been an integrated Nordic battalion in Macedonia (UNPREDEP) for 4 years. A similar arrangement existed during UNPROFOR in Bosnia. Since the introduction of IFOR/SFOR, there has been a Nordic-Polish brigade in the Multinational Division North in Bosnia and Herzegovina. At home, this has inspired the decision to establish the so-called Nordic Co-ordinated Arrangements for Military Peace Support (NORDCAPS). NORDCAPS is to become a modular system for the rapid establishment of joint Nordic units up to the size of a reinforced brigade, to be used for future U.N. or NATO peace operations.

All Nordic countries base their defense on a system of conscription. There are, therefore, no "professional" soldiers to send to international peace operations. Hence, soldiers typically are volunteers who have applied for international service, some during the last stage of their draft, but the vast majority several years after their initial service. Thus the Nordic units have a higher average age than many other counties. Within the Nordic community, it is believed that given the specific tasks to be conducted in peacekeeping operations, some "life experience" is a benefit when the soldiers are, for instance, to negotiate with the local population in tense situations.[4]

The fact that most men have served in the military, combined with the lack of a professional army, implies that there are few signs of a distinct military culture apart from the civilian population. In complex operations, the typical male, humanitarian aid worker has a personal experience with military service, because many military personnel are or have been actively involved in civil society organizations. Cooperation among them therefore is facilitated, an advantage not always prevalent elsewhere. Lately, the close relationship between the military and humanitarian sectors has even led to joint exercises: The military-NGO joint exercise *Nordic Peace* in May 1997 brought together a full ad hoc Nordic battalion with four major relief NGOs in an "ethnic conflict" scenario in Northern Norway. As far as we know, this was the world's first military-civilian exercise of its kind. At *Nordic Peace*, police participants only observed the exercises, but in the next *Nordic Peace* exercise to be held in Finland in 1998, an active police component will be included.

---

[4]A counterargument is that when real fighting starts, there is nothing like a professional unit that has been drilled for such action for years. Several Nordic commanding officers have pointed out that, at least in the first phase of the transition from traditional to "second generation" peacekeeping, their troops were not sufficiently trained to play their part well when combatlike situations occurred. Over the last few years, however, training and preparation for more robust peace operations have been developed.

Norwegian CIVPOL Contributions

When the peacekeeping focus shifted from interstate to intrastate conflict, and the question of a U.N. police force was brought up, Norway decided to contribute some 20 police officers to the UNTAG operation in Namibia. Since then, Norwegian police have participated in ONUSAL (El Salvador) with some 5 officers, the Balkans operations (UNPROFOR, UNCRO, U.N. Transitional Authority in Eastern Slavonia, Baranja and Western Sirmium, IPTF) with some 150 officers, UNTAC (Cambodia) with 31, ONUMOZ (Mozambique) with 11, and MINURSO (Western Sahara) with 5 officers. All in all, approximately 220 of Norway's 8,000 police officers have served with UNCIVPOL in 11 different missions. In addition, others have been involved in planning, support and training for U.N. missions at home and in international organizations. Currently, Norwegian police officers serve with the UNDPKO as well as with the West European Union.

Below, we will first present the way Norway currently recruits and trains its U.N. police personnel. Thereafter, with a basis in Norwegian experiences and thinking in the field, we will discuss some of the general conceptual challenges the United Nations faces in this area, before we go on to discuss possible improvements in the CIVPOL system.

Recruitment and Training

All Norwegian police officers receive 3 years of education and training at the National Police Academy. To enter the Academy, secondary school must be completed, and male candidates must have fulfilled their military service. In addition, a large number of police cadets have completed the military's junior officer course. Among those who serve in CIVPOL, the number of police officers with junior officer training is relatively higher than among police officers in general. This ensures that policemen, like most other Norwegian males, have a basic understanding of the military system. Among women in the police, there is a clear overrepresentation of persons with military background as well, typically a 2-year noncommissioned officer course.[5] The high number of police officers with a military background is seen as an asset in situations where international police have to work closely with military peacekeepers in the field.

International service is based on applications to join specific police missions. No police officer can be commanded to serve internationally.[6] To be selected for U.N. police service, the candidate has to go through a selection process that is tailored to the requirements of the U.N. DPKO training unit. They must have at least 8 years of varied police experience after completing the Academy, good mental and physical health, good driving skills (including four-wheel drive practice), good language skills (English plus the mission language), basic computer knowledge, and the capacity to write good police reports. Furthermore, they must hold values and attitudes toward other cultures consistent with U.N. principles.

A selection team, consisting of one representative of the Ministry of Justice, one of the National Police Academy, and a police chief commissioner, then interviews the applicants. The interview takes not only professional skills into account but also poses questions concerning the family situation of the candidate in order to ensure that a mission abroad does not inflict too much strain on the candidate's private life. As the selection process is relatively strict, a significant number of applicants fail and are not sent to international service.

Those who fulfil the requirements may apply for the basic U.N. course at the National Police Academy. The course adheres to the guidelines issued by the U.N. DPKO Training Unit. It lasts 2 weeks and includes theoretical as well as practical elements. At the end of the

---

[5]Women are normally not drafted but may voluntarily join the armed forces. All positions in the Norwegian Armed Forces are open to women.

[6]This resembles the military system. Recruitment for peacekeeping missions has been based on a voluntary system, where privates and NCOs send in an application in order to join a specific mission; this was the rule for officers as well. Recently, however, Parliament adopted laws to ensure that officers may be assigned to international missions when the number of volunteers proves insufficient. Thus, service in peacekeeping missions is brought more in line with the "normal" military service system.

course, a field exercise is organized. The most recent course was conducted in English primarily to allow foreign participants to be included, but it also serves to familiarize participants with a foreign language milieu prior to deployment. (The most recent course included participants from Africa.)

The second round of training takes place just before deployment. The duration of the training is 1 week, and includes information about the mission mandate; the history, culture and geography of the mission area; and the conflict that triggered the mission. Upon their return, participants take part in a 3-day debriefing.

Training of Norwegian CIVPOL recruits is organized by the Ministry of Justice through the U.N. coordinator's office. (Norway has a national police force but no national police chief; hence the national co-ordinating body is the Ministry.) The Norwegian training model differs from the Swedes, who channel their police through the country's center for military peacekeeping training, the Swedish Armed Forces International Centre (SWEDINT). The argument in favor of this model is that it promotes a higher level of co-operation between the two services. U.N. policemen are administered by the Armed Forces while undergoing training and U.N. service, and then transferred back to their police district after completing their service. A Government white paper has recently suggested, however, that the U.N. police resources in Sweden be transferred to the National Police Board and that courses be held at the National Police Academy.[7] Currently, the Swedish and the Norwegian academies are looking into the possibility of closer co-operation on the basic course model.

---

[7]SOU 1997:108 *Polis i fredens tjänst—Betänkande av utredningen om civilpoliser i internationell verksamhet* [Swedish Official Report 1997:108, "Police in the Service of Peace—A Report About Civilian Police in International Operations"] (Stockholm, 1997). A translation of the report's concluding chapter is included in this volume.

Norwegian CIVPOL
Experiences and Perspectives

Generally, Norwegian experience has indicated that civilian police support is a valuable and constructive extension of international peacekeeping, given the character of contemporary conflicts. However, many lessons have been learned about which approaches work and which do not.

First and foremost, we have learned that there is a high degree of confusion about the CIVPOL concept among member states, the local population in the mission areas, military and civilian "mission colleagues," and even among CIVPOL personnel themselves. Misunderstandings and lack of clarity about the mandate and the mission can at best be a hindrance to an effective peace implementation process and, at worse, prove disastrous for the mission and the people involved. There is a strong need to improve the understanding of what the role of civilian police is in the wider context of peacekeeping operations.

We increasingly experienced a problem related to the very name "civilian police." Whereas the word originally was introduced to distinguish police officers from military police, it might be a flawed concept, as UNCIVPOL operations almost never have executive powers. It is only logical that if foreign people turn up in police uniforms and police vehicles and call themselves police, the local population will expect them to behave as if they were the police. Over and over again, frustrations have been generated when CIVPOL officers have confined themselves to taking notes rather than intervening in situations such as local police harassment of citizens. The local people can hardly be expected to differentiate between the roles of observing and executing police powers. Media are often confused by the concept as well. Repeatedly, international media, like CNN, have reported that "the U.N. police are not doing a proper job," as they, too, seem to expect that UNCIVPOL are there to enforce "the law." Norwegian and other CIVPOL personnel have repeatedly reported that being present and expected to intervene—but without a mandate to do so—has been the most frustrating part of their field work.

The main tasks of international police officers in peacekeeping operations are to monitor the local police (reporting on their activities to international institutions, co-locating with them, etc.) or to train and assist them. Perhaps the role they are to play should be reflected in the very title of their mission. If they are to be police observers or monitors, why not call the mission UNCIVPOL observers or UNCIVPOL monitors.[8] Obviously, performing such roles requires police experience, but other skills may be requested as well (e.g., human rights competence). Here we see a parallel to the existing model of U.N. military observers. A U.N. military observer (UNMO) is often a high-ranking military officer, but he or she operates alone or in small teams, unarmed, and without any executive authority. In contrast to UNCIVPOL, the title UNMO seems better to reflect the actual work being conducted, which basically is reporting on military activity in the mission area. Again, to perform that job requires military knowledge (there is little use in sending someone to report on troop movements who cannot distinguish a tank from an APC), but it is not a military job per se.

Once CIVPOL observers or monitors themselves understand their role, with its implications and limitations, it is of paramount importance to inform other actors about that role and to establish a good working relationship with them. It is of particular importance to make the local population and local authorities aware of why there is a U.N. police mission in their area.

CIVPOL officers are often deployed in very small teams in masses of potentially hostile people and are usually far outnumbered by the local security forces. Only in exceptional cases can they rely on the international military presence to perform "point security" for their benefit. Their personal security, therefore, depends primarily on the co-operation of the local community and secondarily on general "area security" provided by international military forces. When international military forces take on a more proactive role against parts of the local

---

[8]This would also bring the U.N. language more in line with a term occasionally used in the United States—International Police Monitors.

population, the international police become potential "soft targets." Local groups who want to protest an international military action would be prudent to avoid firing on an Abrams tank but would likely seek other ways to take revenge. In such situations, a well-established working relationship with local authorities, as well as maintenance of a clear distinction between the UNCIVPOL and the international military presence, might be the best source of security available.

UNCIVPOL officers are typically unarmed, and calls to provide them with weapons are not heard within the Norwegian peacekeeping community. Introducing arms—even only for self-defense—may incorrectly signal enforcement authority. In a typical immediate postwar situation, small arms are flourishing, particularly automatic rifles, grenade launchers, etc. The typical sidearm of the policeman has little to offer in combat against more heavily armed civilians with recent war experience. It is a common feeling among the Nordic countries that the police officers in peace operations are in fact better protected by not being armed. Heavy weapons, then, should be left for the military presence.

In Norway, the police are unarmed during normal operations, such as patrolling and carrying out arrests. Only in extreme situations is permission given to arm the officers, and each case is later reported and investigated by a special commission in order to keep the use of weapons as limited as possible. Hence, Norwegian policemen come to the mission area prepared mediate disputes. Again, this is perceived as a beneficial experience in UNCIVPOL work.

If the mandate gives international police a more proactive role, on the other hand, one might want to reconsider the armaments question. Theoretically, two paths then become available: Equipping the police with appropriate armaments (possibly of a paramilitary nature in hostile environments), or enhancing the police-military cooperation within the mission, as in the form of joint patrols.

Which path to choose obviously depends on the specific situation of each mission. The first one, arming the U.N. police, would require recruitment from countries with established paramilitary police forces, like the Spanish Guardia Civil, the Italian carabinieri, or the French gendarmerie. There would most likely not be any role for Nordic police forces in such paramilitary operations, because of a lack of experience with this kind of activity. As the potential opponents of such a police force would be well armed and trained, the force would need to be quite heavily armed and protected and might eventually become quite indistinguishable from a military peace enforcement mission.

The other path, integrating more closely with the international military presence while maintaining a clear distinction in the mission mandates, may in many situations be a better solution for the desire to introduce a more proactive public security role. Very interesting developments are currently taking place between NATO's SFOR and the U.N. IPTF in Bosnia-Herzegovina. A system of joint patrolling has developed where the IPTF in fact is "borrowing" enforcement authority from SFOR. A typical joint patrol consists of an IPTF vehicle followed by three SFOR vehicles, of which at least one is an APC. It is still the IPTF officers who, for instance, inspect a local police station for illegal armaments or ask for the removal of a checkpoint, but it is SFOR who represents the enforcement capacity if needed. In many situations, the very presence of SFOR has been sufficient to make the IPTF's possible opponents comply. This model has been developed without having to go beyond the two missions' formal mandates. The IPTF still does not do enforcement, and SFOR already had provisions to "provide a secure environment for the civilian implementation process," to disarm armed civilians, and to "provide freedom of movement in the whole territory of Bosnia-Herzegovina." What has developed is simply a more flexible manner of applying the mandates and of doing it in coordination. It is yet another example of the constructive "mission creep" that has taken place within IFOR/SFOR since the beginning of the Dayton peace process.[9]

---

[9]The model has its drawbacks, however. By appearing together with SFOR, the IPTF is increasingly associated with the military forces that certain local people, not the least within parts of the Republika Srpska, see as an occupation force. This may run contrary to IPTF's wishes to present itself as another mission with another type of mandate. However, earlier experiences have proven that the benefit of representing a mission distinct from the military decreases when the situation deteriorates.

Drawing on the SFOR-IPTF cooperative model, we would suggest that rather than arming the police, the enforcement role is better left to the one institution that can do that effectively in a potentially hostile environment, which is the military peacekeeping force. As military peace forces are rapidly learning—in Bosnia-Herzegovina and elsewhere—many of the tasks they may have to conduct in tense postwar environments resemble tasks that traditionally are associated with police forces. An example may be riot control, for which infantry troops are normally not trained. Possibly future peacekeeping training of military forces may include this kind of operation, and police experience may be drawn upon in the training for and conduct of such operations. For instance, the Norwegian infantry battalion in Multinational Division North in Bosnia has received advice and practical help from IPTF officers in the handling of civilian crowds.

The environment we are talking about here is not one where classical distinctions between combatants and noncombatants are easily applied. Many of the alleged "civilian" crowds that stir up trouble, attack returning refugees, etc., are actually military and police personnel in plain clothes, whereas the "combatants" as such often live a "civilian" life between the battles. Whether a given situation involves armed persons is typically very difficult to determine at the outset. For instance, the status of armed children or armed gangs is not very clear if we try to apply international humanitarian law. The distinction between police and military tasks during a peace operation may have to be reconsidered. ·

The military, at least in more "robust" operations like the one currently underway in Bosnia-Herzegovina, have a completely different degree of escalation control than does a police force. It is often forgotten that in well-functioning societies, the police normally do not need to apply force physically, precisely because the threat is already credible. The perpetrator normally knows that somewhere behind the friendly unarmed Norwegian policeman is the overwhelming power of the state. This "invisible backup" is key to the credibility of his authority even if he does not bring it with him. The other key is that most citizens support the law most of the time and are even prepared to assist the community policeman when necessary. In contrast, in a undefined, partly chaotic, post-civil war situation, the uniform itself does not convey authority. Credibility must be demonstrated locally. One of the reasons NATO troops in Bosnia-Herzegovina have not been drawn into any major combat situation to date, whereas UNPROFOR was repeatedly attacked and actually lost quite a number of lives, is that IFOR made its capacity to escalate credible. From day one, there have been heavy artillery and attack helicopters moving around in pure displays of force. The lesson learned is that if one wants to threaten with force, one had better be prepared to use it when challenged, or credibility will be lost. In the context of international police support, the lesson is that a police officer cannot simply be deployed, without backup, and receive the same respect or reaction as they do "at home." At home, the police officer is the lowest but most visible element of the "authority chain." Abroad, the officer might easily be quite alone on the job.

Law Enforcement Needs a Native Basis

New models of cooperation between international police and military peacekeeping forces may help make the native police comply with the peace accords, and in some situations, avoid local turbulence involving opposing groups of (alleged) civilians. However, as a general rule, law and order functions, including that of policing a local population, must be based on the mission country's own institutions. The idea that international CIVPOL personnel should conduct local policing is futile, except in very exceptional cases.

Enforcement of law and order must be connected to a legitimate judiciary and penal system. There is little use in detaining perpetrators, for instance, if there is no court to take them to or no prison in which to put them. A legitimate and impartial police force needs a native backing, an impartial judiciary, and an impartial prison system. Making such institutions work is a very important element of a postconflict settlement. Hence the United Nations and others put special emphasis on assistance in training, restructuring, and developing such systems. It is hardly desirable to have two such systems operating at cross purposes in the same area, one being international, the other homegrown. We should stick therefore to the principle of monitoring and assisting local police authorities as much as possible and avoid using international cops to police a local population.

There may, however, be cases where law and order cannot be maintained by local authorities, either because they no longer exist, are completely illegitimate, or fractionated. Torn-apart or "failed states" may sometimes represent such a picture of total anarchy. In principle, the international community may decide to introduce certain minimal state functions in such situations, in the interest of the local population and of a long-term return to peace. That route, however, should then go via the establishment of a protectorate or occupation government. It is a dangerous misconception that one can enforce law and order in isolation from the other elements of the public security triad of police, judiciary, and penal system described above. An internationally mandated occupation government may combine these functions. There may be situations where the majority of the local population welcomes such an arrangements as the lesser evil, as it, for instance, keeps war from returning. Still, few people would want such a model to persist for a very long time. It easily becomes very costly to conduct, and public support might easily deteriorate. If economic growth, for instance, is delayed for some time, the population might blame the foreign government, and the cry to expel the foreign occupiers might become an easy rallying ground for native political leaders. The international community may shy away from situations requiring such involvement. The only viable approach, therefore, would be to form a transitional authority that from the very first day starts planning for a future withdrawal and re-establishment of a locally founded government.

As a general proposition, the international community may either assist a local government in its law and order functions or choose to take over the government, but intermediate solutions may prove futile. Involving oneself in actual policing, for instance, including the detention of perpetrators, but then leaving the detainee to the local authorities for punishment may turn out to be disastrous either for the individual in question, the prestige of the international police force, or both. If the international community involves itself in such acts, it must also take the moral responsibility for the future fate of the persons detained. In some settings, this means ensuring that the physical treatment of and legal process for a detainee are consistent with international human rights covenants and legitimate native laws. In other settings, the local detainee might actually have committed an offense but be protected by a corrupt or politically governed local court system and hence be freed instead of being put on trial. Both situations illustrate the problems of having a police force based on an international mandate and a judiciary and penal system based on local political realities.

The failure to understand that there is no "middle ground" here is reflected in a series of unrealistic and ill-informed suggestions about how to improve the CIVPOL system. The idea that the UNCIVPOL as they exist today should take a more proactive role in, for instance, Bosnia-Herzegovina, has frequently been brought up in the discussions both in 1996 and 1997 about a post-IFOR/post-SFOR situation in that country. Both NATO's Secretary-General Javier Solana and U.S. Secretary of Defense William Cohen have suggested an increased U.N. IPTF role as an answer to a reduced NATO role. It is crucial to recognize, however, that this is not simply a matter of swapping one for the other.

Arresting War Criminals

When it comes to arresting suspected war criminals sought by an international tribunal, the case is different. Here, we do not see the same principal objections against international bodies conducting search and arrest, as the legal framework where the court trial and possible punishment will take place itself is internationally mandated. However, this does not in itself give the UNCIVPOL executive powers. Again, the first choice would be to have the local authorities arrest the suspects—as they are obliged to do by international law and often by the peace agreement—or the job must be carried out by international bodies that have both enforcement authority and the actual means to conduct such an operation. This points once again toward a military peacekeeping force.

Norwegian conceptual thinking in the field of developing police support operations, therefore, indicates that a move toward more enforcement power for CIVPOL should be rejected, but that the role of monitoring and training should be enhanced. We see the U.N. mission to El Salvador as a good example of a model to develop further: By concentrating on developing the curriculum and assisting in the training of police recruits at the police academy, CIVPOL concentrates on improving local capabilities and bringing them more in line with international human rights regulations. It also involves a "train the trainers" approach, which is frequently sought by the Nordic governments in order to make the initiatives sustainable. Assistance in the restructuring of local police forces such as in Eastern Slavonia and in Bosnia and Herzegovina are other examples of such models.

This emphasis puts high demands on the police officers who are to conduct the monitoring or training of the local police. It is important to remember that as a general rule, UNCIVPOL officers are professional police officers, not professional police monitors. Being a good police officer, for instance, does not imply that one is also a good educator. More specific tailoring of personnel for the mission seems warranted. If this means fewer people will be available, then quality should take priority over quantity.

Whichever model is chosen, respect for the local population and authorities as well as a high degree of cultural sensitivity is an inescapable dimension of any police support operation. A good understanding of the international human rights system is paramount. Functions like training and monitoring require that local officers trust the sincerity and professionalism of their international counterparts. There have been cases where the skills and experiences of international police officers have been clearly inferior to local officers. Too many stories have been reported about CIVPOL officers deployed in a mission area with no language skills, no driving experience, and no familiarity whatsoever with the concept of human rights. Such cases easily undermine the operation as a whole. The professional quality of the individual officer is particularly important in CIVPOL work because, in contrast to military peacekeepers, CIVPOL deploy in very small teams and operate very close to local police officers.[10]

---

[10]It should also be discussed whether one sends the right signal to the local police force if international monitors represent regimes that themselves are widely known for violating basic human rights.

DPKO has adapted to negative feedback and improved the selection system for international CIVPOL personnel. A system of Selection Assistance Teams and Training Assistance Teams that are sent to the contributing countries before the officers are selected and sent to the mission area has been introduced. Whereas in the first contingents many of the officers provided were clearly below the minimum standards required, the introduction of these measures has substantially improved the picture.

Suggestions for Future Improvements

Norwegian authorities are actively involved in attempts to improve the UNCIVPOL system.[11] The general impression is that the CIVPOL unit is well aware of the possible shortcomings in the system. Authorities in Norway feel that rather than changing the existing procedures and norms, the challenge is to support the work going on at DPKO and to encourage contributing countries to stick to the recommendations that already exist. The Selection Assistance Teams approach could even be considered for the selection of other types of peacekeeping personnel, for instance, UNMOs. Norway also supports the move toward more standard international training, either through the exchange of trainers between different countries' training centers or through actually training future CIVPOL personnel in international settings.

With stricter application of selection principles, a possible consequence may be that fewer people will be eligible for CIVPOL missions. This should not lead to a weakening of the requirements but rather to an open recognition from the United Nations that priority should be given to quality rather than quantity. It may not be the case, however, that everyone involved in, for instance, the establishment of a new national police academy in a war-torn country needs to be a police officer: for instance, those who are to teach human rights could be selected from professional sectors other than the police community.

---

[11]This section is to a large extent based on written contributions from and discussions with the U.N. coordinator's office in the Ministry of Justice.

There is no universal key to how to make good CIVPOL officers. Training courses need further tailoring to meet the specific needs of each mission. However, basic "modules" may be developed according to tasks to be fulfilled. Initiatives are currently underway to increase Nordic co-operation in such training and to open Nordic courses to non-Nordic participants.

Improvements should also be made when it comes to presenting the CIVPOL role and limitations to the local population, local authorities, international military and civilian "colleagues" in the mission area, and the international community. This is increasingly becoming an integral part of international military missions, which by definition are larger and come much better prepared to conduct information campaigns (or, more precisely, psychological operations). It is important to ensure that these also take the information needs of the CIVPOL contingents into account or, as a minimum, seek to avoid contributing to misunderstandings of the role of the U.N. police. It is a fact of life that the CIVPOL often will be the junior partner to the military in complex peace support operations, so one might as well prepare for such situations right from the start.

The time it takes to recruit CIVPOL personnel and equipment and bring them to the theater is often all too long. From the time a mandate is given by the U.N. Security Council until actual deployment in the field may often extend to several months. In the meantime, the local situation might have deteriorated and the operation becomes both more difficult and costly. Norwegian authorities have, therefore, contemplated the idea of establishing a small, rapid deployment capacity within the CIVPOL sector.[12] This could consist of, at the least,

---

[12]The idea of rapid reaction capacity within the U.N. system has been discussed for decades. Although a U.N. Volunteer Force under Security Council or Secretary-General auspices seems far away, individual countries have taken steps to provide resources for such a force. Canada, the Netherlands, and Denmark are currently the lead nations in this discussion on the military side. In May 1997, the Nordic Defense Ministers' meeting in Bardufoss indicated that the emerging NORDCAPS system could be connected to the suggested SHIRBRIG (Standing High-Readiness International Brigade), in which the Danish Government is taking a leading role.

a rapidly deployable headquarters (RDHQ) and some equipment, particularly four-wheel drive vehicles and radio transmitters.

When discussing an increase in CIVPOL activity, one frequently runs into the problem that few countries have many "spare" policemen to send without creating problems in their home institution. Whereas states living in peace keep military forces for the eventuality of other times, police forces are needed every day, and few countries seem to think that they have too many of them. Particularly scarce are those most sought after for U.N. missions (e.g., senior personnel like commissioners and instructors with special skills). Member states with a national police force might establish a reserve available for international service. This has recently been suggested in the Swedish debate, where the government white paper on reforming Sweden's UNCIVPOL contribution includes a suggestion of allocating 150 extra positions in Sweden's police force for CIVPOL contributions.[13] Similar ideas are being discussed in Norway, but no official decision has been taken yet in either country.

The Swedish white paper also suggests that the CIVPOL label be changed to *police monitors* or *police advisers* to better relate to what the international police contingents are actually doing and to avoid misunderstandings and false impressions. It is most likely that a Swedish proposal in this direction at the United Nations would gain Norway's official support.

It seems that international public security assistance has come to stay. More and more peace support operations take place after civil wars, and many typically take place where the previous regime used its police forces for public control rather than for public service. Whereas the classical, first generation peacekeeping operation was about re-establishing something resembling the status quo ante (i.e., the situation preceding the war), today's operations involve managing change. At the same time, the international community is striving to avoid a return to hostilities and assisting in constructing a new political system that is both more democratic and able to stand on its own feet

---

[13]SOU 1997:108 *Polis i fredens tjänst.*

in the long run. A judiciary and prison system is an integral part of achieving a legitimate, sound, and effective police force. It deserves the attention of all those interested in enhancing the international community's ability to achieve and maintain peace. Furthermore, there should be no doubt that such activity should be rooted in the U.N. Charter and co-ordinated by the United Nations. Precisely because international police assistance easily runs the risk of being associated with neo-imperialism or great power interference by its critics, it needs an internationally recognized mandate and provisions to ensure that it does not become a cover-up for less altruistic activity.[14] This principle in no way excludes subcontracting but just ensures that the international community as a collective keeps some kind of track of the contents of such activity.

---

[14]Because of its obvious "internal" nature, police support is even more dangerously balancing on this edge than is military peacekeeping, which can be seen as an extension of international security concerns of U.N. member states.

REPORT OF THE SPECIAL SWEDISH COMMISSION ON INTERNATIONAL POLICE ACTIVITIES

NILS GUNNAR BILLINGER

Background

On December 19, 1996, the Government of Sweden decided to appoint a special commission with the task of proposing guidelines for contributions by civilian police in international activities. As a basis, the commission was tasked to report, analyze, and evaluate the contributions made to date by Swedish civilian policemen in international actions. Further, they were asked to estimate the future international demand for Swedish participation with civilian police. Finally, the commission was expected to present a proposal for how the activity involving Swedish civilian police should be organized and administered.

On January 16, 1997, Minister for Foreign Affairs Hjelm-Wallén appointed the former Under-Secretary of State at the Ministry of Defense, Nils Gunnar Billinger, as special investigator. The Deputy Assistant Under-Secretary at the Ministry of Justice, Helena Lindström; the Directors at the Ministry of Foreign Affairs, Malin Kärre, Elisabeth Borsiin Bonnier, Staffan Carlsson, and Johan Molander; and the Director at the Ministry of Defense, Nils Daag, were assigned as experts to the Commission. The Principal Administrative Officer at the County Administrative Board in Uppsala, Sune Lindh, was appointed secretary.

On May 27, 1997, the Director at the Ministry of Foreign Affairs, Herman af Trolle; the Associate Judge of Appeal, Tomas Zander; the Senior Administrative Officers at the Ministry of Foreign Affairs, Johanna Brismar Skoog, and Cecilia Ruthström-Ruin, the then-Senior

Administrative Officer at the Ministry of Defense; Lars Schmidt; the Chief Superintendent at the National Police Board, Michael Jorsback; the Principal Administrative Officer at the Swedish Defence Command, Nils-Ivar Tetting; and the Program Officers at the Swedish International Development Authority, Margareta Eliasson and Henrik Hammargren, were also assigned as experts, effective as of February 1, 1997. On April 16, 1997, the Senior Clerical Officer at the Foreign Ministry, Margareta Pååg, was assigned to be the assistant of the Commission, effective March 24, 1997.

The Commission submitted its completed report, *Police in the Service of Peace*, in June 1997. The Government of Sweden has kindly given permission for a translation of the concluding chapter of the 12-part report to be included here. The conclusions contain a number of important insights, observations, and recommendations for national governments and the United Nations as to how international police assistance can be enhanced.

CONSIDERATIONS, ESTIMATES, AND PROPOSALS

The Need for Guidelines for Police Work

Peace-promoting efforts during recent years have to an increasing extent taken place in response to internal conflicts where the legal system has been weakened or has collapsed, thus the role and mandate of international police efforts have been subject to discussion and analysis. The task of this investigation is to propose guidelines for the role of the police in peace-promoting activities, to analyze the question of armament, and to consider the responsibility for different tasks concerning civil security and order, while national judicial authorities are being built up or reconstructed.

Several peace-promotion missions since the first Congo operation have included different forms of police activity, from advice to local police forces to active cooperation in maintaining law and order. Most of this work has been carried out by police who have been part of a civilian police unit (CIVPOL) in a peace-promotion mission established by the United Nations. Although police are included as an important element in peace-promotion efforts and although this activity has continued for several decades, guidelines for this type of activity have been deficient or lacking. Mandates give only a general direction, and documents which describe tasks and responsibilities vary in stature from resolutions adopted by the Security Council to local agreements. In Sweden, civilian police activities have been treated only in general terms by the government. Guidelines or doctrines are lacking for how police work shall be designed and how public security shall be maintained in a peace-promotion operation. The responsibility for specifying tasks and guidelines has been given to those who have had active responsibility in each mission. Nor, until most recently, has police work been subject to analysis and intensive international debate about peace-promoting efforts.

A further reason why it is necessary to clarify the concept of police work is that traditional "civilian police efforts" are often hindered by incorrect expectations. The primary aim of traditional civilian police efforts has been to monitor, guide, and educate the local police, not to create security for the local population through direct contributions to the maintenance of law and order, which is often expected.

Most of the conflicts motivating peace-promoting contributions today are domestic. Civil wars are certainly no new phenomenon, but the number of domestic conflicts has increased dramatically during recent years. Many of these *new conflicts* are to a great extent multidimensional. This means that, besides political and armed antagonism between the parties, they have radical social and sometimes also international ramifications, e.g., ethnic purging, other serious crimes against human rights, refugee flows, and actions by irregular military units. In many cases, the conflict has progressed so far that the social structure is close to collapse or has collapsed. The police system and other judicial authorities have ceased to function or have lost the confidence of the people. The consequences for the civil population are in most cases very serious.

Monitoring and ensuring the observance of human rights have become increasingly important tasks in peace-promoting efforts. The security of the civil population is a basic condition for rebuilding a society after a conflict. In all peace-promoting activities, work with such security questions, therefore, assumes a central place. Security can be achieved for the local population through intervention by international peace-promoting forces. These can also in certain cases take responsibility for maintaining law and order before national judicial authorities have been created or reconstructed and before confidence in these has been re-established. If a peace-promoting mission succeeds in the task of creating a stable and secure environment, the possibility of succeeding in other effective and long-term measures improves considerably.

New Concepts

Proposal

A unit with police in peace-promoting or similar activities should be called an International Police Force or where appropriate a U.N. Police Force. The individual police officer should be called a police observer or police adviser or should be given another title which corresponds to the task.

Considerations

The concept of "civilian police activities" is imprecise and should be replaced by the concept of International Police Activities. The force should be designated an International Police Force or where appropriate a U.N. Police Force. In the documents which regulate the activity in the conflict area, a distinction should be made between Police Observer and Police Adviser. These concepts should be used both in multilateral work and within the framework of bilateral work. The Commission notes that developments are already taking place in this direction, and Sweden should act for a continued separation of these concepts. A police presence in peace-promoting activities has during the 1990s become so common that it is no longer justifiable to use the word "civilian" to distinguish these police from military police. In everyday Swedish, the term "civilian police" is not used either.

The Character and Development of Conflicts

Considerations

In connection with the establishment of a peace-promoting mission, the categories currently given by the United Nations and other organs are used to describe the character and purpose of the action. Concepts such as peacekeeping, wider peacekeeping, peace enforcement, and peace building indicate roughly what type of contribution is required and what authority the force has. In the inquiries made to member countries about contributions to peace-promoting activities, military units and police contingents are spoken of in general terms. In certain U.N. operations, forces consisting of police were recruited and sent to the mission area without the decision having been preceded by sufficient analysis of the problems to be solved or tasks to be accomplished. To increase efficiency and the probability of success, better analysis is required both of the problems to be solved and of the contributions and authority required. A comprehensive and long-term view must be developed so that peace-promoting measures and aid measures can be linked together to increase efficiency and minimize the costs.

One part of this task is to analyze the character and development of a conflict. There is no unambiguous way of describing and analyzing a conflict process; all conflicts are unique. It is, however, possible to describe schematically the different levels or different phases of a conflict. Different phases and levels can overlap each other. A crisis development is not linear; setbacks can occur. Nor is a crisis always equally serious in all parts of the crisis area.

Common to the many conflicts subjected to peace-promoting measures is that they require an input of different components with different tasks. The actions thereby become multifunctional. The mission components can vary between different conflicts and over time within a conflict.

The Initial or Chaotic Phase
In a situation characterized by open fighting and fragmentation or dissolution of the national authority or police force, the first important task is to create basic stability and security. This is in general a task for military units. Different armed groups can be separated and disarmed only by units acting under military emergency powers.

Even after open fighting has ceased, military units can be required. The situation can, for example, be disturbed by serious riots and domestic armed groups. Because of the firepower these large or small groups often possess, this is a task for military units. If the legal system is weak, the forces which arrive first may also need to take responsibility for creating law and order.

The Completion or Normalization Phase
In order to be able to complete a peace-promoting effort, a reasonably functioning state governed by law with relevant authorities must have been recreated. In the task of creating a new police and judicial system, an international police force has an important task. Above all, it can supervise the national police and contribute to establishing principles for how a policeman shall act in a just society. The involvement can

take place either as a multinational contribution or as a bilateral contribution. An international police force can also collaborate in the appointment of a new police corps and assist with education and equipment.

The Grey Zone

Between the task of creating security and the task of participating in rebuilding a judicial system there is a grey zone. It can either be described as a gap between different functions or as a gap across time between different contributions. In a situation where a national authority or legal apparatus has not yet begun to function and where individuals or groups use gross violence for political or criminal reasons, international peace-promoting actions are required to maintain security for the local population and for aid workers.

In such a grey zone, the international military units have the given task of monitoring domestic military units and arms depots, maintaining separation zones, etc. The international police force also has a given task in monitoring and participating in the reconstruction of an often weak national police force. The task of assisting in the maintenance of order and security for the population has a tendency in such situations to fall between the task of the military force and that of the police force.

Important Tasks in a Peace-Promoting Mission

In order to specify the type of contribution and the mandate which are required to reach a goal, there is reason to describe, from an analysis of the conflict concerned, the concrete tasks for an international force consisting of military units, police, judicial experts and other specialists. Examples of such tasks are:

Category A
- ☐ To dampen disturbances through a presence
- ☐ To conduct "on-the-spot-diplomacy/mediation."

Category B

- ☐ To carry out measures to repel an attacker
- ☐ To carry out measures to separate fighting parties
- ☐ To establish and man buffer zones between the parties' troops
- ☐ To monitor a cease-fire
- ☐ To monitor the regrouping and demobilization of forces
- ☐ To clear away ammunition (mines, etc.)
- ☐ To collect weapons
- ☐ To guard arms depots
- ☐ To monitor and assist in disarming military companies and paramilitary groups.

Category C (the Grey Zone)

- ☐ To control riots and disturbances
- ☐ To intervene against armed "gangs"
- ☐ To maintain civil law and order
- ☐ To discover and prevent crimes (e.g., plundering)
- ☐ To maintain order and security during election preparations
- ☐ To monitor and assist in disarming civilians
- ☐ To escort civilians in violence-prone areas
- ☐ To protect refugees in refugee camps from armed elements.

Category D

- ☐ To monitor the local police system
- ☐ To participate in the education of the local police force
- ☐ To give advice and support in the establishment or restructuring of a new local police system.

Category E

- ☐ To assist in taking care of refugees and homeless people
- ☐ To integrate disarmed forces into civilian life
- ☐ To promote the repatriation and reintegration of refugees and displaced persons
- ☐ To provide humanitarian help in connection with reconstruction

□ To give support in the rebuilding of a judicial system and other administrative functions

□ To monitor respect for human rights

□ To coordinate support for economic recovery and rebuilding

□ To monitor elections.

Tasks under *Category A* can be carried out by diplomats, military observers, or police observers. For such work, people are often recruited who have a long experience and good skills in mediation and negotiation.

Tasks under *Category B* can only be carried out by military units. For several of these tasks, a mandate is required which allows the use of violence other than in self-defense (i.e., a mandate which is based on Chapter VII in the U.N. Charter).

Tasks under *Category D* are carried out by police. To fulfill these tasks, they have no executive authority but act as monitors, observers, advisers and educators. Other civilian experts within the legal field are also required to rebuild a legal system.

Tasks under *Category E* are carried out by civilian experts, such as monitors of human rights and aid workers. In the Swedish case, recruiting has in certain cases intentionally taken place within the police system. The tasks under *Category E* are under certain conditions carried out together with an international police force which acts in the area.

Tasks under *Category C,* the "grey zone," involve the creation of security and order for the population. The tasks can be carried out by military units, police and soldiers in cooperation or by gendarmes and soldiers in cooperation. Contributions of this kind can require a mandate with certain elements of authorization according to Chapter VII in the U.N. Charter. This argument is developed in a later section.

Legal Basis for Peace-Promoting Work

All exercise of power in a peace-promoting or similar mission must build on a legal foundation connected to international legal regulations [described in "The Legal Basis for International Intervention," of the

Commission's report]. A characteristic feature of a civil war or crisis is that the legal system does not function. The civilian population has often lost confidence in the legal apparatus and in the legislation which exists. The police and military may even be accomplices in serious crimes in violation of both human rights and national legislation. In certain cases, the social structure may have collapsed totally and anarchy may prevail.

In situations where local legal apparatus do not exist or cannot fulfill its task, a peace-promoting force, regardless of whether it consists of military units or police, faces great difficulties. In these situations, it is often unclear whether the authorities indicated in the mandate and Status of Forces Agreement (SOFA) constitute sufficient legal support to intervene and protect the population. It is further often unclear according to which national law one shall act.

In more difficult cases, the international peace-promoting forces must act under emergency powers described in the mandate. When the legal apparatus has collapsed or has otherwise lost its legitimacy, the task can be limited to monitoring respect for human rights. It may even be necessary in certain cases to start from an agreed minimum level regarding law and rights. This can mean intervention against gross violations of human rights and humanity laws such as murder, kidnaping, rape, and gross property crimes. The degree of intervention that can be applied must in such cases rest completely on international law. If it is a question of a U.N. operation, or an operation mandated by the U.N. Security Council, it should be possible to derive this authority from chapter VI or VII in the U.N. Charter. This means that the command lines must be so clear that it is possible to derive the responsibility for measures taken in the field all the way up to the organ that has given the mission its mandate.

In the final phase of a conflict, or in less serious situations in a conflict, there is in general a national law from which to start. The aim of all peace-promoting activity must be that, when the mission is completed, there shall exist a national judicial system that functions and a national law to follow. Even during an ongoing mission, the main rule shall be to start from the national judicial system. The task for the international operation then becomes to monitor local legal authorities' adherence to the established legal order. This is usually a task for police observers and police advisers. Another possibility is that the host country gives an international force the right to exercise authority. In such cases, the individual international police officers act within the legal system of the host country.

The Task of Creating Security and Order

Definitions and Problem Formulation

Considerations. In a previous section [of the Commission Report], it was established that in any decision regarding peace-promoting efforts, it is essential to define at an early stage, and before the mission begins, those tasks are to be addressed. Concurrently, attention should be given to the question of which instruments (components in a peace operation) can tackle the tasks involved. It is important that the organization issuing the mandate (the United Nations) understands that there can be urgent tasks for which none of the traditionally available components is especially trained or suitable. If a decision is made to establish a peace-promoting mission, all participants should be aware of these "grey zones." The organization giving the mandate should make an effort to quickly find, or develop a component which can solve the tasks which arise within the "grey zones." This report will discusses the choice of a component for tackling the task of creating order and security.

Basic Differences: Policeman/Gendarme/Soldier. In Sweden, as in other democracies, the division of responsibility between the police and military is clearly defined in law. The task of the military is to protect the country against external threats. The police are recruited, educated, and organized to maintain law and order within the country. The police have certain forcible means at their disposal. They can, with legal support, employ force which shall, however, always be in proportion to what the situation requires. The police are the only civilian organ that in peacetime can legitimately use violence in its exercise of power. Military personnel have in peacetime such authority only in cases indicated in the Ordinance (1982:756) concerning intervention of the Swedish Military Command organization in the event of a violation of Swedish territory during peace and neutrality (Instruction for the Armed Forces in Peace and Neutrality, the IKFN ordinance).

A judicial state is characterized, for example, by the exercise of power that takes place with the support of laws which are decided upon in a democratic manner. A national police force, therefore, acts in a politically controlled environment where questions about legal authority, power, and control are important elements. For the police to be able to act, they must have the confidence of the people. This can be attained only if there are generally accepted laws and other statutes which control the activity of both the citizens and the police. Further, it is generally required that individual officers have wide experience and good judgement and that they use their intuition in the executive role.

Swedish police who participate in peace-promoting activities have a good insight into and understanding of work within the law. They are accustomed to working singly or in small groups. On the other hand, they have little experience working in units such as platoons or companies or creating security and order in environments characterized by heavy violence.

Swedish police are normally equipped only with pistols. Use of weapons is strictly controlled, and police may use only the degree of violence proportional to the situation. This means that police can use their weapons in certain cases.

Swedish *military units* are trained and organized for fighting under military laws against a military opponent. Military personnel usually work in units, not singly. The units consist of platoons, companies, battalions, and brigades. Military personnel are not assumed to have any knowledge about sections of the law under which general order is maintained during peacetime, nor are they trained in such tasks. Swedish U.N.-units consist mainly of persons who have undergone basic military training later complemented with a shorter period of training for peace-promoting activities.

In several countries, a special form of police force, *gendarmes*, has been created to act outside both the police and military systems. Gendarme forces have evident military characteristics; for example, they are trained to act in units. They are intended to act domestically and are responsible for internal order in situations involving riots or heavy violence.

Grey Zone. Thus, there is no force that can "naturally" be given the task of creating security and order. Experience from several peace-promoting missions in the past decade shows that a grey zone often develops in a situation where none of the components in an international peace-promoting force is trained or otherwise prepared to create order and security. This obstructs and delays the effort to give the subjected country security and conditions for democratic development.

There are several reasons why none of the parties in a peace-promoting mission addresses or is inclined to deal with the urgent task of creating order and security. Often the task is not mentioned in the mandate or in any other tasking document. This can be attributed to a hesitance on the part of the police and troop contributing countries to undertake such a task. The legal basis for executive tasks is often unclear. The creation of order and security also assumes that there is a functioning judicial apparatus (i.e., a prosecutor system, courts, and prisons). A further reason can be an unwillingness in the host country to allow foreign personnel to carry out these tasks. Accordingly, no preparations are made to tackle such tasks by either international police forces or military units.

Among *military personnel,* both within and outside Sweden, there is great reluctance to assume responsibility for security and order in a civil environment. Military personnel lack education, training, and experience in such situations. There is a risk that military methods used in a civil environment may escalate the conflict to uncontrollable proportions. It further conflicts with democratic practice for military personnel to be responsible for civil security and order.

Gendarme forces have never been deployed in international peace-keeping missions. On the other hand, several countries have recruited gendarmes as participants in international police forces. Gendarme tasks and organizational structure differ country to country. This makes it doubtful that an international organization would be able to create an international gendarme force for peace-promoting activities at a reasonable cost.

According to many analysts, a basic condition for police observers and police advisers to monitor, educate, and advise local police successfully is that they are unarmed, live among the population, and are perceived to be impartial. If they were given more arms and had executive tasks in riots and disturbances, their ability to successfully perform ordinary tasks would probably decrease.

Order and Security in Peace-Promoting Work. Nevertheless, it is necessary that a force in certain peace-promoting missions is tasked with participation in the maintenance of order and security. Such efforts must be based on international law. A peace-promoting mission in a failed state ravaged by civil war or plagued by irregular units is placed in a situation where the division of responsibility between military and police, as in a Western state governed by law, is not always applicable.

The task of creating security and order in the initial phase of such a mission can be carried out only by military units. Later phases, when the open fighting has ceased and an internationally supervised peace process has begun, often see violence and lawlessness still occurring during the transition period. Groups that have a lot to lose from a peace can carry out more or less open fighting to regain lost territory. In these situations, national authorities able to oppose this violence are often lacking. Anxiety and fear of reprisals are common among the population.

In such a situation, the task of creating security and order can be at least partly carried out by military units or in collaboration with a deployed international police force *or* by an international gendarme force. On the other hand, the task cannot generally be given to an unarmed or a lightly armed international police force. The heavy armament that is often found in illegal "gangs" and the low threshold that exists for the use of violence make it difficult for an unarmed or lightly armed international police force to have any effect. Such a force runs the risk of being ignored or of provoking the use of violence, because armed civilians or groups command such heavy weapons that only a unit with military training and equipment can challenge the threats. Further, only the military can respond to riots and disturbances arising from these situations. Military units assigned such tasks as a rule have undertaken them without enthusiasm. Sometimes, the mission has not been accomplished, which has led to great suffering for the civilian population.

Increased Preparedness for Police Tasks in Military Units

Proposal. Organizations issuing mandates need to indicate clearly what responsibility the mission components have for maintaining order and security for the population.

Military units involved in peace-promoting work should, to a greater extent, be prepared to cooperate, when required, in maintaining order and security for the local population. They should be trained for this task by instructors who are police officers and include posts which are manned by police officers

Further, it should be possible under certain circumstances to place military personnel in peace-promoting missions who are trained and prepared to maintain order and security in the mission area, under police command when this type of mission is required. The Government should assign to the Swedish Military Command and the National Police Board the task of studying more closely the conditions for giving military units such missions.

Considerations. The Commission concludes that police observers and police advisers should continue to perform the tasks entrusted to them so far (i.e., to monitor, educate, and give advice to the local police). It is not suitable to assign executive [law enforcement tasks] that might jeopardize these missions. Only in a few countries are police educated and trained to act in units, which is necessary to defeat an uprising or to take action against armed "gangs." The number of police from each police-contributing country is usually small enough to allow training for these kinds of tasks in the home country before departure; exercises and training carried out in the conflict area risk taking too much attention away from the main task.

The investigation also establishes that internationally recruited gendarme forces could probably be manned only by countries that have national gendarmes. It would cause considerable problems to coordinate the armament, work methods, and leadership of such a force. If the force were assigned heavy weapons and vehicles, a condition to succeed with this type of task, it would mean that a force would be built largely parallel to the military component in peace-promoting mission. This would mean further costs for the United Nations and other organizations involved.

The Commission further considers that it *is not acceptable* that an internationally composed peace-promoting mission be delayed or even become impossible to carry out as a consequence of violence and terrorism from irregular units or other armed assailants. The "grey zone," where none of the components included in the mission has or perceives itself to have a responsibility for maintaining order and security for the population, must be made as small as possible and preferably be eliminated completely. Because the Commission has already rejected the possibility of giving tasks of this character to international police departments or gendarmes, it remains to test the possibility of giving military units in peace-promoting activities increased preparedness to execute certain tasks that, in a national perspective, are policing duties.

Military units in peace-promoting missions already fulfill some of the requirements of a force tasked to maintain order and security for the local population: the ability to work in a unit, access to weapons and armored vehicles, secured barracks, and an internationally recognized staff and leadership organization comparable among troop-contributing countries. The military units often monitor regular military units and armistice lines and monitor or sometimes disarm one party in the conflict or guard weapon depots. The methods used to perform these tasks could often be applied to irregular units or armed "gangs." It is therefore understandable that military units in peace-promoting missions have already been assigned tasks of this kind. The Commission judges that this also will take place in the future and that this is a suitable task for military units, provided that they are prepared for the task and the mandate permits this.

The Commission concludes that Sweden should train military units recruited to serve in peace-promoting activities so that they can participate in performing certain tasks in the area of maintaining order. It must be clear that this training is intended for use only in work abroad. The task shall be performed within the framework of what the United Nations or some other international organization has decided. Education of this type should not be done during basic military education.

It is natural for the Swedish Military Command to employ experts from the Swedish police to provide this education. Within the police system, there is a documented knowledge of how to handle so-called *special occurrences* such as violent demonstrations, riots, and sports violence. By adding such knowledge to military education, the possibility of using military units in peace-promoting missions to maintain security and order increases, if permitted by the mandate.

A military unit strives to have personnel in its organization who possess required expert knowledge for solving all imaginable tasks. A unit which can be assigned police tasks should, therefore, in its organization include posts intended for police officers. These should be able to participate both in the planning and performance of tasks of a police character. Examples of this can already be found in certain foreign battalions that act in peace-promoting missions. The police's tactical experience and ability to mediate and create confidence among the civilian population should be exploited in military units with responsibility for civil security and order in their mandate. These police officers should be organizationally included in the military unit and consequently wear military uniforms.

Regarding the operational management of a police contribution to a military unit in connection with a riot, careful consideration should be given to whether the regular military commander should temporarily transfer operational control to a police officer. Several considerations should be weighed against each other, for example, the ability to make a professional estimate of the situation and the importance of continuity and consistency in the exercise of command. The Commission estimates that, in most cases, it would be appropriate for the regular commander to retain command, but that the police officials' opinion should be given decisive importance when orders are given. The Commission does not, however, reject the possibility that, in certain situations, it may be more suitable to have command temporarily taken over by a police officer. The conditions for this should be stated in advance, and the police officer who in such a case shall assume command should, of course, have been given the opportunity to carry out training exercises with the unit during the training period in Sweden.

The requirement for this type of measure has been demonstrated in several ongoing and recently completed missions. It is therefore important that Sweden act in an international context so that more countries carry out similar arrangements. This increases prospects for creating more versatile peace-promoting missions by reducing a troublesome "grey zone."

The Commission recommends that the Government ask the Swedish Military Command and the National Police Board to investigate carefully the circumstances when military units assume police tasks, as described above. In this context, the need for additional education for peace-promoting forces and the related costs should also be addressed.

The Responsibility of International Police Forces for Order and Security

Proposal.

☐ Methods should be developed to reinforce the capacity of an international police force to better perform missions regarding order and security for the population in the troubled area.

☐ Police and the military units should develop new and flexible forms of cooperation in peace-promoting activities where the special knowledge of each is allowed to complement the other.

Considerations. Although their main task is to monitor, educate, and guide the local police, police in peace-promoting activities can play a greater role than ever to create and maintain order and security for the population. Police included in an international force often have great experience with negotiation and mediation. Through their presence, they can also contribute to creating order. This can be facilitated through deliberate *proactive* behavior. This means that the police display great mobility within their field and utilize flexible methods to prevent improper action by local police.

In connection with the large refugee flows in parts of Africa during the 1990s, armed militia sometimes infiltrated refugee camps and caused further suffering for already severely tried people. The prospects for handling this and other refugee-related problems should, for example, be an aspect of doctrinal development.

Through good relations with the local population and authorities and through close collaboration with the political components of a mission, conditions for an early identification of local problems and their causes can be improved. Police observers can then be effectively used to mediate between the parties and thereby defuse an uneasy situation. For such tasks, experienced police officers should be recruited.

To reinforce the effect of proactive behavior by the police, military units can use a highly visible presence to support police work in certain situations. The importance of a police force for public security can thus be reinforced through close cooperation with military units. This can take place through joint planning and by having high flexibility and mobility in both the military and the police components of the mission. The responsibility for achieving this in the mission area lies with the senior commander and his staff. Methods should be developed to reinforce the capacity of the police to establish order and security.

Future Tasks and the Estimated Requirement for Police Participation

Estimate

The international requirement for police in peace-promoting activities during the coming decade will at least be of the same magnitude as during 1997. The need will probably increase. This means an increased need for Swedish police. In the future, major tasks for international police forces will be to monitor, educate, and support local police in a conflict area. Gradually, the demand for police officers in posts other than their traditional monitoring role will increase.

Considerations

The Tasks of the Police. An important aim of a peace-promoting mission is to reinforce successively the possibilities for national police to maintain order and security in a democratic manner and with respect for human rights. Long-term stability can only be achieved by national authorities which have the confidence of the population. After a civil war or in a situation where the judicial apparatus is weak or has collapsed, it is (as pointed out previously) essential that international support include comprehensive measures for reconstructing a national system of justice. In the initial phase of this process, the main tasks for an international police force are, as a rule, as follows:

- ☐ To monitor the local police
- ☐ To train and educate the local police
- ☐ To support the local police in their professional work.

Monitoring local police means to check that they respect both national legislation and human rights in their professional conduct. This entails verifying that police observe an impartial behavior, respect minorities, treat arrested and imprisoned persons according to valid international conventions, and document their actions according to recognized standards. (These can be found in Appendix 6 [of the Commission's Report], "U.N. Criminal Justice Standards for Peacekeeping Police.") To determine whether local police respect national laws, the international police force must have a knowledge of these. Because this is often not the case, human rights often becomes the dominating element in monitoring.

Monitoring can take place through a presence at police stations, prisons, places of criminal investigation, on joint patrols, etc. The international police force may also be authorized to carry out its own investigations and patrols. Monitors must report what has been observed. This makes it possible for the representative of the Secretary-General, or in certain situations the Security Council, to take necessary measures.

In some missions, the task is to train and educate the local police. This can take place at special training or education centers or by on-the-job training of local police. In some cases, training can be performed abroad. International police officers can also assist in the recruitment of new police officers when the system of justice is to be rebuilt. This is a discreet but very important task. In many conflicts, the local police have participated in the fighting and may be guilty of serious violations of human rights. In order to create a new national police force which can win the confidence of the people, it is very important that individuals who are guilty of crimes not be permitted to serve.

In addition to recruiting police officers, the re-creation of a judicial system requires the recruitment of lawyers with a variety of specialties. International police officers can, therefore, cooperate with prosecutors, judges and prison personnel. In the initial phase, these persons may need to be internationally recruited. The more successful the international community is in re-establishing legal institutions and authorities in a country hit by a conflict, the greater will be the potential for reaching a long-term solution to the conflict.

International Needs. At present, approximately 3,000 "civilian police" are engaged in peace-promoting missions. About 100 of these are Swedes, 90 of whom are employed in the Foreign Force within the Swedish Military forces. It is probable that the United Nations and other international organizations will decide to establish missions in a large number of acute crises in the future. There are many unstable areas and countries where open conflicts may break out. Furthermore, reverberations from conflicts which have been the cause of peace-promoting missions during recent years will continue to be the subject of international interest and responsibility (e.g., in the Balkans and several African countries). These crises are or will often be of a multinational character which means that the international peace-promoting efforts will probably have a multifunctional character. International police work is expected to continue to be an essential and increasingly required component in this work. This is underlined by the fact that many "new" conflicts have a domestic character.

It is very difficult to estimate the magnitude of future requirements. It is also difficult to indicate exact geographical regions which will be subject to civilian police activities. Practically all conflict centers can become the object of a peace-promoting contribution. The Commission estimates that *the demand will increase* and that the need for countries, such as Sweden, to increase its contribution will continue.

Swedish Participation with Police Officers

Proposal

Sweden should be prepared to have about 125 police officers permanently on call for service in peace-promoting abroad. Sweden should be prepared to temporarily to raise the level to 150 police officers, for a maximum period of 12 months. Sweden should further strive to have at least 75 police officers deployed abroad engaged in this type of international activity.

Special attention should be given to the importance of employing female police officers to create security and confidence in a mission area.

Considerations

The international need for police officers for peace-promoting activities is estimated to increase, as has been shown in the previous section. The demand includes police both for the traditional tasks of monitoring and educating local police and for participating in development activities. The traditional tasks are described in the previous section. The demand for the latter type of activity usually arises in connection with the completion and normalization phase of a conflict. It can also involve participation in international war crime tribunals of the kind active today in the Hague and Arusha.

An important part of Swedish aid policy is to support the democratization process and the promotion of human rights. This involves reinforcing processes and developing institutions within the state and society in general which promote the development of peace, democracy, and respect for human rights. This may require long-term efforts to reinforce key institutions within the state and other parts of society. Especially important are activities that improve the openness, legitimacy, and responsibility of the local administration toward its constituents, so-called good governance. To stabilize the process of building a nation, a functioning police system is very important for the population's trust in national authorities. Experiences from recent activities with Swedish police officers in aid projects are so good that continued involvement is warranted.

In education and training courses, it has been shown that Swedish female police officers have also filled an important function. In an international police force, female officers can play a special role in creating security and confidence for a civil population exposed to traumatic events. This is true especially in relation to women who have been exposed to violence or have witnessed acts of violence toward relatives and, as a result, have lost confidence in men.

Experience shows that monitoring of elections and implementation of a peace agreement by an independent international force is strategically important. The Swedish International Development Co-operation Agency (SIDA) estimates that police often have a professional background that makes them suitable for this type of service. SIDA has, therefore, intentionally recruited police officers for such a purpose. This will probably continue to take place in the future.

Policing contributions that either ameliorate humanitarian crises or contribute to maintenance of law and order within the framework of rebuilding a state governed by law are recognized both in Sweden and internationally as an increasingly recognized function within aid services. This trend is expected to continue. Experience from such police assistance activity should be utilized for methodological development within the field of international aid.

Sweden should have a clear and realistic level of ambition regarding the total number of police officers who should serve abroad in national service in their capacity as police officers. Several factors limit the level of involvement: international demand for Swedish policemen, the total supply of policemen in Sweden, the willingness of Swedish police officers to serve abroad, the lead organization's demands on the police officers who participate and the country's financial situation. Sweden has about 17,000 police officers, of whom about 100 currently serve abroad. The largest number of Swedish policemen who have served abroad at the same time is about 150. This took place during a period in the early 1990s when the number of policemen in the country was greater than it is today. The Commission notes as follows:

☐ There is a clear demand for Swedish policemen in international service.

☐ There is a lack of police officers with sufficient experience and competence for international tasks.

☐ To date, it has not been difficult to recruit police officers for service in peace-promoting activities.

☐ To date, it has not been difficult to finance Swedish police participation.

☐ Swedish policemen as a rule satisfy the requirements of the international organizations.

The Commission considers that there should be budgetary and organizational preparedness to increase Swedish participation from the present level of 100 police officers to about 125. Thereafter, a gradual increase should take place in relation to demand. For a short period (at the most 12 months), it would be possible to increase the level to about 150 police officers. Sweden should make these parameters known in international contexts.

The United Nations will continue to play a dominating role both as the organization issuing the mandate and performing the activities. The demand for police contributions has also increased in relation to U.N. humanitarian activity (e.g., the handling of massive refugee flows). In the long run, regional organizations will also be given a larger role, particularly with regard to police contributions. The Western European Union has already acted in this role, and other international organizations may in the future also play an active role in a police context. Thus, Sweden, as a police-contributing country, must ensure that the organization performing these activities has the required competence and capacity to plan and execute a peace mission involving police officers. Sweden should strive to participate in the formulation of mandates and other basic regulations when an action is planned.

Arming the Police Force

Proposal

Police officers who act as police observers or police advisers in international peace-promoting missions shall as a rule be unarmed. In exceptional cases, these policemen could be armed for self-defense.

Considerations

International Police Observers. The task of police observers is not usually of an executive character. They shall monitor a national police corps, report, mediate and promote stability by showing their presence in sensitive regions, so-called proactive behavior. The ability to perform these tasks is not improved if policemen are armed. International police officers need the confidence of both the local police and the civil population to be able to complete their mission. The experiences of both military observers and police observers suggest that they can complete their task best if they are unarmed. If the police are armed, they may be expected to perform executive tasks which the mandate in general does not permit.

In many missions, the arms possessed by different groups and criminal elements are of such a caliber that arming police observers with sidearms would have no deterrent effect. Light arms usually provide no protection in situations characterized by heavy violence. On the contrary, arms can have a provocative effect and undermine the security for the policemen. The notion of equipping police with heavier weapons than sidearms has been rejected in a previous section. *The main rule therefore should be that police observers are unarmed.*

Sweden should not, however, categorically reject participation in police actions where police observers are armed. In the WEU-led action in Mostar in Bosnia-Herzegovina and in the U.N. mission in Haiti, police observers were armed with firearms. This was because a majority of the police-contributing countries considered arms necessary to give sufficient protection in these difficult situations. Another alternative should be noted in this context. The police observers can be given access to firearms which are stored under lock until the situation is judged to be such that the policemen should be armed.

International Police Advisers. In the case of police advisers, it is even clearer that they fulfill their task best if they are unarmed. Police advisers can act either as teachers in police education or as mentors when local police carry out their tasks. Regardless of whether a police adviser acts together with police observers or in a later phase of the conflict when the reconstruction of a society is in progress, arming of police serves no purpose.

More Efficient Police Work
Within the United Nations

Proposal

☐ The mandate for the police force in a peace-promoting mission should be stated separately from the mandate for the military force.

☐ Involved countries should give experienced police officers the opportunity to participate in drafting the mandate and on subsequent occasions when other documents relating to concrete police tasks are formulated.

☐ Police competence should be included in more units within DPKO.

☐ The Civilian Police Unit within DPKO should be reinforced.

☐ Sweden should act for a higher competence among participating police officers by promoting the following initiatives:

1) Ensure that all police officers who act in peace-promoting missions undergo adequate training in the home country before departure

2) Develop a screening system with relevant proficiency tests

3) Encourage those countries able to do so to make available resources for the education of future police observers and police advisers

4) Increase U.N. capacity to provide information about the purpose and methods of police activities in the conflict area.

Considerations

General. The Swedish attitude has traditionally been that a well-functioning multilateral system is an important guarantee for the creation of international peace and security, especially for small and medium-sized countries. International police activities have proven to be very useful as instruments of conflict resolution in situations where military troops or military observers have not constituted an active tool. Since 1989, the United Nations has initiated several international police missions. Other organizations have also shown an interest in organizing police work. In the foreseeable future, however, the United Nations will be the most important international actor in the field. As shown in chapter 9 of the Commission's report addressing Swedish experiences with previous and continuing missions, there have been many deficiencies in these missions, largely because of U.N. inability to act rapidly and flexibly to solve practical problems and to meet unexpected situations. A further reason for difficulties has been the inability to learn from mistakes. There is, therefore, good reason for Sweden to act to develop, reinforce and improve U.N. potential for using police officers in peace-promoting activities.

Special difficulties have been observed when new missions are established. Proposals and considerations in this regard are provided in the next section.

Mandates and Other Documents That Define the Tasks of the Police. Mandates, which are approved by the U.N. Security Council, are political compromises which are often of a general nature, often intentionally so, to cover situations which are still difficult to predict. They are not always specified in the text of the resolution but are often indicated in a report from the Secretary-General to the Security Council. This report is then referred to in the resolution. From experience, mandates are primarily designed for the military component of a peace-promoting mission. This means that they provide only vague guidance to the U.N. Police Commissioner who must execute police tasks in the field. To facilitate both the initial and continuing mission activity, there should be a separate mandate for the international police force. This applies even in those cases where it is not possible, for reasons of time, to formulate a detailed mandate.

"Police advisers" are not included in U.N. delegations of Member States in the same way as there is often a military adviser. There is reason to believe therefore that police officers are not consulted in the preparation of mandates for a police component. With the aim of avoiding unclear tasks which can be misinterpreted, policemen with experience leading international police forces should be consulted when mandates are formulated. This can, for example, take place if member states, especially members of the Security Council, make room for a police adviser in the national U.N. delegations.

Increased Police Competence in the United Nations. It is common that the concrete tasks for a police force evolve continuously during the mission. This involves standard operating procedures (SOPs), rules of engagement, or operational directives. Regardless of in which document(s) the concrete tasks are specified, qualified police officers must be given the opportunity to participate in the process. This increases the potential that the police force will be used in the best possible way.

A special example of the formulation of tasks for police work is provided in the Dayton Agreement, Annex 11, regarding the International Police Task Force. This text has been declared by several reviewers to be the best example of a task description for a police force. The agreement was prepared under unusual circumstances and over a longer period than is normally available when the U.N. Security Council formulates a mandate.

The Commission encountered difficulties in its attempts to survey the concrete tasks of U.N. police forces. The tasks are dispersed among several documents which have in some cases been difficult to trace.

In relation to the number of military officials within DPKO, the Civilian Police Unit within DPKO is small. In the very important Mission Planning Cell in DPKO, there is only one policeman. The development of U.N. Headquarters does not correspond to the rapid increase in U.N. missions with police elements and the high expectations placed on the police in these missions. Police questions should be afforded greater attention in the planning work within DPKO. Police advisers and administrators should be integrated within more units of DPKO. The Civilian Police Unit should be given a greater role in planning new missions. The unit should also be given increased resources for developing methods and doctrines within this field of expertise.

Greater Competence for the Police in Peace-Promoting Service. It is well documented from various missions that many police officers in international service are not sufficiently experienced and qualified for the tasks they are expected to perform. For example, they lack knowledge of basic human rights and this makes it impossible for them to judge whether the local police follow current conventions. Knowledge of internationally applicable rules regarding the rights of an arrested or imprisoned person is necessary to be able to act as a police observer. Differing tasks in home countries also mean that the requirements of police academies will vary. In countries with a federal form of government there is not always a national police corps with standardized training. The United States, for example, lacks such a national police corps.

Another problem is the lack of knowledge of the national language. The effectiveness of police action is considerably increased if international police officers have a command of the language. This is especially important if they are to have law enforcement authority.

In general, the United Nations strives for broad geographical representation among police-contributing countries. This is an expression of U.N. striving for neutrality and impartiality. It also promotes global community and constitutes a condition for the organization to maintain the broad support required to be able to act. This striving for geographical representation and an equal opportunity for all members to participate has meant that police forces are often composed of police from many countries.

The general level of competence of policemen in peace-promoting service should be increased. An objective should be that the members of the international police force should have at least the same average general education level as the police who are to be supervised. An important additional step is to provide specialized training relating to local conditions in the mission area. In the section on Training and Recruiting, proposals are given for how the such activities in Sweden can be improved. Here a few proposals are provided for increasing general competence during an ongoing mission. (Special difficulties related to new missions are treated separately.)

The United Nations has observed the problems that arise as a consequence of the low competence of international police and certain measures have been adopted to ensure a certain minimum level. This level is in some respects too low to be accepted over the long term. Further measures should be taken. Education for an international mission should in principle be carried out before arrival at the conflict area. This should include a general knowledge of the U.N. system, human rights, and a basic knowledge of the technical equipment included in the mission. Opportunity should be provided for practical training in handling different possible scenarios in the field and in report writing. Further, there should be sufficient training in the mission language and in vehicle driving.

Special attention should also be given to a knowledge of the national laws in the area. The United Nations should collect and distribute to police-contributing countries information about the most important of these laws (e.g., which civil rights apply in addition to the universal human rights). International police officers should also be informed about the cultural, ethnic, and religious traditions of the other police-contributing countries and about the tasks of the police system in each country. Such knowledge facilitates preparations for service.

Sweden and other police-contributing countries should contribute as much as possible to improving the education of their police for international service. This would make U.N. missions much more effective. Screening systems of various kinds should be undertaken before departure from the home country. The United Nations should maintain and enhance the system introduced in 1997 with the Selection Assistance Teams.

The United Nations should continue to perfect its mission-specific police training programs. This should include current information about the situation in the mission area and about the operational routines. Another important aim is to give police from different countries the opportunity to establish contacts with each other prior to deployment.

Screening and predeployment training programs should be maintained for the duration of the mission.

Information to the Population about U.N. Tasks. When a force is established, the United Nations should seek the assurance of the parties to the conflict that it will be permitted to disseminate information to the population about U.N. roles and tasks. Because a recognized and general definition of the concept of "monitor" is lacking, interpretation of the concept becomes dependent on the specific conditions of each individual mission. If a mandate is far reaching and intended to be attained step by step, unless this is clearly expressed the local population may misinterpret U.N. conduct as being overly passive. There are examples where police in a U.N. force have witnessed a criminal act such as assault and have not intervened because the mandate only allows monitoring and reporting. This type of passivity impacts U.N. credibility if it is not clearly explained and justified to the population.

Higher Level of Preparedness for International Police Work

Proposal

Concerning Measures Within the United Nations. The Commission proposes that Sweden should act so that the United Nations:

☐ To a greater extent, allows police personnel to participate in preparations for new missions

☐ Prepares a standardized organization plan for the headquarters in an international police force. The plan should be designed so that it facilitates cooperation with a corresponding military headquarters

☐ Creates so-called "HQ-elements" (key personnel selected in advance and given the possibility to prepare for future missions)

☐ Prepares plans for purchase of standardized materials and for the initial maintenance of police forces

☐ Makes more rapid decisions about the financing of such a force

☐ Encourages its member countries to develop national systems which facilitate rapid recruitment and deployment of police officers trained for international service

☐ Further develops the capacity to evaluate completed missions. By recording and analyzing experiences, the procedures and organizations can be systematically improved

☐ Develops and maintains a roster of police officers who have a documented ability to fill leadership posts.

Regarding Measures in Sweden. The Commission proposes that the Government shall give the National Police Board the task of preparing a system which facilitates the deployment of Swedish police officers in international peace-promoting activities at short notice. Sweden should reinforce its Delegation to the United Nations in New York with a police adviser.

Considerations

General. Recent experiences with peace-keeping missions indicates a need for these to mobilize rapidly and to deploy shortly after the mandate is issued. Another important lesson is that ongoing missions can require rapid reinforcement or quickly change their direction and composition. If a conflict can be frozen at an early stage and momentum turned in a positive direction, this will have the following beneficial effects:

☐ The suffering of the civil population decreases.
☐ The conditions for reconciliation between the parties are improved.
☐ The duration of the peace-promoting mission is reduced.
☐ The cost of the peace-promoting mission is reduced.

This leads to the conclusion that measures should be taken on both the international and national levels to facilitate more rapid establishment of multinational police forces.

Measures Within the United Nations. Good, comprehensive planning for new peace-promoting activities is very important for the rapid establishment of an international police force in a conflict area. In general, police observers act in a conflict situation together with both military and other civil components of a peace-promoting mission. In the early planning process, the focus is usually directed toward military requirements; this reduces the possibility of creating favorable conditions for the police force. In planning, increased consideration should therefore be given to police viewpoints and requirements. An important task for police officers who participate in reconnaissance assessments and preparations for an international police force should be to map out the structure of the local judicial system, especially the organization of the police system, and the local laws. A knowledge of this is important if realistic mission tasks are to be formulated in mandates and other documents. It is also important for the determination of how the international police force is to be composed and organized and how police-contributing countries should plan mission-specific training.

Missions are led more and more often by a Special Representative appointed by the Secretary-General. Directly subordinate to him is the military chief (the Force Commander), the chief of the police force (the Police Commissioner), and possibly other parts of the mission. The largest and therefore dominating component in a mission usually consists of the military force under the command of the Force Commander. A military headquarters has a fixed organization similar to that in most countries. Units from different countries have the same names and the chains of command are clear. A model for a U.N. military headquarters also exists. Similar conditions do not exist for the police. When an international police force is established, a police headquarters must, therefore, be created. This must function in parallel with the military headquarters and cooperate with it in many respects. It is appropriate, therefore, that the police headquarters be given a structure corresponding to that of the military headquarters.

It is vital that a reserve of previously selected and trained personnel be established who can be called upon to staff key positions in the police headquarters. Examples of such posts are Police Commissioner, chief of staff, operations leader, and maintenance chief. By selecting candidates in advance for these posts, persons can be given staff and leadership education. They can be recruited among those who work at the U.N. Headquarters and have positions there which need not be manned when an actual mission is undertaken. The Lessons Learned Unit is a unit where such personnel may be found.

Access to the right equipment during the initial phase of a mission increases efficiency and creates confidence in the United Nations. The United Nations should supply all joint equipment for the police force (e.g., vehicles, means of communication and buildings). Police-contributing countries are expected to contribute only the personal equipment of their police officers. For logistical supplies such as fuel and communications equipment, the police are often obliged to use the resources of the military force. It is important that this is taken into consideration when the military logistics capacity is calculated. The equipment the United Nations selects for police missions should be standardized and user-friendly, to make it possible to train in advance under accurate mission conditions. In order to achieve greater mission capability, however, even more advanced equipment should be available to permit rapid communication. The information transmission used by EU monitors in Bosnia-Herzegovina with the help of portable computers and telephones should also be available to police forces involved in U.N. missions.

The ability of the United Nations to supply suitable equipment rapidly has varied in different missions. Delayed deliveries have caused problems for police activities in the initial stage of the mission. One reason for this is that the budget of a U.N. force is often determined by the General Assembly several months after the Security Council has decided to establish the force. Sweden, together with other troop- and police-contributing countries, should act so that the budget for the U.N. forces is determined more rapidly and is compiled so that a police component is given the same access to suitable resources as the military force in the same mission.

Certain types of conflict require that many police observers be made rapidly available. It is important that police officers placed at U.N. disposal have a good education, the experience necessary for the task, and in other respects meet the requirements of the mission, not least regarding knowledge of the mission language. To make this possible, Sweden should act so that member countries undertake national preparations so they can rapidly make police officers available.

The number of U.N. missions that have included police components is now so large that it is possible to derive general lessons from these experience. The United Nations should study and use these lessons not least when a new mission is being established. The low administrative alert is an example of experience gained about deficiencies that are now being corrected. Documents controlling administrative routines and the police code of behavior (Standard Administrative Procedures and Code of Conduct) have been prepared case by case for each mission, which has made the work more difficult; attempts are now being made to standardize these documents. Sweden should act to develop the capacity of the United Nations to implement lessons learned from previous operations.

There are only a few persons in different countries who have a documented experience of leading international police forces. The United Nations should draw up a roster of these individuals in order to make rapid recruitment possible when a new mission is to be established.

Measures in Sweden. Certain measures have already been taken to improve Sweden's capacity to participate in a broad array of peace-promoting activities. A system is available at the National Rescue Service Board that makes action possible at short notice. This system includes mobilization of personnel, equipment and logistics. The Swedish Parliament has further decided that within the Swedish Military Command a system shall be established which permits rapid deployment of military units for international missions. Experience during the 1990s shows that police observers and police advisers for peace-promoting activities are needed to an increasing extent. There is good reason, therefore, to establish a system within the *police force* which makes it possible for Swedish police officers to be deployed rapidly. At present, it takes about 10 weeks to recruit and train a Swedish police contingent for a new mission. The process includes application, grading, selection, planning of training, training, and equipping. In the case of smaller missions, the process can in certain cases be shortened by making direct contact with police officers with earlier experience.

The Commission proposes that the Government assign the National Police Board the task of developing experimental procedures to rapidly mobilize police officers for peace-promoting purposes. The trial activity should include 20 police officers who are contracted by the National Police Board to participate in the trial for 12 months. The police officers contracted should have undergone the United Nations Police Officers Course (UNPOC) and have completed at least 6 months of foreign service during the previous 5 years. Decisions about foreign service for the contracted person should be made by the Government. Those who are contracted should receive continuous information from the National Police Board about developments in possible conflict areas. The contract should include:

☐ The obligation to report to the Swedish Armed Forces International Centre (SWEDINT) at one week's notice to undergo mission-specific training and to be prepared to serve abroad within a further week

☐ The obligation to provide location and contact information to the National Police Board if the home or workplace is left for more than 48 hours.

For this, remuneration should be a fixed sum per calender month, one-third of which is paid together with the ordinary monthly salary. The remaining two-thirds are paid only if the Government decides on foreign service. In that case, retroactive payment of the sum earned is made.

The payment to those deployed shall be a compensation for sacrifices such as:

☐ The discomfort of not being able to take a holiday or other long trips, which would result in the police officer being unavailable for rapid mobilization

☐ The impact of the uncertainty factor on the officer and his/her family in the planning of their private lives

☐ Possible difficulties at the workplace because one is not entrusted with more important tasks.

The Commission concludes that the level of compensation should be decided after the Commission on Survey of the Rules for the Swedish Military Command's peace-promoting activities abroad (dir. Fö 1997:21) has presented its report. It is important that the benefits for police and military personnel in similar peace-promoting service are calculated according to the same procedures. This also applies to those who pledge themselves to be a member of the rapid deployment force.

Tested and stored equipment should be available for those who are under contract. The system for rapid deployment should be designed so that financing via the Swedish development aid budget is possible.

The Swedish delegation to the United Nations in New York should be reinforced with a police adviser with the aim of looking after police matters and to maintain contact with the Civilian Police Unit and other parts of DPKO. Such a reinforcement would increase the visibility of Sweden's position on the establishment and operation of police activities in peace-promoting missions. This is especially important during the period when Sweden is a member of the Security Council.

The National Police Board Assumes Responsibility

Proposal

The Commission proposes that the National Police Board shall have a total responsibility for all Swedish police officers in peace-promoting service. The National Police Board should take over the state's employer responsibilities and be responsible also for these police officers. A foreign force for the Police System should be established, with conditions of employment similar to those used for personnel deployed abroad by the Swedish Military Command.

Considerations

Reasons for Change. When the responsibility for police in peace-promoting activity is considered, it is suitable to start from the tasks which the police officers will perform.

The Swedish Military Command's responsibility for the police in peace-promoting service today includes not only their time abroad but also the training period in Sweden and the debriefings carried out after the period of service. This means that the National Police Board has no formal, statute-controlled responsibility whatsoever for these police officers. The responsibility for psychosocial measures after the homecoming rests with the home-authority of the individual policeman. For peace-promoting service, Sweden recruits only police officers active in the national police service. Those who are of interest are of such an age that they are expected to return to Swedish service after their period of foreign service. They are recruited because they have a special professional knowledge and common basic police education based on the standards and values characteristic of Swedish public life. Because the employer responsibility for Swedish policemen is now divided, depending on whether they serve in Sweden or abroad, motives (and resources) are lacking both within the police system and the Swedish Military Command to a take a real concentrated hold on this activity. The police activity in peace-promoting service is today not given the attention which it deserves. Neither the National Police Board nor the Swedish Military Command has to a sufficient extent followed the international debate or participated in the doctrine development within the field. Nor has it been possible to handle the experiences gained in a systematic way.

It is further a weakness that the ordinary employer has no formal responsibility for the police officers during their foreign service, even though police in foreign service represent not only the international organization concerned but also the total Swedish police corps. Experiences and knowledge that might be useful and valuable for the continued service of the civilian policeman on his return to Sweden are not systematically added to the police organization, either. The possibilities of observing the merits of foreign service in a promotion context are also made more difficult. Finally, staff welfare aspects related to experiences in foreign service are interrupted under the present system.

The tasks of the police in peace-promoting activities are normally to monitor or assist local police. These tasks are carried out within the framework of the judicial system of the host country. In such cases, the police are placed under the command of a police commissioner appointed by the United Nations and who is subordinate to the representative of the Secretary-General at the location. In these cases, the police officers are not included in a Swedish military force. There is thus no Swedish constitutional requirement that the police officers shall be employed in the Foreign Force of the Swedish Military Command (cf section 8.2). Instead, the employment should take place within a foreign force established within the Police force.

The Meaning of the Proposal. In certain cases, an international police force can, without being integrated into the military component or the military command and control, be given certain executive tasks. These can be, for example, to protect the civil population, aid workers, or prevent plundering. Intervention by the police and the employment of force in such a situation must be derived from a mandate based on Chapter VI or VII of the U.N. Charter. Ultimately, the decisionmaking for each measure must go appropriately through the chain of command. Police under such command conditions may also be assigned to create security and order through proactive behavior.

When police serve abroad under such conditions, a requirement should be made for the same adjustment of their position in Swedish law as applies to the military personnel. The Commission estimates that police officers who act under such conditions should also be employed in the foreign force of the Police System. Employment in the foreign force of the police system should therefore involve certain legal consequences, for example, that Sweden shall have unrestricted penal jurisdiction regarding crimes committed by such personnel (Chapter 2, Section 3.3, of the Swedish Penal Code). Provisions concerning disciplinary responsibility can be necessary in accordance with what is shown more closely in Section 8.2. However, it falls outside the framework of this investigation to propose necessary changes. When police officers serve as police advisers or instructors in a Swedish military unit, they constitute a part of the Swedish Armed Forces. To meet Constitutional requirements and the regulations of Section 2 of the Armed Forces Act, they should thus be employed in the Foreign Force within the Swedish Military Command. Also in cases when police officers in other forms constitute a part of a Swedish military contribution in peace-promoting activities, the employment should be with the Foreign Force within the Swedish Military Command. In pure assistance operations, another form of employment should be considered than within the foreign force of the Police System.

The Commission proposes that the National Police Board shall have total responsibility for Swedish police in peace-promoting service. The proposal means that a foreign force of the Police system is established by amending the instructions of the National Police Board. As a consequence, an amendment is proposed to the Ordinance (1984:309) about the Foreign Force within the Swedish Military Command so that the provisions concerning the civilian police department in Section 3 of the Ordinance are removed. The responsibility for Swedish police officers in international peace-promoting service is thereby transferred to the National Police Board. This includes responsibility for the recruiting, training, maintenance, and staff welfare of the Swedish police officers who participate in peace-promoting activities. The National Police Board should also be given the responsibility of actively following the methodological and doctrinal development within the field. The proposal means that the Government may need to take the initiative to introduce amendments of the type recently indicated and to the Ordinance accounted for below.

The employment conditions for the foreign force of the police force should be the same as those for the personnel in the Foreign Force within the Swedish Military Command. The benefits should be determined in an ordinance. In each individual mission, an estimate should be made as to whether the employment shall take place within the foreign force of the police force or in another form. If police officers are to serve as observers or advisers in a police component led by a Police Commissioner who acts in the same area as a military peace-promoting force, employment in the foreign force of the Police System is suitable. If the service has the characteristics of an aid contribution, such as a teacher at a national police school or as a member of an international tribunal, the employment should take place in the same way as before with the National Police Board as employer with financing from SIDA. The proposal does not influence the possibility of recruiting police officers for service at military posts in the Foreign Force within the Swedish Military Command. In such cases, the police officers shall be given leave of absence from the police force and shall have the Swedish Military Command as employer.

Special attention should be directed toward the tasks that the police are to carry out in the conflict area. If they are to be placed under military command and armed in any way other than for self-defense, employment can take place only in the Foreign Force within the Swedish Military Command. This should not occur often.

The Commission considers it essential that the responsibility of the National Police Board also includes the systematic and long-term work within the field of police in peace-promoting service. Methodological and doctrinal development should, along with a regular followup, be subjected to continual attention.

The Commission's proposal for a change in responsibility need not in itself mean any cost increase. The proposed increase in ambition regarding in particular methodological and doctrinal development means extra costs which must, however, be financed. This should largely be achieved through a coordination and rationalization of all the international activity within the National Police Board.

Today, the responsibility for international police questions within the National Police Board is divided into different units. As shown in Chapter 7 [of the Commission Report], International and National Organization for Police Work, such matters are handled at three different units within the National Police Board: the International Secretariat, the National Criminal Police, and the Police Academy. The National Criminal Police has the operational responsibility for international police activity and has for several years dealt with matters concerning police officers in peacekeeping service. To increase efficiency, the National Police Board should combine overall responsibility for police in peace-promoting activities into a single unit.

As shown previously, the Commission proposes that a system should be established within the police force which permits more rapid police mobilization than is possible at present. It appears technically and practically difficult to handle if those who are affected by this system are contracted, budgeted, and otherwise administered by any other principal than the National Police Board. In the same way, it appears to be unsuitable both administratively and in principle if members of the rapid-deployment system have a different employer than those who serve abroad.

Retain the Benefits of the Present System. There are, however, certain obvious advantages with the system used in Sweden today. The cooperation between the relevant administrators at the National Police Board and the Swedish Military Command on these issues works well according to concordant testimonials. There are well-developed routines and good working relationships among teachers and officials. Education in the form of UNPOC, mission-specific training, and the postmission debriefings is carried out by the Swedish Military Command at the same location as military personnel training.[1] This means that the local knowledge and experience available within the Swedish Military Command to act within a certain conflict area are utilized. In U.N. missions, there has been close and frequent cooperation between the civilian police and military headquarters. In certain missions, such as UNAVEM III in Angola, there was close cooperation in the field. Similar education and training are therefore desirable. It should be observed that the education of policemen and military personnel does not however take place simultaneously at the Swedish Military Command. No contacts of importance for the future are therefore established at the pupil level. This reduces somewhat the importance of the civilian police education taking place at SWEDINT. Only the few policemen educated at the U.N. Staff Officers Course (UNSOC) or at the Nordic U.N. Peace-Keeping Mission Management Seminar (UNMAS) have military course comrades.

---

[1] Military observers are trained at a 3-week joint Nordic course in Finland and spend only a short period at SWEDINT.

Because the police are included in the Foreign Force within the Swedish Military Command, they are automatically subjected to several other laws and regulations, such as the Ordinance (FFS 1984:31) regarding benefits to an employed person in the Foreign Force within the Swedish Military Command, and the Act (1994:1811) regarding disciplinary responsibility within the total defense. The police officers are also awarded the Swedish Military Command's medal for international service. This guarantees that personnel who serve in the same region under similar conditions, as a rule within the same mission, also have the same Swedish employment conditions. This reduces the risk that different Swedish personnel categories in a conflict area will feel that there are "injustices" among different groups.

The joint responsibility for military and police components facilitates the possibility of using the Swedish Military Command's transport resources for service and leave trips. The joint storage of uniforms and other materials provides coordination benefits for the national administration. Through SWEDINT, the Swedish Military Command has an organization specially adapted to international service and with the resources required to meet rapid and unexpected new tasks. For the running operation of the forces located abroad, there is similarly great experience and high competence within the Swedish Military Command. Cashier services, salary routines, and contacts with the United Nations and other international organizations are facilitated by the fact that there is *one* responsible authority in Sweden. Because the home country has no right to give operational instructions during the foreign service, it is not critical that there be police competence at the employment authority in Sweden.

The Commission considers it very important that a change in responsibility aims at assimilating the advantages of the change without losing the advantages of the present system. Several international reporters have considered that the close cooperation existing in Sweden between military and police activity in peace-promoting service is good. Training, equipment, and exercise should therefore also take place at SWEDINT in the future. The fine collaboration already existing between the two authorities should be developed and deepened.

This can take place if the foreign force of the Police System mainly carries out its activity at SWEDINT. An agreement is probably required between the Swedish Military Command and the National Police Board to govern details of this collaboration. It is very important that rules applicable for the Foreign Force within the Swedish Military Command, described more closely in chapter 8 [of the Commission's Report], also apply to the foreign force of the National Police Board.

Training and Recruiting

Proposal

The Commission proposes that elements concerning peace-promoting service are introduced into basic Swedish police training. Recruitment of police officers to the foreign force of the police force should take place more actively than has so far been the case. Special attention should be directed toward those counties which traditionally have a low proportion of police officers serving abroad. The importance of female police officers should be addressed. The present structure with UNPOC and later mission-specific training should be maintained and complemented in certain respects. The need for integration with military units should be given increased attention.

When the foreign force of the Police System is established, the National Police Board should consult with the Coordinator of Training for International Missions, who was appointed in accordance with the Government's decision on the defense of 1996.

Considerations

The Commission establishes that Sweden has a good international reputation as a police-contributing nation. An important reason for this is that Swedish police officers have undergone training that has made them both mentally prepared and qualified to act in a foreign environment.

To develop an understanding of police as an instrument of conflict-resolution at an early stage of professional development, and thereby stimulate an interest in international activities, information should be provided during basic police training about the possibility of

502

participating in peace-promoting missions later in one's career. This can take place in the form of a study visit to SWEDINT during police training or by employing police officers with international experience as lecturers during basic training at the Police Academy.

The circle of police officers who apply for foreign service should be made as large as possible. This increases selection possibilities and quality. A simple comparison of the county-affiliation of police officers who served abroad during the spring of 1997 shows that several counties are not represented. According to information from experienced police officers, this is a common situation. The Commission considers it important that special measures are taken to expand the recruitment base. In recruiting for each mission, the role which female police officers can play in creating confidence in the civil population should be given special consideration. In training police officers—women and men—for peace-promoting activities, special training should be provided in the handling of traumatized women who have been exposed to or have witnessed acts of violence.

Understanding human rights and basic policing skills is ingrained in the police officer, whereas knowledge about ongoing missions needs to be updated continuously. Teachers and instructors at UNPOC and mission-specific training must have the opportunity to continuously update their knowledge. Also, in the future recruiting should take place among those who have personal experience from service abroad. Teachers and instructors should be connected to the National Police Board in a more solid way than before, perhaps for a period of 3 years, to motivate them to keep their knowledge updated. The National Police Board should have continuous contact with the teachers and should supply adequate information. The system should be arranged so that not all teachers are exchanged at the same time. For the Swedish viewpoint to be credible in the international debate on policing issues, a number of confidence-inspiring persons who work with them are required; a sufficient number of voices must be heard in public for the Swedish opinions to be credible. Not least, it is important that teachers and instructors communicate their experiences to the world around. This is also facilitated if the teachers are more firmly connected to the foreign force of the police force than is so at present.

UNPOC is suitable in its length and extent. The course content should be general and continually updated. UNPOC should also be located at SWEDINT, in cooperation with the Coordinator of Training for International Missions, who has been appointed as a result of the latest Governmental decision on defense.

The mission-specific training should be extended to a week and should be directed mainly toward the judicial conditions in the mission country. Knowledge of the local police force and the legal system should be given a prominent place.

In recruiting new personnel for ongoing missions, knowledge of the mission language should continue to be observed. Opportunities should be provided to those who have been selected to carry out studies in relevant languages through individual study courses made available by the foreign force of the police force. The same condition should apply to the mission language. This is especially important when the mission language is not English. It is not reasonable to train police officers in "odd" languages for possible future work.

Managerial training in the form of staff training should be implemented to a greater extent. More police officers should undergo integrated training such as UNSOC and UNMAS.

In Section 12.10 [of the Commission's Report], "More Efficient Police Activities Within the United Nations," viewpoints are given on training on arrival at the mission area. Sweden should further act so that within the United Nations and other performance organizations, budgeting should always ensure that resources are continuously available for training in an ongoing mission. This education should primarily be aimed at providing a complementary knowledge within different fields where a need has been found to exist during the course of the mission.

Sweden should also encourage police-contributing countries to offer each other places in national training courses for peace-promoting police activities. The aim should be to encourage other countries to provide similar education.

It is natural that the National Police Board actively collaborate with the Swedish Military Command in the introduction of the police force's foreign force. Cooperation should also take place with the Coordinator of Training for International Mission.

Financing

Proposal

The Commission proposes that funds for administration in Sweden of the police force's foreign force should be budgeted within the National Police Board's administration appropriation as a special item. The item should be dimensioned so that at least those funds today allocated by the National Criminal Police, the Police Academy, and the Swedish Military Command for recruiting, training, administration, and followup are transferred to the police force's foreign force item, which should be administered by the National Police Board.

Funds budgeted for UNPOC and other aid activities to be executed by police officers should be placed at the disposal of the National Police Board in a so-called regulation letter. Operational costs for activities abroad should continue to be kept separate from the costs in Sweden. The present division of the operational costs according to the type of activity is appropriate and should be continued. In future budgets, the Government should take into consideration that international demand for police officers is expected to increase. In relevant appropriations, funds should be allocated to permit an involvement on at least the level proposed in this investigation.

Considerations

A collected responsibility for international police matters means that economic responsibility must be transferred to the National Police Board. This means, for example, responsibility to prepare the annual budget and annual accounts and to calculate costs in connection with the start of a new mission or extension of an ongoing mission. The *Government* must determine the level of activity and should therefore be budgeted as its own item to prevent funds from being reduced in connection with new priorities in other fields within the activities of the National Police Board.

Responsibility and Method Development. The proposal for a change in responsibility is estimated to be neutral regarding costs to the state. Certain one-time costs in connection with reform can arise, however. The exact size of sums to be transferred to the police force's foreign force from the Swedish Military Command, the National Police Board, and the Police Academy must be calculated before the budget is set. The Commission's proposal for greater attention to the field of methodological and doctrinal development means an increase in ambition, which leads to greater costs than in the present situation. The Commission estimates that resources needed for this purpose can amount to work for approximately one person during 1 year.

Increased Awareness of Police Tasks in Peace-Promoting Military Units. The Commission proposes that the Government should commission the Swedish Military Command and the National Police Board to investigate more closely conditions for an increased awareness of military peace-promoting units for solving certain police tasks. The task should also include an estimate of the economic consequences of such an extended training period.

The Extent of the Swedish Participation. The proposal for a Swedish readiness to make available 125 police officers permanently or 150 police officers temporarily must correspond to a budgetary preparedness within the appropriations concerned to be feasible and credible. A higher long-term ambition level also means higher costs at the National Police Board for administration and training. The average Swedish operational cost for 125 police officers in U.N. service is calculated to be about Swedish Krona (SEK) 75 million, with an annual average cost of SEK 0.6 million per police officer. The cost for those police officers who do not receive a mission subsistence allowance (MSA) from the United Nations is in general higher than for those who have MSA. The budgetary preparedness should be such that it also permits participation in those countries where the costs exceed the average. The Commission establishes that police activities abroad are of different characters and are included in missions with different mandates. Some missions involve aid while others can be regarded as parts of a traditional peace-keeping contribution in close collaboration with military components. To continue to meet new demands rapidly and flexibly, possibilities should exist within the Swedish state budget to use funds from several appropriations. The two appropriations used at present are well suited for the purpose. When the budget is established for a new mission, or the police contribution is reinforced in ongoing missions, it should be noted that an increase also means increased costs for administration and training in Sweden. These costs should also, while awaiting a coming budget, be included in the operational costs for the new or extended mission. The Commission considers that the National Police Board should administer the funds used for the operational costs of the personnel stationed abroad.

System for Higher Awareness of International Work. The costs for a system that makes it possible to recruit personnel rapidly are independent of the number of persons included, the length of the contract period, and the mobilization time. In a previous section, examples have been given of factors which are important when the payment level is calculated. In the same section, reasons are given for why the Commission refrains from making any proposal about the payment level.

Police Advisers at the Swedish Representation in New York. The annual cost for a police adviser at the U.N. Delegation in New York is estimated to amount to nearly one million SEK. This position provides the opportunity to improve an activity, largely aid in character, and should therefore be financed with funds from Swedish development aid grants.

Extended Mission-Specific Training. The mission-specific training is currently financed by funds assigned in a regulation letter or separate Government decision for the operation cost of each action. The Commission's proposal means that the cost for each mission increases with a sum which corresponds to three further service days in Sweden per police officer. This should be observed in the preparation of future budgets.

CONCLUSIONS

ROBERT B. OAKLEY and MICHAEL J. DZIEDZIC

The cases treated in this work offer ample evidence to support the claim that each post-Cold War peace operation has been unique. Our authors have provided the distinct flavor of these experiences in abundant detail and have also drawn operation-specific conclusions. When these experiences are examined together in comparative perspective, however, it also becomes possible to identify recurring themes and commonalities. Such is the burden here: to identify durable lessons and general recommendations to pass on to military and civilian officials who will be responsible for planning and executing public security aspects of future multilateral peace operations. We have organized this discussion into three categories:

- □ General lessons learned
- □ A set of specific recommendations addressing each of the public security gaps identified in this work
- □ Brief reflections on the broader implications of the "new world disorder" and the need for international public security assistance beyond the realm of peace operations.

Authors' note: In this regard, we particularly wish to acknowledge the wealth of insights developed by leading international specialists from Norway and Sweden included above. Although arrived at via their own distinct methodologies, we are encouraged that many of their conclusions overlap with or are identical to our own. A special thanks is also due to the panelists and rapporteurs who made the September 15-16, 1997 National Defense University conference on public security so insightful and productive. They are: Carl Alexandre, Dr. David Bayley, Nils Gunnar Billinger, Colonel James Burger, U.S. Army, Colonel Brian Bush, U.S. Army, Charles T. Call, Antonia Handler Chayes, Dr. Graham Day, Mark Ellis, Charles English, Dr. Ken Eyre, Colonel Karl Farris, U.S. Army (Ret.), Dr. Michele A. Flournoy, Colonel Larry Forster, U.S. Army, Major General Louis A. Geiger, Swiss Army (Ret.), Brigadier General

Lessons Learned

Public Security Reform Is Vital

One of the defining features of post-Cold War peace operations is domestic disorder. Because these are internal conflicts, a lasting resolution will require erstwhile antagonists to live together as part of a single political community with adequate assurances that political disputes will be resolved through peaceful rather than violent means.

Merely restoring order will not be sufficient. Unless attention is also given to establishing effective safeguards against abuse, there is the very real possibility that international assistance for public security could have the perverse effect of reinforcing rather than reforming the repressive capacity of the state. Justice must also be included as an objective, otherwise public security will not be sustainable. Reform does not require creating an ideal society or advanced democracy, but it does require functional mechanisms to deal with abuses of authority within the public security system. These mechanisms need to function well enough so that no significant segment of the political community feels compelled to resort to force once again to demolish an unjust system.

This process takes time, and it will almost assuredly take longer than the United States and other countries are prepared to leave their military forces deployed in significant numbers in some distant land. However, the military contingent can be progressively downsized as law and order are restored and civilian assistance programs come into effect. There are clear operational advantages for the military contingent if international law enforcement assistance is effectively carried out. It can reduce the threat to military peacekeepers, enhance popular support for the ongoing mission, improve respect for human

---

W. C. Gregson, U.S. Marine Corps, Edmund Hull, Lieutenant Colonel Michael J. Kelly, AM, Dr. Otwin Marenin, Major General William Nash, U.S. Army, Colonel David Patton, U.S. Army, Robert Perito, J. O'Neil G. Pouliot, Om Prakash Rathor, Dr. James Schear, Dr. William Stanley, Jan Stromsem, Molly Warlow, Robert Wasserman, and Richard Wilcox. Several of them were also very helpful to us in developing this chapter.

rights, accelerate the reduction and withdrawal of military peacekeepers, and increase prospects for long-term stability.

Public Security Reform is Holistic

The task of rebuilding or reforming the public security apparatus requires that the judicial process, associated legal code, and penal system be addressed during the earliest stages, along with reform of the police force. Compared to policing, judicial reform takes longer and is even more difficult because of its intimate connection with national sovereignty and the distribution of power in any regime. By waiting until the latter stages of a peace operation to come to grips with such shortcomings, the clout of the international community will likely have faded, and a window of opportunity will probably have been lost. This is self-defeating, because police reform is of little value when the judicial process is corrupt and abusive behavior is rampant within the penal system.

In Bosnia, Civil Affairs specialists assigned to IFOR/SFOR and the NGO community (e.g., the American Bar Association) have stressed the need to assist the IPTF and other organizations in reforming the judiciary. This was reflected in a study conducted by IFOR, "The Functioning of the Legal System in Bosnia-Herzegovina as of 1 October 1996," similar to the U.S. Army Civil Affairs survey of Haiti's judicial system. This sort of collaboration is extremely important and should be standard procedure in future operations, especially given the inevitable impact upon military activities and the fate of the overall mission.

Taking a holistic approach to the criminal justice system would entail conducting a detailed assessment of the local judiciary, legal codes, and penal systems, along with the police force; identifying the major deficiencies in each; and engaging in a dialogue with local authorities to determine how the resources of the international community can be applied to overcoming shortcomings. It also means getting an early start on these programs in order to build momentum. None of this will matter, however, unless local authorities manifest a willingness to cooperate and bilateral and multilateral assistance programs give judicial and penal reform adequate priority when resources are allocated.

Sustainable Public Security is Not Always Possible

Not all internal conflicts are ripe for the ministrations of a peace operation. Prior to mounting such a mission, it is absolutely crucial to perform a rigorous assessment of the prospects for a successful intervention. Apart from other pertinent considerations, reform of public security will require two developments: commitment of resources over time that are capable of overcoming deficiencies in the capacity of public security structures, and generating political consensus among the former disputants that these structures should function in a reasonably impartial manner. It is essential to address both if the efforts of the international community are to have lasting beneficial impact. The most daunting of these challenges invariably will be to overcome resistance from powerful political elites who calculate they will be disadvantaged by the outcome of the reform process. A proper job of institution building could undercut the political interests of certain powerful actors whose consent may be required for the peace mission to continue functioning or for its results to be sustained.

These general lessons, viewed in the context of past performance and current capabilities of international law enforcement assistance, lead to a number of specific recommendations (set forth below). These recommendations are directed at the U.N. system, starting with DPKO but also including other U.N. offices and agencies; at member states of the United Nations who participate in its law enforcement assistance activities or who have bilateral assistance programs of their own; and at those NGOs engaged in various aspects of law enforcement assistance (e.g., the American Bar Association).[1]

---

[1]Specific entities that should consider acting upon individual recommendations are identified in parentheses.

Recommendations

The Deployment Gap

There are two basic remedies for this gap. To narrow the gap, *the capacity of the international community to mobilize CIVPOL personnel should be strengthened*, both within contributing states and at the United Nations. Because this gap probably cannot be closed entirely in most cases, *the military also needs to be prepared to discharge this function, on an interim basis,* until the security environment has been sufficiently stabilized and the CIVPOL contingent has become operational. The recommendations developed below are intended to address these two requirements.

A Standby Force of Trained CIVPOL Personnel. *(Key Actors: United Nations and Member States)* The standby force concept currently used to assemble military troop contributions for peace operations should be adapted for use in CIVPOL mobilization. The most significant difference would be that it would almost always be individuals, rather than entire units, who would be designated as potentially available. Member states would have to assume some responsibility for ensuring their volunteers had received the requisite advanced training, either in-country or in certain third countries specializing in international police training (e.g., Norway, Spain, Sweden, etc.). The CIVPOL office within the U.N. DPKO would require additional staffing to establish training standards and procedures, identify the spectrum of specialized skills likely to be required, establish a team to oversee this function, and maintain a data base of standby personnel and organizations (see CIVPOL Resources, below). Also required would be rapid access to the necessary equipment and supplies. The U.N. Interregional Crime Research Institute and the Crime Prevention and Criminal Justice Division should also seek to identify a cadre of judicial experts for standby status, enabling rapid deployment alongside police specialists. Countries such as Sweden and Norway have already taken the initiative to establish a reserve of dedicated civilian police personnel for use in future UNCIVPOL or other multilateral missions. This includes the development of specialized training programs for international policing.

513

Canada and Australia also have established procedures for rapidly mobilizing personnel for CIVPOL missions and providing advanced training for them. The United States and others should follow their example.

CIVPOL in U.N. Assessment Teams and Deployable Headquarters. *(Key Actor: United Nations)* Experienced CIVPOL personnel should be incorporated into the proposed U.N. Rapidly Deployable Mission Headquarters (RDMHQ) and advance U.N. assessment teams. To support the RDMHQ, a cadre of prospective supervisory personnel with experience in international policing and in administering police and judicial organizations need to be identified and maintained in a reserve status by the U.N. Civilian Police office (perhaps as a special category of the CIVPOL standby force recommended above). The assessment team should include civilian law enforcement specialists who are prepared to address the scope of the CIVPOL mission, the viability of the current public security apparatus (police, judiciary/legal code, prisons), the extent of consent among local elites as well as popular acceptance of the peace mission, resources required, and how this activity can be sustained over the long haul. It would also be beneficial to include specialists in the legal tradition and culture of the nation-state involved so that mission-specific planning can be tailored to local circumstances. The assessment should strive to do more than describe the structures of public security and their present capabilities; it should also seek to understand the popular legitimacy of each, the prevailing "legal culture," and the dynamics that determine their actual functioning (e.g., is the system characterized by impunity for a few or equal justice for all).

CIVPOL Training. *(Key Actors: United Nations and Member States contributing to CIVPOL)* Over the past several years there has been significant progress in producing handbooks, field guides, manuals, etc., on international human rights and justice standards for CIVPOL, providing training in these areas, and screening/testing prospective personnel prior to deployment (see section by Broer and Emery). However, there is a need to continue to improve training, including for specialized as well as basic functions. This can be undertaken by individual member states, with CIVPOL supervision. Before deployment, CIVPOL personnel should be familiar with international standards that apply to the broad range of public security and human rights functions; the general differences among legal systems based on the Napoleonic Code, English Common Law, and the Sharia; and techniques for effective monitoring and mentoring. This would be in addition to pre-mission training dealing with the specific cultural traits, contemporary political realities, and security threats in the mission area. English language training should also be made liberally available.

In addition to basic CIVPOL training programs conducted by Member States, there is a need for multilateral training and exercises. This would emulate the considerable number of multilateral military peacekeeping exercises, such as those conducted by NATO and PFP forces and by U.S. and Latin American militaries. This would substantially improve collective civilian capabilities, as it has with military forces. In addition, military planners should give consideration to incorporating CIVPOL elements in their exercise scenarios.

Skills for the CIVPOL Contingent. *(Key Actors: United Nations and Member States)* Until recently, the typical pattern of recruitment by the United Nations had been to solicit volunteers from Member States using a very basic set of criteria, such as a given number of years experience in policing, fluency in the mission language (normally English), and driving ability. Beginning with the second cadre of police monitors in Bosnia, however, the United Nations also asked contributing nations to provide volunteers who have the specific skills needed for that operation. This is a major advance, and recruitment of future CIVPOL contingents should continue to be done in this manner (i.e., on the basis of specific personnel needs). Among the areas of expertise that ought to be considered during recruitment of future CIVPOL contingents (depending on the nature of the mandate) should be the following: specialists in the legal code applicable in the host country, administration of justice, administration of police academies, penal system reform, internal affairs/inspector general, criminal investigations, organized crime, and field training. There should be a special emphasis upon recruiting personnel proficient in the language of the country where the mission is taking place.

Continuing emphasis should be placed on obtaining credible performance evaluations on CIVPOL personnel during the conduct of each mission. The purpose would be both to identify incompetent personnel, so they can be removed, as well as the most qualified, so they can be groomed for supervisory positions in future missions.

CIVPOL Resources. *(Key Actors: United Nations and Member States)* Present requirements for mobilizing, training, equipping, and sustaining CIVPOL field operations greatly outstrip current capabilities. The UNCIVPOL office is currently authorized one full-time position. Even though the office has been supplemented by five specialists seconded from member states at no cost to the United Nations, this is woefully insufficient given that there are some 3,000 CIVPOL personnel in the field under the nominal supervision of this office. Implementation of the recommendations made here, such as a CIVPOL standby force, would require additional staffing, computerization, and financial resources. Yet, there is strong pressure from the Non-Aligned Movement to end the practice of secondment, which would deprive the CIVPOL office of its five pro bono specialists. This would be highly counterproductive and tantamount to abandonment of concern for this function.

The United Nations and Member States need to assign a higher priority to supporting CIVPOL activities. The CIVPOL office has been commendably flexible in welcoming various forms of assistance for CIVPOL activities via bilateral government programs and NGOs. To a limited degree, CIVPOL personnel shortcomings might be ameliorated by greater integration with and support from other elements of DPKO (for equipment, logistics, etc.). However, DPKO also faces severe personnel and budgetary pressures. Thus, an increase in funding for CIVPOL is essential, but not likely until the United States clears up the bulk of its arrears to the United Nations and others increase their contributions.

A Generic Public Security Plan. *(Key Actors: United Nations and Member States contributing to CIVPOL)* To ensure that vital lessons gleaned from previous peace operations are reliably acted upon

516

in the future, a generic public security plan should be developed by U.N. DPKO. This should also be an integral component of the U.S. interagency political-military planning process. This plan would identify the functions to be performed by members of the international community (e.g., UNCIVPOL and bilateral governments); address all elements of the public security "triad"; specify the resources and personnel skills/ranks normally required for each function; list the likely sources for resources and personnel and their likely availability to sustain such missions; and provide general guidance regarding the relationships that should be developed with the local police force and other authorities, the military contingent, and other entities contributing to the mission. Each mission will confront anew various fundamental choices: whether CIVPOL should be armed and have "executive authority" to enforce local law; whether the military and CIVPOL should have common communications and logistics systems and engage in joint patrolling; and how the deployment, enforcement, and institutional gaps will be addressed, especially how civil disturbances and other types of unrest are to be handled.

Other functional issues to be considered would be how former combatants are to be demobilized, disarmed, and reintegrated into civil society; the potential for vigilante activity by police if the judiciary does not function; whether the international community should provide funding for judicial and police salaries until the government can do so adequately; the sanctions and inducements available to encourage compliance with reform of the public security apparatus; possible placement of experienced international advisors within ministries involved in public security; how the safety of CIVPOL personnel will be preserved and, if necessary, how evacuation will be accomplished; and how to adapt to cultural conditions and public expectations in the mission area.

While a generic plan can serve as a rough-and-ready guide, it must be tailored to the circumstances of each contingency. The generic plan would, thus, be the starting point for mission-specific planning for each new operation. A plan covering policing, the judiciary, and prisons is essential before deployment for each mission, ideally integrated with the military plan but valuable by itself if this is not feasible. At a minimum, the relationship between the military and CIVPOL contingents must be addressed, with special attention given to maximizing common communications capabilities and logistics support. Coordination with other elements of the operation (e.g., humanitarian, human rights, economic reconstruction) should also be vigorously pursued. An actual operation plan will be much easier to prepare if there is a generic plan to use as a template. Even after this step has been taken, however, the plan must be reviewed and revised as the mission unfolds, conditions change, and more is learned from exposure to reality on the ground. Rigidity is to be avoided. In addition, there should be a dynamic mechanism for capturing lessons learned after each peace operation and revising the generic plan as warranted.

MPs and Civil Affairs Specialists. *(Key Actors: Military and CIVPOL Planners at the United Nations and Member States)* While steps can and should be taken to accelerate CIVPOL mobilization and overall capacity, there will continue to be a high probability that in most cases there will be a considerable lag between the deployment of the two contingents. Military peacekeepers will need to perform constabulary functions on an interim basis, therefore, during the earliest stages of most peace missions. Additionally, a high threat environment during the initial period of international intervention may militate against effective CIVPOL operations until the military contingent has been able to stabilize the situation (e.g., by beginning the process of cantonment for the former combatants). Consequently, military planners should ensure that adequate military police or gendarme units are incorporated in the initial deployment package. As Brigadier General David Foley pointed out in his speech to the September 1997 National Defense University conference, "Policing the New World Disorder," U.S. Army Military Police are well qualified for this mission, as are constabulary forces from some other countries (see appendix B). Erwin Schmidl points out the frequent past use of constabulary forces for this purpose. As experience in Panama and Haiti demonstrates, when adequate advanced provisions have not been made to have MP units immediately available, the consequences for the peace mission can be decidedly negative.

Careful attention must be given to specification of the mission, tasks, and ROEs for these units. ROEs must be crafted with prudence and precision, indicating circumstances under which military forces are to act to preserve order. Issues to be addressed include responses to violence within the local population, responses to other criminal activity, authority to arrest and detain local citizens and their subsequent disposition, and the extent of training assistance that troops are permitted to provide indigenous police and judicial authorities. Other issues that must be covered are the relationship with local police forces, the process by which CIVPOL will ultimately assume its responsibilities from the military, and their subsequent relationship with each other.

In addition, civil affairs personnel with backgrounds in planning, logistics, and police operations should be assigned to work with the CIVPOL commissioner, as soon as one has been designated, to facilitate CIVPOL deployment and military support to it. Intelligence and public information/psychological operations assets as well as communications and logistics capabilities of the military contingent are vital for restoring the rule of law and should be closely coordinated from the outset with corresponding CIVPOL functions. With proper preparation this can be done within the context of existing policies and capabilities of the United Nations, the United States, and other governments. It is justifiable as a military activity, given the negative effect upon force protection, mission accomplishment, and prospects for withdrawal if there is a delay in restoring public security.

Constabulary Capability and Utilization. *(Key Actors: United Nations and Member States)* Some military establishments already possess very significant constabulary forces—that is, units capable of maintaining public order by performing both law enforcement and light infantry operations. Such units (e.g., the U.S. Military Police and Special Forces, French gendarmerie, Spanish Guardia Civil, Chilean carabineros, Argentine gendarmes, Italian carabinieri, Dutch Royal Mariechaussee, etc.) should be explicitly solicited from donor nations when there is a serious prospect that an impending peace operation will have to cope with significant public disorder. Constabulary forces are better suited for law enforcement functions and for interaction with

CIVPOL than regular military forces. In circumstances where potential for violence is not high or has been greatly reduced, but there is a continuing need for law enforcement, constabulary forces could be considered as a substitute for regular combat forces in peace operations.

This remedy could overtax the finite number of member states currently possessing such a "constabulary" capability. Additional training, manpower, and other resources would undoubtedly be required if there were to be significant and recurring missions for such units. Thus, there are inherent limitations in this approach, unless Member States would be amenable to expanding their constabulary forces and/or assisting other countries to develop an enhanced capability in response to this need. Owing to sensitivities about the possible impact on civil-military relations, assistance to Member States in developing new "constabulary" forces would need to be considered on a case-by-case basis.

The Enforcement Gap

This gap is greatest when political consent with the peace agreement is deficient and the CIVPOL element is unarmed, as is normally the case. To address the existing void in local law enforcement, the most workable option is generally *an interim police force* assembled, after careful screening, from local government security forces.

When the enforcement gap involves a need to promote compliance with provisions of a peace agreement, the most promising approach is to bring all resources of the peace operation to bear in a coordinated fashion. In particular, this entails *integrated and mutually reinforcing operations by the military and CIVPOL contingents*. Absent such unity of effort, this gap in public security can become acute and threaten the success of the entire mission.

An Interim Police Force. *(Key Actors: Special Representative of Secretary-General or Equivalent in Charge of the Peace Mission; CIVPOL; Military Contingent Commander; Local Officials)* In most cases, the local police force will not be held in very high public esteem. Thus, in seeking to fill the law enforcement gap, the challenge will be to convert what may have been a predatory and illegitimate force into at least a visible facade of law enforcement (as in Haiti with the IPSF). This allows local law to be applied and minimizes confrontations between the peace force and the local population. This will entail vetting of notoriously corrupt or sadistic personnel, a retraining program to make those retained on duty aware of their new performance standards, adequate materiel support, supervision by CIVPOL monitors, and, perhaps, joint patrolling with military police, as well. A mechanism for funding salaries and operational expenses of this interim police force must be anticipated, because revenue collection is apt to have broken down along with other government functions. Even if this were not the case, there may be no utility in relying on a police force that has remained totally beholden to those responsible for causing the intervention in the first place. One of the inherent dangers that must be guarded against is the inclination for such interim policemen to exploit what they may view as their final opportunity in a police uniform to enrich themselves through extortion or outright banditry. Stifling this requires a competent, adequately staffed, and fully engaged CIVPOL force, often with military support. It also means holding out opportunities for individuals in the interim force to become members of a permanent force if their current behavior and past records meet proper standards. Throughout this process a public information campaign should keep the general public and specific elite audiences informed about the mission's intentions and the new standard expected from the police.

The Demobilization Dilemma. *(Key Actors: Special Representative of Secretary-General or Equivalent in Charge of the Peace Mission; CIVPOL; Commander of Military Contingent; Local Government Officials; Donor Nations Funding Retraining Programs; ICITAP and Equivalent Government Agencies)* In a postconflict environment, the rates of violent crime, especially assault with automatic weapons, are apt to be soaring. Government security forces are typically demobilized or restricted to cantonments, creating a void in public order after years of harsh and repressive rule. As public alarm mounts, the retention of elite units and a leadership cadre who have had the benefit of extensive training and years of experience becomes very appealing. The dilemma arises because these same individuals and elite units are often guilty of grave human rights abuses and rampant corruption.

Past experience indicates it is generally preferable to disband elite units, vet the personnel, require them to be fully retrained if they wish to re-enter the force, and permit them back only individually to prevent them from coalescing as a group and usurping control over the fledgling police force. Similarly, there will be a great temptation to retain experienced police supervisors because the remainder of the police force will be comprised of rookies. Once again, extreme care must be exercised, because whoever is allowed to name these individuals to senior posts will be in a strong position to monopolize power over the long haul. Prospects for constructing a police force that is both proficient and endowed with an ethos of service to the public hinges on fundamentally altering the police culture. Retaining specialized units or cadres of previous supervisory personnel (especially midlevel supervisors) could constitute an insurmountable barrier to essential change.

Another dimension of the demobilization dilemma is the concern that former security personnel may be unable to find gainful employment and will therefore turn to criminal activity to support themselves. Given their training, discipline, and knowledge of the criminal underworld, this is a realistic possibility. Demobilization or retraining programs are an obvious answer, but as in Haiti, there may be considerable political resistance to providing special assistance to the same nefarious group that had formerly victimized their fellow citizens.

CIVPOL and Military Unity of Effort. *(Key Actors: U.N. DPKO; Special Representative of Secretary-General or Equivalent in Charge of the Peace Mission; CIVPOL and Military Contingent Commanders; Member States Contributing Military or Police Personnel)* The most effective way to deal with an enforcement gap is via mutually reinforcing operations between the international military and CIVPOL contingents. Haiti provides the model. There was a single individual in charge of the operation, to whom both the police and military contingents were subordinated. (For this to function well, key individuals involved must be capable of working together as a team.) At the operational level, police and military command posts were co-located, and both forces used the same communication network, information/intelligence structures, and logistics support system. At the tactical level, military policemen were temporarily assigned to duty in local police stations to accompany CIVPOL and local police on patrols.

The "Haiti model" enhances unity of effort in a variety of areas. First, information about potential threats, forthcoming operations, and other mutual concerns can be passed freely between the military and CIVPOL organizations by virtue of a common communications net, a shared command post, and intermingling of personnel in the field. Second, the presence of military forces serves as a deterrent against armed resistance to CIVPOL and their local counterparts, boosting their morale and effectiveness. Third, the use of common communication and logistics networks allows for economies of scale, interoperability, and other efficiencies. Finally, joint planning by the military and CIVPOL should make the response to contingencies much more timely and effective.

Maximizing unity of effort also requires recognition of the need for Civil Affairs personnel to work with CIVPOL, as well as for effective coordination of public information and intelligence capabilities. CIVPOL personnel can serve as a rich and timely source of raw intelligence data, as demonstrated by the ASF in Somalia and by the IPTF in Bosnia. Assuring a continuous and timely exchange of information should be a high priority. The efficacy of the military's public information campaign in shaping local attitudes toward CIVPOL activities was clearly demonstrated in Haiti. Such capabilities are not found in normal UNCIVPOL deployments, therefore arrangements for military support in this area should be included in military planning. After the military peacekeeping mission has ended, a limited number of military police, Civil Affairs, intelligence, or public information personnel may be required to remain with CIVPOL temporarily to ensure a smooth transition and continuity of effort.

Sanctions and Inducements. *(Key Actors: U.N. DPKO; Special Representative of Secretary-General or Equivalent in Charge of the Peace Mission; CIVPOL and Military Contingent Commanders; Member States Contributing Military or Police Personnel)* Even the most unified and well-coordinated peace mission will not, by virtue of this factor alone, be able to overcome deficient political will on the part of one or more of the parties to comply with obligations of their peace agreement. Assuming the international coalition involved is reasonably unified regarding the desired outcome (or end state), it may be possible to encourage greater compliance through a coordinated package of international sanctions and inducements. One of the dilemmas for those concerned with reforming the instruments of public security is that suspending public security reform programs as a sanction for misconduct might be counterproductive. The lack of effective measures to sanction defiance by Bosnian Serb police and Interior Ministry officials was a chronic liability for IPTF Commissioners.[2]

The Institutional Gap

A blueprint for achieving sustainable security ought to be considered a centerpiece of any peace operation. First, the structural components of indigenous public security (police, judiciary/legal code, and prisons) must achieve at least *a basic capacity to maintain law and order* by capitalizing on the international assistance available to them. This process should begin as soon as possible during the peace operation.

The second and more challenging task is to *imbue these structures of public security with an ethos of public service and impartiality, and to bolster societal mechanisms of accountability.*[3] Achieving law and order with justice under these circumstances is a long-term process requiring international and indigenous mechanisms for generating and sustaining the requisite political will. This process brings a host of additional players to the forefront. Among the more prominent are specialists in public administration, human rights, electoral processes, and journalism.

---

[2]Former IPTF Deputy Commissioner Robert Wasserman was particularly compelling in his discussion of this point during the September 15-16, 1997, conference on international policing at the National Defense University.

[3]This combination of attributes is derived from a presentation by Professor David Bayley to a conference conducted by the Center for Strategic International Studies, October 1997.

Strive for Multilateral Cohesion. *(Key Actors: U.N. DPKO; the SRSG; the CIVPOL Contingent; the Military Contingent; Member States; Relevant International Organizations and NGOs)* The UNCIVPOL office has been commendably flexible in blending available bilateral assistance together with the efforts of CIVPOL operations in the field. This has ranged from ICITAP taking responsibility for creating and operating police and judicial academies and training programs in Haiti, Bosnia and elsewhere, to France and Canada providing personnel for police and judicial activities in parallel with CIVPOL, to Norway and Spain providing training for prospective CIVPOL personnel from other countries. This is constructive and should be continued, especially given CIVPOL's resource limitations. However, it must be more systematic, and more member states should be encouraged to become active if there is to be a positive, long-term impact on the overall law enforcement capability of states being assisted.[4]

Multilateral unity of effort requires a process of coordination embracing not merely Member States but key international organizations and NGOs involved in a peace operation, as well. There needs to be greater integration or coordination by DPKO with the Crime Prevention and Criminal Justice Division, the U.N. Development Program and other elements of the U.N. system, because public safety assistance goes well beyond policing and is a long-term developmental as well as a peacekeeping function. A suitable method for achieving this would be to establish a clearinghouse within the United Nations for premission coordination. While this process could never be mandatory or binding, it should at least identify the international actors expected to be involved, what their anticipated contributions to public security will be, and how they all will interact/coordinate with each other (e.g., CIVPOL contingents have been called upon to assist with human rights

---

[4]For example, which international entity or entities will provide monitoring, mentoring, and equipment and other assistance for indigenous police forces; who will provide near-term and long-term training, and at what levels; and will this cover the foreseeable needs? Similar questions need to be answered for the judiciary (including possible legal code reform) and the penal system.

monitoring, disarmament programs, demobilization of ex-combatants, electoral supervision, etc.).[5] The purpose would be to facilitate the sharing of intentions and coordination of plans among the various actors associated with a pending or ongoing peace mission (public security would not be the only aspect of peace operations to benefit from such a mechanism). A centralized database, perhaps building upon the computerized system used for refugee repatriation and reintegration in Bosnia by SFOR, UNHCR, and the Office of the High Representative could be developed as the centerpiece of this effort.

Once the mission has begun, the CIVPOL Commissioner and the senior international civilian and military representatives should take the initiative to establish a suitable mechanism for communication and coordination with other actors providing assistance in the realm of public security, including NGOs, international organizations, and Member States conducting bilateral assistance programs. The commissioner should also work closely with the military commander and under the unifying direction of the senior civilian authority (e.g., U.N. SRSG, the High Representative) to coordinate with other actors in the areas of human rights, elections, refugee resettlement, and related issues. The value added via coordination can be significant, both in planning and execution.

Follow-on Assistance for Public Security. *(Key Actors: AID, ICITAP, and other Bilateral Assistance Programs; Human Rights Organizations; American Bar Association; Other Relevant NGOs)* Redressing severe deficiencies in the public security system effectively requires a prolonged commitment by the international community. Reformation of the police force alone is normally at least a 5-year proposition; the judiciary requires even more time, because of the extensive educational requirements and experience required for most judicial posts. Public attitudes and expectations toward the legal

---

[5]The U.S. Government recently recognized the need to prepare an interagency plan with the adoption of Presidential Decision Directive 56. Other governments have already instituted similar planning processes. Clearly the U.S. Government must take seriously its recently self-imposed requirement to prepare a comprehensive interagency plan.

system must also be altered, and support for the rule of law must be engendered within civil society (e.g., human rights organizations and free press). These reforms should begin as soon as possible during the peacekeeping phase and continue as a foundation for peace building. Once this has begun to happen and the peace process has become irreversible, there is no further need for the presence of a military intervention force.

One of the areas requiring particular development is follow-on assistance after the departure of military forces. Resources and programs need to be marshaled to sustain and consolidate advances made during the military phase of the peace operation. In the United States, AID, and ICITAP are crucial for this purpose, yet their funding is far from robust. Other bilateral public security assistance programs and NGOs can make a crucial contribution to development of institutions in civil society that will provide accountability for the police, judiciary, and prisons.

Standards for Public Security and Criminal Justice. *(Key Actors: U.N. DPKO; UNHCR; U.N. Crime Prevention and Criminal Justice Division; Member States)* International standards for policing have been prepared by the U.N. Crime Prevention and Criminal Justice Division. However, they are general in nature. The IPTF in Bosnia developed Commissioner's Guidance, which specifies the actual conduct expected of policemen in the Federation and the Serb Republic.[6] UNCPCJD also developed the "Guideline for the Conduct of Public Justice in Cambodia" (even though circumstances militated against practical application). Building on these initiatives, the United Nations should endeavor to refine international standards for policing, judicial affairs, and penal systems. As the Bosnia Commissioner's Guidance has done, emphasis should be on providing specific, observable, and objective measures that can be used by monitors to evaluate the conduct of personnel involved in public security functions. Prior to deployment, CIVPOL monitors should receive training on these

---

[6]"Commissioner's Guidance Notes for the Implementation of Democratic Policing Standard in the Federation of Bosnia-Herzegovina," *Commissioner's Guidance*, Part 1, 1-2.

standards and a field monitoring and training guide should be developed reflecting them. Country-specific Commissioner's Guidance manuals should also be developed with input from the UNCPCJD on judicial and penal matters and legal codes, and from the U.N. High Commissioner on Human Rights and the Center for Human Rights on human rights matters. For example, the Center produced a field guide for Bosnia ("Human Rights and Law Enforcement: International Standards for Monitoring, Training and Advice"); it is also working on universal guidance materials.

Public Security and Criminal Justice Responsibilities. *(Key Actors: U.N. Security Council; U.N. DPKO; Member States; the Military Contingent)* If warranted, authority for CIVPOL and other elements of the peace mission to reform the police, judiciary/legal code, and penal system, in conformance with internationally accepted standards, should be explicitly articulated in the mandate. The mandate should include provision for an international tribunal or other means of dealing with the issues of war crimes, if this is necessary. It should also address whether the military or CIVPOL contingents will have law enforcement powers and whether CIVPOL should be armed. Only under rather unusual circumstances would it be warranted to arm the CIVPOL contingent and assign it law enforcement responsibilities. The Haitian case was just such a partial exception. Even in this case, however, an interim local force (the IPSF) retained primary responsibility for law enforcement and arresting suspects, albeit under international scrutiny. Under normal circumstances, law enforcement activity by CIVPOL would run the risk of seriously antagonizing at least one of the former disputants and potentially the indigenous population, as well. This could easily entangle CIVPOL as a protagonist in local disputes, raising the risk of unacceptable casualties or hostage taking. To avoid such an outcome, the time-honored practice has been to adopt a strictly neutral and unarmed posture. Most of the countries that have a long tradition of contributing to CIVPOL operations prefer this approach, although the Swedish study included in this volume recognizes there may be exceptions.[7]

The more detailed the mandate and peace agreement are about required reforms, the more leverage CIVPOL has to press effectively for compliance. If possible, international standards for public security conduct should also be incorporated into any peace agreement that serves as a basis for the peace operation. A law enforcement plan should subsequently be developed under the guidance of the UNCIVPOL office.[8] Authority to resolve conflicts between local law and international standards should be allocated in the mandate to the Special Representative of the Secretary-General or equivalent. If warranted, the mandate should also include authority to certify the fitness of local police and to cashier those deemed by the CIVPOL commissioner to be responsible for gross human rights abuses or serious corruption, and to establish an indigenous police oversight body to ensure accountability to the public after CIVPOL departs. Provision should be made in both the mandate and the law enforcement plan for civilian assistance to continue after the military phase has concluded.

The early phase of an intervention is likely to be fraught with uncertainty about the willingness of the disputants to cooperate with the intervention force; however, this is also the moment of greatest opportunity to set in motion the dynamics necessary to complete the mission successfully. Those in charge of each peace operation should seek to capitalize on local war weariness, the state of flux, and the positive shock effect of international intervention to obtain necessary concessions and acceptance of a robust interpretation of the mandate. The emphasis ought to be on securing broad freedom of action for the peace force, but great care should be taken in actually exercising this authority until commanders gain a clearer understanding of local political realities. This phase of the intervention should not be

---

[7]Eide and Bratteland, Billinger, and Broer and Emery provide three excellent explanations of this philosophy.

[8]DPKO and member states should ensure that adequate resources, especially qualified personnel, are available for judicial and penal reform from the outset of the operation.

squandered, because military presence in significant numbers and the initial positive impact on public opinion are of limited duration. The longer an external military force remains deployed on the ground, the more it is apt to be perceived as an occupation army.

Civil Society. *(Key Actors: UNDP; U.N. High Commissioner for Human Rights; U.N. Crime Prevention and Criminal Justice Division; CIVPOL; Member States, Relevant NGOs)* In the long run, the objective of sustainable security will be assured only when impunity is no longer the norm and justice is perceived to be available to all, even if not on a totally equal footing. Achieving this aim entails mobilization and development of civil society. This is the only way that institutions of public security will reliably be held accountable for their conduct. Specific functions that are conducive to this outcome are a free press, open elections, availability of pro bono defense counsel for the indigent and minorities, domestic human rights monitoring organizations with effective international sponsorship, an ombudsman or similar mechanism to promote transparency of public security institutions, and public access to police via hot line (a 911 equivalent). The exact form that these take must be carefully crafted so as to be compatible with local culture and tradition.

This process involves arousing a sense of efficacy in the average citizen and a conviction that public security ought to be a public good and not a private privilege. The political culture must be altered, therefore, so repressive behavior by the police is not reinforced, which is probably what the populace expects. Public education is a crucial component of the process of altering expectations. In this regard, the public information resources of the military intervention force, as well as civilian agencies, ought to be put to maximum use. There should be planning for coordinated actions by both military and civilian elements of the peace mission to strengthen civil society as well as to promote good communication with local authorities. It will also be vitally important to nurture public support when sanctions are required to promote needed reform of the police, penal system, or judiciary. At the end of the day, civil society is the constituency that stands to gain if order *with* justice becomes the norm.

Separation of Power Between the Executive and Judiciary.
(Key Actors: Local Government; SRSG; Human Rights Organizations)
Injustice, impunity, and exploitation of the police and legal system to
repress political opponents are often major contributing factors to the
governmental meltdown that causes an international intervention. If
the judicial process has been co-opted by the executive branch, its
primary function invariably becomes perpetuation in power of the
current governing elite. To alter this fundamentally, so justice
ultimately prevails and the cycle of repression and governmental decay
does not repeat itself, the power of the executive over the judiciary
should be checked by other forces, such as the legislative branch and
civil society. This would likely include limiting or balancing executive
prerogatives in such areas as judicial appointments, budgetary
allocations, and physical security.

U.S. Support for Public Security Assistance

Organizational

At present, responsibility for developing and implementing U.S.
bilateral programs is divided between ICITAP (see Call's paper in this
volume) and the State Department's Bureau of International Narcotics
and Law Enforcement (INL). AID, Department of Defense, the
Department of State's Bureau of International Organizations (IO) and
federal, state, and local law enforcement agencies have lesser roles. IO
has the primary responsibility for working with UNCIVPOL, with
important roles for ICITAP and State INL. All the primary agencies
(ICITAP, IO, and INL) are short of personnel in relation to the
magnitude of the bilateral programs involved and the need to
coordinate them closely with UNCIVPOL, other bilateral programs, and
NGOs. ICITAP is the only official agency with an exclusive focus on
providing assistance to public security organizations outside the United
States. However, other agencies also provide assistance to various law
enforcement agencies (e.g., the DEA, FBI, CIA, Bureau of Alcohol,
Tobacco, and Firearms, and Secret Service). In spite of its pivotal role,
ICITAP is only a temporary organization within the Department of
Justice, without permanently funded staff or programs. Another

organizational weakness is that none of the federal-level organizations has much experience, authority, or capacity to assist judicial or penal reform. The alternative of using AID-funded contractors for judicial assistance in Haiti has proven unsatisfactory.

The United States should follow the Swedish example by creating a single, permanent, properly staffed office to coordinate international policing functions currently fragmented among State (INL, IO, AID, etc.), Justice (ICITAP, FBI, DEA, etc.), and other agencies. This would greatly facilitate coordination with local or state police forces and with the United Nations, other governments, and NGOs. The scope of responsibility should include penal and judicial as well as police assistance. This office could be subordinate to the Department of State, but the Department of Justice and the Treasury Department would both need to be actively involved.

Funding

In the past 5 years, concern over and funding for U.S. law enforcement activities abroad have greatly increased, in recognition of the growing threat of international organized crime, narcotics, and terrorism. This has not been reflected in funding to enhance law enforcement capabilities of other countries. In order to better protect the United States and its interests from criminal activity abroad, this needs to be corrected.

Recruitment

At present, recruitment of U.S. personnel for UNCIVPOL missions or "coalitions of the willing" is essentially ad hoc and badly needs improvement. At the September 1997 NDU Conference, Chicago Police Superintendent Matt Rodriguez made specific suggestions for improving ICITAP/INL cooperation with major city police forces (appendix A). It would be a vast improvement if a formal arrangement were established to allow police chiefs to identify their best candidates for CIVPOL duties. Such an arrangement should be put into effect as soon as possible. Additional measures to regularize recruitment of qualified local and state police personnel should also be developed.

Similar action needs to be taken to recruit qualified personnel with backgrounds in penal and judicial reform, working with organizations such as the Bureau of Prisons, state prison systems, and the American Bar Association. An additional, parallel measure could be the establishment of a database within DOD that indicates U.S. Reserve and National Guard personnel with civilian police experience or with military experience as MPs or Special Forces. This database would be a step toward establishing a national CIVPOL standby roster. The next step would be to incorporate volunteers from state and local police forces into this database.

Looking Beyond Peace Operations

This book has dealt primarily with international assistance to public security in the context of peacekeeping operations, although it has also emphasized the need for across-the-board support to the entire public security spectrum after the military peacekeeping mission has ended. The ramifications of the "new world disorder" extend beyond the realm of peace operations, however, and compel us to think more expansively about how the international community can confront these challenges more effectively. Moving outside the peacekeeping context, the United Nations and interested Member States need to look more closely at providing public security assistance to troubled states preemptively to reduce the risk of major crises that might trigger such costly operations. In several of our case studies, it is evident that with more capable (and just) law enforcement institutions, states could well have avoided the crises that precipitated international intervention. It is also evident that unless such institutions are developed and sustained, the situation that caused the intervention could easily return.

The United Nations and interested Member States should also explore prospective measures to assist states with weak police forces and judicial systems that are collapsing under the weight of transnational criminal activities, including narcotics, organized crime, and terrorism. Without expanding here upon the nature and scope of this threat, it is clear that bilateral assistance programs have clear limitations owing to concerns about national sovereignty. If the process of developing universally accepted public security standards gathers momentum, and the capacity of multilateral organizations to render effective assistance develops as a function of repeated experiences acquired during peace operations, there may be an expanding role for the international community in dealing with the transnational crime phenomenon as well. Thus, the question emerges:

Should the United Nations and other multilateral or regional organizations examine the utility and feasibility of more comprehensive law enforcement assistance to troubled states outside of peacekeeping operations?

Finally, there is also a pressing need for greater protection of personnel and assets in international humanitarian missions, given the sharp increase over the past 5 years of violence directed against organizations such as the International Committee of the Red Cross, the U.N. High Commissioner for Refugees, U.N. Children's Fund, and numerous NGOs, as well as violence against refugees and displaced persons. In many instances, there is a reluctance (e.g., for political reasons or expense) to call for full-scale military peacekeeping forces in such situations (e.g., eastern Zaire, 1994-96). There could be an opportunity to use constabulary forces in some of these situations instead of military forces, given their greater political acceptability, particularly if they are deployed before a situation becomes too violent and the floodgates have been opened to the flow of weapons and paramilitary groups. On the other hand, in some instances where civilians have undertaken protective roles, the results have not been as positive as expected (e.g., U.N. civilian guards for northern Iraq; UNHCR guards for eastern Zaire), and some say that this is not a feasible alternative to regular combat forces. Nevertheless, the question needs to be asked:

Is there a need for a standby rapid reaction constabulary for selected humanitarian (or other) operations when military forces are not deemed feasible or necessary?

534

Summary

Even if all the recommendations cited above were to be heeded and all lessons faithfully applied, the outcome of any peace operation will remain hostage to the political will of the parties enmeshed in the internal dispute. No peace force can compel reconciliation if the power brokers involved are unalterably opposed to this, nor can the best efforts of the international community ensure that local law enforcement institutions will use this opportunity for reform to begin functioning according to "international standards" (which are still under development). Careful attention must also be given to the sanctions and inducements available to achieve compliance. Prudence is required when pressing for reforms, because of the potentially confounding influence of local culture, unfamiliar legal traditions, and internal political dynamics. Pressing too hard in the wrong areas may produce a backlash that places the mission in jeopardy and retards the reform process. Even in more promising circumstances, expectations must be realistic, because the clout of the international community is normally insufficient to induce all changes that might be desired in the subject nation's public security apparatus.

Perhaps the most daunting constraint for the United States is the impatient character of the American people, especially when they do not understand why tax dollars and especially lives are being spent in some obscure corner of the globe. On the other hand, policy makers are apt to be bombarded by vocal and well-organized human rights and special interest groups pressing for an aggressive policy to rectify past wrongs immediately and to remake an uncivil culture promptly into an incubator of democracy. If peace operations are going to result in sustainable security over the long haul, the American people must come to a much clearer understanding of what we are about, what interests are at stake, and what our expectations realistically ought to be. It is hoped that this work can contribute modestly to that important task.

APPENDIX A

MATT L. RODRIGUEZ

At the September 15-16, 1997, National Defense University conference on "Policing the New World Disorder: Peace Operations and the Public Security Function" Matt L. Rodriguez, then Superintendent of the Chicago Police Department, gave the luncheon address. Below is an edited version of his remarks and extracts from the question and answer session following the speech.

Civilian Police in International Peace Operations: Local Law Enforcement Perspectives

I want to acknowledge all of you who are here today, who have taken the time and made the investment to be a part of this conference. The use of civilian police in international peace operations is certainly not a new phenomenon. But their role is clearly changing and taking on added significance in this, the post-Cold War era.

Policing the new world disorder is crucial from both a national, military perspective, the perspective that many of you bring here today, as well as from a local law enforcement perspective, a view I hope to share with you.

I speak to you today as a police officer, who has spent nearly 38 years working in Chicago and watching my profession, and the world around it, change dramatically. I am also a police officer who has tremendous respect for our military organizations and for the men and women who serve in our Armed Forces. The military has always been a fertile ground for recruiting police officers, and we continue to benefit from the unique training and experiences that military personnel bring to the job of police officer.

From the perspective of public safety alone, I am struck by the enormous challenges inherent in today's international peace operations. These missions are carried out in the harshest and most unstable of environments. The public's expectations of what these operations can accomplish are extraordinarily high—and the time frames within which they are expected to succeed are unrealistically short. All the while, the media spotlight on the participants can be constant and glaring.

Yet, despite all the attention these missions get, the public's understanding and appreciation of them remain limited. Here at home, so much of the focus rests on the short-term military and political components of these operations that the American public tends to lose sight of the truly profound, long-range issues that are at stake— ideals such as human rights, freedom, domestic tranquillity, and a lasting system of justice rooted in the rule of law.

Civilian police working in concert with military peacekeepers play an important and growing role in achieving these long-term ideals. Their role in contemporary peace operations is something that should be highlighted, studied, reported on, and ultimately improved. This conference is an important step in furthering this discussion, and I am very pleased to be a part of the dialogue.

In reading over the background materials for this conference, I was struck by something I read in chapter one of the draft book, a very simple and straightforward equation attributed to Major General Mark Hamilton on the U.S. Joint Staff. The equation states, "peace equals order plus justice."

For me, those five words deftly describe the two essential but sometimes conflicting goals of a successful international peace operation or, for that matter, a successful domestic policing strategy: securing order in the short-term, while working toward the long-range goal of justice. Increasingly, the success of international peace operations and local policing strategies has come to be defined as achieving both of these conditions, not simply the first step of restoring order.

From a public safety perspective, the "peace equals order plus justice" equation suggests a couple of important considerations. First, there are indeed distinctions between order-restoration on the one hand, and order-maintenance, or justice, on the other. In general, the order-restoration function fits more closely with the military tradition of securing a quick victory—no holds barred—in a highly charged and combative situation. The order-maintenance function, on the other hand, is more akin to the role that police departments in the United States typically perform: promoting and enforcing the rule of law within a community structure that the police are a part of.

These descriptions may be overly simplistic, and there will always be gray areas between the two functions, but there is also a very real line separating them, a line that is important for those planning peace operations and those carrying them out, to recognize and respect. At some point, order-restoration must be phased out, and order-maintenance must become the predominant activity, if the ultimate goal of peace is to be achieved.

The order of terms in the "peace equals order plus justice" equation also has significance. It is no coincidence that the equation places "order" before "justice." Long-term change cannot occur unless and until basic order has been restored and some semblance of stability established. This is as true in international peace operations, as it is in domestic law enforcement situations.

Police in the United States recognize that we cannot build up and restore a crime-ridden neighborhood until we have reclaimed that community from the dominant criminal element. Civilian police officials involved in international peace operations must also recognize that their desire for long-term change must "follow" the restoration of order and must not compromise this short-term imperative.

By the same token, order-restoration efforts must support and complement the long-range goal of building lasting public safety and justice. Whether in international peacekeeping or local policing, it is never too early to start planning for long-range change.

Few people today would dispute the fact that civilian police are an integral part of modern-day international peace operations and that their role will likely grow in importance in the years ahead. So the question then becomes, what can planners and managers of these international operations learn from the domestic police experience that will assist them in integrating and better managing the civilian police function? A discussion of some of the basic tenets or principles of modern-day policing that will likely impact the changing role of civilian police in international peace operations may answer that question.

In many ways, it is difficult to be specific about how these principles translate into the design and operation of any one peace mission. The source of the conflict, the degree of instability, and the strength of the existing justice infrastructure—these and other factors will necessarily impact the particular role of the civilian police and their relationship with military peacekeepers.

Nevertheless, there are some overarching issues or considerations that will be present in all instances. I want to explore three of them today: the police mandate, the approach or style in carrying out that mandate, and the police role in the larger justice system. A better appreciation and understanding of these three considerations will help the planners and managers of international peace operations better integrate and manage civilian police activities under their control.

The police mandate is important to consider because, as I alluded to earlier, it does differ from the traditional mandate of the military. It is the difference between immediate victory, or "order," usually secured by vanquishing the enemy, and long-term change, or "justice," within a larger context.

The police mandate—to protect the lives, property, and the rights of all people, including, at times, those people accused of committing a crime—is markedly different from the military mandate. And these differences must be considered in planning and implementing peace operations that include both traditions.

Another important consideration is the manner in which police agencies fulfill their mandate. This is particularly important now, because there has been such dramatic change in our implementation strategies and approaches in recent years. I believe it is important to recognize that community policing does represent a dramatic expansion of the police officer's role in society. This expansion of the police role beyond narrow law enforcement represents a major change for policing. For international peace operations, the change has two important implications.

First, it means that civilian police officers involved in such operations will likely have at least an understanding of community policing, if not a full orientation to this new approach or style of policing. Second, and perhaps more important, the community policing perspective can help guide peace operations toward the long-term goal of creating an indigenous and independent police force, one that is responsive to the community it serves and enjoys the respect of that community.

One thing community policing does very effectively is force the police to consider, and respond to, the concerns of the community—both the emergency calls for service and the broader quality-of-life concerns that often create a climate of fear in the community. If the long-term success of international peacekeeping lies in winning the hearts and minds of the local populace, then community policing approaches should be studied, planned for, and implemented, where possible.

The third consideration involves the police role in the larger criminal justice system, an extremely difficult and complex issue. Stop to think about it. As if the challenge of developing an indigenous police capacity were not difficult enough, peace operations often face the even more daunting challenge of helping to build an indigenous prosecutorial, judicial, and penal capacity as well. In many instances, these latter agencies and institutions may be even more closely aligned with one of the existing political factions and, therefore, even more resistant to reform.

But the fact remains that the police are just one part of a larger system of justice, and the police cannot be effective without the cooperation and support of these other components. Even in developed countries such as ours, where justice agencies and processes are well established, coordination between the police and other elements of the system remains a challenge.

I raise this issue not because I have a "magic bullet" for solving the coordination problem, but rather to remind you that achieving justice in these nations will require much more than reforming or reinventing an indigenous police force. That's not to suggest that local police reform should wait for the rest of the justice system to come on board.

The police are the first step in the justice process, and they play a pivotal role in maintaining order and building public support and confidence in the rule of law. What I am suggesting is that reform of the entire justice system will be a lengthier, more difficult process, and the results may never be ideal.

I hope my observations on the police organization are helpful as you continue to contemplate and redefine the role of civilian police in international peace operations. I would like to briefly turn my attention to a few of the more practical matters involved in organizing and staffing the civilian police function.

Staffing civilian police operations is a sticky issue, both for the people commanding these police forces and for those of us in U.S. law enforcement who are asked to supply many of the officers. You must recognize that just as nations are reluctant to commit military troops to open-ended peacekeeping commitments, so, too, are local police agencies reluctant to commit extensive resources to civilian police operations.

Faced with tight budgets and tremendously high political and community expectations of our own, police executives tend to view releasing our officers for months at a time for international peacekeeping duty to be a costly, no-win endeavor. And this is true not only for small departments, but for large ones as well. We are willing to do our part—police departments have done so for decades by accommodating those officers in the military reserves. But we also need to see more tangible benefits when our departments do commit officers to international efforts.

The military must make it easier and more attractive for police departments to commit officers to these operations, not just through monetary reimbursement, but also through such benefits as specialized training for program participants.

Rigorous recruiting and screening processes are essential, as officers are sought who have the skills, demeanor, and cultural sensitivity and awareness to handle these types of missions. And, in addition to police officers, peacekeeping missions should recruit from the prosecutorial, judicial, and correctional ranks as well, to assist in developing those parts of an indigenous justice system. Beyond personnel, U.S. police agencies can offer other resources to these operations—resources such as training, technical assistance, and executive-level mentoring. The International Criminal Investigative Training Assistance Program provides a good framework for this transfer of information and knowledge to take place.

Questions and Answers

Chuck English: I am from the State Department and am directly involved in recruiting U.S. personnel for CIVPOL missions. We've now had to do this in reactive mode for Haiti, Bosnia, and Eastern Slovonia, and that's not the way we want to work it. We want to work it in a much more partnership-oriented approach, with major police departments such as your own. As a matter of fact, in thinking this through, to design the sort of cooperative program that we'd like to see take place, I would very much like to work with a designee of yours, so that we could do it in a way that makes sense for Chicago and other major police agencies, as we set up what might be a new concept in approaching civilian policing overseas. So my question is: Can I look to your agency as partner?

Superintendent Rodriguez: Yes, you can, and I'll tell you why. You can look to our agency to continue to be cooperative in the future no matter what the needs are. We'll toss and turn and cry and what have you, but we'll provide assistance wherever we can. Sometimes as little as we can, depending on the circumstances in the city. But my point is: we will cooperate.

William O'Neill: Going back to recruiting, not only enough people but the right people. What about retired police officers? Would it be possible for you, or for any police force to keep a roster of retired police officers that you already have vetted at some point? Somehow keep them on call or available to use when it came time to recruit?

Superintendent Rodriguez: I think it's an excellent idea. With the liberal pensions being provided in the United States today, a good many officers leave after 20-25 years of service and have accomplished a great deal and have an excellent record and might be perfect for the kind of situation you just described. I think again we need to establish the medium. We need to institutionalize, "standardize" because you don't want just any retired officer. You're looking for someone who meets the standards. I'm looking to send, and have represented, from a local criminal justice perspective, the finest officer possible.

Jeffery Ross: Jeffrey Ross, National Institute of Justice. At the risk of sounding crass, what benefit does your organization get from sending officers abroad? Can you think of something that might sweeten the pot?

Superintendent Rodriguez: Well, the most important thing, first if all, is standardizing procedures. I'm interested in a good beat officer being on the beat. It's important that we have somebody who meets certain standards: your standards and our standards. It's important that there is some benefit returned to us, whether its the experiences that were acquired during this operation, or something meaningful that can be conveyed to other officers, I'm not certain. We haven't really sat down to talk about it. I'll tell you what we're getting right now: nothing directly or, to my knowledge indirectly, from *any* of the returnees. They go back to their former assignments, [and] in some instances if they're gone at the wrong time they've lost promotional opportunities, they may have a new commanding officer who doesn't know who they are, or where they came from, and who is looking to bring on other individuals and looking for someone who's replaceable. It may create a whole lot of problems. And so when you ask me the benefits, they're more intangible than tangible. What is needed is some process to certify achievement of identifiable standards, so that when that person leaves, and is gone for 3 months or 6 months, and returns to the Department, he or she comes back with some identifiable certification of recognition, as achieving that kind of a standard, and that they went off and did the service. This may even be career-enabling, to some degree. But typically that does not occur. And an award or certification is only as important as the individual who receives it, reviews it, and recognizes the laudatory intent of this thing, and that this is indeed a fine officer. But there is no such present recognition. You may get a certificate that you served with the State Department in a peacekeeping operation, but you know what's absent is the indication that there was some kind of standard that you met. Or some standards that you *exceeded*, and for those reasons were chosen. That's the kind of thing that I think is probably the most rewarding thing that you can provide any of the individuals who were chosen from our departments to serve.

Jan Stromsem: Jan Stromsem with ICITAP. I feel compelled to make a few comments. First, let me share some of the concerns that my colleague Chuck English expressed a few minutes ago, about the great challenge and difficulty we face in recruiting very talented police officers to go on these foreign missions. We at ICITAP probably need less in terms of numbers than the Department of State when they're looking at fulfilling a CIVPOL type of mission. Let me describe some of the types of positions that we are looking to fill when we are approaching a foreign mission. It's not only trainers, but we found perhaps the best way to approach instituting fundamental change and reoriented change in a country is placing what we call "technical advisors" or "senior advisors" at the highest level of the police that's trying to undergo that change. By and large there's absolutely no opportunity at all to train the executive level of a new policing service, whether it's Haiti, or Albania. And, actually I'm looking for two people for Albania, by the way, at this very high, executive level. Using Albania as an example, what we try to do is place the senior executive with the Minister of the Interior, who's in charge of implementing this whole change. The person will be involved in not only writing laws, but coming up with a new structure. How should the police operate? The fact is, they need to instill elements of accountability and community policing aspects [in their assignments].

APPENDIX B

David W. Foley

Brigadier General David W. Foley, Commandant of the U.S. Army Military Police School, gave the keynote address at the September 15-16, 1997, National Defense University conference, "Policing the New World Disorder: Peace Operations and the Public Security Function." Below is an edited version of his remarks and extracts from the question and answer session following the speech.

The Military Police Corps

As the Commandant of the Military Police Corps, my responsibilities span doctrine development, training, leader development, organizations, materiel development, and soldier concerns relative to military police soldiers. Today, the Military Police Corps focuses on the demands of the 21st century. We are posturing our capabilities to meet the requirements of full dimensional operations. "Full dimensional operations" speak to the application of our capabilities to accomplish missions decisively and at least cost. This application spans the full range of operations—from providing law enforcement training support to providing a combat capable response force.

We are a capabilities-oriented force. Our organizations are modular and can be tailored to meet the functional security requirements in the area of operations. We can operate as a squad or as a brigade. Our brigades operate in joint, multinational, or interagency environments, either embedded in larger organizations, as with IFOR in Bosnia or, when augmented, as a command and control headquarters. An example of the latter was Operation *Sea Signal* in Guantanamo Bay, Cuba, where the 89th MP Brigade conducted Haitian migrant and Cuban refugee operations.

Military police (MPs) are especially useful in contingency operations involving the stabilization or support to the local populace and

547

infrastructure. Our usefulness is predicated upon our capabilities that reflect how we have been trained, think, and operate. MPs represent an acceptable force to the international community, U.S. citizens, and the indigenous population in these operations. They project an image of "assist, protect, and defend," and present a low force signature. This was illustrated when an MP brigade was sent into Panama prior to the ousting of Noriega. The brigade was accepted as a force protecting U.S. citizens, not an invasion force. When the situation deteriorated to open warfare, MPs added their combat capability to the general effort.

Organizations conducting stability and support operations today face a changed threat. Belligerents are often criminal elements who may enjoy support from corrupt government officials. These criminal elements may have "rights" that constrain how we deal with them. MPs routinely operate in this environment in cooperation with other forces and agencies.

MP functional capabilities are focused in five general areas:

☐ **Maneuver and mobility support operations.** MPs provide information on route conditions and regulate traffic on routes. This is done on a routine basis or pursuant to damage to routes from natural or manmade disasters.

☐ **Area security operations.** MPs provide a mobile security force to facilities, populations, and resources on an area basis.

☐ **Internment and resettlement operations.** MPs safeguard, segregate, shelter, sustain, secure, and account for prisoner, detainee, and dislocated civilian populations.

☐ **Law and order operations.** MPs and the Criminal Investigation Command (CID) support law enforcement operations, as well as the training and mentoring of local security forces.

☐ **Police intelligence operations**. MPs and CID are an effective human intelligence source. They provide criminal intelligence and police information gathered from the local populace and joint police efforts.

The following tables depict MP capabilities to fill the deployment gap in stability operations. We are a force protection resource and provide mobile area security. MPs and CID provide security for information facilities, resources, and technologies. We provide physical security and law enforcement guidance and expertise. We combat terrorism and we provide personal security to VIP.

STABILITY OPERATIONS

Force protection resource
HUMINT and information resource
Cooperate with other security forces
Apply force without threatening
Understand consequences of individual and small
    unit actions
Apply force selectively
Act decisively to prevent escalation

MILITARY POLICE CAPABILITIES

Execute/train/mentor
Rules of Interaction (ROI)
Interpersonal communications skills
Nonlethal/lethal
Crowd control
Force protection

MPs and CID usually conduct these activities in cooperation with other security forces and in close proximity to the local populace. MPs and CID are therefore a reliable HUMINT source.

Because of our law enforcement training, we can apply force without threatening. We understand the consequences of inappropriate, individual, and small-unit actions upon mission success. Our law enforcement training also reinforces the selective and judicious use of force. We execute our functions under restrictive rules of engagement, aided in this role by our training in interpersonal communications skills.

These skills lend a human dimension to our activities. We also appreciate the supportive role that rules of interaction play in lessening the friction generated by differing ideologies, customs, and beliefs.

We routinely employ lesser means, such as nonlethal technologies (pepper spray, batons, and military working dogs) before resorting to deadly force, but when overwhelming force is required to prevent escalation of conflict, we act decisively.

MP and CID can execute all the above functions in a stability operation to offset the deployment security gap while CIVPOL and ICITAP are deploying. To offset the enforcement gap, MPs and CID continue executing their functions while local security forces are being trained by outside agencies. MPs and CID can support this training effort by mentoring local security forces. Additionally, MPs can provide reaction forces (for incidents such as civil disturbances) and modular capabilities such as military working dogs, investigations, and force protection teams to bolster emerging local law enforcement capabilities. During the institutional gap, MPs and CID have a lesser role as this stage marks the transition to civilian control and responsibility.

Questions and Answers

Colonel David Patton: I would argue against *ever* putting CIVPOL in the military mission for one basic reason. I think, when we talk about changing the culture of a country, and a lot of the countries that we go into have a history of having a police force that was part of the military, if we're going to start changing that culture and introducing them to Western methods of policing, they need to see the role model of a civilian controlled force, as opposed to a military controlled force.

Question from Audience: However, we are in a situation where you see military forces for internal order within a country already, so the fact that they'd be operating with police support should not be entirely surprising to the population. They want *their* army to be for external defense, but the troops that the international community has sent there are *for* internal order in their own country as well.

Brigadier General Foley: I think it's a consideration. I would just guard against saying, "This is what we *should* do," because I can think of more cases where we wouldn't do it than where we might think it would be a legitimate way to perform things for the reasons that Col. Patton listed.

Question from Audience: In the immediate aftermath of the intervention in Haiti, the U.S. military was tasked to perform certain policing duties. Was the division of labor established between the military police and conventional army units, or did the army units perform these duties on an ad hoc basis?

Brigadier General Foley: I'll let Colonel O'Brien answer that.

Colonel Howard O'Brien: Haiti was not a good example, because we went in with the attitude that we were not going to do civil law enforcement. You recall the sight of an infantryman standing with a 9mm pistol, with a 1,000-mile stare, as there was Haitian-on-Haitian violence. The President said the next day, "I want 1,000 MPs." Well, he said it and the next morning I was trying to find them and put them on the planes to get them down there. They were so far down the airlift list we couldn't get them in there in sufficient time. Mike Sullivan, who was the brigade commander on the ground, just took control of the situation, went into the police stations and took them over. Thank goodness we had an experienced guy; he did the same thing in Panama some years before. We didn't have the planning mechanism, but as was explained this morning with PDD-56, I think we've got the interagency process at least together. But we didn't have it at *that* time and it was done very ad hoc and planned very poorly, at least the police part was from the military police perspective.

Brigadier General Foley: We went into that far enough that we had planned on a contingency basis for what we would have to do in the training of those forces, through Mike Sullivan, how we were going to form some cadre battalions, in Haiti. We didn't know whether ICITAP was going to get the mission or whether we were going to have to assign the mission to the military police. Sullivan's the guy who you saw put General Cedras on the airplane. He's just a terrific guy and, as Howie said, when they hit the ground with a whole brigade, then that provided a police presence in the cities, and the special operations forces provided that kind of capability out in the countryside.

APPENDIX C
CASE STUDY FRAMEWORK

Authors who contributed cases studies to this volume were asked to address the following issues (if applicable) in their drafts:

Background

□ Briefly, what was the situation that precipitated international intervention?

□ Describe the indigenous capacity for self-governance, the strength of armed opposition groups, the condition of the economy and infrastructure, and extent of societal disruption (e.g., was this a "failed state"?).

□ What was the status of the domestic public security apparatus? How capable was it of maintaining public order? How did the indigenous police force relate to other elements of the local power structure (e.g., Army, Ministry of Interior, Prime Minister/President)? How did the general population view the indigenous police establishment(s) (e.g., as an instrument of state repression and control, a defender of factional interests, or a basically impartial and dedicated protector of the people)? What was the condition of the judicial and prison systems?

The Mandate and Resources

□ What was the mandate? Did this mandate spring from a peace accord among major combatants or exclusively from a resolution adopted by the UNSC or a regional security organization? What were the ROEs? Was public security an explicit, initial responsibility of the peace mission or was this task adopted later by the peace mission? If the latter, was this done only after careful consideration or as a result of "mission creep?"

□ How was the peace mission organized? Was there unity of command among the various components of the mission (e.g., humanitarian, human rights, CIVPOL, and military)? Did any predeployment training or team-building activity take place among the various elements that were to comprise the mission?

☐ Describe the size and composition of CIVPOL, International Police Monitors or equivalent elements, and, if they contributed to policing, military components of the peace mission. Were any standards used to screen CIVPOL members, during recruitment? What special considerations (such as the need for sensitivity to gender issues, language ability, historical considerations) impinged upon the composition of CIVPOL?

☐ What resources (financial, logistical, equipment) were allocated for the public security function and from what sources? Were the resources adequate for the job and available on a timely basis?

☐ Describe the phases through which the peace mission was designed to pass? Was this the result of a peace accord or some other planning process?

☐ What advance planning was done, by the United States or the United Nations, regarding public security? Who had the lead for the United States?

The Mission

☐ Did the mission unfold as planned? At the outset, was there a "public security gap" that the military component of the peace mission had to fill? If not, how was this avoided? To what extent did the peace mission assume responsibility for enforcing domestic law? Did the populace view the presence of and public security functions performed by the peace mission as legitimate?

☐ How did CIVPOL relate to the indigenous police force (Monitoring, mentoring, joint patrolling, passive observation, training, etc.)? Did MPs, Special Forces, or other regular military units become involved in public security matters? How did the military element of the mission relate to the indigenous public security force? Was there a direct relationship or did CIVPOL serve as intermediary? Did indigenous military or paramilitary forces become a factor?

☐ Was the peace mission charged with controlling weapons and demobilization of existing military and/or paramilitary forces? Did

CIVPOL have a role in this? For ex-combatants (e.g., soldiers, paramilitary elements, guerrillas) who were not allowed to join or remain in the police force or military, was an effort made to reintegrate them into civil society? To what extent did former combatants continue as armed opposition or become transformed into criminal elements? What factors influenced these outcomes?

□ Was vetting the existing police establishment and/or establishing a new force part of the peace mission's responsibility? Who provided the background data, training, equipment, and funding? Was it adequate and timely? Did military personnel or other ex-combatants become part of a reconstituted police force? Was a leadership cadre developed for the new police force? How? If applicable, how long did it take to recruit, train, and deploy a new police cadre? Did CIVPOL or others provide effective mentoring and on-the-job training to the new police force? How long before their operation became reasonably effective?

□ Was CIVPOL given responsibility for assistance to penal and judicial systems? What resources did it have for these tasks? What other entities provided assistance (e.g., governments, NGOs, international organizations)? What were their programs? Were these efforts adequate and well coordinated? What impact did shortcomings in the judiciary and penal systems have on public security?

□ Were CIVPOL, the military division, and local police forces used to assist with or protect elections and human rights observers? How did they perform?

□ Was the creation of a new or reconstituted police force an integral part of the exit strategy? Did police assistance continue after the military phase of the mission ended? By whom and to what effect?

Coordination and Cooperation

□ Was there a coherent philosophy or mandate that governed conduct of the CIVPOL (e.g., regarding use of force and exercise of police powers, authority to carry a weapon, community policing, respect for human rights)? How did it relate to the overall philosophy of the peace mission?

☐ Describe the working relationship between the military and CIVPOL (i.e., command, planning, information sharing, logistics, communication, operations center, joint or coordinated patrolling, QRF arrangements, liaison with local police for training). How effective was this? Were psychological operations or civil affairs specialists involved in this operation? How were their contributions coordinated with the remainder of the mission and how effective were they?

☐ Describe the working relationship between CIVPOL and other components of the mission (e.g., Human Rights, Electoral, Humanitarian)?

☐ Was there coordination with and support for CIVPOL from the political leadership of the mission, U.N. HQ, and contributing governments? Were the contributions of the United States, other governments, NGOs, and the United Nations effectively coordinated? How? Was coordination between CIVPOL and local authorities accomplished effectively?

Evaluation/Conclusions

☐ How successful was the peace mission in establishing a climate of public security and, if part of its mandate, institutionalizing the rule of law? Was this central to the success of the overall peace mission? Did maintenance of public order contribute to force protection and reduction of conflict with elements of the local population (or vice versa)?

☐ Were the human rights of the general population and suspected criminals respected by the local police during and after the departure of the peace mission?

☐ What factors were most important in determining these outcomes? How competent were the CIVPOL contingents (and related elements) to perform their duties (e.g., as policemen, mentors, monitors)? What were the most troubling deficiencies? What actions were taken to enhance CIVPOL capabilities? How successful were they?

☐   What were the principal issues that arose during this peace mission and the most important lessons learned? Have these problems been corrected by the United States and the United Nations or are they still unresolved today?

ACRONYMS

1 RAR	First Battalion, Royal Australian Regiment
ABA	American Bar Association
ABiH	Army of Bosnia-Herzegovina
ACOM	U.S. Atlantic Command
AID	U.S. Agency for International Development
AMGOT	Allied Military Government of Occupied Territory
ANSP	National Public Security Academy
AOJ	AID Administration of Justice Project
APC	armored personnel carrier
ARENA	National Republican Alliance
ASF	Auxiliary Security Force
ATP	principal technical advisor
BAID	Bosnian Agency for Investigation and Documentation
CA	Civil Affairs
CAO	chief administrative officer
CARBG	Canadian Airborne Regiment Battle Group
CARBG BOI	Canadian Airborne Regiment Battle Group Board of Inquiry
CCEADM	Joint Commission for Formation of the Mozambique Defense Force
CCF	Cease-fire Commission
CCG	community consultative groups
CEELI	Central and Eastern European Law Initiative
CENTCOM	U.S. Central Command
CEP	Provisional Electoral Council
CID	Criminal Investigation Division
CJCPD	Criminal Justice and Crime Prevention Division
CMOC	Civil-Military Operations Center
COMCMOTF	Commander, Civil-Military Operations Task Force
COMPOL	National Police Affairs Commission
COPAZ	Commission for the Consolidation of Peace
CORE	Reintegration Commission

CPP	Cambodian People's Party
CRHB	Croatian Republic of Herceg-Bosna
CSC	Supervision and Control Commission
CTV	Canadian Television
DAN	Anti-Narcotics Division
DEA	Drug Enforcement Administration
DENI	Departamento Nacional de Investigaciones
DIC	Criminal Investigations Division
DOD	Department of Defense
DOJ	U.S. Department of Justice
DPA	Dayton Peace Accords
DPKO	Department of Peacekeeping Operations
EC	European Community
ECHR	European Convention on Human Rights
EPLF	Eritrean People's Liberation Front
EPRDF	Ethiopian People's Revolutionary Democratic Front
FAA	Foreign Assistance Act
FAd'H	Haitian Armed Forces
FBI	Federal Bureau of Investigation
FMLN	Farabundo Martí National Liberation Front
FPP	Fuerza Publica de Panama
FRAPH	Front for Haitian Advancement and Progress
FRELIMO	Frente de Libertação de Moçambique
FTO	field training officer
FUNCINPEC	Front Uni National pour une Cambodge Indépendent, Neutre, Pacifique et Coopératif
GOH	Government of Haiti
GOP	Government of Panama
GPA	General Peace Agreement
HNP	Haitian National Police
HNPTC	Haitian National Police Training Center
HOC	Humanitarian Operations Center
HR	High Representative
HRS	Humanitarian Relief Sector
HVO	Bosnian Croat Army
I MEF	I Marine Expeditionary Force

ICITAP	International Criminal Investigative Training Assistance Program
IEBL	Inter-Entity Boundary Line
IFOR	Implementation Force
IG	Inspector General
INL	Department of State Bureau of International Narcotics and Law Enforcement
IO	Department of State Bureau of International Organizations
IPM	International Police Monitors
IPSF	Interim Public Security Force
IPTF	International Police Task Force
IUDOP	Instituto Universitario de Opinión Publica
JCS	Joint Chiefs of Staff
JNA	Yugoslav Army
JOTC	Jungle Operations Training Center
JTF	Joint Task Force
KPNLF	Khmer People's National Liberation Front
KR	Khmer Rouge
LAC	Latin American and the Caribbean
LCY	League of Communists of Yugoslavia
MAT	Military Assistance Team
MFO	Multi-National Force and Observers
MICIVIH	UN/OAS International Civilian Mission
MINURSO	U.N. Mission for the Referendum in Western Sahara
MINUSAL	U.N. Mission in El Salvador
MIST	military information support team
MNF	Multinational Force
MP	military police
MSA	mission subsistence allowance
MSG	Military Support Group
MUP	Ministry of Interior Special Police
NGO	nongovernmental organization
NORDCAPS	Nordic Coordinated Arrangements for Military Peace Support

OAS	Organization of American States
OAS-EOM	Organization of American States—Electoral Observer Mission
OFOF	orders for opening fire
OHR	Office of the High Representative
OIE	State Intelligence Agency (Organo de Inteligencia del Estado)
ONUC	Opérations des Nations Unies au Congo
ONUCA	United Nations Observer Group in Central America
ONUMOZ	U.N. Mission in Mozambique
ONUSAL	U.N. Observer Mission in El Salvador
ONUV	U.N. Verification Office
OPDAT	Overseas Prosecutorial Development, Assistance, and Training (formerly known as the Office of Professional Development and Training)
OPL	Lavalas Political Organization
OPR	Office of Public Responsibility
OPS	Office of Public Safety
OSCE	Organization for Security and Cooperation in Europe
PAT	Auxiliary Transitory Police
PC	police commissioner
PDF	Panama Defense Force
PKO	peacekeeping operation
PM	Provost Marshal
PN	National Police
PNC	National Civilian Police
PNP	Panamanian National Police
PRM	Mozambican police
PSU	Presidential Security Unit
PTJ	Judicial Technical Police
QRF	quick reaction force
RCMP	Royal Canadian Mounted Police
RDHQ	rapidly deployable headquarters
RENAMO	Resistência Nacional Moçambicana
ROE	rules of engagement

ROI	Rules of Interaction
RS	Serb Republic
SAT	U.N. Selection Assistance Team
SCR	Security Council Resolution
SDA	Party for Democratic Action
SDS	Serb Democratic Party
SF	special forces
SFOR	Stabilization Force
SHIRBRIG	Standing High-Readiness International Brigade
SIDA	Swedish International Development Cooperation Agency
SIU	Special Investigative Unit
SNC	Supreme National Council
SOC	State of Cambodia
SOFA	Status of Forces Agreement
SOP	standard operating procedure
SPO	Special Prosecutor's Office
SRSG	Special Representative of the Secretary-General
SWAPOL	South West Africa Police
SWEDINT	Swedish Armed Forces International Centre
TNA	training needs assessment
UEA	Executive Anti-Narcotics Unit
UNAMIC	U.N. Advance Mission in Cambodia
UNAVEM	U.N. Angola Verification Mission I, II, III
UNCIVPOL	U.N. Civilian Police
UNCRO	U.N. Confidence Restoration Operation
UNDP	U.N. Development Programme
UNEF	U.N. Emergency Force
UNFICYP	U.N. Peace-keeping Force in Cyprus
UNGCI	U.N. Guards Contingent in Iraq
UNHCR	U.N. High Commissioner for Refugees
UNITA	National Union for the Total Independence of Angola
UNITAF	United Task Force
UNMAS	Nordic U.N. Peace-Keeping Mission Management Seminar

UNMIBH	U.N. Mission in Bosnia-Herzegovina
UNMIH	U.N. Mission in Haiti
UNMO	U.N. Military Observer
UNOSOM	U.N. Operation in Somalia I, II
UNPA	U.N. Protected Area
UNPOC	U.N. Police Officers Course
UNPREDEP	U.N. Preventive Deployment Force
UNPROFOR	U.N. Protection Force
UNSCR	U.N. Security Council Resolution
UNSMIH	U.N. Support Mission in Haiti
UNSOC	U.N. Staff Officers Course
UNTAC	U.N. Transitional Authority in Cambodia
UNTAES	U.N. Transitional Authority in Eastern Slavonia, Baranja and Western Sirmium
UNTAG	U.N. Transition Assistance Group
UNTAT	U.N. Training Assistance Team
UNTEA	U.N. Temporary Executive Authority
USARSO	U.S. Army South
USCINCSO	U.S. Commander-in-Chief, Southern Command
USIP	U.S. Institute for Peace
USLO	U.S. Special Envoy Office
VRS	Army of the Serb Republic
WEU	Western European Union
WFP	World Food Program
ZOS	Zone of Separation

ABOUT THE EDITORS

AMBASSADOR ROBERT B. OAKLEY was retired from the Department of State in 1991 after 34 years of diplomatic service. He served as Ambassador to Pakistan, Zaire, and Somalia; Coordinator for Counterterrorism; Assistant to the President for Middle East and South Asia, National Security Council staff; and Deputy Assistant Secretary of State for East Asia Affairs. Ambassador Oakley subsequently served Presidents Bush and Clinton as Special Envoy to Somalia during UNITAF and UNISOM II. He is currently directing the Public Security Project as a Distinguished Visiting Fellow at the Institute for National Strategic Studies, National Defense University.

COLONEL MICHAEL J. DZIEDZIC, U.S. Air Force, is a Senior Military Fellow specializing in peace operations and security affairs in the Western Hemisphere at the Institute for National Strategic Studies, National Defense University. Previously, he was a member of the faculty at the National War College, served as Air Attache in El Salvador during the implementation of the peace accords, and was a professor in the Department of Political Science at the U.S. Air Force Academy. His writings include *Mexico: Converging Challenges* and articles on Mexican defense policies, the transnational drug trade, and hemispheric security matters.

ELIOT M. GOLDBERG is Project Manager for the Public Security Project at the Institute for National Strategic Studies, National Defense University. He previously worked on Middle East security issues with Search for Common Ground's Initiative for Peace and Cooperation in the Middle East. In 1994-1995 he was a Fulbright Fellow in Jordan, researching the Kingdom's national security policy.

ABOUT THE
CONTRIBUTING AUTHORS

LIEUTENANT COLONEL MICHAEL BAILEY, U.S. Army, has served as one of the military advisors to the office of Peacekeeping and Humanitarian Operations, U.S. Department of State, since February 1996. Previously, LTC Bailey served as Chief of Election Support/Training on the U.N. Mission in Haiti (UNMIH), from April 1995 until January 1996. Prior, he was the operations planner on the UNMIH Advanced Team, where he authored the rules of engagement and the operations plan. LTC Bailey has also served on the Department of the Army staff as the Peacekeeping Policy Analyst for the Chief of Staff of the Army, and spent over a year in Cambodia as a Military Observer Team Chief and Executive Officer for an Observer Sector. LTC Bailey holds an M.A. in National Strategic Studies from Cal State, San Bernardino.

ANDREW BAIR serves as Senior Advisor to the Special Representative of the President and Secretary of State for Implementation of the Dayton Peace Accords. Previously, he served two tours with the United Nations in the former Yugoslavia as a political officer, first during 1993 in the U.N. protected areas in Croatia and, most recently, in Bosnia during 1995-1996 as the Special Assistant to the U.N. Chief of Mission there. Afterward, Mr. Bair served as the Political Advisor to the Commissioner of the U.N. International Police Task Force. From 1988 to 1994 Mr. Bair was Senior National Security Analyst and Manager of the Center for National Security Negotiations of Science Applications International Corporation. Mr. Bair holds an M.A. from and is currently a doctoral student at The George Washington University, Washington, DC.

NILS GUNNAR BILLINGER is a former State Secretary for both the Ministry of Defense and the Cabinet of the Prime Minister in Sweden. Over the past decade he has held a number of high level positions in the Swedish Government. He is currently head of the official inquiry into civilian police on international assignments and the Euro-coordinator for Sweden's practical preparations for conversion to a common European currency.

COLONEL HARRY BROER (Netherlands) was stationed in New York from February 1994 till July 1997 as Deputy Police Advisor in the Civilian Police Unit in the U.N. Department of Peacekeeping Operations. Since September 1997, Colonel Broer has served as Special Consultant on police matters in the Criminal Justice and Crime Prevention Division in the U.N. office in Vienna.

THORSTEIN BRATTELAND is a Police Commissioner currently seconded to work on the Civilian Police in Peace Operations Project at the Norwegian Institute of International Affairs. Trained both as a lawyer and at the National Police Academy, he has held various positions within the Norwegian police. Mr. Bratteland also served 2 years in the ONUSAL mission in El Salvador.

CHARLES T. CALL is a National Security Education Fellow currently finishing his doctorate in political science at Stanford University. He has written several articles on policing in Latin America, human rights, and democratization, and in 1996 was a Peace Scholar at the U.S. Institute of Peace. He has been a consultant to the U.S. Departments of Justice and Defense and to international human rights organizations.

ESPEN BARTH EIDE is a researcher at the Norwegian Institute of International Affairs and Director of the Institute's U.N. Program. He has written on peacekeeping, conflict prevention, and postconflict peace-building in general, with a particular emphasis on Bosnia-Herzegovina and Macedonia.

MICHAEL EMERY worked with the United Nations for several years initially in Liberia, then as Chief of Training for the U.N. Protection Force in the former Yugoslavia. In recent years Mr. Emery has worked closely with the Civilian Police Unit in U.N. Headquarters New York, assisting with the establishment of selection standards and training guidelines for U.N. Civilian Police and working with national trainers in Member States to improve the quality of predeployment training of UNCIVPOL monitors.

COLONEL KARL FARRIS, U.S. Army (Ret.), established the U.S. Army's Peacekeeping Institute at Carlisle Barracks, Pennsylvania, and served as its first Director from 1993 to 1996. He also served with UNTAC in Cambodia as Chief, Strategic Investigations, assisted in planning and preparing for the U.N. Mission in Haiti and directed Civil-Military Operations during the U.S. humanitarian intervention in Rwanda. Though retired from active duty, Colonel Farris remains engaged in developing procedures for improving component coordination in multidimensional peace operations.

DR. ANTHONY WHITFORD GRAY, JR., has served on the faculty of the Military Strategy and Logistics Department of the Industrial College of the Armed Forces since 1993. Dr. Gray is a retired naval officer with extensive experience in inter-American affairs. From 1983 to 1993 he served as Deputy Director of Inter-American Affairs and subsequently as Director of Humanitarian Assistance and Refugee Affairs in the Office of the Undersecretary of Defense for Policy. He received his doctorate in International Relations from the American University in 1982. His publications include "The Evolution of U.S. Naval Policy in Latin America" (doctoral dissertation, 1982), "Latin American Military Institutions" (Hoover Institute, 1986-contributing author), and *The Big L: American Logistics in World War II* (National Defense University Press, 1997, contributing author).

LIEUTENANT COLONEL MICHAEL J. KELLY, AM, is an operations law officer in the Australian Army. He has served and worked in Somalia, Bosnia, the Middle East, and Kenya. He has recently published a book, *Peace Operations: Tackling the Military, Legal and Policy Challenges*, and is completing a Ph.D. in international law on the subject of the interim administration of justice in peace operations.

SPECIAL AGENT ROBERT LOOSLE is an 11-year veteran of the FBI, of which 6 years were spent detailed to the Department of Justice's International Criminal Investigative Assistance Program (ICITAP). He spent some 2 years as the Program Manager responsible for all development activities in Central America and the Dominican Republic. For 4 years he served as Project Manager for El Salvador ICITAP, where he developed a new police institution following the signing of the Peace Accords. Agent Loosle previously worked as a Special Assistant to the Assistant Secretary of State for International Organization Affairs at the State Department. He is currently assigned as the Supervisory Senior Resident Agent at the Beaumont, Texas, office of the FBI.

COLONEL F. M. LORENZ is currently the Marine Corps Chair and Professor of Political Science at the Industrial College of the Armed Forces, National Defense University. Between December 1992 and May 1993, he was the senior legal advisor for Operation *Restore Hope* in Somalia. During the first 4 months of 1996 he participated in Operation *Joint Endeavor* in Sarajevo on the legal staff of Admiral Leighton Smith. He has lectured at a number of international conferences on the subject of operational law and published a series of articles and papers for professional journals around the world.

DR. ROBERT MAGUIRE, a specialist on Haiti, has been involved with that country for over two decades through his work at the Inter-American Foundation, the Foreign Service Institute, and Johns Hopkins, Brown, and Georgetown Universities. He has written extensively on issues of development, security, and state/civil society relations and is principal author of *Haiti Held Hostage: International Responses to the Quest for Nationhood, 1986-1996* (Providence, RI: Watson Institute for International Studies and the United Nations University, 1996).

DR. MAXWELL G. MANWARING is a retired U.S. Army Colonel and is currently a political-military affairs consultant based in Carlisle, Pennsylvania. He has served in various positions, including the U.S. Army War College, the U.S. Southern Command's Small Wars

Operations Research Directorate, the Defense Intelligence Agency, and the Southern Command's Directorate for Plans, Policy, and Politico-Military Affairs. Dr. Manwaring is the author of several articles on political-military affairs and is co-editor of the prize-winning *El Salvador at War: An Oral History* (Washington, DC: Government Printing Office, 1989) and *Managing Contemporary Conflict: Pillars of Success* (Boulder, CO: Westview Press, 1997).

J. O'NEIL G. POULIOT, Royal Canadian Mounted Police (Ret.), is a retired Chief Superintendent, with 34 years of diverse law enforcement experience. He has been involved in numerous international criminal investigations, and supervised onsite undercover operations in Europe, the Caribbean, and Asia. During the U.N. Mission in Haiti, Mr. Pouliot welded the highly diverse UNCIVPOL force of 21 countries, 9 languages, and 8 religions into a cohesive and focused organization. Mr. Pouliot is currently a faculty member of the Lester B. Pearson Canadian International Peacekeeping Center in Ottawa, Nova Scotia.

DR. JAMES A. SCHEAR is the Deputy Assistant Secretary of Defense (Peacekeeping and Humanitarian Affairs) in the Office of the Assistant Secretary of Defense (Strategy and Requirements). Prior to this appointment, Dr. Schear served as a Resident Associate and Abe Fellow at the Carnegie Endowment for International Peace. He has worked as a consultant on peacekeeping and humanitarian operations with the United Nations on missions in Cambodia and the former Yugoslavia. He has also held research appointments at the International Institute for Strategic Studies (1982-83), Harvard University's Center for Science and International Affairs (1983-87), and the Brookings Institution (1987-1988).

DR. ERWIN A. SCHMIDL, is historian with the Austrian Ministry of Defence's Bureau of Military Research in Vienna. He received his Ph.D. from the University of Vienna in 1981 and then worked in the Austrian Army Museum (Research Department). Seconded to the Ministry of Foreign Affairs (U.N. Section) in 1991-92, he was an observer with the U.N. Observer Mission in South Africa in 1994 and a Senior Fellow at

571

the U.S. Institute of Peace in 1995-96, where he organized the first conference on police in peace operations. The author of numerous studies on political, military, and colonial history, he is currently working on a major study on the evolution of peace operations, 1897-1997.

LIEUTENANT COLONEL STEVE SPATARO, U.S. Army, was the UNITAF Provost Marshal during Operation *Restore Hope*. He is a U.S. Army Military Police Officer, with extensive experience in tactical MP and Law Enforcement operations and a veteran of Operations *Desert Shield* and *Desert Storm*. He commanded the MP Battalion at the U.S. Disciplinary Barracks and the 24th Division's Ft. Stewart Law Enforcement Command. Currently he works in the Deputy Chief of Staff, Operations, at Headquarters, Department of the Army.

DR. WILLIAM STANLEY has published a book on civil military relations and state violence in El Salvador (Temple University Press 1996), as well as numerous articles, book chapters, and policy reports on police reform, U.N. peace building, political violence, and refugee issues in Central America. His research has been supported by the U.S. Institute of Peace. Currently, he is Assistant Professor of Political Science at the University of New Mexico.

LYNN THOMAS worked on public security issues in Somalia during UNITAF, while on loan to the United Nations from CARE. As a 1997 Women in International Security fellow, she was assigned to the State Department, where she managed the Africa and Latin America portfolio in the Political-Military Bureau Office of International Security and Peacekeeping. She completed her fellowship at the American Embassy in Sarajevo working on legal system reform. Ms. Thomas has an M.A. in Strategic Studies and International Economics from the Johns Hopkins University School of Advanced International Studies. She is currently with the consulting firm of Cohen and Woods International.

About the Contributing Authors

JAMES L. WOODS is Vice President of Cohen and Woods International, Inc., a consulting firm specializing in African Affairs. Mr. Woods served in the Office of the Secretary of Defense for 34 years, the latter half of them concentrating exclusively on Africa. Mr. Woods was involved in all crises and programs in sub-Saharan Africa from 1979 onward, retiring in 1994 as Deputy Assistant Secretary for African Affairs. He has been actively involved in lecturing and writing on Africa as well as on conflict resolution and peacekeeping issues. A Senior Associate at the Center for Strategic and International Studies (CSIS) African Studies Program, Mr. Woods holds B.A. and M.A. degrees from Ohio State and is currently engaged in graduate study in international relations at Cornell University.